The Archaeology of Athens and Attica under the Democracy

Proceedings of an International Conference celebrating 2500 years since the birth of democracy in Greece, held at the American School of Classical Studies at Athens, December 4–6, 1992

Edited by

*W.D.E. Coulson, O. Palagia,
T.L. Shear, Jr., H.A. Shapiro and F.J. Frost*

Oxbow Monograph 37
1994

Published by
Oxbow Books, Park End Place, Oxford OX1 1HN

ISBN 0 946897 67 0

This book is available direct from
Oxbow Books, Park End Place, Oxford OX1 1HN
(Phone: 0–865–241249; Fax: 0–865–794449)

and

The David Brown Book Company
PO Box 5605, Bloomington, IN 47407, USA
(Phone: 812–331–0266; Fax: 812–331–0277)

Published with the assitance of the A. G. Leventis Foundation

Printed in Great Britain by
The Short Run Press, Exeter

Contents

Foreword

THE PAPERS IN THIS VOLUME are based on an international conference which was organized by the American School of Classical Studies at Athens on December 4–6, 1992, to celebrate the 2500th anniversary of the birth of democracy in ancient Athens. They illustrate well the interplay between archaeology and history and address broadly such questions as, "Did the political organization of the Athenian city-state in the fifth and fourth centuries B.C. affect its physical remains," "What aspects of the archaeological record are peculiarly democratic," and "To what extent were the form and content of late archaic and classical art conditioned by the constitution". The authors offer a fresh look at the art and architecture of Athens, as well as at the Athenian way of life in both city and country. The opportunity is also provided to publish the results of recent Greek and American excavations both in the heart of Athens and in the rural demes.

Since the American governmental system was inspired by the Greek democratic ideal, it was particularly appropriate that the American School organize a conference in Greece to commemorate the anniversary of one of the most important events in western history: the democratic reforms of the Greek statesman, Kleisthenes. The present conference, however, was not the only event organized by the American School in celebration of democracy. The others consisted of an exhibition and a second conference which was held in Washington, DC, between April 16 and 18, 1993. This second conference brought together ancient historians and modern political theorists to speak about such issues as citizenship, freedom, equality, law and education. The exhibition, entitled "The Birth of Democracy," opened first in the Gennadius Library of the American School on March 9, 1993, and ran for two months until May 9 (see *Η γέννηση της δημοκρατίας, Κατάλογος έκθεσης* [Athens 1993]). After that, it was sent to Washington, where it opened on June 15 in the Rotunda of the National Archives, in the same room where the constitution of the United States is displayed (see *The Birth of Democracy, An Exhibition Celebrating the 2500th Anniversary of Democracy* [Washington, DC 1993]). This emphasizes again the close connection that has always existed between Greece and America in both political ideals and social values.

Our conference was held under the auspices and with the cooperation of the Ministry of Culture of Greece and with the special support of Katerina Rhomiopoulou, Director of the Department of Prehistoric and Classical Antiquities. It was funded by the A.G. Leventis Foundation, and we would like to thank the Foundation for its generous support. It could never have taken place without the help of the staff of the American School. We thank them warmly, especially the Secretary of the School, Robert Bridges, the Administrative Assistant, Maria Pilali, the Secretary, Maria Michalopoulou, and the Residence Manager, Niamh Michalopoulou. We are deeply grateful to Maria Pilali for long hours spent in entering manuscripts into the computer, thus facilitating the prompt publication of this volume, and for general troubleshooting.

The post conference excursion, under the leadership of John Traill, visited the demes of southeastern and eastern Attica, including Rhamnous, Marathon, Brauron, and Sounion. We are particularly indebted to Vasilios Petrakos for his kindness in allowing the participants entry to his excavations at Rhamnous and to the other sites. We would also like to thank Iphigeneia Dekoulakou and the staff of the Second Ephoreia of Prehistoric and Classical Antiquities for helping with the arrangement of the visits to the sites and museums. Steven Diamant's help also ensured that the excursion went smoothly.

The authors were invited to participate by the Chairs of the individual sessions (see Program, page vii), who also edited the papers of their sessions. Further editing was done by Olga Palagia, who read all the papers, and by William Coulson.

Abbreviations of bibliographical references follow the guidelines of *American Journal of Archaeology* 95 (1991) 4–16.

William Coulson *Olga Palagia*

Program

Friday, December 4, 1992

8:00–9:15 a.m.	Registration
9:15–9:30 a.m.	Opening Remarks: Katerina Rhomiopoulou and William Coulson

Session I: The Archaeology of Democracy

Chair:	T. Leslie Shear, Jr.
9:30–10:15 a.m.	William Childs, "The Dating of the Old Temple of Athena."
10:15–11:00 a.m.	John Camp, "Before Democracy: the Alkmaionidai and Peisistratidai."
11:00–11:30 a.m.	Coffee/Tea Break
11:30–12:15 p.m.	Stefan Brenne, "Ostraka and the Process of Ostrakophoria."
12:15–12:40 p.m.	Πέτρος Καλλιγάς, "Το ιερό του Διονύσου, το θέατρο και η αναστήλωση της ανατολικής παρόδου του καθώς και το Ωδείο του Περικλέους."
12:40–1:00 p.m.	Άλκηστις Χωρέμη – Κων. Καζαμιάκης, "Η αρχαία οδός των Τριπόδων και τα χορηγικά Μνημεία."
1:00–1:25 p.m.	Καλλιόπη Παπαγγελή, "Το νεκροταφείο της οδού Λένορμαν."
1:25–1:45 p.m.	Ευσταθία Μπαζιωτοπούλου-Βαλαβάνη, "Αθηναϊκά κεραμικά εργαστήρια του 6ου και 5ου αι. π.Χ."

Session II: The Sculpture of Democracy

Chair:	Olga Palagia
4:20–4:30 p.m.	Olga Palagia, Introductory Remarks.
4:30–5:00 p.m.	Όλγα Αλεξανδρή, "Πολιτικές προσωποποιήσεις."
5:00–5:30 p.m.	Carol Mattusch, "The Eponymous Heroes: the Making of Sculptural Groups."
5:30–6:00 p.m.	Ισμήνη Τριάντη, "Γλυπτά της εποχής του Κλεισθένη."
6:00–6:30 p.m.	Coffee/Tea Break
6:30–7:00 p.m.	Reinhard Stupperich, "The Iconography of Athenian State Burials in the Classical Period."
7:00–7:30 p.m.	Valtin von Eickstedt, "Bemerkungen zur Ikonographie des Frieses vom Ilissos-Tempel."
7:30–8:00 p.m.	Olga Palagia, "No Demokratia."
8:00 p.m.	Reception for speakers and participants in Loring Hall of the American School of Classical Studies.

Saturday, December 5, 1992

Session III: Cult and Festival in Democratic Athens

Chair:	Alan Shapiro
9:00–9:30 a.m.	Alan Shapiro, Introductory Remarks on Religion and Politics in Classical Athens.
9:30–10:15 a.m.	Μιχάλης Τιβέριος, "Θησεύς και Παναθήναια."
10:15–11:00 a.m.	Robin Osborne, "Democracy and Imperialism in the Panathenaic Procession: the Parthenon Frieze in its Context."
11:00–11:30 a.m.	Coffee/Tea Break

11:30–12:15 p.m.	Jenifer Neils, "Tribal Contests and Tribal Organization after Kleisthenes."
12:15–1:00 p.m.	Kevin Clinton, "The Eleusinian Mysteries and Panhellenism in Democratic Athens."

Session IV: Town and Countryside

Chair:	Frank Frost
5:00–5:30 p.m.	Frank Frost, Introductory Remarks.
5:30–6:00 p.m.	Γιώργος Σταϊνχάουερ, "Το έργο της αρχαιολογικής υπηρεσίας στην Αττική."
6:00–6:30 p.m.	Ιωάννα Ανδρέου, "Η αρχαιολογική έρευνα του δήμου των Αιξωνίδων Αλών."
6:30–7:00 p.m.	Herman Mussche, "Thorikos during the Last Years of the Sixth Century B.C."
7:00–7:30 p.m.	Gregory Stanton, "The Rural Demes and Politics."
7:30–8:30 p.m.	Plenary talk by T. Leslie Shear, Jr., "'Ισονόμους τ' 'Αθήνας ἐποιησάτην: The Agora and the Democracy."
9:00 p.m.	Dinner for chairmen and speakers in Loring Hall of the American School of Classical Studies.

Sunday, December 6, 1992

Excursion to southeastern and eastern Attica led by John Traill.

The Date of the Old Temple of Athena on the Athenian Acropolis

William A.P. Childs

With the exception of two articles by Klaus Stähler in the 1970's[1] very little has been published on the Old temple of Athena on the Acropolis of Athens since Hans Riemann's study of its architecture in 1950.[2] Although Stähler convincingly redated the Gigantomachy pediment to the end of the sixth century, his date has not been universally accepted, and further consideration of the temple and its architectural sculpture has not been forthcoming.[3] In this paper I wish to propose that not only is Stähler's date for the Gigantomachy pediment correct but also that the whole temple was most likely built after 510 B.C., not in the 520's.

In most accounts of the architecture of the Old Athena Temple it is linked closely with the temple of Apollo at Corinth, dated around 540 B.C.[4] The main reason for this comparison is the fact that both temples have a double cella. The temple of Apollo at Delphi, the date of which is controversial but here will be accepted as *ca.* 530 B.C., is also considered closely linked with the other two temples.[5] Whereas the Delphi temple shares with the temple at Corinth the long and narrow plan of six by sixteen columns and its dimensions are extremely close also, the Old Athena Temple has a peculiarly short and broad plan of six by twelve columns, an arrangement it shares with distinctly late Doric temples such as Aphaia at Aigina,[6] Athena Pronaia at Delphi,[7] and Hera ("Tavole Paladine") at Metapontum.[8]

The actual dimensions of the stylobate of the Old Athena Temple as given by Gruben are 21.30 × 43.15 m[9] which compare closely with those of the Apollo temple of Corinth of 21.49 × 53.82 m., except in the length.[10] On the other hand, the temples of Athena Pronaia, Aphaia at Aigina and Hera at Metapontum are all much smaller, in the range of 13 to 16 m. wide by 27 to 33 m. long.[11] The Old Athena Temple shares, therefore, the large size of the earlier temples while adopting proportions in plan that link it with the late temples.

A complication in the analysis and evaluation of the plan of the Old Athena Temple has been the argument that it replaced on the same foundations the Hekatompedon or H architecture, which is dated to the second quarter of the sixth century and associated with the reorganization of the Panathenaia.[12] Dinsmoor rejected this proposition and argued that the H architecture occupied the south side of the Acropolis, its foundations hidden in the platform built for the older Parthenon.[13] After decades of gradual erosion of this theory, it appears to be regaining popularity at the present time.[14] Although I have favoured the interpretation that the Old Athena Temple was the successor of the H architecture on the north side of the Acropolis, the point is not crucial to my thesis.

One feature of the Old Athena Temple does appear so strange as to require an explanation out of past precedent: the lack of the canonical three steps up to the stylobate. The Old Athena Temple has but one step. Since the temple of Hera at Olympia had only one or two steps up to the stylobate,[15] the most plausible theory to explain this idiosyncracy in the much later Old Athena Temple is that it replaced an earlier building that did not have three steps, and some continuity with the preceding building was sought. This building could have been a seventh-century temple of which some terracotta tiles survive.[16] On the other hand, the very different proportions of the plan of the Old Athena Temple in comparison with the normal long and narrow archaic temple are a startling innovation. The likely explanation of the plan is the unusual combination of old cults in a single structure which also resulted a hundred years later in a highly individual plan for the Erechtheion. So the plan of the Old Athena Temple could *a priori* be of any date, because it derives in large part from a unique function of the building. Yet it seems clear that two buildings dedicated to Athena around or shortly after 500 B.C. copy the proportions of the Old Athena Temple: the temples of Athena Pronaia at Delphi and Aphaia at Aigina.[17] That both are only slightly later than the Old Athena Temple will be demonstrated below. Accordingly, the Old Athena Temple occupies an important position in the development of the Doric order on the Greek mainland and a highly interesting position in the history of Athens. Whatever explanation of the genesis of its forms one adopts, I lay emphasis on the reverence for past patterns in the design of the Old Athena Temple, a factor which comes out particularly strongly in its sculptural decoration and is evident from the later name for the

Erechtheion, ὁ ἀρχαῖος νεώς. (See J. M. Paton [ed.], *The Erechtheum* [Cambridge, Mass. 1927] 434 and *s.v.* νεὼς [ἀρχαῖος].)

The imitation of the plan of the Old Athena Temple by two temples of Athena that date around or after 500 B.C. is certainly suggestive for the date of the temple. Several features of its architectural detail tend to confirm that the whole temple was built at the end of the sixth century, not just the Gigantomachy pediment as argued by Stähler. Much attention is usually attributed to the profile of the echinus of the Doric capitals. La Coste-Messelière, in particular, tried to argue that the capitals of the Old Athena Temple are earlier than those of the temple of Apollo at Delphi, which he dated after 514 B.C.[18] Such a judgement is based on the theory that the profile of the echinus becomes steeper and less everted with time.[19] The published drawings of capitals belonging to buildings of the end of the sixth century and the beginning of the fifth are not so precise that one can draw absolutely certain conclusions from them.[20] Nonetheless, the study of Auberson agrees with my own analysis that the profile of a capital from the Old Athena Temple has a steeper, less everted echinus than one from the temple of Apollo at Delphi (Fig. 1a-b).[21] Steeper still is the profile of the capital of the temple of Aphaia at Aigina, which is almost the same as one from the temple of Athena Pronaia (Fig. 1c-d).[22] Translation of the relative series into absolute dates has only a rough value but does suggest that the Old Athena Temple comes after the temple of Apollo at Delphi (*ca.* 530 B.C.) and before the two short and broad temples in Aigina and Delphi, which does allow a date in the last decade of the sixth century.

The impressive painted sima of the Old Athena Temple was studied by Shoe and, though she dates the moulding to the then conventional date for the temple of 527 B.C., she notes that it resembles more closely mouldings of the end of the century.[23] The form of the painted palmettes of the sima can be related closely to those of the temple of Aphaia at Aigina, though the old drawings of the latter disagree with each other in detail (Fig. 2a-b).[24] Stewart draws another apt comparison with the palmettes on the calyx-shaped capital on which a statue of Athena signed by Pythis stood.[25] The statue is generally dated around 500 B.C. Comparison with palmettes on vases is not particularly rewarding, but the pattern does appear to be later rather than earlier.[26]

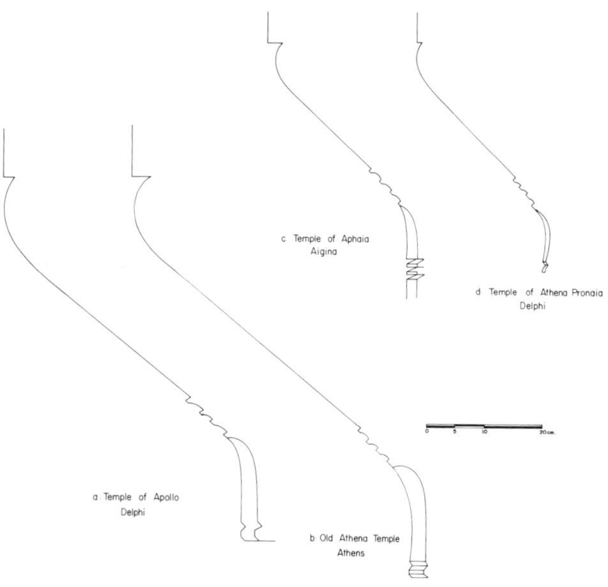

Fig. 1. Profiles of capitals of a) Temple of Apollo, Delphi (after La Coste-Messelière); b) Old Athena Temple, Athens (by Tasos Tanoulas, 1993); c) Temple of Aphaia at Aigina (after Cockerell); d) Athena Pronaia, Delphi (after Demangel).

Fig. 2. Sima decoration of a) Old Athena Temple, Athens (after Wiegand); b) Temple of Aphaia at Aigina (after Cockerell).

Though the weight of evidence for a date close to 500 B.C. for the Old Athena Temple is not great, it is nonetheless far stronger in favour of such a date than for one in the 520's. Stähler's arguments for the date of the Gigantomachy pediment agree completely with the above observations on the architecture. I need only paraphrase his and my own observations published elsewhere.[27] The himation of the statue of Athena has its closest links with Kore 685 and the Kallimachos Nike (Acropolis 690).[28] The lunging Giants of the left and right angles of the pediment twist their torsos almost 90 degrees in contrast to the one Giant in a similar position in the west pediment of the temple of Apollo at Delphi, who is shown in simple profile.[29] The reclining Giant of the Old Athena Temple, often called Enkelados, has his closest associate in the wounded warrior of the west pediment of the temple of Aphaia on Aigina.[30] The rudimentary attempt to show the actual displacement of the abdominal muscles is similar to the patterns of the figures on the "Cat and Dog Base" from the Kerameikos in the National Museum.[31]

If the Gigantomachy can be dated securely in the late archaic period, close to 500 B.C., the sorry fragments of the other pediment of the Old Athena Temple, two lions killing a bull, provide little to go on.[32] However, several fragments of the manes of the lions are preserved, and there can be little doubt that these suggest a late rather than an early date. The locks of the manes are depicted overlapping in several layers, and the individual locks are plastically rendered with sinuous curves.[33] Some are presented as more rigid tufts with incised lines (Fig. 3).[34] In all cases these must be contrasted with the flat surfaces and isolated character of the tufts of the manes of the lions in the east pediment of the temple of Apollo at Delphi.[35]

Fig. 3. Lion mane of presumed east pediment of Old Athena Temple, Acropolis Museum (after Schrader, Die archaischen Marmorbildwerke der Akropolis *[Frankfurt 1939] fig. 477).*

The various lions from the Athenian Agora published by Harrison confirm the observations made here. The manes of the Agora lions 91 and 95 are fully plastic and contrast with the linear treatment of the mane of lion 94.[36] Harrison dates the former shortly before and after 500 B.C., the latter in the second quarter of the sixth century. The more plastic treatment of the lion mane begins as early as the Siphnian Treasury frieze,[37] develops through Agora lion 91, a pair of lions on the Acropolis,[38] the marble lion-bull group divided between the National Museum in Athens and the Metropolitan Museum in New York,[39] and culminates in Agora lion 95.

Various absolute dates have been proposed for these lions.[40] The lion water-spout of the Megarian Treasury at Olympia gives perhaps the best point of departure.[41] Bol considers the pediment of the treasury to be close to the west pediment of the temple of Aphaia at Aigina, that is, probably in the decade 500–490 B.C.[42] If this date is also valid for the lion water spout, Agora lion 95 must fall in about the same period, probably near its end. The marble group in New York and Athens is earlier, perhaps around 500 B.C. Details of the fragmentary manes of the lions in the pediment of the Old Athena Temple compare well with this marble group, though the group may be slightly later.

If there is any doubt about these observations, the lion head water spout of the Old Athena Temple serves as confirmation.[43] The balance of plastic rendering of the face[44] and linear elements of the mane make it, on the one hand, a clear precursor of the lion water spout of the Megarian Treasury at Olympia and, on the other hand, a contemporary of the face and drapery of the Athena of the Gigantomachy pediment.[45]

The Old Athena Temple was probably begun after the triumph of Kleisthenes over Isagoras in 508/7 B.C. Its sculptural decoration should date around 500 B.C.[46] The two pediments are of great interest both in terms of subject and composition. It is unknown to which end each pediment is to be assigned, though Lapalus enunciated the principle that hieratic pediments belong in the east and narrative or action pediments in the west.[47] This certainly applies at Delphi and later at Olympia, though it does not apply to Aigina.[48] If applied to the Old Athena Temple, the Gigantomachy belongs in the west and the lion-bull pediment in the east.[49] On the Acropolis there is an added advantage in this arrangement: the entrance through the Propylaia would have presented the Gigantomachy to view and this may have had particular significance as we shall see below.

Stähler has attributed two horse protomes to the center of the Gigantomachy pediment, which must have belonged to the chariot of Zeus set frontally in the center of the pediment.[50] His arguments are persuasive. The resulting composition is close to that of both the east and west pediments of the temple of Apollo at Delphi, in both of which frontal chariots occupied the center.[51] According to Vian, however, after the end of the sixth century, Zeus' chariot was no longer a regular part of the Gigantomachy on vases.[52] This underscores the somewhat old-fashioned arrangement of a frontal chariot *per se*, which represents an old schema known from a votive relief on the Acropolis and one of the metopes of temple C at Selinus.[53]

The east pediment of the Old Athena Temple was even more old-fashioned: it repeated the ancient motif of the lion and bull contest that decorated the pediment of the H architecture of the second quarter of the sixth century.[54] It is interesting to note that a column krater in Geneva presents the paired scenes of Gigantomachy (with chariot of Zeus in profile) and lion-bull.[55] Dated between 530 and 520 B.C., it has long been thought a reflection of the pediments of the Old Athena Temple. It and two relatives must, however, be about two decades earlier than the temple pediments and attest the importance of the motifs. The lion-bull motif is a relative of the great Gorgon in the center of the pediment of the temple of Artemis at Corfu,[56] and must reflect an older archaic type of divine image of the power of

Athena.[57] This pediment stands in stark contrast to the appearance of Apollo himself in the east pediment of the Alkmaionid temple in Delphi, Athena in both pediments of the temple of Aphaia at Aigina, and Zeus in the east pediment of Olympia.

The motif of lions and bull in the east pediment of the Old Athena Temple can only be a purposeful repetition of the earlier pediments. The probable location in the east pediment, the more hieratic location, is reasonable. The double reference to earlier pediments, that is, the lions and bull referring to the old H architecture and the Gigantomachy referring back to the pediments of the Alkmaionid Apollo temple at Delphi with frontal chariots, is significant. Since the temple occupies a particularly sacred part of the Acropolis and must have incorporated within its walls the oldest and most sacred cults on the Acropolis, the pediments display elemental divine powers.

There is another and important point to be made concerning the Gigantomachy pediment and its presumed location on the west end of the temple. Pinney has argued from a fragment of Aristotle that the Panathenaia was established in commemoration of the Gigantomachy.[58] The visitor to the late archaic Acropolis would have seen the west pediment of the Old Athena Temple on passing through the Propylaia and been aware of the connection between the Gigantomachy and the truly "national" procession in honor of Athena.[59]

The possible political significance of the pediment has long been a topic of discussion.[60] Even if we can imagine that the appearance of the theme in the west pediment of the temple of Apollo at Delphi was the choice of the Alkmaionidai (which is doubtful), the Gigantomachy on the prominent north frieze of the Siphnian Treasury[61] and in the pediment of the Megarian Treasury at Olympia[62] indicate a broader meaning of the subject in the late sixth century than primarily a local political banner. Indeed, the close connection of the Gigantomachy with the Panathenaia could easily suggest that the subject had Peisistratid overtones. It seems more likely, however, that the Gigantomachy, like the deeds of Herakles, had a more general meaning than any "political" group could claim for their own.[63]

There is also evident in the Gigantomachy pediment an important shift in the nature of temple sculpture. The narrative element implicit in the representation was relatively new. The isolated scenes of the terracotta metopes of the temple of Apollo at Thermon[64] and in the corners of the pediment of the temple of Artemis on Corfu[65] were first elaborated into dominant narratives in the small poros pediments of the Acropolis and then transferred to a monumental temple at Delphi around 530 B.C.[66] The narrative compositions of both pediments of the temple of Aphaia on Aigina and the temple of Zeus at Olympia are natural developments out of the late sixth-century temples and underscore the real continuity of evolution from archaic into early classical sculpture.

The size, proportions and sculptural decoration of the Old Athena Temple mark the building as truly transitional between the earlier archaic period and the new structures of the classical. This, of course, applies metaphorically to its historical context: the end of tyranny and the beginning of a new form of government that will lead to democracy. The short and stubby proportions of the temple's ground plan are in sharp contrast to the elongated earlier temples whose origins are in the seventh century. The new proportions, whatever pragmatic forces may have led to their adoption, mark an aesthetic revolution that had to be adjusted before the harmonious classical plan was discovered. The imitation and partial modernization of the ground plan by slightly later buildings[67] demonstrates the strength of Attic influence as the fifth century dawns. Finally, the combination of a narrative and hieratic pediment looks both backward and forward and suggests that the leading artistic position Athens was to have in the fifth century was not yet clearly established. Perhaps most interesting is the almost seamless evolution from the Peisistratid tyranny to the nascent democracy, which is equally visible in the dedication of statues of korai on the Acropolis.

The weight we should like to put on the relationship of artistic forms to historical events and developments is rarely as clear as we might wish. But it is not only from the perspective of the historical context that the correct date of the Old Athena Temple at the end of the sixth century is important. Its character, architectural and sculptural, puts it in a singularly important, pivotal position in the evolution of mainland Greek art and architecture.

Notes

1 K. Stähler, "Zur Rekonstruktion und Datierung des Gigantomachiegiebels von der Akropolis," in *Antike und Universalgeschichte, Festschrift Hans Erich Stier* (Münster 1972) 88–112; *id.*, "Der Zeus aus dem Gigantomachiegiebel der Akropolis?" *Boreas* 1 (1978) 28–31, pl. 4.

2 H. Riemann, "Der peisistratidische Athenatempel auf der Akropolis zu Athen," *MdI* 3 (1950) 7–39. The original publication is T. Wiegand, *Die archaische Poros-Architektur der Akropolis zu Athen* (Kassel and Leipzig 1904) 115–26. See also J. Travlos, *Pictorial Dictionary of Ancient Athens* (London 1971) (=*PDA*) 143, figs. 196–199; G. Gruben, *Die Tempel der Griechen* (Munich 1966) 154.

3 J. Boardman, *Greek Sculpture: The Archaic Period* (London 1978) 155; K. Schefold, *Götter- und Heldensagen der Griechen in der spätarchaischen Kunst* (Munich 1978) 64 and n. 143; J. Floren in W. Fuchs and J. Floren, *Die griechische Plastik* I: *Die geometrische und archaische Plastik* (Munich 1987) 246; and H. Knell, *Mythos und Polis: Bildprogramme griechischer Bauskulptur* (Darmstadt 1990) 41, maintain the old date of 520 B.C.; M. Oppermann, *Vom Medusabild zur Athenageburt* (Leipzig 1990) 58, allows the decade 520/510 B.C. Stähler is followed by A. Stewart, *Greek Sculpture, An Exploration* (New Haven 1990) 129–30, and in part by B.S. Ridgway, *The Archaic Style in Greek Sculpture* (Princeton 1977) 205–208. *Cf.* A. Delivorrias, *Attische Giebelskulpturen und Akrotere des fünften Jahrhunderts* (Tübingen 1974) 178–79.

4 R. Stillwell, "The Temple of Apollo," in H.N. Fowler and R. Stillwell (eds.), *Corinth* I: *Introduction, Topography, Architecture* (Cambridge, Mass. 1932) 124–25; Riemann (supra n. 2) 38; Gruben (supra n. 2) 154.

5 F. Courby, *FdD* II.1: *Topographie et architecture: La terrasse du temple* (Paris 1915) 111. The author has argued the date of 530 in *JdI* 108(1993) 399–441.

6 A. Furtwängler (ed.), *Aegina: Das Heiligtum der Aphaia* (Munich 1906) pls. 31–32.

7 R. Demangel, *FdD* IIB: *Topographie et architecture*, 1: *Le sanctuaire d'Athéna Pronaia, Les temples de tuf* (Paris 1923) 2–26; dated shortly before 500 B.C.: 23–25; H. Berve and G. Gruben, *Griechische Tempel und Heiligtümer* (Munich 1961) 339 (dated to the end of the sixth century), figs. 32–34 on 340.

8 R. Koldewey and O. Puchstein, *Die griechischen Tempel in Unteritalien und Sicilien* (Berlin 1899) 36–37, pl. 5 top; E. Galli, "Metaponto: Esplorazioni archeologiche e sistemazione dell'area del tempio delle Tavole Palatine," in *Campagne della Società Magna Grecia (1926 e 1927)* (Rome 1928) 63–79; W.B. Dinsmoor, *The Architecture of Ancient Greece*[3] (London 1950) 97–98 (dated ten years after the temple of Demeter at Paestum, or *ca.* 500 B.C.); Gruben (supra n. 2) 256–57, fig. 192 on p. 255; D. Mertens, "Zur archaischen Architektur der achäischen Kolonien in Unteritalien," in U. Jantzen (ed.), *Neue Forschungen in griechischen Heiligtümern* (Tübingen 1976) 170–71; F.G. LoPorto, "Ricerche e scoperte nell'Heraion di Metaponto," *Xenia* 1 (1981) 24–44.

9 Gruben (supra n. 2) 154.

10 Gruben (supra n. 2) 96; the measurements for the temple of Apollo at Delphi are given by Gruben (p. 72) as 21.68 × 58.18 m.

11 Gruben (supra n. 2) 89, 112, 256: Athena Pronaia 13.25 × 27.46 m.; Aphaia at Aigina 13.77 × 28.815 m.; Hera at Metapontum 16.06 × 33.46 m. LoPorto (supra n. 8) 27 gives the measurements of the stylobate of the Heraion at Metapontum as 16.06 × 33.30 m.

12 C. Weickert, *Typen der archaischen Architektur in Griechenland und Kleinasien* (Augsburg 1929) 145–46, with earlier literature; W.-H. Schuchhardt, "Die Sima des Alten Athenatempels der Akropolis," *AM* 60–61 (1935–1936) 1–111; Riemann (supra n. 2) 14–16; and generally F. Preisshofen, "Zur Topographie der Akropolis," *AA* 1977, 74–84.

13 W.B. Dinsmoor, "The Hekatompedon on the Athenian Acropolis," *AJA* 51 (1947) 109–151; Travlos, *PDA* 143; Gruben (supra n. 2) 154.

14 Both Tessa Dinsmoor and Judith Binder supported this view to me in conversations at the conference in Athens. In a later conversation with Manolis Korres, he informed me that he has taken cores through the platform of the Parthenon, which suggest the possible existence of a structure beneath it.

15 Wiegand (supra n. 2) 1; Dinsmoor (supra n. 8) 53.

16 Travlos, *PDA* 143, figs. 194–95.

17 It is notable, however, that they do not share the same method of laying out the plan, but adopt a more modern method: J.J. Coulton, "Towards Understanding Doric Design: The Stylobate and Intercolumniations," *BSA* 69 (1974) 65, 70, 74, 75, 80, 83. The Old Athena Temple appears to look back to the temple of Apollo at Corinth (p. 74), while the two small Athena temples are linked with their sister temple of Hera at Metapontum (pp. 80, 83). It is interesting to note that there appear to be cross-influences between all these temples and the Older Parthenon (pp. 65, 76).

18 P. de la Coste-Messelière, "Chapiteaux doriques de Delphes," *BCH* 66–67 (1942–1943) 29–31; *id.*, "Les Alcméonides à Delphes," *BCH* 70 (1946) 274–75; *cf.* Weickert (supra n. 12) 146. A new fragment of a capital of the Apollo temple is published by P. Amandry, *BCH* 105 (1981) 689, fig. 11.

19 Dinsmoor (supra n. 8) 54; Gruben (supra n. 2) 38. The wise reservation expressed by P. Auberson, *Eretria, Fouilles et Recherches* I: *Temple d'Apollon Daphnéphoros, architecture* (Bern 1968) 24, must be kept in mind: "les ordres architecturaux ne représentent pas des règles figées et contraignantes, mais des canons idéaux, susceptibles d'être interprétés de manière très diverse."

20 My comparison of the published profiles indicate slight variations among the publications of the "same" profile. These are, however, small and do not alter the general sense of development.

21 Auberson (supra n. 19) 19–20, pl. IX. I am deeply indebted to Petros Kalligas, Ephor of the Acropolis, for permitting a new drawing of one of the capitals of the Old Athena Temple to be made, and to Tasos Tanoulas for making the drawing. When Dr. Tanoulas set out to make the new drawing he discovered discrepancies with previously published measurements of the capitals and wrote me in a letter of 6 September, 1993: "There are four ... poros capitals in the Chalkotheke area, but the best preserved is one lying by the northern Akropolis wall, near the Belvedere, and I decided to draw the profile of this one. The capital height given by the French and German scholars is 1.083m, but the highest capital I could find is 1.07m high, and the one I measured is only 1.050m." The measurement Dr. Tanoulas refers to is given in Wiegand's publication (supra n. 2). 122, fig. 118. My Figure 1a-b shows very little difference between the capitals of the Apollo and Old Athena temples, while the drawings of Auberson cited above indicate far more difference. Clearly a more intense study of the evidence is needed than could be accomplished here. The drawing of the capital of the Apollo temple in Delphi is from La Coste-Messelière, *BCH* 66–67 (1942–1943) 56, fig. 12.

22 *Cf.* Auberson (supra n. 19) pl. IX. My drawings are made after Furtwängler (supra n. 6) pl. 42; Demangel (supra n. 7) 33, fig. 41. The capital of the Heraion at Metapontum is unrelated to those of its sister temples: LoPorto (supra n. 8) 31, fig. 9.

23 L.T Shoe, *Profiles of Greek Mouldings* (Cambridge 1936) 34; *cf.* p. 104. My thanks to John Camp for pointing out this discrepancy to me.

24 The palmettes of Aigina published by C.R. Cockerell, *The Temples of Jupiter Panhellenius at Aegina and of Apollo Epicurius at Bassae near Phigaleia in Arcadia* (London 1860) pl. XIII, fig. 3, are less sinuous and less pointed than the drawing of the same palmettes given by Furtwängler (supra n. 6) pl. 42. It is Cockerell's version (illustrated here) that most closely resembles the palmettes of the Old Athena Temple.

25 Stewart (supra n. 3) 130. Acropolis Museum 136: H. Schrader (ed.), *Die archaischen Marmorbildwerke der Akropolis* (Frankfurt 1939) pl. 111, lower left; M.S. Brouskari, *The Acropolis Museum* (Athens 1974) 54–55.

26 The placement and context of palmettes on vases appear to have a great influence on their form. Double palmette chains on the necks and upper borders of panels seem to have a standardized form that is unrelated to the anthemion. The basic pattern of the palmettes on the sima of the Old Athena Temple may be characterized as light and slightly flexible. That is, the fronds of the palmettes have open space about them, and the lower fronds bend slightly down at their ends. There are two different palmettes on the sima, one with seven petals, one with nine, but otherwise the forms are very similar. The earliest palmette of similar form that I have found occurs on an oinochoe in the Louvre (F 116): Beazley, *ABV*, 230; P. Jacobsthal, *Ornamente griechischer Vasen* (Berlin 1927) pl. 30b; which may be as early as 525: I. Wehgartner, *Attisch weissgrundige Keramik* (Mainz 1983) 5–6. But the forms of the fronds are distinctly different on this vase, in that the stems are attenuated and the ends bulbous. The best, but not wholly convincing parallels, are on black-figured vases of the Leagros period and contemporary red-figured vases, that is in the decade 510–500: J. Boardman, *Athenian Black Figure Vases* (New York 1974) figs. 210, 231; *id.*, *Athenian Red Figure Vases: The Archaic Period* (London 1975), figs. 24.1, 32.2, 33.1, 34.1 *etc.*

27 Stähler 1972 (supra n. 1) 103–107; author, *JdI* 108(1993) 399–441.

28 E.B. Harrison, "The Victory of Kallimachos," *GRBS* 12 (1971) 5–24, with earlier literature. Kore 685: H. Payne, *Archaic Marble Sculpture from the Acropolis*[2] (London 1950) pls. 72–74; Schrader (supra n. 25) 97–98, no. 47, pl. 70; G.M.A. Richter, *Korai, Archaic Greek Maidens* (London 1968) figs. 573–77.

29 Schrader (supra n. 25) pls. 193–97; P. de la Coste-Messelière, *FdD* IV: *Monuments figurés, sculpture* 3: *Art archaïque: Sculptures des temples* (Paris 1931) 19–20, pl. IV, fig. 6 on p. 27.

30 Schrader (supra n. 25) pl. 188; temple of Aphaia at Aigina: R. Lullies and M. Hirmer, *Greek Sculpture*[2] (New York 1960) pls. 74–75.

31 Lullies - Hirmer (supra n. 30) pl. 62, bottom; dated "Kleisthenic," *i.e.* post 510 B.C., by F. Willemsen, *AM* 78 (1963) 135; see also Floren (supra n. 3) 293–94; Stewart (supra n. 3) 130 and figs. 206, 139, both of which resemble closely the depiction of an athlete on a krater by Euphronios in Berlin (F2180: P.E. Arias, M. Hirmer and B.B. Shefton, *A History of Greek Vase Painting* [London 1962] pl. 112), dated shortly before 500 B.C.

32 Schrader (supra n. 25) 377–87, nos. 471–73; H. Gabelmann, *Studien zum frühgriechischen Löwenbild* (Berlin 1965) 52, no. 37; F. Hölscher, *Die Bedeutung archaischer Tierkampfbilder* (Würzburg 1972) 72–73.

33 Schrader (supra n. 25) 383, figs. 487–90.

34 Schrader (supra n. 25) 381, fig. 477.

35 *FdD* IV.3 (supra n. 29) 34–40, pl. V (XIIa-b); *FdD* IV (Paris 1927) pls. XXXII-XXXIII; P. de la Coste-Messelière and G. de Miré, *Delphes* (Paris 1943) pls. 146–49; Boardman (supra n. 3) fig. 203.2; Stewart (supra n. 3) fig. 203.

36 E.B. Harrison, *Agora* XI: *Archaic and Archaistic Sculpture* (Princeton 1965) 28–29, 31–36, pls. 12, 14–16.

37 Lullies - Hirmer (supra n. 30) pl. 52; F. Willemsen, *Die Löwenkopf-Wasserspeier vom Dach des Zeustempels*, *OlForsch* IV (Berlin 1959) pl. 1 top.

38 Schrader (supra n. 25) pls. 166–68; Willemsen (supra n. 25) pls. 2–3 top, dated on p. 38 in the last decade of the sixth century.

39 G.M.A. Richter, *Catalogue of Greek Sculptures: Metropolitan Museum of Art* (Cambridge, Mass. 1954) 5–6, no. 7, pl. X, dated *ca.* 500–495 B.C.

40 Harrison (supra n. 36) 29.

41 Willemsen (supra n. 37) pl. 1 bottom left.

42 P.C. Bol, "Die Giebelskulpturen des Schatzhauses von Megara," *AM* 89 (1974) 73–74.

43 Wiegand (supra n. 2) pl. X; Schrader (supra n. 25) pl. 180; Travlos, *PDA*, fig. 197; Brouskari (supra n. 25) fig. 104.

44 Though Harrison (supra n. 36) 35, notes correctly that the eyes of the earlier lions are set at a slight angle, while those of her lion 95 and the other late lions of the group are set horizontally.

45 Compare Schrader (supra n. 25) pl. 181 (lion) to pl. 187 (Athena head).

46 Judith Binder suggested to me that the Gigantomachy could be even later, falling in the decade 500–490. The Athena does appear to me to be very advanced and allow such a date. However, comparisons with the west pediment of Aigina suggest that the latter is the more advanced. Ridgway (supra n. 3). 212 n. 37 maintains her date for the west pediment *ca.* 490 B.C., and the comparison here suggested confirms that the figure from the Athena Temple is the earlier of the two. Equally, the comparison of the capitals of the two buildings assures a definite sequence. Accordingly, I continue to advocate a date for the Gigantomachy of the Old Athena Temple of *ca.* 500 B.C.

47 E. Lapalus, *Le fronton sculpté en Grèce* (Paris 1947) 373–85.

48 Delphi pediments: (supra n. 47) figs. 20–22 after p. 142; Olympia: *ibid.* pls. XIV-XV; Aigina: *ibid.* pl. XI.

49 Stähler 1972 (supra n. 1) 109–110.

50 (Supra n. 49) 98–99; *Boreas* 1 (1979) 28–31 with drawing on p. 30, horse on pl. 4; Schrader (supra n. 25) 242–44, figs. 271–73; Payne (supra n. 28) pl. 135.2; Brouskari (supra n. 25) fig. 3, pp. 17–18 (no. 6454), dated *ca.* 500 B.C. (p. 18), but she attributes them to a votive monument.

51 See above n. 48 and *FdD* IV.3, figs. 7–8, after p. 32.

52 F. Vian, *La guerre des géants: Le mythe avant l'époque hellénistique* (Paris 1952) 104.

53 Votive relief: Brouskari (supra n. 25) no. 577, fig. 79; metope of Temple C at Selinus: L. Giuliani, *Die archaischen Metopen von Selinunt* (Mainz 1979) pl. 5.1; *cf.* pl. 8, a metope from the earlier temple Y.

54 R. Heberdey, *Altattische Porosskulptur* (Vienna 1919) 87–100, figs. 70, 72–75 on pp. 91–93; Boardman (supra n. 3) fig. 190.

55 *CVA* Suisse 3, Genève 2 (Bern 1980) 28–29, pls. 59, 61.2 (C. Dunant and L. Kahil).

56 K. Schefold, *Myth and Legend in Early Greek Art* (New York n.d.) 52, fig. 16; Boardman (supra n. 3) fig. 187.1. J.L. Benson, "The Central Group of the Corfu Pediment," in *Gestalt und Geschichte: Festschrift Karl Schefold* (Bern 1967) 48–60. Benson's emphasis on the "narrative" character of the central group is, to my mind, misleading. Artemis is present in the form of the Gorgon; the "narrative" elements of running and Medusa's children on either side are mere attributes. John Boardman's ingenious interpretation of the poros "Bluebeard" group of the H architecture as "the body politic" (*RA* 1972, 71–72) is less difficult to believe. Surely he is right to point to the snake-kings of early Attica as the source of the image; *cf.* Hölscher (supra n. 32) 93. The attributes of "Bluebeard" are likely to have more elemental significance than political or geographic, though the two types of meaning may not have been distinguishable.

57 Hölscher (supra n. 32) 93, believes that there is a difference; the lions represent the nature of Athena, not herself in the "primitive" manner of earlier examples.

58 G.F. Pinney, "Pallas and Panathenaea," in J. Christiansen and T. Melander (eds.), *Proceedings of the 3rd Symposium on Ancient Greek and Related Pottery, Copenhagen August 31–September 4 1987* (Copenhagen 1988) 471. This was already recognized by Vian (supra n. 52) 103–104, 255–59.

59 The attribution of several fragments of frieze blocks to the Old Athena Temple has always enjoyed some support, though there is no evidence for the proposal: Stewart (supra n. 3) 130; Brouskari (supra n. 25) 52, 60, 68, nos. 1340, 1342, 1343, figs. 92, 107, 127; Payne (supra n. 28) 47–48; Schrader (supra n. 25) 387–399, pls. 198–200. The subject of the frieze might be the Panathenaic procession, which, if it did indeed belong to the Old Athena Temple, would underscore the iconography of the Gigantomachy pediment. There is, however, too little evidence on either the provenance of the frieze fragments or their subject to warrant renewed discussion here.

60 E. Thomas, *Mythos und Geschichte* (Cologne 1976) 24–25, with earlier literature.

61 Schefold (supra n. 3) 58–59, figs. 67–69.

62 Bol (supra n. 42) 65–74, pls. 31–35.

63 H.A. Shapiro, *Art and Cult under the Tyrants in Athens* (Mainz 1989) 39. On p. 38 Shapiro remarks that all but one of the early representations of Gigantomachies in Attic pottery come from the Acropolis of Athens.

64 Schefold (supra n. 64) 35–38, pls. 18–21.

65 *Ibid.* pls. 42–43.

66 On the poros pediments see Brouskari (supra n. 25) figs. 15–17, 27–29, 47, 74; Boardman (supra n. 3) figs. 194–98.

67 Supra n. 17.

Before Democracy: Alkmaionidai and Peisistratidai

John McK. Camp, II

The origins of Athenian democracy are to be found in the struggles for power among the great aristocratic families which flourished in Athens in the sixth century B.C. As described by Herodotos (1.59) and Aristotle (*Ath.Pol.* 13.4) these families controlled large and separate areas of Attica: those in the plain led by Lykourgos, those on the coast led by Megakles, son of Alkmaion, and those of the hills led by Peisistratos. Almost all power and authority, whether political, religious, or economic, was under their control. Discord among the aristocracy opened the door to democracy as the various factions found it necessary to turn to the populace for support. In other states with a unified aristocracy or a single dominant family in power, the opportunities for the people to play an active political role were far less than at Athens. Any gain in our understanding of two families in particular, the Alkmaionidai and Peisistratidai, is likely to shed light on the Kleisthenic reforms and the rise of Athenian democracy. The written record is largely confined to a handful of passages. It will be the purpose of this paper to examine some archaeological evidence which may supplement the meager and familiar literary tradition.

The Alkmaionidai in Exile

On at least four occasions in the sixth century the Alkmaionidai were driven or went into exile. Once in around 599 B.C. when they were charged with sacrilege for their actions during the Kylonian conspiracy (*Ath.Pol.* 1). Again after 546 B.C., on the occasion of the third, final, successful attempt by Peisistratos to establish a tyranny (Hdt. 1.64). Once more during the final years of the Peisistratid tyranny (Hdt. 5.62), and, finally, in 508 B.C. during the conflict between Kleisthenes on the one hand and Isagoras and King Kleomenes of Sparta on the other (Hdt. 5.72). Where did the Alkmaeonidai go in exile? The ancient sources provide no direct information, but there are three indications that the family had especially close ties with Delphi and Phokis in the sixth century. The first occurs in Plutarch's *Life of Solon* (2.2) where he tells us that although Solon persuaded the Athenians and other Greeks to take part in the First Sacred War, it was Megakles the Alkmaionid who was chosen to lead the Athenian forces which took part in the destruction of Chrysso. The second instance is the anecdote in Herodotos (6.125) of Alkmaion's visit to Sardis and his reward by King Kroisos of as much gold as he could carry for having acted as the king's agent in consulting the oracle at Delphi. The third instance is, of course, the best known: the Alkmaionidai, during their third exile, took the contract from the Amphikteony to rebuild the temple of Apollo at Delphi and finished the façade in marble rather than the limestone called for in the contract (Hdt. 5.62). In view of these three instances, it can be suggested that the Alkmaionidai settled in Phokis during those times in the sixth century when they were unwelcome in Athens. These ties with Phokis, Athenian and presumably Alkmaionid, deserve further scrutiny.

Athens and Phokis

Mythologically, traditionally, and historically, the ties between Athens and the Phokians were extraordinarily close.

In myth, Kephalos, son of Deion, king of Phokis, married Prokris, daughter of Erechtheus, and they lived together in Thorikos. Regardless of what we may think of the reliability of this tradition of dynastic intermarriage between Athens and Phokis, it is clear the classical Athenians believed it. Kephalos was the eponymous hero of the nearby deme of Kephale, and both he and Prokris were worshipped in Thorikos in the fourth century. The sacred calendar from Thorikos, first published by Eugene Vanderpool and now in Malibu, records that the members of the deme sacrified a ram to Kephalos and set a sacred table for Prokris every year in the month of Boedromion.[1]

Phokian connections with Thorikos appear in another context as well. According to an account preserved in Nikolaos of Damaskos, written in the first century A.D. (*FGH* 90 fr. 51): the "Phokians in a war against the Orchomenians carried out raids on their country and made off with numerous female prisoners. Making them their concubines, they had children by them. When the bastards had grown up and made a not negligible group of youths, the legitimate sons took fear and expelled them from the country. The exiles took refuge at

Thorikos in Attica, chose leaders and left by sea with the Ionians." Pausanias, in two presumably related passages (7.2.4, 7.3.10), records that the Phokians who settled Phokaia in Asia Minor were led by two Athenians, Philogenes and Damon.

Other traditions concern specific Phokian towns. Prokne, daughter of King Pandion and sister of Erechtheus, was married to King Tereus, who ruled the Phokian town of Daulis. On the Acropolis of Athens Pausanias recorded (1.24.3) having seen a statue of Prokne with her son Itys, usually associated with Acropolis Museum 1358,[2] and at Daulis, according to Pausanias (10.4.9) there was "a sanctuary of Athena with an ancient statue: the still older xoanon is said by the Daulians to have been brought by Prokne from Athens."

Next to Daulis is Panopeus, a city full of Athenian associations. According to Plutarch (*Theseus* 20), Theseus fell in love with Aigle, daughter of Panopeus, the eponymous founder of the town. And Pausanias, in his account of Panopeus (10.4.3), discusses an Athenian connection which had, at first, puzzled him:
"I could not understand why Homer spoke of the fair dancing-grounds of Panopeus till it was explained to me by the women whom the Athenians call Thyiads. These Thyiads are Attic women who go every other year with the Delphian women to Parnassos and there hold orgies in honor of Dionysos. It is the custom for these Thyiads to dance at various places on the road from Athens, and one of these places is Panopeus."

A third connection between Panopeus and the Athenians is to be found on the acropolis of the city. On a cliff face near one of the gates there is a series of rock-cut votive niches, first seen by Edward Dodwell, who noted inscriptions which he could not decipher. With more time, five of us from the American School were able to read the inscription under the largest niche.[3] Suprisingly, it reads: "Dexios the Athenian dedicated this to Herakles." The worship of Herakles elsewhere in Phokis is almost unattested, whereas in Athens he is virtually a national hero. His worship is attested in no less than 25 of the 140 demes of Attica.[4] For Panopeus, then, we have Athenian connections through Theseus, the Athenian Thyiads dancing on their way to worship Dionysos on Parnassos with Phokian women, and an Athenian dedication to Herakles carved into the very bedrock of the citadel.

A third Phokian town has close Athenian connections. According to Pausanias (10.35.8): "The people of Stiris say they are not Phokians, but Athenians originally, and came from Attica with Peteos, son of Orneus, when he was chased from Athens by Aigeus; and because most of the people came with Peteos from the deme of Stiria, the city was called Stiris." This tradition, too, has been greatly enhanced by the publication by Eugene Vanderpool (*AAA* 4[1971] 439–443) of an Athenian decree, found built into the refectory of the church of Hosios Loukas, which lies just above the ancient site.

These instances will perhaps suffice to explain the traditional ties of friendship between Athens and the Phokians which are attested by Thucydides (3.95.1), Xenophon (*Hell.* 6.3.1), Demosthenes (19.61–62), Diodorus Siculus (16.29), Plutarch (*Perikles* 21) and Pausanias (10.3.3). Most telling of all, perhaps, is the testimony of Polemon (Preller I,h), who wrote in the second century B.C. an entire book, now lost, entitled: "The foundation of cities in Phokis and concerning their kinship with the Athenians": "κτίσεις τῶν ἐν Φωκίδι πόλεων καὶ περὶ τῆς πρὸς Ἀθηναίους συγγενείας αὐτῶν."

The cumulative evidence of these various passages and inscriptions would seem to indicate close Athenian/Phokian ties and it further seems likely that these ties were created or maintained by the Alkmaionidai.

This suggestion of strong influence in a given area by a specific Athenian family, in this case the Alkmaionidai in Phokis, might lead one to consider a complementary influence by a rival family, such as the Peisistratids, in other areas of Greece inimical to the Phokians. Throughout the archaic period the abiding enemies of the Phokians were the Thessalians, as is attested by Herodotos (7.176; 8.27–30), Pausanias (10.13), and Plutarch (*Moralia* 244B). If the Alkmaionidai were allied with the Phokians, we might well expect good relations between the Peisistratids and Thessaly and that is precisely the case. First, the tyrant's youngest son bore the name Thessalos. Second, when the Peisistratids were under attack by the Spartans, between Leipsydrion and their final downfall, the Thessalians sent 1,000 cavalry to fight on their behalf (Hdt. 5.63–64). They were successful at first against the Spartan general Anchimolios at Phaleron, but were then routed and driven back to Thessaly by Kleomenes before his final siege of the Acropolis. Finally, when overthrown and exiled, Hippias was offered the city of Iolkos by the Thessalians (Hdt. 5.94).

The Alkmaionidai in Attica

In short, there is reason to suppose that the two large Athenian families had their own traditional ties with other regions of Greece, the Peisistratids with Thessaly and the Alkmaionidai with Phokis. Having noted those cities in Phokis with especially strong Athenian ties, we may reverse the equation and try to determine from which part of Attica these Athenians, presumably Alkmaionidai, came. As described above, the two demes for which we have specific Athenian/Phokian connections attested in the tradition are Thorikos and Stiria, both of which lie in southeast Attica, not far from each other. Just south of the Attic deme of Stiria, sharing the bay of modern Porto Raphti, was the deme of Prasiai. Although we have no specific testimony of a Phokian connection, one of the few things known about Prasiai is that there was a shrine of Athena Pronaia there, reminding us, of course, of the lower sanctuary at Delphi. The last coastal deme in southeast Attica is Potamioi Deiradiotai; like Prasiai, it has no specific tradition of association with Phokis though there is one prosopographical note worth mentioning. The fourth century statesman Phokion, whose father's name was Phokos, is thought to have come from the deme of Potamioi.[5]

The traditions concerning Athenian and Phokian kinship concentrate in southeast Attica and essentially provide new and welcome evidence to confirm and expand the known areas of Alkmaionid control. We know, for instance, that the Alkmaionidai were among the people of the coast (*Ath.Pol.* 13.4 and Hdt. 1.59), and all these are coastal demes. They should be added to the old suggestions, based on prosopography and the kouros bearing the name Kroisos, that the family was settled on the coast of southwest Attica.[6] It can now be argued on the basis of the Phokian connections that Alkmaionid control of the coast included not just the west coast with the demes of Alopeke and Anaphlystos, but also southeast Attica from Stiria to Thorikos. Certainly the deme of Thorikos with its Bronze Age traditions, its two tholos tombs, its extensive geometric cemetery and an archaic theater was for centuries a rich deme, though its representation of five councillors in the *boule* indicates that it was not particularly large. This is of considerable interest because it virtually ensures that the family also controlled the silver mines of southern Attica and the wealth they provided. It leads us to note also the extraordinary wealth of the sanctuaries of Poseidon and Athena at Cape Sounion, where no fewer than 13 kouroi were dedicated, several of them of colossal size.[7] They are far more lavish than the archaic votives from the Attic sanctuaries of Brauron or Eleusis, or any other sanctuary, other than the Acropolis itself. Just as the Peisistratids lived near Brauron and are said by one ancient source (Photios *s.v.* Brauron) to have built the temple there, so we might suggest that the Alkmaionidai were the primary benefactors of Athena and Poseidon at Sounion.

The role played by the aristocratic families in the development of Athenian cults is worth pursuing a bit further. The traditional and hereditary priesthoods presumably reflect accurately the virtually total control over specific cults by the various families. One thinks immediately of the Eumolpidai and Kerykes and their control over the cult of Eleusinian Demeter or the Eteoboutadai and their responsibility for the cult of Athena Polias. In addition to their activity at Brauron, the Peisistratids were also responsible for starting the temple of Olympian Zeus and for building the altar of the twelve gods in the Agora and another to Apollo Pythios. In later times, several cults were founded on private initiative; for example, Themistokles and Artemis Aristoboule, Kimon and the Theseion, and Telemachos and the Asklepieion.[8] If anything, such private initiative may well have been more prevalent before the founding of the democracy. If so, then we should look anew at the archaic acropolis. W.A.P. Childs at this conference has shown reason for dating the Athena temple to the period of the democracy.[9] What, however, are we to make of the small treasury-like buildings, richly decorated with sculpture, which adorned the citadel? Who built them, and why? Their usual identification as treasuries seems a problem, given the fact that treasuries are generally confined to Panhellenic sites and are designed to hold offerings of individual city states. It is hard to see how such an arrangement would work in sixth-century Athens, and some other use should perhaps be proposed. With their elaborate sculpted decoration, they might best be identified as small temples. Another obvious suggestion for their use is that they served as dining halls. One thinks of the small chambers, both rectangular and circular at the Kabeirion at Thebes, or the numerous separate family dining chambers in the sanctuary of Demeter at Corinth. Whether treasuries, dining halls, temples, or something else it seems to me probable that these small buildings are not to be thought of as the work of the Athenian state, but more probably were built on the initiative of the great families who controlled so much of Athenian cult activity in the archaic period.

If Alkmaionid control, as suggested above, included the silver mines at Laurion, then we have confirmation that they represented more wealth, were perhaps more conservative and were presumably more powerful than the Peisistratids, as is suggested by Herodotos. The Alkmaionidai as a family had been influential at the time of the Kylonian conspiracy late in the seventh century and during the First Sacred War at the beginning of the sixth century, whereas Peisistratos himself is said to have created the faction from which he drew support. According to Aristotle (*Ath.Pol.* 13.4–5) Peisistratos "was thought to be an extreme advocate of the people. And on the side of this party were also arrayed, from the motive of poverty, those who had been deprived of the debts due them and from the motive of fear, those who were not of pure descent." Is there anything in the archaeological record to indicate that Peisistratos was, in fact, as Aristotle labels him: δημοτικώτατος?

One place to start would be the Agora. My colleague, Leslie Shear has shown that the public area of the Agora was greatly expanded in the course of the middle of the sixth century, during the tyranny of Peisistratos.[10] Numerous wells, indicative of private houses, went out of use in the area during the second and third quarters of the sixth century. This important observation can be enhanced by a look at the buildings of the archaic Agora as well. Throughout much of antiquity and perhaps until the construction of the Stoa of Attalos, the eastern limit of the public area was ill-defined. Wells and cisterns under the library of Pantainos suggest the location of private houses or small commercial establishments until well into the Hellenistic period. In effect, the Agora square is in fact a triangle, with the Panathenaic Way forming the eastern limit (p. 232, Fig. 4). Three important public buildings lie at the three apices of this triangle, and all were built at the time Peisistratos or his sons were in power. In the southwest corner is a structure designated by the excavators as Building F (p. 233, Fig. 5). It has the form of a house, with rooms grouped around a central courtyard and provisions for cooking, but it is built on a much larger scale, measuring 18 by 26 m. Leslie Shear (here p. 231), returning to an old hypothesis made by Homer Thompson, has suggested that Building F served as the "palace" of the tyrants, a suggestion consistent with the scale, plan, date, and location of the building.

In the southeast corner of the Agora, alongside the Panathenaic Way, the excavations have brought to light the poorly preserved remains of an archaic fountain house (p. 230, Fig. 3) in just the spot where Pausanias (1.14.1) saw the famed Enneakrounos or nine-spouted fountain house built by the Peisistratids. This identification is dubious, however, in view of the information preserved by Thucydides (2.15) to the effect that the Enneakrounos lay south of the Acropolis, at the Kallirhoe springs in the bed of the Ilissos River. Whether or not these pitiful remains are those of the Enneakrounos is of no great concern here for the fountain house is certainly Peisistratid in date: the polygonal masonry in Kara limestone, the Z-clamps used to hold the blocks together, and pottery beneath the floor of the building all suggest a date in the years around 530–520 B.C. The construction of such a fountain house was surely of great benefit to many, especially those who did not have slaves, and will have encouraged people to congregate, rather than discourage them. Indeed, a series of handsome black-figured hydrias of the period show young women lining up to collect their water, and Aristophanes describes the crowds at a fountain house in the opening lines of the *Lysistrata*. The addition of a large public fountain house with its substantial supply aqueduct represents a major transformation of the area, which hitherto had only been supplied by means of wells. It should be emphasized that water for this fountain was piped in over a long distance, indicating that the siting of the building was both deliberate and important, presumably placed so as to supply a large number of people in this specific location.[11] Finally, the northern tip of the triangle was adorned in 522/1 B.C. by an altar dedicated to the twelve gods, established by Peisistratos the Younger in the year of his archonship (Thuc. 6.55). That this altar was very much a focal point in the life of the city is clear from the fact that according to both Herodotos (2.7) and an inscription of the late fifth century B.C. (*IG* II^2, 2640), the sanctuary served as the central milestone of the city, the point from which all distances were measured. Thus we find in the latter half of the sixth century the public area of the Agora (p. 232, Fig. 4) was not only enlarged under the Peisistratids but that they also defined the area architecturally by means of three important structures: Building F, which the tyrants may well have used as their headquarters, the southeast fountain house which for the first time provided abundant water in this area for large numbers of people, and the altar of the twelve gods which represented the physical center of the city. Although it comes as a shock to those of us who think of the Agora as the essence of democratic Athens, the archaeological evidence seems clear: much of the laying out of the great public square should be attributed to the tyrants. There are several possible reasons why a large open area was deemed desirable or necessary to the Peisistratids.

1) One possibility, offered by F. Kolb, is that the early Greek agora derives from the rise of theatrical performances. For Athens, this suggestion is especially attractive in that the orchestra was located in the Agora until a collapse of the wooden bleachers led to a shift of the theatrical performances to the south slope of the Acropolis and the sanctuary of Dionysos Eleutherios.[12]
2) Another possibility is that the area was used for athletics at this early date, before the development of gymnasia: here one can point to Peisistratos' association with the founding or aggrandizement of the Panathenaic festival in 566 B.C., and three sixth-century inscriptions which refer to a *dromos*, perhaps the Panathenaic Way itself which was used both as race course and processional route. The fifth-century Agora certainly had a running track, the starting line for which was found in 1980, adjacent to the altar of the twelve gods. It is worth noting that two other early agoras, at Corinth and Argos, also had running tracks and starting lines.[13]
3) A third possible use for a large open area was for military drill and training. Peisistratos was, after all, a military leader of some skill: he made his reputation by seizing Nisaia in a war against Megara (Hdt. 1.59), he defeated his opponents at Pallene at the time of his third tyranny (Hdt. 1.62–3), and he held power by means of an armed bodyguard (Hdt. 1.59) and mercenaries (Hdt. 1.64). A large open space would be useful for practising military drill.[14] Certainly in later times the Agora was used for military training: the cavalry practised along the Panathenaic Way as late as the fourth century B.C. according to a fragment of the comic poet Mnesaichmos, "Go Manes to the Agora, to the Herms, the place frequented by phylarchs, and to their handsome pupils whom Pheidon trains in mounting and dismounting."[15] The Agora of Elis was known as the hippodrome, because it, too, was used for training horses (Paus. 6.24).
4) A fourth possibility is that which started us on our review of the archaic Agora, namely that Peisistratos was in fact δημοτικώτατος and that the laying out of a large public square designed to accommodate many people represents the democratic tendencies of a tyrant who ruled, according to Aristotle (14.3), "in a manner more constitutional than tyrannical" and whose tenure was described as follows: (16.7–9) "And in all other matters too he gave the multitude no trouble during his rule, but always worked for peace and safeguarded tranquillity; so that men were often to be heard saying that the tyranny of Peisistratos was the Golden Age of Kronos; for it came about later when his son succeeded him that the government became much

harsher. And the greatest of all the things said of him was that he was popular and kindly in temper. For he was willing to administer everything according to the laws in all matters, never giving himself any advantage ... Both the notables and the men of the people were most of them willing for him to govern, since he won over the former by his hospitality, and the latter by his assistance in their private affairs, and was good-natured to both." Herodotos (1.59) also portrayed Peisistratos' reign in a positive light: "he administered the state according to the established usages, and his arrangements were wise and salutary." Thucydides' account (6.54.5–7) of the tyranny is equally favorable.

However one chooses to interpret it, the archaeological evidence suggests that the Agora, the focal point of Athenian public life, was, in the first instance, the work largely of Peisistratos and his sons. It may well be that Peisistratos in enlisting the support of the poorer element of Athenian society to counterbalance the richer, more established, and conservative Alkmaionidai merely set the stage for a similar revolt by Kleisthenes, using a similar tactic, several decades later. When one turns to the dedications on the Athenian Acropolis the evidence is slight but interesting. There are no dedications which preserve the name of any of the Peisistratids. Those dedications which preserve the names in this period often include professions sounding not much like landed aristocracy: an architect, a shipbuilder, and several potters.[16]

Kleisthenes, an Alkmaionid, was said to have been the man who thought to bribe the Delphic oracle (Hdt. 5.66) and then contended with Isagoras for power after the overthrow of the Peisistratids. He fared ill at first and in the end, like Peisistratos, drew his support from the common people according to Herodotos (5.66;69). The creation of the ten new tribes and its impact on the development of democracy needs no recitation here, where we meet to celebrate this remarkable achievement. The Kleisthenic reforms represent one step in a series of events stretching from Solon to Perikles which led to a democratic Athens. It has been suggested here that some of the first steps may have been taken by Peisistratos and his sons, and later the creation of the Athenian fleet under Themistokles was certainly an important step as well. Kleisthenes' great contribution was, of course, the breaking of control by the land-based aristocracy and the dissolution of the spheres of influence based on geography of the sort we have been examining.

What is impressive about the Kleisthenic reforms is the speed with which the democracy took root. This may best be appreciated from the monuments of the city. I have suggested above that in the sixth century much if not all of the religious architecture in Athens and Attica should be seen as sponsored not by the state, but by wealthy individuals or by the great families. The concept of the 'people' as the sponsors of public works is a result of the Kleisthenic reforms. The great temple of Athena Polias on the Acropolis as we have seen may well have been the first building built by the Athenians. Of 394 dedications recorded by Raubitschek in his *Dedications of the Athenian Acropolis*, a total of three seem to have been public. The earliest is the chariot group set up to commemorate the victory over the Boiotians and Chalcidians in 506 B.C., just a year or so after the Kleisthenic reforms. Herodotos (5.78), in describing this monument, offered one of the most telling assessments of the new form of government: "Thus did the Athenians increase in strength. And it is plain enough, not from this istance only, but from many everywhere, that freedom is an excellent thing; since even the Athenians, who, while they continued under the rule of tyrants, were not a whit more valiant than any of their neighbours, no sooner shook off the yoke than they became decidedly the first of all. These things show that, while undergoing oppression, they let themselves be beaten, since then they worked for a master; but so soon as they got their freedom, each man was eager to do the best he could for himself. So fared it now with the Athenians."

The new government had other requirements and the lower city was soon transformed. Started soon after Kleisthenes' reforms was the *Bouleuterion* (p. 235, Fig. 10), built to house the new *boule* of 500. The assembly of citizens was provided with a meeting place on the Pnyx. The early date originally proposed of ca. 500 B.C. seems to me correct, despite a recent challenge in favor of the more nebulous reforms of 462 B.C. under Ephialtes.[17] The Pnyx in a sense represents, along with the *Bouleuterion*, the essence of Athenian civic awareness as a result of the Kleisthenic reforms, built specifically to house the thousands of citizens who henceforth would decide the future of the city.

Given the rambling nature of this presentation, it might be well to conclude with a brief review of how archaeology may shed light on the origins of Athenian democracy. The evidence seems first to emphasize the extraordinary degree of control the aristocracy exercised over all aspects of Athenian life in the archaic period. From Aristotle, we have long known that political power, in the form of the highest magistracies, was the preserve of the great families. The Alkmaionid associations with Phokis and, perhaps, corresponding Peisistratid relations with Thessaly would seem to suggest further that foreign policy, too, was in the hands of the great families. In economic matters it seems clear that most of the wealth was concentrated in the hands of a few; though if the Alkmaionidai in fact controlled the silver of south Attica, then we have evidence for a substantial discrepancy between Alkmaionidai and Peisistratidai, a disadvantage which led Peisistratos to draw support from the common people, a move which may well be reflected in the early development of the Agora as a civic center. In religious matters, it seems likely that the Alkmaionidai controlled the cult of Poseidon at Sounion, an association which might explain the extraordinary prominence of the god on the Acropolis in the fifth century.[18]

Seen against this background of aristocratic monopoly of political power, economic resources, and cult activity, the success of the Kleisthenic reforms is all the more remarkable. The concepts of full and equal citizenship, of civic awareness, and a sense of the corporate identity of the demos are phenomena of the late sixth century, with meager antecedents. By redrawing the political map of Attica with his ten new tribes, Kleisthenes created an entirely new Athenian society, one which endured in reality for two hundred years and which has remained an ideal for twenty-five hundred. The archaeological evidence would seem to provide a coherent picture of the origins of this extraordinary achievement.

Notes

1. E. Vanderpool, in *Miscellanea Graeca I: Thorikos and the Laurion in Archaic and Classical Times* (Ghent 1975) 33–42. See also G. Dunst, *ZPE* 25 (1977) 243–264. The references to Kephalos and Prokris are in lines 16 and 17.
2. Acropolis 1358: M. Brouskari, *The Acropolis Museum, A Descriptive Catalogue* (Athens 1974) 165–166.
3. E. Dodwell, *A Classical and Topographical Tour Through Greece* (London 1819) I, 209 and G. Umholtz and J. McInerney, "A Sanctuary of Herakles on the Sacred Way to Delphi," *AJA* 95 (1991) 330.
4. For Herakles in Attica: S. Woodford, "Cults of Heracles in Attica," *Studies Presented to George M.A. Hanfmann* (Cambridge, Mass. 1971) 211–226, and A. Matthaiou in *Πρακτικά τῆς Δ' Επιστημονικῆς Συνάντησης ΝΑ. Αττικῆς* (Kalyvia 1993) 81–90.
5. For Prasiai and Athena Pronaia: Bekker, *Anecdota Graeca* 299 and for Phokion from Potamioi: L.A. Tritle, *Phocion the Good* (London 1988) 36–38.
6. On the homeland of the Alkmaionidai see: *Historia* (1960) 143; *BSA* 56 (1961) 189–219; *BSA* 57 (1962) 143–144; *Historia* 12 (1963) 23; *Historia* 16 (1967) 279–286; and Bicknell, *Hist. Einz.* 19 (1972) 4.
7. For Thorikos see H.F. Mussche in this volume, pp. 211–216. For the kouroi of Sounion: G. Papathanasopoulos, *Σούνιον ἱρὸν* (Athens 1983).
8. Artemis Aristoboule: Plutarch, *Themistokles* 22 and J. Threpsiades and E. Vanderpool, "Themistocles' Sanctuary of Artemis Aristoboule," *ArchDelt* 19 (1964) 26–36. The Theseion: Pausanias 1.17.6 and Plutarch *Theseus* 36. The Asklepieion: *IG* II^2, 4960 and L. Beschi, "Il Monumento di Telemachos fondatore dell' Asklepieion ateniese," *ASAtene* N.S. 29/30 (1967/8) 381–426 and 511–517.
9. Here pp. 1–6. A late date was also suggested long ago by Wiegand on the basis of the profiles of the capitals (*Die Archaische poros-Architektur der Akropolis zu Athen* [1904]) and hinted at by L. Shoe on the basis of the profile of the sima: *The Profiles of Greek Mouldings* (Cambridge, Mass. 1936) 34 and pl. XVIII.15.
10. T.L. Shear, Jr., "Tyrants and Buildings in Archaic Athens," in W.A.P. Childs (ed.), *Athens Comes of Age: From Solon to Salamis* (Princeton 1978) 1–19.
11. Note that other early Athenian fountains such as the Enneakrounos at the Kallirhoe springs and Klepsydra represent embellishments of pre-existing springs at their source.
12. F. Kolb, *Agora und Theater* (Berlin 1981). For the orchestra see R.E. Wycherley, *Agora* III, *Literary and Epigraphical Testimonia* (Princeton 1957) 162–163 and 220.
13. Peisistratos and the Panathenaia: W.B. Dinsmoor, *AJA* 37 (1934) 446, nn. 6 and 7 and *Schol.* Aristides, *Panathenaikos* (Dindorf, Vol. III, 323, ll. 27 ff). For the early inscriptions referring to the *dromos*, perhaps our earliest attested state-sponsored public works: A.E. Raubitschek, *Dedications from the Athenian Acropolis* (Cambridge, Mass. 1949) nos. 326–328, on pp. 350–358. Agora racetrack: T.L. Shear, Jr., "The Athenian Agora: Excavations of 1973–1974," *Hesperia* 44 (1975) 362–365; Corinth racetrack: C.K. Williams, "Corinth: Excavations of 1980," *Hesperia* 50 (1981) 2–15 (note that Williams does not believe this area to be the classical agora of Corinth: *Hesperia* 39 [1970] 32–39); Argos racetrack: *BCH* 111 (1987) 585–588. As a result of work in the 1980's, it begins to look as though a running track is the *sine qua non* of the classical agora.
14. In view of Peisistratos' attested association with the Panathenaia (supra n. 13) it is interesting that many of the Panathenaic events not found in the Panhellenic games have a distinctly military character: pyrrhic dance, javelin throw on horseback, apobates, and anthippasia. Note also the special rubric "for warriors" (line 58) for several events in *IG* II^2, 2311, the list of prizes in the Panathenaic games. For an excellent recent treatment of the Panathenaia: J. Neils (ed.), *Goddess and Polis* (Hanover, New Hampshire 1992), especially D. Kyle on the games: 77–102. In the absence of other venues it seems probable that most if not all the events of the Panathenaia, both athletic and musical, will have been held in the Agora in the sixth century B.C.
15. For cavalry archives found in the northwest corner of the Agora see J. Kroll, *Hesperia* 46 (1977) 83 ff. and *Hesperia* 49 (1980) 89–91.
16. Raubitschek (supra n. 13) 464–465.
17. H.A. Thompson, "The Pnyx in Models," *Hesperia* Suppl. 19 (1982) 136–137.
18. For Poseidon on the Acropolis: L.H. Jeffery, "Poseidon on the Acropolis," *Praktika of the 12th International Congress on Classical Archaeology, 1983* 3 (Athens 1988) 124–126.

Ostraka and the Process of Ostrakophoria

Stefan Brenne

Ostracism has always been considered a strange, exceptional institution within the Athenian democracy.[1] Once a year it gave the Athenians the opportunity to expel one fellow-citizen without a trial, a fact already stigmatized in antiquity. Between 487 and 416 B.C. personalities like Aristeides, Themistokles and Kimon were thus expelled, others like Perikles, Alkibiades or Nikias were in danger. But then ostracism seems not to have functioned any longer and went out of use, although maybe not yet abandoned at the time of Aristotle. Its purpose is just one of the unanswered questions concerning ostracism. Some progress on the literary testimonia can be expected from a project at Vienna,[2] but in recent times another source has gained much more attention, the sherds on which the votes were written.[3] In 1853 the first ostrakon was identified.[4] Many ostraka have since turned up in the Kerameikos Excavations and in the Agora Excavations and by 1966 a total of 1,658 ostraka was known.[5] Then a hoard of some 8,500 ostraka was uncovered in the filling of an abandoned Eridanos River bed in the Kerameikos Excavations and stimulated new studies on ostracism.[6] In this paper I shall try to demonstrate how the ostraka supplement the literary evidence for the events before and during the ostrakophoria.

Ostraka and Comedy

According to the *Athenaion Politeia* the question whether an ostrakophoria should be held or not was put to the vote at the κυρία ἐκκλησία of the 6th prytany.[7] If a simple majority agreed, another day was fixed for the ostrakophoria, perhaps before the 8th prytany.[8] It is obvious that the interval was used for propaganda. A considerable number of remarks on ostraka have the same tone as personal attacks in comedies. Therefore the *phallika* at the rural Dionysia in the middle of the month Posideon, if celebrated after the preliminary vote, may have been a platform for defamations; and also the Lenaia in the middle of Gamelion, presumably provided with some sort of forerunner to the comedies later introduced, could have antedated the ostrakophoria. Obviously this kind of propaganda was forceful enough to find its way onto the sherds themselves.[9]

One ostrakon reads: Μεγακλε̄ς ¦ hιπποκράτο̄ς ¦ μοῖχος — "Megakles Hippokratous, adulterer" (Figs. 1–2).[10] Adultery of course was a serious moral and legal offence and as such was prosecuted.[11] But it also was a topic common in the comedies and may have been used as a means of attack in politics as it is today. In this context I

Figs. 1–2. Ostrakon against Megakles Hippokratous. Kerameikos.

Figs. 3–4. Ostrakon against Kimon. Kerameikos.

mention two other ostraka against Megakles in which the voters explained their decision with νέα κόμε̄ — "new hair".[12] One of the possible interpretations is connected with adultery, for in Aristophanes' *Acharnians* we find the note that the hair of adulterers was cut off.[13] Do the ostraka tell about Megakles' fictitious haircut for adultery?

Many of the remarks on ostraka are very difficult to interpret, but this one is not: Κίμων ¦ Μιλτιάδο̄ ¦ 'Ελπινίκην ¦ λαβὼν ¦ ἴτω — "Kimon Miltiadou, take Elpinike and go!" (Figs. 3–4).[14] We know that Kimon and his half-sister were suspected of living as man and wife,[15] and Pseudo-Andokides even hints that this incestuous relationship was the reason for Kimon's dismissal.[16] Later, when Kimon was accused in court, it was Elpinike who tried to intervene and to influence Perikles.[17] The ostrakon proves that Elpinike was a public figure and even, perhaps, that the rumor of her affair with Kimon was contemporary — by the way, just the sort of thing comedy writers exploited. The scholiast on Aristeides even holds them responsible, particularly Eupolis[18] — a misjudgement as far as Eupolis is concerned, but he might be essentially right.

This ostrakon is even more explicit: Θεμιστοκλε̄ς ¦ καταπύγο̄ν ¦ Νεοκλέο̄ς (Figs. 5–6), described by Mattingly as: "... unprintable — or would once have been".[19] It accuses Themistokles of lewdness or more concretely and literally of being presumably the passive partner in practising anal homosexuality. Parallels on contemporary graffiti have been found in the Agora Excavations,[20] and the word is, as we could have expected, in the repertory of Aristophanes.[21] Pederasty was or had been a part of aristocratic upbringing, but the role here attributed to Themistokles did not fit an adult man.[22] Political leaders have to have a clean slate, and morality is always an easy target in satire and comedy.[23]

Plutarch's Anecdote

At the fixed day for the ostrakophoria the citizens gathered in the agora to cast their vote. Not much is said about the

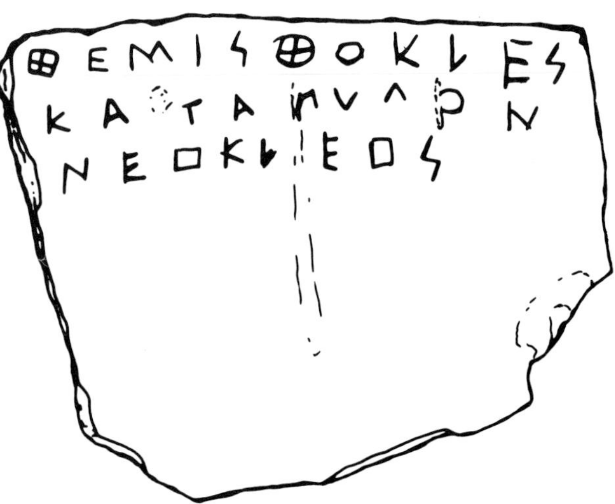

Figs. 5–6. Ostrakon against Themistokles.

Fig. 7. Ostrakon against Leagros.

time before the voting or where, when and how the ostraka were inscribed, but we do have Plutarch's lovely andecdote about the illiterate peasant. At the day of the voting he came to Athens and asked Aristeides, whom he did not recognize, to inscribe a sherd against Aristeides himself just because he did not like his being called "the Just". Aristeides wrote — and once again deserved his nickname.[24] We get some impressions:

— The individual motivation of the voters could have been merely private rather than political.

— The time immediately before the voting was used by the voters for discussing the subject.

— Each person was responsible for bringing his own voting sherd and for the inscription.

— At this stage of the voting secrecy regarding the ballots was not intended.

Let us have a look, whether these points can be confirmed by the ostraka.

There are remarks on ostraka that must express personal grudges although we cannot recapture the specific occasion, like: Λέαγρος ¦ Γλαύκονος ¦ βάσκανος – "Leagros Glaukonos, slanderer" (fig. 7)[25] or: [Μεγα]κ̣λέε̄ς ¦ hιπποκράτο̄ς ¦ Ἀλο̄πεκε̄θεν ¦ δρυμο̄ ¦ h<έ>νεκα – "Megakles Hippokratous from Alopeke, on account of the coppice" (Figs. 8–9).[26] In the first example someone must have felt insulted by Leagros, in the second a loss of property caused by Megakles seems to be the reason for the vote. Like the examples given above most of the remarks on ostraka belong to low-level slogans easily propagated, so that they can hardly be used for the reconstruction of the political background of the law as such, not even of the individual events.[27] They should rather be considered as the view of the man in the street, perhaps best shown in the gossipy pseudo-Andokidean speech, comparable with today's tabloid press.

Besides Elpinike the other woman appearing on ostraka is Koisyra: Μεγακλε̄ς ¦ hιπποκράτο̄ς ¦ καὶ Κοισύρας (Fig. 10), characterized as Megakles' mother by the genitive

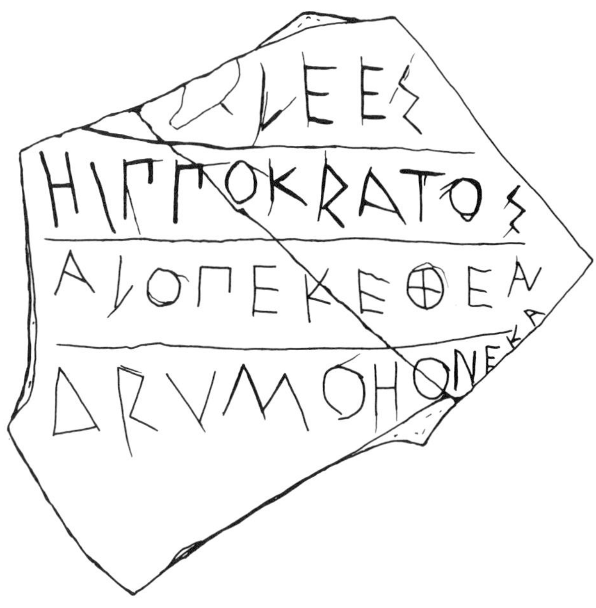

Figs. 8–9. Ostrakon against Megakles. Kerameikos.

ending.[28] I shall not enter the discussion of how many women named Koisyra there were and who they were.[29] Her association with Megakles on ostraka certainly is to be explained by her luxurious life-style that became a byword for arrogance. In this context it is interesting that at least five writers thought about that topic, so either it was a common one or it was discussed while the ostraka were being inscribed.

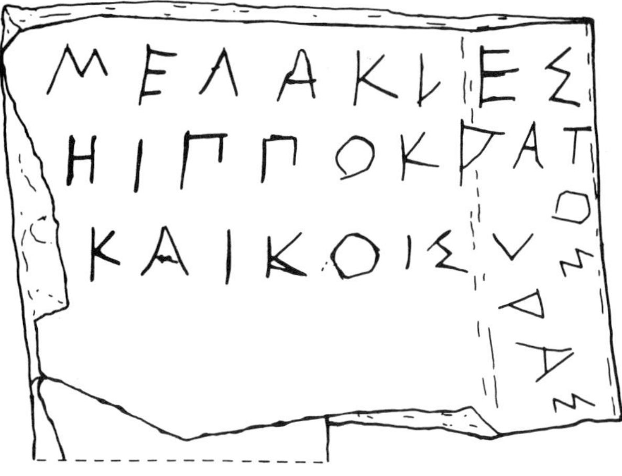

Fig. 10. Ostrakon against Megakles. Kerameikos.

On the reverse of one of the Koisyra ostraka we find the drawing of a knight, obviously a representation of Megakles himself,[30] perhaps a reaction against the knights as a social class and political group, but mainly alluding to the high-living Koisyra and the aristocratic connotations of the equestrian context. Just remember Pheidippides in Aristophanes' *Clouds*: The second part of his name is explicitly explained as alluding to the aristocratic love for names with "horse" and to his uncle Megakles, Olympic winner of the chariot race, who, as Pheidippides says later, would not leave him without a horse.[31] Note the parallel to Megakles' ostracized ancestor, who is called a horse-rearer on two sherds: Μεγακλε̄ς | hιπποκράτο̄ς | hιπποτρόφος (Figs. 11–13).[32] Both ostraka seem to be written by the same hand. So we can add the observation, that even such exceptional ostraka could have been prepared in advance and distributed.

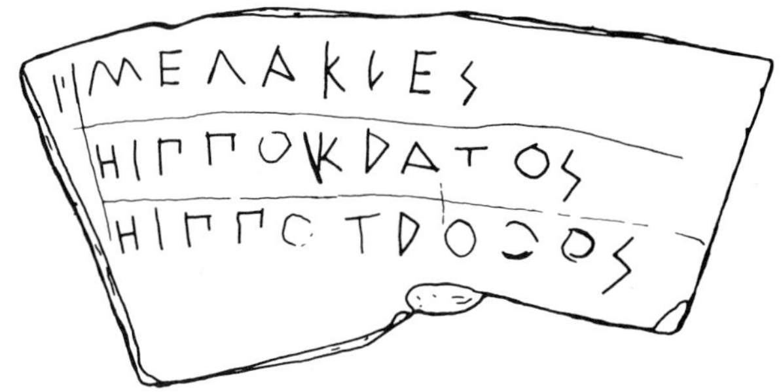

Fig. 11. Ostrakon against Megakles. Kerameikos.

In this connexion another ostrakon is even more interesting: Μεγακλέε̄ς | hιπποκράτο̄( ) | ἀλειτε̄ρός — "Megakles Hippokratous, cursed" (Fig. 14),[33] which means, with the Kylonian curse burdening the Alkmeonidai[34] as proven by another ostrakon: Μεγακλε̄ς | hιποκράτ( )| Κυλο̄νε<ι>ος — "Megakles Hippokratous, descendant of Kylon" (Figs. 15–16).[35] The inscription of the ostrakon with ἀλειτε̄ρός, although regular spacing seems to be intended, is of lesser quality than the joining sherd that is written neatly and stoichedon. But with this model we can restore the fourth, scratched-out line of the second ostrakon as identical with the first: Μεγακλέα | hιπποκράτο̄ς | 'Αλο̄πεκε̄θεν | [[ἀλ̣ε̣ιτε̄ρ]]ο̣( ) (Fig. 17).[36] Obviously two voters obtained their sherds together and had a discussion about their candidate. Who copied whom we cannot tell, the one attempting to imitate the stoichedon or the other adopting the remark and changing his mind without having finished, but we can almost see them sticking their heads together and hear them exchanging gossip about the accursed Megakles.

The ostraka confirm that there was no rule for the procedure before the voters entered the voting-place.[37] Some ostraka definitely were prepared in advance, such as the lot of unused Themistokles ostraka from a well on the Acropolis

Figs. 12–13. Ostrakon against Megakles. Kerameikos.

14.

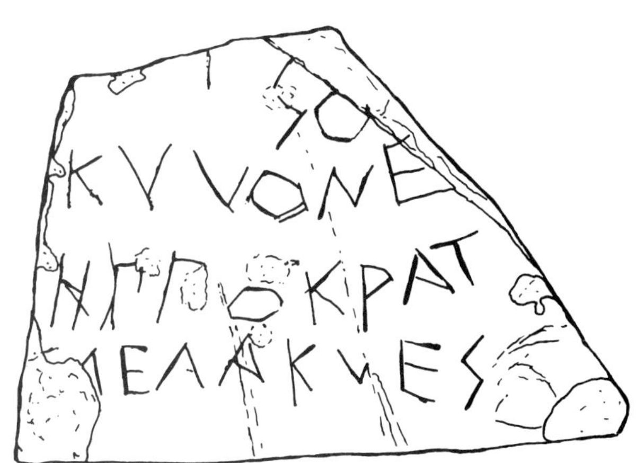

15. 16.

17.

Figs. 14–17. Ostraka against Megakles. Kerameikos.

North slope,[38] or those written with glaze and fired in a potter's kiln, one of which has been found in the Agora against Kallixenos,[39] another in the Kerameikos against Menon.[40] The great variety of vessels or tiles from which the sherds came and the variety of hand-writings demonstrate that the ostraka were prepared individually, but there are exceptions. The prepared Themistokles ostraka were inscribed by just a few writers, and Lang recognized a group of seven ostraka against Kallixenos as having been produced by only one writer.[41] Another scribe may be added, who wrote Kallias Didymiou with black ink on fragments of clay discs. This suggestion was already made by E. Vanderpool and M. Lang for the single one in the Agora[42] and is now confirmed by another two in the Kerameikos Excavations (Figs. 18–19).[43] A second hand might have been involved, because two more ostraka against Kallias Didymiou are written with ink on the same sort of sherds, but with taller letters and a thinner writing instrument.[44] Note also the

18

19

Figs. 18–19. Ostraka against Kallias Didymiou. Agora P 5946; Kerameilos.

difference between the curved and straight-line forms of *upsilon*. The question was raised by D. J. Phillips and M. Lang, whether those scribes were interested in distributing ostraka with certain names and therefore politically motivated or whether they could also be uninvolved, simply selling prepared ostraka or paid for lettering ostraka with different names.[45] The question can now be answered, for the Kerameikos ostraka provide new evidence and a new starting point through many joins made by F. Willemsen.

In contrast to research in identifying hands on stone inscriptions,[46] we are dealing with very short texts and often non-diagnostic letters and therefore have to develop criteria similar to those used in modern graphology.[47] The exceptional circumstance that 190 unused Themistokles ostraka were found together enabled O. Broneer to isolate several different hands. In the huge Kerameikos Deposit one has to depend on joins of ostraka against the same person[48] as, for example, the four joining sherds against Megakles (Fig. 20),[49] obviously inscribed by the same hand.

Now we can be sure that there are ostraka against different persons inscribed by the same hand, for example,

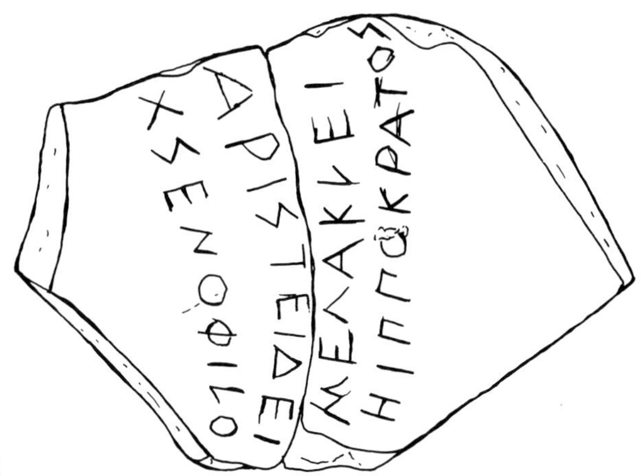

Figs. 21–22. Ostraka against Megakles and Aristeides Xenophilou. Kerameikos.

two sherds against Megakles and Aristeides Xenophilou (Figs. 21–22),[50] the latter a victorious choregos in 477/6 B.C. He may have come from Alopeke like Aristeides the Just[51] and been the Archon of 489/8 B.C.[52] One hand wrote two joining ostraka, one against Megakles and one against Kallikrates Lamprokleous (Fig. 23),[53] against whom six ostraka are directed, but who is otherwise unknown to us.[54] In this case yet another joining ostrakon against Kallikrates and another ostrakon against Megakles, which comes from the same vessel, show similiarities and may therefore have been copied, but seemingly by another writer (Fig. 24).[55] Note the similar distribution of the letters but the rounded *omicron* and the untailed *rho*, although letters as different as these can also be used together on one single sherd. So here we seem to deal with neutral scribes. I would not go further, because in other such cases the writing is not always as neat as one would expect for a professional and trained scribe.

But what if joining sherds are inscribed by different writers like the two ostraka against Megakles and one each

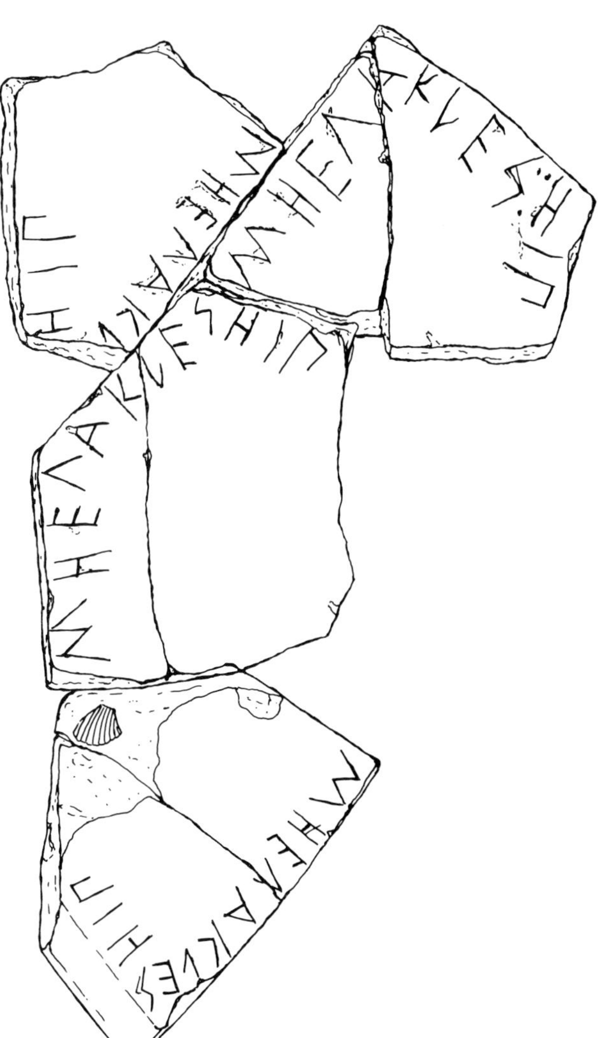

Fig. 20. Ostraka against Megakles. Kerameikos.

Fig. 23. Ostraka against Megakles and Kallikrates Lamprokleous. Kerameikos.

Fig. 24. Ostrakon against Megakles. Kerameikos.

Fig. 25. Ostraka against Hippokrates Anaxileo, Megakles and Themistokles. Kerameikos.

against Themistokles and Hippokrates Anaxileo (Fig. 25)?[56] Leaving aside the not very probable assumption that uninscribed sherds were handed out to the voters by the officials, we have to imagine a quite interesting scene: a vessel or a fragment too big to serve as a single ostrakon was broken up shortly before the voting and distributed among voters with different targets. These examples give the impression that the voters were not separated into well organized political groups. Thus we have seen parallels to almost every aspect of Plutarch's anecdote.[57]

Entering the Polling-station

A place in the Agora was fenced off for the voting itself. The findspots of the ostraka provide no information for the location of this περισχοίνισμα, but it is thought to have been somewhere in front of the Stoa Basileios and might be connected with the archaic orchestra.[58] The voters entered, separated by tribes,[59] checked by the boule and archons, who presided over the voting. According to Philochoros they carried the ostraka with the inscription turned over.[60] There must have been some kind of control, certainly that everyone entering had a vote and maybe that he carried just one sherd. As we see from the ostraka of different sizes, such a precaution might indeed have been necessary. How easy it would have been to hide a small and unobtrusive sherd under a bigger one, if you carried them in the flat hand! Therefore

Fig. 26. Ostrakon against "Limos". Kerameikos.

in my mind's eye I see the voters carrying the sherds with the hand open and holding it between two fingers only.

The idea of turning the inscription over suggests that some secrecy was intended now that the voters were facing the officials, but this rule cannot have been handled too strictly or might have been optional. There are some ostraka inscribed on both sides or even all over so that the inscription could not have been hidden easily. One ostrakon calls Kallias a Persian on one side and illustrates this statement on the other side with the sketchy drawing of a bearded Persian warrior, wearing tiara, long trousers, pointed shoes and holding a bow.[61] No less than 16 ostraka relating Kallias to Persia show that this topic was well known. So we are forced to assume that the drawing was enough to recognize Kallias even if the written name was not visible. And it is even more confusing that the remark Με̄δος is scratched out. Is it possible that there were restrictions after all on what was allowed in the text and what not? Perhaps the writer was afraid to spoil his vote and decided to replace the remark with the drawing. Compare the scratched-out remark ἀλειτερός for Megakles. Some voters for sure wasted their votes and put Λιμός on their ostrakon, no person but the personification of hunger:[62] τὸν Λιμὸν ὀστρακίδō — "The hunger I expel" (Fig. 26).[63]

Most of the over 700 ostraka against Kallias Kratiou from the Kerameikos were found apart from the main bulk of ostraka which are directed mostly against Megakles and Themistokles.[64] Therefore it was assumed that Kallias was voted against in a separate ostrakophoria, and he was even taken for the unknown man ostracized in 485 B.C. with far-reaching consequences for the history of this time.[65] Now that F. Willemsen has found joins between Kallias ostraka and those against Megakles (Figs. 27–29)[66] and Themistokles

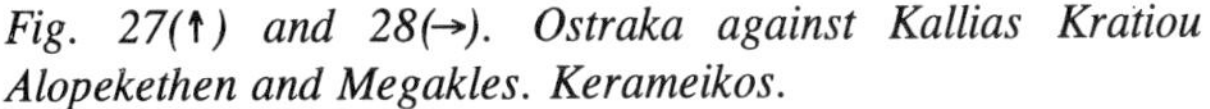

Fig. 27(↑) and 28(→). Ostraka against Kallias Kratiou Alopekethen and Megakles. Kerameikos.

Fig. 29. Ostraka against Kallias Alopekethen and Megakles. Kerameikos.

(Fig. 30),[67] and now that the dispute over the date of the Kerameikos ostraka seems to be settled in favour of the 470s,[68] the Kallias ostraka must also be dated after the Persian wars.

Fig. 30. Ostraka against Kallias and Themistokles. Kerameikos.

Counting the Ostraka and the Consequences

After the ostraka were cast they were counted. Maybe the procedure is shown on a cup of the Pan Painter around 470 B.C.[69] Much has been said about the problem whether a quorum of 6,000 votes was required for the voting to be valid or whether someone had to receive 6,000 votes to be exiled.[70] The ostraka are of no help in this problem, not even the more than 4,400 ostraka against Megakles,[71] a number quite close to 6,000 for a single person, but the evidence for a quorum of 6,000 votes is better and should be accepted. The counting must have been done by all nine archons simultaneously, for one person counting to 6,000 would have lasted at least two hours, and deciphering and sorting the votes must have been a time-consuming business. In spite of this technical problem Plutarch seems to indicate that the ostraka were counted twice,[72] first to make sure the quorum was fulfilled and second to determine the result. Probably the idea was that in this way if the vote was invalid nobody would know who had the most votes. It would have been more practical if the voters were counted at the entrances to assure that the required number of votes was reached, or even, that the space of the περισχοίνισμα was calculated for a certain number of persons as was assumed for the Pnyx.[73]

The man who lost had to leave Attica within ten days for ten years without losing his property. After that, or having been recalled sooner, he took his place as a responsible citizen as if nothing had happened. He just had to leave Attica for the set time. When the ostracized were recalled in 480 B.C., while Xerxes' army was on the march, they were gathered on Salamis, near enough to be at hand and on Attic property, but outside of the politically organized area, for Salamis was not a deme. After the war the restricted area was redefined. The ostracized had to live outside the southern capes of Euboia and Troizen that marked the entrance to the Saronic Gulf, so obviously the ostracized were expected to leave by ship.[74] Even after this law was passed, Eretria for example, although less than one hour away from Attica across the Euripus, could have been thought of as a place of exile as shown by an ostrakon against Megakles: [Μεγ]ακλε̄ς ¦ [hιπ]οκράτο̄ς ¦ [1–2 πά]λι ἔχσο ¦ [3–4] εἰσέλθεις : ΜΕρετρ[ί]αζε.[75] This conclusion can be drawn independently from the two different possibile readings of the text: "Megakles out again where he came from, to Eretria" or: "Megakles out again where he came from, but not to Eretria".[76]

There must have been an official procedure, marking the stages of holding the ostrakophoria. We might seek a reflection of this on the ostraka and look at the distribution of the cases in which the names are given. Of the identified cases 87.4% are in the nominative, 0.1% in the genitive, 9.8% in the dative and 2.7% in the accusative, leaving aside some possible slight revisions in the final publication of the Kerameikos ostraka. So there is some probability that the inscriptions responded to a question something like this: "Who shall be ostracized?" or "Who shall go?" rather than "Whose sherd is this?", "To whom do we give the ostrakon?" or "Whom do we want to be ostracized?", but now we may be stretching the possibilities of interpreting the ostraka.

Certainly there are more questions the ostraka could be asked, as: who attended the voting, can the social status of the voters be ascertained, can their home districts be determined by the quality of the writing or the provenience of the candidates on scattervotes? But I think we have seen enough to create a vivid picture of the process of ostrakophoria and of political and personal interaction, a contribution to our unterstanding of the routine in the developing Athenian democracy.

Acknowledgements

I wish to thank F. Willemsen for unlimited access to the Kerameikos material, the Agora Excavations for the permission to study and draw the ostrakon against Kallias Didymiou, P. Siewert for the suggestions he made and J. Binder for reading and correcting the paper. Illustrations by the author.

Abbreviations

Lang — M. Lang, *Agora* XXV: *Ostraka* (Princeton 1990).

Mattingly — H.B. Mattingly, "Facts and Artifacts: the Researcher and his Tools," *University of Leeds Review* 14 (1971) 277–97.

Phillips — D.J. Phillips, "Athenian Ostracism," in G. H. R. Horsley (ed.), *Hellenika. Essays on Greek Politics and History* (North Ryde 1982) 21–43.

Vanderpool — E. Vanderpool, "Ostracism at Athens," *Lectures in Memory of L.T.Semple* II (Cincinnati 1973) 215–70.

Notes

1. The brief outline by Phillips and the report on the literature by M. Martin, "L'ostracisme athénien," *REG* 102 (1989) 125–43 are very helpful. Most recently: E. Stein-Hölkeskamp, *Adelskultur und Polisgesellschaft* (Stuttgart 1989) 193–204; D. Stockton, *The Classical Athenian Democracy* (Oxford 1991) 33–41; C. Schubert, *Die Macht des Volkes und die Ohnmacht des Denkens* (Wiesbaden 1993) 20–31.
2. Begun by A. E. Raubitschek and now supervised by P. Siewert. The first volume on the prehellenistic authors is announced for 1994.
3. The first systematic approach to the ostraka was made by A. E. Raubitschek, "Ostracism," *Actes du deuxième congrès international d'épigraphie grecque et latine, 1952* (Paris 1953) 59–74 = "Athenian Ostracism," *CJ* 48 (1953) 113–22. The most complete treatment to date is that of Vanderpool.
4. G. Chrysides, *ArchEph* (1853) 777–8, no. 1300 bis; *IG* I^3 915.
5. R. Meiggs and D. Lewis, *A Selection of Greek Historical Inscriptions to the End of the Fifth Century B.C.*^{2} (Oxford 1988) 40–47, no. 21; 311, no. 21. The Agora ostraka are now published by Lang.
6. F. Willemsen, "Die Ausgrabungen im Kerameikos 1966," *ArchDelt* 23 (1968) Chron. 24–32; R. Thomsen, *The Origin of Ostracism* (Gyldendal 1972) 61–108; F. Willemsen and S. Brenne, "Verzeichnis der Kerameikos-Ostraka," *AM* 106 (1991) 147–56. For a bibliography on the Kerameikos ostraka: F. D. Harvey, "Bibliographical Note," *Klio* 66 (1984) 72–73; Willemsen and Brenne 147, n. 5.
7. Arist. *Ath. Pol.* 43.5.
8. Philochoros, *FGrHist* 328 F 30; Phillips 34 n. 8.
9. S. Brenne, ""Portraits" auf Ostraka," *AM* 107 (1992) 161–185. On the chronology J. D. Mikalson, *The Sacred and Civic Calendar of the Athenian Year* (Princeton 1975) 97, 110.
10. Kerameikos, unpublished. Mentioned by Mattingly 283.
11. W. Erdmann, *Die Ehe im alten Griechenland* (Munich 1934) 286–99. A. R. W. Harrison, *The Law of Athens* I (Oxford 1968) 32–38; K. J. Dover, "Classical Greek Attitudes to Sexual Behaviour," *Arethusa* 6 (1973) 61–62; S. G. Cole, "Greek Sanctions Against Sexual Assault," *CP* 79 (1984) 97–113.
12. Brenne (supra n. 9).
13. Ar. *Ach.* 849.
14. Kerameikos, unpublished. Mentioned by Mattingly 284 with n. 9.
15. Nep. *Cim.* 1.2; Plut. *Kim.* 4.7, 15.3; Schol. Aristeides 515 (Dindorf) and the following note.
16. [Andok.] 4.33; Ath. 13.589E.
17. Plut. *Kim.* 14.4, *Per.* 10.6; Ath. 13.589E.
18. Schol. Aristeides 515 (Dindorf), obviously derived from Eupolis F 221 (Kassel — Austin, *PCG*).
19. Kerameikos, unpublished. Mattingly 285.
20. M. Lang, *Agora* XXI: *Graffiti and Dipinti* (Princeton 1976) 14, no. C 22, 24–27.
21. Ar. *Ach.* 79, *Vesp.* 687. K. J. Dover, *Greek Homosexuality* (London 1978) 141–3.
22. Dover (supra n. 21) 100–109, 142–8.
23. V. Hunter, "Gossip and the Politics of Reputation in Classical Athens," *Phoenix* 44 (1990) 309–16.
24. Plut. *Aristeides* 7.7–8.
25. Kerameikos, unpublished. Mentioned by Mattingly 286.
26. Kerameikos, unpublished.
27. For such attempts, e.g.: J. H. Schreiner, "The Origin of Ostracism Again," *ClMed* 31 (1970) 84–97; P. Siewert, "Accuse contro i "candidati" all'ostracismo per la loro condotta politica e morale," in M. Sordi (ed.), *L'Immagine dell'uomo politico: vita pubblica e morale nell'antichità, Contributi dell'Istituto di storia antica* 17 (Milan 1991) 3–14.
28. Kerameikos, unpublished. Mentioned by Mattingly 283 and quoted by P. J. Rhodes, *A Commentary on the Aristotelian Athenaion Politeia* (Oxford 1981) 204.
29. T. L. Shear, Jr., "Koisyra: Three Women of Athens," *Phoenix* 17 (1963) 99–112; J. K. Davies, *Athenian Propertied Families 600 — 300 B.C.* (Oxford 1971) 380–1; R. D. Cromey, "On Deinomache," *Historia* 33 (1984) 389–90; B. M. Lavelle, "Koisyra and Megakles, the Son of Hippokrates," *GRBS* 30 (1989) 503–13.
30. Kerameikos, Brenne (supra n. 9) 162–164.
31. Ar. *Nub.* 60–74, 124–5.
32. Kerameikos, unpublished. Mentioned by Mattingly 283. There are more ostraka connecting Megakles with his horses.
33. Kerameikos, unpublished. Mentioned by D. M. Lewis, "Postscript 1984," in A. R. Burn, *Persia and the Greeks*^{2} (Stanford 1984) 605.

34. G. W. Williams, "The Curse of the Alkmaionidai," *Hermathena* 78 (1951) 32–49, 79 (1952) 3–21, 80 (1953) 58–71; M. W. Dickie, "Pindar's 7th Pythian Ode and the Status of the Alkmeonidai as *Oikos*," Phoenix 33 (1979) 196–203.
35. Kerameikos, unpublished.
36. Kerameikos, unpublished. The last omikron is unfinished.
37. Vanderpool 219–27.
38. O. Broneer, "Excavations on the North Slope of the Acropolis, 1937," *Hesperia* 7 (1938) 228–43; Lang 142–58, pls. 4–11.
39. A. Stamires and E. Vanderpool, "Kallixenos the Alkmeonid," *Hesperia* 19 (1950) 379–81, 390, no. 34, pl. 112; Lang 78, no. 468.
40. Willemsen (supra n. 6) 28, pl. 19 e.
41. Lang 161, fig. 30.
42. Vanderpool 240, fig. 57; Lang 65, no. 311, fig. 11.
43. Kerameikos, unpublished.
44. Kerameikos, unpublished.
45. D. J. Phillips, "Observations on some Ostraka from the Athenian Agora," *ZPE* 83 (1990) 133–6; Lang 161.
46. Some recent studies: H. Mattingly, "Some Fifth-Century Attic Epigraphic Hands," *ZPE* 83 (1990) 110–22; S. V. Tracy, *Attic Letter-Cutters of 229 - 86 B.C.* (Berkeley - Los Angeles - Oxford 1990) 2–6, with reflections on the methods.
47. L. Michel, *Gerichtliche Schriftvergleichung* (Berlin - New York 1982).
48. Broneer (supra n. 38). On the difficulties in such an attempt on sherds without a *tertium comparationis*: S. Dow, "Introduction: The Study of Lettering," in S. V. Tracy, *The Lettering of an Athenian Mason*, *Hesperia* Suppl. 15 (1975) XXI; Lang 161.
49. Kerameikos, unpublished.
50. Kerameikos, unpublished.
51. J. Kirchner, *PA*, no. 1687; Davies (supra n. 29) 52 V.
52. E. Badian, "Archons and Strategoi," *Antichthon* 5, 1971, 12; P. J. Bicknell, "The Archon of 489/8 and the Archonship of Aristeides Lysimachou Alopekethen," *RivFil* 100 (1972) 166–7. Against that view: L. Piccirilli, "Demetrio Falereo e l'arcontato di Aristide — una testimonianza "scomoda"," *AnnPisa* 3.13.3 (1983) 661–4.
53. Kerameikos, unpublished.
54. Willemsen and Brenne (supra n. 6) 152.
55. Kerameikos, unpublished.
56. Kerameikos, unpublished. Mentioned by D. M. Lewis, "The Kerameikos Ostraka," *ZPE* 14 (1974) 4.
57. On a sherd against Aristeides obviously corrected by a more able writer: T. L. Shear, "The Campaign of 1935," *Hesperia* 5 (1936) 39; Vanderpool 230, figs. 41–42.
58. Discussion of the location: F. Kolb, *Agora und Theater, Volks- und Festversammlung* (Berlin 1981) 53–57; B. M. Lavelle, "A Note on Perischoinisma," *RivFil* 10 (1982) 129–39.
59. On the procedure and the sources: Phillips 22 with nn. S. Dow has announced a major study on the ostrakophoria.
60. Philochoros, *FGrHist* 328 F 30: ... ἐτίθεσαν τὰ ὄστρακα, στρέφοντες τὴν ἐπιγραφήν.
61. Kerameikos, Brenne (supra n. 9) 173–177.
62. Willemsen, quoted by Thomsen (supra n. 6) 104 n. 342. Willemsen and Brenne (supra n. 6) 153: Λιμὸς Εὐπ{ρ}ατρίδε̄ς.
63. Kerameikos, unpublished.
64. Willemsen (supra n. 6) 28.
65. G. Daux, *BCH* 92 (1968) 732; G. M. E. Williams, "The Kerameikos Ostraka," *ZPE* 31 (1978) 110–13; id., "Athenian Politics 508/7 - 480 B. C.: a Reappraisal," *Athenaeum* 60 (1982) 533–43; H. A. Shapiro, "Kallias Kratiou Alopekethen," *Hesperia* 51 (1982) 69–73.
66. Kerameikos, unpublished.
67. Kerameikos, unpublished.
68. Lewis (supra n. 56) 1–4; P. J. Bicknell, "Was Megakles Hippokratous Alopekethen Ostracised Twice?" *AntCl* 44 (1975) 172–5; F. Willemsen, "Ostraka einer Meisterschale," *AM* 106 (1991) 141–4.
69. *ARV*[2] 559, no. 152; T. B. L. Webster, *Potter and Patron in Classical Athens* (London 1972) 142, pl. 16 b.
70. Discussed by Phillips 24–25 with nn. On the value of *Cod. Vat. gr.* 1144 for this aspect: G. A. Lehmann, "Der Ostrakismos-Entscheid in Athen," *ZPE* 41 (1981) 95.
71. Willemsen and Brenne (supra n. 6) 153.
72. Plut. *Aristeides* 7.5; Phillips 22.
73. M. H. Hansen, "The Athenian "Ecclesia" and the Assembly-Place on the Pnyx," *GRBS* 23 (1982) 241–2
74. Phillips 23 with nn.; discussed in detail by T. J. Figueira, "Residential Restrictions on the Athenian Ostracized," *GRBS* 28 (1987) 281–305.
75. Kerameikos, Willemsen (supra n. 68) 144, pl. 26.3. Lines 1–4 stoichedon. The fifth line is added in somewhat smaller letters beside the first, but there is no reason to assume a different writer, as indicated by D. M. Lewis, "Megakles and Eretria," *ZPE* 96 (1993) 51. The complete name is given just *exempli gratia* and could also have been [Μhεγ]ακλε̃ς [hιππ]οκράτο̄ς, leaving more space for restorations in the third and fourth lines.
76. A. E. Raubitschek "Nicht nach Eretria (Kerameikos Ostrakon 3469)," *ZPE* (forthcoming).

Η περιοχή του ιερού και του θεάτρου του Διονύσου στην Αθήνα

Πέτρος Γ. Καλλιγάς

Η ευρύτερη περιοχή του θεάτρου του Διονύσου στην Αθήνα, ενώ ήταν μία από τις σημαντικώτερες της αρχαίας πόλης, είναι συγχρόνως παραμελημένη ακόμη ανασκαφικά και ερευνητικά (εικ. 1). Αποτέλεσμα αυτής της παραμέλησης είναι η δυσχέρεια στην ορθή ερμηνεία των μνημείων της περιοχής, στην ορθή χρονολόγησή τους και στην διασάφηση της αρχαίας τοπογραφίας. Το γεγονός είναι παράδοξο, καθώς η περιοχή υπήρξε πάντοτε, μαζί με τα παρακείμενα ιερά και ιδίως το θέατρο, χώρος συγκεντρώσεως του αθηναϊκού λαού, κυρίως κατά την περίοδο της ακμής της αθηναϊκής δημοκρατίας, και εκεί παίχθηκαν τα άφθαστα έργα των αρχαίων τραγωδών και κωμωδών.

Η ανάγκη για την έρευνα στην περιοχή γίνεται σήμερα ακόμη πιο επιτακτική λόγω της προοπτικής ανέγερσης του νέου Μουσείου της Ακρόπολης στο ΝΑ. άκρο του χώρου αυτού, στο σημερινό οικόπεδο του Μακρυγιάννη. Τα σχέδια για το νέο Μουσείο προβλέπουν την ενοποίηση του χώρου του Μουσείου με τον αρχαιολογικό χώρο στα βόρειά του, με την κατάργηση της σημερινής οδού, της Διονυσίου Αρεοπαγίτου, τουλάχιστον σε αυτό το τμήμα.[1] Με τον τρόπο όμως αυτόν ο χώρος στα νότια του αρχαίου θεάτρου, που ήταν μέχρι πρόσφατα η παραμελημένη άκρη του αρχαιολογικού χώρου του θεάτρου, αποκτά πρωτεύουσα σημασία και θα απαιτήσει διαμόρφωση προσβάσεων προς και από το νέο Μουσείο. Είναι φανερό ότι απαιτείται σύντομα ένα μεγάλο πρόγραμμα ανασκαφών από την περιοχή του οικοπέδου Μακρυγιάννη μέχρι τα ριζά του Ιερού Βράχου στα βόρεια. Η προς έρευνα περιοχή θα εκτείνεται, σε πλάτος, από την ΝΑ. γωνία του βράχου μέχρι την περιοχή του Ασκληπιείου στα δυτικά του θεάτρου. Η συντομία του διαθέσιμου χρόνου για την ανακοίνωση επιτρέπει μια σύντομη μόνο περιδιάβαση του χώρου με την βοήθεια του πολύτιμου παλαιού περιηγητή, του Παυσανία (1.20–21), και την επισήμανση των προβλημάτων και των για την ώρα συμπερασμάτων.

Κατ' αρχήν πρέπει να σημειωθεί ότι μεγάλο τμήμα του χώρου αυτού μέχρι πριν από λίγες δεκαετίες καταλαμβάνονταν από ολόκληρο τμήμα του νεώτερου οικισμού της Πλάκας. Τα μικρά σπίτια με την δαιδαλώδη ρυμοτομία έφθαναν μέχρι την άκρη του ιερού του Διονύσου και την ανατολική πρόσβαση του θεάτρου. Από το 1961 άρχισε εκτεταμένο πρόγραμμα απαλλοτριώσεων και στη συνέχεια κατεδαφίσεων, ώστε να αποδοθεί ο χώρος για αρχαιολογική έρευνα.[2] Αλλά ενώ στις αρχές της δεκαετίας αυτής ο ρυθμός των κατεδαφίσεων ήταν αργός και επέτρεπε την περισυλλογή και καταγραφή των αρχαίων καταλοίπων που ήταν εντοιχισμένα στα νεώτερα σπίτια, στη συνέχεια ο ρυθμός επιταχύνθηκε και χρησιμοποιήθηκαν και μηχανικά μέσα. Αποτέλεσμα ήταν η αποκάλυψη αρχαίων ερειπίων στο μέσον του χώρου χωρίς την καταγραφή των ανασκαφικών στοιχείων και η απομάκρυνση των αρχαίων επιχώσεων. Σήμερα η περιοχή οριοθετείται από την οδό Θρασύλλου.

Το ιερό του Διονύσου Ελευθερέως είναι το σημαντικώτερο και αρχαιότερο ιερό της περιοχής. Στην αρχική του μορφή, στα τέλη του 6ου αι. π.Χ., περιελάμβανε μικρόν λίθινο ναό εν παραστάσι αφιερωμένο στον Διόνυσο Ελευθερέα και τον παρακείμενο προς βορράν θεατρικό χώρο, με απλή διαμόρφωση της ορχήστρας και του κοίλου στην πλαγιά του λόφου της Ακρόπολης.[3] Περιορισμένες βελτιωτικές εργασίες στην περιοχή της ορχήστρας και του κοίλου στον 5ο αι. π.Χ. επέτρεψαν την ανετώτερη διαρρύθμιση του χώρου με ξύλινα ικριώματα. Στον χώρο αυτόν ακούστηκαν για πρώτη φορά τα αξεπέραστα αριστουργήματα του Φρυνίχου, του Αισχύλου, του Σοφοκλή, του Ευριπίδη και του Αριστοφάνη καθώς και των άλλων τραγωδών και κωμωδών του "χρυσού αιώνα." Ο σκηνικός διάκοσμος ήταν απλά ζωγραφισμένοι πίνακες. Το ιερό πάντως του Διονύσου θα απέκτησε την εποχή αυτή περίβολο και πρόπυλο. Στα νότια του χώρου υπήρχε ήδη οδός και παρά αυτήν μικρό παρόδιο ιερό.[4]

Στα χρόνια του Περικλή οικοδομήθηκε στην περιοχή ένα ακόμη κτίσμα. Ήταν ένα παράδοξο κτίσμα, ο Παυσανίας (1.20.4) το χαρακτηρίζει "κατασκεύασμα", και είχε την κυκλοτερή, προφανώς, μορφή της περσικής βασιλικής σκηνής. Ο Πλούταρχος (*Βίος Περικλέους* 13) το περιγράφει ως "περικλινὲς καὶ κάταντες ἐκ μιᾶς κορυφῆς πεποιημένον" και η ξύλινη οροφή του ήταν κατασκευασμένη από τμήματα

Εικ. 1.Ακρόπολη Αθηνών. ΝΑ. κλιτύς. Σχέδιο Κ. Καζαμιάκη.

περσικών πλοίων, λάφυρα του περσικού στόλου που κατανίκησαν οι Αθηναίοι. Ο ρωμαίος αρχιτέκτων Βιτρούβιος (5.21) που ονοματίζει το κτίσμα Ωδείον, το τοποθετεί στα αριστερά της εξόδου του θεάτρου του Διονύσου, δηλαδή στα ανατολικά του. Την ονομασία "Ωδείον" είχε λάβει φαίνεται από νωρίς το κτίσμα, όπως προκύπτει από τη ζωντανή περιγραφή που μας δίνει ο Ανδοκίδης (*Περί Μυστηρίων* 1.38): ένας από τους μάρτυρες της ιερόσυλης πράξης του ακρωτηριασμού των ερμαϊκών στηλών το 415 π.Χ., ο Διοκλείδης, διηγείται πως ενώ ήταν ακόμη νύχτα, αλλά είχε πανσέληνο, βρέθηκε στο πρόπυλο του ιερού του Διονύσου όταν διαπίστωσε πολλούς ανθρώπους να κατεβαίνουν από το Ωδείον προς την ορχήστρα του θεάτρου του Διονύσου και να σχηματίζουν μικρούς κύκλους. Επειδή φοβήθηκε, κρύφτηκε πίσω από τον κίονα του προπύλου και το βάθρο πάνω στο οποίο ήταν στημένο χάλκινο άγαλμα στρατηγού, και παρακολούθησε αθέατος τα γενόμενα, αναγνωρίζοντας όμως μέσα στο φεγγαρόφωτο τα πρόσωπα των δραστών. 'Ολα αυτά τα στοιχεία τοποθετούν αρκετά καλά τη θέση του κτίσματος του Ωδείου του Περικλή, στα ανατολικά του θεάτρου αλλά ψηλότερα από αυτό και μαρτυρούν για την κυκλική μορφή του.

Μετά τα μέσα του 4ου αι. π.Χ., στα χρόνια του ρήτορα Λυκούργου, το θέατρο και το ιερό του Διονύσου υπέστησαν μεγάλες και ριζικές αλλαγές. Τα ξύλινα ικριώματα του κοίλου καταργήθηκαν και το θέατρο επενδύθηκε όλο με λίθινα εδώλια. Διαρρυθμίστηκε η ορχήστρα και σχηματίστηκαν οι πάροδοι του θεάτρου, ανατολικά και δυτικά, με χαρακτηριστικά τους ψηλούς τοίχους, που ως αναλήμματα συγκρατούσαν στα μέρη αυτά το θέατρο. Η βάση και τα θεμέλια του θεάτρου κατασκευάστηκαν από σκληρό (τότε) κροκαλλοπαγή λίθο, ίσως από την περιοχή του Υμηττού, ενώ οι όψεις επενδύθηκαν με μαλακώτερο αλλά ωραίο πωρόλιθο, εξορυγμένο από την περιοχή της ακτής του Πειραιά, τον λεγόμενο γι' αυτό ακτίτη λίθο. Το μεγάλο λίθινο θέατρο του Λυκούργου ανοιγόταν σαν ένα τεράστιο ριπίδιο χωρισμένο σε κερκίδες με κλίμακες ανόδου ενδιάμεσα και φαίνεται ότι έφθανε ψηλά μέχρι που συναντούσε στα ριζά του βράχου τον αρχαίο δρόμο, τον λεγόμενο περίπατο, χωρίς ενδιάμεσο διάζωμα.[5] Ενώ όμως η ακτινωτή ανάπτυξη του κοίλου του θεάτρου είναι ομαλή σε όλες τις πλευρές του, στο ΝΑ. άκρο δημιουργείται ανωμαλία με μία βαθειά ορθογώνια εντομή. Μόνη λογική εξήγηση για το γεγονός αυτό είναι η ύπαρξη ενός προγενέστερου μεγάλου ορθογώνιου κτηρίου στο σημείο αυτό, που εμπόδιζε την κανονική ανάπτυξη του κοίλου και το οποίο ήθελε να διαφυλάξει ο αρχιτέκτων του θεάτρου. Η ερμηνεία αυτή βρήκε τη λύση της όταν στις δεκαετίες 1910–20 ο αρχαιολόγος Π. Καστριώτης διεξήγαγε μακροχρόνιες αλλά περιορισμένες σε έκταση ανασκαφές.[6] Ο Καστριώτης απεκάλυψε μέσα στην εντομή του θεάτρου την βόρεια πλευρά ενός μεγάλου κτίσματος, του οποίου ανέσκαψε και μέρος του δυτικού τοίχου. Η ύπαρξη ακόμη τότε του σύγχρονου οικισμού παρεμπόδιζε την εκτεταμμένη ανασκαφή που έπρεπε να γίνει σε επιχώσεις βάθους περίπου 7 μ.[7] Η απομάκρυνση των νεώτερων οικιών στην περιοχή αυτή στη δεκαετία του 1960 αποκάλυψε συμπληρωματικά μια σειρά ορθογωνίων βάθρων από μαλακό πωρόλιθο που θεωρήθηκε ότι οριοθετεί το κτίσμα στα νότια.[8] Τούτο μαρτυρείται και από μια παράλληλη σειρά βάθρων χορηγικών μνημείων στο σημείο αυτό, που περιορίζουν την έκταση του κτίσματος και επιβεβαίωναν συγχρόνως τη διαδρομή της αρχαίας οδού των Τριπόδων.[9] Τα στοιχεία αυτά μας δίνουν ένα μεγάλο τετράπλευρο κτίσμα (κάθε πλευρά μήκους πάνω από 60 μ.), του οποίου το εσωτερικό είναι ακόμη άσκαφο στο μεγαλύτερό του μέρος. Ο Καστριώτης είχε σπεύσει πάντως να χαρακτηρίσει το κτίσμα ως το Ωδείο του Περικλή, παρά την αντινομία στην μορφή, και η ονομασία έγινε γενικά αποδεκτή μέχρι σήμερα.

Ο κροκαλλοπαγής λίθος που είχε χρησιμοποιηθεί στο λυκούργειο θέατρο, χρησιμοποιήθηκε επίσης στα θεμέλια του δεύτερου ναού του Διονύσου που οικοδομήθηκε στα χρόνια αυτά νότια από τον υστεροαρχαϊκό μικρό ναό, καθώς και της μακράς στοάς στα βόρεια του ιερού, που στραμένη στα νότια έκλεινε πια την επικοινωνία του θεάτρου με το ιερό. Από πωρόλιθο αντίθετα κατασκευάστηκε ο περίβολος του ιερού, που στο ΝΑ. του άκρο, πριν από την κάμψη του προς βορράν σχημάτιζε μία κόγχη για να προστατεύσει το σωζόμενο προφανώς παλαιότερο μικρό παρόδιο ιερό. Πιθανόν ο περίβολος να απέκτησε νέο πρόπυλο στα ανατολικά, όπως και το παλαιότερο της εποχής του Ανδοκίδη, στο σημείο απ' όπου άρχιζε η σημαντική αρχαία οδός που κατευθυνόταν στην περιοχή της πόλης, ακολουθώντας στα πρανή τον βράχο της Ακρόπολης, η οδός των Τριπόδων. Η αρχαία αυτή οδός ήταν άρρηκτα δεμένη με το θέατρο του Διονύσου, αφού οι τρίποδες που στήνονταν δεξιά και αριστερά απ' αυτήν — και απ' όπου έλαβε το όνομά της — ήταν τοποθετημένα πάνω σε αξιόλογα πολλές φορές χορηγικά μνημεία και μνημόνευαν νίκες σε θεατρικούς αγώνες.[10] Αυτή ήταν γενικά η εικόνα που είχαμε για τον χώρο μέχρι το 1980 και οι προτεινόμενες λύσεις είχαν γίνει γενικά αποδεκτές, με εξαίρεση ίσως το χαμήλωμα της χρονολογίας του νεώτερου ναού του Διονύσου και της στοάς στον 4ο αιώνα (αντί στα τέλη του 5ου αι. π.Χ.), που είχε προτείνει ο υποφαινόμενος από το 1962 και κάλυψε με το κύρος του ο αρχιτέκτων Ιωάννης Τραυλός,[11] αλλά συνάντησε ορισμένες αντιρρήσεις και αμφιβολίες.[12]

Το 1980 ένα αναπάντεχο εύρημα ήλθε να διαταράξει τα λιμνάζοντα ύδατα της έρευνας και να τοποθετήσει την τοπογραφία της περιοχής σε νέα βάση. Κατά τη διάρκεια εργασιών διευθετήσεων ψηλά στην ρίζα του βράχου κατά την ανατολική πλευρά, κάτω από το μεγάλο ορατό σπήλαιο, ο τότε έφορος των αρχαιοτήτων Ακροπόλεως Γ. Δοντάς βρήκε κατά χώραν μία μικρή ενεπίγραφη στήλη που φέρει ψηφισματική επιγραφή του 3ου αι. π.Χ. προς τιμή της Τιμοκρίτης, ιέρειας της Αγλαύρου.[13] Τα ολίγα υπόλοιπα ευρήματα επιβεβαιώνουν το γεγονός ότι πρόκειται για ιερό και η στήλη ήταν στερεωμένη πάνω σε βάση και σαφώς βρισκόταν στην αρχική της θέση. Η επιγραφή μνημονεύει την εντολή της λάξευσης *μίας* στήλης με το κείμενο του ψηφίσματος και του στησίματός της στο ιερό της Αγλαύρου, του οποίου έτσι βεβαιώνεται η τοποθεσία. Αναγκαίες μελλοντικές ανασκαφές θα δώσουν ασφαλώς περισσότερα στοιχεία για το ιερό αυτό, που είναι μικρό σε έκταση, σπουδαίο όμως για την τοπογραφία της περιοχής. Η ύπαρξη του ιερού ήταν γνωστή από τις φιλολογικές πηγές, κυρίως τον Ηρόδοτο (8.52–53) και τον Παυσανία (1.18.2–3), αλλά η ακριβής του θέση ήταν άγνωστη και οι μελετητές μέχρι σήμερα το τοποθετούσαν στο μέσον περίπου της διαδρομής του βόρειου τείχους της Ακρόπολης κοντά στο Αρρηφόρειο.

Οι επιπτώσεις όμως από την ταύτιση του Αγλαυρείου στη νέα του θέση, είναι αλυσσιδωτές όπως επισημαίνει ο Γ. Δοντάς, που δημοσίευσε αμέσως το εύρημα. Οι φιλολογικές πηγές αναφέρουν ότι λίγο χαμηλώτερα από το ιερό της Αγλαύρου ήταν το ιερό των Διοσκούρων (το Ανάκειον), ενώ επίσης κοντά ήταν το Πρυτανείο (Παυσανίας 1.18.3: “πλησίον”). Ακόμη, ότι ανάμεσα στο Πρυτανείο και το Ολυμπιείο βρίσκεται το ιερό του Σάραπι. Η αναζήτηση του Πρυτανείου στη νέα του θέση, στα ΒΑ. του θεάτρου του Διονύσου, απέχει πολύ από την μέχρι σήμερα υποστηριζόμενη άποψη, που το 1978 παρουσίασε αναλυτικά ο Stephen Miller, δηλαδή της τοποθέτησής του στα βόρεια της Ακρόπολης.[14] Τώρα, αντίθετα, είναι πια βεβαιωμένο και φανερό ότι θα πρέπει το Πρυτανείο να αναζητηθεί κάπου στην περιοχή ανάμεσα από το θέατρο του Διονύσου και την ΝΑ. γωνία του βράχου της Ακρόπολης, όπου οριστικά το ιερό της Αγλαύρου.[16]

Ως πιθανότερη θέση για το Πρυτανείο, έχω να προτείνω την θέση, όπου μέχρι σήμερα τοποθετείται το κτήριο που ονοματίζεται “Ωδείο του Περικλή,” και σε αυτό βασίζομαι στον Παυσανία που ρητώς αναφέρει (1.20.1), ότι από την περιοχή του Πρυτανείου αρχίζει η οδός των Τριπόδων: “ἔστι δὲ ὁδὸς ἀπὸ τοῦ Πρυτανείου καλουμένη Τρίποδες.” Η άποψη αυτή, εκτός από τα στοιχεία που δίνει για τη θέση ο Miller,[16] επικουρείται και από τη διαπίστωση ότι παρόμοια κτήρια συνδέονται με τα θέατρα, όπως π.χ. το βουλευτήριο (το Θερσίλιον), μπροστά από το θέατρο της Μεγαλόπολης (Παυσ. 8.32.1) ή ο θεατρικός χώρος που διαμορφώνεται παρά το πρυτανείο στη Λατώ της Κρήτης.[17] Επίσης παρουσιάζει ενδιαφέρον το ότι κατά τα μέσα του 4ου αι. π.Χ. με νόμο οι πρυτάνεις χρησιμοποιούν μία φορά το χρόνο το θέατρο του Διονύσου για σύγκληση της εκκλησίας του δήμου για να εξετάζει θέματα που έχουν σχέση με παραβάσεις των θρησκευτικών εορτών, όπως μαθαίνουμε από τον *Κατά Μειδίου* λόγο του Δημοσθένη (21.8–9).[18] Εάν γίνει βέβαια αποδεκτή αυτή η θέση[19] θα πρέπει να αναζητηθούν πλησίον και τα άλλα ιερά, ιδίως των Διοσκούρων, του Σάραπι κτλ. και να βρεθεί νέα θέση για το κυκλικό Ωδείο του Περικλή, ψηλότερα πάντως από την είσοδο του θεάτρου.[20] Είναι φανερό, ότι μόνο με την εκτέλεση οργανωμένων ανασκαφικών ερευνών θα μπορέσουν να βρούν τη λύση τους τα πιο πάνω ενδιαφέροντα τοπογραφικά θέματα, που έχουν σχέση με την οργάνωση και λειτουργία της πόλης της αρχαίας Αθήνας.[21]

Μέχρι τότε πάντως αξίζει να αναφερθούν οι επιμέρους εργασίες που εκτελούνται από την Υπηρεσία στον χώρο κατά τα τελευταία έτη: κατά τα έτη 1978–80 ο γερμανός αρχιτέκτων-μηχανικός W. Würster με τη συνεργασία του τοπογράφου Κ. Καζαμιάκη συνέταξε νέα ακριβή σχέδια της ορχήστρας, του κοίλου και του ανατολικού αναλήμματος του θεάτρου σε κλίματα 1:20.[22] Κατά τα έτη 1980–83 εργάστηκε στο χώρο ο αρχιτέκτων Μ. Κορρές. Σημαντικώτερες συμβολές του ήταν η αναδιάταξη της πλακόστρωσης της ορχήστρας, η ταύτιση και ανασύνταξη βάθρων αναθημάτων στις δύο παρόδους, ιδίως την δυτική, η αναγνώριση και ταύτιση ομοίων προπύλων στις δύο παρόδους, η ανασύνθεση και στήριξη τμημάτων χορηγικού μνημείου με μεγάλο ενεπίγραφο επιστύλιο, η αναγνώριση και σχεδίαση μεγάλου αριθμού αρχιτεκτονικών μελών, ορισμένα από τα οποία αποδίδονται και σε γνωστά μνημεία, κ.α.[23]

Η καταστροφή στην ανατολική πάροδο, που προκλήθηκε από τον σεισμό του 1981, ανάγκασε την Υπηρεσία να αντιμετωπίσει δραστικώτερα το θέμα της στήριξης τμημάτων του θεάτρου. Από το 1984 συστήθηκε ομάδα εργασίας, με πρόεδρο τον Α. Δεληβορριά, για την ανάθεση της μελέτης και την παρακολούθηση της εργασίας. Το έργο ανατέθηκε στην αρχιτέκτονα Ε. Μακρή και την άνοιξη του 1987 οι προτάσεις αποκατάστασης παρουσιάστηκαν σε διεθνές συνέδριο που έγινε στην Αθήνα.[24] Μετά την έγκριση της μελέτης αποκατάστασης, από το καλοκαίρι του 1990, την εκτέλεσή της ανέλαβε η αρχιτέκτων Α. Σαμαρά μετά την αποχώρηση της Ε. Μακρή, κάτω πάντοτε από την εποπτεία της ομάδας εργασίας με πρόεδρο τώρα τον υποφαινόμενο. Παράλληλα με τις εργασίες αυτές ο αρχιτέκτων της Υπηρεσίας Θ. Παπαθανασόπουλος προέβει σε διευθέτηση και καθαρισμό καθώς και νέα μέτρηση του χώρου του κοίλου του θεάτρου και στην κατασκευή στεγάστρου στην άκρη του χώρου, όπου μεταφέρθηκαν για προστασία τα αξιόλογα γλυπτά από την περιοχή του θεάτρου. Ενδιαφέρον παρουσίασε μικρή ανασκαφική έρευνα το 1985 από τον τότε έφορο αρχαιοτήτων Κ. Τσάκο στην περιοχή του κοίλου του θεάτρου πίσω από το ανατολικό ανάλημμα. Η έρευνα έδωσε στοιχεία για την επαναχρονολόγηση του μεσαιωνικού οχυρωματικού έργου του Ριζόκαστρου στα μέσα του 13ου αι. μ.Χ.[25]

Το έργο της αποκατάστασης της ανατολικής παρόδου βαίνει πλέον ικανοποιητικά, παρά τις καθυστερήσεις που οφείλονται κυρίως στην αδυναμία προμήθειας του κατάλληλου υλικού γιά τις αναγκαίες συμπληρώσεις. Μετά από προσπάθειες προμήθειας φυσικού κροκαλλοπαγούς λίθου και την διαπιστούμενη ανομοιογένεια του νέου με το παλαιό υλικό, επελέγει η λύση της κατασκευής τεχνιτού λίθου. Η προμήθεια όμως ακτίτη πωρόλιθου για την επένδυση απέβει πολύ δύσκολη, αφού όλα τα λατομεία του Πειραιά έχουν παύσει από μακρού χρόνου να λειτουργούν και δεν είναι δυνατός ο προσπορισμός παρόμοιου υλικού. Η λύση δόθηκε χάρη στην κατανόηση του Χατζηκυριάκειου Ιδρύματος που στον μεγάλο περιβάλλοντα χώρο του, σώζεται και τμήμα αρχαίου λατομείου.[26] Το αρχαίο λατομείο διαφυλάχτηκε και σχεδιάστηκε και σε απόσταση ανοίχτηκε από μας νέο. Ο προσποριζόμενος πωρόλιθος είναι άριστης ποιότητας και παρά τις αναπόφευκτες καθυστερήσεις, άρχισαν ήδη να αποθηκεύονται στο εργοτάξιο του θεάτρου οι απαραίτητοι λίθοι. Ελπίζεται ότι σύντομα θα μπορέσουνε να επέμβουμε σωστικά στο μνημείο απομακρύνοντας τον κίνδυνο μιας νέας, μεγαλύτερης καταστροφής αυτού του τμήματος. Παράλληλη εργασία συντελείται στον ευρύτερο αρχαιολογικό χώρο και στις αρχαιολογικές αποθήκες, όπου καταλογραφούνται τα διάσπαρτα αρχιτεκτονικά μέλη, με την ελπίδα της σύνταξης ενιαίου ευρετηρίου και της ένταξης των μελών σε μηχανογραφημένο πρόγραμμα.[27]

Το πρόγραμμα της ευρύτερης ανασκαφικής έρευνας πρέπει πάντως να συνδυαστεί και με την αναγκαία διαμόρφωση του χώρου κάθε μνημείου και την απαραίτητη κατάχωση των σήμερα εκτεθειμένων θεμελίων. Η κατάχωση και η προστασία των μερών αυτών από το χώμα είναι η μόνη πρακτική λύση για την διατήρηση των ευπαθών αυτών αρχιτεκτονικών καταλοίπων. Προστασία και συντήρηση απαιτείται και για τα γλυπτά που βρίσκονται κατά χώραν και κυρίως για εκείνα του βήματος του Φαίδρου. Ελπίζεται επίσης ότι όλο το σχετικό εποπτικό υλικό (σχέδια, προπλάσματα, κτλ.) και πληροφορίες για τον χώρο και ιδιαίτερα το μνημείο του θεάτρου του Διονύσου, θα γίνει κατορθωτό να παρουσιαστεί και προβληθεί για το ελληνικό και ξένο κοινό στο παρακείμενο οίκημα της Υπηρεσίας στην οδό Θρασύλλου, παρά τις κακόβουλες προσπάθειες που καταβάλλονται τελευταία να αφαιρεθεί η χρήση του από την Εφορεία μας και να παραδοθεί για άσχετη χρήση σε άλλους. Εφ' όσον θα επιτευχθούν οι πιο πάνω στόχοι, πιστεύουμε ότι θα γίνει κατανοητός και παιδευτικά χρήσιμος ένας από τους πιο σημαντικούς αρχαιολογικούς χώρους της αρχαίας Αθήνας.

Σημειώσεις

1. Προκήρυξη αρχιτεκτονικού διαγωνισμού για το κτήριο και εναλλακτικές λύσεις: *Νέο Μουσείο Ακρόπολης. Διεθνής αρχιτεκτονικός διαγωνισμός*, Υπουργείο Πολιτισμού (Αθήνα 1989). Τα αποτελέσματα του διαγωνισμού: *Νέο Μουσείο Ακρόπολης*, Υπουργείο Πολιτισμού (Αθήνα 1991) (ελληνικά και αγγλικά).
2. Αναφορά στα ευρήματα των κατεδαφίσεων: Π. Καλλιγάς, *ΑρχΔελτ* 18 (1963) Χρονικά 18; Ν. Πλάτων, *ΑρχΔελτ* 19 (1964) Χρονικά 34–37; Ι. Παπαποστόλου, *ΑρχΔελτ* 22 (1967) Χρονικά, 35–6; Γ. Δοντάς, *ΑρχΔελτ* 25 (1970) Χρονικά 30.
3. Travlos, *PDA* 537–552. Για τις διαδοχικές φάσεις του θεάτρου βλ. και πρόσφατα: L. Polacco, *Il Teatro di Dioniso Eleutereo ad Atene* (Roma 1990), αν και ορισμένες θέσεις του συγγραφέα δεν συμφωνούν με τα σωζόμενα στοιχεία.
4. Για τον μικρό πώρινο ναΐσκο: Π. Καλλιγάς, *ΑρχΔελτ* 18 (1963) Χρονικά 16, πίν. 10γ. Ελπίζεται ότι σύντομα μικρή ανασκαφική έρευνα στην περιοχή θα αποσαφηνίσει τη ΝΑ. γωνία του περιβόλου και την διαδρομή του κατά την ανατολική πλευρά του ιερού του Διονύσου.
5. Την απουσία διαζώματος, σε αντίθεση με τους παλαιότερους ερευνητές, υποστηρίζουν οι Μ. Κορρές, *ΑρχΔελτ* 35 (1980) Χρονικά 10–11, σχεδ. 1 και Θ. Παπαθανασόπουλος, *Το θέατρο του Διονύσου — Η μορφή του κοίλου* (Αθήνα 1987) εικ. 47.
6. Πρώτη έρευνα Π. Καστριώτη *Πρακτ* (1914) 81–124 (= *ΑρχΕφ* [1914] 143–166). Βιβλιογραφία για το Ωδείο: Travlos, *PDA* 387–391.
7. Μικρή συμπληρωματική έρευνα από τον Α. Ορλάνδο: *Πρακτ* (1931) 25–36 και *Πρακτ* (1932) 27–8.
8. Πρβλ. Μ. Κορρές, *ΑρχΔελτ* 35 (1980) Χρονικά 16.
9. Μ. Κορρές, *ΑρχΔελτ* 35 (1980) Χρονικά 14 κ.επ. Επίσης σχέδιο του ιδίου στο *Αθήνα — Προϊστορία και Αρχαιότητα*, Υπουργείο Πολιτισμού (Αθήνα 1985) 37.
10. Για τα χορηγικά μνημεία και την οδό Τριπόδων βλ. την ανακοίνωση των Α. Χωρέμη — Κ. Καζαμιάκη στον παρόντα τόμο, σελ. 31–44. Για τις μαρμάρινες ενεπίγραφες βάσεις των τριπόδων των Διονυσίων βλ. P. Amandry, "Trépieds d' Athènes: I. Dionysies," *BCH* 100 (1976) 15–93. Η τριγωνική καμπυλόγραμμη βάση του Δρακοντίδη, που βρέθηκε στις ανασκαφές του "Ωδείου" το 1931 (Ορλάνδος, *Πρακτ* [1931] 35–6, εικ. 12–13) είναι σήμερα στην περιοχή του θεάτρου: Ε. Στίκας, "Τρίπλευρα κιονόκρανα, κορυφώματα και μνημεία," *ΑρχΕφ* (1961) 163, εικ. 9 και Amandry 28–30, εικ. 12–13. Επίσης στα ανατολικά του ιερού του Διονύσου βρίσκεται σήμερα το τμήμα ορθογώνιου ενεπίγραφου χορηγικού βάθρου από τον τοίχο της Αγ. Παρασκευής: Π. Καλλιγάς, *ΑρχΔελτ* 18 (1963) Χρονικά 18, πίν. 14α και Amandry 48–50, εικ. 26–27.
11. Π. Καλλιγάς, *ΑρχΔελτ* 18 (1963) Χρονικά 14–15. Travlos, *PDA* 537.
12. F.E. Winter, "The Stage of New Comedy," *Phoenix* 37 (1983) 38 κ.επ.
13. G. Dontas, "The True Aglaurion," *Hesperia* 52 (1983) 48–63, του ιδίου στα *Πρακτικά του Η' Διεθνούς Συνεδρίου Ελληνικής και Λατινικής Επιγραφικής* 2 (Αθήνα 1987) 147–150. Δες και την ανακοίνωση του T.L. Shear, Jr. στον παρόντα τόμο, σελ. 225–248.
14. S.G. Miller, *The Prytaneion* (Berkeley 1978) 38 κ.επ. Δες και την ανακοίνωση του T.L. Shear, Jr. στον παρόντα τόμο, σελ. 225–248.
15. Τον σύγχρονο προβληματισμό για την πιθανή θέση της αρχαϊκής Αγοράς, του Πρυτανείου και των παρακειμένων κτηρίων ύστερα από την οριστική ταύτιση του Αγλαυρείου, θέτει ο N. Robertson, "Solon's Axones and Kyrbeis, and the Sixth-Century Background," *Historia* 35 (1986) 147–176. Ο μελετητής συνδέει τους "άξονες" των νόμων του Σόλωνα με το Πρυτανείο στην αρχαϊκή αγορά και προσπαθεί να τοποθετήσει τα αναφερόμενα ως παρακείμενα ιερά και κτήρια: σελ. 157–168, εικ. 1. Παράλληλα, ενδιαφέρον παρουσιάζει και η από μέρους του Ι. Δημακόπουλου το 1984 (έγγρ. αναφ.), απόδοση στο αρχαίο Πρυτανείο ενός καλά

σωζόμενου τμήματος αναλημματικού τοίχου, στο βάθος του ακινήτου της σημερινής οδού Τριπόδων 28 (της Ελληνικής Εταιρείας) (p. 38, Figs. 7-8). Ανασκαφή που ακολούθησε τότε από μέρους της Α΄ Εφορείας Αρχαιοτήτων (*ΑρχΔελτ* 44 [1989] Χρονικά, υπό έκδοση) δεν επιβεβαίωσε την υπόθεση του Δημακόπουλου, αλλά κατά την γνώμη μου, ο τοίχος είναι δυνατόν να συνδέεται με τα κτήρια και την εν γένει σε άνδηρα διαμόρφωση της περιοχής της αρχαϊκής Αγοράς. Ελπίζεται ότι οι συνεχιζόμενες, διερευνητικές ανασκαφές της Εφορείας στην περιοχή αυτή της Πλάκας θα οδηγήσουν τελικά σε κάποια πιο συγκεκριμένα συμπεράσματα.

16. Miller (σημ. 14) 45. Πρβλ. και το μεταγενέστερο Σχόλιο στον Θουκυδίδη (2.15.2) όπου το Πρυτανείο χαρακτηρίζεται ως "οἶκος μέγας" (Miller 177, A.242). Για την εσωτερική μορφή του ανασκαφέντος κτίσματος θα πρέπει να σημειωθεί ότι το αποδιδόμενο στο "Ωδείο" μαρμάρινο εδώλιο με ανάγλυφες γλαύκες (Π. Καστριώτης, *Πρακτ* [1914] 110-116, εικ. 18) τώρα αποδίδεται με βεβαιότητα στο Παναθηναϊκό Στάδιο (Μ. Κορρές, *ΑρχΔελτ* 35 [1980] Χρονικά 16 — πρβλ. και Μ. Κορρές *ΑρχΔελτ* 37 [1982] Χρονικά 18). Ο αποδιδόμενος επίσης στο εσωτερικό του "Ωδείου" σπόνδυλος μεγάλου αρράβδωτου κίονα με την αναθηματική επιγραφή στον Αριοβαρζάνη (*Πρακτ* [1914] 108-110, εικ. 17) είναι αμφίβολο εάν συνδέεται πραγματικά με το κτήριο αυτό. Αξιοσημείωτη είναι η τοιχογράφηση των τοίχων του "Ωδείου" (Ορλάνδος, *Πρακτ* [1931] 25, εικ. 2), με στέφανο δάφνης και μικρό αμφορέα.

17. Miller (σημ. 14) 81, εικ. 5.

18. 'Εργο των πρυτάνεων ήταν και ο καθορισμός του χώρου των συνεδριάσεων της Βουλής και της Εκκλησίας του Δήμου: Αριστ. *Αθ.Πολ.* 43.3 ("ὅπου καθίζειν οὗτοι"). Ο P.J. Rhodes, *The Athenian Boule* (Oxford 1972) 16 σημ. 5 επισημαίνει ότι το Πρυτανείο ήταν κυρίως χώρος υποδοχής των τιμωμένων Αθηναίων και ξένων και όχι έδρα των πρυτάνεων, που θα ήταν η Θόλος στην Αρχαία Αγορά. Γενικά για την λειτουργία του Πρυτανείου και για τους δικαιούχους δωρεάν σίτησης βλ. P. Schmitt - Pantel, "Les repas au Prytanée et à la tholos dans l' Athènes classique. Sitesis, trophé, misthos," *Annali - Istituto Universitario Orientale — Archeologia e Storia Antica*, Napoli (1980) 55-68 *και* M.J. Osborne, "Entairtainment in the Prytaneion at Athens," *ZPE* 41 (1981) 153-170.

19. Με το πρυτανείο πρέπει να συνδέεται και μεγάλη μαρμάρινη διπλή ερμαϊκή στήλη με ανάγλυφο υδρίας και κηρυκείου, εύρημα των πρώτων ανασκαφών (Καστριώτης, *Πρακτ* [1914] 103-5, εικ. 5) που σώζεται σήμερα στην περιοχή του θεάτρου του Διονύσου. Είναι γνωστό από τις φιλολογικές πηγές ότι οι κήρυκες και οι πρέσβεις μετά την άφιξή τους στην πόλη προσέρχονταν πρώτα στους πρυτάνεις (Αριστ. *Αθ.Πολ.* 43.5) και ότι το κηρύκειο συσχετίζετο με το πρυτανείο (Πολυδεύκης 8.138). Με το κηρύκειο του αναγλύφου, πιθανότατα, υποδηλώνεται το πρυτανείο, όπως και σε σφράγισμα πήλινης κεραμίδας, εύρημα των ερευνών του Ορλάνδου (*Πρακτ* [1931] 31, εικ. 9), και όχι παρακείμενο ιερό του Ερμή. Αλλά και η υδρία πρέπει να συνδέεται με το πρυτανείο, υποδηλώνοντας την σε αυτό δωρεάν σίτηση των αρχόντων, κηρύκων και των επισήμων ξένων. Ο Καστριώτης λανθασμένα ονοματίζει το σκεύος στάμνο και το συνδέει με τη λατρεία του Διονύσου, αλλά για τη νεώτερη τοποθέτηση στο θέμα βλ. B. Philippaki, *The Attic Stamnos* (Oxford 1967) XIX-XXI. Για τους τόπους των δημοσίων συσσιτίων βλ. πρόσφατα: S. Rotroff and J. Oakley, "Debris from a Public Dining Place in the Athenian Agora," *Hesperia* 25 (1992) 36 κ.επ. Στην σελ. 39 σημ. 27, επισημαίνεται η νέα θέση του Αγλαυρείου και η εξ αυτής αναζητούμενη θέση του Πρυτανείου. 'Αξιο έρευνας επίσης είναι, εάν το τμήμα μαρμάρινου αναθήματος με την επιγραφή *'Αγαθῆι Τύχηι*, που βρέθηκε σε επιχώσεις του μεσαιωνικού Ριζόκαστρου στην πάροδο του θεάτρου του Διονύσου (Ν. Πλάτων, *ΑρχΔελτ* 21 [1966] Χρονικά 39, πίν. 61α = αρ. ευρ. Ακρ. 14.902), έχει σχέση με την ύπαρξη αγάλματος της Αγαθής Τύχης, που αναφέρεται ότι ήταν στημένο κοντά στο Πρυτανείο (Αιλιανού *Ποικίλη Ιστορία* 9.39). Για το άγαλμα αυτό δες την ανακοίνωση της O. Palagia στον παρόντα τόμο, σελ. 113-122.

20. 'Ισως η θέση οικοδόμησης του Ωδείου, κατασκευασμένου από τα ξύλα των κατανικηθέντων περσικών πλοίων, να πρέπει ακριβώς να συνδεθεί με την άμεση περιοχή της καταστροφικής ανόδου των Περσών στην Ακρόπολη το 480 π.Χ. (Ηροδ. 8.53).

21. Αξιοσημείωτη η σχέση του πρυτανείου και με το ιερό της Αρτέμιδος Αγροτέρας, μέσω των εφήβων: οι έφηβοι, σύμφωνα με επιγραφικά τεκμήρια του τέλους του 2ου αι. π.Χ. (Miller [σημ. 14] 16 και Α.196-202), αφού έθυαν πάνω στην κοινή εστία στο Πρυτανείο έκαμαν, ένοπλοι, πομπή στο ιερό της Αρτέμιδος Αγροτέρας (ταυτίζεται με τον εκτός των τειχών "ναό του Ιλισσού," στις ανατολικές όχθες του ποταμού: Travlos, *PDA* 112-120). Με τη λατρεία αυτή της Αρτέμιδος πιθανόν να συνδέονται ευρήματα από τις παλαιές ανασκαφές στο "Ωδείο": α) μικρή μαρμάρινη κεφαλή Αρτέμιδος (Καστριώτης, *ΑρχΕφ* [1915] 146, εικ. 5) και β) μαρμάρινο αγαλμάτιο Αρτέμιδος (Ορλάνδος *Πρακτ* [1931] 31-2, εικ. 10) σήμερα στο Εθν. Αρχ. Μουσείο (3714): Β. Θεοφανείδου, "Νέα Προσκτήματα," *ΑρχΕφ* (1939-41) Αρχ. Χρονικά, 10, αρ. 35 και *LIMC* II (1984) 645, αρ. 257.

22. W. Würster, *Architectura* 9 (1979) 58-76; Μ. Κορρές, *ΑρχΔελτ* 35 (1980) Χρονικά 9 κ.επ.

23. Μ. Κορρές, *ΑρχΔελτ* 35 (1980) Χρονικά 9-20; *ΑρχΔελτ* 36 (1981) Χρονικά 4; *ΑρχΔελτ* (1982) Χρονικά 15-18; *ΑρχΔελτ* 38 (1983) Χρονικά 10-11.

24. H. Makri, *The Theatre of Dionysos, Athens: The Rehabilitation of the Auditorium Retaining Walls Along and Adjoining the Eastern Parodos* (Summary) (Athens 1987).

25. Κ. Τσάκος, *ΑρχΔελτ* 40 (1985) Χρονικά 9-11 και Ε. Μακρή, Κ. Τσάκος, Α. Βαβυλοπούλου-Χαριτωνίδου, "Το Ριζόκαστρο, Σωζομενα υπολείμματα: Νέες παρατηρήσεις και επαναχρονολόγηση," *Δελτίο Χριστιαν. Αρχ. Εταιρείας* 14 (1987-88) 329-366.

26. Α. Τσαραβόπουλος, *ΑρχΔελτ* 36 (1981) Χρονικά 44.

27. Την ανάγκη παράλληλης συνθετικής έρευνας θραυσμάτων γλυπτών, αρχιτεκτονικών μελών, επιγραφών, κ.λ.π. από τον αρχαιολογικό χώρο, σε σχέση με τα φυλασσόμενα σήμερα σε άλλα Μουσεία μαρτυρούν και πρόσφατες αναγνωρίσεις και αποδόσεις, όπως εκείνες ενεπίγραφων θραυσμάτων από τους μεγάλους καταλόγους νικητών στα Διονύσια, που βρίσκονται στο Επιγραφικό Μουσείο, D. Peppas-Delmousou, *AM* 92 (1977) 229-243, και *AM* 93 (1978) 109-118.

Η οδός των Τριπόδων και τα χορηγικά μνημεία στην αρχαία Αθήνα

Άλκηστις Χωρέμη-Σπετσιέρη

Χάρις σε ορισμένες νομοθετικές ρυθμίσεις που έκανε ο Κλεισθένης το 508/7 π.Χ., μετά την διαίρεση των Αθηναίων πολιτών σε δέκα φυλές, λειτούργησε συστηματικά ο θεσμός της χορηγίας, ο οποίος προϋπήρχε ήδη από την εποχή των Πεισιστρατιδών.[1] Η χορηγία, ως γνωστόν, ήταν μία από τις λειτουργίες,[2] η οποία υποχρέωνε τους εύπορους πολίτες κάθε φυλής να αναλαμβάνουν με έξοδά τους την προετοιμασία ενός χορού για τους διθυραμβικούς ή δραματικούς αγώνες σε διάφορες εορτές της πόλεως, κυρίως όμως κατά τα Μεγάλα ή εν Άστει Διονύσια, προς τιμήν του Διονύσου Ελευθερέως, τον μήνα Ελαφηβολιώνα. Ο νικητής χορηγός, εκπροσωπώντας την φυλή του, έπαιρνε από την πολιτεία ως βραβείο έναν τρίποδα, τον οποίο με δαπάνη του έστηνε επάνω σε ένα μνημείο, που θα έφερε και την κατάλληλη επιγραφή.[3]

Οι τρίποδες ήταν χάλκινοι, καμιά φορά επίχρυσοι ή επάργυροι, και στήνονταν ψηλά, επάνω σε απλές ορθογώνιες βάσεις τον 5ο αι. π.Χ.,[4] σε πιο περίτεχνες τον 4ο αι. π.Χ. Όπως π.χ. σε πρισματικές βάσεις με ανάγλυφες παραστάσεις καμμιά φορά στις κοίλες πλευρές τους[5] ή επάνω στην στέγη κτηρίων σε σχήμα ναΐσκου, όπου συχνά ετοποθετούντο περισσότεροι του ενός τρίποδες.[6] Τα μνημεία αυτά, που είχαν και γλυπτά κάτω από τον τρίποδα ή στο εσωτερικό τους,[7] ήταν αφιέρωμα του χορηγού στον τιμώμενο θεό, αλλά συγχρόνως "μνᾶμα χοροῦ," "μάρτυς ἀέθλων Βακχίων," όπως μας πληροφορούν σχετικά επιγράμματα,[8] διαρκές μνημείο της νίκης της φυλής και της προσφοράς του χορηγού στον θεό και στην πολιτιστική παράδοση της πόλης.

Χορηγικά μνημεία ανεγείρονταν στον χώρο γύρω από το Διονυσιακό θέατρο, αλλά κυρίως σε έναν από τους επισημότερους δρόμους της αρχαίας Αθήνας, την οδό των Τριπόδων ή απλά Τρίποδες, που πήρε το όνομά της από τους χορηγικούς τρίποδες.[9] Σύμφωνα με τον Παυσανία ο δρόμος ξεκινούσε από το Πρυτανείο,[10] που κατά τους περισσότερους μελετητές, πρέπει να βρισκόταν στην Β. κλιτύ,[11] παρέκαμπτε την Α. κλιτύ της Ακρόπολης, σε μήκος 800 μ. κατά τον υπολογισμό του Τραυλού,[12] και κατέληγε στο ιερό του Διονύσου στη Ν. κλιτύ, ΝΔ. από το Ωδείο του Περικλέους.[13] Πρόκειται για πολύ παλαιό δημόσιο δρόμο που συνέδεε δύο διονυσιακά ιερά: το ένα στην πλατεία της Αρχαίας Αγοράς,[14] όπου τον 6ο αι. π.Χ. γίνονταν και δραματικοί αγώνες,[15] με το ιερό του Διονύσου Ελευθερέως στη Ν. κλιτύ της Ακρόπολης, όπου επίσης διεξάγονταν δραματικοί αγώνες από τον 6ο αι. π.Χ., αλλά ιδίως τον 5ο αι. π.Χ., αφού ιδρύθηκε εδώ το Διονυσιακό θέατρο για τον σκοπό αυτό.[16]

Αν και δεν παραδίδεται από τις πηγές η ακριβής πορεία που ακολουθούσαν οι πομπές κατά τα Μεγάλα Διονύσια, δεν αποκλείεται να ακολουθούσαν την οδό Τριπόδων, όπως μπορεί να υποθέσει κανείς με βάση ορισμένες φιλολογικές πληροφορίες. Συγκεκριμένα ο Ξενοφών[17] αναφέρει χορούς γύρω από βωμούς και ιερά, ιδίως των δώδεκα θεών, στην Αγορά, κατά τις πομπές των Μεγάλων Διονυσίων, χωρίς όμως να διευκρινίζει ποιές πομπές εννοεί. Έτσι ορισμένοι μελετητές συνδέουν τους χορούς αυτούς με την πομπή των εφήβων κατά την προκαταρκτική τελετή της "εἰσαγωγῆς" τοῦ ἀγάλματος τοῦ Διονύσου "ἀπὸ τῆς ἐσχάρας" στο Διονυσιακό θέατρο (σε ανάμνηση της αρχικής μεταφοράς του ξοάνου του θεού από τις Ελευθερές),[18] ενώ άλλοι τους συνδέουν με τη μεγάλη θρησκευτική πομπή της πρώτης ημέρας των εορτών, κατά την οποία οδηγούνταν ο ταύρος και τα άλλα προς θυσίαν ζώα στο Διονυσιακό θέατρο από εφήβους, μαζί με πλήθος κόσμου και επισήμων, μεταξύ των οποίων και οι χορηγοί με τα πορφυρά χρυσοκέντητα ενδύματά τους.[19] Μετά τους χορούς και τις τελετές αυτές η πιθανότερη διαδρομή που μπορεί να ακολουθούσαν οι πομπές, ήταν η οδός των Τριπόδων, η οποία είναι σαφώς ο φυσικότερος και συντομότερος δρόμος από την Αγορά προς το Διονυσιακό θέατρο.

Με την καθιέρωση του εθίμου της ανεγέρσεως χορηγικών μνημείων από τον 5ο αι. π.Χ. και μετά, και ιδίως τον 4ο αι. π.Χ., η οδός των Τριπόδων διαμορφώθηκε κατάλληλα με αναλήμματα και πλαισιώθηκε σταδιακά από τα λαμπρά μνημεία σε σχήμα ναού με τους περίτεχνους χάλκινους τρίποδες και τα γλυπτά μεγάλων καλλιτεχνών, τα οποία σώζονταν ως τις μέρες του Παυσανία. 'Ετσι, εκτός από σημαντική πομπική οδός, έγινε και χώρος περιπάτου και αναψυχής, όπως μας πληροφορεί ο Αθήναιος.[20]

Ήδη από το 1921 είναι γνωστή η θέση και η πορεία της οδού κατά τις Α. υπώρειες της Ακρόπολης, χάρις στις ανασκαφές που κατά καιρούς έγιναν στη σημερινή Πλατεία Λυσικράτους[21] και την οδό Τριπόδων,[22] ενώ χάρις στους επιφανειακούς καθαρισμούς, που έγιναν στην περιοχή του Διονυσιακού θεάτρου το 1979, γνωρίζουμε και το τέρμα της οδού.[23] Συγκεκριμένα οι ανασκαφές στην Πλατεία Λυσικράτους αποκάλυψαν τα θεμέλια από κροκαλοπαγείς λιθόπλινθους οκτώ χορηγικών μνημείων κατά μήκος της Δ. πλευράς της οδού: έξι Ν. από το μνημείο του Λυσικράτους και δύο Β., εκ των οποίων το ένα ήταν μεγάλων διαστάσεων και πιθανόν στήριζε μνημείο σε σχήμα ναΐσκου (εικ. 1). Ανάμεσα σε αυτό και το μνημείο Λυσικράτους διαπιστώθηκε ότι περνούσε άλλη, λίγο στενότερη οδός, πολύ ανηφορική, με κλίση 20%, η οποία οδηγούσε από την οδό των Τριπόδων στον Περίπατο και το άνω διάζωμα του Διονυσιακού θεάτρου (εικ. 2).[24]

Η ανασκαφή του Ι. Μηλιάδη το 1956 έφερε στο φως για πρώτη φορά λείψανα μνημείου και στην Α. πλευρά της αρχαίας οδού[25] και έτσι έγινε γνωστό το συνολικό πλάτος της οδού, που φθάνει τους 20 αρχαίους πόδες, 6–6.50 μ. Λείψανα ενός ακόμη μικρού απλού βάθρου αποκάλυψε το 1981 η ανασκαφή κάτω από την οδό Επιμενίδου,[26] που αποτελεί το Ν. όριο της Πλατείας Λυσικράτους. Τα περισσότερα μνημεία ήταν τοποθετημένα στην Δ. πλευρά της οδού, μπροστά από την κατατομή του βράχου ή μπροστά από αναλήμματα, που είχαν κατασκευαστεί σε διάφορα σημεία για την συγκράτηση των χωμάτων της κλιτύος. Στην Α. πλευρά υπήρχαν λίγα ή δεν βρέθηκαν, γιατί κατολίσθησαν και καταστράφηκαν λόγω της κλίσεως του εδάφους. Στις ανασκαφές της Πλατείας Λυσικράτους εντοπίστηκε και το επίπεδο των οδοστρωμάτων της κλασικής εποχής, του 5ου αι. π.Χ., και ιδίως του 4ου αι. π.Χ., το οποίο ορίζεται με ακρίβεια από την κατώτατη βαθμίδα της κρηπίδας του μνημείου του Λυσικράτους (εικ. 1). Η αποκάλυψη επαλλήλων πήλινων αγωγών κατά την πορεία της οδού μαρτυρεί την σταδιακή ανύψωση του αρχαίου δρόμου στους ρωμαϊκούς και βυζαντινούς χρόνους. Τη βυζαντινή περίοδο (11ος - 12ος αι.) και τους χρόνους της Φραγκοκρατίας (13ος - 14ος αι.) τον χώρο κατέλαβε εκτεταμένο χριστιανικό κοιμητήριο, ενώ τον 17ο αι. (1669) χτίστηκε εδώ η μονή των Καπουτσίνων, που ενσωμάτωσε το μνημείο.[27]

Εικ. 1. Το μνημείο του Λυσικράτους και δεξιά η κρηπίδα ενός μεγάλου χορηγικού μνημείου (από ΝΑ.).

Σύμφωνα με τις στάθμες που ελήφθησαν σε διάφορα σημεία του οδοστρώματος του 4ου αι. π.Χ. στο Β. και Ν. μέρος της Πλατείας, διαπιστώθηκε κλίση της αρχαίας οδού προς Ν. (4,6%), μεγαλύτερη από την αντίστοιχη της σημερινής οδού.

Μετά την γωνία των οδών Βύρωνος και Βάκχου η αρχαία οδός των Τριπόδων κάμπτεται ελαφρά προς τα ΝΔ. Η πορεία της παρακολουθείται με ακρίβεια από το σημείο αυτό ως το τέρμα της στο Διονυσιακό ιερό και το θέατρο, χάρις στον εντοπισμό θεμελίων και άλλων χορηγικών βάθρων. Συγκεκριμένα στο ακίνητο οδού Βάκχου 4, ιδιοκτησίας Ι. Στράτου, αποκαλύφθηκε η κρηπίδα δύο εφαπτομένων βάθρων, ενώ στο υπόγειο της οικίας οδού Βάκχου και Θρασύλλου γωνία, μία πωρόπλινθος προφανώς ήταν κατά χώραν κατάλοιπο μνημείου, συνδετικός κρίκος ανάμεσα στα προηγούμενα μνημεία και σε ένα άλλο που εντοπίστηκε πρόσφατα ακριβώς μέσα από τον περίβολο του αρχαιολογικού χώρου του ιερού του Διονύσου. Η κρηπίδα του τελευταίου βρίσκεται σε ευθεία γραμμή με σειρά λειψάνων χορηγικών βάθρων κατά μήκος του Ν. ανδήρου του Ωδείου του Περικλέους, που αποκαλύφθηκαν με επιφανειακούς καθαρισμούς (εικ. 2).[28] Τα δύο καλλίτερα σωζόμενα είναι: το άνω μέρος της κρηπίδας ενός ορθογωνίου βάθρου από ακτίτη λίθο, διαστ. 4.50 x 2.30 μ. και τα λείψανα ενός άλλου μνημείου σε σχήμα ναού "έν παραστάσι", πλ. 5 μ., βάθ. 4 μ., που είναι το παλαιότερο σωζόμενο ναόσχημο μνημείο, όπως μαρτυρεί ο τύπος του.[29]

Στη ΝΔ. πλευρά του ανδήρου του Ωδείου σώζονται

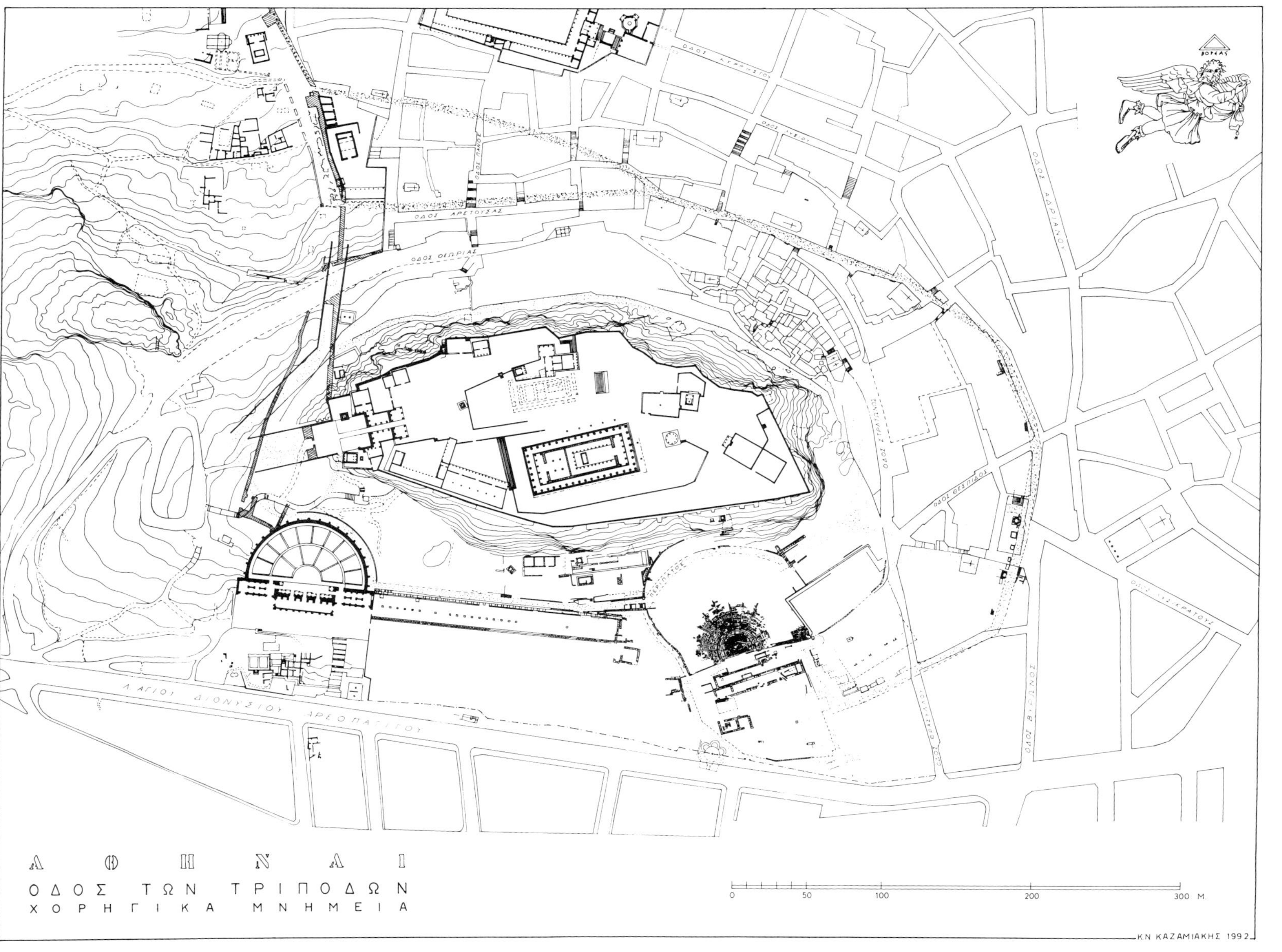

Εικ. 2. Γενικό τοπογραφικό σχέδιο περιοχής Ακρόπολης-Διονυσιακού θεάτρου-Πλάκας-Αρχαίας Αγοράς, με σημειωμένη την πορεία της αρχαίας οδού Τριπόδων. (Σχέδιο Κ. Καζαμιάκη 1992).

κατάλοιπα ενός άλλου μνημείου με κροκαλοπαγή πυρήνα και επένδυση από ακτίτη λίθο, διαστ. 11 x 7.50 μ., το οποίο κατά τον αρχιτέκτονα Μ. Κορρέ πρέπει να είχε μορφή στοάς.[30] Ν. ακριβώς από τη σειρά αυτή των μνημείων περνούσε η οδός των Τριπόδων (εικ. 4). Σειρά θεμελίων άλλων βάθρων σώζονται επιφανειακά και κατά μήκος της Δ. πλευράς του Ωδείου του Περικλέους, πράγμα που μαρτυρεί ότι η οδός των Τριπόδων εκάμπτετο και οδηγούσε και στην Α. πάροδο του Διονυσιακού θεάτρου (εικ. 2).[31] Σημειωτέον ότι η επιμήκης κατασκευή στα δεξιά της παρόδου δεν ανήκει σε χορηγικό μνημείο, όπως εθεωρείτο παλαιότερα, αλλά σε πρόπυλο που ελάμπρυνε την πάροδο του θεάτρου, όπως απέδειξε πρόσφατα ο Μ. Κορρές.[32] Στην αριστερή πλευρά της παρόδου ο Κορρές συνάρμοσε πάνω σε χαμηλούς πεσσούς από τεχνητό λίθο τα κομμάτια της ιωνικής ανωδομής του μνημείου του αγωνοθέτη Ξενοκλή, τόσο εκείνα που ήταν γνωστά από τον περασμένο αιώνα, όσο και τα νεώτερα, που ταύτισε ο ίδιος.[33] Πάνω στο τριταινιωτό επιστύλιο σώζεται η παλαιότερη επιγραφή (307/6 π.Χ.), στην οποία αναφέρεται ο δήμος ως χορηγός, και ο αγωνοθέτης, ο οποίος εποπτεύει τους δραματικούς αγώνες και αναθέτει το μνημείο μόνον, σύμφωνα με το νόμο του Δημητρίου Φαληρέα του 316/5 π.Χ.[34] Ο Κορρές θεωρεί ότι το μνημείο είχε την μορφή ελεύθερης πύλης με πεσσούς πεπλατυσμένους και άνοιγμα 2.70 μ. και ότι πιθανόν έστεκε σε κάποιο σημείο της οδού των Τριπόδων προς το Διονυσιακό θέατρο.[35]

Άλλα χορηγικά μνημεία είχαν στηθεί γύρω από το θέατρο, μερικά με μνημειώδη μορφή, όπως εκείνο του Νικία (319 π.Χ.) στα ΒΔ. της Δ. παρόδου,[36] του οποίου σώζονται μόνον τα θεμέλια στην θέση τους, ενώ τα αρχιτεκτονικά του μέλη αναγνωρίστηκαν εντειχισμένα στην πύλη Beulé από τον Dinsmoor.[37] Επάνω από το θέατρο επίσης, στον βράχο, στην γνωστή "κατατομὴ" των αρχαίων,[38] στήνονταν χορηγικοί τρίποδες πάνω σε απλές βάσεις ή σε μεγάλα μνημεία, όπως του Θρασύλλου (319 π.Χ.).[39] Ο χώρος ήταν κατάλληλος για τέτοια μνημεία, γιατί ήταν πολυσύχναστος, μια και λίγο πιο χαμηλά περνούσε ο άλλος σημαντικός δρόμος που περιέτρεχε την Ακρόπολη, ο Περίπατος.[40]

Ας έλθουμε τώρα στο τμήμα της αρχαίας οδού Τριπόδων Β. από την Πλατεία Λυσικράτους. Σε απόσταση 45 μ. περίπου, στο υπόγειο του ακινήτου στην σημερινή οδό Τριπόδων 34 και Θέσπιδος γωνία, σώζεται η Α. πλευρά του βάθρου ενός μεγάλου χορηγικού μνημείου του 4ου αι. π.Χ., που είχε αποκαλυφθεί το 1875 (εικ. 3).[41] 'Οπως διαπιστώθηκε σε πρόσφατη έρευνα, η υποθεμελίωσή του από κροκαλοπαγείς λίθους εδράζεται σε λάξευμα του φυσικού βράχου.[42] Το βάθρο αυτό αποτελούσε μέχρι πρόσφατα το βορειότερο βεβαιωμένο άκρο της αρχαίας οδού, της οποίας το επίπεδο στο σημείο αυτό είναι 82.20 μ. περίπου από την επιφάνεια της θάλασσας, 0.20 μ. ψηλότερα από εκείνο στο βορειότερο άκρο της Πλατείας Λυσικράτους. Παρατηρείται δηλαδή μια ελαφρά ανηφορική πορεία της αρχαίας οδού, η οποία συμπίπτει σχεδόν με τη σημερινή οδό.

Πρόσφατες έρευνες σε άλλα ακίνητα προς τα Β.-ΒΔ. έφεραν στο φως και άλλα τμήματα της αρχαίας οδού, καθώς και λείψανα μεγάλου κτηρίου, το οποίο πρέπει να είναι χορηγικό μνημείο. Συγκεκριμένα στο ημιϋπόγειο του ακινήτου αρ. 28, ιδιοκτησίας της "Ελληνικής Εταιρείας", 36 μέτρα βορειότερα από το

Εικ. 3. Βάθρο χορηγικού μνημείου στο υπόγειο καταστήματος οδού Τριπόδων 34 και Θέσπιδος γωνία (από ΝΑ.).

προηγούμενο μνημείο, ανασκάφηκε τμήμα της αρχαίας οδού Τριπόδων σε μήκος 12.50 μ. και στη Δ. πλευρά της η ΝΑ. γωνία μεγάλου μνημείου.[43] Σώζεται η υποθεμελίωσή του από κροκαλοπαγείς λίθους και τμήματα της Α. και Ν. όψης (διαστ. 9.50 μ. και 5.50 μ. αντίστοιχα) σε ύψος τριών δόμων από πειραϊκό ακτίτη. Η Ν. πλευρά του είχε ενσωματωθεί σε εσωτερικό τοίχο του νεοκλασικού κτηρίου, ενώ τμήμα της Α. πλευράς έχει καταστραφεί από μικρό λιοτρίβι νεωτέρων χρόνων. Σύμφωνα με την κεραμεική και τον τρόπο δομής του πρέπει να χρονολογηθεί στο δεύτερο μισό του 4ου αι. π.Χ. (εικ. 4–6).

Πίσω από το μνημείο αυτό, σε απόσταση 20 μ. περίπου από την Α. όψη του, υψωνόταν ισχυρότατος αναλημματικός τοίχος από κροκαλοπαγείς λιθόπλινθους, ο οποίος ήταν ενσωματωμένος στον πίσω τοίχο του νεοκλασικού κτηρίου, στο όριό του προς την οδό Ραγκαβά. Ο μνημειώδης αυτός τοίχος, τμήμα του οποίου αποκαλύφθηκε και στο προς Ν. όμορο ακίνητο αρ. 30, σώζεται σε μήκος 25 μ. και σε ύψος 6 ανισοϋψών δόμων, που φθάνουν τα 4 μ. (εικ. 4, 7–8). Το χορηγικό μνημείο, αν κρίνει κανείς από το σωζόμενο τμήμα του, πρέπει να είναι ένα από τα μεγαλύτερα, ίσως του μεγέθους του μνημείου του Νικία, στο μέσον περίπου της διαδρομής της αρχαίας οδού. Από το σημείο αυτό αρχίζει ανηφορική πορεία. Σε απόσταση 25 μ. περίπου Β.-ΒΔ., στο ακίνητο της σημερινής οδού Τριπόδων αρ. 22, ιδιοκτησίας Ι. Μεντζικώφ, αποκαλύφθηκαν σε σωστική ανασκαφή πέντε επάλληλα οδοστρώματα της αρχαίας οδού, της οποίας η στάθμη στο σημείο αυτό είναι 85 μ. (από την επιφάνεια της θάλασσας), 93 εκ. ψηλότερα από το Β. σημείο στο ακίνητο οδού Τριπόδων αρ. 28 (κλίση 7.3%).

Ενώ έως εδώ παρακολουθούμε με ακρίβεια την πορεία, τις κάμψεις και τις κλίσεις της αρχαίας οδού Τριπόδων σε μήκος 380 μ., σε τριπλάσιο μήκος περίπου από εκείνο του 1971,[44] την συνέχειά της στην ΒΑ. και Β. κλιτύ του λόφου της Ακρόπολης γνωρίζαμε μέχρι πρόσφατα μόνον από τοπογραφικούς χάρτες διαφόρων μελετητών, κυρίως του Τραυλού, όπου σημειωνόταν υποθετικά η πορεία της. Σε χάρτη του 1968 ο Τραυλός εικονίζει την αρχαία οδό, μετά το ακίνητο αρ. 20, να κάμπτεται ομαλά προς τα ΒΔ., να ακολουθεί την πορεία της σημερινής οδού Ερωτοκρίτου, Β. από τον Αγ. Ιωάννη τον Θεολόγο, να ανηφορίζει στην σημερινή οδό Θόλου στην Β. κλιτύ και να προχωρεί ως την διασταύρωση της τελευταίας με την οδό Κλεψύδρας.[45] Στο σημείο αυτό διακλαδώνεται σε δύο σκέλη, τα οποία οδηγούν προς την Αγορά, πλαισιώνοντας από Β. και Ν. το Ελευσίνιο (εικ. 9). Σε χάρτη του 1976 ο Τραυλός σημειώνει μίαν άλλη πορεία (εικ. 10).[46] Από το ακίνητο αρ. 20 της σημερινής οδού Τριπόδων η αρχαία οδός ανηφορίζει προς τα ΒΔ., στην οδό Πρυτανείου, περνάει από την ΒΔ. γωνία της εκκλησίας του Αγ. Νικολάου του Ραγκαβά, προχωρεί ΒΔ.-Δ. ακολουθώντας πάντοτε την οδό Πρυτανείου έως την διασταύρωσή της με την οδό Πανός, όπου διακλαδώνεται σε δύο σκέλη, ΝΔ. από την αντίστοιχη διακλάδωση στον προηγούμενο χάρτη (πρβλ. εικ. 9 και 10).

Χάρις στη συνεχή παρακολούθηση των οικοδομικών εργασιών στην Πλάκα τα τελευταία χρόνια, την διενέργεια σωστικών ανασκαφών από αρχαιολόγους της Εφορείας Ακροπόλεως, τον εντοπισμό επιφανειακών αρχαίων καταλοίπων στους δρόμους και τις σύγχρονες οικίες, συγκεντρώθηκαν αρκετά αρχαιολογικά στοιχεία, με βάση τα οποία τώρα μπορούμε να ορίσουμε με αρκετή ακρίβεια την πορεία της αρχαίας οδού στην Β. κλιτύ. Αυτό κατέστη δυνατόν με την εκπόνηση ενός γενικού τοπογραφικού χάρτη της Πλάκας, στον οποίο σημειώθηκαν και συσχετίστηκαν όλα τα μέχρι στιγμής αρχαιολογικά δεδομένα, παλαιά και νέα, από τον αρχιτέκτονατοπογράφο Κ. Καζαμιάκη. Έτσι διαπιστώθηκε ότι επιβεβαιώνεται κατά το μεγαλύτερο μέρος η δεύτερη πορεία του Τραυλού, με μόνη διαφορά την θέση της διακλάδωσης της οδού. Αυτή σύμφωνα με τα σημερινά δεδομένα πρέπει να τοποθετηθεί ανατολικότερα, στην διασταύρωση των οδών Πρυτανείου και Θόλου, ακριβώς Α. από το Παλαιό Πανεπιστήμιο (εικ. 2).

Σε όλη την διαδρομή από το ακίνητο αρ. 20 της σημερινής οδού Τριπόδων και στη συνέχεια στην σημερινή οδό Πρυτανείου έχουν εντοπισθεί κροκαλοπαγείς και πώρινες λιθόπλινθοι, οι περισσότερες παρόμοιων διαστάσεων με εκείνες των σωζομένων χορηγικών μνημείων: άλλες τοποθετημένες κατά μήκος των πεζοδρομίων, άλλες εντειχισμένες στους τοίχους των συγχρόνων οικιών ή εγκατάσπαρτες σε αυλές. Στη γωνία των οδών Πρυτανείου και Ραγκαβά είναι ορατή μία γωνία κάποιου αρχαίου κτίσματος, πάνω στην οποία εδράζεται το σύγχρονο σπίτι, ενώ στο πεζοδρόμιο ΝΑ. απέναντι σώζεται μία μεγάλη πωρόπλινθος. Προφανώς πρόκειται για κατάλοιπα *in situ* χορηγικών μνημείων, δεδομένου ότι βρίσκονται στη γραμμή της Δ. πλευράς της αρχαίας οδού. Πολλές πωρόπλινθοι από ακτίτη λίθο είναι εντειχισμένες στους τοίχους της εκκλησίας του Αγ. Νικολάου Ραγκαβά. Είναι πολύ πιθανόν ότι στη θέση της εκκλησίας προϋπήρχε κάποιο μεγάλο χορηγικό μνημείο, που έδωσε άφθονο οικοδομικό υλικό για το χτίσιμο του χριστιανικού ναού.

Στην οδό Πρυτανείου και Επιχάρμου γωνία, στο ακίνητο ιδιοκτησίας Ν. Στάη βρέθηκαν κροκαλοπαγείς λιθόπλινθοι χτισμένες σε τοίχο μεσαιωνικών χρόνων σε δεύτερη χρήση, καθώς και μαρμάρινα αρχιτεκτονικά μέλη, (τμήματα μικρών κιόνων και ιωνικών βάσεων) που προέρχονται πιθανόν από κάποιο ναόσχημο μνημείο.[47] Κατάλοιπα *in situ* άλλων μνημείων ή αναλημμάτων της αρχαίας οδού Τριπόδων πρέπει να είναι οι πωρόπλινθοι κατά μήκος της οικοδομικής γραμμής έξω από τα ακίνητα οδού Πρυτανείου 5 και 9, απέναντι από το Μετόχι του

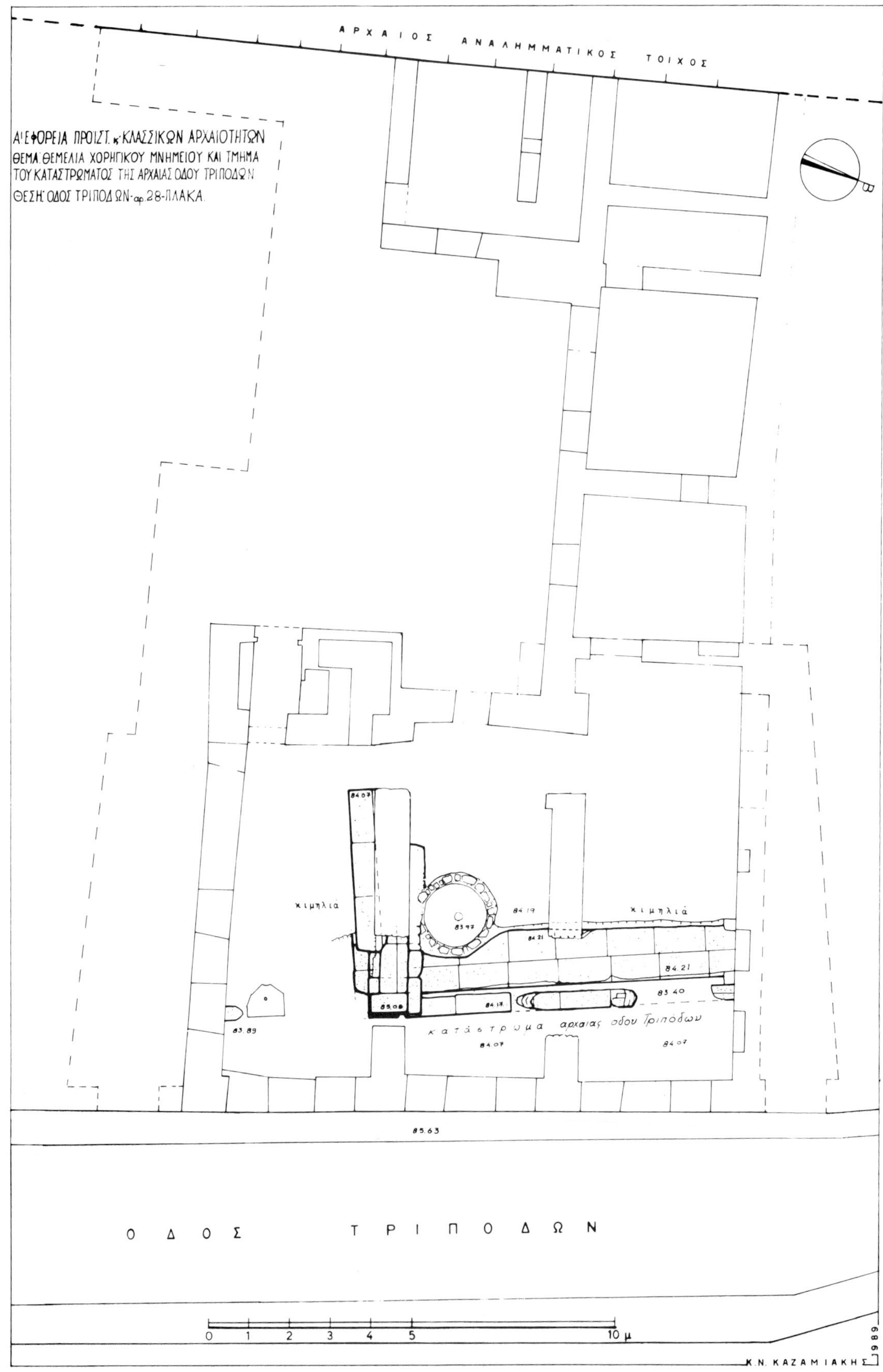

Εικ. 4. Κάτοψη ανασκαφέντος χορηγικού μνημείου μπροστά σε μεγάλο αναλημματικό τοίχο στην οδό Τριπόδων 28, στο κτήριο της "Ελληνικής Εταιρείας". (Σχέδιο Κ. Καζαμιάκη 1989).

Εικ. 5. Τμήμα μεγάλου χορηγικού μνημείου στο υπόγειο του ακινήτου οδ. Τριπόδων 28 (από Β.).

Εικ. 6. Ο Ν. τοίχος του μεγάλου χορηγικού μνημείου στην οδό Τριπόδων 28.

Εικ. 7. Μνημειώδης αναλημματικός τοίχος στο Δ. όριο του ακινήτου οδού Τριπόδων 28, προς την οδό Ραγκαβά.

Εικ. 8. Τμήμα του μνημειώδους αναλημματικού τοίχου στην αυλή του ακινήτου οδού Τριπόδων 28.

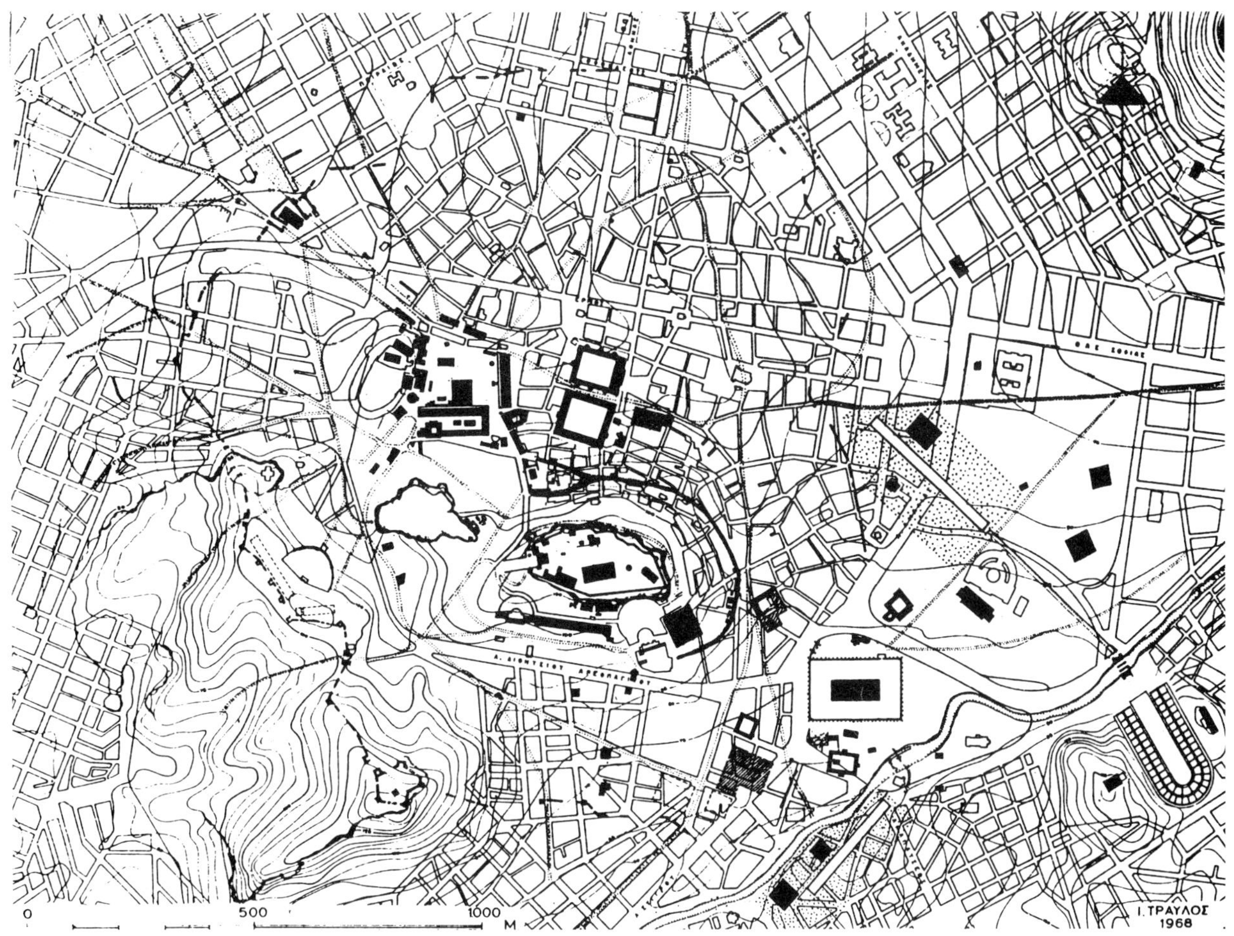

Εικ. 9. Τοπογραφικό σχέδιο του Ι. Τραυλού (1968), όπου σημειώνεται η πορεία της αρχαίας οδού των Τριπόδων στην Β. κλιτύ της Ακρόπολης δια της σημερινής οδού Ερωτοκρίτου.

Παναγίου Τάφου (εικ. 2).[48] Διαγωνίως απέναντι, στο ακίνητο ιδιοκτησίας Κωνσταντίνας Μακκαίηπ, οδός Πρυτανείου 10, αποκαλύφθηκαν σε σωστική ανασκαφή μεγάλες πωρόπλινθοι χτισμένες σε δεύτερη χρήση σε τοίχο μεσαιωνικών χρόνων.[49] Οι πωρόπλινθοι αυτές πιθανόν προέρχονται από τα συμπαγή θεμέλια που αναφέρει ο Leak ότι αποκαλύφθηκαν εδώ το 1835, στις εκσκαφές θεμελίων της παλαιάς οικίας, η οποία συνόρευε με την προϋπάρχουσα στο σημείο αυτό εκκλησία της Παναγίας Βλαστού ή Σαρρή.[50] Τα κατάλοιπα αυτά θεώρησε ο Άγγλος περιηγητής ότι ανήκαν στο Πρυτανείο, χωρίς όμως άλλα συγκεκριμένα στοιχεία που να επιβεβαιώνουν την ταύτιση.[51] Η φράση "massive foundations" που χρησιμοποιεί μαρτυρεί ότι μάλλον πρόκειται για την υποθεμελίωση κάποιου χορηγικού μνημείου κατά μήκος της αρχαίας οδού των Τριπόδων παρά για θεμέλια τοίχων άλλου κτηρίου.

Το πιο σημαντικό στοιχείο για τον προσδιορισμό του Δ. τμήματος της οδού Τριπόδων στην Β. κλιτύ ήταν η αποκάλυψη διαδοχικών οδοστρωμάτων αρχαίας οδού με κατεύθυνση από Α. προς Δ., η οποία διακλαδώνεται σε δύο σκέλη. Το Β. σκέλος έχει κατεύθυνση και μεγάλη κλίση προς τα ΒΔ. Σημειωτέον ότι οι κλίσεις των οδοστρωμάτων των δύο σκελών της αρχαίας οδού παρουσιάζουν σαφή αντιστοιχία με τις κλίσεις των σημερινών οδών Πρυτανείου και Θόλου, που συναντώνται στο σημείο αυτό ακριβώς Β. από την ανωτέρω οικία. Είναι άλλωστε γνωστό, ότι οι σύγχρονοι δρόμοι ακολουθούν σε γενικές γραμμές την πορεία και τις κλίσεις των αρχαίων. Πλήν των οδοστρωμάτων βρέθηκαν εδώ και πωρόπλινθοι από πειραϊκό ακτίτη που πιθανότατα προέρχονται από κάποιο μνημείο ή ανάλημμα. Στο σημείο αυτό προφανώς έχουμε την διακλάδωση της αρχαίας οδού Τριπόδων, Α. όμως από το σημείο που την σημειώνει ο Τραυλός (πρβλ. εικ. 2 και 9). Πιστεύουμε ότι το Β. σκέλος, που ακολουθεί την οδό Θόλου, στην συνέχεια περνάει από το Δ. άκρο της οδού Θρασυβούλου, όπου σώζεται πωρόπλινθος *in situ* έξω από το ακίνητο αρ. 19,[52] και τέλος Β. από το Ελευσίνιο, είναι το σκέλος που οδηγούσε στην περιοχή της Αρχαίας Αγοράς, όπου ήταν ο ορχήστρα, ο αρχικός χώρος τελέσεως δραματικών αγώνων (εικ. 2).

Το έθιμο της ανεγέρσεως χορηγικών μνημείων συνεχίστηκε επί μακρόν όχι μόνο στην οδό των Τριπόδων στην Β. κλιτύ, όπου τα είδε ο Παυσανίας, αλλά και στο

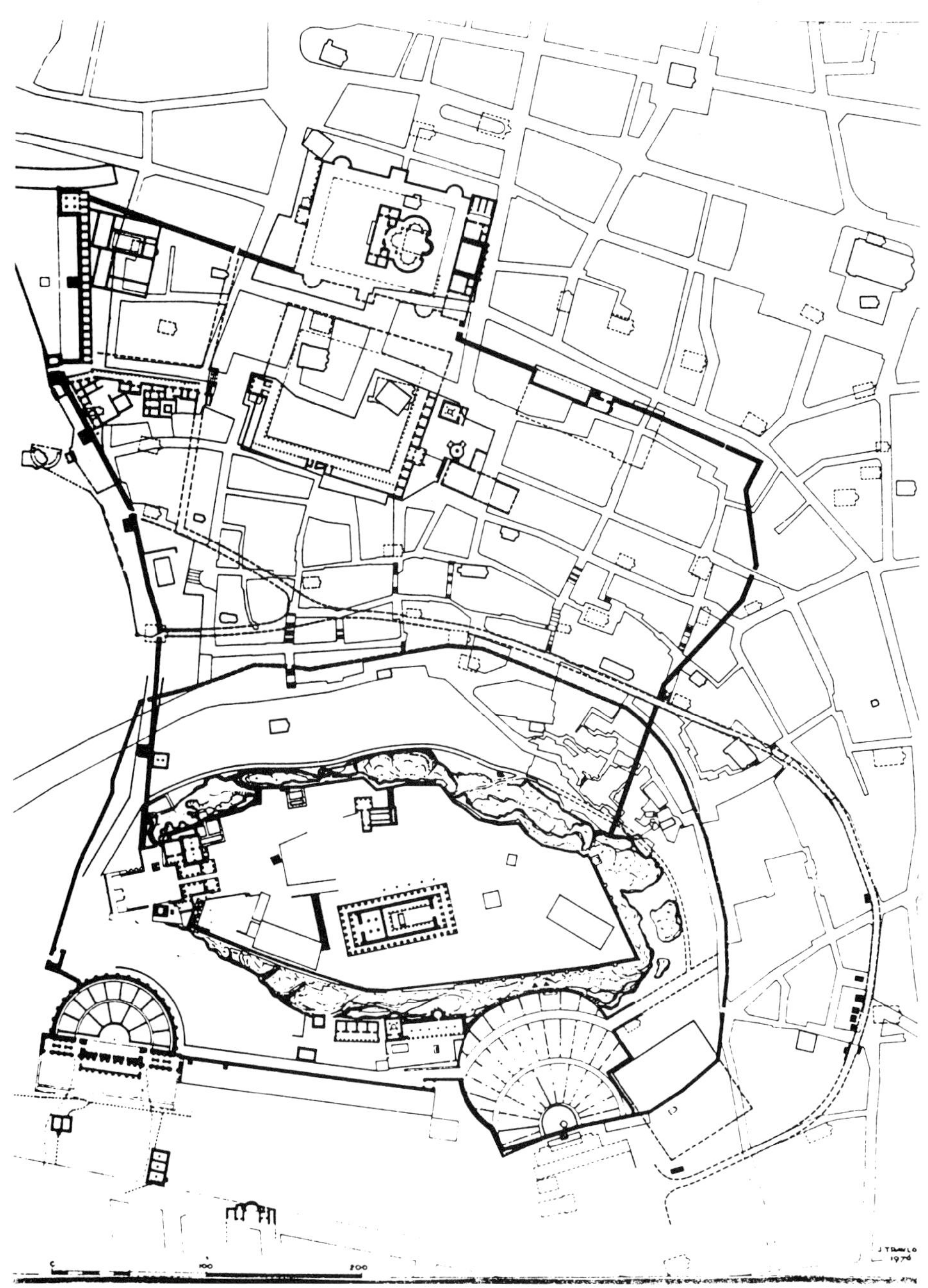

Εικ. 10. Τοπογραφικό σχέδιο του Ι. Τραυλού (1976), όπου σημειώνεται η πορεία της αρχαίας οδού των Τριπόδων δια της σημερινής οδού Πρυτανείου.

συνεχόμενο με αυτήν τμήμα της οδού Παναθηναίων, όπως μαρτυρούν μνημεία και χορηγικές επιγραφές ελληνιστικών και ρωμαϊκών χρόνων που βρέθηκαν στην Αρχαία και την Ρωμαϊκή Αγορά.[53] Αυτό μαρτυρεί πόσο έντονα διατηρήθηκε αφ' ενός η ανάμνηση του αρχικού χώρου της τελέσεως των δραματικών αγώνων στην Αγορά, αφ' ετέρου η σημασία της οδού των Τριπόδων ως επίσημου δρόμου, που συνδέει δύο τόσο σημαντικούς για την πολιτιστική ιστορία της αρχαίας Αθήνας χώρους, τον χώρο όπου γεννήθηκε η δημοκρατία με τον χώρο όπου γεννήθηκε το αρχαίο δράμα.

Ευχαριστώ τον Προϊστάμενο της Α' Εφορείας Ακροπόλεως, Έφορο κ. Π. Καλλιγά που μου ανέθεσε να μιλήσω για το θέμα αυτό στο παρόν συνέδριο, παραχωρώντας όλο το σχετικό αρχαιολογικό υλικό. Επίσης ευχαριστώ την συνάδελφο Σ. Ελευθεράτου για την παροχή στοιχείων από τις πρόσφατες ανασκαφικές έρευνες που διεξήγαγε η ίδια στα ακίνητα της οδού Τριπόδων αρ. 20, 22, 34 και Πρυτανείου 19, καθώς και τον αρχιτέκτονα-τοπογράφο κ. Κ. Καζαμιάκη για την εκπόνηση των δύο σχεδίων, ιδίως του γενικού τοπογραφικού.

Σημειώσεις

1. *RE* III (1899) λ. Χορηγία, 2409–2410 (E. Reisch). Ο Αριστοτέλης (*Οικ.* 2.2.1347α) αναφέρει χορηγία επί Ιππία, ενώ ο Δημοσθένης (*Πρὸς Φαίνιππον. Περὶ Ἀντιδόσεως* 42.1) αναφέρει ότι ο περί αντιδόσεως νόμος υπήρχε ήδη επί Σόλωνος.
2. *RE* XII (1925) λ. Λειτουργία, 1873 (J. Oesler) και *RE* III 2 (1899) Χορηγεία, 2409–2418 (E. Reisch).
3. *RE* ο.π. 2414. Πλουτ. *Ἀριστείδης*, 1.3.
4. Πρβλ. μαρμάρινη πλίνθο από κάποιο μνημείο του 5ου αι. π.Χ. με χορηγική επιγραφή του 415 π.Χ., που αναφέρει τη νίκη της Αιγηΐδος φυλής με χορηγό τον Πυθόδωρο, γιό του Επιζήλου, πρόσωπο γνωστό και από άλλες επιγραφές. Η επιγραφή είχε βρεθεί στις ανασκαφές της Αρχαιολογικής Εταιρείας του 1885 στα Δ. της Μεγάλης Παναγιάς στον χώρο της Βιβλιοθήκης Αδριανού. Ενώ είχε πολλές φορές δημοσιευθεί, δεν ήταν γνωστό, πού βρισκόταν. (Βλ. J.K. Davies, *Athenian Propertied Families 600–300 B.C.* [Oxford 1971] 481). Εντοπίστηκε πρόσφατα από την υπογράφουσα και φυλάσσεται στον χώρο της Βιβλιοθήκης Αδριανού (αρ. ευρ. ΒΑ 594). Ταυτίστηκε από τον επιγραφολόγο Ἀγγελο Ματθαίου, τον οποίο ευχαριστώ.
5. *LIMC* III (1986) λ. Dionysos, 431 αρ. 88. Σ. Καρούζου, *Εθνικό Αρχαιολογικό Μουσείο. Συλλογή Γλυπτών* (Αθήνα 1967) 155, αρ. 1463, πίν. 51α,β.
6. Πλουτ. *Νικίας* 3.3.4. Ναός "τρίποσιν ὑποκείμενος χορηγικοῖς" αποκαλείται από τον Πλούταρχο το χορηγικό μνημείο του Νικία στα Δ. του Διονυσιακού θεάτρου. J. Travlos, *Pictorial Dictionary of Ancient Athens* (= *PDA*) (New York 1971) 357, εικ. 461–463.
7. Παυσ. 1.20.1. πρβλ. καί 1.21.3.
8. *Anthologia Graeca* 13.28. *Anthologia Palatina* 6.140.
9. *RE* Suppl. 8 (1956) λ. Tripodes, 861 (H. Hermann).
10. Παυσ. 1.20.1
11. Travlos, *PDA* 566, εικ. 711, 713, 540. H.A. Thompson and R.E. Wycherly, *Agora* XIV (Princeton 1972) 46. S.G. Miller, *The Prytaneion* (Berkeley 1978) 42–49, εικ. I, όπου σημειώνονται οι κατά καιρούς προταθείσες θέσεις για το Πρυτανείο στην Β. κλιτύ της Ακρόπολης. Δες και τις ανακοινώσεις των T.L. Shear, Jr. και Π. Καλλιγά στον παρόντα τόμο, σελ. 227–228, 28.
12. Travlos, *PDA* 566.
13. Πρβλ. Ανδοκ. *Περὶ Μυστηρίων* 1.38.
14. Κατά τους Τραυλό και Thompson το ιερό αυτό πιθανόν ήταν το Λήναιον (Ι. Τραυλός, *Πολεοδομικὴ ἐξέλιξις τῶν Ἀθηνῶν* [Ἀθῆναι 1960] 23, 40). *PDA* 566. Thompson-Wycherley, *Agora* XIV 128.
15. Πρβλ. Φώτιος λ. ὀρχήστρα. Τραυλός, *Πολεοδομικὴ ἐξέλιξις* 23, 40. *PDA* 537–539. Thompson-Wycherley, *Agora* XIV 126–129, ιδίως 127.
17. Ξεν. *Ἱππ.* 3.2.
18. A. Pickard-Cambridge, *The Dramatic Festivals of Athens* (Oxford 1953) 59–61, σημ. 2.
19. Ο.π. (σημ. 18) 61–62.
20. Αθην. 12.60. Για τα χορηγικά μνημεία της Αθήνας επραγματεύετο ο Ηλιόδωρος στο έργο του *Περὶ τῶν Ἀθήνησιν Τριπόδων*, το οποίο δεν σώζεται. (Ἁρποκρ. λ. Ὀνήτωρ).
21. Travlos, *PDA* 348 και 566, όπου η σχετική βιβλιογραφία για τις ανασκαφές από το 1878 έως το 1971. Για το μνημείο Λυσικράτους βλ. H. Bauer, "Lysikrates-Denkmal. Baubestand und Rekonstruktion," *AM* 92 (1977) 197–227, εικ. 1–7, πίν. 91–96, Beil. 5–10.
22. *AZ* 33 (1875) 162. W. Judeich, *Topographie von Athen* (München 1931) 305–306 *σημ.* 1. S.G. Miller, "Old Discoveries from Old Athens," *Hesperia* 39 (1970) 223–227, εικ. 1–3.
23. Μ. Κορρές, "Περίκλειο Ωδείο και τα πλησίον χορηγικά μνημεία," *ΑρχΔελτ* 35 (1980) Β1, 14–18, σχ. 1 και 4.
24. Judeich (σημ. 22) 306, σημ. 1, σχ. 1. Α. Φιλαδελφεύς, "Ἀνασκαφὴ παρὰ τὸ Λυσικράτειον," *ΑρχΕφ* (1921) 84, εικ. 2–3. G. Welter, "Die Tripodenstrasse in Athen," *AM* 47 (1922) 72, 75, αρ. 2. Πρβλ. O. Broneer, "Excavations on the Slopes of the Acropolis, 1939," *AJA* 44 (1940) 252, εικ. 2.
25. E. Vanderpool, "News Letter from Greece," *AJA* 61 (1957) 281. Τραυλός, *Πολεοδομικὴ ἐξέλιξις* 81 σημ. 3.
26. Μ. Κορρές, "Πλατεία Λυσικράτους," *ΑρχΔελτ* 36 (1981) Β1 5–7, σχ. 1. Τα λείψανα των χορηγικών μνημείων και της αρχαίας οδού Τριπόδων της Πλατείας Λυσικράτους έχουν αποτυπωθεί και τοποθετηθεί σε γενικό τοπογραφικό σχέδιο της περιοχής σε κλίμακα 1:100 από τους αρχιτέκτονες Μ. Κορρέ και Κ. Καζαμιάκη. Εδώ πρέπει να σημειωθεί ότι ο Κ. Καζαμιάκης, που είναι και τοπογράφος, έχει εγκαταστήσει στην περιοχή του Διονυσιακού θεάτρου και της Πλατείας Λυσικράτους καθώς και στην ευρύτερη περιοχή της Πλάκας μεγάλης έκτασης και πυκνότητας δίκτυο σταθερών σημείων σε συνάρτηση με το Κρατικό Σύστημα Αναφοράς (Κ.Σ.Α.). Ἐτσι έχουμε μεγάλη ακρίβεια στις συναρτήσεις της στάθμης των μνημείων και των αρχαίων οδοστρωμάτων που βρίσκονται στην περιοχή, καθώς και στον προσδιορισμό των κλίσεων της αρχαίας οδού στα διάφορα τμήματά της.
27. Τραυλός, *Πολεοδομικὴ ἐξέλιξις* 190 σημ. 4, εικ. 128–129.
28. Βλ. σημ. 23.
29. Κορρές (σημ. 23) 16, αρ. 8, σχ. 1 και 4.
30. Ο.π. (σημ. 23) 16, αρ. 7, σχ. 1.
31. Ο.π. (σημ. 23) σχ. 1.
32. Μ. Κορρές, "Πρόπυλο κλασικής εποχής στην ανατολική πάροδο και το ανατολικό άκρο της σκηνής (του Διονυσιακού θεάτρου)" ό.π. (σημ. 23) 11–14, σχ. 1, 2, πίν. 9.
33. *IG* II², 3073. *RE* Suppl. 8 (1956) 873–874, λ. Tripodes (H. Hermann). Μ. Κορρές, "Διονυσιακό Θέατρο (χορηγικό μνημείο *IG* II², 3073)," *ΑρχΔελτ* 38 (1983) 10, πίν. 15α.
34. *RE*, ό.π. 874. E. Bayer, *Der Athener Demetrius Phalereus* (Darmstadt 1969) 69–71.
35. Κορρές (σημ. 33).
36. Travlos, *PDA* 357, εικ. 459–463.
37. W.B. Dinsmoor, "The Choragic Monument of Nicias," *AJA* 14 (1910) 459–484.
38. Harpokration λ. κατατομή.
39. Travlos *PDA* 562, εικ. 705–708.
40. Judeich (σημ. 22) 181. Τραυλός, *Πολεοδομικὴ ἐξέλιξις* 21, 61, 120. *PDA* 228, 562, εικ. 71.
41. Miller (σημ. 22) 223–231, πίν. 59.
42. Η μικρή ανασκαφική έρευνα γύρω από την υποθεμελίωση του μνημείου έγινε από την συνάδελφο Σ. Ελευθεράτου. Φωτογράφηση και αποτύπωση από τον Κ. Καζαμιάκη.
43. Την ανασκαφική έρευνα διενήργησε η συνάδελφος Ε. Μώρου, *ΑρχΔελτ* 44 (1989) Β1 (υπό έκδοση).
44. Travlos, *PDA* 566.
45. Travlos, *PDA* εικ. 219.
46. Travlos, "Athens after the Liberation. Planning the New City and Exploring the Old," *Hesperia* 50 (1981) εικ. 7.
47. Την ανασκαφική έρευνα διενήργησε ο συνάδελφος Α. Μάντης το 1984. Κατά την αρχιτέκτονα Ε. Μακρή, ο αποκαλυφθείς εδώ τοίχος ανήκει σε πύργο του Ριζόκαστρου, το οποίο, όπως απέδειξε η πρόσφατη ανασκαφή του Κ. Τσάκου, ακολουθεί την οδό Επιχάρμου (Ε. Μακρή-Κ. Τσάκος-Α. Βαβυλοπούλου-Χαριτωνίδου, "Το Ριζόκαστρο. Σωζόμενα υπολείμματα: Νέες παρατηρήσεις και επαναχρονολόγηση," *Δελτίον της Χριστιανικής Αρχαιολογικής Εταιρείας* [1987–88] 329–336, 342–344, 350–363, ιδίως 363, εικ. 52–58). Το πάχος και η δομή όμως του τοίχου σαφώς δεν είναι οχυρωματικού πύργου.
48. Τις πωροπλίνθους αυτές η Ε. Μακρή θεωρεί κατάλοιπα του Ριζόκαστρου, το οποίο, κατά τη γνώμη της, μετά την οδό Επιχάρμου ακολουθούσε τη Ν. οικοδομική γραμμή της οδού Πρυτανείου. Τα κατάλοιπα όμως του τείχους που έχουν βρεθεί στο υπόγειο του Μουσείου Κανελλοπούλου, στην οδό Θεωρίας (Γ. Δοντάς, "Νεοκλασική οικία παρά τας οδούς Πανός και Θεωρίας," *ΑρχΔελτ* 26 [1971] Β1, 29, σχ. 1, πίν. 40α) και πρόσφατα στο Ν. μέρος της αυλής της οικίας Λ.

Καρρά, στην οδό Πρυτανείου 19, στο προς την οδό Θεωρίας όριο του ακινήτου, μαρτυρούν ότι η πορεία του περνάει υψηλότερα, νοτιότερα, στην κλιτύ της Ακρόπολης όπως σημειώνεται και στο σχέδιο του Τραυλού του 1976 (εικ. 10).

49. Την έρευνα έκανε η συνάδελφος Ε. Μώρου.

50. W. Leak, *Topography of Athens 2* (London 1841) 270 σημ. 1.

51. Leak (σημ. 50) και Miller (σημ. 11) 51.

52. Η σωστική ανασκαφική έρευνα στο ακίνητο οδού Θρασυβούλου 19, ιδιοκτησίας Χ. Μοάτσου, διενεργήθηκε από την συνάδελφο Χ. Βλασσοπούλου. Αποκαλύφθηκαν και εδώ πωρόπλινθοι καθώς και τμήμα μικρού πώρινου κίονα εντειχισμένα σε τοίχο νεοτέρων χρόνων.

53. Βλ. υψηλό πρισματικό χορηγικό βάθρο με επιγραφή του τέλους του 1ου π.Χ. αι. (*IG* II^2, 3114), Travlos, *PDA* 566, εικ. 711, 713. *The Athenian Agora, Guide*[4] (Αθήνα 1990) 130–133. Χορηγική επιγραφή από τη Ρωμαϊκή Αγορά (αρ. ΡΑ 744), όπου αναφέρεται νίκη της Κεκροπίδος φυλής σε χορό παίδων, με χορηγό τον Δήμο και αγωνοθέτη, του οποίου δεν σώζεται το όνομα. (Σ.Ν. Κουμανούδης, "Ἐπιγραφαί ἐξ Ἀθηνῶν," *ΑρχΔελτ* 25 [1970] Μελέται, 57; 3ος αι. π.Χ.). Πρισματικό βάθρο (ΡΑ 394), που βρέθηκε στη Ρωμαϊκή Αγορά, με το κάτω μέρος ανάγλυφης παράστασης και χορηγική αρχαϊστική επιγραφή (Φ. Σταυρόπουλος, "Ἀνασκαφὴ Ρωμαϊκῆς Ἀγορᾶς," *ΑρχΔελτ* [1930–31] Παρ. 7, εικ. 7).

Η οδός των Τριπόδων - τεχνικά και κατασκευαστικά στοιχεία

Κ. Ν. Καζαμιάκης

Το θέατρο του Διονύσου, η οδός Τριπόδων και τα χορηγικά μνημεία αποτελούν ιδιαίτερη θεσμική ενότητα του δημοσίου βίου αλλά και μία κεντρική συνιστώσα στη χωροταξία της αρχαίας Αθήνας. Στη σύντομη αυτή αναφορά παρατίθενται τα μέχρι σήμερα γνωστά τεχνικά και κατασκευαστικά στοιχεία της οδού. Το τμήμα της οδού που είχε αποκαλυφθεί μέχρι το 1988, είχε μήκος 320 μ. Οι έρευνες που διεξήχθησαν έκτοτε[1] μας επέτρεψαν να τεκμηριώσουμε ακόμη 80 μ. της πορείας της οδού,[2] καθώς επίσης να συμπληρώσουμε την οριζοντιογραφία και μηκοτομή της οδού από το Διονυσιακό θέατρο μέχρι περίπου τον Άγιο Νικόλαο Ραγκαβά (σελ. 33, εικ. 2).[3]

Η διατομή της οδού είναι μεικτή: εν εκχώσει και εν επιχώσει. Σ' όλο το μήκος της οδού, το εν εκχώσει τμήμα είναι προς την πλευρά του βράχου της Ακρόπολης (ανάντι), όπου ακριβώς κτίστηκαν όλα τα μέχρι σήμερα γνωστά χορηγικά μνημεία, εδραζόμενα στο βράχο.[4] Ο θεατής που φεύγει από το θέατρο, κατευθυνόμενος προς την Αγορά, βλέπει πάντα αριστερά του τα χορηγικά μνημεία και ψηλότερα την Ακρόπολη.

Ερείσματα, αναλημματικούς τοίχους, ορύγματα και αποχετευτικούς αγωγούς[5] δεν έχουμε σε επαρκή βαθμό, ώστε να τεκμηριωθεί η πλήρης εγκάρσια διατομή της οδού. Για τα παραπάνω τεχνικά στοιχεία η έρευνα είναι σε εξέλιξη. Η εγκάρσια κλίση, όπου εντοπίσθηκε, είναι περίπου της τάξεως 5% το δε πλάτος φθάνει τους 20 πόδες (6-6.50 μ.).[6]

Υποδομή και επιδομή της οδού. Στις θέσεις Πρυτανείου 10, Τριπόδων 20, 22 και 28, οι ανασκαφές απεκάλυψαν επάλληλα οδοστρώματα της οδού, αντιστοιχούντα σε χρονολογικές φάσεις. 'Εχουν πάχος 0.03-0.09 μ. και αποτελούνται από πεπιεσμένο αργιλόχωμα, άμμο, λεπτά θραύσματα κιμηλιάς και μικρά χαλίκια. Είναι χαρακτηριστικό το παράδειγμα της οδού Τριπόδων 22 όπου εντοπίσθηκαν έξι επάλληλα οδοστρώματα, πάχους, από πάνω προς τα κάτω, 0.04, 0.04, 0.05, 0.06, 0.03 και 0.03 μ. Το τελευταίο στρώμα απλώνεται πάνω στο υπόστρωμα της οδού που αποτελείται από επίχωση, πάχους 0.33 μ., με σύνθεση διαβαθμισμένη προς τον φυσικό μαλακό βράχο: χώμα, χαλίκια και θραύσματα κιμηλιάς. Σε κανένα σημείο της οδού δεν βρέθηκε πλακόστρωση[7] ή ίχνη από ρόδες άμαξας.[8] Η οδοποιία ως τέχνη δεν απασχόλησε τους κατασκευαστές των κλασικών και ελληνιστικών πόλεων, με εξαίρεση τις ιερές/πομπικές οδούς (Δήλος, Δίδυμα, Αθήνα: Παναθηναίων-Τριπόδων).Με το μεγάλο πλάτος και τη μνημειώδη όψη που όφειλαν στη θρησκευτική τους λειτουργία δημιούργησαν πρότυπο για τις λεωφόρους της ρωμαϊκής εποχής, οπότε η οδός απέκτησε μεγάλη σημασία στην πολεοδομική αισθητική.

Σημειώσεις

1. Στις 11 Νοεμβρίου 1988, κατά τις εργασίες αποκατάστασης οικίας στην οδό Τριπόδων 28 (ιδιοκτησία Ελληνικής Εταιρείας), εντοπίσθηκε από τον υπογράφοντα αρχαία οικοδομή στο υπόγειο, στη θέση ακριβώς όπου υπολογίζαμε ότι περνά η αρχαία οδός. 'Οπως έδειξε η ανασκαφή που ακολούθησε, επρόκειτο για χορηγικό μνημείο (σελ. 37, εικ. 5-6). Λίγες μέρες αργότερα, στις 14 Νοεμβρίου 1988, κατά τις εργασίες αποκατάστασης οικίας στην οδό Βάκχου 4 (ιδιοκτησία Στράτου), εντοπίσθηκαν ομοίως αρχαία θεμέλια τα οποία ανήκαν σε δύο χορηγικά μνημεία, όπως έδειξε η ανασκαφή που διενήργησε ο έφορος κ. Κωνσταντίνος Τσάκος. Τα παραπάνω μνημεία καθώς και όλες οι θέσεις όπου βρέθηκαν τμήματα της αρχαίας οδού μετρήθηκαν και σχεδιάστηκαν λεπτομερώς, εξαρτήθηκαν υψομετρικώς από το γεωειδές και οριζοντιογραφικώς από το Κρατικό Σύστημα Αναφοράς.
2. Το πιθανό συνολικό μήκος της οδού είναι περίπου 850 μ. Μέχρι το 1988 γνωρίζαμε το 37% ενώ σήμερα προσεγγίζουμε το 50% του όλου μήκους.
3. Η οριζοντιογραφία της οδού άλλαξε σαφώς στο σημείο όπου εντοπίσθηκαν τα νέα χορηγικά μνημεία (Βάκχου 4), καθώς επίσης στο τμήμα από Τριπόδων 34 μέχρι τον 'Αγιο Νικόλαο Ραγκαβά (θέσεις: Τριπόδων 28, 22 και 20).
4. Η ανασκαφή Μηλιάδη (1955), λίγο νοτιότερα του μνημείου του Λυσικράτους, απεκάλυψε το Α. άκρο της οδού και ερείπια οικιών του 5ου π.Χ. αιώνα. Δεδομένου ότι τα ανασκαφικά στοιχεία κατάντι της οδού και καθ' όλο το μήκος της είναι ελλιπή, παραμένει θεωρητική η άποψη ότι τα χορηγικά μνημεία στήθηκαν μόνον από τη μια πλευρά της οδού, οι δε οικίες της άλλης πλευράς με τον χρόνο κατεδαφίστηκαν, ώστε να διευρυνθεί η οδός και να αναδειχθούν τα μνημεία.
5. Στην Αθήνα, ήδη από το τέλος του 6ου αι. π.Χ., έχουμε σημαντικά αποχετευτικά συστήματα και πυκνό δίκτυο πήλινων αγωγών κάτω από τα οδοστρώματα, αν και το σύστημα των ανοικτών αγωγών δεν εγκαταλείφθηκε τελείως.
6. Πριν τη ρωμαϊκή εποχή και σε πόλεις όπως η Αθήνα που δεν

ρυμοτομήθηκαν εξ αρχής με το σύστημα των ορθογωνίων αξόνων αλλά σταδιακά και σε απόλυτη εξάρτηση από το φυσικό ανάγλυφο, το πλάτος των δρόμων ήταν 3–4.50 μ. κατά μέσο όρο. Στις συνοικίες επικρατούσαν τα στενά δρομάκια πλάτους 1.50–3 μ. ενώ κάποιες μεγαλύτερες αρτηρίες που συνέδεαν την Αγορά με τις πόλεις, έφθαναν τα 9 μ. Εξαίρεση αποτελούσαν η οδός Παναθηναίων που έφθανε τα 12 μ. προκειμένου να εξυπηρετήσει συγκεκριμένες θρησκευτικές λειτουργίες (πομπές, αγώνες κ.λ.π.) και η οδός Τριπόδων, που έφθανε τα 6 μ. προφανώς για παρεμφερείς λόγους.

7. Η πλακόστρωση δεν φαίνεται να συνηθιζόταν στην αρχαία Αθήνα. Το έδαφος παρέμενε άστρωτο ή σκεπαζόταν με λεπτή στρώση χαλικιών, έτσι ώστε το πέρασμα του νερού, από βροχή ή οικιακή χρήση να δημιουργεί χαντάκια, ακόμα και στην οδό Παναθηναίων, και να απαιτεί συνεχή φροντίδα. Η συντήρηση και επισκευή των δρόμων, μέχρι κάποια απόσταση από την πόλη, ήταν έργο των *όδοποιῶν* καθώς επίσης η χάραξη και η κατασκευή/επιπέδωση των οδών. Οι *άστυνόμοι* φρόντιζαν μεταξύ άλλων για τη διατήρηση της καθαριότητας στους δρόμους και την αποκατάσταση των ζημιών και καταπατήσεων, που εθεωρούντο σοβαρές παραβάσεις.

8. Πιθανό ίχνος "ροδιάς" βρέθηκε στην οικία Καρρά (Πρυτανείου 19).

Ανασκαφές σε αθηναϊκά κεραμικά εργαστήρια αρχαϊκών και κλασικών χρόνων

Έφη Μπαζιωτοπούλου-Βαλαβάνη

Στους αρχαιολόγους της Γ′ Εφορείας

Είναι πράγματι αξιοπερίεργο το γεγονός ότι συγκριτικά με τη διάρκεια, την ποιότητα και το πλήθος των προϊόντων της αττικής κεραμικής παραγωγής, ελάχιστα μας είναι γνωστά για τους χώρους όπου ασκούνταν αυτή η τέχνη.[1] Τα κεραμικά εργαστήρια με τις ταπεινές πλινθόκτιστες εγκαταστάσεις τους ήταν εύκολο να εξαφανιστούν σε μια πόλη με συνεχή οικοδομική δραστηριότητα από την αρχαιότητα, που έφτασε σε εξοντωτικούς για τα μνημεία ρυθμούς τα τελευταία τριάντα χρόνια. Συγχρόνως όμως τα κεραμικά εργαστήρια, έχοντας συγκεκριμένα αρχιτεκτονικά γνωρίσματα που δεν συναντώνται σε άλλες κατασκευές, δίνουν τη δυνατότητα στον ανασκαφέα να επισημάνει την ύπαρξή τους μέσω κυρίως κεραμικών κλιβάνων, δεξαμενών καθαρισμού του πηλού, αποθέσεων καθαρού πηλού, καθώς και αποθέσεων με προϊόντα τους που ποτέ δεν έφθασαν στο εμπόριο, όπως σπασμένα, κακοψημένα ή μισοτελειωμένα αγγεία, όστρακα δοκιμής, στηρίγματα αγγείων, μήτρες και άλλα εργαλεία της δουλειάς των κεραμέων.

Η Γ′ Εφορεία Αρχαιοτήτων στις δεκάδες ανασκαφές που διεξάγει κάθε χρόνο στην περιοχή της αρχαίας πόλης είχε τη δυνατότητα να διαπιστώσει την ύπαρξη αρκετών κεραμικών εργαστηρίων, από τα οποία θα εξετάσουμε εδώ αυτά που χρονολογούνται στα αρχαϊκά και κλασικά χρόνια.[2] Το αρχαιότερο, με τις μέχρι σήμερα γνώσεις μας, κεραμικό εργαστήριο, που ανάγεται στο β′ μισό του 6ου π.Χ. αιώνα, επισημάνθηκε από δύο αποθέτες στην οδό Προφήτου Δανιήλ, στον αρχαίο δρόμο προς την Ακαδημία, περίπου 700 μ. από το Δίπυλο (εικ. 1, αρ. 1).[3] Οι ενδείξεις εργαστηριακής χρήσης προέρχονται από όστρακα δοκιμής με τη χαρακτηριστική οπή, στηρίγματα αγγείων, κακοψημένα αγγεία και μήτρα ανθεμίου. Ενδιαφέρον παρουσιάζει μικρός μελανόμορφος πίνακας του τρίτου τέταρτου του 6ου αι. με παράσταση Αρτέμιδος σε τέθριππο και Απόλλωνα, θέμα γνωστό στην αττική αγγειογραφία κυρίως από τις επόμενες δεκαετίες.[4] Στην πίσω όψη του πλακιδίου διακρίνεται σπουδή αλόγων και ίσως τεθρίππου με απλές μελανές και λευκές πινελιές. Η απόδοση της ελεύθερης κίνησης των αλόγων στη σπουδή αυτή φαίνεται πρωτοποριακή για την εποχή. Από τα προϊόντα του εργαστηρίου υπερτερούν τα όστρακα από μελανόμορφες κύλικες και σκύφους των ομάδων Κροκωτού, Chariot-Courting και Cock Group ή του ζωγράφου των Αθηνών 581 και χρονολογούνται από το β′ μισό του 6ου και κυρίως από το τρίτο τέταρτο του αιώνα μέχρι και τις δύο πρώτες δεκαετίες του 5ου.[5] Τέλος, σε πήλινους δακτυλίους[6] εμφανίζονται διάφορα εγχάρακτα γράμματα, αρχικές συλλαβές προφανώς ονομάτων, που ίσως αποδίδουν ονόματα κεραμέων ή ιδιοκτητών εργαστηρίου, χωρίς να αποκλείονται και άλλες ερμηνείες. Υπερτερούν εδώ τα αρχικά ΣΙΣ.

Αρκετά κεραμικά εργαστήρια φαίνεται ότι δραστηριοποιούνται στα υστεροαρχαϊκά και κλασικά χρόνια στην περιοχή της σημερινής συνοικίας Ακαδημία Πλάτωνος.[7] Σε οικόπεδο στη γωνία των οδών Μοναστηρίου και Φαιάκων (εικ. 1, αρ. 2) διασώθηκαν και οικοδομικά λείψανα, αφού εκτός των αποθετών βρέθηκαν και θεμέλια τοίχων που σχηματίζουν ορθογώνιους χώρους, μία δεξαμενή, αυλάκια λαξευμένα στην κιμηλιά, λάκκοι με καμμένες μάζες πηλού και υπαίθριος χώρος, προφανώς αυλή.[8] Τις ενδείξεις παρουσίας του εργαστηρίου ενισχύουν κι εδώ όστρακα δοκιμής, πήλινοι δακτύλιοι, μάζες καθαρού πηλού, τμήμα εργαλείου και κακοψημένα αγγεία, σε ένα από τα οποία διακρίνουμε σπουδή με λευκό επίθετο χρώμα που απολεπίστηκε.[9] Από τα προϊόντα του εργαστηρίου που καλύπτουν χρονικά όλο τον 5ο αιώνα υπερτερούν τα όστρακα μελαμβαφών κυλίκων, σκύφων και σκυφοειδών κυλίκων, ενώ αρκετά προέρχονται και από υστεροαρχαϊκές μελανόμορφες κύλικες και σκύφους. Τα ερυθρόμορφα όστρακα είναι ελάχιστα, κυρίως από κρατήρες του β′ μισού του 5ου αι. Όστρακα ενεπίγραφων πήλινων δακτυλίων βρέθηκαν αρκετά, από τα οποία τα περισσότερα φέρουν τα γράμματα ΣΤΡΑ. Σε μερικούς από τους αποθέτες υπάρχουν ενδείξεις λειτουργίας του εργαστηρίου μέχρι και τη δεύτερη δεκαετία του 4ου αιώνα με ανοιχτά σχήματα που φέρουν έντυπη διακόσμηση και πρώιμο rouleting. Ένα στρώμα καταστροφής του 4ου αιώνα κάλυψε τους εργαστηριακούς χώρους προκαλώντας και τη διακοπή της δραστηριότητάς τους. Τον 3ο π.Χ. αιώνα στο στρώμα αυτό ανοίχτηκαν τάφοι και ο χώρος χρησιμοποιήθηκε ως νεκροταφείο μέχρι τον 4ο μ.Χ. αιώνα. Το κάτω τμήμα κυκλικού κεραμικού κλιβάνου που

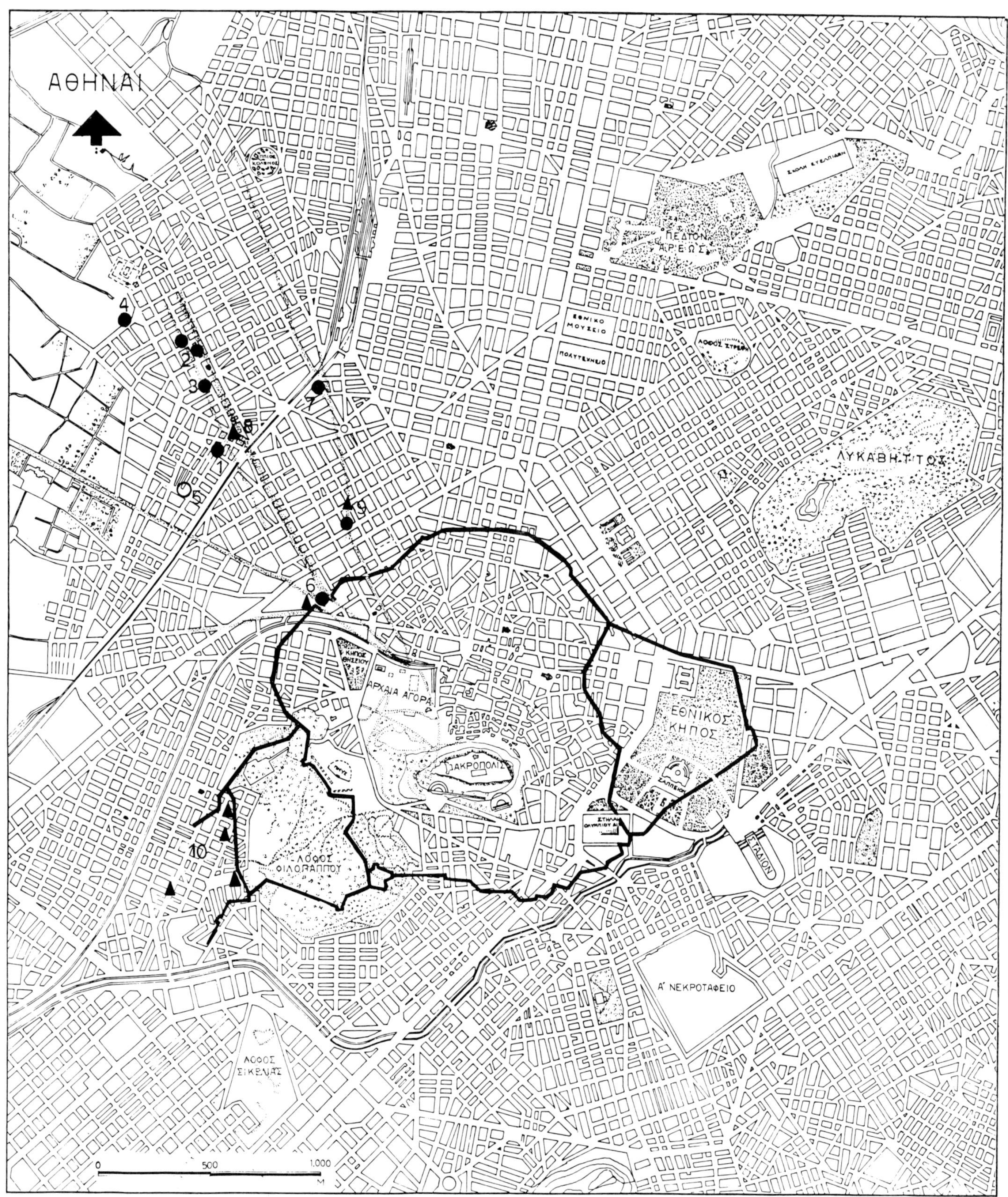

Εικ. 1. Κάτοψη της πόλης των Αθηνών με σημειωμένες τις θέσεις εύρεσης λειψάνων κεραμικών εργαστηρίων. Με κύκλο τα εργαστήρια του 6ου και 5ου αι. π.Χ., με τρίγωνο του 4ου. Ο αρ. 5 δηλώνει θέση εργαστηρίου κοροπλαστικής.

βρέθηκε πρόσφατα στο απέναντι οικόπεδο και χρονολογήθηκε στα κλασικά χρόνια, θα πρέπει να ανήκει στο ίδιο εργαστηριακό συγκρότημα.[10]

Στην ίδια γειτονιά και την ίδια περίπου εποχή ένα άλλο εργαστήριο ή το κατάστημά του άφησε τα προϊόντα του σε τμήμα αποθέτη που ερευνήθηκε στην οδό Παλαμηδίου (εικ. 1, αρ. 3). Σε λάκκο διαστάσεων 1 × 0,50 μ. βρέθηκαν 262 μελαμβαφείς οξυπύθμενοι αμφορίσκοι με εμπίεστη διακόσμηση, που χρονολογούνται από το τρίτο τέταρτο του 5ου μέχρι τις αρχές του 4ου αιώνα.[11] Στην ίδια περιοχή τέλος, σε οικόπεδο επί των οδών Μητροδώρου και Γεμηνού (εικ. 1, αρ. 4), εκτός των γεωμετρικών εγχυτρισμών και των κλασικών ταφών, βρέθηκαν ένα πηγάδι και τρεις αποθέτες.[12] Από τους τελευταίους ο ένας περιείχε μελαμβαφή κεραμική του 5ου αιώνα, κυρίως του τρίτου τέταρτου, με συντριπτικό το ποσοστό των αττικών σκύφων και κυλίκων. Ανάμεσά τους όστρακα δοκιμής, αρκετά άλλα με ανομοιομερή όπτηση, πήλινοι δακτύλιοι διαφόρων τύπων αλλά και κομμάτια ψημμένου και άψητου πηλού.

Σχετικά κοντά στα τείχη της πόλης προς την πλευρά των λεγόμενων Ηρίων πυλών, στη σημερινή οδό Μαραθώνος 2 (εικ. 1, αρ. 9, κύκλος), αποκαλύφθηκαν το 1967 τρεις αποθέτες του εργαστηρίου του Βρύγου.[13] Λόγω της ανορθόδοξης ανασκαφικής διαδικασίας, αφού οι αρχαιολόγοι έφτασαν μετά την παράνομη διάνοιξη των θεμελίων, δεν γνωρίζουμε αν πρόκειται για τρεις αποθέτες ή για ενιαία απόθεση, όπως δείχνει η ομοιογένεια του υλικού και ως προς τα σχήματα και ως προς την τεχνοτροπία των παραστάσεων τους. Ο Maffre που έχει την τύχη να μελετά αυτό το υλικό, επισημαίνει ότι σε μεγάλο σύνολο τμημάτων ερυθρόμορφων αγγείων τα 200 ανήκουν σε κύλικες και μόνο τα 20 σε σκύφους. Τα 13 καλύτερα της τελευταίας κατηγορίας τα χρονολογεί γύρω στο 480 και αποδίδει 3 σκύφους στο ζωγράφο του Βρύγου, άλλους 3 στον ίδιο με πιθανότητα, 5 στο ζ. της Βρησηίδος, 1 στο ζ. του Τριπτολέμου και 1 γενικώς στον κύκλο του ζ. του Βρύγου. Επιβεβαιώνεται δηλαδή και ανασκαφικά ότι σημαντικοί ζωγράφοι εργάζονταν κάτω από την ίδια στέγη, υπό τον ίδιο προφανώς εργοδότη.

Εκτός των ερυθρόμορφων υπάρχουν και μερικά όστρακα ύστερων μελανόμορφων κυλίκων και σκύφων, ενώ σπανιότερα είναι τα λυχνάρια, οι λήκυθοι και τα κύπελλα, καθώς και τα αβαφή αγγεία. Ανομοιομερή όπτηση βλέπουμε σε κύπελλα, καθώς και σε μελαμβαφή σκυφοειδή κύλικα και κύλικα με αποτυχημένη ερυθρή βαφή από μίλτο στο εσωτερικό. Από την ίδια ανασκαφή προέρχονται ερυθρόμορφα όστρακα δοκιμής, το γνωστό πλακίδιο με τις λαβές σκύφων,[14] διάφοροι τύποι δακτυλίων και σπουδή ανθεμίου σε απλό όστρακο. Μάζες πηλού και τεφρές επιχώσεις συμπληρώνουν την εικόνα των αποθέσεων του εργαστηρίου, που οι εγκαταστάσεις του θα πρέπει να βρίσκονταν στην αμέσως γειτονική περιοχή. Το εργαστήριο του Βρύγου παραμένει μέχρι σήμερα το σημαντικότερο από πλευράς ποιότητος εύρημα του αθηναϊκού Κεραμεικού.

Ο ίδιος ο Κεραμεικός δεν έχει δώσει μέχρι σήμερα προϊόντα αντάξια της φήμης του, τουλάχιστον για την εποχή που μας απασχολεί (εικ. 1, αρ. 6).[15] Τα παλιότερα ίχνη που χρονολογούνται γενικά στον 5ο και στον πρώιμο 4ο π.Χ. αιώνα, εντοπίστηκαν κάτω από τα πρώτα ταφικά οικοδομήματα στα αριστερά της μεγάλης οδού του Διπύλου και φαίνεται ότι μετατοπίστηκαν από τα μέσα του 5ου αιώνα με την αλλαγή της χρήσης του χώρου για τη δημιουργία του δημοσίου σήματος. 'Αλλα υπολείμματα κλασικών εργαστηρίων θα πρέπει να βρίσκονται κάτω από την εκκλησία της Αγίας Τριάδος, ενώ τμήματα κλιβάνων και ενδείξεις κεραμικής δραστηριότητας στην περιοχή του Μουσείου και μπροστά στην τάφρο υποδηλώνουν συνεχή εργαστηριακή χρήση του χώρου συγχρόνως με την ταφική μέχρι το τέλος της αρχαιότητας.

Με την περιοχή του αρχαιολογικού χώρου του Κεραμεικού μπορεί όμως να συνδεθεί η εύρεση απόθεσης από το κεραμικό εργαστήριο όπου εργαζόταν ένας σημαντικός αγγειογράφος του τελευταίου τέταρτου του 5ου π.Χ. αι., ο ζωγράφος του Δίνου των Αθηνών.[16] Εκατοντάδες όστρακα από κωδωνόσχημους κρατήρες, μεταξύ των οποίων και αρκετά αποτυχημένα, καθώς και όστρακα δοκιμής, βρέθηκαν στις αρχές του 20ου αι. κατά την ανοικοδόμηση σπιτιού "in der nähe des Piräus Bahnhofs," και κατέληξαν στη Βόννη.[17] Η μαρτυρία για σταθμό του Πειραιώς, όπως ονομαζόταν τότε ο σταθμός του ηλεκτρικού σιδηροδρόμου στο Θησείο, υποδηλώνει σαφέστατα ως τόπο εύρεσης την περιοχή Δ.-ΝΔ. του αρχαιολογικού χώρου του Κεραμεικού, μια δηλαδή περιοχή που θα πρέπει να ανήκε στον δήμο των Κεραμέων. Επειδή όμως η μαρτυρία είναι γενική και επισφαλής, δεν επαρκεί για να τεκμηριώσει την τοποθέτηση του συγκεκριμένου εργαστηρίου σε περιοχή εντός των τειχών.

Η εικόνα των κεραμικών εργαστηρίων του 5ου π.Χ. αιώνα, συμπληρώνεται με τα ευρήματα της μεγάλης σωστικής ανασκαφής για την κατασκευή του ανισόπεδου κόμβου των οδών Λένορμαν και Κωνσταντινουπόλεως (εικ. 1, αρ. 7).[18] Στην ανασκαφή εκτός των νεκροταφείων εντοπίστηκαν 3 δρόμοι, 4 κλίβανοι, 1 δωμάτιο και τμήματα άλλων, αγωγοί και 11 αποθέτες. Ο πυρήνας του εργαστηριακού χώρου βρίσκεται στο νότιο τμήμα της ανασκαφής, ενώ οι αποθέτες, κατεσπαρμένοι σε όλη την έκτασή της, δείχνουν εκτεταμμένη εργαστηριακή χρήση μιας ολόκληρης γειτονιάς κεραμέων.[19]

Το δυτικό τμήμα του εργαστηριακού χώρου (εικ. 2) ορίζει ο αρχαίος δρόμος Ι με συνεχή χρήση τουλάχιστον από το τελευταίο τέταρτο του 6ου έως και τον 2ο μ.Χ. αιώνα. Πρόκειται για τη βασική οδική αρτηρία της αρχαίας πόλης που οδηγούσε από τις Ηρίες πύλες στον Ίππιο Κολωνό. Με βάση τα αρχιτεκτονικά κατάλοιπα διακρίνονται δύο φάσεις λειτουργίας των εργαστηρίων. Στην πρώτη (εικ. 3), ο δρόμος, ένα δωμάτιο και τμήμα δεύτερου ορίζουν υπαίθρια αυλή, το δάπεδο της οποίας βρέθηκε σε δύο σημεία, έτσι ώστε να είμαστε βέβαιοι ότι έφτανε μέχρι την επιφάνεια του δρόμου και αντιστοιχούσε σε ένα από τα οδοστρώματά του. Στον

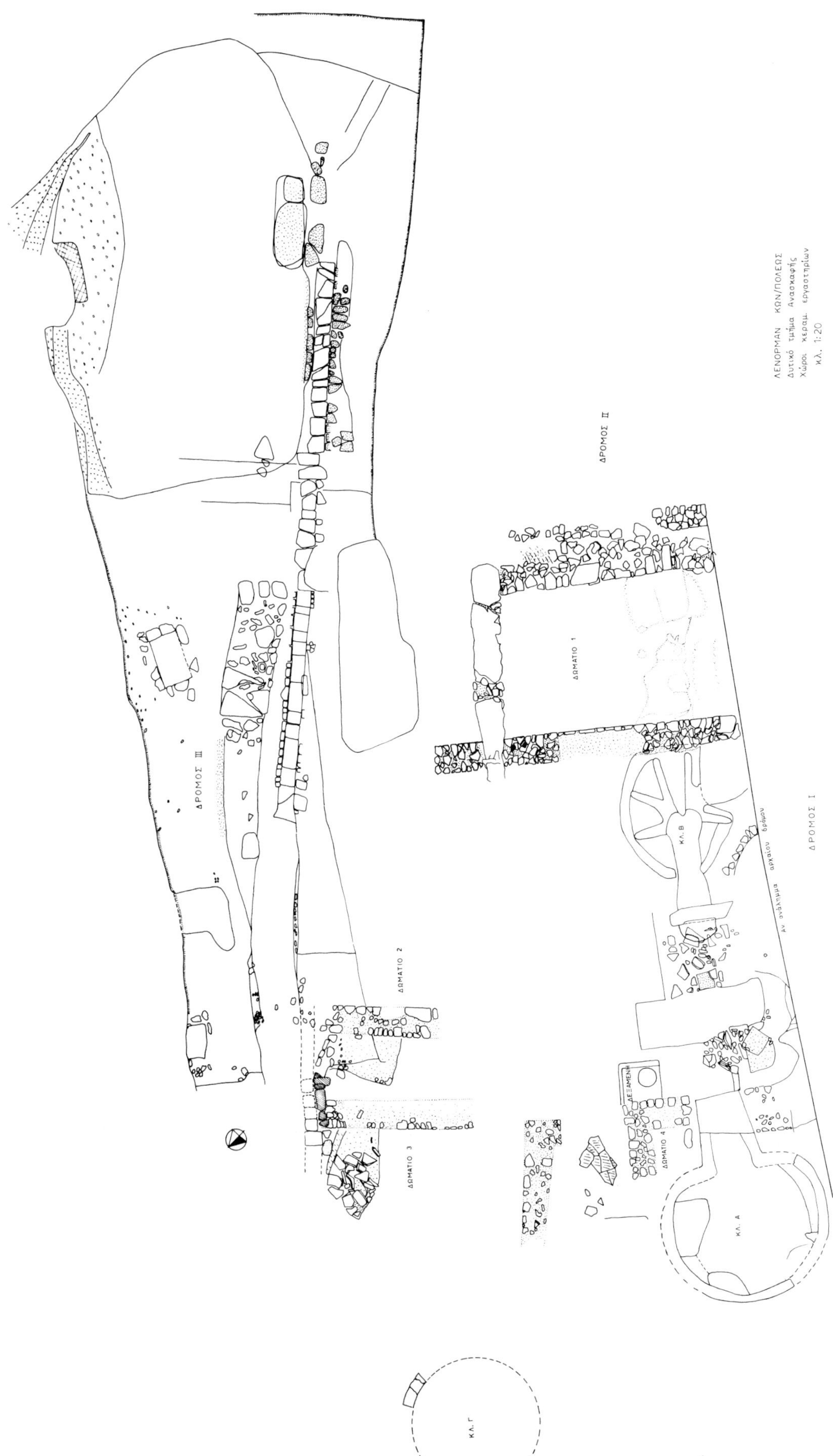

Εικ. 2. Ανασκαφή Λένορμαν και Κωνσταντινουπόλεως. Το τμήμα της ανασκαφής με τα οικοδομικά λείψανα των κεραμικών εργαστηρίων.

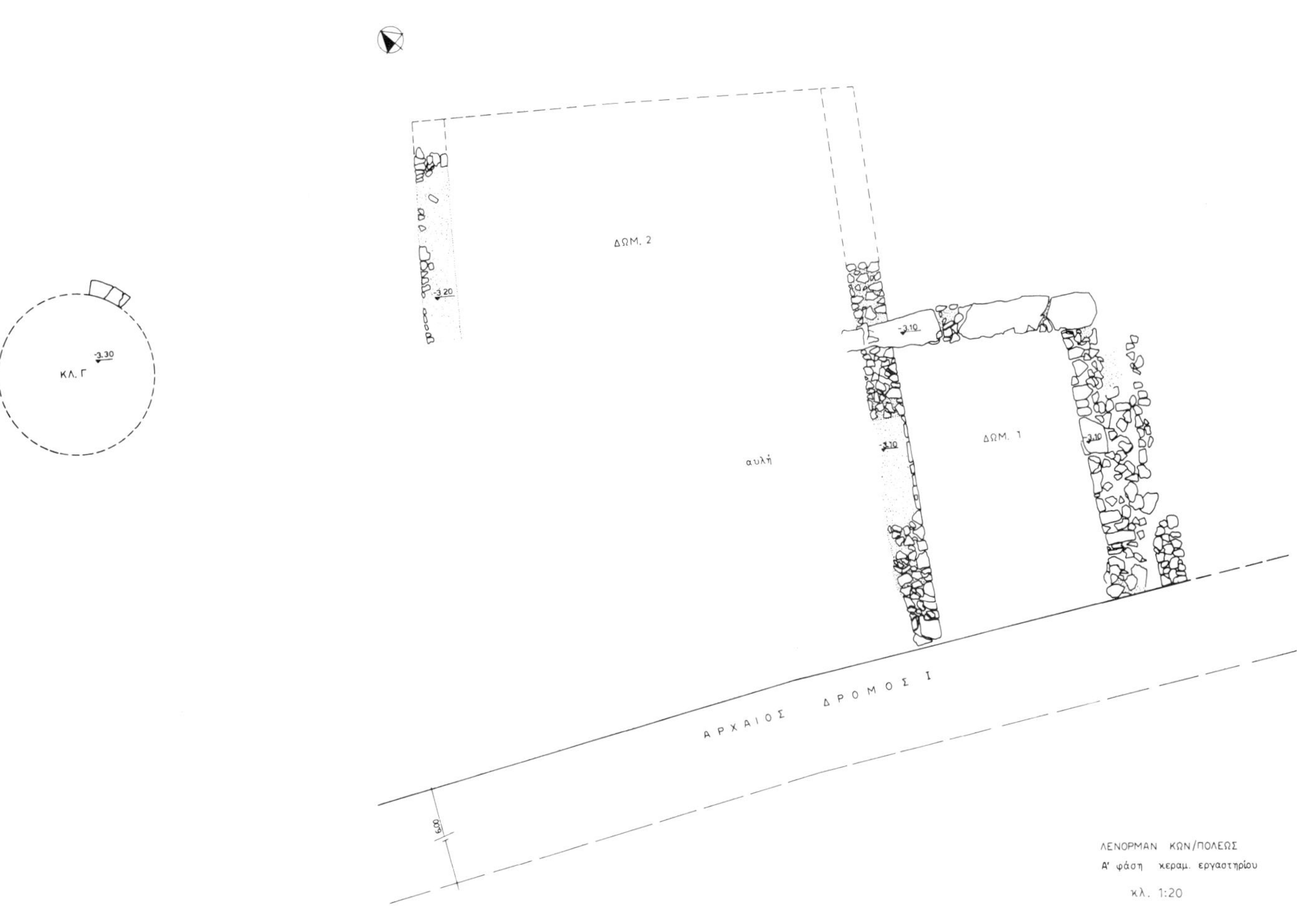

Εικ. 3. Ανασκαφή Λένορμαν και Κωνσταντινουπόλεως. Α΄ φάση των κεραμικών εργαστηρίων.

ελεύθερο αυτό χώρο φαίνεται ότι λειτουργούσε και ο κυκλικός κλίβανος Γ, με το θάλαμο θέρμανσης θεμελιωμένο στην κιμηλιά. Στο τελευταίο τέταρτο του 5ου αιώνα, μια καταστροφή είχε ως αποτέλεσμα εκτεταμμένη απόθεση 20 περίπου τετραγωνικών μέτρων και πάχους 0,60 μ. που κάλυψε και το δωμάτιο, σταματώντας τη λειτουργία του ως χώρου κατασκευής αγγείων και φύλαξης αγγείων και πηλών.

Το πλούσιο υλικό κεραμικών προϊόντων που βρέθηκε στην απόθεση αυτή χρονολογείται σε όλη τη διάρκεια του 5ου αι. και κυρίως στο β΄ τέταρτό του. Η ποικιλία των σχημάτων είναι σημαντική αλλά κυριαρχούν οι μελανόμορφες σκυφοειδείς κύλικες, καθώς και σκύφοι και των δύο τύπων. Αρκετά είναι και τα όστρακα κυλίκων τύπου Ρήνειας, ληκύθων, ολπών, αλατοδοχείων και πινακίων. Τα ερυθρόμορφα όστρακα είναι λίγα, κυρίως από κρατήρες και κλειστά αγγεία των μέσων του αιώνα. Πολλά είναι και τα τεκμήρια εργαστηριακής δράσης όπως μάζες καθαρού πηλού, δοκιμαστικά όστρακα όπτησης, ίχνη μίλτου σε πυθμένα σκύφου και σε βότσαλο-τριπτήρα, μήτρες ειδωλίων και ανθεμίου και λίγα σιδερένια αντικείμενα, βελόνες και μαχαιρίδια, ίσως εργαλεία των ίδιων των κεραμέων. Ιδιαίτερο ενδιαφέρον παρουσιάζουν πολλά μικρά κομμάτια άψητου πηλού, που όπως δείχνει το σχήμα και τα δακτυλικά αποτυπώματα που φέρουν, θα πρέπει να χρησίμευαν στη στήριξη των υγρών ακόμη αγγείων. Τέλος, στο ίδιο στρώμα βρέθηκαν όστρακο με εγχάρακτα αριθμητικά σύμβολα για καταγραφή κάποιας μέτρησης και ένα σύνολο μικύλλων αβαφών αγγείων, ίσως κάποια παραγγελία.

Αμέσως μετά την καταστροφή των εργαστηρίων που ίσως οφείλεται σε έναν από τους σεισμούς του τελευταίου τέταρτου του 5ου αιώνα που αναφέρει ο Θουκυδίδης, ο χώρος αναδιοργανώνεται (εικ. 4).[20] Δύο ακόμη δρόμοι, ο ΙΙ και ο ΙΙΙ κατασκευάζονται και μαζί με τον Ι ορίζουν τώρα από τρεις πλευρές το νέο εργαστηριακό χώρο που αναπτύσσεται στην ίδια περιοχή.[21] Δύο τουλάχιστον δωμάτια και μικρή τετράγωνη δεξαμενή με φρεάτιο αποτελούν χώρους εργαστηρίου που καταλαμβάνει τη θέση της προηγούμενης αυλής. Δύο κυκλικοί κλίβανοι χτίζονται δίπλα στο δρόμο Ι (εικ. 4, 5) και πιθανότατα ως αυλή χρησιμοποιείται ο ελεύθερος χώρος πάνω από το παλιό

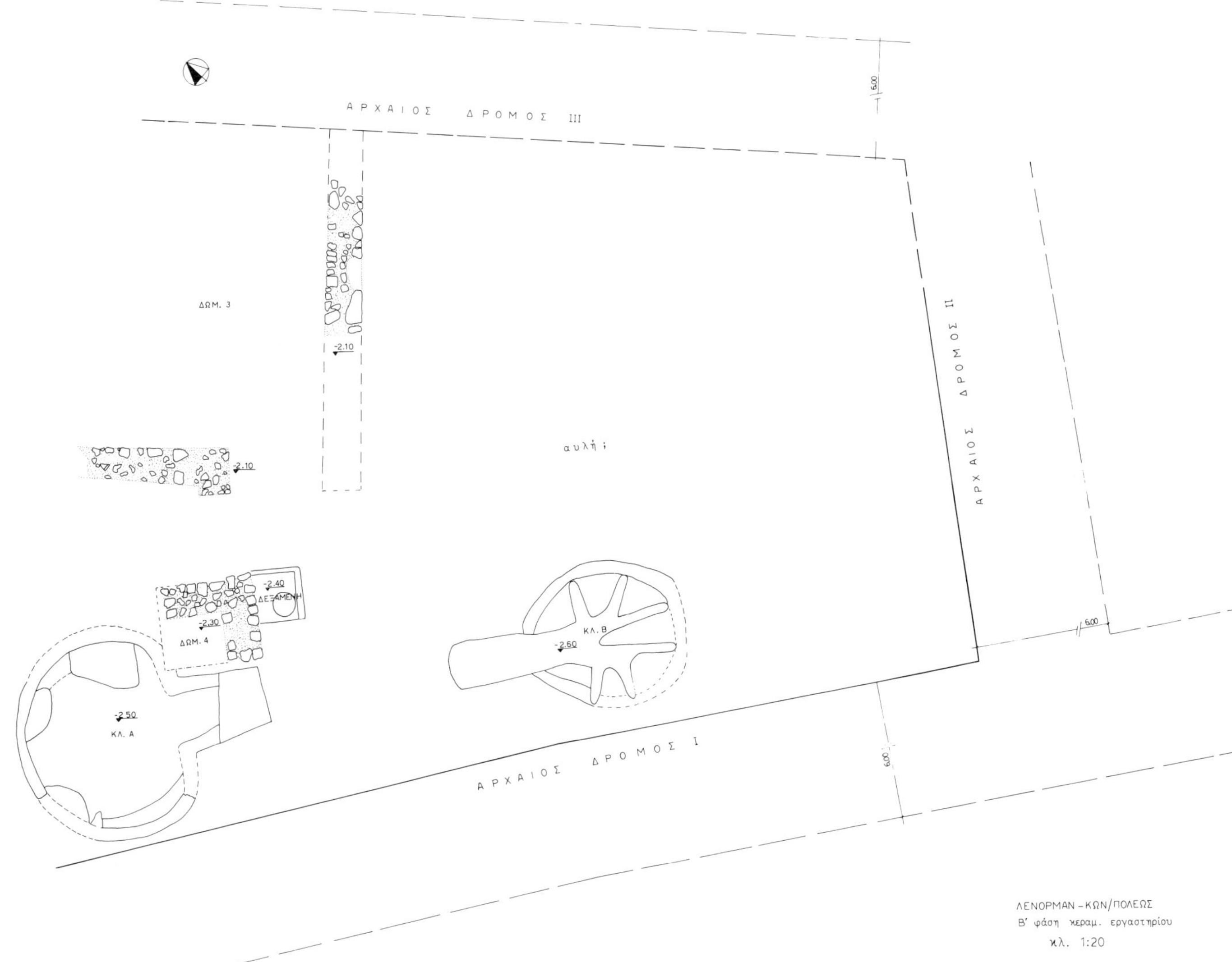

Εικ. 4. Ανασκαφή Λένορμαν και Κωνσταντινουπόλεως. Β΄ φάση των κεραμικών εργαστηρίων.

δωμάτιο. Η διάρκεια λειτουργίας της δεύτερης φάσης του εργαστηρίου ήταν αρκετά σύντομη: ήδη στον πρώιμο 4ο π.Χ. αιώνα μια άλλη ξαφνική καταστροφή πρέπει να διέκοψε οριστικά τη λειτουργία του, αφού στην εξωτερική γωνία της δεξαμενής βρέθηκε *in situ* ένα σύνολο πήλινων δακτυλίων (εικ. 6).[22] Τέλος, τμήμα ορθογώνιου κεραμικού κλιβάνου θεμελιωμένου στην κιμηλιά που βρέθηκε προς το κέντρο της ανασκαφής σε διαταραγμένη επίχωση θα μπορούσε να συσχετισθεί με την κλασική φάση του εργαστηρίου.

Τις σημαντικότερες όμως πληροφορίες για την παραγωγή των εργαστηρίων αντλούμε από τους αποθέτες τους, που σε γενικές γραμμές μπορούν να διακριθούν σε τρεις κατηγορίες: α. Σ' αυτούς που έχουν υλικό εργαστηρίων αλλά και απορρίμματα από τον καθαρισμό της περιοχής που έγινε μετά την καταστροφή.[23] β. Σε ορύγματα που έχουν δεχθεί σχεδόν αποκλειστικά, υλικό από απορρίμματα εργαστηρίων, όπως πηλούς, στηρίγματα αλλά και σπασμένα προϊόντα τους.[24] Χαρακτηριστικά ευρήματα από τους αποθέτες αυτούς είναι ιδιότυπες μήτρες και πήλινοι δακτύλιοι με εγχάρακτα γράμματα ή λιγκατούρες. Ο πληρέστερος αναγράφει το πρώτο τμήμα του ονόματος ενός Ναυκράτη ή Ναυκρατίδα, μερικοί τα γράμματα ΝΑΥ και πολλοί άλλοι φέρουν γραπτό μόνο το αρχικό του Ν. γ. Στην τρίτη κατηγορία αποθετών είχαν απορριφθεί μεγάλα σύνολα όμοιων αγγείων, τα περισσότερα καλής ποιότητας, που μάλλον αποτελούν παραγγελίες που για κάποιο λόγο δεν πρόλαβαν να πουληθούν ή να προωθηθούν σε μακρινές αγορές.[25]

Μεγάλες ποσότητες οστράκων, που φθάνουν περίπου τα 20 κιβώτια, ανήκουν κυρίως σε μελανόμορφους μαστοειδείς σκύφους και κύπελλα, σε οφθαλμωτές κύλικες, καθώς και σε ληκύθους και κύλικες του ύστερου μελανόμορφου ρυθμού. Η πιθανότητα μιας παραγγελίας είναι ιδιαίτερα μεγάλη στους μαστοειδείς σκύφους και τις οφθαλμωτές κύλικες, οι οποίες μάλιστα βρέθηκαν όλες μαζί σε ξεχωριστό αποθέτη χωρίς την παρεμβολή άλλων σχημάτων. Τα εργαστήρια επομένως της οδού Λένορμαν λειτουργούν στο μεγαλύτερο διάστημα του 5ου π.Χ. αιώνα με εντονότερη παραγωγική δραστηριότητα στο α΄ μισό του. Τα προϊόντα τους, αποτέλεσμα μαζικής παραγωγής είναι δεύτερης ποιότητας, χαρακτηριστικό του ύστερου μελανόμορφου και αποτελούνται κυρίως από τις γνωστές στυλιστικές ομάδες των "χωρίς φύλλα κλαδιών" (Leafless Group) και του Αίμονα.[26] Η μελέτη του υλικού αυτού αναμένεται να δώσει μια ποικιλία καλλιτεχνικών χεριών, καθώς και γενικότερες πληροφορίες για την παραγωγή του αθηναϊκού Κεραμεικού στην κλασική περίοδο.

Τα εργαστήρια του 4ου π.Χ. αιώνα περιέργως δεν φαίνεται να διαδέχονται τους ήδη εγκαταλελειμμένους χώρους του 5ου,[27] αλλά από τα μέσα κυρίως του αιώνα δημιουργούν νέες εγκαταστάσεις, κοντά στα τείχη της πόλης. Η τοπογραφική αυτή συρρίκνωση φαίνεται ανάλογη με την κεραμική παραγωγή της Αθήνας αυτήν την εποχή. Στην αρχή του 4ου π.Χ. αιώνα χρονολογείται και το εργαστήριο του ζ. της Ιένας, που προϊόντα του βρέθηκαν το 1853 κατά την ανοικοδόμηση σπιτιού στην οδόν Ερμού, χωρίς να γνωρίζουμε ακριβέστερη ένδειξη τοποθεσίας.[28] Η πιθανότερη υποψήφια περιοχή είναι το κατώτερο τμήμα της οδού, δίπλα στον αρχαιολογικό χώρο του Κεραμεικού, που ανήκε στον δήμο των Κεραμέων, χωρίς να μπορούμε να διαπιστώσουμε αν ήταν εκτός του τείχους ή πολύ κοντά στο εσωτερικό του. Προσωπικά και με βάση τα δεδομένα των άλλων κεραμικών εργαστηρίων, θεωρώ πιθανότερο το πρώτο. Η συνέχεια της παραγωγής διαπιστώνεται και από ευρήματα των γερμανικών ανασκαφών του Κεραμεικού, ενώ πρόσφατες ανασκαφές της Γ΄ Εφορείας επεσήμαναν δύο νέα εργαστήρια στην οδό Χαλκιδικής και στη γωνία των οδών Αγησιλάου και Μυλλέρου (εικ. 1, αρ. 8 και 9).[29]

Τελευταίες έρευνες στα σημερινά Άνω Πετράλωνα επιβεβαιώνουν τη δημιουργία στο β΄ μισό του 4ου π.Χ. αιώνα μιας νέας συνοικίας κεραμέων εκτός του οχυρωματικού περιβόλου αλλά εντός των σκελών των Μακρών Τειχών (εικ. 1, αρ. 10). Στα εργαστήρια αυτά, εκτός των συνηθισμένων καταλοίπων, βρέθηκαν και σύνολα όμοιων αγγείων που υποδηλώνουν παραγγελίες ή τρόπους λειτουργίας των εργαστηρίων. Η λειτουργία τους παύει στο τέλος του αιώνα και ο χώρος, τουλάχιστον εντός των Μακρών Τειχών, δεν ξαναχρησιμοποιείται μέχρι τον 2ο π.Χ. αιώνα, οπότε και δημιουργείται νεκροταφείο που λειτουργεί συνεχώς μέχρι το τέλος της αρχαιότητας.[30]

Από μια πρώτη εξέταση των ανασκαφικών δεδομένων των μέχρι σήμερα γνωστών κεραμικών εργαστηρίων της κλασικής Αθήνας και πριν τη διεξοδική μελέτη του υλικού τους, μπορούμε να κάνουμε τις ακόλουθες γενικές παρατηρήσεις.

α. Τα εργαστήρια λειτουργούν γενικά εκτός των τειχών.[31] Οι πληροφορίες ότι δύο απ' αυτά, δηλαδή του ζ. του Δίνου και του ζ. της Ιένας, βρίσκονταν στο εσωτερικό της πόλης αλλά πολύ κοντά στο τείχος, είναι επισφαλείς για να μπορούν να τεκμηριώσουν μια τέτοια άποψη, χωρίς όμως να είναι και απίθανη.[32]

β. Τα κεραμικά εργαστήρια του τέλους του 6ου και του 5ου αιώνα αναπτύσσονται κυρίως προς την ΒΔ. πλευρά της πόλης, στον ευρύτερο Κεραμεικό αλλά πολλές φορές σε μεγάλη απόσταση από το Άστυ, προς την Ακαδημία Πλάτωνος και τον ΄Ιππιο Κολωνό. Τόσο από τις γραπτές πηγές όσο και από

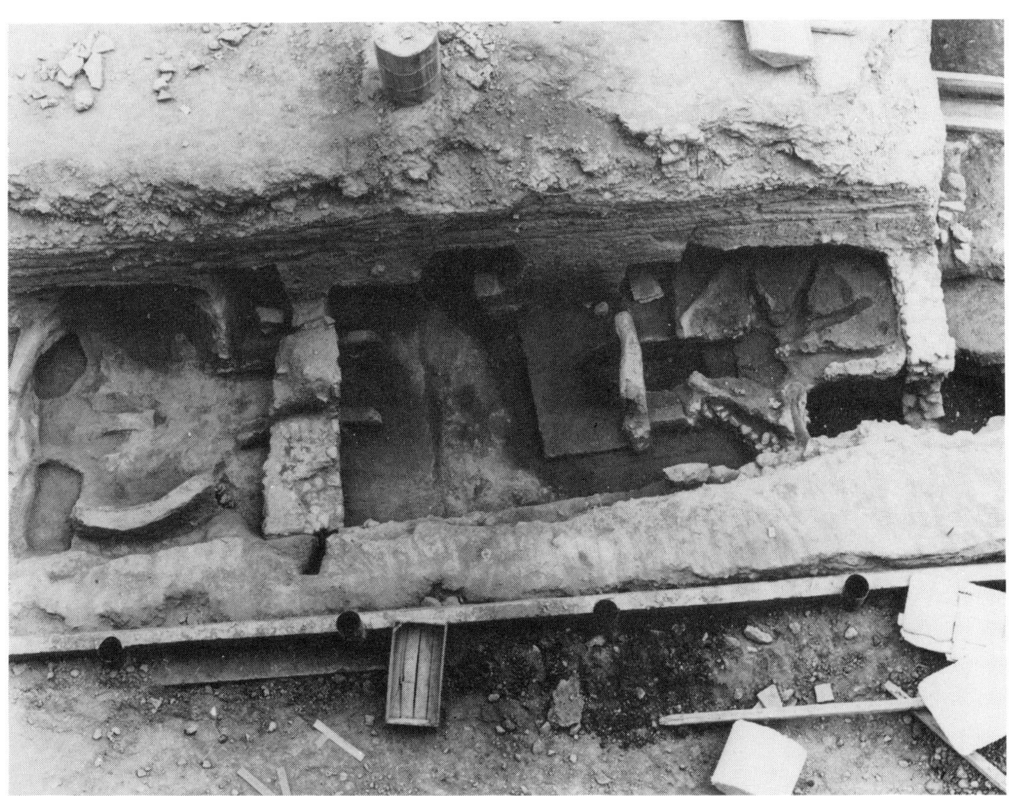

Εικ. 5. Ανασκαφή Λένορμαν και Κωνσταντινουπόλεως. Το νότιο τμήμα της ανασκαφής με τα λείψανα των δύο κλιβάνων.

τις ανασκαφές προκύπτει ότι η περιοχή αυτή, χωρίς μεγάλη οικιστική πυκνότητα, διέθετε ένα πυκνό δίκτυο δρόμων και φιλοξενούσε νεκροταφεία, κεραμικά εργαστήρια και μερικά ιερά. Ο Σοφοκλής, στον *Οἰδίποδα ἐπὶ Κολωνῷ* (24 κ.ε.), περιγράφει δια στόματος της Αντιγόνης έναν ειδυλλιακό τόπο. Ακόμη κι αν δεχθούμε κάποια ποιητική υπερβολή, δεν υπάρχει αμφιβολία ότι εκεί τα νερά ήταν άφθονα και η βλάστηση πυκνή, υπήρχαν δηλαδή οι βασικές προϋποθέσεις για τη λειτουργία των εργαστηρίων.[33] Η καύσιμη ύλη από την περιοχή και τα βουνά της Πάρνηθας και του Αιγάλεω, καθώς και πηλός ίσως από τις αποθέσεις του Κηφισού ήταν αμέσως προσιτά. Επίσης, το πυκνό οδικό δίκτυο της περιοχής εξυπηρετούσε την σύντομη και άνετη διακίνηση των προϊόντων προς το Άστυ και το λιμάνι δια της Πειραϊκής οδού.

γ. Η οργάνωση των εργαστηρίων φαίνεται να γίνεται σε μικρές συνοικίες, στην κυριολεξία γειτονιές κεραμέων, κοντά σε μεγάλες οδικές αρτηρίες.

δ. Οι περιπτώσεις της Λένορμαν και της Μαραθώνος αποδεικνύουν ότι και σε άλλα σημεία εκτός του Κεραμεικού, έχουμε συνύπαρξη και ταυτόχρονη λειτουργία κεραμικών εργαστηρίων και νεκροταφείων, με εύλογη συνέπεια ότι προϊόντα των πρώτων εξυπηρετούσαν τα δεύτερα.

ε. Από τα προϊόντα που βρέθηκαν στις ανασκαφές των συγκεκριμένων εργαστηρίων προκύπτει ότι μερικά απ' αυτά παρήγαν συγκεκριμένα είδη αγγείων και ως προς το σχήμα και ως προς τη διακόσμηση, τουλάχιστον σε ορισμένες περιόδους, όπως για παράδειγμα στο τέλος του 6ου και στο α΄ τέταρτο του 5ου π.Χ. αιώνα, οπότε παρατηρείται και η μεγαλύτερη τυποποίηση στη μελανόμορφη αττική αγγειογραφία. Χαρακτηριστικό είναι το γεγονός ότι τα σύγχρονα εργαστήρια του Βρύγου και του Αίμονα παράγουν το καθένα τα ιδιαίτερά τους αγγεία.

στ. Ενδιαφέροντα στοιχεία για τη δομή των εργαστηρίων δίνουν και τα γράμματα που εμφανίζονται σε πήλινους δακτυλίους, αφού σε κάθε κεραμικό εργαστήριο διαπιστώνεται υπεροχή ενός συγκεκριμένου ονόματος.

ζ. Τέλος, εντύπωση προξενεί το γεγονός ότι μέσα σε τόσα κεραμικά εργαστήρια του 6ου και του 5ου αιώνα δεν βρέθηκαν πουθενά, εκτός από το εργαστήριο του Βρύγου και δευτερευόντως του ζ.

Εικ. 6. Ανασκαφή Λένορμαν και Κωνσταντινουπόλεως. Σύνολο πήλινων δακτυλίων in situ.

του Δίνου, τα μεγάλα αγγεία και τα μεγάλα ονόματα των καλλιτεχνών του μελανόμορφου και του ερυθρόμορφου ρυθμού. Πάντως, φαίνεται πάρα πολύ πιθανό, κι αυτά να βρίσκονταν στον δήμο των Κεραμέων, έξω από τα τείχη της πόλης, ίσως στις περιοχές μεταξύ Διπύλου και Ηρίων Πυλών, καθώς και Ιεράς Πύλης και Πειραϊκών Πυλών, σε μια δηλαδή περιοχή απολύτως πρόσφορη όχι μόνο για την παραγωγή και για τη διάθεση των προϊόντων στην ίδια την πόλη αλλά και στις μακρυνές αγορές, αφού ο προσανατολισμός των εργαστηρίων αυτών ήταν σε μεγάλο ποσοστό της παραγωγής τους εξαγωγικός.

Θερμές ευχαριστίες οφείλω σε όλους τους συναδέλφους της Γ΄ Εφορείας, που από το 1960 μέχρι σήμερα με τις έρευνές τους έφεραν στο φως λείψανα κεραμικών εργαστηρίων. Στον καθένα χωριστά και συγχρόνως σε όλους αφιερώνεται η προκαταρκτική αυτή μελέτη, δείγμα εκτίμησης και ευχαριστίας για την αυθόρμητη βοήθειά τους στην πληρέστερη αξιοποίηση των ανασκαφικών δεδομένων. Ιδιαίτερες ευχαριστίες οφείλονται στην προϊσταμένη της Εφορείας Θ. Καράγιωργα-Σταθακοπούλου για την παρότρυνσή της και τις διευκολύνσεις στην πορεία της μελέτης, καθώς και στις συναδέλφους Ε. Λυγκούρη και Ε. Χατζηπούλιου για την πρόθυμη παροχή στοιχείων από πρόσφατες ανασκαφές τους. Τέλος, είμαι βαθιά υποχρεωμένη στους Μ. Τιβέριο και Π. Βαλαβάνη για το συνεχές ενδιαφέρον τους και τις χρήσιμες υποδείξεις τους.

Σημειώσεις

1. Βλ. γενικά J.D. Beazley, *Potter and Patron in Ancient Athens* (London 1946) 5 και I. Scheibler, *Griechische Töpferkunst* (München 1983) 107 κ.ε.
2. Για λείψανα παλιότερων κεραμικών εργαστηρίων στην Αθήνα, ιδιαιτέρως στην περιοχή της Αγοράς, βλ. J.M. Camp, *The Athenian Agora. Excavations in the Heart of Classical Athens* (London 1986) 138.
3. *ΑρχΔελτ* 34 (1979) Β1 Χρον. 21.
4. Για τον εικονογραφικό αυτόν τύπο βλ. *LIMC* II (1984) 265 κ.ε., αρ. 683–684 και *LIMC* II, 715, αρ. 1210–1214.
5. *ABV* 205 κ.ε. (Krokotos Group), 617 κ.ε. και 711 (CHC Group), 466 κ.ε. και 699 (Cock Group).
6. Για πήλινους δακτυλίους βλ. τελευταία J.K. Papadopoulos, "ΛΑΣΑΝΑ, Tyères and Kiln Firing Supports," *Hesperia* 61 (1992) 203 κ.ε., πίν. 47 κ.ε.
7. Πρβλ. την ύπαρξη στην περιοχή και λειψάνων κεραμικού εργαστηρίου ήδη από τα υστερογεωμετρικά χρόνια. *ΑρχΔελτ* 35 (1980) Β1 Χρον. 36.
8. *ΑρχΔελτ* 34 (1979) Β1 Χρον. 20.
9. Πρόκειται για το εσωτερικό μιας σκυφοειδούς κύλικας (cup-skyphos), όπου πάνω στο μελανό γάνωμα εξίτηλη λευκή βαφή άφησε ίχνη μεγάλων φυλλόσχημων κοσμημάτων, που κάλυπταν όλη σχεδόν την εσωτερική επιφάνεια του αγγείου.
10. Την πληροφορία οφείλω στη συνάδελφο Ε. Λυγκούρη.
11. *ΑρχΔελτ* 27 (1972) Β1 Χρον. 132 και Π. Καπετανάκη, "Νεκροταφεῖον τοῦ 4ου αἰ. π.Χ. εἰς Ἀθήνας παρὰ τὴν Ἱερὰν Ὁδόν," *AAA* 6 (1973) 150 κ.ε.
12. *ΑρχΔελτ* 34 (1979) Β1 Χρον. 24.
13. Τις πρώτες αναφορές στο εύρημα βλ. *ΑρχΔελτ* 23 (1968) Β1 Χρον. 75. Επίσης, *BCH* 94 (1970) και *CRAI* (1971) 531 κ.ε. Παρουσίαση μερικών από τα αγγεία του ευρήματος βλ. J.J. Maffre, "Quelques scènes mythologiques sur des fragments de coupes attiques de la fin du style sévère," *RA* (1982) 195 κ.ε. Το όστρακο της κύλικας της εικ. 1 στη σελ. 196 φέρει χαρακτηριστική οπή που το κατατάσσει στα όστρακα δοκιμής. Νομίζω πως το υλικό της ανασκαφής δεν αφήνει αμφιβολία ότι πρόκειται για κατάλοιπα κεραμικού εργαστηρίου. Βλ. επίσης J.J. Maffre, "Une gigantomachie de la première décennie du Ve siècle," *RA* (1972) 221 κ.ε.
14. A. Kaloyeropoulou, "From the Techniques of Pottery," *AAA* 3 (1970) 429 κ.ε.
15. Συνοπτικές πληροφορίες για τα κεραμικά εργαστήρια που έχουν βρεθεί μέσα στον αρχαιολογικό χώρο του Κεραμεικού βλ. U. Knigge, *The Athenian Kerameikos. History, Monuments, Excavations* (Αθήνα 1990) ιδ. 39, 163. Παλιότερη βιβλιογραφία ό.π. 189.
16. Για το εύρημα βλ. J.H. Oakley, "An Athenian Red-figure Workshop from the Time of the Peloponnesian War" στο διεθνές συνέδριο "Les ateliers de pottiers dans le monde grec aux époques géometrique, archaïque et classique," που οργάνωσε η Γαλλική Αρχαιολογική Σχολή στις 2–3 Οκτωβρίου 1987: *BCH* Suppl. 23 (1992) 195 κ.ε
17. Βλ. *CVA* Bonn 1, 31.
18. Γενικά για την ανασκαφή βλ. Ο. Ζαχαριάδου, Δ. Κυριακού, Ε. Μπαζιωτοπούλου, "Σωστική ανασκαφή στον ανισόπεδο κόμβο Λένορμαν - Κωνσταντινουπόλεως," *AAA* 18 (1985) 39 κ.ε. Θ. Καράγιωργα - Σταθακοπούλου, "Δημόσια έργα και ανασκαφές στην Αθήνα τα τελευταία πέντε χρόνια," *HOROS* 6 (1988) 87 κ.ε., ιδ. 93 κ.ε. Αναφορά στο εύρημα υπάρχει και στα πρακτικά του συνεδρίου της Γαλλικής Σχολής ό.π. (σημ. 16) 53 κ.ε.
19. Γενική κάτοψη της ανασκαφής βλ. Ο. Ζαχαριάδου - Δ. Κυριακού - Ε. Μπαζιωτοπούλου (σημ. 18) 40, εικ. 1.
20. Ο Θουκυδίδης αναφέρει τρεις σεισμούς μεταξύ 430 και 420: 3.87.4 (427/6), 4.52.1 (424) και 5.45.4 (420 π.Χ.).
21. Ο χώρος των εργαστηρίων δεν ανασκάφηκε ενιαία αλλά σε λωρίδες, ανεξάρτητα από τη θέληση των ανασκαφέων. Ἐτσι, ενώ έγινε δυνατή η εξακρίβωση της γωνίας των αρχαίων οδών I και II, δεν είμαστε βέβαιοι για τη γωνία των οδών II και III, αφού στο υποτιθέμενο σημείο της συνάντησής τους υπήρχαν νεότερες επεμβάσεις. Λόγω αβεβαιότητας, η πορεία των οδών και τα όριά τους αποδόθηκαν στο σχέδιο με διακεκομένη γραμμή.
22. Η πλειονότητα της κεραμικής φθάνει μέχρι το α΄ τέταρτο του 4ου π.Χ. αιώνα, αν και μερικά όστρακα ίσως θα μπορούσαν να χρονολογηθούν μέχρι τα μέσα του αιώνα.
23. Στην κατηγορία αυτή ανήκει πηγάδι – αποθέτης που εντοπίστηκε στο δυτικό τμήμα της ανασκαφής, σε αρκετή απόσταση από τους περιγραφόμενους εργαστηριακούς χώρους. Στον αποθέτη αυτόν είχαμε και το φαινόμενο νεώτερα όστρακα, ρωμαϊκών χρόνων, να βρίσκονται βαθύτερα από τα όστρακα της κλασικής εποχής, ένδειξη ότι η απόθεση προήλθε από καθαρισμό της περιοχής, που πραγματοποιήθηκε το ενωρίτερο στα ρωμαϊκά χρόνια.
24. Στην Αθήνα έχουν βρεθεί αρκετοί αποθέτες τέτοιου τύπου, κυρίως από μεταγενέστερες της κλασικής περιόδους. Βλ. π.χ. το εργαστήριο σκύφων μεγαρικού τύπου στις οδούς ΄Οθωνος και Ξενοφώντος κοντά στην πλατεία Συντάγματος. *ΑρχΔελτ* 20 (1965) Β1 94 και *ΑρχΔελτ* 21 (1966) Β1 80.
25. Η καλή κατάσταση των αγγείων, η ομοιομορφία τους τόσο στο σχήμα όσο και στη διακόσμηση, καθώς και ο μεγάλος αριθμός τους, είναι πιθανόν να υποδηλώνει μία ή περισσότερες "φουρνιές" στον κλίβανο. Από πουθενά όμως δεν προκύπτει υποψία αποτυχημένης όπτησης. Αν έσπασαν πριν πουληθούν, κάτι που δεν φαίνεται πιθανό από τη μορφή των οστράκων, αυτό θα οφειλόταν σε ατύχημα που δεν είχε καμμιά σχέση με την όπτηση.
26. *ABV* 632 κ.ε., 711 κ.ε. 716 (Leafless Group) και *ABV* 538–9. 706–7 (Haimon P.) και 539 κ.ε. 705 κ.ε. 716 (Haimon Group).
27. Από τις μέχρι σήμερα ενδείξεις, όπου βέβαια έγινε δυνατό να εντοπισθούν ανασκαφικά, όπως π.χ. στις ανασκαφές Λένορμαν και Κωνσταντινουπόλεως, καθώς και Μοναστηρίου και Φαιάκων, φαίνεται ότι στο τέλος του 5ου ή στις αρχές του 4ου αιώνα π.Χ.

ένα στρώμα καταστροφής καλύπτει τα κεραμικά εργαστήρια. Η αιτία της καταστροφής τους δεν μπορεί μέχρι σήμερα να τεκμηριωθεί. Με βεβαιότητα πάντως μπορούμε να ισχυριστούμε ότι από το β΄ τέταρτο του 4ου αιώνα δεν επισημάνθηκε εργαστηριακή δραστηριότητα στις ανωτέρω ανασκαφές.

28. Βλ. σχετ. J.D. Beazley, στην βιβλιοκρισία του για το *CVA* της συλλογής Mouret (France 6), στο *JHS* 48 (1928) 127, όπου και η παλιότερη βιβλιογραφία.

29. Βλ. *ΑρχΔελτ* 33 (1978) Β1 Χρον. 25. Στη γωνία των οδών Σερρών και Χαλκιδικής, σε ανασκαφή ορύγματος του ΟΤΕ το 1990, βρέθηκε αποθέτης με χαρακτηριστική απόθεση κεραμικού εργαστηρίου. Ενδείξεις παρόμοιου εργαστηρίου του 4ου π.Χ. αιώνα, υπάρχουν και σε ανασκαφή της οδού Χαλκιδικής το 1990.

30. Για την περιοχή βλ. *ΑρχΔελτ* 36 (1981) Β1 Χρον. 22, 23. *ΑρχΔελτ* 37 (1982) Β1 Χρον. 24. *ΑρχΔελτ* 34 (1979) Β1 Χρον. 18. *ΑρχΔελτ* 29 (1973/4) Β1 Χρον. 86. *ΑρχΔελτ* 25 (1970) Β1 Χρον. 69. *ΑρχΔελτ* 24 (1969) Β1 Χρον. 37. *ΑρχΔελτ* 18 (1963) Β1 Χρον. 42. Επίσης ενδείξεις ύπαρξης εργαστηρίου προέκυψαν από σχετικά πρόσφατες ανασκαφές της ίδιας περιοχής στις οδούς Βαλαβάνη 4, Βαλαβάνη 6 και Παμφίλης γωνία, Κυκλώπων 21, Βαλαβάνη και Γκίκα γωνία και Καλλισθένους 36. Τα χρονικά των ανασκαφών αυτών στους υπό εκτύπωση τόμους του *Αρχαιολογικού Δελτίου*. Ενδείξεις κεραμικών εργαστηρίων στην ίδια περιοχή προκύπτουν και από ευρήματα της ανασκαφής του Σ. Χαριτωνίδη στον Λουμπαρδιάρη. Βλ. σχετ. Σ.Ι. Χαριτωνίδη, "᾿Ανασκαφὴ παρὰ τὸν Ἅγιον Δημήτριον Λουμπαρδιάρην ἐν ᾿Αθήναις," *ΑρχΕφ* (1979) [1981] 161 κ.ε., ιδ. πιν. 47.

31. Σύμφωνα με τις παρατηρήσεις και τα συμπεράσματα του E.L. Schwandner, "Handwerkerviertel in Gründungsestätten des 5. und 4. Jahrhunderts," *Πρακτικά του XII Διεθνούς Συνεδρίου Κλασικής Αρχαιολογίας* 4 (Αθήνα 1988) 183 κ.ε., αντίστοιχη *extra muros* εγκατάσταση εργαστηρίων δεν παρατηρείται σε νεοϊδρυμένες, άρα οργανωμένες πολεοδομικά πόλεις του 5ου και 4ου π.Χ. αιώνα, αφού οχληρά εργαστήρια επισημαίνονται και σε κεντρικές συνοικίες, όπως π.χ. στην Κασσώπη. Πάντως αυτό θα πρέπει να ισχύει μόνον για πόλεις με συνήθη και περιορισμένη σε τοπικά πλαίσια βιοτεχνική δραστηριότητα. Για περιπτώσεις όπου η βιοτεχνική παραγωγή ήταν τέτοια που απαιτούσε μεγάλους αριθμούς εργαστηρίων, όπως η Αθήνα και η Κόρινθος για την κεραμική παραγωγή, θα πρέπει να δεχόμαστε ως φυσιολογική τη συγκέντρωσή τους σε συγκεκριμένες περιοχές. Βέβαια, η "οργάνωση" αυτή δεν είναι απαραίτητο να προήλθε από πολεοδομικό περιορισμό αλλά ίσως να επιβλήθηκε και από τις ανάγκες προμήθειας πρώτων υλών και διάθεσης των προϊόντων.

32. Πρβλ. και την εγκατάσταση κεραμικών εργαστηρίων εντός των τειχών στην περιοχή του οικοδομήματος Υ, κατά τα υστερορρωμαϊκά χρόνια (3ο-6ο αιώνα μ.Χ.). Βλ. σχετ. U. Knigge - A. Rügler, "Die Ausgrabungen im Kerameikos 1986/87," *AA* (1989) 81 κ.ε.

33. Τα νερά του Ηριδανού, του Σκίρου, του Κηφισού και των παραποτάμων τους, καθώς και οι πολυπληθείς αγωγοί από όλη τη διάρκεια της αρχαιότητας που έχουν βρεθεί στις ανασκαφές, δεν αφήνουν καμμιά αμφιβολία για την ύπαρξη πολλών νερών στην περιοχή.

Πολιτικές προσωποποιήσεις

Όλγα Τζάχου-Αλεξανδρή

Στον Ευάγγελο

κύριον μὲν γὰρ πανταχοῦ τὸ πολίτευμα τῆς πόλεως, πολίτευμα δ' ἐστὶν ἡ πολιτεία. λέγω δ' οἷον ἐν μὲν ταῖς δημοκρατικαῖς κύριος ὁ δῆμος, οἱ δ' ὀλίγοι τοὐναντίον ἐν ταῖς ὀλιγαρχίαις

(Αριστοτέλης, *Πολιτικά* III.4. 1278 Β'.1)

Οι πολιτικές προσωποποιήσεις[1] που συναντάμε στην τέχνη είναι η Δημοκρατία, η Ολιγαρχία, η Βουλή και ο Δήμος. Δημιουργήθηκαν ως έκφραση της δημοκρατίας κι αυτές στην Αθήνα του 5ου αι. π.Χ.[2] Οι απεικονίσεις τους αναγνωρίζονται κυρίως σε παραστάσεις ψηφισματικών αναγλύφων.[3] Οι γραπτές πηγές και οι επιγραφικές μαρτυρίες που αναφέρουν πίνακες και αγάλματά τους, ή διασώζουν πληροφορίες σχετικές με τη λατρεία τους, μας κάνουν γνωστά μνημεία χαμένα και ταυτόχρονα προσφέρουν στοιχεία πολύτιμα στην έρευνα.

Η ταύτιση των προσωποποιήσεων αυτών είναι βέβαιη όταν στην παράσταση αναγράφεται το όνομά τους, ή ακόμη όταν το μνημείο είναι ακέραιο, ώστε η ερμηνεία της παράστασης να είναι δυνατή από την ανάγνωση του κειμένου. Επειδή όμως τα περισσότερα ψηφισματικά ανάλυφα με παραστάσεις πολιτικών προσωποποιήσεων είναι ελλιπή και στο σύνολό τους λίγα, η έρευνα για την ταύτιση των απεικονίσεών τους στηρίζεται ως επί το πλείστον σε συγκρίσεις και σε συνδυασμούς των παρεχομένων πληροφοριών. Προς αυτή την κατεύθυνση η έρευνα είναι ιδιαίτερα χρήσιμη, και προς αυτή θα στραφούμε κι εμείς, προτείνοντας μια νέα ταύτιση. Προηγουμένως θα αναφερθούμε με συντομία σε καθεμιά από αυτές τις προσωποποιήσεις προκειμένου να εντάξουμε την πρότασή μας σε ένα γενικότερο πλαίσιο.

Μολονότι η μνεία της δημοκρατίας στην αρχαία ελληνική φιλολογία είναι συχνή,[4] οι αναφορές στην εικονογράφησή της είναι σπάνιες. Γι'αυτό δεν είναι δυνατόν να προσδιοριστεί ακριβώς χρονικά πότε δημιουργήθηκε η προσωποποίηση της Δημοκρατίας.[5] Θεωρείται όμως πολύ πιθανό ότι αυτό έγινε στο τέλος του 5ου αι. π.Χ. μαζί με την ίδρυση της λατρείας της, η οποία, όπως υποστήριξε ο J.H. Oliver, θεσπίστηκε το 403 π.Χ. για τον εορτασμό της απελευθέρωσης των Αθηνών από τους Τριάκοντα τυράννους και την παλινόρθωση της δημοκρατίας.[6] Μια γνωστή μαρτυρία, που μπορούμε να επικαλεστούμε για την προσωποποίηση της Δημοκρατίας στα τέλη του 5ου αι. π.Χ. είναι το σχόλιο στον Αισχίνη, από το οποίο πληροφορούμεθα ότι οι Τριάκοντα τύραννοι τοποθέτησαν επάνω στον τάφο του Κριτίου γλυπτό σύμπλεγμα, που απεικόνιζε την Ολιγαρχία με μία δάδα να βάζει φωτιά στη Δημοκρατία.[7] Βέβαια, αναρωτάται κανείς αν θα ήταν δυνατόν αμέσως μετά το 403 π. Χ. να επιτραπεί η ανέγερση ενός τέτοιου μνημείου. Εάν δεν είναι κάποια φιλολογική επινόηση, οπωσδήποτε η μαρτυρία αυτή πρέπει να είναι κάπως μεταγενέστερη.

Το ψηφισματικό ανάγλυφο εναντίον της τυραννίδος στην Αρχαία Αγορά αρ. Ι 6524, του 337/6 π.Χ., επί άρχοντος Φρυνίχου, διασώζει τη μόνη βεβαιωμένη παράσταση της Δημοκρατίας (εικ. 1).[8] Η Δημοκρατία εικονίζεται όρθια με άνετο το δεξί πόδι, και φοράει ψηλά ζωσμένο πέπλο, ιμάτιο και σανδάλια. Στο δεξί χέρι κρατάει στεφάνι για να στέψει το Δήμο, ο οποίος παριστάνεται ένθρονος, τυλιγμένος στο ιμάτιό του από τη μέση και κάτω, μέ υψωμένο το αριστερό χέρι στο οποίο θα κρατούσε το σκήπτρο. Ο γλυπτικός τύπος της Δημοκρατίας είναι αυτός που συναντάμε και σε άλλες γυναικείες θεότητες.[9] Μπορεί επίσης να συγκριθεί με τις γυναικείες μορφές επιτυμβίων[10] και αναθηματικών αναγλύφων[11] της ίδιας περιόδου. Μαζί με τον κάπως προγενέστερο πίνακα του Ευφράνορος, στη Στοά του Ελευθερίου Διός, που μνημονεύει ο Παυσανίας 1.3.3,[12] αποτελούν την απόδειξη για μια συνειδητή διάκριση μεταξύ της Δημοκρατίας, ως πολιτεύματος και του Δήμου ως κυβέρνησης.

Τμήμα από τη βάση του αγάλματος της

Εικ. 1. Αρχαία Αγορά αρ. I 6524, του 337/6 π.Χ.

Δημοκρατίας, που ήταν στημένο στην Αρχαία Αγορά, βρίσκεται σήμερα στο Επιγραφικό Μουσείο (ΕΜ), αρ. 3913,[13] και αποτελεί ένα από τα σημαντικότερα μνημεία για την τεκμηρίωση της προσωποποίησης και της λατρείας της.[14] Είναι αφιέρωμα της Βουλής του 333/2 π.Χ., όπως πληροφορούμαστε από την ίδια την επιγραφή της (το αριστερό τμήμα της έχει χαθεί):

[ΔΗ]ΜΟΚΡΑΤ[Ι]Α
[Η ΒΟΥΛΗ Η]ΕΠΙ ΝΙΚΟΚΡΑΤΟΥΣ Α[Ρ]ΧΟΝΤΟΣ
[ΑΝΕΘΗΚ]ΕΝ ΣΤΕΦΑΝΩΘΕΙΣΑ ΥΠ[Ο] ΤΟΥ ΔΗΜΟΥ
[ΑΡΕΤ]ΗΣ ΕΝΕΚΑ ΚΑΙ ΔΙΚ[ΑΙ]ΟΣΥΝΗΣ

Ο A.E. Raubitschek, που έχει ταυτίσει τη βάση αυτή, πρότεινε ως θέση του αγάλματος της Δημοκρατίας το ιερό του Δήμου και των Χαρίτων στην βορειοδυτική κλιτύ του Αγοραίου Κολωνού.[15] Την πρότασή του αυτή στηρίζει στο συνδυασμό των τριών επιγραφών που σώζονται στα δύο μαρμάρινα έδρανα του θεάτρου του Διονύσου, *IG* II^2, 5029a, του 3ου αι. π.Χ., τα οποία αναφέρουν: ιερέα Δημοκρατίας, ιερέα Δήμου και Χαρίτων, ιερέα Πτολεμαίου Ευεργέτου και Βερενίκης. Η συμπλήρωση αυτών των επιγραφών έγινε με τη βοήθεια μιας άλλης επιγραφής, που βρίσκεται στο Επιγραφικό Μουσείο με αριθμό 8896 και πιστεύεται ότι αποτελεί το ερεισίνωτο των εδράνων αυτών.[16] Αλλες δύο επιγραφές αναφέρονται στο άγαλμα της Δημοκρατίας: το διάταγμα του ΕΜ αρ. 12749, του 306/5 π.Χ. και η εφηβική επιγραφή *IG* II^2, 1011, 62, του 106/5 π.Χ.[17] Το άγαλμα της Δημοκρατίας στην Αρχαία Αγορά δεν είναι το μόνο που μαρτυρείται. Η εφηβική επιγραφή Αγορά Ι 7484 του έτους 214/3 αναφέρει άγαλμα της Δημοκρατίας στη Σαλαμίνα.[18] Μία ακόμη επιγραφή αναφέρει την ύπαρξη αγάλματος της Δημοκρατίας στη Σαλαμίνα.[19]

Για την προσωποποίηση της Ολιγαρχίας[20] δεν έχουμε άλλα στοιχεία εκτός από το γνωστό και αμφιβόλου ακριβείας σχόλιο στον Αισχίνη, σύμφωνα με το οποίο στο ταφικό μνημείο του Κριτίου, του ενός εκ των Τριάκοντα τυράννων, παριστανόταν η Ολιγαρχία, η οποία έβαζε φωτιά στη Δημοκρατία.[21] Η έλλειψη ενδιαφέροντος για την εικονογράφηση της Ολιγαρχίας δείχνει και τη σαφή άποψη των Αθηναίων για το πολίτευμα, που αντιπροσωπεύει.

Η βουλή και ο δήμος εμφανίζονται ήδη μαζί στις επιγραφές στα μέσα του 5ου αι. π.Χ. ως αλληλοσυμπληρούμενα όργανα.[22] Για την προσωποποίηση του πολιτικού θεσμού της βουλής των πεντακοσίων,[23] ή των τοπικών αντιστοίχων σωμάτων, οι πληροφορίες είναι φτωχές. Για την ύπαρξη λατρείας της Βουλής δεν υπάρχουν επαρκή αποδεικτικά στοιχεία. Σε επιγραφή του 4ου αι. π.Χ. αναφέρεται ιεροποιός βουλής, αλλά αυτό το στοιχείο δεν αποδεικνύει τη λατρεία της.[24] Οι ιεροποιοί δεν υπηρετούσαν στη λατρεία μιας συγκεκριμένης θεότητας, αλλά στη διοργάνωση των λατρειών, των θυσιών και των τελετουργιών γενικώς. Οι ταυτίσεις της Βουλής περιορίζονται σε τρία μόνον παραδείγματα, από τα οποία στο ένα αναγράφεται το όνομά της. Πρόκειται για το ελλιπές γλυπτό του Εθνικού Αρχαιολογικού Μουσείου (ΕΑΜ) αρ. 1473 (εικ. 2), του 320 π.Χ. περίπου.[25] Εικονογραφείται σε αυτό μια επίσημη πράξη, η απονομή τιμής σε έναν πολίτη για τις υπηρεσίες του στην πόλη της Αθήνας, την οποία ενσαρκώνει η Αθηνά. Στο δεξί τμήμα του αναγλύφου που έχει χαθεί, η C.L. Lawton συμπληρώνει τη μορφή του Δήμου πίσω από τον τιμώμενο. Ομως είναι δύσκολο να πιστέψει κανείς ότι ο καλλιτέχνης απεικόνισε το Δήμο πίσω από την πλάτη του τιμωμένου. Πιστεύω ότι εάν ο καλλιτέχνης είχε την πρόθεση να απεικονίσει το Δήμο σε αυτή τη θέση, θα παρίστανε τον τιμώμενο κατ' ενώπιον. Επίσης η συμπλήρωση του κενού ανάμεσα στον τιμώμενο και στη δεξιά παραστάδα είναι περισσότερο αποδεκτή, όπως θα αναπτύξω παρακάτω, με τη μορφή ενός ακόμη θνητού, σύνθεση την οποία βλέπουμε εξάλλου και σε άλλα τιμητικά ανάγλυφα. Η Βουλή παρακολουθεί στα δεξιά της, ή συμμετέχει στην πράξη της απονομής. Είναι ντυμένη με πέπλο και ιμάτιο και έχει τον εικονογραφικό τύπο των γυναικών που βλέπουμε και στα σύγχρονα επιτύμβια μνημεία.[26] Στο ανάγλυφο του Βρετανικού Μουσείου αρ. 771, του 320 π.Χ., η Βουλή εικονίζεται μαζί με την Αθηνά να στεφανώνουν έναν πολίτη.[27] Επίσης στο ανάγλυφο του Επιγραφικού Μουσείου αρ. 7180+2811 (εικ. 4), των ετών 323/2 π.Χ., η δεύτερη γυναικεία μορφή της παράστασης ερμηνεύεται συνήθως ως Βουλή.[28]

Η προσωποποίηση που εμφανίζεται με τη μεγαλύτερη συχνότητα είναι του Δήμου.[29] Ο δήμος

Εικ. 2. Εθνικό Αρχαιολογικό Μουσείο αρ. 1473.

Εικ. 3. Εθνικό Αρχαιολογικό Μουσείο αρ. 1473 (συμπλήρωση).

στην πολιτική ζωή αντιπροσωπεύει το σύνολο του πληθυσμού της Αττικής, είναι αυτός που λαμβάνει μέρος στις συνελεύσεις της εκκλησίας, είναι αυτός που αποφασίζει.[30] Ανάλογη είναι και η σημασία του στα αντίστοιχα τοπικά σώματα.[31] Οι πρωϊμότερες μαρτυρίες αφορούν τη λατρεία του. Το πρώτο ιερό του ιδρύεται σε χώρο ιερό, στο λόφο των Νυμφών,[32] ο οποίος γειτνιάζει άμεσα με τον πολιτικό πυρήνα της αθηναϊκής δημοκρατίας, που είναι η Πνύκα.[33] Η ταύτιση του ιερού οφείλεται στην U. Kron, η οποία διάβασε και συμπλήρωσε σωστά τη χαραγμένη στο βράχο επιγραφή, την οποία και χρονολογεί στα μέσα του 5ου αι. π.Χ., περίοδο ακμής της δημοκρατίας.[34] Τήν εποχή αυτή, που ο λαός των Αθηνών αποκτά

Εικ. 4. Επιγραφικό Μουσείο αρ. 7180+2811, του 323/2 π.Χ.

μεγάλη ισχύ, ο δήμος γίνεται κυρίαρχος. Η επιγραφή αποτελείται από τρεις λέξεις σε τρεις στίχους: ΙΕΡΟΝ/ΝΥΜΦΩΝ/ΔΗΜΟ.[35]

Ενα δεύτερο ιερό Δήμου με κοινή λατρεία και αυτό, το ιερό του Δήμου και των Χαρίτων, υπάρχει στην Αρχαία Αγορά, το δεύτερο ενδιαφέρον κέντρο της πολιτικής ζωής στην Αθήνα.[36] Ενας μεγάλος μαρμάρινος βωμός, ο οποίος βρέθηκε στη θέση του, προσδιορίζει με ακρίβεια τη θέση του ιερού.[37] Ο βωμός αυτός βρίσκεται στο Εθνικό Αρχαιολογικό Μουσείο, αρ. 1495.[38] Είναι αφιερωμένος στην Αφροδίτη και τις Χάριτες, επί ιερέως Μικίωνος, γιού του Ευρυκλείδου από την Κηφισιά το 197/6 π.Χ. Η χρονολογία ίδρυσης του ιερού αυτού δεν μας είναι γνωστή, γιατί τα αρχιτεκτονικά λείψανά του καταστράφηκαν με την κατασκευή της σιδηροδρομικής γραμμής στις αρχές του 20ου αι. Στο ψήφισμα των Χερρονησιτών, το οποίο μνημονεύεται στο λόγο του Δημοσθένη *Περί του στεφάνου* 92, περιέχεται η πληροφορία ότι οι κάτοικοι της Χερρονήσου απεφάσισαν να ιδρύσουν βωμό στη Χάριν και στο Δήμο των Αθηναίων, επειδή τους συμπαραστάθηκαν στους αγώνες τους εναντίον του Φιλίππου, δηλαδή το 340 π.Χ.[39] Το πιθανότερο είναι ότι το αναφερόμενο ψήφισμα είναι στο σύνολό του μεταγενέστερη επινόηση, διαφορετικά θα πρέπει να υποθέσουμε ότι το ιερό της Αγοράς των Αθηνών υπήρχε ήδη πριν από τα μέσα του 4ου αι. π.Χ. Οι επιγραφικές μαρτυρίες που έχουν σχέση με το ιερό αυτό έχουν συγκεντρωθεί από τον R.E. Wycherley,[40] και οι προγενέστερες από αυτές χρονολογούνται μετά το 229 π.Χ.[41] Γι' αυτό πιστεύεται ότι η ίδρυση της λατρείας του Δήμου και των Χαρίτων είναι άλλο ένα χαρακτηριστικό της προσπάθειας για την παλινόρθωση της δημοκρατίας στα κρίσιμα χρόνια μετά το 230 π.Χ.[42]

Η μνεία της προσωποποίησης του Δήμου στην αρχαία ελληνική φιλολογία είναι σπάνια. Ο Αριστοφάνης τον παρουσιάζει στη σκηνή στους *Ἱππεῖς* (40–43) το 424 π.Χ.:

νῷν γάρ ἐστι δεσπότης
ἄγροικος ὀργήν, κυαμοτρώξ, ἀκράχολος,
Δῆμος Πυκνίτης, δύσκολον γερόντιον
ὑπόκωφον.

Η πρωϊμότερη απεικόνιση του Δήμου που μας σώζεται δεν χρονολογείται πριν από την τελευταία δεκαετία του 5ου αι. π.Χ. Σύγχρονος περίπου θα ήταν και ο πίνακας του Παρρασίου, με παράσταση του Δήμου και του Θησέως, που μας παραδίδει ο Πλίνιος.[43] Το ψηφισματικό ανάγλυφο του Μουσείου του Λούβρου αρ. ΜΑ. 831, του έτους 410/9 π.Χ., απεικονίζει την Αθηνά και έναν ώριμο γενειοφόρο άνδρα δεξιά και αριστερά από την ιερή ελιά.[44] Η ερμηνεία του άνδρα ως του Δήμου των Αθηνών στηρίζεται στο περιεχόμενο του ψηφίσματος, το οποίο αναφέρεται στην τήρηση των λογαριασμών του θησαυροφυλακίου στον οπισθόδομο του Παρθενώνος.[45] Εδώ εικονογραφείται μία από τις λειτουργίες του δήμου, αυτή που αφορά στις οικονομικές αρμοδιότητές του. Ο εικονογραφικός τύπος είναι αυτός του αστού της Αττικής που βλέπουμε σε

Εικ. 5. Εθνικό Αρχαιολογικό Μουσείο αρ. 1467.

σύγχρονα γλυπτά,[46] ο οποίος έχει την καταγωγή του στους ήρωες των δέκα φυλών της Αττικής στην ανατολική ζωφόρο του Παρθενώνος (σελ. 75, εικ. 1-3),[47] και συναντάται στις απεικονίσεις θεών, όπως του Ασκληπιού ή του Δία.[48]

Μια άλλη αρμοδιότητα της εκκλησίας του δήμου, αυτή των εξωτερικών υποθέσεων, εικονογραφείται στο ψηφισματικό ανάγλυφο του Εθνικού Αρχαιολογικού Μουσείου αρ. 1467 (εικ. 5),[49] το οποίο αναφέρεται στη σύναψη συνθήκης με την Κέρκυρα του έτους 375 π.Χ.[50] Ο Δήμος των Αθηνών, ο οποίος αναγνωρίζεται στην καθιστή ανδρική μορφή, αντιπροσωπεύει την πολιτεία. Είναι τυλιγμένος στο ιμάτιό του από τη μέση και κάτω. Και εδώ παραλληλίζεται με τους αστούς των ταφικών μνημείων,[51] αλλά και με τις καθιστές μορφές θεών, όπως του Δία και του Ασκληπιού.[52] Η μεσαία πεπλοφόρος μορφή ταυτίζεται με την Κέρκυρα.[53] Η Αθηνά παριστάνεται ντυμένη με πέπλο και ιμάτιο, φοράει το κράνος της, και κρατάει με το δεξί την ασπίδα και με το αριστερό το δόρυ, που θα ήταν ζωγραφισμένα.[54]

Το ανάγλυφο του Εθνικού Αρχαιολογικού Μουσείου αρ. 2407 (εικ. 6),[55] μολονότι ελλιπές, σπασμένο και με φθαρμένη την επιφάνειά του, έχει ιδιαίτερη σημασία γιατί οι τρεις μορφές της παράστασης κατονομάζονται με επιγραφές, από τις οποίες πληροφορούμαστε ότι τα απεικονιζόμενα πρόσωπα είναι η Αθηνά, ο Ηρακλής και ο Δήμος.[56] Η παρουσία του Ηρακλή, προστάτη του δήμου της Μελίτης, στην οποία υπάγεται ο λόφος των Νυμφών[57] και η γύρω περιοχή όπου βρέθηκε και το ανάγλυφο, οδήγησε την U. Kron να προσδιορίσει περισσότερο το περιεχόμενο της παράστασης και να αναγνωρίσει σ'αυτήν τον τοπικό Δήμο της Μελίτης.[58]

Τα περισσότερα όμως από τα ψηφισματικά ανάγλυφα στα οποία αναγνωρίζεται η μορφή του Δήμου, αφορούν την απονομή τιμής σε κάποιον πολίτη για τις υπηρεσίες που προσέφερε στο κράτος.[59] Στον κατάλογο των γνωστών αναγλύφων της κατηγορίας αυτής πιστεύω ότι μπορούμε να συμπεριλάβουμε άλλο ένα, το ανάγλυφο του Εθνικού Αρχαιολογικού Μουσείου αρ. 2986 (εικ. 7), το οποίο απεικονίζει τρεις μορφές.[60] Ως τόπος εύρεσής του αναφέρεται η Αθήνα, χωρίς όμως περισσότερες λεπτομέρειες. Το μάρμαρο είναι πεντελικό και δεν

Εικ. 6. Εθνικό Αρχαιολογικό Μουσείο αρ. 2407.

Εικ. 7. Εθνικό Αρχαιολογικό Μουσείο αρ. 2986.

διατηρεί ίχνη χρωμάτων. Επάνω και κάτω είναι ελλιπές. Ένα σπάσιμο διασχίζει λοξά το ανάγλυφο σε όλο το ύψος του.[61] Σε πολλά σημεία διακρίνονται ίχνη των εργαλείων που μεταχειρίστηκε ο καλλιτέχνης.[62] Στο έδαφος του αναγλύφου διακρίνονται ίχνη λίμας (εικ. 8) για την λείανση της επιφάνειάς του, ενώ στα περιγράμματα των μορφών μικρές εκβαθύνσεις δηλώνουν τη χρήση αρίδας ή τρυπανιού (εικ. 9). Με ποντίλι ή λαμάκι (εικ. 10) δημιουργούνται οι πτυχώσεις και το βάθος του αναγλύφου. Ίχνη λάμας (εικ. 11) φαίνονται στις επίπεδες επιφάνειες και στο κυμάτιο. Οι πλάγιες

Εικ. 8. Εθνικό Αρχαιολογικό Μουσείο αρ. 2986 (ίχνη από λίμα).

Εικ. 9. Εθνικό Αρχαιολογικό Μουσείο αρ. 2986 (ίχνη από αρίδα ή τρυπάνι).

Εικ. 10. Εθνικό Αρχαιολογικό Μουσείο αρ. 2986 (ίχνη από ποντίλι ή λαμάκι).

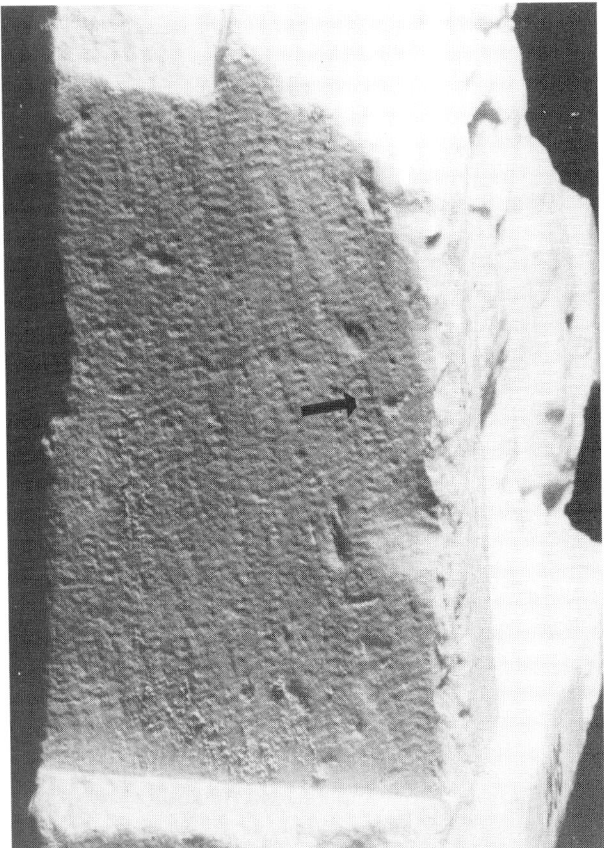

Εικ. 12. Εθνικό Αρχαιολογικό Μουσείο αρ. 2986 (ίχνη από ντισιλίδικο).

πλευρές των παραστάδων φέρουν σαφή ίχνη επεξεργασίας με ντισιλίδικο (εικ. 12). Στην πίσω πλευρά διακρίνονται ίχνη από το βελόνι (εικ. 13) που χρησιμοποιήθηκε για την αφαίρεση του υλικού και τη διαμόρφωση της πλευράς αυτής. Από το αρχιτεκτονικό πλαίσιο του αναγλύφου σώζονται τμήματα των δύο πλευρικών παραστάδων. Η στήλη της επιγραφής, της οποίας διατηρείται ελάχιστο τμήμα μόνο, στέφεται με ιωνικό κυμάτιο και ταινία, που λειτουργεί και ως βάση της παράστασης. Το

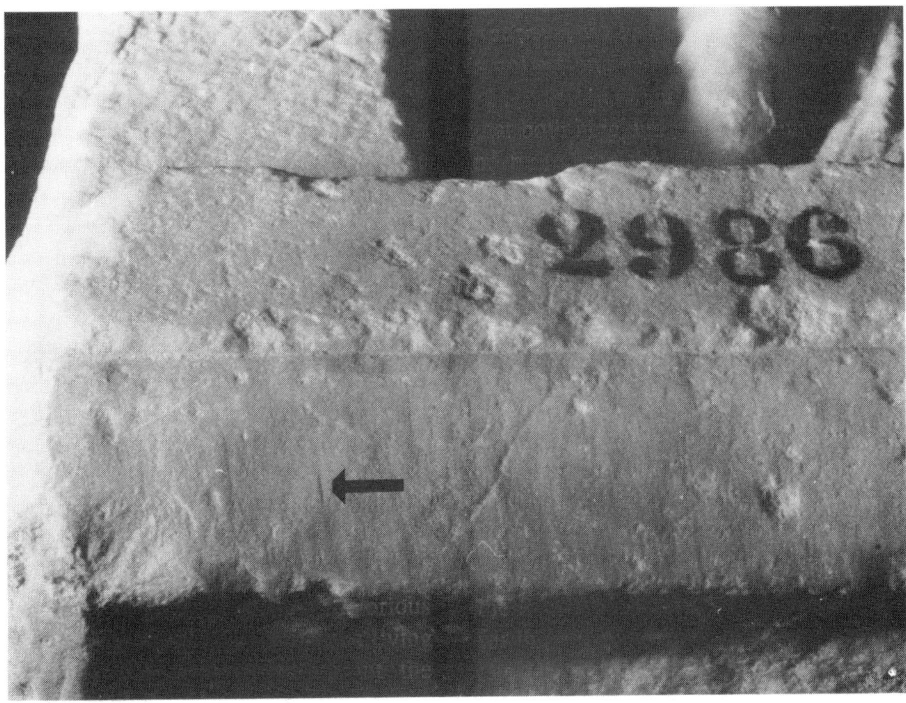

Εικ. 11. Εθνικό Αρχαιολογικό Μουσείο αρ. 2986 (ίχνη από λάμα).

Εικ. 13. Εθνικό Αρχαιολογικό Μουσείο αρ. 2986 (ίχνη από βελόνι).

σπάσιμο κάτω από τη βάση της παράστασης διασχίζει τη στήλη σε όλο το μήκος της (εικ. 14) και δείχνει ότι η στήλη θα συνεχιζόταν αντίστοιχα και προς τα κάτω. Τα λίγα δυσανάγνωστα γράμματα, ύψ. 0, 05 μ., που μόλις διακρίνονται στο σωζόμενο τμήμα της στήλης, επιβεβαιώνουν με το μικρό μέγεθός τους ότι το γλυπτό αποτελούσε την επίστεψη ενός ψηφίσματος χαμένου σήμερα.[63] Μολονότι το ύψος της ενεπίγραφης στήλης δεν μας είναι γνωστό, μπορούμε να υποθέσουμε ότι αυτή θά είχε ένα ύψος ανάλογο με εκείνο άλλων ψηφισματικών αναγλύφων παρόμοιων διαστάσεων, και να προτείνουμε αντίστοιχα μία υποθετική αναπαράσταση του μνημείου (εικ. 15).[64]

Την παράσταση συνθέτουν τρεις μορφές, μία γυναίκα και δύο άνδρες, από τους οποίους ο ένας, στα δεξιά της παράστασης εικονίζεται σε μικρότερη κλίμακα. Την κεντρική θέση κατέχει η γυναίκα. Λείπουν το κεφάλι, από τη βάση του λαιμού, και το αριστερό χέρι από τον ώμο. Στέκεται σε μετωπική στάση και στηρίζεται στο δεξί πόδι, ενώ σύρει το αριστερό, λυγισμένο προς τα πίσω και στο πλάι. Το δεξί χέρι, λυγισμένο, στηρίζεται στο αντίστοιχο ισχίο, ενώ το αριστερό θα ήταν υψωμένο. Η μορφή είναι ντυμένη με τον αττικό πέπλο, ζωσμένο στη μέση. Το ιμάτιο, διαμορφωμένο σαν εσάρπα, συγκρατείται με το δεξιό βραχίονα, αναδιπλώνεται και πέφτει στο πλάι, ενώ στα αριστερά πέφτει από το ύψος του ώμου και φτάνει στο ύψος των γονάτων, όπως και στα δεξιά, πλαισιώνοντας τη μορφή. Η αριστερή ισοϋψής μορφή του άνδρα είναι και αυτή ακέφαλη, και της λείπει το δεξί χέρι από τον ώμο. Η στήριξη του άνδρα είναι αντίστροφη από εκείνη της γυναίκας. Το αριστερό χέρι ακουμπάει στην οσφύ, ενώ το δεξί θα ήταν υψωμένο. Το ιμάτιο τυλίγει το κάτω μέρος του κορμού, αφήνοντας το στήθος ακάλυπτο. Η μία άκρη του σχηματίζει τριγωνική αναδίπλωση επάνω απο την κοιλιά και φτάνει ώς τη μέση του αριστερού μηρού, ενώ η άλλη άκρη περνάει επάνω από τον αριστερό ώμο, καλύπτει το βραχίονα και πέφτει προς τα κάτω σε μία δέσμη πτυχών. Ο άνδρας στα δεξιά εικονίζεται μικρότερος και σε στροφή τριών τετάρτων, με το κεφάλι στραμμένο προς τα αριστερά. Μολονότι η επιφάνεια του προσώπου του είναι φθαρμένη, από το περίγραμμά του συμπεραίνεται ότι θα είχε γένι. Στηρίζεται στο δεξί του πόδι, έχει το δεξί χέρι λυγισμένο στον αγκώνα με λοξή κατεύθυνση προς τα επάνω, ενώ το αριστερό φέρεται κάτω από το στήθος. Και οι τρεις μορφές έχουν ραδινές αναλογίες.

Οι κινήσεις των απεικονιζομένων παραμένουν σε ένα επίπεδο. Οι μορφές δεν αναπτύσσονται σε βάθος. Το άνω τμήμα του σώματος των μεγάλων μορφών αποδίδεται μετωπικά και είναι ευθυτενές. Και στις τρεις μορφές η θέση του άνετου σκέλους τονίζει το άνοιγμα της μορφής προς τα κάτω. Στη γυναίκα ο πέπλος είναι ζωσμένος ψηλά. Στον άνδρα το σταύρωμα του ιματίου γίνεται στο ύψος της οσφύος. Ο όγκος του σώματος και το ύφασμα αποδίδονται μαζί ως ενιαίο σύνολο. Τα ενδύματα εφάπτονται στο σώμα και δημιουργούν έντονες πτυχώσεις με βαθιές αυλακώσεις. Ο καλλιτέχνης σχεδιάζει τις μορφές του με κάθετους και λοξούς άξονες ακολουθώντας πραξιτέλειους κανόνες.

Η τεχνοτροπία του θυμίζει το αναθηματικό ανάγλυφο του Ασκληπιείου των Αθηνών, το οποίο έχει συντεθεί[65] από τρία τεμάχια, τα δύο του ΕΑΜ αρ. 2501[66] και 2935[67] και εκείνο του Μουσείου Ακροπόλεως αρ. 2584.[68] Το συγκολλημένο αυτό ανάγλυφο εμφανίζει πραξιτέλεια χαρακτηριστικά και αποδίδεται σε αττικό εργαστήριο, όπως εξάλλου ένας

Εικ. 14. Εθνικό Αρχαιολογικό Μουσείο αρ. 2986 (κατώτερη επιφάνεια).

Εικ. 15. Εθνικό Αρχαιολογικό Μουσείο αρ. 2986 (συμπλήρωση).

σημαντικός αριθμός αττικών αναγλύφων του β' μισού του 4ου αι. π.Χ. Η στάση και η σιγμοειδής διαμόρφωση του κορμού του αριστερού άνδρα της παράστασης του γλυπτού του ΕΑΜ αρ. 2986 είναι ίδια με αυτήν του Ασκληπιού του τεμαχίου ΕΑΜ αρ. 2501.[69] Επίσης η διαμόρφωση του υφάσματος γύρω από τον αριστερό βραχίονα της μορφής που εξετάζουμε μοιάζει με αυτήν του ιματίου του Ασκληπιάδη στο ανάγλυφο του ΕΑΜ αρ. 2935,[70] αντίστοιχα με αυτήν της ανδρικής μορφής στο ανάγλυφο του ΕΑΜ αρ. 4465[71] και του νέου στο ανάγλυφο του Μουσείου Ακροπόλεως αρ. 4675.[72]

Για τη χρονολογική κατάταξη του γλυπτού μας χρήσιμη είναι η σύγκρισή του με άλλα καλά χρονολογημένα μνημεία. Το ανάγλυφο του Μουσείου Ελευσίνος αρ. 5115,[73] του έτους 330 π.Χ., στο οποίο η Δήμητρα και η Κόρη κρατούν ένα στεφάνι για να το απονείμουν στο Σμικυθίονα από την Κεφαλή, πού εικονίζεται στα δεξιά της παράστασης, παρουσιάζει βασικές ομοιότητες, μολονότι η τεχνοτροπία του διαφέρει. Και εδώ οι μορφές δεν αναπτύσσονται σε βάθος, οι κινήσεις τους γίνονται επίσης σε ένα επίπεδο, το άνοιγμα του άνετου σκέλους των παριστανομένων δεν επιφέρει την αντίστοιχη στροφή του επάνω τμήματος του κορμού, όπως είδαμε και στις μορφές του αναγλύφου του ΕΑΜ αρ. 2986. Επίσης το ψηφισματικό ανάγλυφο της Γλυπτοθήκης Ny Carlsberg στην Κοπεγχάγη αρ. 462, του έτους 329/8, με το οποίο τιμώνται δύο επιμελητές των οργεώνων της Βενδίδος, παρουσιάζει την ίδια γλυπτική αντίληψη στη δομή των σωμάτων, στη στάση τους, καθώς και στις πτυχώσεις των ενδυμάτων.[74] Τα χαρακτηριστικά αυτά συναντώνται σε γλυπτά μετά το 330 π.Χ., ενώ στα γλυπτά της προηγούμενης δεκαετίας επικρατούν άλλες τάσεις. Στο ανάγλυφο του Εθνικού Αρχαιολογικού Μουσείου αρ. 2407 (εικ. 6), στο οποίο αναφερθήκαμε και προηγουμένως, και το οποίο χρονολογείται στα 340 π.Χ., η κίνηση των μορφών και η αίσθηση του βάθους επιτυγχάνεται με στροφή ολοκλήρου του σώματος.[75] Βλέπουμε επίσης ότι το ύφασμα έχει δικό του όγκο και αποδίδεται χωριστά από το σώμα: μικρές βαθιές πτυχώσεις προσδίδουν πλαστικότητα και δημιουργούν την εντύπωση ενός ακόμη επιπέδου.

Ακόμη αργότερα, γύρω στα 320 π.Χ., οι τάσεις της γλυπτικής πάλι αλλάζουν. Στο ψηφισματικό ανάγλυφο του Μουσείου της Ελευσίνος αρ. 5114, των ετών 319/8 π.Χ., το οποίο παριστάνει τη Δήμητρα να δίνει ένα στεφάνι στον Δερκύλο από τον Αγνούντα, οι μορφές δεν είναι πλέον μετωπικές, αλλά στρέφονται γύρω από τον άξονά τους.[76] Η πτύχωση των ενδυμάτων είναι πλουσιότερη και αποκτά δική της κίνηση. Οι μορφές τώρα έχουν ένα ρυθμό και μια κίνηση, που δεν υπήρχε προηγουμένως. Σύμφωνα με αυτές τις συγκρίσεις η χρονολόγηση του γλυπτού αρ. 2986 προσδιορίζεται στα 330 π.Χ. περίπου. Η ευσυνείδητη και επιμελημένη εργασία, τα καθαρά περιγράμματα των μορφών, η δομή, η στάση και η ισορροπία των σωμάτων, καθώς και η αρμονική σύνθεση της παράστασης προδίδουν προικισμένο τεχνίτη αθηναϊκού εργαστηρίου.

Η αθηναϊκή προέλευση του γλυπτού, η απόδοσή του σε αθηναϊκό εργαστήριο, καθώς και το σημαντικό μέγεθός του, μας επιτρέπουν να προτείνουμε το χαρακτηρισμό του ως κρατικού ψηφισματικού.[77] Ειδικότερα μπορεί να χαρακτηριστεί ως τιμητικό, αφού στην παράστασή του απεικονίζεται ένας θνητός, όπως είναι φανερό από τη μικρότερη κλίμακα με την οποία απεικονίζεται η μία μορφή, που ενσαρκώνει τον τιμώμενο του ψηφίσματος.[78] Ο τιμώμενος του ψηφισματικού αναγλύφου αρ. 2986 δεν διαφέρει τυπολογικά από τους σεβίζοντες των αναθηματικών αναγλύφων,[79] ή τους τιμωμένους των άλλων ψηφισματικών.[80] Οπως και αυτοί, εικονίζεται γενειοφόρος με μακρύ ιμάτιο και χωρίς προσφορές. Στα τιμητικά ψηφίσματα η χειρονομία της ύψωσης[81] του δεξιού χεριού συναντάται και όταν γίνεται στεφάνωση,[82] και όταν παραδίδεται το στεφάνι στο χέρι,[83] αλλά και όταν η απόδοση τιμής δεν συνοδεύεται με στεφάνωση.[84] Βέβαια, η χειρονομία της ύψωσης της δεξιάς δεν είναι υποχρεωτική για τον τιμώμενο.[85] Ως προς το δικό μας ανάγλυφο, δεν είναι φανερό, αν η απονομή της τιμής συνοδεύεται και με στεφάνωση. Επίσης δεν έχομε κανένα στοιχείο για την ταύτιση του τιμωμένου, αν δηλαδή είναι πολίτης της Αττικής ή άλλης πόλης.

Η έλλειψη επιγραφικών δεδομένων, αλλά και η ελλιπής διατήρηση των δύο σε μεγαλύτερη κλίμακα μορφών του γλυπτού 2986, δυσχεραίνουν ακόμη περισσότερο την ταύτισή τους. Η C.L. Lawton θεωρεί τη γυναικεία μορφή ως την προσωποποίηση της Βουλής, αλλά δεν αιτιολογεί την ερμηνεία της αυτή.[86] Ομως ο εικονογραφικός τύπος της Βουλής, όπως τουλάχιστον μας παραδίδεται στο γλυπτό του ΕΑΜ αρ. 1473 στο οποίο αυτή κατονομάζεται (εικ. 2), είναι διαφορετικός από εκείνον της γυναικείας μορφής του αναγλύφου 2986. Η M.T. Fortuna πάλι, η οποία θεωρεί το ανάγλυφο ως αναθηματικό, ερμηνεύει τις δύο μεγάλες μορφές ως το Δία και την Ηρα.[87] Παραπάνω εξετέθησαν οι λόγοι για τους οποίους το ανάγλυφο αυτό ανήκει στην κατηγορία των ψηφισματικών, επομένως και η ερμηνεία της Fortuna δεν στηρίζεται. Η ίδια μελετήτρια πάντως συγκρίνει επιτυχώς τη γυναικεία μορφή του αναγλύφου με τα δύο γυναικεία αγάλματα του Μουσείου της Κυρήνης αρ. C.14092[88] και αρ. C.14093.[89] Η L. Kahil συμπεριλαμβάνει τα αγάλματα της Κυρήνης ανάμεσα στους τύπους της Αρτέμιδος, όμως χαρακτηρίζει την απόδοση αυτή ως αβέβαιη.[90] Τα αγάλματα αυτά ανήκουν στον ίδιο κύκλο με τα πραξιτέλεια έργα, την Αρτέμιδα του Βατικανού,[91] την Αθηνά Castra Praetoria,[92] ή ακόμη τον Απόλλωνα Πύθιο της Γόρτυνος.[93]

Η γυναικεία μορφή που κατέχει το κέντρο της σύνθεσης εμφανίζεται ως η σημαντικότερη μορφή της παράστασης, εκείνη που απονέμει την τιμή. Ο τύπος του ενδύματος, ο αττικός πέπλος[94] και το ιμάτιο ριγμένο στους ώμους[95] είναι συνήθη χαρακτηριστικά της Αθηνάς. Επίσης ο εικονογραφικός τύπος της πεπλοφόρου με το δεξί χέρι στο ισχίο και υψωμένο το αριστερό συνηγορούν για την ταύτιση της γυναίκας ως Αθηνάς, όπως θα δούμε παρακάτω, μολονότι εδώ λείπουν τα σύμβολα της θεάς. Αλλά, το γοργόνειο και η ασπίδα δεν εικονίζονται πάντα στα γλυπτά[96] επίσης κάποια από τα σύμβολα της θεάς αποδίδονται ζωγραφικά,[97] όπως πιστεύω ότι συμβαίνει και σε αυτή την παράσταση. Ο εικονογραφικός τύπος εμφανίζεται σε ένα πλήθος μνημείων. Η πρώτη Πρόμαχος πεπλοφόρος, η Αθηνά του Μουσείου Ακροπόλεως αρ. 140,[98] έχει το ένα χέρι στο ισχίο και υψώνει το άλλο για να κρατήσει το δόρυ. Ηδη η Αθηνά του αναγλύφου του Μουσείου Ακροπόλεως αρ. 695,[99] του 470-460 π.Χ., εμφανίζεται με τον ίδιο εικονογραφικό τύπο. Αλλά και στα σύγχρονα αγγεία απεικονίζεται η Αθηνά με αυτό τον τύπο.[100] Σε τέσσερα τουλάχιστον ψηφισματικά ανάγλυφα του 4ου αι. π.Χ. η Αθηνά απεικονίζεται με το δεξί χέρι στο αντίστοιχο ισχίο, ενώ με το υψωμένο αριστερό κρατάει το δόρυ. Το προγενέστερο είναι το ανάγλυφο του ΕΑΜ αρ. 1481 + ΕΜ αρ. 7044, των ετών 362/1.[101] Λίγο μεταγενέστερο είναι το ανάγλυφο του Fitzwilliam Museum αρ. Gr. 13.1865, του 350 π.Χ.[102] Ακολουθούν τα δύο ανάγλυφα του ΕΑΜ αρ. 1473,[103] του 320 και αρ. 1482, του 318/7.[104] Στα δύο πρώτα την Αθηνά συνοδεύει η ασπίδα της, η Αθηνά του αναγλύφου 1473 έχει τον τύπο της Αθηνάς της Φλωρεντίας στο Palazzo

Corsini,[105] και η Αθηνά του αναγλύφου 1482 έχει τον τύπο της Αθηνάς Castra Praetoria.[106] Στη συγκεκριμένη περίπτωση η σύγκριση της γυναικείας μορφής του αναγλύφου αρ. 2986 με την Αθηνά του αναγλύφου αρ. 1473, στο οποίο αναφερθήκαμε και προηγουμένως, είναι αποφασιστική για την τάυτισή της, γιατί σε αυτό το γλυπτό η Αθηνά έχει τον ίδιο εικονογραφικό τύπο, και παράλληλα η λειτουργία της ως η απονέμουσα την τιμή είναι φανερή. Θα μπορούσαμε λοιπόν να αποκαταστήσουμε τη γυναικεία μορφή του αναγλύφου αρ. 2986 προσθέτοντας το κεφάλι της θεάς και το δόρυ της (εικ. 16).

Την ερμηνεία της γυναικείας μορφής ως Αθηνάς ενισχύουν και οι λόγοι τους οποίους προαναφέραμε για τον χαρακτηρισμό του αναγλύφου μας ως κρατικού ψηφισματικού. Ο τύπος της απονομής τιμής και της στεφάνωσης στα κρατικά ψηφισματικά ανάγλυφα είναι συνηθέστερος με τη μορφή της Αθηνάς, η οποία ενσαρκώνει την εξουσία: οι θεοί χαρίζουν στον συγκεκριμένο θνητό, διαμέσου του ψηφίσματος, την τιμή που αποφασίστηκε από τους θνητούς. Με αυτό το σκεπτικό η ταύτιση της πεπλοφόρου με μια θεότητα άλλης πόλης, ή με την προσωποποίησή της δεν έχει ερείσματα, εφόσον η θέση της πεπλοφόρου στην εικόνα κοντά στον τιμώμενο προσδιορίζει και το ρόλο της: ενσαρκώνει την πόλη που απονέμει την τιμή, και όχι μια άλλη πόλη, είτε ο τιμώμενος είναι Αθηναίος πολίτης, είτε είναι πολίτης άλλης πόλης.

Εφόσον η ερμηνεία της γυναικείας μορφής του αναγλύφου μας ως Αθηνάς είναι βεβαία, και αφού ο γλυπτικός τύπος μοιάζει με αυτόν των αγαλμάτων της Κυρήνης που προαναφέραμε, τότε το πρωτότυπο των αγαλμάτων αυτών παρίστανε την Αθηνά, και η δημιουργία του προσδιορίζεται γύρω στα 330 π.Χ. Οπως είναι γνωστό οι καλλιτέχνες των ψηφισματικών

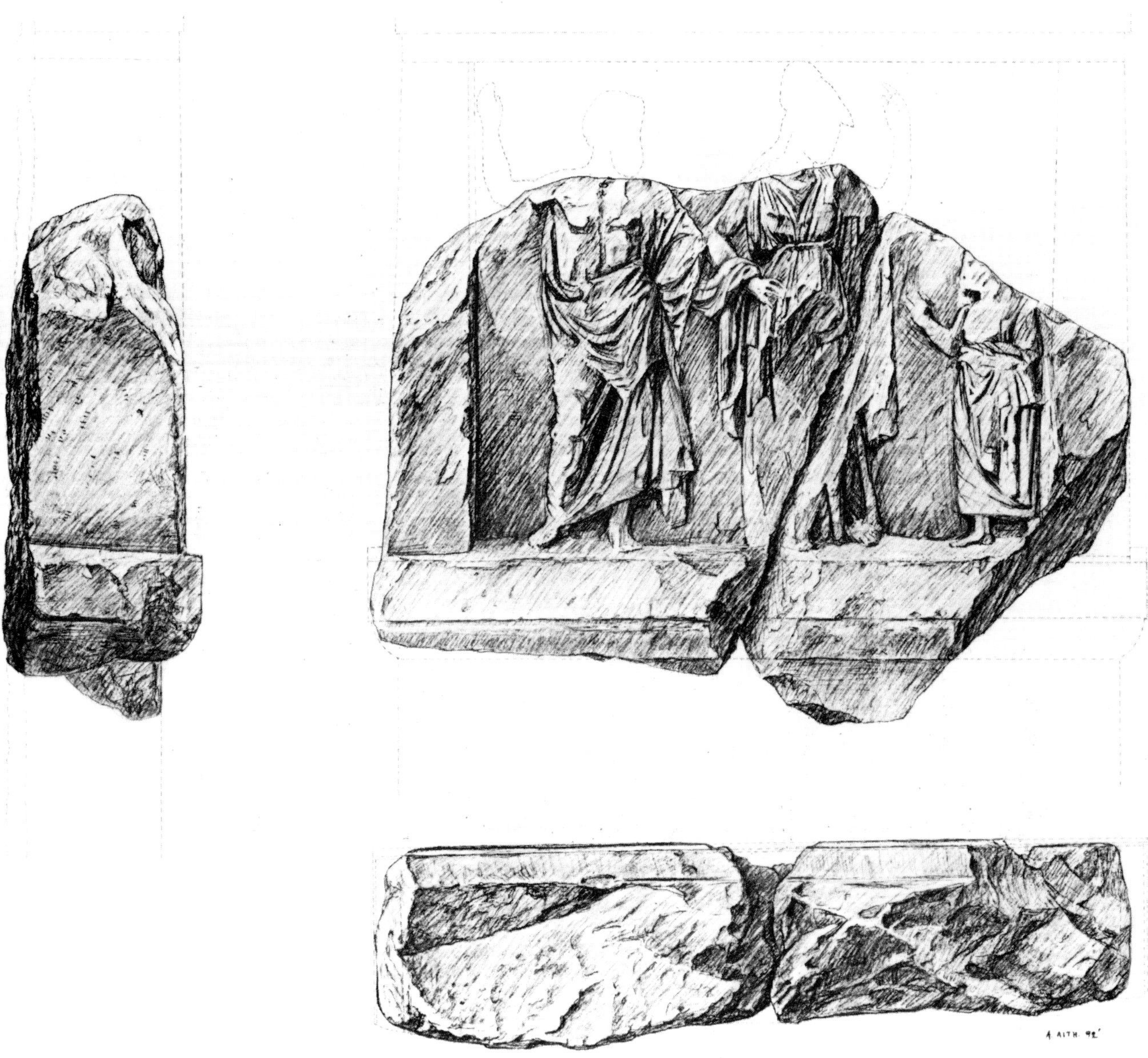

Εικ. 16. Εθνικό Αρχαιολογικό Μουσείο αρ. 2986 (συμπλήρωση).

αναγλύφων ακολουθούσαν τις στυλιστικές εξελίξεις και οι μορφές τους είχαν εξάρτηση από τα έργα της μεγάλης γλυπτικής και της αρχιτεκτονικής γλυπτικής της εποχής τους.[107] Επομένως μπορούμε να πούμε, ότι με την ερμηνεία της γυναικείας μορφής του αναγλύφου του ΕΑΜ αρ. 2986 ως Αθηνάς προσθέτομε στους ήδη γνωστούς τύπους του γ' τετάρτου του 4ου αι. π.Χ. έναν ακόμη αγαλματικό τύπο, αυτόν που διασώζουν τα αγάλματα της Κυρήνης, τον τύπο "της Αθηνάς του Εθνικού Αρχαιολογικού Μουσείου αρ. 2986".[108]

Η έρευνα για την απόδοση του πρωτοτύπου σε συγκεκριμένο καλλιτέχνη δεν εντάσσεται στα πλαίσια της παρούσας μελέτης. Ομως εδώ θα μπορούσαμε να προσδιορίσουμε την πρόθεση του καλλιτέχνη, ο οποίος φαίνεται ότι δημιούργησε έναν τύπο λατρευτικού αγάλματος και όχι αναθηματικού, αφού αυτός ο αγαλματικός τύπος της Αθηνάς χρησιμοποιήθηκε για την εικονογράφησή της σε κρατικό ψηφισματικό ανάγλυφο. Για να στηρίξουμε αυτήν την άποψη, θυμίζουμε ότι στα ψηφισματικά ανάγλυφα η παρουσία της Αθηνάς έχει πολιτική σημασία, δίνει έμφαση στη σύνδεση του τιμωμένου με την πόλη των Αθηνών, η Αθηνά παρίσταται ως η θεϊκή αντιπρόσωπός της, αποτελεί μέρος του πολιτικού συστήματος της αθηναϊκής δημοκρατίας. Βέβαια, η σύνδεση της Αθηνάς με την αθηναϊκή δημοκρατία διήρκεσε δύο εκατονταετηρίδες, ώς το τέλος του 4ου αι. π.Χ.

Η ανδρική μορφή στα αριστερά της παράστασης παρουσιάζει περισσότερες δυσκολίες για την ταύτισή της. Στά τιμητικά ανάγλυφα μαζί με την Αθηνά ως ομόλογη μορφή εμφανίζεται η κύρια θεότητα της πόλης του τιμωμένου, ή μία τοπική προσωποποίηση, ή μία πολιτική προσωποποίηση. Η ταύτιση αυτής της ομόλογης μορφής είναι πολύ δύσκολη, όταν δεν υπάρχουν επιγραφικές μαρτυρίες, όπως συμβαίνει εδώ. Η ανδρική μορφή του αναγλύφου αρ. 2986 παρουσιάζει τον εικονογραφικό τύπο του Δήμου, ο οποίος όμως, όπως προαναφέραμε, είναι ίδιος με αυτόν του Ασκληπιού ή του Διός, ή των ηρώων των δέκα φυλών της Αττικής, ή ακόμη του αστού της Αττικής.[109] Η ερμηνεία της ανδρικής μορφής ως του Διός, ή του Ασκληπιού δεν ευνοείται, αφού η λειτουργία της απονομής τιμής με τη συμμετοχή τους δεν μαρτυρείται σε αυτή την κατηγορία των μνημείων. Επιπλέον η παρουσία της Αθηνάς θα ήταν δεσμευτική.[110] Αλλά δεν θα ήταν πειστική ούτε και η ερμηνεία ως ενός των ηρώων των δέκα φυλών,[111] αφού σε κανένα τιμητικό ανάγλυφο δεν βεβαιώνεται η παρουσία τους μαζί με την Αθηνά. Τέλος, η πιθανότητα ταύτισης του ώριμου άνδρα της εικόνας μας ως προσωποποίησης της πόλης του τιμωμένου, ή της κύριας θεότητάς της, εάν ο τιμώμενος είναι ξένος, περιορίζεται και αυτή από τον εικονογραφικό τύπο που παριστάνει, του αστού της Αττικής, αλλά και από την αιτία που απεικονίζεται. Εφόσον όμως οι επιγραφικές μαρτυρίες έχουν χαθεί, θα στηριχτούμε στη σύνθεση της εικόνας και συγκεκριμένα στη θέση του άνδρα σ' αυτήν, κοντά στην Αθηνά και όχι κοντά στον τιμώμενο. Η εντύπωση την οποία δίνει αυτός ο άνδρας εδώ είναι ότι μοιράζεται με την Αθηνά την απονομή της τιμής, ή ότι παρακολουθεί τα τελούμενα, και όχι ότι συνοδεύει τον τιμώμενο. Συνήθης είναι η παρουσία της θεότητας της πόλης του τιμωμένου, ή της προσωποποίησής της στα προξενικά ανάγλυφα, όπως στο ανάγλυφο του Προξενίδη από την Κνίδο,[112] του 420 π.Χ., σε αυτό του Σοτίμου από την Ηράκλεια, της τελευταίας δεκαετίας του 5ου αι. π.Χ.,[113] στο ανάγλυφο του Πολύπου από την Γόρτυνα, του 405/4 π.Χ.,[114] ή στο ανάγλυφο του Μουσείου Ακροπόλεως αρ. 3006 του 370-60 π.Χ.[115] Αλλά στα ανάγλυφα αυτά ο τιμώμενος απεικονίζεται στο μέσον της παράστασης.

Η ταύτιση της ανδρικής μορφής του αναγλύφου μας ως του Δήμου του 'Αστεως είναι η πιθανότερη, αφού η απόφαση για την απονομή τιμής σε έναν πολίτη για τις υπηρεσίες που προσέφερε στην πόλη που τον τιμά λαμβάνεται από το δήμο και τη βουλή. Η παρουσία τους στα τιμητικά ανάγλυφα αντικατοπτρίζει την τάση των Αθηναίων να αντιπροσωπεύεται το κράτος από τους διοικητικούς θεσμούς. Επομένως η παρουσία του Δήμου κοντά στην Αθηνά σε αυτό το ανάγλυφο είναι μέσα στα πλαίσια των αρμοδιοτήτων του και ανταποκρίνεται στη γνωστή εικονογραφία του. Το γεγονός ότι στο τελευταίο τρίτο του 4ου αιώνα, περίοδο χρονολόγησης του αναγλύφου μας, αυξάνεται ο αριθμός των τιμητικών ψηφισμάτων, καθώς και η συμμετοχή του Δήμου στις παραστάσεις τους, όπως θα δούμε παρακάτω, ενισχύει την ερμηνεία αυτή.

Ως το πρωϊμότερο τιμητικό ανάγλυφο με απεικόνιση του Δήμου του 'Αστεως θεωρεί η Μ. Meyer το ελλιπές ανάγλυφο του Επιγραφικού Μουσείου αρ. 7024, του έτους 363/2 π. Χ.[116] Στα δεξιά αναγνωρίζεται η Αθηνά από την ασπίδα της και στα αριστερά ο τιμώμενος Μενέλαος από την Πελαγωνία, ο οποίος παριστάνεται σε μικρότερη κλίμακα. Η τιμή που ορίζεται στο ψήφισμα, απονέμεται από την κεντρική μορφή, η οποία ταυτίζεται με το Δήμο.

Παραστάσεις του τελευταίου τρίτου του αιώνα, που εικονογραφούν τη λειτουργία του Δήμου ως απονέμοντος μια τιμή με την παρουσία της Αθηνάς, έχουμε πέντε, από τις οποίες οι δύο πρώτες ταυτίζονται από το περιεχόμενο του σωζόμενου ψηφίσματος. Το ανάγλυφο του Επιγραφικού Μουσείου αρ. 7180+2811 (εικ. 4) εικονογραφεί το ψήφισμα του 323/2 π.Χ. για τους πρέσβεις των Φωκαίων.[117] Παριστάνει τη στεφάνωση του αντιπροσώπου τους εκ μέρους της Αθηνάς, του Δήμου και μιας τρίτης μορφής, πιθανότατα της Βουλής, όπως προαναφέρθηκε. Το ανάγλυφο του Εθνικού Αρχαιολογικού Μουσείου αρ. 1482 (εικ. 17) εικονογραφεί το ψήφισμα του 318/7, με το οποίο τιμάται ο Εύφρων από τη Σικυώνα.[118] Ο Εύφρων και ο ιπποκόμος του εικονίζονται σε μικρότερη κλίμακα. Το στεφάνι που

Εικ. 17. Εθνικό Αρχαιολογικό Μουσείο αρ. 1482, του 318/7 π.Χ.

δίνει ο Δήμος στον Εύφρονα, θα ήταν ζωγραφισμένο. Η Αθηνά στην άκρη της παράστασης μοιράζεται, ή παρακολουθεί τη στεφάνωση. Μολονότι η λειτουργία των δύο θεϊκών μορφών στο γλυπτό αυτό είναι αντίστροφη από εκείνη των δύο αντίστοιχων μορφών στο γλυπτό αρ. 2986, αφού στο πρώτο η τιμή απονέμεται από το Δήμο, ενώ στο δεύτερο από την Αθηνά, εντούτοις η μεγάλη ομοιότητα ανάμεσα στα δύο ζεύγη συνηγορεί για την ταύτιση της ανδρικής μορφής του γλυπτού 2986 ως του Δήμου των Αθηνών.

Για τα άλλα τρία ανάγλυφα, των οποίων το ψήφισμα έχει χαθεί, η ερμηνεία της ανδρικής μορφής που στεφανώνει, ως του Δήμου του ΄Αστεως, στηρίζεται σε συγκρίσεις. Το γλυπτό του ΕΑΜ αρ. 2952+2961, του 340 π. Χ. απεικονίζει την Αθηνά και έναν ισοϋψή με αυτήν άνδρα να στεφανώνουν ο καθένας τους από έναν πολίτη.[119] Το γλυπτό του ΕΑΜ αρ. 2946, του 330 π.Χ, απεικονίζει τη στεφάνωση ενός οπλίτη από έναν άνδρα μεγαλύτερης κλίμακας από αυτόν, και την Αθηνά ως συμμετέχουσα στην τελετή.[120] Το γλυπτό του Μουσείου Ακροπόλεως αρ. 7231, του 320 π.Χ., απεικονίζει την Αθηνά και μία ανδρική μορφή ισοϋψή με αυτήν να στεφανώνουν ένα θνητό.[121] Και για τα τρία αυτά ανάγλυφα έχει διατυπωθεί και η άποψη ότι η ανδρική μορφή, που απεικονίζεται να στεφανώνει, παριστάνει έναν από τους ήρωες των δέκα φυλών της Αττικής. Αλλά, στην εικονογραφία των τιμητικών αναγλύφων οι ήρωες αυτοί δεν απεικονίζονται μαζί με την Αθηνά. Εξάλλου ο καθένας τους αντιπροσωπεύει ένα μέρος του πληθυσμού της Αττικής, ενώ ο Δήμος του ΄Αστεως το σύνολο, όπως και η Αθηνά.

Σε δύο άλλα τιμητικά ανάγλυφα ο Δήμος εμφανίζεται χωρίς την Αθηνά. Στο προξενικό ανάγλυφο του ΕΜ αρ. 7155, του έτους 332/1, εικονίζονται δύο ανδρικές αντιμέτωπες μορφές σε διαφορετική κλίμακα η καθεμιά, από τις οποίες σώζονται μόνον τα πόδια.[122] Ο τιμώμενος, η μικρότερη μορφή, είναι ο ΄Αμφις από την ΄Ανδρο, όπως πληροφορούμεθα από την επιγραφή, και η δεύτερη μορφή ταυτίζεται με το Δήμο. Στο ψηφισματικό ανάγλυφο του ΕΜ αρ. 2791, του 310 περίπου, το όνομα του Δήμου γράφεται επάνω στην ταινία όπου πατούν τα πόδια του, το μόνο μέρος του σώματός του που σώζεται.[123] Τα πόδια μιας δεύτερης μορφής σε μικρότερη κλίμακα σώζονται επίσης, του τιμωμένου προφανώς, καθώς και η κατάληξη του ονόματός του: ΔΡΩΝ. Σε άλλο ένα ανάγλυφο του ΕΜ αρ. 2809, το οποίο χρονολογείται γύρω στο 310, αναγνωρίζεται η μορφή του Δήμου.[124] Αλλά εφόσον η προέλευση του γλυπτού είναι άγνωστη, δεν μπορούμε να πούμε εάν ο εικονιζόμενος Δήμος είναι ο Δήμος του ΄Αστεως, αυτός που αντιπροσωπεύει το αθηναϊκό κράτος, ή ένας τοπικός Δήμος της Αττικής. Με το δεξί χέρι κρατάει το σκήπτρο και με το αριστερό στεφανώνει. Πάντως, μαζί με εκείνο της Σάμου αρ. J187,[125] των ετών

314-306 π.Χ., είναι τα μόνα γλυπτά στα οποία ο Δήμος παριστάνεται να στεφανώνει καθισμένος.

Σε όσα από τα ανάγλυφα που είδαμε σώζεται η παράσταση, απεικονίζεται η στιγμή της στεφάνωσης, ή της απονομής τιμής, στην οποία ο Δήμος λαμβάνει ενεργό μέρος. Αντίθετα, στο ανάγλυφο του ΕΑΜ αρ. 2986 η μορφή που ταυτίζουμε με το Δήμο δεν παριστάνεται σε δράση. Πιστεύω ότι η παράσταση αποδίδει μιαν άλλη καλλιτεχνική σύλληψη.[126] Ως προς το σημείο αυτό χρήσιμη είναι η σύγκριση του αναγλύφου μας με αυτό του ΕΑΜ αρ. 1473, το οποίο είδαμε και πριν, γιατί και τα δύο έχουν παρόμοια σύνθεση. Η απεικόνιση δύο τιμωμένων στο αρ. 1473,[127] όπως πιστεύω ότι συμπληρώνεται το γλυπτό στο ελλείπον τμήμα του (εικ. 3), αντί του ενός που απεικονίζεται στο 2986, δεν αλλάζει την έννοια της σύνθεσης: στο ανάγλυφο 2986 ο Δήμος εικονίζεται στη θέση που κατέχει η Βουλή στο ανάγλυφο 1473.

Σε πολλά από τα ανάγλυφα που απεικονίζεται, ο Δήμος παριστάνεται να κρατάει στο χέρι του ραβδί, ή σκήπτρο,[128] σύμβολο της εξουσίας του. Η θέση του δεξιού χεριού της ανδρικής μορφής του γλυπτού 2986 επιτρέπει την συμπλήρωσή του με την προσθήκη του σκήπτρου. Ετσι οι δύο ομόλογες μορφές εμφανίζονται με μια συμμετρία (εικ. 16). Από την επισκόπηση που προηγήθηκε και τα συγκριτικά στοιχεία που παραθέσαμε, νομίζω έγινε φανερό ότι η ανδρική μορφή του αναγλύφου μας απεικονίζει το Δήμο του ´Αστεως.

Αυτή η ολιγάριθμη ομάδα των γλυπτών που είδαμε συνθέτει την κατηγορία των κρατικών ψηφισματικών αναγλύφων, στην οποία ο Δήμος εμφανίζεται ως αντιπρόσωπος του αθηναϊκού λαού στην απόφασή του για την απονομή μίας τιμής. Σε αυτή την κατηγορία κατατάσσουμε και το ψηφισματικό ανάγλυφο του ΕΑΜ αρ. 2986. Τα μνημεία αυτά, όλα του 4ου αι. π.Χ., αποτελούν μια παραστατική επιβεβαίωση του ενδιαφέροντος των πολιτών και της συμμετοχής τους στα πράγματα της πόλης, αλλά και των συμμάχων πόλεων, αυτού του ενδιαφέροντος το οποίον εξήρε ο Περικλής στην περίοδο της γέννησης και εδραίωσης της δημοκρατίας.

Για τις διευκολύνσεις που μου παρεσχέθησαν στο Επιγραφικό Μουσείο, αλλά και για τις ενδιαφέρουσες υποδείξεις επιθυμώ να εκφράσω και από τη θεση αυτή τις θερμές ευχαριστίες μου στη διευθύντριά του Δρ. Ντίνα Δελμούζου-Πέππα, και στην επιμελήτριά του Χαρά Μολιζάνη-Καράπα. Επίσης ευχαριστώ την Δρ. Ιφιγένεια Λεβέντη για τη διόρθωση του κειμένου, όπως και για τις πολύτιμες παρατηρήσεις της. Τέλος, ευχαριστώ θερμά τη γλύπτρια του Εθνικού Αρχαιολογικού Μουσείου Αφροδίτη Λίτη τόσο για τα ωραία σχέδιά της όσο και για τις χρήσιμες τεχνικές πληροφορίες που μου έδωσε. Οι φωτογραφίες προέρχονται από τα αντίστοιχα Μουσεία.

Συντομογραφίες

Hamdorf	F.W.Hamdorf, *Kultpersonifikationen der vorhellenistischen Zeit* (diss. Mainz 1964)
Kron	U.Kron, "Demos, Pnyx und Nymphenhugel," *AM* 94 (1979) 49–75
Kron, *Phylenheroen*	U.Kron, *Die zehn attischen Phylenheroen, AM-BH* 5 (1976)
Lawton	C.L. Lawton, *Attic Document Reliefs of the Classical and Hellenistic Periods* (diss. Princeton 1984)
Meyer	M.Meyer, *Die griechischen Urkundenreliefs, AM-BH* 13 (Berlin 1989)
Palagia	O.Palagia, *Euphranor* (Leiden 1980)
Παπαδάκη-Αγγελίδου	Β.Παπαδάκη-Αγγελίδου, *Αἱ προσωποποιήσεις εἰς την ἀρχαίαν ἑλληνικὴν τέχνην* (Αθήνα 1960)

Σημειώσεις

1. Για το θέμα γενικά δες Παπαδάκη-Αγγελίδου 41–48. Hamdorf 30–32, 57. H.A. Shapiro, *Personifications in Greek Art* (Zurich 1993). Palagia 3, 23, 42, 50, 57–63. *LIMC* III (1986) λ. Boule (V. Komninos). *LIMC* III (1986) λ. Demokratia, Demos (O. Alexandri-Tzahou). Kron 49–75. Kron, *Phylenheroen* 101, 192 κ.ε., 237–38. Lawton. Meyer.
2. Για την Αθηναϊκή Δημοκρατία και την εδραίωση των δημοκρατικών θεσμών δες A.H.M. Jones, *Athenian Democracy* (Oxford 1957). V. Ehrenberg, *The Greek State* (Oxford 1960). R. Meiggs, *The Athenian Empire* (Oxford 1972). J. Bleicken, *Die athenische Demokratie* (Paderborn 1985). M.H. Hansen, *The Athenian Assembly* (Oxford 1987). R. Osborne, *Demos: The Discovery of Classical Attika* (Cambridge 1985). Ch. G. Starr, *The Birth of Athenian Democracy: the Assembly in the Fifth Century B.C.* (Oxford 1990). D. Kagan, *Pericles of Athens and the Birth of Democracy* (New York 1991). P.J. Rhodes, *The Athenian Boule* (Oxford 1972).
3. Δες κυρίως Lawton. Meyer. I. Kasper-Butz, *Die Göttin Athena im klassischen Athen: Athena als Repräsentantin des demokratischen Staates* (Frankfurt A/M 1990).
4. Η λέξη δημοκρατία συνηθίζεται τον 5ο αι. π. Χ. Η πρωϊμότερη μνεία της εμφανίζεται στον Ηρόδοτο 6.43.3 "τοὺς γὰρ τυράννους τῶν 'Ιώνων καταπαύσας πάντας ὁ Μαρδόνιος δημοκρατίας κατίστα ἐς τὰς πολίας." Η πρωϊμότερη επιγραφική μαρτυρία της δημοκρατίας αναφέρεται σε μία επιγραφή της αρχαίας Αγοράς με αριθμό I 7169, στ. 6, του τέλους του 5ου αι. π.Χ.: R.S. Stroud, "Greek Inscriptions: Theozotides and the Athenian Orphans," *Hesperia* 40 (1971) 280 κ.ε., αρ. 7. Palagia 59 σημ. 334.
5. Παπαδάκη-Αγγελίδου 44. Hamdorf 57, αρ. Τ 448. Palagia 57–63. Της ιδίας, "A Colossal Statue of a Personification from the Agora of Athens," *Hesperia* 51 (1982) 99–113. *LIMC* III, λ. Demokratia. Meyer 138, 193 κ.ε., 256 κ.ε. Kasper-Butz (σημ. 3) 127, 205.
6. J.H. Oliver, *Demokratia, the Gods and the Free World* (Baltimore 1960) 105–106. Ο συγγραφεύς μνημονεύει την επιγραφή *IG* II², 1496, στ. 131–32, 140–41, των ετών 332/1 και 331/0 π.Χ., η οποία αναφέρεται σε θυσία στη Δημοκρατία, που λαμβάνει χώρα στο χρονικό διάστημα 12–17 Βοηδρομιώνος, την επέτειο της επιστροφής των ανδρών από το φρούριο της Φυλής και τον εορτασμό για τα "χαριστήρια ελευθερίας." Δες επίσης, E. Schweigert, "Greek Inscriptions," *Hesperia* 9 (1949) 328–30. A.E. Raubitschek, "Demokratia," *Hesperia* 31 (1962) 239 σημ. 10.
7. Schol. Aischines, I, 39, εκδ. Dindorf (Oxford 1852), 16. "δεῖγμα δὲ τῆς τῶν λ πολιτείας καὶ τόδε ἐστὶν Κριτίου γὰρ ἑνὸς τῶν λ ἀποθανόντος ἐπέστησαν τῷ μνήματι 'Ολιγαρχίαν δᾷδα κατέχουσαν καὶ ὑφάπτουσαν Δημοκρατίαν, καὶ ἐπέγραψαν τάδε: Μνῆμα τόδ' ἐστι ἀνδρῶν ἀγαθῶν, οἱ τὸν κατάρατον δῆμον 'Αθηναίων ὀλίγον χρόνον ὕβριος ἔσχον." Δες επίσης Palagia 61.
8. B.D. Meritt, "Greek Inscriptions," *Hesperia* 21 (1952) 355 κ.ε., αρ. 5, πίν. 89, 90. *SEG* XVIII (1962) 12. U. Hausmann, *Griechische Weihreliefs* (Berlin 1969) 42 κ.ε., εικ. 21, 22.

Παπαδάκη-Αγγελίδου 44, 46, αρ. 1. Hamdorf αρ. T254k, 448c. H.A. Thompson-J.Mck Camp II, *The Athenian Agora Guide*[4](Αθήνα 1990) 248 κ.ε., εικ. 153. Kron 59, πίν. 8, 2. Palagia 23, 58 κ.ε., 61, αρ. 2, 63, αρ. 3, εικ. 43. Της ιδίας, *Hesperia* 51 (1982) 109, πίν. 36c. *LIMC* III, λ. Demokratia, αρ. 7. Lawton αρ. 50. Meyer αρ. A97, πίν. 30, 2.

9. Για την παρομοίωση του εικονογραφικού τύπου με αυτόν της Υγείας, ή Νύμφης δες Palagia 61. Της ιδίας, "A Draped Female Torso in the Ashmolean Museum," *JHS* 95 (1975) 180 κ.ε. Δες επίσης, Meyer 240 σημ. 1713. Πρβλ. επίσης *LIMC* V (1990) λ. Hygieia, αρ. 64 (F. Croissant).

10. Δες τη στήλη του ΕΑΜ αρ. 737 των Προκλή και Προκλείδη: H. Diepolder, *Die attischen Grabreliefs des 5. und 4. Jahrhunderts v. Chr.* (Berlin 1931) 50, 54, πίν. 46. K.F. Johansen, *The Attic Grave -Reliefs* (Copenhagen 1951) 46 κ.ε., εικ. 25.

11. Οπως η Υγιεία του αναθηματικού αναγλύφου του ΕΑΜ αρ. 1345: *LIMC* II (1984) λ. Asklepios, αρ. 344 (B. Holzmann). *LIMC* V, λ. Hygieia, αρ. 147. Επίσης η Υγιεία του αναγλύφου του Μουσείου του Λούβρου αρ. MA. 755: *LIMC* II, λ. Asklepios, αρ. 64. *LIMC* V, λ. Hygieia, αρ. 32. M. Hamiaux, *Louvre. Catalogue: les sculptures grecques* I (Paris 1992) 218, αρ. 227.

12. Παυσανίας 1.3.3-4. "ἐπὶ δὲ τῷ τοίχῳ τῷ πέραν Θησεύς ἐστι γεγραμμένος καὶ Δημοκρατία τε καὶ Δῆμος. Δηλοῖ δὲ ἡ γραφὴ Θησέα εἶναι τὸν καταστήσαντα 'Αθηναίοις ἐξ ἴσου πολιτεύεσθαι." Δες σχετικά Palagia 3, 50, 57-60. Επίσης T.B.L. Webster, *Art and Literature in Fourth Century Athens* (London 1956) 48. Palagia, *Hesperia* 51 (1982) 111. T. Hölscher, *Griechische Historienbilder* (Würzburg 1973) 119 σημ. 650.

13. Είναι κατασκευασμένη από ελευσίνιο λίθο, έχει ύψος 0,34μ. και διατηρείται σε πλάτος 0, 20μ. και πάχος 0, 35μ. Το αριστερό της τμήμα έχει χαθεί: *IG* II[2], 2791. *SEG* XXXII (1982) 238. Raubitschek (σημ. 6) 242, πίν. 86d. Palagia, *Hesperia* 51 (1982) 111, πίν. 36 κ.ε. *LIMC* III, λ. Demokratia, αρ. 1. Γιά την επιγραφή αυτή δες και την ανακοίνωση της O.Palagia στον παρόντα τόμο, σελ. 116-117.

14. Σημ. 6.

15. Raubitschek (σημ. 6) 240, πίν. 86.

16. M. Maass, *Die Prohedrie des Dionysostheaters in Athen* (München 1972) 108-13, 121, πίν. 7, 8, 12.

17. Raubitschek (σημ. 6) 241.

18. S.V. Tracy, "Greek Inscriptions from the Athenian Agora," *Hesperia* 48 (1979) 174-78, στ. 18, πίν. 59.

19. *SIG*[3], 694, 30-31. Raubitschek (σημ. 6) 243.

20. Παπαδάκη-Αγγελίδου 45. Hamdorf 57, αρ. T448d. R. Stupperich, *Staatsbegräbnis und Privatgrabmal im klassischen Athen* (diss. Münster 1977) 252 σημ. 2. *LIMC* III, λ. Demokratia, αρ. 5.

21. Σημ.7. Δες την ανακοίνωση του R.Stupperich στον παρόντα τόμο, σελ. 99.

22. Π.χ.: *IG* I[3], 10 (469-450 π.Χ.), *IG* I[3], 17 (451/0 π.Χ.), *IG* I[3], 40 (446-5 π.Χ.). Ομως η προγενέστερη εμφάνιση των δύο μαζί απαντά στην επιγραφή *IG* I[3], 5 (περίπου 500 π.Χ.).

23. *LIMC* III, λ. Boule. Παπαδάκη-Αγγελίδου 41 κ.ε., 46, 55. Hamdorf 32, αρ. T258. Meyer 5, 9, 110, 139 κ.ε., 148, 160, 193 κ.ε., 202, 217, 228 κ.ε., 257.

24. *IG* II[2], 1, 330.

25. N.J. Svoronos, *Das Athener Nationalmuseum* (Athen 1908-1937) 616, αρ. 251, πίν. 109, 2. H.K. Süsserott, *Griechische Plastik des 4 Jhs. v. Chr.* (Frankfurt A/M 1938) 64 κ.ε. σημ. 120, 202 σημ. 22. Παπαδάκη-Αγγελίδου 43, αρ. 2. Hamdorf αρ. T258a. E. Mathiopoulos, *Zur Typologie der Göttin Athena im 5. Jh v. Chr.* (diss. Bonn 1968) 43 κ.ε. Palagia (σημ. 13) 109, πίν. 36d. *LIMC* III, λ. Boule, αρ. 1. Lawton αρ. 115. Meyer, αρ. A 136, πίν. 41, 1. Kasper-Butz (σημ. 3) αρ. K18.

26. Πρβλ. τη στήλη του Μουσείου του Κεραμεικού αρ. P 687: Diepolder (σημ. 10) 53 κ.ε., πίν. 51, 1. W.K. Kovacsovics, *Die Eckterrasse an der Gräberstrasse des Kerameikos, Kerameikos* XIV (Berlin 1990) 80 κ.ε., αρ. 2, πίν. 17.

27. A. H. Smith, *Sculpture* I (London 1892) 354 κ.ε., αρ. 771. *Ancient Marbles in the British Museum* IX (London 1842) 154 κ.ε., πίν. 35, εικ. 4. A. Michaelis, *Der Parthenon* (Leipzig 1871) 281. Mathiopoulos (σημ. 25) 31 σημ. 143. E. Mitropoulou, *Five Contributions to the Problems of Greek Reliefs* (Αθήνα 1976) 43 κ.ε., 49 κ.ε., αρ. 1α, εικ.1. Lawton αρ. 134. Meyer αρ. A135, πίν. 39, 2. Kasper-Butz (σημ. 3) αρ. K23.

28. Svoronos (σημ. 25) 666, αρ. 438, πίν. 213. R. Binneboessel, *Studien zu den attischen Urkundenreliefs des 5. und 4. Jahrhunderts* (Kaldenkirchen 1932) αρ. 67. Süsserott (σημ. 25) 218, πίν. 9, 3. Mathiopoulos (σημ. 25) 33. A. Giuliano, "Rilievo da Aphrodisias in onore di ΖΩΙΛΟΣ," *ASAtene* 37/38 (1959/1960) 399, 401, εικ. 15. Παπαδάκη-Αγγελίδου 42 κ.ε., αρ. 1, 46, αρ. 2. Hamdorf αρ. T254n. H. Rauscher, *Anisokephalie* (Wien 1971) 162 κ.ε. C. Schwenk, "The Relief of *IG* II[2], 367," *AntK* 19 (1976) 64 κ.ε., πίν. 14. Mitropoulou (σημ. 27) 52 κ.ε., αρ. 5, εικ. 9. Kron, *Phylenheroen,* 237 κ.ε., 281, αρ. 7. Palagia 62, αρ. 6. N. Eschbach, *Statuen auf Panathenäischen Preisamphoren des 4. Jhs. v. Chr.* (Mainz am Rhein 1986) 125 κ.ε. *LIMC* III, λ. Boule, αρ. 3 και λ.Demos, αρ. 57. Lawton αρ. 61. Meyer αρ. A125, πίν. 35, 2. Kasper-Butz (σημ. 3) αρ. T31.

29. Παπαδάκη-Αγγελίδου 45-48. Hamdorf 30-32, 93, αρ. T253-57. Kron 49-75. Palagia 3, 42, 50, 52, 57-63. *LIMC* III, λ. Demos. Meyer 5, 9, 25, 36, 37, 56, 65, 69 κ.ε., 77 κ.ε., 110, 116, 122, 126, 138, 146, 148, 160, 177-87, 189, 190 κ.ε., 193 κ.ε., 197 κ.ε., 200, 210, 212 κ.ε., 231, 237, 239 κ.ε., 252, 255 κ.ε. Lawton 46 κ.ε. Kasper-Butz (σημ. 3) 36 κ.ε.

30. Η αναδιοργάνωση του αθηναϊκού πολιτεύματος που έκανε ο Κλεισθένης στα 508 π.Χ. βασίστηκε στην ανακατάταξη των εκλογικών περιφερειών της Αττικής. Τότε, ο πληθυσμός της διαιρέθηκε σε δέκα φυλές, η κάθε φυλή αποτελέστηκε από τρεις τριττύες (μία μέσα στη πόλη και δύο σε αγροτικές περιοχές). Επίσης η κάθε τριττύς αποτελέστηκε από έναν, ή περισσότερους δήμους, οι οποίοι στο σύνολό τους ήταν 140. Δες σχετικά, J.S. Traill, *Demos and Trittys* (Toronto 1986). D. Whitehead, *The Demes of Attica, 508/7-ca 25 B.C.* (Princeton 1986).

31. Π.χ. σε δήμους της Αττικής: στο ψηφισματικό ανάγλυφο του δήμου των Αχαρνών της ιδιωτικής συλλογής Λυδάκη, του 330 π.Χ.: Meyer αρ. A119, πίν. 34, 1, ή σε ένα άλλο του δήμου Ευωνύμου: Meyer αρ. A 182, πίν. 52, 4. Επίσης δήμων άλλων πόλεων: Της Τρωάδος, στο Cambridge, Μουσείο Fitzwilliam, αρ. Gr.13.1865, περί το 350 π.Χ., *CIG* 3635: L. Budde-R. Nicholls, *A Catalogue of the Greek and Roman Sculpture in the Fitzwilliam Museum* (Cambridge 1964) 11 κ.ε., αρ. 27, πίν. 5. Meyer αρ. A81, πίν. 26, 1. Της Τροιζηνίας στο Μουσείο Πόρου, αρ. 575, περί το 320 π.Χ., *IG* IV, 748: *SIG* [3], 162. *IG* IV2, XX. A. Frickenhaus -W. Müller, "Aus der Argolis. Bericht uber eine Reise von Herbst 1909," *AM* 36 (1911) 33 κ.ε., εικ. 5. Meyer αρ. N10, πίν. 54, 1 και 55, 1. Της Σάμου, στο Μουσείο του Ηραίου της Σάμου, αρ. J.187, των ετών 314-306 π.Χ.: R. Horn, *Hellenistische Bildwerke auf Samos, Samos* XII (Bonn 1972) 125 κ.ε., αρ. 102, πίν. 67, Beil. 3. Παπαδάκη-Αγγελίδου 46. Hamdorf αρ. T.257. Kron 61, πίν. 8, 1. Palagia 63, αρ. 6. *LIMC* III, λ. Demos, αρ. 64. Meyer αρ. N 12.

32. W. Judeich, *Topographie von Athen*[2] (München 1931) 398.

33. H.A. Thompson, "The Pnyx in Models," στο *Studies Presented to E. Vanderpool, Hesperia* Suppl. 19 (Princeton 1982) 136-37.

34. Kron 63 κ.ε.

35. Kron 63 κ.ε., εικ. 1, πίν. 10, 11.

36. H.A. Thompson - R.E. Wycherley, *The Agora of Athens, Agora* XIV (Princeton N.J. 1972) 159, 223, πίν. 7. *LIMC* III, λ. Demos, 376.

37. Judeich (σημ. 32) 363. G. Welter, "Datierte Altäre in Athen," *AA* 1939, 35-36, εικ. 8-9. J. Travlos, *Bildlexikon zur Topographie des antiken Athen* (Tübingen 1971) 79.

38. *IG* II[2], 2798. R.E. Wycherley, *Agora* III, *Literary and Epigraphical Testimonia* (Princeton 1957) αρ. 130.

39. Δες, H. Wankel, *Demosthenes. Rede für Ktesiphon über den Kranz* (Heidelberg 1976) I 499-500.
40. Wycherley (σημ. 38) αρ. 125-31.
41. *IG* II², 834 και 4676 και του Επιγραφικού Μουσείου αρ. 8896. Ολες συνδέονται με τον ιερέα Ευκλείδη από την Κηφισιά.
42. Oliver (σημ. 6) 106.
43. *HN* 35. 69 (Overbeck 52, αρ. 1710). A. Rumpf, "Parrhasios", *AJA* 55 (1951) 7-11. Hamdorf 31, 94, αρ. T255a. M. Robertson, *A History of Greek Art* (Cambridge 1975) 434. Kron 59. Palagia 61, αρ. B1. *LIMC* III, λ. Demos, αρ. 47.
44. J. Charbonneaux, *La sculpture grecque et romaine au Musée du Louvre* (Paris 1963) 124, αρ. 831. Binneboessel (σημ.28) αρ. 14. E. Mitropoulou, *Corpus I: Attic Votive Reliefs of the 6th and 5th centuries B.C.* (Αθήνα 1977) αρ. 17, εικ. 162. Diepolder (σημ. 10) 23, εικ. 4. Süsserott (σημ. 25) 27 κ.ε., 216, πίν. 1, 1. W.H. Schuchhardt, *Die Epochen der griechischen Plastik* (Baden-Baden 1959) 85, εικ. 68 και σ. 92. Παπαδάκη-Αγγελίδου 47, αρ. 3. E. Berger, "Eine Athena aus dem späten 5. Jhr. v. Chr.," *AntK* 10 (1967) 85, αρ. 11, πίν. 24, 3. F. Hiller, *Formgeschichtliche Untersuchungen zur griechischen Statue des späten 5. Jhs v. Chr.* (Mainz 1971) 21, 50, 54, 63, πίν. 7, εικ. 17. W. Fuchs, *Die Skulptur der Griechen*³ (München 1983) 521, εικ. 608. Kron, *Phylenheroen*, 209, 259, πίν. 29. Palagia 58, 62, αρ.1. *LIMC* II, λ. Athena, αρ. 608 (P. Demargne). *LIMC* III, λ. Demos, αρ. 43. Lawton αρ. 13. Meyer αρ. A16. Kasper-Butz (σημ. 3) αρ. T13. Hamiaux (σημ. 11) 140, αρ. 132.
45. *IG* I², 304. *IG* I³, 375, 377. B.D. Meritt, "The Reverse Face of the Choiseul Marble," *ΑρχΔελτ* 25 (1970) *Μελ.*, 5 κ.ε. W.K. Pritchett, *Choiseul Marble* (Berkeley, Los Angeles 1970).
46. Για τα επιτύμβια Stupperich (σημ. 20) 97 κ.ε., 101 κ.ε. Για τα ψηφισματικά Meyer 179 κ.ε.
47. Kron, *Phylenheroen*, 206-208.
48. Meyer 186, σημ. 1284.
49. Svoronos (σημ. 25) 588 κ.ε., αρ. 240, πίν. 103. Σ. Καρούζου, *Εθνικό Αρχαιολογικό Μουσείο: συλλογή γλυπτών* (Αθήνα 1967) 130. Binneboessel (σημ. 28) αρ. 34. H. Brunn, *Denkmäler griechischer und römischer Skulptur in historischer Anordnung* (München 1888-1911) 533c. O. Walter, "Zu attischen Reliefs," *ÖJh Beibl.* 18 (1915) 90. H. Speier, "Zweifiguren-Gruppen im fünften und vierten Jahrhundert vor Christus," *RM* 47 (1932) 56 κ.ε., πίν. 20, 2. Diepolder (σημ. 10) 36 κ.ε., εικ. 9. Süsserott (σημ. 25) 217, πίν. 3, 2. G. Lippold, *Die griechische Plastik* (*Handbuch d. Alt.* VI, 3, München 1950) 230, πίν. 88, 2. Παπαδάκη-Αγγελίδου 24, 47, αρ 3. Hamdorf 94, αρ. T254e. K. Schefold, *Die Griechen und ihre Nachbarn, PropKg* I (Berlin 1967) 188, πίν. 94b. J. Charbonneaux - R. Martin - F. Villard, *Das klassische Griechenland* (Paris 1971) 207, εικ. 239. Hiller (σημ. 44) 27, 52, 56 κ.ε., 63, 66. B. R. Brown, *Anticlassicism in Greek Sculpture of the 4th Century B.C.* (New York 1973) 25 κ.ε., εικ. 79. H. Jung, "Zur Eirene des Kephisodot," JdI 91 (1976) 113 κ.ε., εικ. 4. Kron 52 κ.ε. Της ιδίας, *Phylenheroen*, 262, αρ. K 31. Fuchs (σημ. 44) 527, εικ. 619. Palagia 63 αρ. 2. *LIMC* II, λ. Athena, αρ. 609. *LIMC* III, λ. Demos, αρ. 53. Lawton αρ. 30. Meyer αρ. A51, πίν. 16, 2.
50. *IG* II², 97. *SEG* XXI (1965) 235. J. Pouilloux, *Choix d'inscriptions grecques* (Paris 1960) αρ. 28. M.N. Tod, *A Selection of Greek Historical Inscriptions* II (Oxford 1948) αρ. 127. H. Bengston, *Die Staatsverträge des Altertums* II (München-Berlin 1962) αρ. 263. M. Guarducci, *Epigrafia Greca* II (Roma 1969) 543 κ.ε., εικ. 170, 607 κ.ε.
51. Σημ. 46, 47.
52. Meyer 186 σημ. 1284, 183 σημ. 1260.
53. Meyer 183 σημ. 1261. *LIMC* VI (1992) λ.Korkyra, αρ. 8 (G. Dontas).
54. Meyer 170-71.
55. Svoronos (σημ. 25) 640, αρ. 371, πίν. 148, 4. Süsserott (σημ. 25) 113 κ.ε., πίν. 18, 3. Παπαδάκη-Αγγελίδου 47, αρ. 3. Kron 49 κ.ε., πίν. 7. Palagia 63, αρ. 4. *LIMC* III, λ. Demos, αρ. 46. Lawton αρ. 106. Meyer αρ. A94, πίν. 28, 2. Kasper-Butz (σημ. 3) αρ. T38.
56. *IG* II², 4630.
57. Kron 49 κ.ε., πίν.9.
58. Σημ.57.
59. Το συνηθέστερο είδος τιμής είναι η στεφάνωση. Δες σχετικά M. Blech, *Studien zum Kranz bei den Griechen* (Berlin 1982). Ειδικότερα δες Meyer 132 κ.ε.
60. Δες Svoronos (σημ. 25) 662, αρ. 421, πίν. 197. M.T. Fortuna, "Grande statua feminile acefala," στο *Sculture greche e romane di Cirene: Scritti di L. Polacco ... presentati da Carlo Anti* (Padova 1959) 240 κ.ε., εικ. 82. L. Beschi, "Rilievi votivi attici ricomposti," *ASAtene* 47/48 (1969/1970) 103 σημ. 6.
61. Οι διαστάσεις του μνημείου είναι: σωζ. ύψ. 0, 487μ., σωζ. μήκ. 0, 65μ. και 0, 70μ. (στην ταινία), πάχ. 0, 165μ. και 0, 17μ. (στην ταινία). Το πλάτος των παραστάδων είναι 0, 08μ., το εξωτ. πάχ. 0, 127μ. και το εσωτ. πάχ. 0, 047μ. Το σωζ. ύψ. των δύο μεγάλων μορφών είναι 0, 315μ. και 0, 328μ. τις συμπληρώνομε στο ύψος 0, 39μ. και 0, 412μ. περίπου. Το εσωτερικό ύψος του πλαισίου αποκαθίσταται ενδεικτικά σε 0.415μ. Το πάχος του αναγλύφου φτάνει έως 0, 048μ. Το ύψος της ταινίας της βάσης είναι 0, 055μ.και του κυματίου 0, 034μ.
62. Για την τεχνική και τα εργαλεία στην γλυπτική δες S. Adam, *The Technique of Greek Sculpture in the Archaic and Classical Periods* (Oxford 1966) 3-79, εικ. 1.
63. Στην προαναφερθείσα μελέτη της Fortuna (σημ. 60) 242 σημ. 12, δημοσιεύονται κάποια γράμματα, τα οποία διαβάστηκαν από τον W. Peek και δόθηκαν στη συγγραφέα από τον Χ. Καρούζο. Αριστερά, κάτω από την ανδρική μορφή στην ταινία ΟΦΗΥ. Δεξιά, στον πρώτο στίχο ΙΜΑΕ και στο δεύτερο ΔΙΑ.
64. Το σχέδιο που δημοσιεύουμε είναι έργο της γλύπτριας του Μουσείου Αφροδίτης Λίτη.
65. Beschi (σημ. 60) 101 κ.ε., εικ. 9.
66. Svoronos (σημ. 25) 641, αρ. 376, πίν. 151. K.A. Neugebauer, "Asklepios," 78. *BWPr* (Berlin 1921) 33, εικ. 11. U.Hausmann, *Kunst und Heiltum* (Potsdam 1948) 170 σημ. 58. Lippold (σημ. 49) 191 σημ. 12. G. Heiderich, *Asklepios* (diss. Freiburg 1966) 26 κ.ε., 145. *LIMC* II, λ. Asklepios, αρ. 210.
67. Svoronos (σημ. 25) 656, αρ. 411, πίν. 188. Hausmann (σημ.66) 179 σημ. 155. Süsserott (σημ. 25) 119. Ch. Picard, *Manuel d'archéologie grecque. La sculpture*, IV, 2 (Paris 1963) 1211 σημ. 5.
68. O. Walter, *Beschreibung des Reliefs im kleinen Akropolismuseum in Athen* (Wien 1923) αρ. 92, 54. Hausmann (σημ. 66) 171 σημ.68.
69. Σημ. 66.
70. Σημ. 67.
71. Hausmann (σημ. 8) 60, εικ. 3. Καρούζου (σημ. 49) 91, πίν. 36.
72. Walter (σημ. 68) 133 σημ. 282.
73. *IG* II², 1193. *SEG* XXII (1967) 119. J. Kirchner -G.Klaffenbach, *Imagines Inscriptionum Atticarum*² (Berlin 1948) αρ. 69, πίν. 31. F.W. Mitchel, "Derkylos of Hagnous and the Date of *IG* II², 1187," *Hesperia* 33 (1964) 343 σημ. 26, πίν. 65b. H.J. Mette, *Urkunden dramatischer Aufführungen in Griechenland* (Berlin 1977) 101, αρ. 3. K. Κάντα, *Ελευσίνα* (Αθήνα 1979) 108, αρ. 5115. O. Kern, "Das Kultbild der Göttinnen von Eleusis," *AM* 17 (1892) 131, εικ. 7. A. Peschlow-Bindokat, "Demeter und Persephone in der attischen Kunst des 6. bis 4 Jhs.," *JdI* 87 (1972) 152, αρ. R 46. I. Jucker, "Hahnenopfer auf einem späthellenistischen Relief," *AA* (1980) 462, εικ. 22. Palagia 30 αρ. 10. *LIMC* IV (1988) λ. Demeter, αρ. 279 (L. Beschi). Lawton αρ. 127. Meyer αρ. A117, πίν. 38, 1.
74. G. Lippold, *Antike Skulpturen der Glyptotek Ny Carlsberg* (Leipzig 1924) 17, εικ. 15. F. Poulsen, *Catalogue of Ancient Sculpture in the Ny Carlsberg Glyptotek* (Copenhagen 1951) 168 κ.ε., αρ. 231. Binneboessel (σημ.28) αρ. 66. P. Hartwig, *Bendis* (Leipzig-Berlin 1897) 4 κ.ε., πίν. 1, εικ. 1. Speier

(σημ. 49) 69, 72, πίν. 28, 1. R. Feubel, *Die attishen Nymphenreliefs* (Heidelberg 1935) XII, αρ. 20, 37. Süsserott (σημ. 25) 218, πίν. 9, 2. S. Karusu, "Alkamenes und das Hephaisteion," *AM* 69/70 (1954/55) 75 κ.ε. Rauscher (σημ. 28) 165. Brown (σημ. 49) εικ. 85. M.A. Zagdoun, *Monuments figurés: sculpture. Reliefs. FdD* IV, 6 (Paris 1977) 52, εικ. 34, 35, 55. *LIMC* II, λ. Asklepios, αρ. 211. Lawton αρ. 59. N. Himmelmann, "Eine frühhellenistische Dionysos-Statuette aus Attika," *Studien zur klassischen Archäologie. Festschrift für F. Hiller* (Saarbrücken 1986) 48 σημ. 19. Meyer αρ. A107, πίν. 32, 2.

75. Σημ. 55.

76. Kern (σημ. 73) 130 κ.ε., εικ. 6. G. Mylonas, *Eleusis and the Eleusinian Mysteries* (Princeton 1961) 190, εικ. 64. A. Peschlow-Bindokat (σημ. 73) 154, αρ. R 53. B. Schmaltz, *Untersuchungen zu den attischen Marmorlekythen* (Berlin 1970) 50 σημ. 66. Κάντα (σημ. 73) 108. Jucker (σημ. 73) 462, εικ. 22. Lawton αρ. 126. Meyer αρ. A133, πίν. 38, 2.

77. Παρουσιάζει αναλογίες με τα ψηφισματικά ανάγλυφα του ΕΑΜ αρ. 1467, ή αρ. 1482 αλλά και με άλλα.

78. Για την απεικόνιση των τιμωμένων στα ψηφισματικά ανάγλυφα δες Meyer 211 κ.ε.

79. Π.χ. το αναθηματικό αναγλυφο του ΕΑΜ αρ. 1407: Hausmann (σημ. 66) αρ. A33, πίν. 7. *LIMC* II, λ. Asklepios, αρ. 202.

80. Πρβλ. π.χ. α) το ανάγλυφο του ΕΑΜ αρ. 1892: Svoronos (σημ. 25) 573 κ.ε., αρ. 225, πίν. 95. Meyer αρ. N5, πίν. 54, 2. β) Το ανάγλυφο του ΕΑΜ αρ. 1478: Svoronos 616, αρ. 252, πίν. 109, 3. Kron, *Phylenheroen*, 188 κ.ε., 237, 279, αρ. 0 5. Lawton αρ. 135. Meyer αρ. A149, πίν. 43, 2. γ) Το ανάγλυφο του ΕΑΜ αρ. 1473: Svoronos 616, αρ. 251, πίν. 109, 2. Lawton αρ. 115. Meyer αρ. A136, πίν. 41, 1. δ) Το ανάγλυφο του Μουσείου Ελευσίνος, αρ. 5115: Meyer αρ. A117, πίν. 38, 1.

81. Η χειρονομία της ύψωσης της δεξιάς συχνά συναντάται και σε τιμωμένους που απεικονίζονται κατ' ενώπιον, όπως π.χ. στο ανάγλυφο του ΕΑΜ αρ. 2952+2961: Meyer αρ. A95, πίν. 30, 1.

82. Δες π.χ. το ανάγλυφο του ΕΜ αρ. 2809: Meyer αρ. A144, πίν. 43, 1. Για τα στεφάνια και τη στεφάνωση γενικά δες Blech (σημ. 59).

83. Δες π.χ. το ψηφισματικό ανάγλυφο του Κρατικού Μουσείου του Βερολίνου, αρ. Sk 808: C. Blümel, *Die klassisch griechischen Skulpturen der Staatlichen Museen zu Berlin* (Berlin 1966) 80, αρ. 93, εικ. 127. Kron, *Phylenheroen*, 186 κ.ε., 238, 280 κ.ε., αρ 4. Lawton 107. Meyer αρ. A89, πίν. 36, 1.

84. Δες π.χ. το ανάγλυφο του ΕΑΜ αρ. 1473: Meyer αρ. A136, πίν. 41, 1.

85. Δες π.χ. το ανάγλυφο του Μουσείου Πόρου αρ. 575, του 320 π.Χ.: Meyer αρ. N10, πίν. 54, 1.

86. Lawton αρ. 98. Η ίδια χαρακτηρίζει το γλυπτό ως ψηφισματικό, αλλά με ερωτηματικό.

87. Fortuna (σημ. 60) 240 κ.ε.

88. Fortuna (σημ. 60) 229 κ.ε., εικ. 76–78.

89. Fortuna (σημ. 60) 236, εικ. 79–80

90. *LIMC* II, λ. Artemis, αρ. 521 (Μουσείο Κυρήνης αρ. 14092) και αρ. 523 (Μουσείο Κυρήνης αρ. 14093) (L. Kahil).

91. Μουσείο Βατικανού αρ. 2834 (τύπος Αρτέμιδος Βηρυτού-Βενετίας): W. Amelung, *Die Skulpturen des Vatikanischen Museums* I (Berlin 1905) 51, αρ. 38, πίν. 5. II, 742. G. Lippold, III (Berlin 1956) 407. *LIMC* II, λ. Artemis, αρ. 129.

92. Ρώμη, Μουσείο Conservatori, αρ. 1829: L. Mariani, *BullCom* 35 (1907) 1 κ.ε., πίν. 1 κ.ε. D. Mustilli, *Il Museo Mussolini* (Roma 1939) 93–95, αρ. 17, πίν. 54, 55. R. Horn, *Stehende weibliche Gewandstatuen in der hellenistischen Plastik* (*RM-EH* 2, München 1931) 8–9, πίν. 2, 2. G.M.A. Richter, "Two Greek Statues," *AJA* 48 (1944) 237, εικ. 15. M. Bieber, *The Sculpture of the Hellenistic Age*[2] (Princeton 1961) εικ. 210–212. G.B. Waywell, "Athena Mattei," *BSA* 66 (1971) 378, πίν. 72a. *LIMC* II, λ. Athena/Minerva, αρ. 159 (F. Canciani). L.J. Roccos, "Athena from a House on the Areopagus," *Hesperia* 60 (1991) 400 σημ. 16.

93. Μουσείο Ηρακλείου αρ. 326 (τύπος Απόλλωνος Barberini): L. Savignoni, "Apollon Pythios," *Ausonia* 2 (1907) 16, πίν. IV-V. *LIMC* II, λ. Apollon, αρ. 146c (O. Palagia). Για διαφορετικές απόψεις για τον αγαλματικό τύπο και τις παραλλαγές του δες L.J.Roccos, *The Shoulder-pinned Back Mantle in Greek and Roman Sculpture* (diss. New York 1986, Ann Arbor 1988) 45 κ.ε. M.Fuchs, Glyptothek München, Katalog der Skulpturen VI, Römische Idealplastik (München 1992) 203–207.

94. Ο αττικός πέπλος φορέθηκε για πρώτη φορά από την Αθηνά στην πρωϊμη κλασσική περίοδο: M. Bieber, *Griechische Kleidung* (Berlin 1928) 18. N. Leipen, *Athena Parthenos: A Reconstruction* (Toronto 1971) 27–28. B.S. Ridgway, "The Fashion of the Elgin Kore," *GettyMusJ* 12 (1984) 30–36, 46–50.

95. Το βλέπομε στην Αθηνά του αναγλύφου της λίμνης των Ρειτών, του Μουσείου της Ελευσίνος αρ. 5093: Meyer αρ. A5. Στα ψηφισματικά ανάγλυφα του 4ου αι. π.Χ. είναι συνηθισμένο χαρακτηριστικό του ενδύματός της.

96. Π.χ. α) το ανάγλυφο του Μουσείου Ακροπόλεως αρ. 695: G. Dickins, *Catalogue of the Acropolis Museum*, I, *Archaic Sculpture* (Cambridge 1912) 258. B.S. Ridgway, *The Severe Style in Greek Sculpture* (Princeton 1970) 48 κ.ε., εικ. 69. M. Μπρούσκαρη, *Μουσείον Ακροπόλεως* (Αθήνα 1974) 129, εικ. 237. *LIMC* II, λ. Athena, αρ. 625. β) Η Αθηνά του Μύρωνος: *LIMC* II, λ. Athena, αρ. 623. γ) Το ανάγλυφο του ΕΑΜ αρ. 1481 + ΕΜ αρ. 7044: Meyer αρ. A58, πίν. 17, 2. Kasper-Butz (σημ. 3) αρ. T10, πίν. 15 (για το γοργόνειο). Το ανάγλυφο του ΕΑΜ αρ. 1482: Meyer αρ. A134, πίν. 39, 1. Kasper-Butz, αρ. T32, πίν. 30 (για την ασπίδα).

97. Π.χ. ανάγλυφο ΕΑΜ αρ. 1467: Meyer αρ. A51, πίν. 16, 2. Kasper-Butz (σημ. 3) αρ. T9, πίν. 14.

98. *LIMC* II, λ. Athena, αρ. 144. Εδώ το άνετο σκέλος είναι το δεξί και το χέρι που ακουμπάει στο ισχίο είναι το αριστερό.

99. Σημ. 96, α.

100. Π.χ. η λευκή λήκυθος του Μουσείου της Βασιλείας, αρ. Ka 416, του Ζωγράφου του Βουνί: *ARV*[2] 744, 3. *Para* 413, 3. *Add*[2] 284. *LIMC* II, λ. Athena, αρ. 37.

101. Svoronos (σημ. 25) 598, αρ. 245, πίν. 106. Süsserott (σημ. 25) 217, πίν. 4, 1. Παπαδάκη-Αγγελίδου 24 κ.ε. A. Peschlow-Bindokat (σημ. 73) 142 κ.ε. Brown (σημ. 74) 26, εικ. 81. Jung (σημ. 49) 123 κ.ε., εικ. 6. S. Dusanič, "Arkadika," *AM* 94 (1979) 128 κ.ε., πίν. 38. Lawton αρ. 34. Meyer αρ. A58, πίν. 17, 2. Kasper-Butz (σημ. 3) αρ. T10, πίν. 15.

102. Budde -Nicholls (σημ. 31) 11 κ.ε., αρ. 27, πίν. 5. K. Stemmer, *Untersuchungen zur Typologie, Chronologie und Ikonographie der Panzerstatuen* (*AF* IV, Berlin 1978) 135 σημ. 431. Meyer αρ. A81, πίν. 26, 1. Kasper-Butz (σημ. 3) αρ. K15.

103. Σημ. 25.

104. Svoronos (σημ. 25) 607 κ.ε., αρ. 249, πίν. 108. Παπαδάκη-Αγγελίδου 47. Hamdorf αρ. T254o. Palagia 62, αρ. 7. Eschbach (σημ. 28) 127, 137. Lawton αρ. 66. Meyer αρ. A134, πίν. 39, 1. Kasper-Butz (σημ. 3) αρ. T32, πίν. 30. Εδώ ο τιμώμενος είναι νεκρός: *IG* II[2], 448. *SEG* XXVI (1976/1977) 82. Schwenk (σημ. 28) 167 κ.ε.

105. Roccos (σημ. 92) 408, αρ. 2, πίν. 109.

106. Τη σύγκριση αυτή προτείνει η Lawton 36. Για την Αθηνά Castra Praetoria δες σημ. 92.

107. Lawton 82 κ.ε.

108. Η Αθηνα Rospigliosi είναι ο τελευταίος γνωστός τύπος και εμφανίζεται γύρω στα 330 π.Χ. Waywell (σημ. 92) 377, 381. *LIMC* II, λ. Athena/Minerva, αρ. 155.

109. Σημ. 46, 47.

110. Meyer 138 κ.ε.

111. Meyer 187 κ.ε.

112. MA αρ. 2996 + ΕΜ αρ. 2634+2635+6854β+6854γ+-6829+6626 + Αγορά αρ. I 2806: Meyer αρ. A6, πίν. 2. Kasper-Butz (σημ. 3) αρ. T17, πίν. 22.

113. ΕΜ αρ. 6609: Meyer αρ. A31, πίν. 12, 2. Kasper-Butz (σημ. 3) αρ. T18, πίν. 23.

114. ΕΜ αρ. 3169+2792+255:Meyer αρ. A23, πίν. 12, 1. Kasper-Butz (σημ. 3) αρ. T19, πίν. 24.

115. Meyer, αρ. A55, πίν. 18, 2. Kasper-Butz (σημ. 3) αρ. T21, πίν. 26.

116. Svoronos (σημ. 25) 665, αρ. 434, πίν. 209, 2. Binneboessel (σημ.28) αρ. 36. Süsserott (σημ. 25) 217. Lawton αρ. 33. Meyer αρ. A56, πίν.17, 1. Kasper-Butz (σημ. 3) αρ. T28.
117. Svoronos (σημ. 25) 666, αρ. 438, πίν. 213. Binneboessel (σημ.28) αρ. 67. Süsserott (σημ. 25) 218, πίν. 9, 3. Mathiopoulos (σημ. 25) 33. Giuliano (σημ.28) 399, 401, εικ. 15. Παπαδάκη-Αγγελίδου 42 κ.ε., αρ. 1, 46, αρ. 2. Hamdorf αρ. T254n. Rauscher (σημ.28) 162 κ.ε. Schwenk (σημ.28) 64 κ.ε., πίν.14. Mitropoulou (σημ.27) 52 κ.ε., αρ. 5, εικ. 9. Kron, *Phylenheroen*, 237 κ.ε., 281, αρ. 7. Palagia 62, αρ. 6. *Eschbach* (σημ.28) 125 κ.ε. *LIMC* III, λ. Demos, αρ. 57. Lawton αρ. 61. Meyer αρ. A125, πίν. 35, 2. Kasper-Butz (σημ.3) αρ. T31, πίν. 29.
118. Σημ. 104.
119. Svoronos (σημ. 25) 658, αρ. 416, πίν. 192, 1 και 659, αρ. 417, πίν. 193, 6. Walter (σημ. 49) 92, εικ. 34. K. Schefold, *Untersuchungen zu den Kertscher Vasen* (Berlin-Leipzig 1934) 114. Hamdorf αρ. T254g. Mathiopoulos (σημ.25) 32 κ.ε. N. Himmelmann, *Gnomon* 40 (1968) 632. Kron, *Phylenheroen*, 237, 281, αρ. 8. Mitropoulou (σημ. 27) 52 κ.ε. αρ. 4, εικ. 8. Palagia 62, αρ. 3. *LIMC* III, λ. Demos, αρ. 56. Lawton αρ. 109. Meyer A95, πίν. 30, 1. Kasper-Butz, αρ. K21.
120. Svoronos (σημ. 25) 567, αρ. 413, πίν. 190, 1. Michaelis, (σημ.27) 280 κ.ε. αρ. 16, πίν. 15. R. Schöne, *Griechische Reliefs aus athenischen Sammlungen* (Leipzig 1872) αρ. 76, πίν. 16. O. Walter, "Neugewonnene Reliefs der athenischen Museen," *ÖJh Beibl.* 14 (1911) 60. Hamdorf αρ. T254p. Rauscher (σημ.28) 162 σημ. 30. Palagia, *JHS* 95 (1975) 182, πίν. 22c. Mitropoulou (σημ.27) 51, αρ. 2b, εικ. 6. Kron, *Phylenheroen*, 237 κ.ε., 281, αρ. 5. Palagia 63, αρ. 11, εικ. 68. *LIMC* III, λ. Demos, αρ. 60. Lawton αρ. 124. Meyer αρ. A115, πίν. 34, 2. Kasper-Butz (σημ. 3) αρ. K20.
121. Walter (σημ.68) αρ. 13. Mathiopoulos (σημ.25) 31 σημ. 145. Rauscher (σημ. 28) 162. Horn (σημ.31) 127 σημ. 5. Kron, *Phylenheroen*, 237 κ.ε., 280, αρ 3. Mitropoulou (σημ.27) 50 κ.ε., αρ. 2a, εικ. 5. Lawton αρ. 144. Meyer αρ. A138, πίν. 35, 1. Kasper-Butz (σημ. 3) αρ. K14.
122. Svoronos (σημ. 25) 666, αρ. 440, πίν. 215, 1. Binneboessel (σημ.28) αρ. 61. Lawton αρ. 57. Meyer αρ. A103, πίν. 50, 2. C.J. Schwenk, *Athens in the Age of Alexander* (Chicago 1985) αρ. 38.
123. *IG* II^2, 160. Svoronos (σημ. 25) 671, αρ. 457, πίν. 227, 4. Hamdorf αρ. T254r. Kron, *Phylenheroen*, 238 σημ. 1158. Palagia 58, 62, αρ. 9. Lawton αρ. 103. *LIMC* III, λ. Demos, αρ. 69. Meyer αρ. A146, πίν. 40, 2.
124. Svoronos (σημ. 25) 669, αρ. 448, πίν. 221, 2. Hamdorf αρ. T254d. Kron 61 σημ. 64. Palagia 63, αρ. 5. Lawton αρ. 133. *LIMC* III, λ. Demos, αρ. 65. Meyer αρ. A144, πίν. 43, 1.
125. Horn (σημ.31) 6, 125 κ.ε., αρ. 102, πίν. 67, παρένθ. πίν. 3. Παπαδάκη-Αγγελίδου 46. Hamdorf αρ. T257. Kron 61, πίν. 8, 1. Palagia 63, αρ.6. *LIMC* III, λ. Demos, αρ. 64. Meyer αρ. N12.
126. Αρχικά το κείμενο και η παράσταση των ψηφισματικών αναγλύφων ήσαν κάτω από την μέριμνα του γραμματέως της Βουλής και εκοσμούντο πιθανότατα σύμφωνα με τις δικές του υποδείξεις. Στο δεύτερο μισό του 4ου αι. που χρονολογείται το ανάγλυφο ΕΑΜ 2986, κάποια από τα τιμητικά ανάγλυφα εχρηματοδοτούντο από τον τιμώμενο του οποίου η γνώμη θα ελαμβάνετο υπόψει στη διακόσμηση, με αποτέλεσμα την ποικιλία των παραστάσεων. Δες σχετικά Meyer 13–18.
127. Η απεικόνιση περισσοτέρων του ενός τιμωμένων στα ψηφισματικά ανάγλυφα είναι συχνή. Δες Κοπεγχάγη, Ny Carlsberg Glyptotek αρ. 462: Meyer αρ. A107, πίν. 32, 2 (με δύο τιμωμένους). Μουσείο Ακροπόλεως αρ. 2756: Meyer αρ. A163, πίν. 46, 2 (με τρεις τιμωμένους). ΕΑΜ αρ. 2949+2-960: Meyer αρ. A82, πίν. 26, 2 (με τέσσερις τιμωμένους). Βέβαια δεν αποκλείεται ο καλλιτέχνης να είχε απεικονίσει στο ΕΑΜ αρ. 1473 πίσω από τον τιμώμενο, εάν αυτός ήταν ξένος, τη θεότητα της πόλης του ή την προσωποποίησή της. Ωστόσο για την άποψη αυτή δεν συνηγορεί η στάση του τιμωμένου, που θα έστρεφε τα νώτα του προς την υποθετική συνοδευτική του μορφή.
128. Π.χ. ΕΜ αρ. 2809. Σάμου αρ. J.187 (σκήπτρο). Λούβρου αρ. MA. 831 (ραβδί).

The Eponymous Heroes: The Idea of Sculptural Groups

Carol C. Mattusch

Before considering what is known of the monuments representing the Athenian Eponymous Heroes which were erected in Athens and in Delphi, it is useful to review some Athenian foreign affairs and domestic policies of the late sixth and fifth centuries, so as to approach the two statue-groups in context. Of equal interest are the public monuments which were set up by Kimon and by Perikles while each was in power, particularly those relating to Phidias, who worked for both men.

After the expulsion of the Peisistratids in 510 B.C., Kleisthenes abolished the four old Ionian tribes and instituted ten new ones. The new tribes were named after ten different heroes, whose names were chosen by the Pythia at Delphi from a list of 100 names that were submitted to her. Coincidentally, at the same time, Antenor made bronze statues commemorating two different heroes, the Tyrannicides, which were erected at public expense in the Athenian Agora.[1]

Kimon was born at about this time, probably in 508/7 B.C. His father, Miltiades, was one of the victorious Athenian generals at Marathon in 490.[2] The 192 Athenians who died there were buried on the battlefield; stelai were erected on the tomb, the Soros, listing their names by tribe, and each year a ceremony was held at the tomb.[3] Pausanias mentions the marble trophy and a monument to Miltiades at Marathon.[4] However, in 489 B.C., after an unsuccessful expedition to Paros, Miltiades was fined fifty talents for having deceived the people, and then died. Kimon, who was about eighteen years old, paid his father's fine.[5]

In 480, the Persians sacked Athens, before being decisively defeated by the Greek forces at Salamis and at Plataia. The Delian League was established in 479–8, and the walls of Athens were rebuilt. In 477, Kritios and Nesiotes were commissioned to make a second group of the Tyrannicides to replace Antenor's pair, which had been carried off by the Persians in 480.

In 476/5, Kimon defeated the Persians at Eion near the mouth of the River Strymon; three herms were dedicated in the Agora to celebrate the victory.[6] Kimon brought back from Skyros the bones of Theseus, which were enshrined to the east of the Agora. Kimon financed extensive public works which were intended to enhance the city's center: he planted trees in the Agora and in the Academy, and had shady paths and a racetrack laid out.[7] The Tholos, which was also built in Athens at about this time, was to serve as a focal point for Athenian government via its tribal organization.

After another victory over the Persians in 470/69, on the Eurymedon River, Kimon fortified the south wall of the Acropolis, and, according to Plutarch, he started construction of the Long Walls.[8] In 465, the Stoa Poikile was begun, with the battle of Marathon painted inside, and with Miltiades represented.[9] It was surely also during the 460's that the statues of the Eponymous Heroes were set up at Delphi, with the addition of several other statues, among them Miltiades and Theseus, both important figures for Kimon.[10]

In 461, Kimon was ostracized, and though he was recalled to Athens a few years later, we know little more of him than that he made one last expedition against the Persians, this time to Cyprus, where he died in 449 at about the age of 59. The Peace of Kallias was achieved in the same year.[11]

Perikles, who was born around 490, about twenty years after Kimon, belonged to the next generation, one whose chief external concerns were with Sparta, not with Persia. It was Perikles who, at about the age of 29, effected the ostracism of Kimon, despite his military, political, and financial achievements.[12]

Perikles directed his energy and his rhetorical skill towards glorifying the city of Athens. Around 449, the Assembly rescinded the Plataian oath not to rebuild those buildings which had been destroyed by the Persians, and Perikles argued successfully that the money from the Delian treasury, which had already been moved to Athens, should be used to construct new Athenian temples and public buildings.[13] Before his death in 429, Perikles could claim responsibility for the third Long Wall, for the Odeion in Athens, for the Telesterion at Eleusis, and for the Acropolis building program, including the Parthenon and its chryselephantine cult statue.

Phidias was probably born within ten years of Perikles, in 500 or in 490. Phidias's early commissions came when he would have been in his twenties or thirties, while Kimon was still in power, during the 460's. At the beginning of this decade, the Athenians had defeated the Persians at the Eurymedon River; thereafter, they commissioned a number of Marathon monuments.[14] It was upon these public monuments that Phidias seems to have built his reputation. Already between 470 and 465, he made the colossal akrolithic Athena Areia at Plataia.[15]

It was surely during the 460's, under Kimon, that Phidias made his statues of the Eponymous Heroes of Athens for the sanctuary of Apollo at Delphi, financed by spoils from Marathon.[16] They stood near three other monuments commemorating victory in the Persian wars: the Athenian Treasury; the Athenian Stoa; and the Serpent Column.[17] Pausanias reports that the heroes stood on a base below the statue of the Wooden Horse, and he names seven of them, omitting Hippothoon, Ajax, and Oineus, and adds that they were joined by statues of Athena and Apollo, by Miltiades, and by Kodros, Theseus, and Neleus/Phileus/Philaios, and later by Antigonos, Demetrios, and Ptolemy.[18] Pausanias does not describe the appearance of any of these individuals.

The statue-group at Delphi served as a memorial to the victory at Marathon, and certainly also as a reminder of the 192 Athenians who had died there. Were the names of the dead listed here, as at Marathon? If so, they would have been listed by tribe, as at Marathon.[19] By this time, Miltiades' reputation had been rehabilitated, which must have happened during the 460's, while his son was in power. The inclusion of that single historical figure - Miltiades — is surely a reflection of Kimon's wish to reaffirm his father's heroism at Marathon.[20] The statue of Miltiades would have been heroized -mature, bearded, helmeted, armed, and nude warrior, rather like the Riace bronzes. The statue of Theseus was surely a reminder that Kimon had brought back that legendary hero's bones to Athens.[21]

It is entirely possible that the statue of Athena on the Delphi monument resembled one of the other two Athena statues which Phidias made in Athens during the 460's. One of them was a Marathon monument, a colossal bronze Athena for the Acropolis, which was begun around 465, and finished nine years later. The goddess was fully armed, wore a shield on one arm, and was so tall that the tip of her upright spear could be seen by those sailing in from Cape Sounion. The other one was a bronze Athena Lemnia, dedicated about 450 on the Acropolis, a statue whose great beauty was still being admired in the second century A.D.[22]

By the 450's, Kimon was out and Perikles was in power. Phidias, however, did not suffer: his reputation was such that he could work for both men, and he probably also completed a major commission at Olympia after the death of Perikles. His statues and his war memorials appealed to all Athenians, not just to one party or to one generation. Phidias knew how to use his sculpture to make highly visible public statements with wide appeal. Dionysios of Halikarnassos stressed the majesty, sublimity, and dignity of his work.[23] Obviously, Perikles made the right choice in hiring Phidias to oversee the rebuilding of the Acropolis. When the building of the Parthenon began, Phidias was in his early 40's or 50's.[24] Ten years later, the frieze and the cult statue, which was at least his fifth statue of Athena, were in place. When the Peloponnesian War began in 431, either Phidias and Perikles were both about 59, or Phidias was ten years older than his friend and patron. Two years later, when Perikles died, Phidias must have left Athens for Olympia.

Although Phidias was a great friend of Perikles, and was probably closer in age to him than to Kimon, his commissions spanned the regimes of both men. Some of his major early works, started under Kimon, were victory monuments, including the Athena Areia, the bronze Athena for Athens, and the Eponymous Heroes for Delphi. Later, under Perikles, the tone shifted from glorifying victories to glorifying the city of Athens. The bronze Athena bridged the gap between the careers and the concerns of the two political leaders, and it embodied the interests of each, as it was both a victory monument and an ornament for the city.

In planning the sculpture for the Parthenon, Phidias had to reach not just one generation of viewers, but the entire population, whatever their ages. The audience needed to recognize the sculpted figures, not necessarily each one individually, but certainly some individuals and some major groups of figures. Therefore, the types had to be familiar ones. Groups could be identified by certain types of figures, by their relative sizes and places, and by their actions.

Noone has ever had difficulty distinguishing the group of seated gods on the east frieze of the Parthenon by their placement, by their size, and by their godlike detachment. They can be interpreted as an updated version of the seated gods on the Siphnian Treasury at Delphi, which Phidias could have seen a short way up the hill from his Marathon monument. There is today some argument over the standing men on either side of the gods of the Parthenon frieze (figures 18–23, 43–46) (Figs. 1–3). Are they meant to be invisible to the procession beside them?[25] Are they and the gods unaware of each other? Some of the men have beards and some do not, but all are idealized. They all wear sandals and cloaks, they are relaxed, evidently chatting, and carrying or leaning on staffs. They have no other attributes. Their role is tied to their being a group: they are deliberately generic. We are clearly intended to read them as such, and not to try to identify them as individuals. Whom would the Athenians have been most likely to recognize in them — nine archons and their secretary, judges, Athenian citizens, spectators, or the Eponymous Heroes?[26] Let us assume that they represent the Eponymous Heroes, as most scholars believe, and turn to the statues in the Agora.[27]

A mid-fourth-century B.C. statue base in front of the Metroon is all that remains of the monument of the

Fig. 1. Parthenon, east frieze, figures 11-19. Courtesy Trustees of the British Museum.

Fig. 2. Parthenon, east frieze, figures 20-24. Courtesy Trustees of the British Museum.

Fig. 3. Parthenon, east frieze, figures 43-47. From a cast. Courtesy Trustees of the British Museum.

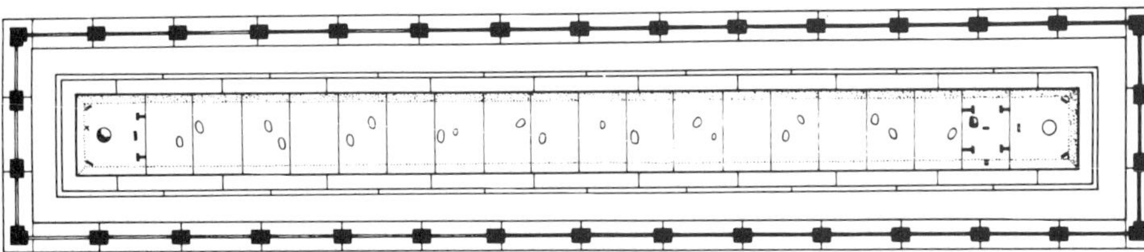

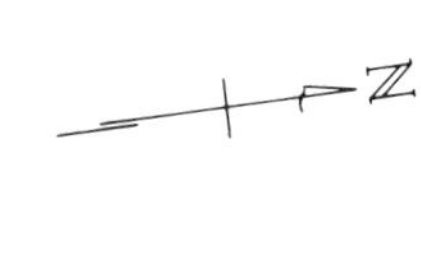

Fig. 4. *Plan and cross-section of the monument of the Eponymous Heroes in the Athenian Agora. Courtesy American School of Classical Studies at Athens: Agora Excavations.*

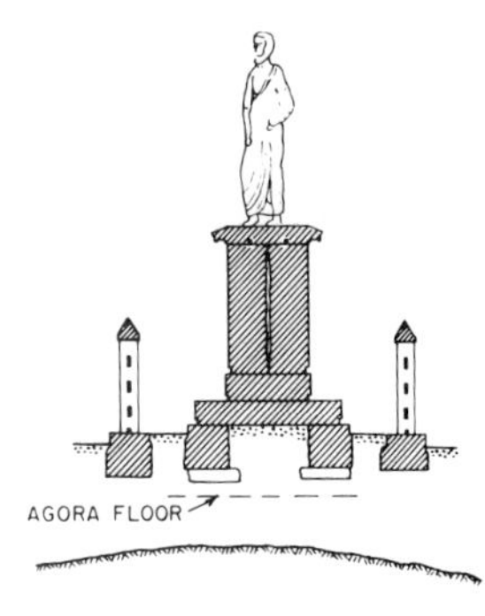

Eponymous Heroes (Fig. 4). More than sixteen meters in length, the high base held ten statues, and a tripod at either end. It was fenced with stone posts and wooden railings. Statues of Antigonos and Demetrios were added to the group in the late fourth century B.C., and removed 100 years later. Attalos I and Ptolemy III were added in the late third century B.C., and Hadrian joined the group in the second century A.D. Throughout their history, public notices were posted on wooden tablets in front of the Eponymoi, where citizens read about their tribes' proposed laws, corrected laws, and lawsuits, and found lists of ephebes, lists for military service, and announcements of honors.[28]

The first reference to the monument of the Eponymous Heroes was made by Aristophanes in 424 B.C., 75 years before the extant statue-base was erected in front of the Metroon. Aristophanes simply mentioned the place where lawsuits were displayed.[29] The audience would have known where that was. As a major bulletin-board, the monument to the Eponymous Heroes would have been well-known and frequently visited.

A foundation about 50 meters south of the fourth-century statue-base, beneath the south aisle of the Middle Stoa, measuring 9.70 m. in length, has been identified tentatively as a base for an earlier monument to the Eponymous Heroes. The pottery excavated here dates between about 430–425 and 350 B.C., which is when the later monument of the Eponymoi was built.[30] However, there is little evidence beyond the foundation itself, and we might wonder whether a base only 9.70 meters long could have held all ten heroes, let alone ten heroes and two tripods, like the later base.

We cannot really be certain, then, when or where the first monument to the Eponymous Heroes was erected. There are no descriptions of it, only references to its important function as a notice-board for tribal information. However, this monument and the statues of the Tyrannicides were the earliest actual commemorative monuments to be erected within the limits of the Agora proper. Like the Tyrannicides, the monument to the Eponymoi should have existed from near the time of the Kleisthenic reforms. After all, important tribal matters were posted there. Certainly, a monument would have been set up when the rebuilding of the Agora began in the fifth century, perhaps about the same time as the installation of the second group of the Tyrannicides, during the 470's. There was a great deal of building activity in the Agora during the second quarter of the fifth century, under Kimon, with the plane trees, the Painted Stoa, the herms, and the Tholos being put up, and with work probably also being done on the Royal Stoa and the Old Bouleuterion.[31] A suitable place could have been selected during this time for the Eponymous Heroes, and it would have been appropriate to line them up near the Old Bouleuterion and the Tholos, in the same region where we later hear of them. In the 420's, Aristophanes took it for granted that everyone knew where lawsuits were displayed. Aristotle specifically identified the Eponymoi as being in front of the Bouleuterion,[32] and, much later, Pausanias put them farther up from the Tholos.[33]

The long monument base in front of the Bouleuterion is dated by pottery to the mid-fourth century B.C. There is no evidence for an earlier structure on this spot. Wherever they stood before, there is no reference to the earlier group being moved, but it is quite possible that the statues from the earlier group were reused on the fourth-century base.

When Pausanias mentions the monument, he names all ten of the original Eponymous Heroes of Athens: Hippothoon, Antiochos, Ajax, Leos, Erechtheus, Aigeus, Oineus, Akamas, Kekrops, and Pandion, adding that there is another statue of Pandion on the Acropolis, one that is well worth seeing. He goes on to say that the statues of Attalos and Ptolemy and Hadrian were added later.[34] Because Pausanias does not describe any of the individual statues of the Eponymoi in the Agora, we must assume that there is nothing noteworthy about any of them. In fact, nobody ever describes them. This must be because everyone knew what the Eponymous Heroes looked like, and nothing stood out about any of them. They simply stood in a row, and they represented the tribes. They were always defined as a group. They were not individualized, but were distinguished from one another only by their names, which Pausanias could have read on the tops of the notice-boards posted in front of the statues.

Although the group of statues retained their function in the Agora for hundreds of years, they are never

Fig. 5. Red-figure rhyton attributed to the Triptolemos Painter, ca. 480 B.C. Virginia Museum of Fine Arts 79.100. Courtesy Virginia Museum of Fine Arts.

mentioned for their great antiquity or for their old-fashioned appearance. They must have conformed to some standard which endured over the centuries. Where did the inspiration for the Eponymous Heroes come from? They were probably the same familiar type of figure which had become popular in both vase-painting and sculpture during the late sixth and early fifth centuries. The type would have been that of the cloaked man, normally bearded, who usually appears at the edges of scenes, apparently as a bystander, not as an active participant. This type served as the model for the ten standing figures on the east frieze of the Parthenon, whether or not we can reach agreement as to which individuals are represented.

Three vases of the early fifth century are of particular interest in this connection. A ram's head rhyton in Richmond, Virginia by the Triptolemos Painter, decorated with a scene of five reclining symposiasts, clearly names Kekrops and Theseus, and preserves the ...ON of a third name, probably Pandion (Fig. 5).[35] Theseus and one other figure are beardless, but the other three are bearded, including Kekrops, and the one who may be Pandion has white hair and beard.[36] Apart from the beards and the white hair, all of the figures could be of about the same age. In Malibu, on a kylix by Douris, the names of two out of three bearded cloaked onlookers with staffs are inscribed: they are Pandion and Kekrops, both youthful, to either side of Eos and Kephalos (Fig. 6). Two unidentified bearded men on the other side of the cup frame and observe Zeus, Ganymede, and an escaping friend.[37] Hippothoon is also named on a dinos in Malibu which is attributed to the Syleus Painter (Fig. 7). Hippothoon is mature and bearded, wears a chiton and cloak, and leans on a staff. He is watching an apparent ceremony involving Demeter and Persephone.[38]

Figures like these appear on many vases of the early

Fig. 6. Red-figure kylix by Douris, ca. 480 B.C. J. Paul Getty Museum 84.AE.569. Courtesy J. Paul Getty Museum.

Fig. 7. Red-figure dinos attributed to the Syleus Painter, ca. 470 B.C. J.Paul Getty Museum 89.AE.73. Courtesy J.Paul Getty Museum.

fifth century, and they are usually identified as observers. The two bearded cloaked men on the Berlin Foundry Cup seem not to be participants in the activities, but they are important enough to be as large as the statue of the warrior which is shown (Fig. 8). Generalized figures like these also appeared in statuary, and were likely to be the type upon which the statues of the Eponymoi were based. We might ask whether these bearded cloaked individuals

Fig. 8. Red-figure kylix attributed to the Foundry Painter, 490–480 B.C. Antikensammlung, Staatliche Museen zu Berlin F 2294, side B. Photo G. Platz. Courtesy Antikensammlung, Staatliche Museen zu Berlin.

are not more than observers. This generic type of figure, so often repeated, could have served as a general tribal reference, a familiar reminder of a flourishing and smoothly-functioning Athenian society.[39]

The Eponymoi, when mythic, are individualized and have attributes. For instance, when Pausanias describes the vast paintings of the Trojan War in the Lesche at Delphi, he mentions Akamas, the son of Theseus, and describes him as wearing a crested helmet.[40] Evidently, the statue of Akamas in the Marathon dedication at Delphi was not wearing a helmet or anything else that distinguished him from the other statues on the base.

During the last third of the fifth century, the Athenian Eponymous Heroes are sometimes named on vases, where they exist as part of the narrative. Akamas is a bearded king or an elder; Kekrops is a king with coils; Pandion, Oeneus, and Hippothoon are young warriors or travelers who arrive, depart, or inhabit a kind of Attic paradise; and in one case, a young Pandion sits with a bird on his wrist.[41] Beazley has observed that "there is a tendency to youthen everyone [on vases] in the late fifth century and the fourth ... and many rather colourless Attic heroes find their way into art at this period."[42]

From the beginnings, Greek freestanding sculpture adhered to certain fixed types, and sculptures of heroes were no exception. The Tyrannicides are a good example of a familiar Archaic genre, that of the striding attacking god or hero. The type survives into the Classical period, but becomes more naturalistic with, for example, the bronze god from Artemision. The Tyrannicides fit easily into this class, although their ages are differentiated. Actually, they embody two forms of the attacking hero, both of them being at the peak of their physical ability, but one youthful, and the other mature.

On a stamnos in Würzburg, the Tyrannicides wear cloaks, and there is a certain naturalism to their anatomy (p. 123, Fig. 1). But the standard heroic features are all present: one is bearded and one is not; both are barefoot, right arms striking, left arms down.[43] Except for the daggers, attributes are not necessary, since their actions identify them. The two are also represented in vase painting as the famous statue-group.[44] Nobody actually describes the two groups of the Tyrannicides, but we know that two groups were made, about thirty years apart. All Pausanias says is that some were the work of Kritios, but that Antenor made the old ones.[45] Were there no stylistic differences between them? They stood side by side in the Agora, giving ample opportunity for comparisons to be made. Which group was copied by the Romans (Fig. 9) ? The figures are not individualized, but heroized, with formulaic striding poses, one arm raised, the other down. Are these copies of the first or of the second group?[46] Perhaps there was little difference between the two groups. Did Kritios and Nesiotes simply repeat Antenor's famous statues, following the accepted type for an attacking figure?

Different types could have called for different styles, and so on the Berlin Foundry Cup we see the simultaneous production of two statues to which, stylistically, we might today assign different dates but which have different styles because they have different functions (Figs. 8 and 10). One is an "Archaic" striding warrior (Fig. 8), the other is a far more naturalistic "Early Classical" athlete (Fig. 10).[47]

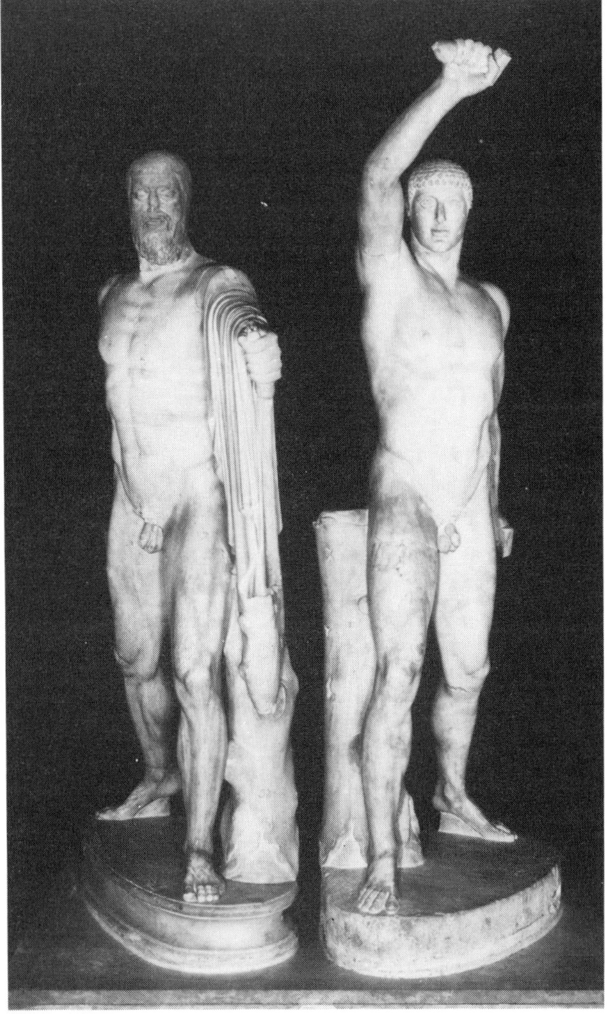

Fig. 9. Roman marble copy of statue-group of the Tyrannicides. Naples, Museo Nazionale inv. 6009, 6010. Courtesy of Soprintendenza Archeologica delle Province di Napoli e Caserta.

Like the Tyrannicides, the Eponymoi were conceived of as a group, but they were certainly not represented in the Agora as mythic figures. Instead, they would have been standardized to fit their generic role as representatives of the tribes. Maybe some were differentiated by age, as on the Parthenon. Probably they all wore the same mantle and sandals, and maybe they carried staffs.[48] They were as familiar as was the type in vase painting: it would have been inappropriate to distinguish members of the group by assigning them additional attributes. The names of the tribes would have been sufficient identification.[49] If the original statues adhered to this approved format, there would have been no need to make new ones on the occasion of moving the monument in the fourth century. They were simply moved, unremarked, from one place to another.

Fig. 10. Red-figure kylix attributed to the Foundry Painter, 490–480 B.C. Antikensammlung, Staatliche Museen zu Berlin F 2294, side A. Photo G. Platz. Courtesy Antikensammlung, Staatliche Museen zu Berlin.

As for how the group was made, we need only consider the Riace Bronzes, whose measurements and technique show clearly that they were based upon a single model, even though they turned out quite differently.[50] This was a perfect approach for a group of ten statues. Of course, all of the Eponymous Heroes would have been draped, some bearded and some not, and perhaps they carried staffs, as do the figures on the Parthenon frieze. Two models for the statues would have ensured plenty of variety in their poses, such as alternating the weight-bearing and the free legs. But the point of such statues was not individuality: on the contrary, it was their close resemblance to one another. When Phidias made the Eponymous Heroes for Delphi, the type was already well-established, as was that for Kimon's warrior-father, who would simply have been armed and nude. When the Parthenon frieze was carved, everyone would have recognized instantly, as a group, the standing men on the east frieze. The formula for them had been widely used in painting and sculpture for nearly forty years: the Athenians knew it by heart.

Notes

1. See Hdt. 5.66 and 5.69; Arist. *Ath. Pol.* ch. 21; and Pliny *HN* 34.17.
2. For discussion of the chronology of Miltiades, see H.T. Wade-Gery, "Miltiades," *JHS* 71 (1951) 212–221.
3. Hdt. 6.117; Paus. 1.32.3. See F. Jacoby, "Some Athenian Epigrams from the Persian Wars," *Hesperia* 14 (1945) 177.
4. Paus. 1.32.4,5. See also E. Vanderpool, "A Monument to the Battle of Marathon," *Hesperia* 35 (1966) 93–106.
5. For a summary of the events and an analysis of the literary sources, see N.G.L. Hammond, "The Campaign and the Battle of Marathon," *JHS* 88 (1968) 13–57.
6. Plut. *Cim.* 7.
7. Plut. *Cim.* 13.
8. Plut. *Cim.* 13.
9. Paus. 1.15.1, 3; Ael. *NA* 7.38; Aeschin. 3,186; Plut. *Cim.* 4; *Schol.* Aristid. 46.174. Pausanias also refers to statues of Miltiades and of Themistokles at the Prytaneion, 1.18.3.
10. See Paus. 10.10.1.
11. For the suggestion that Kimon died in 456, and that the Peace of Kallias was concluded in 456/5, shortly before the transfer of the treasury of the Delian League to Athens in 454, see A.E. Raubitschek, "The Peace Policy of Pericles," *AJA* 70 (1966) 37–41.
12. Plut. *Per.* 9.
13. Plut. *Per.* 12–14.
14. P. Amandry dates all of the important Marathon monuments to the time of Kimon: "Sur les Epigrammes de Marathon," *Théoria, Festschrift für W.-H. Schuchhardt* (Baden-Baden 1960) 1–8.
15. Paus. 9.4.1.
16. E. Kluwe argues that this was a private dedication by Kimon: "Das perikleische Kongressdekret, das Todesjahr des Kimon und seine Bedeutung für die Einordnung der Miltiadesgruppe in Delphi," *Festschrift Gottfried von Lücken* (Rostock 1968) 677–683.
17. W. Gauer has suggested an earlier date of 494 for the Athenian Treasury, after the fall of Miletos and before Marathon: "Das Athenerschatz und die marathonischen Akrothinia in Delphi," *Forschungen und Funde: Festschrift Bernhard Neutsch* (Innsbruck 1980) 127–136.
18. Paus. 9.10.1–2. A.E. Raubitschek suggests that the monument which Pausanias saw had been moved up the hill while being expanded in Hellenistic times, and that it had first stood by the Athenian Treasury: "Zu den zwei attischen Marathondenkmälern in Delphi," *Mélanges Helléniques offerts à Georges Daux* (Paris 1974) 315–316.
19. For explanations as to why Pausanias does not list Hippothoon, Ajax, and Oeneus at Delphi, or whether Kodros, Theseus, and Neleus/Philaios/Phileus actually replaced them, and, if so, why, see J.G. Frazer, *Pausanias' Description of Greece* 5 (repr. New York 1965) 265–267; J.-F. Bommelaer, *Guide de Delphes: Le Site* (Paris and Athens 1991) 110–111; P. Vidal-Naquet, *The Black Hunter*, trans. A. Szegedy-Maszak (Baltimore and London 1986) 302–324; E. Kearns, *The Heroes of Attica*, *BICS* Suppl. 57 (1989) 81 and n. 8. See also W. Gauer, *Weihgeschenke aus den Perserkriegen* (Tübingen 1968) 65–70, and U. Kron, *Die zehn Attischen Phylenheroen*, *AM-BH* 5 (Berlin 1976) 217–219.
20. K. Stähler does not believe that this was the Miltiades who was victorious at Marathon, but identifies him as that man's uncle,

who ruled the Athenian colony in the Thracian Chersonesos: "Zum sog. Marathon-Anathem in Delphi," *AM* 106 (1991) 191–199.

21. E. Berger identifies a young helmeted warrior from Tivoli as Theseus, and suggests that the image is based upon the one in the Delphi group: "Das Urbild des Kriegers aus der Villa Hadriana und die Marathonische Gruppe des Phidias in Delphi," *RM* 65 (1958) 6–32. W. Fuchs argues that the Riace bronzes must come from Delphi, and wonders whether they might actually be the statues of Miltiades and Theseus from this monument: "Zu den Grossbronzen von Riace," *Praestant Interna, Festschrift für Ulrich Hausmann* (Tübingen 1982) 34–40.
22. Paus. 1.28.2. For the evidence for the bronze Athena, see J. Overbeck, *Die antiken Schriftquellen* (Leipzig 1868) 118–119, nos. 637–644; C.C. Mattusch, *Greek Bronze Statuary* (Ithaca 1988) 168–172; G. Zimmer, *Griechische Bronzegusswerkstätten* (Mainz 1990) 62–71. For the Athena Lemnia, see Overbeck, 137–138, nos. 758–764.
23. *Isoc.* 3.
24. Pliny actually dates Phidias to the 83rd Olympiad: 448–444 B.C.: *HN* 34.49.
25. As F. Brommer, *The Sculptures of the Parthenon* (London 1979) 44.
26. Archons: M.C. Root, "The Parthenon Frieze and the Apadana Reliefs at Persepolis: Reassessing a Programmatic Relationship," *AJA* 89 (1985) 105–106; I.D. Jenkins, "The Composition of the So-Called Eponymous Heroes on the East Frieze of the Parthenon," *AJA* 89 (1985) 125–127. Judges: B. Nagy, "Athenian Officials on the Parthenon Frieze," *AJA* 96 (1992) 62–69. Athenian citizens: B.S. Ridgway, *Fifth Century Styles in Greek Sculpture* (Princeton 1981) 78–79. Spectators: K. DeVries, "The 'Eponymous Heroes' on the Parthenon Frieze," *AJA* 96 (1992) 336.
27. Eponymous Heroes: M. Robertson, *A History of Greek Art* (Cambridge 1975) 308; J. Boardman, *Greek Sculpture: The Classical Period* (London 1985) 108; Brommer, (supra n. 25) 44; R.E. Wycherley, *The Stones of Athens* (Princeton 1978) 119; E.G. Pemberton, "The Gods of the East Frieze of the Parthenon," *AJA* 80 (1976) 114; and M. Robertson, *The Parthenon Frieze* (New York 1975) pl. IV east. T. Hölscher summarizes many of the earlier proposed identifications and concludes that ten figures so much alike, who obviously belong together, are most likely to be the tribal heroes: "Ein attischer Heros," *AA* 84 (1969) 416 n. 22.
28. See R.E. Wycherley, *Agora* III, *Literary and Epigraphical Testimonia* (Princeton 1957) 85–90, nos. 229–240; T.L. Shear, Jr., "The Monument of the Eponymous Heroes in the Athenian Agora," *Hesperia* 39 (1970) 145–222. Shear proposes (169) that the notices were posted inside the fence during the fourth century B.C. However, they would have been easier to post and easier to read if they were hung on the fence itself, which would explain the need for a fence.
29. *Eq.* 977–980.
30. Shear (supra n. 28) 205–222.
31. Kron suggests that public notices were first posted near the herms: (supra n. 19) 234–236.
32. *Ath. Pol.* 53,4.
33. 1.5.5. Whatever Pausanias meant by ἀνωτέρω, we know where the monument was located in the second century A.D. See Shear (supra no. 28) 181–186.
34. 1.5.1–5.
35. Virginia Museum 79.100. See R. Guy, "A Ram's Head Rhyton Signed by Charinos," *Arts in Virginia* 21 (1981) 2–15, who interprets the figures on the vase more specifically as Attic kings, with reference to the Persian Wars.
36. Perhaps the white hair and beard refer to his being the father of Kekrops. See Paus. 9.33.1.
37. J. Paul Getty Museum 84.AE.569, side B. The other figures in the scene are Eos and Kephalos. *GettyMusJ* 13 (1985) 169 no. 23.
38. J. Paul Getty Museum 89.AE.73. I am grateful to Kevin Clinton for bringing this vase to my attention. See his paper in this volume, pp. 166–168, Figs. 7–9. See also K. Clinton, *Myth and Cult* (Stockholm 1992) 106, fig. 46.
39. Berlin Antikensammlung F2294. For other possible identifications of the figures on the kylix, see C.C. Mattusch, "The Berlin Foundry Cup," *AJA* 84 (1980) 440–441.
40. 10.26.2.
41. For complete listing, see Kron (supra n. 19) *passim*. Akamas as a mature individual and/or king: bell-krater by the Dinos Painter, Syracuse 30747. See *ARV*[2] 1153.17; J.D. Beazley, "Some Inscriptions on Vases.III," *AJA* 39 (1935) 486–488. Kekrops as a king with coils: lekythos by the Selinus Painter, Hamburg, Schauenburg. *ARV*[2] 1201.4. See W. Hornbostel et al., *Kunst der Antike: Schätze aus norddeutschem Privatbesitz* (Mainz 1977) 329, no. 281. Calyx-krater by the Kekrops Painter, Adolphseck, Landgraf Philipp of Hesse 77. *ARV*[2] 1346.1. *CVA* Germany 11, Schloss Fasanerie 1, pl. 20. *EAA* II, sv. Cecrope, 450. Pandion and Oeneus as youths: bell-krater by the Dinos Painter, Syracuse 30747. *ARV*[2] 1153.17; Beazley, *AJA* 39 (1935) 487–488. Pandion as youth: oinochoe by the Eretria Painter, Palermo 12480. *ARV*[2] 1249.21. E. Brabici, "Vasi greci inediti dei musei di Palermo e Agrigento," *AttiPal* 15 (1929) 16–19, pl. II. Beazley, *AJA* 39 (1935) 487. Young Pandion with a bird, and young Antiochos: lekanis by the Meidias Painter, Naples Santangelo 311. *ARV*[2] 1314.17; L. Burn, *The Meidias Painter* (Oxford 1987) 99, pl. 10. Mature Akamas, youthful Hippothoon, Antiochos, and Oineus: hydria by the Meidias Painter, London British Museum E224. *ARV*[2] 1313.5; P.E. Arias and M. Hirmer, *A History of 1000 Years of Greek Vase Painting* (New York n.d.) 375–377, pls. 214–215; Burn 16–19.
42. Beazley, "Some Inscriptions on Vases. V," *AJA* 54 (1950) 321.
43. Würzburg, Martin von Wagner Museum L.515. *ARV*[2] 256.5. See also Mattusch (supra n. 22) 126.
44. See Mattusch (supra n. 22) 122–125.
45. 1.8.5.
46. For discussion of this question, see S. Brunnsåker, *The Tyrant-Slayers of Kritios and Nesiotes*[2] (Stockholm 1971) 45–83 with bibliography. On the Tyrannicides see also H.A.Shapiro in this volume, pp. 123–129.
47. See Mattusch (supra n. 39) 442–444.
48. A base found in Rome, with the Greek inscription Pandion, has one bare foot on it, but it is impossible to tell whether the statue was of Pandion in his mythic or his heroic role. See U. Kron, "Eine Pandion-Statue in Rom," *JdI* 92 (1977) 139–168; Hölscher (supra n. 27) 410–427, and figs. 1–6, who identifies marble bearded heads in Naples and in Millesgården, Stockholm, as Roman copies of tribal heroes, probably owned by admirers of Attic culture.
49. E.B. Harrison prefers "a balanced mixture of soldiers and civilians" in "The Iconography of the Eponymous Heroes on the Parthenon and in the Agora," *Greek Numismatics and Archaeology: Essays in Honor of Margaret Thompson* (Wetteren 1979) 83.
50. See C.C. Mattusch, "The Casting of Greek Bronzes: Variation and Repetition," *Small Bronze Sculpture from the Ancient World* (Malibu 1990) 135–138.

Παρατηρήσεις σε δύο ομάδες γλυπτών του τέλους του 6ου αιώνα από την Ακρόπολη

Ισμήνη Τριάντη

I. Τα τρία αγαλμάτια καθιστών ανδρών του Μουσείου Ακροπόλεως (εικ. 1)[1] θεωρήθηκαν εξ αρχής ως ομάδα ξεχωριστή από τις άλλες καθισμένες αρχαϊκές μορφές.[2] Η ιδιαιτερότητά τους οφείλεται και στο γεγονός ότι κρατούν στα γόνατά τους ένα τετράπλευρο αντικείμενο, ενδεικτικό της ιδιότητάς τους. Τα τρία αγαλμάτια, παρόλο που είναι του ίδιου τύπου, είναι διαφορετικών διαστάσεων. Το μεγαλύτερο (Ακρ. 629) έχει ύψος 61.50 εκ., το δεύτερο (Ακρ. 144) είναι 44.50 εκ. και το ελάχιστα μικρότερο, από το οποίο σώζεται μόνο το κάτω μέρος του σώματος (Ακρ. 146) είναι 29.30 εκ. Είναι κατασκευασμένα και τα τρία από το ίδιο ψιλόκοκκο, γκριζωπό, υμήττιο μάρμαρο.[3] Κάθονται σε δίφρο, του οποίου τα πόδια στο μεγαλύτερο άγαλμα δηλώνονται ανάγλυφα, ενώ στα άλλα δύο μόνο ζωγραφιστά.[4] Και οι τρεις φορούν μακρύ ιμάτιο από τον αριστερό ώμο, το οποίο τυλίγεται στο σώμα, λίγο υψηλότερα από τη μέση και καλύπτει τα σκέλη τους. Υπολείμματα από χρωματιστούς ιμάντες στα πόδια δείχνουν ότι φορούσαν σαντάλια. Το κεφάλι τους θα είχε κοντά μαλλιά, αφού δεν υπάρχουν βόστρυχοι στη ράχη και θα έστρεφε ελαφρώς προς τα δεξιά, όπως δείχνουν οι μυς του λαιμού.

Ένα θραύσμα κεφαλής του Μουσείου Ακροπόλεως (Ακρ. 306) (εικ. 2–3)[5] μπορεί να συσχετιστεί με το μεγαλύτερο αγαλμάτιο Ακρ. 629. Σώζεται το πάνω μέρος του κρανίου, το μέτωπο, τα φρύδια και η αρχή του δεξιού βλεφάρου, καθώς και το πάνω μέρος του δεξιού αυτιού. Η κάτω επιφάνειά του (εικ. 4) δουλεμένη με το βελονάκι και λεπτή ταινία λειασμένη γύρω-γύρω, δείχνει ότι το θραύσμα έχει προετοιμαστεί για προσθήκη. Η επιφάνεια της κόμης, που οι λεπτομέρειές της αποδίδονται αδρά με βελονιές, είναι καλυμμένη με κόκκινο χρώμα.[6]

Οι λόγοι που με οδήγησαν να συσχετίσω το θραύσμα Ακρ. 306 με τον καθιστό άνδρα Ακρ. 629 είναι η ίδια ποιότητα του μαρμάρου που είναι γκριζωπό ψιλόκοκκο, το κόκκινο χρώμα που έχει το θραύσμα της κεφαλής και όμοιο έχει κυλίσει στα

Εικ. 1. Οι γραφείς Ακρ. 629, 144 και 146.

Εικ. 2. Το θραύσμα της κεφαλής Ακρ. 306, μπροστά.

Εικ. 3. Το θραύσμα της κεφαλής Ακρ. 306, η δεξιά πλευρά.

πλάγια του λαιμού του αγαλματίου 629, η εργασία προσθήκης που μοιάζει με την εργασία προσθήκης του αριστερού βραχίονα[7] και τέλος η στροφή που δείχνει ότι έχει η κεφαλή προς τα δεξιά, στροφή που δείχνει και ο λαιμός του αγαλματίου Ακρ. 629.

Η κεφαλή της Ακροπόλεως έχει πολλά κοινά γνωρίσματα με την κεφαλή του Μουσείου του Λούβρου 2718, τη γνωστή ως κεφαλή Fauvel (εικ. 5).[8] Μοιάζει ο τρόπος που αποδίδονται τα μαλλιά με βελονιές και κόκκινο χρώμα, ο τρόπος που χωρίζονται τα μαλλιά από το μέτωπο, ο τρόπος που σχηματίζονται τα φρύδια με λοξό επίπεδο και οξεία ακμή, ο τρόπος που σχηματίζεται το μάτι με το επίπεδο του βλεφάρου προς τα έξω, όπως αρχίζει να σχηματίζεται στο θραύσμα της Ακροπόλεως, τέλος ο τρόπος που σχεδιάζεται και αποδίδεται το αυτί μέσα στον όγκο των μαλλιών.

Η κεφαλή του Λούβρου αποκτήθηκε από τον Fauvel στην Αθήνα γύρω στα 1800, αλλά η προέλευσή της δεν είναι γνωστή.[9] Ο Langlotz[10] την συγκρίνει με τα γλυπτά του Θησαυρού των Μασσαλιωτών, την θεωρεί κεφαλή πολεμιστού και κάνει μια σκέψη μήπως προέρχεται από τους Δελφούς. Το μάρμαρό της λέει ότι δεν είναι παριανό, ούτε πεντελικό, αλλά πολύ ψιλόκοκκο, πιθανώς μικρασιατικό. Η περιγραφή του μαρμάρου ταιριάζει με το μάρμαρο των τριών αγαλματίων και το ύψος της με το λαιμό που είναι 11 εκ. ταιριάζει με το ύψος της κεφαλής που θα είχε ο καθιστός άνδρας 629. Η κεφαλή Fauvel είναι φωτογραφημένη πάντα από το αριστερό προφίλ, πράγμα που έδωσε λαβή να θεωρηθεί ότι μπορεί να προέρχεται από έξεργο ανάγλυφο. Παρόλο που δεν έχει γραφτεί αν έχει υπολείμματα από εργασία προσθήκης στο πάνω μέρος, οι συμπτώσεις του ελλείποντος πάνω τμήματος της κεφαλής Fauvel με το θραύσμα του Μουσείου Ακροπόλεως ήταν τέτοιες, που δεν άφηναν πολλές αμφιβολίες ότι το θραύσμα 306 της Ακροπόλεως είναι το πάνω τμήμα της κεφαλής του Λούβρου που λείπει. Και πράγματι οι δοκιμές που έγιναν αρχικά στο Λούβρο με τα γύψινα εκμαγεία της σπασμένης επιφάνειας του λαιμού του αγαλματίου 629 και της κάτω επιφάνειας της κεφαλής 306 και στη

Εικ. 4. Το θραύσμα της κεφαλής Ακρ. 306, η κάτω επιφάνεια.

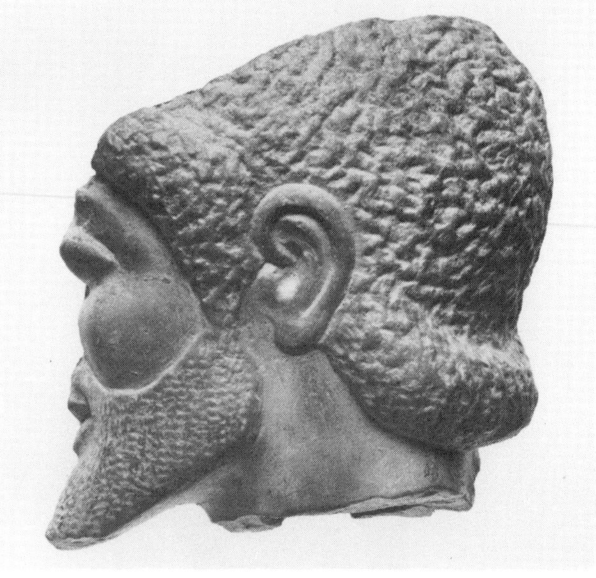

Εικ. 5. Η κεφαλή Fauvel από γύψινο αντίγραφο.

συνέχεια με το γύψινο αντίγραφο της κεφαλής στην Ακρόπολη, επιβεβαίωσαν ότι ο καθιστός άνδρας 629, η κεφαλή Fauvel και το πάνω τμήμα της κεφαλής 306 συνανήκουν όπως φαίνεται στην εικ. 6.[11]

Εικ. 6. Ο γραφέας Ακρ. 629 με την κεφαλή Fauvel και το θραύσμα Ακρ. 306.

Η ερμηνεία των τριών αυτών καθιστών αγαλματίων της Ακροπόλεως βασίστηκε στο τετράπλευρο αντικείμενο που έχουν πάνω στα πόδια τους οι μορφές, το οποίο στις δύο μικρότερες είναι συμφυές, ενώ στη μεγαλύτερη ήταν πρόσθετο, πιθανώς ξύλινο.[12] Το αντικείμενο αυτό αναγνώρισε πρώτος ο Furtwängler ως δίπτυχον δελτίον, πυξίον ή πινάκιον και ερμήνευσε τις μορφές ως γραφείς ή γραμματείς ή πιθανότερα ως ταμίες των θησαυρών της θεάς.[13] Το πτύχιον ή πτυχίον[14] δεν είναι ίδιο στα δύο μικρότερα αγαλμάτια, ως προς τον αριθμό των πινακίων. Στο 144 χωρίζεται με δύο κόκκινες ταινίες σε πέντε και ένα το ανοιχτό έξι, στο 146 τα πινάκια είναι δύο και ένα το ανοιχτό τρία. Τόσο το ανοιχτό προς τα έξω πινάκιο, όσο και αυτό που έχουν μπροστά τους, έχουν ένα περιθώριο λευκό, ενώ το εσωτερικό τους είναι κόκκινο. Η κόκκινη επιφάνεια είναι προφανώς η αλειμμένη με το κερί, πάνω στην οποία έγραφαν με τον στύλο.[15] Στύλο θα κρατούσε στην κλειστή παλάμη του που την διαπερνά μιά οπή και ο καθιστός 629. Στύλοι οστέϊνοι έχουν βρεθεί στην Ακρόπολη (εικ. 7).[16] Παλαιά ευρήματα εντοπίστηκαν πρόσφατα από τη συνάδελφο Χριστίνα Βλασσοπούλου. Το ένα τους άκρο, με το οποίο έγραφαν, είναι οξύ, το άλλο είναι πλατύ για να ισιώνουν το κερί ή και να το αφαιρούν. "Δελτίον δίπτυχον λαβών, τὸν κηρόν αὐτοῦ ἐξέκνησε καὶ ἔπειτα ἐν τῷ ξύλῳ τοῦ δελτίου ἔγραψεν" λέει ο Ηρόδοτος.[17]

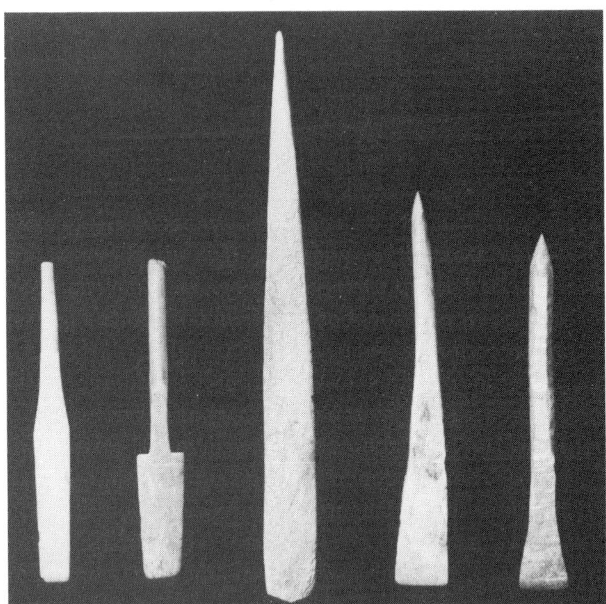

Εικ. 7 Στύλοι από την Ακρόπολη (Ακρ. 14569, 14575, 14576, 14578, 14579).

Τα ίδια σύνεργα, δηλαδή στύλο και πτυχίο θα είχε ανάγκη και ένας ταμίας, όπως υπέθεσε ο Furtwängler.[18] Η σκέψη αυτή οδήγησε τον Raubitschek να συσχετίσει τον κίονα με το κιονόκρανο του αναθήματος του Αλκιμάχου με το μεγαλύτερο αγαλμάτιο.[19] Ο ενεπίγραφος κίονας με τη μολυβδοχόηση και το κιονόκρανο βρέθηκαν από τον Καββαδία στην ανασκαφή του 1886, κοντά στο βόρειο τείχος, μεταξύ Ερεχθείου και Προπυλαίων και είναι από παριανό μάρμαρο.[20] Η επιγραφή συμπίπτει με τη στενή πλευρά του κιονόκρανου, πράγμα που δείχνει ότι αυτή ήταν η κύρια όψη του αναθήματος. Η εγκοπή στην πάνω επιφάνεια του κιονοκράνου είναι στενόμακρη, θα μπορούσε δηλαδή να δεχτεί το καθιστό άγαλμα (εικ. 8). Εκτός από τα δύο παραπάνω στοιχεία, η απόδοση του αγάλματος 629 στο βάθρο του Αλκιμάχου βασίστηκε και σε μια σειρά συλλογισμών του Raubitschek που αφορούν την επιγραφή, η οποία λέει:

᾿Αλ¦κίμαχος μ᾿ ἀνέ{σ}θεκε Διός κόρει τόδ᾿ ἄγαλμα
ε¦ὐ¦χολὲν ἐσθλõ δὲ πατρὸς hῦς Χαιρίονος ἐπεύχεται
<ε̃>νạ[ι].

Ο Αλκίμαχος ανέθεσε αυτό το άγαλμα στην κόρη του Δία ως τάμα και καυχάται που είναι γιός σπουδαίου πατέρα, του Χαιρίονος. Ένας Χαιρίων, γιός του Κλειδίκου, είναι γνωστός από επιγραφή των μέσων του 6ου αιώνα ως ταμίας της θεάς Αθηνάς.[21] Αυτόν τον συσχετίζει ο Raubitschek με έναν Χαιρίονα που αναφέρεται σε μια επιτύμβια στήλη που βρέθηκε στην

Εικ. 8. Ο γραφέας Ακρ. 629 πάνω στη βάση του Αλκιμάχου.

Ερέτρια και φέρει την επιγραφή "Χαιρίων 'Αθηναῖος Εὐπατριδῶν ἐνθάδε κεῖται."[22] Αν ο πατέρας του Αλκιμάχου είναι ο ταμίας Χαιρίων, ο ίδιος που πέθανε στην Ερέτρια, τότε το ανάθημα μπορεί να εικόνιζε έναν ταμία, που θα μπορούσε να είναι το αγαλμάτιο 629.

Κατά της συσχέτισης αγάλματος και βάσης είναι τεχνικά γνωρίσματα, όπως η εγκοπή για την υποδοχή της πλίνθου του αναθήματος, η οποία φαίνεται μεγαλύτερη από ό, τι θα χρειαζόταν για τη μολυβδοχόηση του αγάλματος. Αλλά και το διαφορετικό μάρμαρο και μάλιστα παριανό για τη βάση και υμήττιο για το άγαλμα δεν είναι υπέρ του να συνανήκουν.[23]

Μια άλλη ερμηνεία πρότεινε ο Cahn.[24] Βασιζόμενος στην παράσταση μίας κύλικας του τέλους του 6ου αιώνα, στην Ελβετία, με πομπή νέων και ίππων που κατευθύνονται προς έναν όρθιο άνδρα που κρατά πεντάπτυχο, στο οποίο γράφει με τον στύλο, νομίζει ότι εικονίζεται η δοκιμασία και ότι ο άνδρας με το πεντάπτυχο είναι ο καταλογεύς που αναφέρει ο Αριστοτέλης.[25] 'Ενας καθιστός σε βράχο καταλογεύς εικονίζεται επίσης σε μια νεώτερη κύλικα του ζωγράφου της Δοκιμασίας, στο Βερολίνο.[26] Διερωτάται λοιπόν ο Cahn μήπως και οι τρεις γραφείς, που είναι σύγχρονοι με την κύλικα της Ελβετίας, εικονίζουν καταλογείς. Την άποψή του δέχεται και η Alford.[27]

Τα τρία αγαλμάτια των καθιστών ανδρών, που είναι σύγχρονα, έχουν χρονολογηθεί από τους διάφορους μελετητές από το 530 ως το 500 π.Χ.[28] Η χρονολόγησή τους προς το τέλος του αιώνα γίνεται πιο πειστική με τη σύγκρισή τους με έργα της τελευταίας δεκαετίας του αιώνα, όπως ο ιματιοφόρος νέος 633 της Ακροπόλεως[29] και σχεδόν βέβαιη μετά τη συγκόλληση της κεφαλής Fauvel.[30] Κάποια σκληρά στοιχεία στην απόδοση της πλαστικής τους δεν είναι ένδειξη υψηλότερης χρονολόγησης, αλλά σχετίζονται με το στύλ του καλλιτέχνη που κατασκεύασε και τις τρεις μορφές.

Τα τρία αγαλμάτια φαίνεται ότι εικονίζουν αξιωματούχους. 'Οπως δείχνουν οι πινακίδες και οι στύλοι, στοιχεία προσδιοριστικά της εργασίας τους και της ιδιότητάς τους, μπορεί να είναι γραμματείς ή ταμίες ή καταλογείς. Θα μπορούσε όμως να έχει περισσότερες πιθανότητες η ερμηνεία τους ως γραμματέων, αν συσχετιζόταν με την αλλαγή του πολιτεύματος σε δημοκρατία και την καθιέρωση του γραμματέως της βουλής και του δήμου.[31]

II. Μια δεύτερη ξεχωριστή ομάδα γλυπτών του Μουσείου Ακροπόλεως αποτελούν οι δύο γονατιστοί νέοι Ακρ. 160 και Ακρ. 168 (εικ. 9-10).[32] Από τη μορφή 160 σώζεται η πλίνθος με το αριστερό πόδι και το λυγισμένο ισχυρά στο γόνατο δεξιό σκέλος. Η συγκόλληση του σκέλους αυτού με το ιμάτιο που πέφτει πλάι του οφείλεται στον Schrader, ο οποίος και συσχέτισε ως αντιθετική, τη μορφή στην οποία ανήκει η πλίνθος με άκρο αριστερό πόδι και ιμάτιο Ακρ. 168.[33] Το αριστερό σκέλος των μορφών θα ήταν λυγισμένο στο γόνατο σε ορθή γωνία. Προφανώς θα ήταν γυμνοί, αφού δεν υπάρχει ίχνος από ένδυμα πάνω στο μηρό και θα είχαν στην πλάτη τους ένα μικρό ιμάτιο, τα άκρα του οποίου σώζονται δεξιά και αριστερά πάνω στην πλίνθο. Ο Schrader θεώρησε την εξαιρετική τέχνη των μορφών εμπόδιο στην απόδοσή τους σε γλυπτό διάκοσμο κτιρίου, όπου αρχικά πήγε ο νούς του, και αναζήτησε μια ελεύθερη σύνθεση για να τις εντάξει. Με βάση το μοτίβο τους, τους συσχέτισε με τους ήρωες που παίζουν πεσσούς, όπως αυτοί εμφανίζονται πολύ συχνά στην αγγειογραφία.[34] Σε μερικές από τις παραστάσεις των αγγείων, όπως π.χ. στην κύλικα του Ιέρωνα του 480 π.Χ. στη Φλωρεντία,[35] εικονίζεται ανάμεσα στους ήρωες η Αθηνά και κατ' αναλογία πρότεινε για το μέσο της σύνθεσης την Αθηνά Ακρ. 142 (εικ. 11)[36] από παριανό μάρμαρο και αυτή, όπως οι δύο γονατιστοί νέοι. Η Αθηνά φορά χιτώνα, ιμάτιο και μακριά αιγίδα με έξεργο γοργόνειο στο στήθος. Η ασπίδα της καλύπτει μεγάλο μέρος της ράχης της. Για την απόδοση της Αθηνάς 142 στο σύνολο βασίστηκε ο Schrader στην ομοιότητα της κυματιστής παρυφής του ιματίου της, με την παρυφή του ιματίου των δύο νέων, αλλά και στη γενικότερη συγγένεια της πλαστικής τους.

Εικ. 9. Ο γονατιστός νέος Ακρ. 160.

Λίγα χρόνια αργότερα ο Dickins[37] απέρριψε την ερμηνεία του Schrader, αποσυσχέτισε ως παλιότερη την Αθηνά και θεώρησε πιθανό οι δύο νέοι να είναι αντίπαλοι σε κοκκορομαχία, φέροντας ως σχετικό παράδειγμα το ανάγλυφο στο θρόνο του ιερέως του Διονυσιακού θεάτρου.[38] Ο Picard[39] δέχτηκε τις τρεις μορφές ως ανάθημα, ερμήνευσε τους γονατιστούς νέους ως αστραγαλίζοντες και συσχέτισε το θέμα με την αστραγαλομαντεία. Ως αστραγαλίζοντες ή ως ιπποκόμοι μέσα σε ένα αέτωμα συζητήθηκαν διεξοδικά από τους

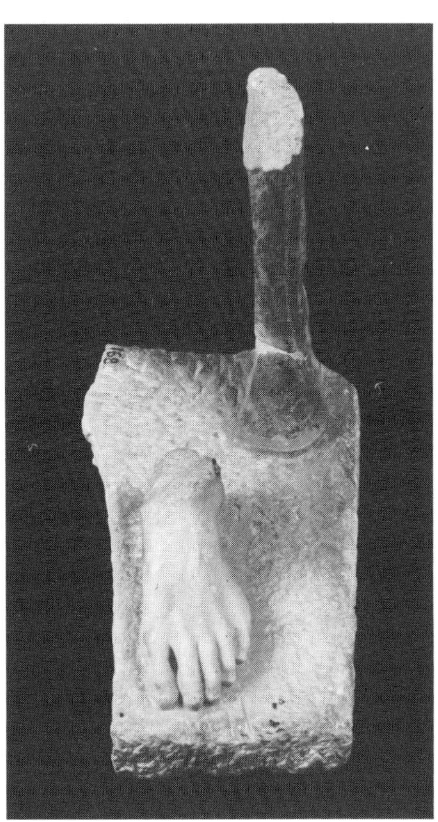

Εικ. 10. Ο γονατιστός νέος Ακρ. 168.

Εικ. 11. Η Αθηνά Ακρ. 142.

Deonna[40] και De la Coste-Messelière.[41] Τις προτάσεις τους συγκέντρωσε ο Lapalus,[42] ο οποίος δέχεται ότι ανήκουν σε αέτωμα. Τέλος, ο Schuchhardt[43] αποσυνέδεσε πάλι τους γονατιστούς νέους από την Αθηνά και τους θεώρησε ανάθημα. Την άποψή του συμμερίζεται και η Μπρούσκαρη.[44]

Με τους δύο νέους όμως, νομίζω, ότι μπορούν να συσχετιστούν και άλλα γλυπτά, όπως το θραύσμα του Μουσείου Ακροπόλεως Ακρ. 571 από παριανό μάρμαρο (εικ. 12).[45] Είναι τμήμα πλίνθου πάνω στην οποία σώζονται τα πόδια ενός νέου προς δεξιά και το πόδι ενός αλόγου προς τα αριστερά. Το αριστερό πόδι του νέου είναι μπροστά και πατά με όλο το πέλμα πάνω στην

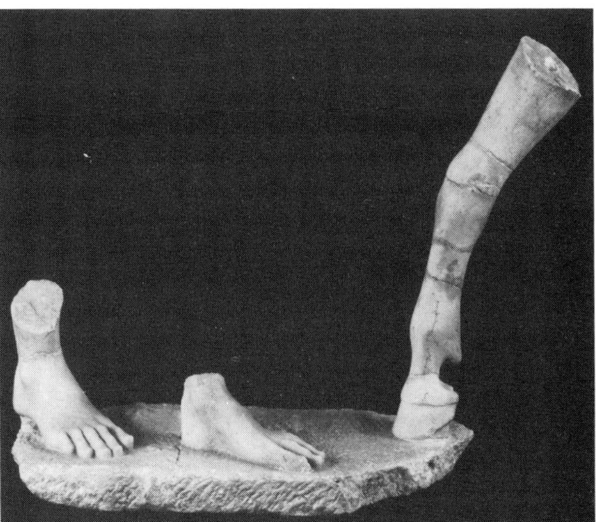

Εικ. 12. Η πλίνθος με νέο και ίππο Ακρ. 571.

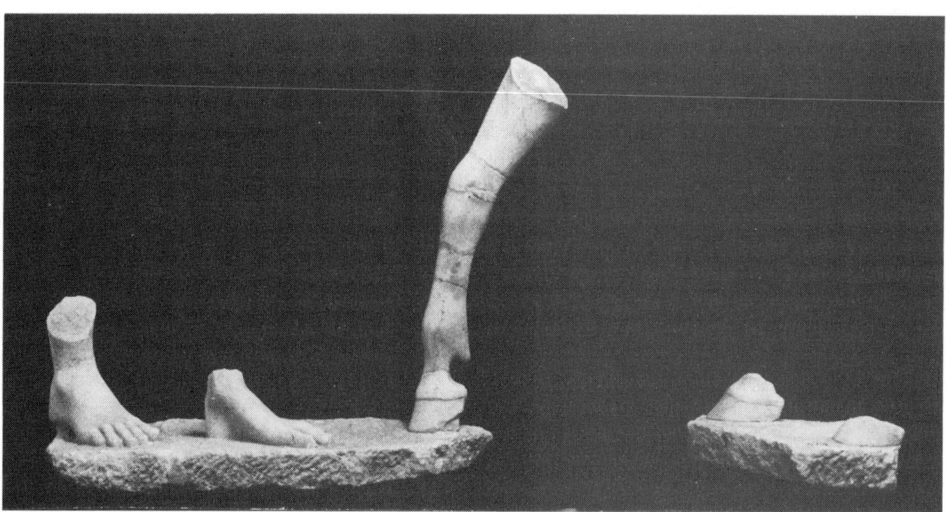

Εικ. 13. Η πλίνθος με νέο και ίππο Ακρ. 571 και 574.

πλίνθο, ενώ το δεξιό, πίσω και πλάγια, είναι ανασηκωμένο. Στο ίδιο σύμπλεγμα ανήκει και ένα τμήμα πλίνθου με τις πίσω οπλές του αλόγου Ακρ. 574 (εικ. 13).[46] Ο Raubitschek είχε θεωρήσει ότι ο νέος που οδηγεί το άλογο μπορεί να ανήκει στη βάση του Ναύκλου, που σώζεται σε θραύσματα στο Επιγραφικό Μουσείο.[47] Σε δοκιμή που έγινε το 1984 με γύψινο εκμαγείο, όπως με πληροφόρησε ο συνάδελφος Ντίνος Κίσσας, διαπιστώθηκε ότι γλυπτό και βάση δεν συνανήκουν.

Η στυλιστική συγγένεια του νέου με το άλογο με τους γονατιστούς νέους έχει ήδη επισημανθεί από τον Schuchhardt,[48] όπως φαίνεται όμως από τη σύγκρισή τους, τα στοιχεία είναι περισσότερα. Τα πόδια δείχνουν ότι οι μορφές έχουν κατασκευαστεί από έναν γλύπτη, ο οποίος φτιάχνει μακρόστενα δάχτυλα χωρίς νύχια, με δηλωμένες πλαστικά τις δύο φάλαγγες. Το μεγάλο δάχτυλο το κάνει κοντύτερο και τα δύο επόμενα, που είναι σχεδόν ενωμένα μεταξύ τους, μακρύτερα, το δεύτερο λίγο μακρύτερο από το τρίτο. Το ξεχώρισμα των δακτύλων είναι χαρακτηριστικό επίσης· με βαθύτερη αυλακιά ανάμεσα στο μεγάλο και το δεύτερο δάκτυλο, μια πιο ρηχή ανάμεσα στο δεύτερο και το τρίτο, και μια λίγο πιο βαθειά ανάμεσα στα υπόλοιπα. Ίδιες είναι και οι φτέρνες των ποδιών με έντονη δήλωση του αχίλλειου τένοντα. Το μήκος των ποδιών από τη φτέρνα ως το δεύτερο μακρύτερο δάχτυλο είναι 14 εκ. στους γονατιστούς νέους, 14.5 εκ. στον νέο με το άλογο. Το πλάτος των ποδιών στο πλατύτερο σημείο του μεταταρσίου είναι 5.9 εκ. στους γονατιστούς νέους, 6.1 εκ. στο νέο με το άλογο. Οι ομοιότητες όμως δεν σταματούν εδώ. Και οι πλίνθοι τους είναι σχετικές και ως προς το ύψος τους, και ως προς την εργασία με το βελονάκι στην πάνω πλευρά, στα μέτωπα και στην κάτω. Ίδια είναι και μια λειασμένη ταινία γύρω από τα πέλματα των ποδιών των γονατιστών νέων και του νέου με το άλογο. Υπάρχει μια λεπτομέρεια ακόμη που κάνει πιο πιθανή τη συσχέτιση. Μπροστά στα δάχτυλα του ποδιού του νέου Ακρ. 168 υπάρχουν 4 χαρακιές, οι οποίες

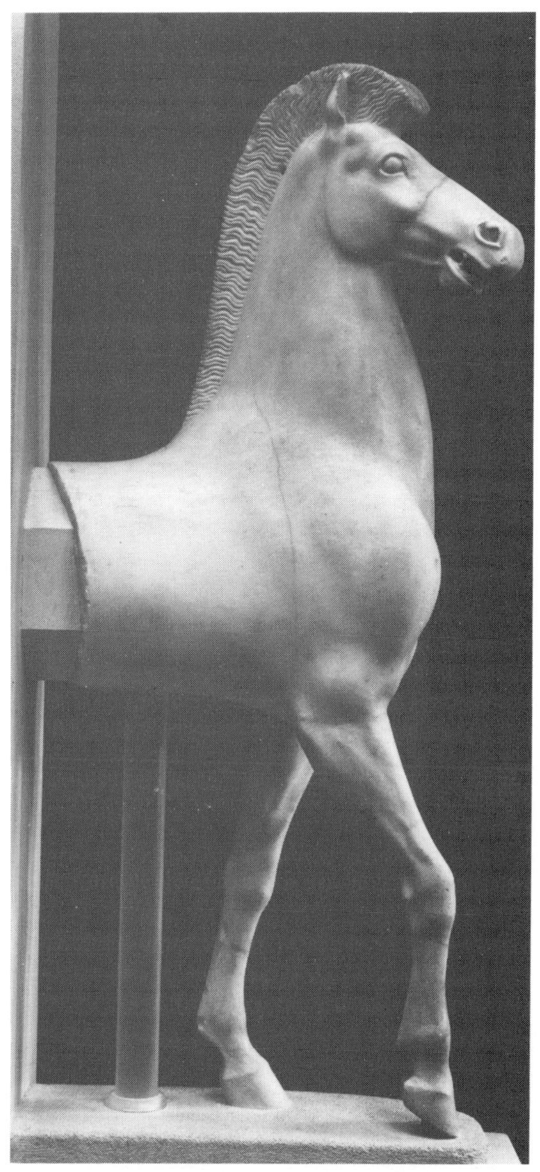

Εικ. 14. Ο ίππος Ακρ. 697.

Εικ. 15. Η οπλή Ακρ. 572 του ίππου Ακρ. 697.

κατά τον Casson[49] δείχνουν ότι τα αυλάκια μεταξύ των δαχτύλων έγιναν με σμιρίγδι σαν τροχό (εικ 10). Δύο υπολείμματα από χαρακιές υπάρχουν στο μπροστινό μέρος του αριστερού ποδιού του νέου με το άλογο, που τις διέκρινε ο Casson.

Το πόδι του αλόγου του θραύσματος Ακρ. 571 και οι οπλές που σώζονται πάνω στην πλίνθο είναι ίδια με το πόδι του αλόγου χωρίς αναβάτη του Μουσείου Ακροπόλεως (Ακρ. 697) και τις οπλές που αποδίδονται σε αυτό (Ακρ. 572 και 573) (εικ. 15–16).[50] 'Ομοια είναι και η πλίνθος, δουλεμένη σε όλες τις πλευρές με ψιλό βελονάκι, η οποία έχει ύψος 4 εκ. και βάθος 19.5, όσο ακριβώς και η πλίνθος του νέου με το άλογο. 'Ιδιος είναι ο τρόπος που αποδίδονται οι μικροί όγκοι των οστών της κλείδωσης και οι λεπτομέρειες της κνήμης στα σκέλη των δύο ίππων. Ο ίππος Ακρ. 697, επίσης από παριανό μάρμαρο, δεν έχει ιππέα και έχει υποτεθεί ότι θα συνοδευόταν από έναν νέο που θα τον κρατούσε από τα ηνία. Η απουσία του ιππέα θεωρήθηκε μάλιστα ενδεικτική για την αλλαγή αντίληψης μετά την επικράτηση της δημοκρατίας, ότι δηλαδή δεν έχουμε πια αναθήματα ιππέων, τα οποία ήταν συχνά παλαιότερα, αλλά νέων που οδηγούν ίππους. Ο ίππος 697 κατευθύνεται προς δεξιά, έχει δηλαδή κίνηση αντίθετη από την κίνηση του ίππου του θραύσματος 571.

Εικ. 16. Η οπλή και το στήριγμα Ακρ. 573 του ίππου Ακρ. 697.

'Ιδια δάχτυλα και ίδιες λεπτομέρειες της πλίνθου έχει ένα θραύσμα που βρίσκεται στις αποθήκες του Εθνικού Μουσείου, χωρίς ένδειξη για την προέλευσή του (αρ. ευρ. 6138) (εικ. 17).[51] Πρόκειται για μια στενόμακρη πλίνθο ύψους 3–4 εκ., στο ένα άκρο της οποίας σώζεται το μπροστινό μέρος ενός άκρου δεξιού ποδιού. 'Εχουμε και εδώ εργασία της πλίνθου με το βελονάκι σε όλες τις πλευρές, δάχτυλα λεπτά και μακριά χωρίς δηλωμένα νύχια, το δεύτερο και το τρίτο δάχτυλο πιο ενωμένα. Είναι πολύ πιθανόν λοιπόν και το θραύσμα του Εθνικού Μουσείου να προέρχεται από την Ακρόπολη και να ανήκει στο ίδιο σύνολο.

'Εχοντας ένα δεύτερο ζευγάρι αντιθετικών μορφών και άλλα θραύσματα στο ίδιο σύνολο, είναι δύσκολο να αμφισβητηθεί πια, η απόδοσή τους σε μια αετωματική σύνθεση. Για την απόδοση συνηγορούν και τεχνικές λεπτομέρειες, όπως η ανόμοια αφημένη πάνω επιφάνεια της πλίνθου στα θραύσματα 571 και 574 του νέου με το άλογο, που σχηματίζει βαθμίδα ύψους 1.5 εκ. προς τα πίσω, ή, μια διάβρωση στην κάτω επιφάνεια μπροστά, που μοιάζει σαν νεροφάγωμα (εικ. 18).

Η παρουσία της Αθηνάς Ακρ. 142 μέσα στο σύνολο, νομίζω, ότι με τα νέα δεδομένα ενισχύεται. Εκτός από τα όσα ανέπτυξε ο Schrader, μπορεί να προσθέσει κανείς ότι υπάρχει μια κοινή αντίληψη στην απόδοση των βοστρύχων της κόμης της Αθηνάς μπροστά και στους μικρούς βοστρύχους της χαίτης του ίππου Ακρ. 697. Επιβεβαιώνεται επίσης η πλαστική συγγένεια των δύο έργων με τη σύγκριση των επί μέρους μορφών τους. Αυτές οι ομοιότητες μπορούν βέβαια να θεωρηθούν ως στυλιστική σχέση. 'Εχουμε όμως μια Αθηνά σε κίνηση, όχι έντονη αλλά σαφή, όπως δείχνει το αριστερό λυγισμένο πόδι της, η διαφορά στη θέση του στήθους της και οι βόστρυχοι πάνω σε αυτό, που είναι οι μεν αριστεροί πιο κοντοί και τοποθετημένοι προς το μέσο, οι δε δεξιοί μακρύτεροι και τοποθετημένοι προς τα πλάγια. Ταιριάζει να βρίσκεται μέσα με μια αετωματική σύνθεση. Υπάρχει βέβαια μια δυσκολία, αν δεχτούμε ότι καταλάμβανε το μέσο του αετώματος. Θα την περίμενε κανείς λίγο μεγαλύτερη. Το ύψος της, που υπολογίζεται σε 1.15 μ. είναι 15 εκ. περισσότερο από το ύψος του νέου, που υπολογίζεται σε 1 μ. και μόλις 2 ή 3 εκ. από το ύψος του ίππου Ακρ. 697. Η κατασκευή των γλυπτών αυτών θα πρέπει να έγινε στα τελευταία χρόνια του 6ου ή στα πρώτα χρόνια του 5ου αιώνα. Η ολιγόχρονη

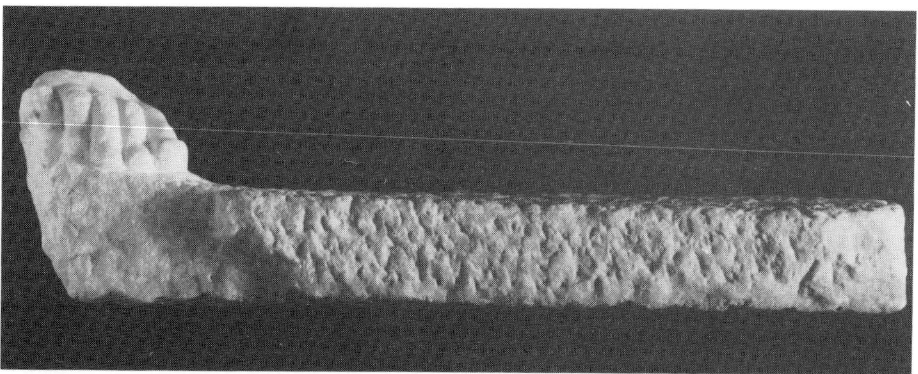

Εικ. 17. Η πλίνθος με το άκρο πόδι Εθν. Μουσ. 6138.

Εικ. 18. Η κάτω πλευρά της πλίνθου Ακρ. 571.

παραμονή τους στο κτίριο ως τα περσικά δικαιολογεί την καλή διατήρηση της επιδερμίδας και των χρωμάτων τους. Με τα νέα κομμάτια δεν κλείνει η συζήτηση γύρω από τους γονατιστούς νέους που άρχισε από τον Schrader το 1909, αλλά η σύνθεση γίνεται ευρύτερη, ανοιχτή στην απόδοση και άλλων θραυσμάτων και τα στοιχεία για την αναζήτηση του θέματος πολλαπλασιάζονται.

Σημειώσεις

1. H. Schrader, *Die archaischen Marmorbildwerke der Akropolis* (Frankfurt am Main 1939) 207–212, αρ. 309–311, πίν. 132–133, εικ. 204–209 (Schuchhardt). H. Payne, *Archaic Marble Sculpture from the Acropolis* (London 1936) 47, πίν. 118. Μ. Μπρούσκαρη, *Ὁδηγός τοῦ Μουσείου Ἀκροπόλεως* (Ἀθῆναι 1974) 65–66, εικ. 112 και 107, εικ. 207. W. Fuchs/J. Floren, *Die Griechische Plastik* I (München 1987) 261, σημ. 46. H.L. Alford, *The Seated Figure in Archaic Greek Sculpture* (Diss. Los Angeles 1978) 398, αρ. 67, 68, 69. J. Boardman, *Greek Sculpture. The Archaic Period*[2] (1991) 86, εικ. 164.
2. H. Möbius, "Form und Bedeutung der Sitzenden Gestalt," *AM* 41 (1916) 169. Payne, ό.π. 47. Schuchhardt στο Schrader (σημ. 1) 211.
3. Το μάρμαρο έχει θεωρηθεί από τον A. Furtwängler, "Marmore von der Akropolis," *AM* 6 (1881) 179 και από τον F. Studniczka, "Zusammensetzungen im Akropolismuseum," *AM* 11 (1886) 359 ως όμοιο με του Μοσχοφόρου, δηλαδή υμήττιο, από τον Schuchhardt στον Schrader (σημ. 1) 207, 209 και 210 ως πεντελικό. Το θεωρώ υμήττιο γιατί είναι γκριζωπό, ψιλόκοκκο, μουντό και σπάει κατά φύλλα, όπως δείχνει και η κατακόρυφη ρωγμή από το λαιμό ως τη μέση στα αγαλμάτια 629 και 144.
4. G.M.A. Richter, *The Furniture of the Greeks, Etruscans and Romans* (London 1966) 39–41. H. Kyrieleis, *Throne und Klinen* (Berlin 1969) 118–120.
5. Schuchhardt στο Schrader (σημ. 1) σημ. 1 247, αρ. 326, εικ. 275.
6. Ο Schuchhardt συγκρίνει το θραύσμα 306 με την κεφαλή του Ερμού του αναγλύφου με τις Χάριτες Ακρ. 702, το χρονολογεί στο τέλος του 6ου αι. και το θεωρεί όπως και το ανάγλυφο έργο νησιωτικο-ιωνικού εργαστηρίου. Βλ. Schrader (σημ. 1) 247, σημ. 1, αρ. 326 και 311, αρ. 430, πίν. 178.
7. Η εξωτερική πλευρά του αριστερού βραχίονα ήταν πρόσθετη από ξεχωριστό κομμάτι μαρμάρου και συνδεόταν με κόλλα, χωρίς σύνδεσμο. Η επιφάνεια έχει προετοιμαστεί με βελονιές και λεπτή ταινία λειασμένη γύρω-γύρω, όπως η κάτω επιφάνεια του θραύσματος της κεφαλής Ακρ. 306.
8. J. Charbonneaux, *La Sculpture grecque et romaine au Musée du Louvre* (Paris 1963) 10. E. Langlotz, *Die frühgriechischen Bildhauerschulen* (Nuremberg 1927) 173, πίν. 63. E. Langlotz, *Studien zur Nordostgriechischen Kunst* (Mainz 1975) 130, πίν. 48, 1. M. Hamiaux, *Louvre, Les Sculptures Grecques* I (Paris 1992) 93, αρ. 84.
9. Η κεφαλή αγοράστηκε από το Μουσείο του Λούβρου το 1817. Βλ. Hamiaux (σημ. 8) 93, αρ. 84.
10. Langlotz (σημ. 8) 130.
11. Ευχαριστώ θερμά το φίλο καθηγητή Luigi Beschi που πηγαίνοντας τον Ιανουάριο του '93 στο Λούβρο προθυμοποιήθηκε να πάρει τα εκμαγεία μαζί του και να κάνει τη δοκιμή. Ευχαριστώ επίσης τον Δ/ντή του Τμήματος Ελληνικών, Ετρουσκικών και Ρωμαϊκών Αρχαιοτήτων του Μουσείου του Λούβρου, Alain Pasquier, που διευκόλυνε την εργασία μου το Μάρτιο του '93 και μου έδωσε το γύψινο αντίγραφο της κεφαλής Fauvel.
12. Η εργασία πάνω στους μηρούς και την κοιλιά και οι δύο οπές,

που είναι ανοιγμένες λοξά προς τα αριστερά, δεν φαίνεται να έγιναν για την προσθήκη αντικειμένου από μάρμαρο.

13. Furtwängler (σημ. 3) 174–180.
14. Βλ. W. Schubart, *Das Buch bei den Griechen und Römern* (Leipzig 1961) 28–34. Ch. Karuzos, "Stelenfragment aus Amorgos," *AM* 76 (1961) 118–120.
15. Για τους στύλους βλ. H. Payne, *Perachora* II (Oxford 1962) 445–6, πίν. 189 (J.M. Stubbings). H. A. Thompson, "Buildings on the West Side of the Agora," *Hesperia* 6 (1937) 13, εικ. 6 και 14. E. Vanderpool, "The Rectangular Rock-cut Shaft," *Hesperia* 15 (1946) 335, πίν. 69. P. Corbett, "Attic Pottery of the Later Fifth Century," *Hesperia* 18 (1940) 131–132, 340, πίν. 101.
16. Από τον Payne (σημ. 15) αναφέρονται 21 στύλοι από την Ακρόπολη στο Εθνικό Μουσείο (αρ. ευρ. 2026–2042 και 2146–2147) και άλλοι 4 στο Μουσείο Ακροπόλεως.
17. Ηρόδοτος 7.239.
18. Furtwängler (σημ. 13).
19. A. Raubitschek, *Dedications from the Athenian Akropolis* (Cambridge, Mass. 1949) 10–12, αρ. 6, εικ. 5.
20. Π. Καββαδία, "Ἀνασκαφαὶ ἐν τῇ Ἀκροπόλει," *ΑρχΕφ* (1886) 79, αρ. 1, πίν. 6,1.
21. Raubitschek (σημ. 19) 364, αρ. 330.
22. *IG* I², 273, 96 κε.
23. Ενδεικτικό είναι επίσης το γεγονός ότι τα θραύσματα του κίονα βρέθηκαν στο βορειοδυτικό τμήμα του βράχου (Καββαδίας [σημ. 20]) ενώ τα θραύσματα των αγαλματίων στο νοτιοανατολικό (Κ. Μυλωνάς, "Εὑρήματα τῆς ἐν τῇ Ἀκροπόλει ἀνασκαφῆς," *ΑρχΕφ* [1883] 40).
24. H. Cahn, "Dokimasia," *RA* (1973) 3–12, πίν. 1–6.
25. Αριστ. *Αθην. Πολιτ.* 49.1.
26. Cahn (σημ. 24) πίν. 7–8. *CVA* 2, πίν. 75. *ARV*² 412.1.
27. Alford (σημ. 1) 121.
28. Στα 530–520 π.Χ. τα χρονολογεί ο Floren (σημ. 1), στα 520–510 π.Χ. ο Schuchhardt (σημ. 1), ο Payne (σημ. 1), ο Καρούζος, *Αριστόδικος* (Αθήνα, επανέκδ. 1982) 54, και γύρω στα 500 π.Χ. ο Boardman (σημ. 1) και η Alford (σημ. 1) 95.
29. Schuchhardt στο Schrader (σημ. 1) 204–207, αρ. 308, πίν. 128–129.
30. Η κεφαλή χρονολογείται από τον Charbonneaux (σημ. 8) στα 525 π.Χ., από τη Hamiaux (σημ. 8) στα 510.
31. Ο γραμματεύς σε ψήφισμα της βουλής και του δήμου αναφέρεται για πρώτη φορά σε μια επιγραφή που αφορά θυσίες στα Ελευσίνια και χρονολογείται γύρω στα 500 π.χ. *IG* I³, 5. R. Develin, *The Athenian Officials 684–321 B.C.* (Cambridge 1989) 60.
32. Schuchhardt στο Schrader (σημ. 1) 284–287, αρ. 412, πίν. 160. Payne (σημ. 1) 73, πίν. 124, 3 και 6.
33. H. Schrader, *Archaische Marmor-Skulpturen im Akropolis-Museum zu Athen* (Wien 1909) 67–71, εικ. 66–68.
34. Α. Πιλάλη-Παπαστερίου, "Ἥρωες πεττεύοντες," *Ελληνικά* 27 (1974) 12–38.
35. P. Hartwig, *Die griechischen Meisterschalen* (Berlin 1893) 274, πίν. 28.
36. Schrader (*σημ.* 33) 68–71, εικ. 59 και Schuchhardt στο Schrader (σημ. 1) πίν. 159 και εικ. 331.
37. G. Dickins, *Catalogue of the Acropolis Museum* I (Cambridge 1912) 104–105.
38. Ph. Bruneau, "Le motif des coqs affrontés dans l' imagerie antique," *BCH* 89 (1965) 112–113, εικ. 21.
39. C. Picard, "Les antécedents des 'astragalizontes' polyclètéens," *REG* 42 (1929) 121 κε.
40. W. Deonna, "Astragalizontes? Groupe isolé ou fronton," *REG* 43 (1930) 384 κε.
41. P. De la Coste-Messèlière, "Le fronton des astragalizontes," *REG* 44 (1931) 279–289.
42. E. Lapalus, *Le fronton sculpté en Grèce* (Paris 1947) 132–134 και εικ. 17.
43. Schuchhardt (σημ. 1) 287.
44. Μπρούσκαρη (σημ. 1) 106, εικ. 201.
45. Schuchhardt (σημ. 1) 291–291, αρ. 416, εικ. 337.
46. Schuchhardt (σημ. 1) 291–291, αρ. 416, εικ. 336.
47. Raubitschek (σημ. 19) 69–70, αρ. 66.
48. Schuchhardt (σημ. 1) 291.
49. S. Casson, "Some Technical Methods of Archaic Sculpture," *JHS* 50 (1930) 319–320 και S. Casson, *The Technique of Early Greek Sculpture* (Oxford 1933) 199–200, εικ. 77.
50. Schuchhardt (σημ. 1) 240–241, εικ. 267, πίν. 147–150.
51. Το πλάτος του ποδιού στο μετατάρσιο είναι 5 εκ., ίδιο περίπου με το πλάτος του μεταταρσίου στις υπόλοιπες μορφές, αν λάβουμε υπόψη μας και την κίνηση του ποδιού που είναι ανασηκωμένο. Το μήκος του μεγάλου δακτύλου είναι 3 εκ., όσο και των γονατιστών νέων.

The Iconography of Athenian State Burials in the Classical Period

Reinhard Stupperich

In the ancient Greek *polis* as in modern states, public burials, especially war burials, could be abused by being made to serve as a means to an end. Thucydides in his famous ἐπιτάφιος λόγος of Perikles, as well as in his introduction to it, however, implies that the Athenian state burial was a purely democratic custom.[1] Probably after the reforms of Kleisthenes,[2] the demos of Athens began to honor certain select individuals with public burials situated along the road running from the Dipylon Gate to the Academy. Single burials were made possible by means of a special decree. Communal burials of the war dead took place annually following a certain ritual.

Though scholars disagree about the origin of this custom, there is sufficient evidence in favor of the Kleisthenic date; the arguments against such a date are weak.[3] Certainly burials at public expense were known earlier in Athens and elsewhere. It is equally true that not all public burials were confined to the road leading to the Academy. Location seems to have been of secondary importance; nevertheless, the Academy Road was soon embellished with monuments that became typical of Athenian democracy. The separate burials in ten larnakes and the casualty lists on ten stelai, one for each tribe, speak clearly in favor of this custom originating with the Kleisthenic tribal reforms. State burials would have been an adjunct to the main reforms, such as, for example, ostracism.[4] The earliest attested public burials on the Academy Road belong to the period of the Tyrannicides and Kleisthenes himself;[5] the earliest known war monument is associated with the war against Chalkis and other neighbors immediately after the reforms of Kleisthenes in 506 B.C.;[6] whether those war dead were buried on the battlefield like the Marathon dead in 490 B.C., or whether they were brought back to the Kerameikos is another question. In favor of a Kleisthenic date can also be cited the almost simultaneous appearance of the state burial with the Athenian sumptuary law, both being mentioned together by Cicero.[7] This decree can be dated around 500 B.C., since this date marks the last appearance of private grave monuments in Attica. We need only compare "the last grave kouros" of Aristodikos[8] with pedimental sculptures from the last decade of the sixth century, for example, the gigantomachy from the Old Temple of Athena on the Athenian Acropolis or the Theseus-Amazon group from the temple of Apollo Daphnephoros at Eretria.[9]

The parallel origins of public burial and sumptuary decree as complementary institutions can serve to highlight the significance of state burials. All large mounds and grave buildings, stelai and statues, which used to evoke the continuous hero-like existence of the aristocratic dead and which supported the political influence of their families by visual suggestion, suddenly come to an end.[10] The large grave mounds in the Kerameikos are given over to all people.[11] Private funerary sculptures of great magnificence would soon be used as readily available building material and embedded into the new city walls.[12] The large mounds — tumulus and stele as γέρας θανόντων in the Homeric sense[13] — would be reserved for the casualties of war and the dead especially honored by the demos. Thus the demos of Athens replaces the Attic gentry: an interpretation supported by the *topoi* of the *laudes Atticae*.[14]

The iconography of Athenian state burials at Athens is not well documented, although the topography of the *demosion sema* is known from literary sources.[15] Apart from Thucydides' account, our main source is Pausanias, whose description of tombs in a roughly topographical order has been tentatively chartered in a series of maps by Clairmont.[16] As for the forms of state funerary monuments, the sources give no indication except for a few enigmatic hints, such as, for example, Pausanias' mention of the otherwise unknown horsemen Melanoppos and Makartatos.[17] Archaeological finds are scanty and the area is now more or less inaccessible to archaeologists being largely built over in modern times. No discussion of the iconography of these tombs and its meaning is possible without knowledge of their sculptured decoration and its position on the tomb; here the evidence is rather fragmentary, since there are no complete tombs of this sort.

The few public burials which survive directly in front of the Dipylon Gate in the Kerameikos are probably not quite representative. The demos honored certain proxenoi with public burials; their stelai, set on stepped bases,[18] are reminiscent of earlier representations of tombs on white-ground lekythoi about the middle of the fifth century. One must also mention the tombs of the victims of political unrest immediately after the end of the Peloponnesian War.[19] As they were killed on the spot in the Kerameikos, they did not require cremation as was the custom for war casualties transported to Athens to wait for the annual ceremony; instead, they were inhumed. As for the tomb of the Lacedaemonians who tried in vain to help the Thirty Tyrants, the retrograde inscription is preserved on an upper row of blocks of the funerary building.

Even less representative in comparison to the tombs of the war dead may be the few examples of individual public burials; their types were less set by custom and could be determined by individual taste as other private tombs. A possible example of a single public burial may be a circular tomb with rectangular wings projecting on each side.[20] The circular mound was crowned by a marble Panathenaic amphora and the two wings by a pair of Molossian dogs (a marble cauldron with griffin *protomai* also belongs here). In this case, along with the archaic type of round tumulus, heroic or aristocratic connotations have been integrated into the rectangular type of funerary building. The question arises whether circular tumuli, as at Marathon, or rectangular enclosures were usual in the beginning. The simple rows of ten stelai for the ten democratic tribes of Attica require rectangular precincts.[21] But in years with fewer casualties all names could be fitted into a single stele. Thus we may suppose that most of the annual burials were rectangular precincts with stelai and reliefs on top of the front walls similar to later family precincts on the south side of the Eridanos River; and that they flanked both sides of the Academy Road, with an open space of thirty meters in between to accommodate the crowds for the ceremony and the funeral oration and especially the ἐπιτάφιος ἀγών.

There are few additional finds from the ancient Academy Road that tell us much. Some elements do certainly come from the area of the *demosion sema*; others have been found elsewhere having been carried away in ancient or modern times for building material; still others were even transported farther away, obviously on account of their historical value. Some elements can only be ascribed to the *demosion sema* on the basis of probability. Whereas fragments of the stelai with casualty lists, many of which have been found in other places, can easily be recognized and ascribed,[23] it is rather more difficult to identify iconographic material from the *demosion sema*, since we are not even certain of the themes that were represented. In cases where just the epigrams are preserved, it is impossible to draw conclusions from any of the names mentioned. But from key words in the epigrams and epitaphs, which are related to one another, we do know of some categories of iconographic material. We can also draw more or less convincing conclusions for people buried in public tombs from additional burial monuments (i.e. *kenotaphia*) sometimes prepared for them in private family tombs.

The representation of a lion on the tomb of a hero represents a long tradition.[24] Lions, therefore, are used not only on private burials, but also on the tombs of those who fell in war, as was the case, for instance, at Chaironeia and Amphipolis. In the Kerameikos a double-sided lion stele from the middle of the fifth century B.C. was found in the area of the *demosion sema*.[25] On the fragmentary neck of a red-figure loutrophoros of the third quarter of the fifth century, also from the Kerameikos, is represented a grave stele topped by the figure of a lion.[26] On some unpublished red-figure sherds that were found at the beginning of this century in tombs of the east side of the Academy Road just outside the Dipylon, felines are also represented. We may conclude, therefore, that lions formed part of the sculptural equipment of public tombs, just as they were used in some private monuments of the fourth century B.C., in the same way as the Molossians were used on the circular tomb with projecting wings.

There are no indications as yet for actual statues in state burials, as had been usual before on aristocratic tombs in the form of *kouroi* and *korai*. We know of only stelai and reliefs. Two pieces come from the year 394 B.C.; earlier ones cannot be dated with certainty. A question that arises is whether the reliefs were set on public tombs right from the beginning or whether they stem from a later date and perhaps belong to the reintroduction of private grave reliefs at the beginning of the Peloponnesian War. Sometime at least in the late fifth century B.C. they must have been adorned by rich *anthemia* with motifs of scrolls with flowers or palmettes of the kind normal at that time, as is attested by two examples, one from the year 394 B.C.[27]

The theme best documented in state burials is the battle scene, usually of a warrior, often on horseback, in the decisive moment of his fight. Such a scene is representative of both aristocratic ideals and the *andragathia*. *Andres agathoi*, not heroes, was the usual denomination in Athens for those fallen in war. Variations of this motif of fighting were used on reliefs of different kinds. Similar to the public tomb reliefs are, for example, the votive relief of the *hipparch* Pythodoros in Eleusis[28] and some of the smaller temple friezes.

A fragment of a late archaic stele in Copenhagen with two warriors fighting to the left[29] might point to the existence of a predecessor, since the scene is oriented contrary to the normal direction; but without certain provenance it is too difficult to tell. The most important relief is the so-called Albani relief,[30] which had been brought to Rome in antiquity; stylistically it can be dated to the beginning of the Peloponnesian War. Other such reliefs include the fragment of a frieze with fighting scenes in Oxford,[31] which preserves the heading of a casualty list in large letters, and the relief with the casualty list of 394 B.C. already mentioned. A fighting relief documented by Fauvel has been lost and therefore cannot be considered in this study.[32]

There are also a number of private reliefs with horsemen and foot soldiers fighting. One of them is that of Dexileos, who fell in 394 B.C., and whose name is written on the stele of the state burial of that year (Fig. 1).[33] The inscription on the base of the relief provides more detailed information about his dates than any other classical Greek tomb inscription. The situation of the family tomb may illustrate how such reliefs may have been placed in a state burial. To the Dexileos relief several other private monuments can be added.[34] Their iconography helps to reconstruct and identify a fragment found a few years ago in secondary use in Roman foundations on the corner of Plataion and Kerameikos Streets, exactly in the area of the *demosion sema*. The scene is of a man being overrun by a horse and is similar to that of the Dexileos relief. Since it can be dated to the later fourth century B.C., it has been suggested that it could belong to the monument of the year of the battle of Chaironeia.[35] To the same category belong representations of warriors storming forwards, but without an enemy shown, as have been found in Attica and Boeotia on stelai from the time of the Peloponnesian War.[36] The Boeotian flat stelai with faint patterns to be filled in with colors follow a scheme that had obviously been developed in Attica.

Fig. 1. Grave relief of Dexileos. Kerameikos Museum. Photo German Archaeological Institute (Athens) Ker. 5976.

A fragmentary relief of Pentelic marble, dating from the end of the fifth century B.C., in Rome in the nineteenth century, but now in New York, shows fighting between Greeks and barbarians.[37] Since no inscription is preserved, it cannot be stated with certainty that the relief belonged to a state burial. The fact that it was brought, perhaps in antiquity, to Rome may point to a situation analogous to that of the Albani relief. What is left of the figures in the fragment are the opponents, in flight, just at the moment of being struck by the victor, and a foot soldier who is not preserved except for his knee. The barbarian he kills is reminiscent of an amazon. The oblong format of the frieze and the number of enemies allow one to postulate that there was at least a second victor involved. It is thus probable that it belonged to a state burial, although a solitary warrior can deal with a number of enemies, as occurs on the private marble loutrophoros of Philon in Athens.[38]

A sculptured base with the bedding for a stele on top comes from the Academy Road; it may have carried a casualty list.[39] The Dexileos motif on the front of the base is repeated on both sides in such a way as if it was being regarded from both sides, just as a piece of sculpture in the round. The Tyrannicides are represented in the same way on a contemporary red-figure cup with Theseus' exploits by the Kodros Painter in London.[40] The reliefs on the base suggest that there were also statues of men on horseback at the top. Red-figure loutrophoroi with such battle scenes, some of which were reported to have been found in the area in the nineteenth century, seem to have been used as part of the burial cult in the *demosion sema*.[41] A red-figure loutrophoros, formerly in the possession of Schliemann, shows the dead warrior as a horseman standing calmly in the midst of his relatives.[42]

Representations of warriors standing calmly might have been borrowed from the iconography of state burials, as seems to be the case with scenes of fighting. The horse which accompanies a soldier is an indication of his social status or rank, just as it is in votive reliefs for heroes. The great relief of a horse guided by a small black boy (Fig. 2), which was found near the Larissa Railway Station in Athens, is likely to be a supplementary relief of a big sepulchral monument. It is probably better dated to the late fourth century B.C., rather than to the Hellenistic period as has been proposed several times.[43] The fragmentary relief from the area of the *demosion sema* which repeats the motif of the Dexileos relief is stylistically similar to it.[44] Just like the latter, this horse relief might have originally belonged to a late fourth century public tomb and have been removed at some time in antiquity.

Judging from the accompanying epigram, the stele of Athenokles, found in the Agora excavations and showing the warrior standing quietly, comes from a state burial.[45] We may thus imagine a big stele with a warrior, like that which was said to have been found on the street from Athens to Megara,[46] to have formed part of the *demosion*

Fig. 2. Grave relief with horse and groom. Athens National Museum 4464. Photo German Archaeological Institute (Athens) NM 69/40.

Fig. 3. Grave relief of Chairedemos and Lykeas. Piraeus Museum. Photo German Archaeological Institute (Athens) Pir. 204.

sema. The same scheme of a warrior standing quietly is used for one of the brothers on the relief of Chairedemos and Lykeas (Fig. 3), which is dated to 412/11 B.C. by mention of Lykeas in a casualty list.[47] Warriors standing side by side give the impression that they are part of a phalanx.

Two warriors on an extraordinary grave relief from the Taman peninsula on the Black Sea wear Corinthian helmets (Figs. 4–5).[48] Normally soldiers depicted on the earlier classical Attic grave reliefs wear a pilos and light weapons; later on the pilos is replaced by the Attic helmet or even by the Macedonian type. The Corinthian helmet is rarely worn and may indicate a hero. Single helmets represented on grave stelai as a symbolic crowning motif are of the Corinthian type.[49] Since the Taman relief is influenced by Attic art, its prototype may well have belonged to a state burial.

Often two soldiers are united with one another by a hand clasp. Some of the earliest examples of this famous standard motif occur in classical Attic grave stelai, the oldest example with Corinthian helmets;[50] this scene later becomes popular in family group reliefs. Few reliefs with *dexiosis* are earlier than the reintroduction of grave reliefs in Attica, and these have been found outside Attica. This suggests that the theme of warriors in *dexiosis* may have been selected as a symbol of *homonoia* in order to visualize the unanimity of the democrats with regard to state burials.[51] The *dexiosis* of soldiers with their relatives, who are regularly mentioned in the *epitaphios logos*, also represents this *homonoia*.

It has been suggested that sepulchral rites may have been represented on Attic tombs and thus might also have been depicted in state burials.[52] A fragmentary relief, for example, from the Kerameikos showing two old men on a cart has been suggested to represent the *ekphora* of the phylai larnakes.[53] The evidence for this interpretation, however, is quite slender. An athlete with a torch running past a stele on a white-ground lekythos has been interpreted as one of the participants in the torch race on the Academy Road which took place every year as part of the ἐπιτάφιος ἀγὼν in honor of the dead warriors.[54] The vase, thus, should have been intended for use at the *demosion sema*. The running athlete, however, can be more easily understood as the figure of a dead sportsman who may have won a torch race.

The case is completely different with the relatives who are left behind mourning and who are addressed and consoled by the speaker of the *epitaphios logos*. They are shown on the back side of an early warrior lekythos that might derive from a state burial.[55] These mourning figures are symbols of the grief and sorrow felt by the relatives and by all Athenians for their casualties. We cannot exclude, therefore, the idea that the relatives may well have played a role in the iconography of the state burial. They are to be found standing in sorrow between several different grave stelai on a red-figure loutrophoros from Athens;[56] three women sitting in sorrow are depicted on a metope found in the area of Hadrian's

Fig. 4. Relief from the Taman Peninsula. Moscow, Pushkin Museum. Photo author.

Fig. 5. Relief from the Taman Peninsula (detail). Moscow, Pushkin Museum. Photo author.

Library.[57] The inspiration for the sarcophagus of mourning women from Sidon may even be Attic.[58]

Grief caused by the casualties of war can also be shown by the figure of the soldier himself, as can be seen on a number of grave reliefs and white-ground lekythoi.[59] One of these is the small grave relief of Demokleides who is sitting on the bow of a ship (Fig. 6).[60] It is interesting to note that the navy, despite its importance for Athenian democracy, does not play a role in the iconography of the state burial. Rowers and marines were closely linked to the new democracy; yet, there was no tradition of their representation in funerary art. The traditional formulae inherited by the early democracy may well have been felt to be sufficient. Both trierarchs and thetes may well have thought it much more imposing and desirable to have a victorious aristocratic or heroic horseman as the symbol on their tombs rather than a ship on which they had been continuously rowing.

A great number of vases for sepulchral rites, especially loutrophoroi, will have been needed for those fallen in war, since many of the young soldiers were unmarried. That these vases were prepared specifically for the state burials can be seen from their iconography, especially in the fighting scenes which sometimes take place in front of the tombs. The fighting does not take place over the tombs by ghosts at midnight, as Langlotz once implied.[61] Rather, the individual pictorial elements must be read as symbols: death is indicated by the tombs themselves, and the fighting warriors despite their death, symbolize victory and glory for the defenders of Athens and the right cause. It may well be that the monumentalizing of these vases in marble was inspired by the public tombs, since some of the earliest examples of marble loutrophoroi and loutrophoros stelai show warriors shaking hands.[62]

The representation of myths seems to have played only a small part in the iconography of state monuments in comparison with that played in the *epitaphioi*. In the annual burial speech, the praise of Attica and of its constitution was followed regularly by a recounting of the mythical fights of the Athenians for the right of the weak and against the *hybris* of the strong, a theme which the Athenians also loved to quote in their political speeches.[63] Based on later historical events, they are divided typologically into fights against barbarian invaders, such as the Persians, symbolized by amazons, centaurs, Thracians, and the Greeks' enemies *par excellence*, the Trojans, and by fights against other rival Greek states who in the eyes of the Athenians were tyrannizing over their less strong neighbors. These themes are well known from vase painting and temple friezes. Yet, only the amazonomachy occurs on late classical sepulchral

Fig. 6. Grave relief of Demokleides. Athens National Museum 752. Photo German Archaeological Institute (Athens) N.M. 404.

monuments and heroa.[64] As such, it may also have been depicted on the friezes of the monuments of the state burials. There is, however, no certain evidence for this. The analogy of the fighting scenes on the Nereid Monument at Xanthos[65] to amazonomachies does not help any more than the fighting Scythians on a monumental relief from the Taman peninsula.[66] But there are amazons fighting on the red-figure loutrophoros already mentioned, once in the possession of Schliemann, as well as on the main frieze of three others, one said to have been found in the Kerameikos.[67]

One theme, however, does irresistibly evoke the idea of the Athenian state burial, that of a dead warrior being brought home by Thanatos and Hypnos. This story, used in the epic cycle of the Trojan War in connection with the deaths of both Memnon and Sarpedon,[68] occurs in early Attic red-figure vase painting at the end of the sixth century B.C., about the time of the Kleisthenic reforms.[69] It may perhaps reflect the Athenians' discussion about the idea of transporting war casualties back to Attica. The warriors represented on the vases are given names as though they were Athenian citizens. The same scheme was also used for the scene of the return of Patroklos' body,[70] which evokes even more the impression of Athenian citizens collecting their dead after the battle. The scene with Thanatos and Hypnos reappears in Athenian vase painting in the late fifth century on the sepulchral genre of white-ground lekythoi; this motif may have been adopted from its use in state burials.[71] By bringing the dead home, Athens gives the same honors to her *andres agathoi* as are given to the heroes in the *Iliad*. In *epitaphios* speeches of the late fourth century, the fallen warriors are addressed as ones who have departed to the islands of the blessed.[72] In some versions of the Thanatos-Hypnos story, both in literature and in painting, Hermes Psychopompos is involved. He also appears on occasion in Attic sepulchral iconography together with the deceased, a motif which may indicate heroic immortality. Compared to his appearance on ceramic lekythoi Hermes does not occur on many tomb reliefs; examples of the latter consist of the marble lekythos of Myrrhine (Fig. 7) and a small pediment from a sepulchral naiskos of uncertain provenience in Zurich.[73]

Fig. 7. Grave lekythos of Myrrhine. Athens National Museum 4485. Photo German Archaeological Institute (Athens) N.M. 5251.

On the base of a marble grave vase in Athens are depicted a young couple picking apples on the front, Hermes (or a light armed soldier) on the left, and an old priest with a knife on the right.[74] This scene recalls the Hesperides relief from the so-called three-figure reliefs.[75] They depict stories concerning victory over death, a theme that seems to be more suited to a sepulchral context than to religious or votive contexts.[76] The original reliefs may have formed the four sides of a freestanding base, perhaps belonging to a state burial.

A sepulchral epigram of two hexameters for Kritias and those fallen with him in the fight for the regime of the Thirty Tyrants suggests that personifications were also represented on the monuments of the Athenian state burials.[77] In the epigram, Oligarchia is described as setting fire to Demokratia. It seems impossible, however, to imagine this as belonging to a relief erected in the Kerameikos; rather, it may have been a caricature from after the time of the Thirty Tyrants or even a mere literary invention. It seems satiric in nature and fits better the style of the fourth century, when Demokratia occurs more often. Though such personifications do occasionally appear in the fifth century B.C., such as the representation of Dike and Adikia fighting with one another on a late Attic black-figure vase in Vienna.[78]

On a small jug found as a sepulchral offering for Dexileos, the famous statues of the Tyrannicides are represented (p. 79, Fig. 9),[79] obviously used as a paradigm of democratic attitude and civil courage. They had in fact been used few years earlier as the shield emblem of Athena Promachos on a Panathenaic prize amphora of 402 for the festival following the democratic victory over the Thirty Tyrants.[80] But this motif did not belong to the standard iconography of the public tombs. The Tyrannicides themselves were buried in the *demosion sema* not far from the Academy and received their cult in this place;[81] their famous statues, however, were not located there, but in the Agora.[82] Yet, the victor in the Albani relief and the victorious Stratokles on a grave stele in Boston,[83] who are both shown contrary to the usual direction of the victor as moving from right to left, adopt the stance of Harmodios. Like the Tyrannicides, therefore, the victorious fighters of the Athenian state burials appeal to the spectator to follow the example they provide.

Whereas Philip II of Macedon obviously acknowledged the custom of the Athenian state burial after the battle of Chaironeia in 338/7 B.C.,[84] some of the democrats may not have held it in so high esteem on account of the imperialism of Athenian naval politics. The state burial is never mentioned in connection with the reforms and building policies, despite the military and patriotic bias of these reforms. They had instead a strong emphasis on democratic buildings, especially on localities for law courts.

At the beginning of the fifth century, it would have been impossible to create new "democratic" ideals or even pictorial formulae and symbols and to allow the spectator to realize their meaning immediately. Those fallen in war, although not called heroes, were treated like heroes. One of the ways in which this was accomplished was the creation and adornment of the state burial. The iconography for these burials was taken, at least partly, from that used by the archaic nobility; this was done on purpose, since sumptuary legislation forbade the aristocracy from such elaborate grave monuments as they had in the past. But not all the aristocratic conventions were adopted. Sculpture in the round, which emphasizes the bodily presence of the deceased in much the same way as the cult images of the gods, seems not to have been used. Karouzou has suggested that the Hermes Ludovisi originally stood on top of the burial mound of 446 B.C., but this idea has generally not found favor.[85] The sculptures found during the course of the excavations in the Kerameikos do not necessarily have to be associated with state burials.[86] All the evidence, therefore, points to the fact that state burials, until the time when private grave stelai were reintroduced, were left as simple as the private burial precincts.

In summary, we can say the following about the iconography of Athenian state burials. Symbolic animals, such as lions, do occur but they are supplemental and do not constitute a major element of the iconography. Scenes of fighting, especially with horsemen, are restricted to the tombs of fallen warriors (in public as well as private monuments). To what extent other motifs of warriors on grave reliefs belong to the repertory of public tombs is debatable. The theme of the warrior carried home by Death and Sleep would be especially suitable for a public burial. Soldiers united by a hand clasp, or with relatives left behind, would represent in pictorial form a motif often repeated in funeral orations. This may in fact have been a theme created by the new democracy for the state burial.

The state burial was essentially a democratic event. Nobody was admitted for burial except according to public vote, as, for example, was Lycurgus' grandfather who had been murdered by the Thirty Tyrants. The custom of the state burial for those fallen in war on behalf of their city was in correspondence with the *isonomia* of the new democracy. The demos took over the part played by the father of the family; the tomb of the soldier who had died far from home became available to his relatives; although it was not part of the family plot, it was adorned with hero-like glamor. All fallen soldiers were honored in the same way; they were listed on the stelai with their simple names in accordance with their phylai; sometimes the names of foreigners, metics, and even in a few cases of slaves, were added. This form of listing was copied in other cities, as for instance, in Boeotia or at Tegea. The relatives were consoled and the widows and orphans taken care of by the demos. After the reappearance of rich tombs, cenotaphs began to be added to family precincts as a means of symbolizing the heroism of the deceased warrior. All fallen soldiers were brought home for state burial and treated like heroes. Even though their heroization was never explicit, it underlined the iconography of public grave monuments.

Abbreviations

The following will be cited by author's name:

Ch.W. Clairmont, *Patrios Nomos*, *BAR-IS* 161 (Oxford 1983)

H. Diepolder, *Die attischen Grabreliefs des 5. und 4. Jahrhunderts v. Chr.* (Berlin 1931)

R. Stupperich, *Staatsbegräbnis und Privatgrabmal im klassischen Athen* (diss. Münster 1977)

Notes

1. Thuc. 2.34.
2. A Kleisthenic date for the custom of the state burial was first suggested by G. Hirschfeld, "Athenische Pinakes im Berliner Museum," *Festschrift für Johannes Overbeck* (Leipzig 1893) 12f. Cf. also Diepolder 7; H. Möbius, *Die Ornamente der griechischen Grabstelen klassischer und nachklassischer Zeit*² (Munich 1968) 9; 101f.; K. Schefold, *Orient, Hellas und Rom* (Bern 1949) 104; id., "Die Thronende, Euthesion und Antigenes," *AntK* 13 (1970) 107; J. Kleine, *Untersuchungen zur Chronologie der attischen Kunst von Peisistratos bis Themistokles*, *IstMitt-BH* 8 (Tübingen 1973) 64; Stupperich 206–224. J. Neils in this volume, p. 151.
3. An earlier date is suggested by the interpretation of certain sources, sometimes in favour of Solon (to whom is attributed the origin of the ἐπιτάφιος λόγος, cf. e.g. Schol. Thuc. 2.35.1; Plut. *Solon* 31.3). Cic. *de leg.* 2.26.64 is erroneously attributed here by L. Weber, *Solon und die Schöpfung der attischen Leichenrede* (Frankfurt 1935) 58f.; 66f.; P. Schmidt, *Staatliche Gefallenenehrung im klassischen Zeitalter Athens* (diss. Tübingen 1944) 52f.; 64; 66f.; Nilsson, *GGR* I² 191f.; I. Th. Hill, *The Ancient City of Athens* (London 1953) 217. Others ascribe the custom on very slight evidence to Peisistratos: cf. K. Kübler, *Kerameikos* VII 1, *Die Nekropole der Mitte des 6. bis Ende des 5. Jahrhunderts* (Berlin 1976) 201 (around 560 B.C.); G.M.A. Richter, *The Archaic Gravestones of Attica* (London 1961) 38f. (around 530), followed by M. Bieber, *AJA* 49 (1945) 385; H. Berve, *Die Tyrannis bei den Griechen* (München 1967) 551; J. Boardman, "Painted Funerary Plaques and Some Remarks on Prothesis," *BSA* 50 (1955) 53; D.C. Kurtz — J. Boardman, *Greek Burial Customs* (London 1971) 89f.; 121f. Some scholars have opted for Themistokles or a later statesman as the founder: e.g. F. Jacoby, "Patrios Nomos," *JHS* 64 (1944) 38f.; 47f.; 51, voting for 465 B.C., assuming an error by Thucydides; V. Zinserling, *Wiss. Zeitschr. Jena* 14 (1965) 29–34, which E. Kluwe, *Die Tyrannis der Peisistratiden und ihr Niederschlag in der Kunst* (diss. Jena 1966) 234–239 tried to corroborate with lists of monuments dated too low; followed also by Clairmont, 12f.; id., *Gravestone and Epigram* (Mainz 1970) 12 n. 45; D. Metzler, *Porträt und Gesellschaft* (Münster 1971) 361; 362 n. 4.
4. Cf. the contemporary origin of ostracism, which has been pointed out by both followers of a Kleisthenic and a later date, the latter dating the origin of ostracism accordingly, cf. Ch. Karusos, *Aristodikos* (Stuttgart 1961) 43; Metzler (supra n. 3) 362 n. 4; Kleine (supra n. 2) 64. Being in accordance with his system of downdating most sculptures on the subjective evidence of style, this provided a welcome opportunity for a late dating to T. Dohrn, *Attische Plastik vom Tode des Phidias bis zum Wirken der grossen Meister des 4. Jahrunderts v. Chr.* (Krefeld 1957) 85f. For the downdating of ostracism, see A.E. Raubitschek, "The Origin of Ostracism," *AJA* 55 (1951) 221; cf. D.W. Knight, *Some Studies in Athenian Politics in the Fifth Century B.C.*, *Historia Einzelschriften* 13 (Wiesbaden 1970) 21–23; 29–30; R. Thomsen, *The Origin of Ostracism. A Synthesis* (Copenhagen 1972). See also S. Brenne in this volume, pp. 13–24.
5. Paus. 1.29.6 and 15. See map of the early tombs prepared by Clairmont fig. 1.
6. Epigram on the fallen against Chalkis in 506 B.C.: *Anth. Pal.* 16.26; E. Diehl (ed.), *Anthologia Lyrica Graeca* 2, 92, Simonides no. 87; W. Peek, *Griechische Vers-Inschriften* I: *Griechische Grab-Epigramme* (Berlin 1955) no. 1; Clairmont 9; 88f., no. 2.
7. Cic. *de leg.* 2. 26.4–65.
8. Athens NM 3938, Karusos (supra n. 4); cf. the so-called Poulopoulos bases, A. Philadelpheus, "Reliefs von attischen Statuenbasen," *AA* (1922) 56f; id., "Bases archaïques d' Athènes," *BCH* 46 (1922) 1–35, figs. 2–3, 6–7, pls. 1–6; id., "Archaische Grabmalbasen aus der Athener Stadtmauer," *AM* 78 (1963) 105f., Beil. 64–66; J. Travlos, *Bildlexikon zur Topographie des antiken Athen* (Tübingen 1971) 311, figs. 404f.
9. For the gigantomachy pediment of the Old Temple of Athena, see K. Stähler, "Der Zeus aus dem Gigantomachiegiebel der Akropolis ?" *Boreas* 1 (1978) 28–31 and W.A. P. Childs in this volume, pp. 1–6; for the Theseus-Antiope group from the pediment of the temple of Apollo Daphnephoros at Eretria see R.

Lullies — M. Hirmer, *Die griechische Plastik*[4] (Munich 1975) figs. 66–68; E. Touloupa, "Die Giebelskulpturen des Apollon Daphnephorostempels in Eretria," in H. Kyrieleis (ed.), *Archaische und klassische griechische Plastik* 1 (Mainz 1986) 144–145, pl. 59, 1–2.

10. Cf. Karusos (supra n. 4) 59–71; L.H. Jeffery, "The Inscribed Gravestones of Archaic Attica," *BSA* 57 (1963) 115f.; Stupperich 77f. A dating of about 20 to 30 years later, as suggested by Kluwe (supra n. 3), is too low.

11. See Kübler (supra n. 4) 22; U. Knigge, *Kerameikos* IX, *Der Südhügel* (Berlin 1976) 14. For plain tomb markers, cf. Kübler 188; 193; Knigge 32f.

12. Their destruction may be due not to the "democrats", as is still claimed by R. Garland, *The Greek Way of Death* (London 1985) 122, but to the Persian occupation army and could have been decisive for their secondary use. Cf. now M. Salta, *Attische Grabstelen mit Inschrift* (diss. Tübingen 1991) 8f.

13. Hom. *Il.* 7.86–91; 16.457; *Od.* 11.76; 24. 80f. M. Andronikos, *Archaeologia Homerica* III, *Totenkult* (Göttingen 1968) 32–34; 107–121; A. Schnaufer, *Frühgriechischer Totenglaube*, *Spudasmata* 20 (Hildesheim 1970) 175–176 nn. 494–496.

14. Stupperich 226f.; N. Loreaux, *L' invention d' Athènes. Histoire de l' oraison funèbre dans la "cité classique", Civilisations et Sociétés* 65 (Paris — Le Haye — New York 1981) especially 150f.

15. Clairmont 46f.; S. Kaempf-Dimitriadou, "Ein attisches Staatsgrabmal des 4. Jahrhunderts v. Chr.," *AntK* 29 (1986) 31–34; S. Ensoli, *L' Heroon di Dexileos nel Ceramico di Atene*, *MemLinc* Ser. 8, 29.2 (Rome 1987) 246f.

16. Paus. 1.29. 3–16. Clairmont 42f., maps figs. 1–5. Cf. S. Wenz, *Studien zu attischen Kriegergräbern* (diss. Münster 1913) 26–32; Jacoby (supra n. 3) 47–55; 66; Stupperich 26–29.

17. Paus. 1.29.6. An inscription mentioning Melanopos was dated to c. 410 B.C. by B.D. Meritt, "Greek Inscriptions," *Hesperia* 16 (1947) 147f., pl. 23, whereas L.H. Jeffery, *JHS* 78 (1958) 145; ead., "The *Battle of Oinoe* in the Stoa Poikile," *BSA* 60 (1965) 52f. n. 58 dated it to the middle of the fifth century, more in accordance with the usual dating. Clairmont 31; 140f., no. 21e considers a later replacement as possible. 457 B.C. is suggested in the commentaries on Pausanias by Hitzig-Blümner I, 320 and Frazer II, 381; cf. *SEG* X, no. 426; D.W. Bradeen, *Agora* XVII, *Inscriptions, The Funerary Monuments* (Princeton 1974) no. 1029a.

18. A. Brückner, *Der Friedhof am Eridanos* (Berlin 1910) 6f.; U. Knigge, "Untersuchungen bei den Grabstelen im Kerameikos," *AA* (1972) 584–629; W. Höpfner, "Das Grabmonument des Pythagoras aus Selymbria," *AM* 88 (1973) 146f.; Clairmont 61f.

19. K. Gebauer, "Ausgrabungen im Kerameikos," *AA* (1938) 612f. and "Ausgrabungen im Kerameikos," *AA* (1940) 355 takes them to be tombs of the allies of 403 B.C., a suggestion repeated by F. Willemsen, "Zu den Lakedaimoniergräbern im Kerameikos," *AM* 92 (1977) pl. 53, Beil. 4. Tomb of the Lacedaemonians: A. Brückner, "Bericht über die Kerameikosgrabung 1914–1915," *AA* (1915) 118f.; G. Karo, "Attika," *AA* (1930) 90f.; K. Gebauer — H. Johannes, "Ausgrabungen im Kerameikos," *AA* (1937) 200–203 (pottery: figs. 13–15); D. Ohly, "Kerameikos-Grabung. Tätigskeitbericht 1956–1961," *AA* (1965) 314–322; La Rue Van Hook, "On the Lacedaemonians Buried in the Kerameikos," *AJA* 36 (1932) 290–292. Following series of tombs: K. Gebauer — H. Johannes, "Ausgrabungen im Kerameikos,"*AA* (1936) 212; Gebauer — Johannes, *AA* (1937) 196f.; Gebauer, *AA* (1938) 612–616; Gebauer, *AA* (1940) 345–357 (355f. some structures not funerary); K. Gebauer, "Ausgrabungen im Kerameikos," *AA* (1942) 206–220 (some structures again not funerary), 220–224, 250–251.

20. "Neue Funde am Kerameikos," *AA* (1914) 94; Brückner, *AA* (1915) 119; Gebauer, *AA* (1940) 358–362; Gebauer, *AA* (1942) 204–206; Ohly (supra n. 19) 322–327; Willemsen (supra n. 19) pls. 6f. (identification of Panathenaic amphorae); A. Mallwitz, in *Kerameikos* XII, *Die Rundbauten* (Berlin 1980) fig. 9, pls. 30f., Beil. 29f.

21. See P. Wolters, *Eine Darstellung des athenischen Staatsfriedhofs*, *SBMünchen* (1913) no. 5; D.W. Bradeen, "The Athenian Casualty List of 464 B.C.," *Hesperia* 36 (1967) 324f., pl. 70d; Clairmont 62, pl. 3c.

22. Another theory was proposed by A. Brückner, "Kerameikos-Studien," *AM* 35 (1910) 183f.; 189 with drawing on p. 188. It was supported by Schmidt (supra n. 3) 21; W. Judeich, *Topographie von Athen*[2] (Munich 1931) 405 and K. Kübler, "Die Ausgrabungen im Kerameikos," *AA* (1943) 339f., who excavated another trial trench in this area and indicated no finds, but in *Kerameikos* VI 1 Tafeln, *Die Nekropole des späten 8. bis frühen 6. Jahrhunderts* (Berlin 1959) Beil. 44 he drew a hatched area on the spot of the subsequent discovery of a Hellenistic tomb in the middle of the road. Brückner's theory that the public tombs formed an enormous spina in an imaginary circus for the ἐπιτάφιος ἀγών and were thus surrounded by the contestants, is incorrect. Perhaps the suggestion was due to an unreported glimpse (during the pre-World War I excavations of Brückner) into the Hellenistic tomb in the middle of the road. This tomb was found in 1961 in a test trench by Ohly (supra n. 19) 277f.; 301–332. A.v. Domaszewski, *Der Staatsfriedhof der Athener*, *SBHeid* (1917) no. 7, with drawing on p. 21, developed Brückner's hypothesis further with a fanciful reconstruction which has no support in the ancient literature. Cf. *contra*, Wenz (supra n. 16) 17f.; Stupperich 27f.; 30; Clairmont 32.

23. Bradeen (supra n. 17) 3–34 nos. 1–25; *IG* II[2], 928–969; *IG* II[2], 5221–5222; Clairmont 20f.; 46f.

24. For lions on polyandria, see O. Broneer, *The Lion Monument at Amphipolis* (Cambridge, Mass. 1941) 42–47; Clairmont 65 n. 23.

25. Athens, National Museum 3709: K. Kübler, "Eine attische Löwenstele des 5.Jahrhunderts," *AM* 55 (1930) Beil. 65f., pl. 13; U. Knigge, *Der Kerameikos von Athen* (Athens 1988) 40, fig. 38.

26. G. Karo, "Archäologische Funde im Jahre 1915," *AA* (1916) 160 (found in 1916 in front of the *proteichisma* in the Kerameikos excavations); *ARV*[2] 1059, 124; Stupperich 156 n. 3, no. 9; Clairmont pl. 6.

27. NM 754: A. Brückner, "Ein Reiterdenkmal aus dem Peloponnesischen Kriege," *AM* 14 (1889) 405–408; A. Conze (ed.), *Die attischen Grabreliefs* (Berlin 1893–1900) no. 1157, pl. 317; Möbius (supra n. 2) 24, pl. 9d; Clairmont no. 68b, pl. 3. — Piraeus Museum inv. no. 1452. For a piece of sculpture in the round suggested for the public tombs cf. the Hermes Psychopompos, see infra nn. 29 and 86.

28. T. Hölscher, *Griechische Historienbilder des 5. und 4. Jahrhunderts v. Chr.* (Würzburg 1973) 99f., pl. 8.2; S. Wegener, *Funktion und Bedeutung landschaftlicher Elemente in der griechischen Reliefkunst archaischer bis hellenistischer Zeit* (Frankfurt — Bern — New York 1985) 88–90; 284, no. 56, pl. 15.1; K. Stähler, *Griechische Geschichtsbilder klassischer Zeit*, *Eikon* 1 (Münster 1992) 96f., pl. 9.2.

29. Copenhagen, Ny Carlsberg Glyptotek 2787, Cat. no. 13a (said to be from Athens): F. Poulsen, "Fragment eines attischen Grabreliefs mit zwei Kriegern," *JdI* 44 (1929) 139f.; K.F. Johansen, *The Attic Grave Reliefs* (Copenhagen 1951) 102, fig. 54; Clairmont 68, takes it to be private because there are no reliefs on state burials at this time. This is surprising since he accepts (p. 73) the relief of the "Mourning Athena" in the Acropolis Museum and (p. 63f.) the statue of Hermes Ludovisi (as suggested by S. Karousou, "ΕΡΜΗΣ ΨΥΧΟΠΟΜΠΟΣ," *AM* 76 [1961] 91f., Beil. 64f.) as possibly part of state burials.

30. Rome, Villa Albani 985: Conze (supra n. 27) no. 1153; W. Fuchs, in Helbig[4] IV 231–233, no. 3257; Lullies — Hirmer (supra n. 9) figs. 172–174; Hölscher (supra n. 28) 109f.; Stähler (supra n. 28) 94f., pl. 8.1.

31. R. Stupperich, "Staatsgrabfragment in Oxford," *Boreas* 1 (1978) 87f., pl. 14.

32. *IG* I[3], 1179; cf. Stupperich 16 n. 5.

33. Athens, Kerameikos Museum: Conze (supra n. 27) no. 1158, pl. 248; Brückner (supra n. 18) 57f., figs. 29–33; Johansen (supra n. 29) 48–50; Lullies — Hirmer (supra n. 9) fig. 188; Ensoli (supra

n. 15) 155f., dealing with the iconography 246f.; G. R. Bugh, *The Horsemen of Athens* (Princeton 1988) 137f., fig. 12.

34. E.g. Berlin, Staatl. Mus. K 30 (from Chalandri): Conze (supra n. 27) no. 1160; C. Weickert, *Kunstwerke aus den Berliner Sammlungen* 3 (Berlin 1946) 31, pl. 29; Clairmont (supra n. 3) 43; 100f., no. 28, pl. 14. Of the same class may be the stele in Budapest, Mus. of Fine Arts 4744: A. Hekler, *Die Sammlung antiker Skulpturen* (Wien 1929) 28–31, no. 20; Stupperich 176, no. 412. This is usually regarded as representing a hunt, a rare theme on Attic grave reliefs as opposed to battles.

35. Kaempf-Dimitriadou (supra n. 15) 23–26, pl. 2f.; reconstruction drawing on p. 26, fig. 1.

36. Stele of Lisas from Tegea: Conze (supra n. 27) no. 1148, pl. 244; F. Studniczka, *Die griechische Kunst an attischen Kriegergräbern* (Leipzig — Berlin 1915, also in *NeueJahrb* 35 [1915] 285–311) pl. 17, 30; stele of Silanion: Conze (supra n. 27) no. 1155, pl. 244; lekythos of Timonax: Conze (supra n. 27) no. 1147, pl. 244; fragmentary stele in New York: G.M.A. Richter, *Catalogue of Greek Sculpture, Metropolitan Museum of Art, New York* (Oxford 1954) no. 81, pl. 66; fragmentary loutrophoros stele Athens, Agora: G. Kokula, *Marmorlutrophoren*, *AM-BH* 10 (1984) pl. 3,2; stele of Ktesikrates, Paris, Louvre 3382: Diepolder pl. 28,1; fragment of stele, Copenhagen, Ny Carlsberg Glyptotek 206: Studniczka pl. 17, 26; stele of Aristonautes: Conze (supra n. 27) no. 1151, pl. 245; A.v. Salis, *Das Grabmal des Aristonautes*, *BWPr* 1926; Diepolder 52f., pl. 50; B.S. Ridgway, "Aristonautes' Stele, Athens Nat. Nus. 738," in *Kotinos, Festschrift für E. Simon* (Mainz 1992) 270–275. Boeotian stelai: Studniczka pl. 16; A. Keramopoulos, "Πολεμισταὶ τῆς ἐν Δηλίωι μάχης," *ArchEph* (1920) 9–36; A. Kalogeropoulou, "Nuovo aspetto della stele di Saugenes," *AAA* 1 (1968) 92–96; K. Demakopoulou — D. Konsola, *Museum Theben, Führer durch die Ausstellung* (Athens 1981) 73–75, nos. 43. 54–56; 240, pl. 39; P. Moreno, *Pittura Greca* (Milan 1987) 8, fig. 1. Turned in the opposite direction and with a dead adversary, see stele of the Phokian Alkias from Corinth: Athens NM, Studniczka pl. 17, 28. Cf. also the white-ground lekythos by the Painter of Munich 2335: F. Felten, "Weissgrundige Lekythen aus dem Athener Kerameikos," *AM* 91 (1976) pl. 29, 2.

37. Richter (supra n. 36) no. 81, pl. 66a; Hölscher (supra n. 28) 91–98, pl. 9,2.

38. Athens NM: Y. Nikopoulou, "Ἐπιτύμβια μνημεῖα παρὰ τὰς πύλας τοῦ Διοχάρους," *AAA* 2 (1969) 331–333, fig. 3; E. Papastavrou, "Η επιτύμβια στήλη 5280 του Μουσείου του Πειραιά," *ArchEph* (1988) 65f.

39. G. Karo, "Archäologische Funde 1930–1931," *AA* (1931) 217f., figs. 1–3; G.M.A. Richter, "Calenian Pottery and Classical Greek Metalware," *AJA* 63 (1959) 242, pl. 52; J. Frel and B.M. Kingsley, "The Attic Sculptural Workshops of the Early Fourth Century B.C.," *GRBS* 11 (1970) 200, pl. 11, 1.

40. London BM: W. Real, *Studien zur Entwicklung der Vasenmalerei im ausgehenden 5. Jahrhundert v. Chr.* (Münster 1973) 19f., pl. 3f.; cf. J.H. Oakley, *The Phiale Painter* (Mainz 1990) 31f.; 93, no. 7bis, pls. 138f.

41. J.D. Beazley, "Battle-Loutrophoroi," *MusJ* 23 (1932) 4–22; B. Van den Driessche, "Fragments d' une loutrophore à figures rouges illustrant une amazonomachie," *Revue des archéologues et historiens d' art de Louvain* 6 (1973) 19–37; Stupperich 156 n. 3 with a list; Clairmont 76f., pl. 8b; see e.g. the loutrophoros by the Talos painter in Amsterdam: *CVA* Musée Scheurleer, Le Hague 2 III Id, pl. 4, 1–3, *ARV*[2] 1339, 4; but cf. E. Böhr-Olshausen, *CVA* Tübingen 4 (1984).

42. G. Bakalakis, "Die Lutrophoros Athen (ex Schliemann)-Berlin 3209," *AntK* 14 (1971) 74–83, pl. 25–29.

43. Athens, NM 4464: U. Hausmann, "Hellenistische Neger," *AM* 77 (1962) 274f. no. 70 (as a late Hellenistic memorial to Mithradates VI); W.H. Schuchhardt, "Relief mit Pferd und Negerknaben im Nationalmuseum in Athen N.M. 4464," *AntP* 17 (Berlin 1976) 75–99, pl. 41f. (as a monument to a horse, second half of second century B.C.); G. Despinis ap. E. Voutiras, "Ηφαιστίων ήρως," *Egnatia* 2 (1990) 145–147 (c. 320 B.C.).

44. Kaempf-Dimitriadou (supra n. 15) 23f., pls. 2f.

45. Athens, Agora I 3845: Bradeen (supra n. 17) 133f., no. 697, pl. 3.

46. Worcester, Mass., formerly in Cairness House: J.D. Beazley, "Stele of a Warrior," *JHS* 49 (1929) 1f., figs. 1–2; Diepolder 21f., fig. 3; R. Vasić, "Das Grabrelief des Chairedemos," *AntK* 19 (1976) 27 n. 10, pl. 6, 3; Clairmont 71f.; C.C. Vermeule, *Greek and Roman Sculpture in America* (Berkeley and Los Angeles 1981) 94, no. 63.

47. P.A. Fourikis, "Ἀρχαῖοι τάφοι ἐν Σαλαμῖνι," *ArchEph* (1916) 1, pl. 2; Karo (supra n. 26) 141 with fig.; Diepolder 21, pl. 16; Lullies — Hirmer (supra n. 9) fig. 184; Vasić (supra n. 46) 24–29, pl. 6, 1–2. For the family, see J.K. Davies, *Athenian Propertied Families* (Oxford 1971) 344f.

48. E. Savostina, "Reliefs attiques du Bosphore cimmérien," *RA* (1987) 22f., figs. 11–16; E.R. Knauer, "Mitra and Kerykeion," *AA* (1992) 392–395, fig. 11.

49. E.g. a triangular stele in the Piraeus Museum and three Attic examples: Conze (supra n. 27) no. 1658; Möbius (supra n. 2) 31 nn. 19 and 25; 110. Cf. on the Black Sea coast: G. Sokolov, *Antique Art on the Northern Black Sea Coast* (Leningrad 1974) 37 with bibl., pl. 15. Helmet on top of stele on white-ground lekythos with Thanatos and Hypnos, British Museum D 58: *ARV*[2] 1228, 12; D.C. Kurtz, *Athenian White Lekythoi* (Oxford 1975) pl. 32, 4. For Corinthian helmets worn by warriors on Attic grave reliefs, see e.g. lekythos Athens NM 835: Conze (supra n. 27) no. 1073, pl. 218f.; Clairmont 84 n. 60; id., "The Grave Lekythos Athens NM 835," *Meded* 48 (1980) 71–75; fragment Ny Carlsberg Glyptotek 437; cf. stele of Alkias from Corinth (supra n. 36).

50. E.g. Erasippos and Meixias, Paris, Louvre 3063: Diepolder 10, pl. 2, 2; Johansen (supra n. 29) fig. 16. Sosias and Kephisodoros, Berlin, Staatl. Mus. K 29: Johansen (supra n. 29) fig. 17; C. Blümel, *Die klassisch griechischen Skulpturen* (Berlin 1966) 25f., no. 17, pl. 25.

51. Stupperich 183f.

52. E.g. J. Thimme, "Die Stele der Hegeso als Zeugnis des attischen Grabkults," *AntK* 7 (1964) 16–29.

53. Gebauer, *AA* (1942) 255 n. 28, fig. 28; cf. B.S. Ridgway, *Fifth Century Styles in Greek Sculpture* (Princeton 1981) 153, no. 4; Clairmont 29.

54. Brückner (supra n. 22) 202f.; L. Deubner, *Attische Feste* (Berlin 1932) 230, pl. 26, 1–2; Clairmont 25 with n. 37; *contra* Wenz (supra n. 16); Kurtz (supra n. 49) 137f., pl. 45, 2; Stupperich 54 n. 5.

55. This is improbable, as the lekythos Athens NM 835 was found in Syntagma Square: Conze (supra n. 27) 1073; Clairmont 60f., id. (supra n. 49) 71f.

56. *ARV*[2] 1146, 50; R. Weisshaeupl, "Ἐρυθρόμορφα ἀγγεῖα ἀττικῶν τάφων," *ArchEph* (1893) pl. 2. Compare the Schliemann loutrophoros (supra n. 42). It is reminiscent of the two women on a white-ground lekythos sherd from Athens: B. Philippaki, "Ἀττικαὶ λευκαὶ λήκυθοι," *AAA* 2 (1969) 304, fig. 10; Kurtz (supra n. 49) pl. 50.3.

57. Athens NM 1688: P. Wolters, "Sepulkrales Relief aus Athen," *AM* 18 (1893) 1f., pl. 1; Conze (supra n. 27) no. 1486, pl. 306; J.N. Svoronos, *Das Athener Nationalmuseum* (Athens 1903–1937) 628f., no. 324, pl. 128; Wegener (supra n. 28) 67 n. 278; 277, no. 30, pl. 11.1; R. Fleischer, *Der Klagefrauensarkophag aus Sidon*, *IstForsch* 34 (Tübingen 1983) 54, pl. 48, 1.

58. Lullies — Hirmer (supra n. 9) figs. 211–213; Fleischer (supra n. 57) *passim*.

59. Marble lekythos Leiden RO1A5: Conze (supra n. 27) no. 627, pl. 147; Frel — Kingsley (supra n. 39) 206, no. 32, pl. 14, 2; Clairmont, "Gravestone with Warriors in Boston," *GRBS* 13 (1972) 49f., pl. 2, 3. Cf. the fragment of a stele, inscribed "Theokles" in Cambridge, Fitzwilliam Museum GR.12.1885: Conze (supra n. 27) no. 912; L. Budde — R. Nicholls, *Catalogue of Greek and Roman Sculpture* (Cambridge 1964) 13f., no. 30, pl. 7. Hoplites in sorrow are to be found on many white-ground

lekythoi of the late fifth century, e.g. among those of group R, see Kurtz (supra n. 49) pls. 48.4–49.3; cf. pls. 51–53.

60. Athens NM 752: Conze (supra n. 27) no. 623, pl. 122; Wenz (supra n. 16) 83–86, fig. 7; Studniczka (supra n. 36) pl. 9.
61. E. Langlotz, *Wiss. Zeitschrift Rostock* 16 (1967) 475.
62. Cf. Kokula (supra n. 36) pl. 2.14.
63. Cf. Stupperich 39f., different topical themes 42–53; Loreaux (supra n. 14) 147f.; cf. 245f.
64. Athens NM 3614, found in 1926: E. Tsirivakos, "Ergebnisse der Ausgrabung," *AAA* 4 (1971) 110; Piraeus Mus.: Tsirivakos, "*Εἰδήσεις ἐκ Καλλιθέας*," *AAA* 1 (1968) 108f.; id., *AAA* 4 (1971) 108–110, figs. 1–2; id., *AntK* 15 (1972) 147. Cf. the blocks in Svoronos (supra n. 57) 639, no. 2378, pl. 146; 649, no. 1691, pl. 165; 650, no. 1007 (and cf. 2636), pl. 169. Cf. the fragments of a battle, perhaps an amazonomachy, from a private tomb in the Kerameikos: U. Knigge, "Marmorakroter und Fries von einem attischen Grabbau?" *AM* 99 (1984) 231–234, pl. 39. For amazons on Athenian lekythoi, see D. v. Bothmer, *Amazons in Greek Art* (Oxford 1957) 204, no. 171, pl. 84, 2; 202, no. 153, pl. 84, 1; 229, no. 85 bis; 92, no. 18; 195f., no. 113; 191, no. 143; 199, no. 145; 182, no. 69; 193, no. 107, pl. 81, 8; for amazons fighting on loutrophoros Athens NM 13032: G.M.A. Richter, "Distribution of Attic Vases," *BSA* 11 (1904–5) 238–241, figs. 1–3; *ARV*[2] 1099, 47. Louvain University: Van den Driessche (supra n. 41); *ARV*[2] 230, 49. New York, MMA 09.286.53/55/58: Beazley (supra n. 41); *ARV*[2] 1059, 128; v. Bothmer 162, no. X 14.
65. London, British Museum: W.H. Schuchhardt, "Die Friese des Nereidenmonuments," *AM* 52 (1927) 94–161; W.A.P. Childs — P. Demargne, *Fouilles de Xanthos* VIII, *Le Monument des Néréides, le décor sculpté* (Paris 1989).
66. Moscow, Pushkin Museum: Savostina (supra n. 48) 18f., figs. 6–10.
67. Cf. Bakalakis (supra n. 42) pl. 29, 4.6; Van den Driessche (supra n. 41) 19f., esp. 31f., figs. 1–4 and 6; Stupperich 158f.; 156 n. 3, nos. 3–4, 13, 17.
68. *Roscher* II 2, 2653 f., especially 2676–79, s.v. Memnon; 411, s.v. Sarpedon; V, 498–515, s.v. Thanatos.
69. D. v. Bothmer, "Der Euphronioskrater in New York," *AA* (1976) 485–512; id., *Greek Vase Painting, An Introduction* (New York n.d.) no. 15 and cover illustration; K. Schefold, *Götter und Heldensagen der Griechen in der spätarchaischen Kunst* (Munich 1978) 224f., fig. 303 (Sarpedon); red-figure cup by the Nikosthenes Painter: 244, fig. 329 (Memnon); cf. Stupperich 152 n. 2.
70. Krater of the Pezzino group in Agrigento, around 500 B.C.: Schefold (supra n. 69) 229f., fig. 309.
71. Cf. e.g. the lekythoi *CVA* Athens Jc, pl. 20, 1; III Jd, pls. 11, 8 and 14, 1; pls. 16, 7 and 18; A.S. Murray, *White Athenian Vases in the British Museum* (London 1896) pls. 9 and 11; Studniczka (supra n. 36) pl. 8; Kurtz (supra n. 49) pl. 32, 4; C.M. Robertson, *Greek Painting* (Geneva 1959) 150f.; E. Simon — M. Hirmer, *Die griechischen Vasen*[2] (Munich 1981) fig. 204; and elsewhere, cf. Stupperich 152 n. 2. For the group crowning a stele on a white-ground lekythos, see E. Curtius, "Fragmente einer polychromen Lekythos im Berliner Museum," *JdI* 10 (1895) pl. 2.
72. Demosthenes 60.34; cf. Hypereides 6.35–39.
73. Myrrhine, Athens NM 4485: Conze (supra n. 27) no. 1146, pls. 242f.; Diepolder (supra n. 2) 19, pl. 13, 1; Johansen (supra n. 29) 160, fig. 82; Karousou (supra n. 29) 92f., Beil. 59–62, pl. 3. Zurich University 2135: H. Blümner, *Aus der archäologischen Sammlung der Universität Zürich* (Zurich 1916) pl. 12; Fleischer (supra n. 57) 54f., pl. 47.
74. Athens NM 4502: A. Mantis, *Προβλήματα της εικονογραφίας των ιερειών και των ιερέων στην αρχαία ελληνική τέχνη* (Athens 1990) 85, no. 4; 89, pl. 37.
75. H. Götze, "Die attischen Dreifigurenreliefs," *RM* 53 (1938) 189–280, pls. 32–38; W.H. Schuchhardt, *Das Orpheus-Relief*[2] (Stuttgart 1964) 22f. (as the tomb of Sophokles); Stupperich 115f.
76. H.A. Thompson, "The Altar of Pity in the Athenian Agora," *Hesperia* 21 (1952) 47f.; E.B. Harrison, "Hesperides and Heroes: a Note on the Three-Figure Reliefs," *Hesperia* 23 (1964) 76; H. Möbius, *Die Reliefs der Portlandvase und die griechischen Dreifigurenreliefs, Abhandlungen Bayer. Akad. der Wiss.* NF 61 (Munich 1965) 15–25, esp. 18.
77. Th. Preger, *Inscriptiones Graecae Metricae* (Leipzig 1891) 217, no. 270 (from *Schol.* Aischines 1.39, ed. Dindorf); cf. Stupperich 252; O. Palagia, *Euphranor* (Leiden 1980) 60f. A real epigram should have had a pentameter as a second line instead of another hexameter. See also O. Tzachou-Alexandri in this volume, pp. 55–56.
78. *CVA* Vienna 2, pl. 51.1; H.A. Shapiro, "The Origins of Allegory in Greek Art," *Boreas* 9 (1986) 6f., pl. 1.1.
79. E. Vermeule, "Five Vases from the Grave Precinct of Dexileos," *JdI* 85 (1970) 94f.; S. Brunnsåker, *The Tyrant-Slayers of Kritios and Nesiotes*[2] (Stockholm 1971) 105f., no. 7, pl. 24.1; B. Fehr, *Die Tyrannentöter oder: Kann man der Demokratie ein Denkmal setzen?* (Frankfurt 1984) fig. 1.
80. Brunnsåker (supra n. 79) 104f., no. 6, pl. 23. 6; Simon — Hirmer (supra n. 71) 157, color pl. LI.
81. Cf. Stupperich 222f. with n. 3; the sacrifices on their tombs were the responsibility of the *polemarchos*, commander-in-chief of the Athenian army in the first years after the Kleisthenic reforms. We may infer that this duty stemmed from these early times and that it was a military affair; similar rites must have been performed for the army casualties, an additional indication that this custom originated in the same time, i.e. the end of the sixth century.
82. Brunnsåker (supra n. 79); Hölscher (supra n. 28) 85f.; Fehr (supra n. 79).
83. For the Albani relief, supra n. 30; Stratokles, Boston, Museum of Fine Arts: Clairmont (supra n. 59) 49f., pl. 1.
84. Plut. *vit. decem orat.* 9.10; Polyb. 5.10.1–5; Justin 9.4.4.6.
85. Karousou (supra n. 29) 91f., Beil. 64f.; Clairmont 63f.
86. Different sculptures have been suggested, some from the Kerameikos excavations; for example, the head Kerameikos Museum inv. P. 313: H. Riemann, *Kerameikos* II, *Die Skulpturen vom 5. Jahrhundert bis in römische Zeit* (Berlin 1940) 87f., no. 116 pl. 26; a Severe Style male head: U. Knigge, "Ein Jünglingskopf vom Heiligen Tor in Athen," *AM* 98 (1983) 45f.; 53f.; ead. (supra n. 25) 87f.; a fighting group in Boston: K. Stähler, "Zur Reiterkampfgruppe in Boston," *AA* 91 (1976) 58–72; cf. in general Clairmont 63f.; M. Salta, *Attische Grabstelen mit Inschrift* (diss. Tübingen 1991) 9 n. 42; but these may well come from other sites, see e.g. convincingly A. Delivorrias, *Attische Giebelskulpturen und Akrotere des fünften Jahrhunderts* (Tübingen 1974) 118f.: 154f., pls. 36–38; 164f., pls. 56b-57.

Bemerkungen zur Ikonographie des Frieses vom Ilissos-Tempel

Klaus-Valtin von Eickstedt

Forschungsgeschichte

Am Ufer des Ilissos stand bis zum Jahre 1778 ein kleiner ionischer Tempel, der von Stuart & Revett noch um 1751/3 aufgenommen worden war. Vor Ort sind heute nur noch spärliche Reste der Tempelstützmauer erhalten.[1]

Mehrere Friesplatten, die aus italienischem Besitz in Museen in Berlin und Wien gelangt waren, wurden von F. Studnizcka dem Ilissos-Tempel zugewiesen.[2] Die Deutung dieser Platten hat die archäologische Forschung schon vor Studnizcka, aber auch noch bis in die jüngere Zeit beschäftigt.[3] Bedingt durch den fragmentarischen Erhaltungszustand des Frieses und die z.T. ungewöhnliche Darstellung konnte bisher keine in der Forschung allgemein akzeptierte Deutung vorgelegt werden.[4] Problematisch waren vor allem die Versuche, die Friesplatten einer fortlaufenden, zusammengehörigen Darstellung zuzuweisen[5] und einen direkten Bezug auf den Tempelinhaber herzustellen,[6] der zudem nicht mit völliger Sicherheit zu bestimmen ist.[7]

Unter der Annahme, dass den Friesplatten keine einheitliche Erzählung zugrunde gelegen hat,[8] werde ich mich hier auf die Behandlung der Platte D (Abb. 1) beschränken.[9]

Die Darstellung

Dargestellt ist ein Frauenraub. Von links hat ein Mann in Chlamys eine Frau im Chiton von hinten ergriffen und in die Höhe gehoben. Von rechts verfolgt ein Mann, ebenfalls in Chlamys, eine nach links fliehende Frau im Chiton, die er bereits am Gewand gepackt hat. Am rechten Bildrand, vor dem nach links eilenden Mann, steht unbewegt eine kleine mädchenhafte Gestalt.

Frauenraub kam in der griechischen Mythologie häufig vor und ist in der griechischen Kunst auch häufig

Abb. 1. Platte D des Ilissos-Frieses. Antikensammlung, Staatliche Museen zu Berlin — Preussischer Kulturbesitz, Inv. Nr. Sk 1483, Neg. Nr. Sk 3276.

dargestellt worden.[10] So wiederholt der Frauenraub auf dem Ilissos-Fries bekannte Schemata.[11]

Auffällig an den Figuren des hier dargestellten Frauenraubes ist zunächst das Fehlen jeglicher Attribute.[12] So kann es sich nicht um Boreas und Oreithyia, Hades und Persephone, Theseus und Antiope oder Theseus und Helena handeln, da diesen Gestalten eine eigene Ikonographie zugrunde liegt, die hier nicht zu erkennen ist.[13]

Bereits 1903 wurde von R.v. Schneider[14] die Deutung des Leukippidenraubes vorgeschlagen, der sich jüngst noch einmal C.A. Picón[15] anschloss, die aber in der Forschung, insbesondere von Studnizcka[16] abgelehnt wurde.

Gegen die Leukippiden-Deutung wurden vor allem zwei Argumente vorgebracht: Studnizcka vermisste in der Darstellung die für die Dioskuren als Kennzeichen zu erwartenden Viergespanne. Felten nimmt einen Zusammenhang mit der Platte E in Wien an, auf der seiner Auffassung nach ebenfalls ein Frauenraubgeschehen zu beobachten sei; durch die zu hohe Zahl der beteiligten Personen sei deshalb eine Deutung auf den Leukippidenraub nicht möglich.[17]

Darstellungen des Leukippidenraubes sind in der antiken Bildkunst nicht sehr häufig.[18] Der übliche Typus war in der Tat der des Raubes mit einer Quadriga (Abb. 2–4).[19] Allerdings wurde eine Veränderung im ikonographischen Schema der Dioskuren in frühklassischer Zeit kürzlich von M. Prange beobachtet, wonach neben dem Raub mit dem Wagen auch die Verfolgung zu Fuss auftritt.[20] Der Einwand Studnizckas wird dadurch entkräftet. Gegen den Einwand Feltens lässt sich hingegen vorbringen, dass eine Forderung nach der Zusammengehörigkeit der Platten D (Abb. 1) und E (Abb. 5) vor allem durch eine Deutung der Darstellung begründet werden müsste. Allein die Tatsache, dass auf beiden Platten Geschehen dargestellt sind, die mit Frauenraub zu tun haben, muss nicht zu der Folgerung zwingen, dass beide Platten zu derselben Szene gehören. Insbesondere spricht aber die Tatsache, dass die männlichen Gestalten auf Platte E nackt dargestellt sind und sich somit grundlegend von denen auf Platte D unterscheiden, gegen die Deutung einer einheitlichen Frauenraubszene. Die mittlere männliche Gestalt auf Platte E kann zudem, da sie offensichtlich ein Kind auf dem Arm trägt, kaum mit einem Frauenraub in Verbindung gebracht werden. Eine überzeugende Deutung für eine kontinuierliche Darstellung auf den Platten D und E ist bislang nicht vorgelegt worden.[21]

Löst man Platte D aus der nur vermuteten Zusammengehörigkeit mit Platte E, lösen sich auch die bisher vorgebrachten Widersprüche gegen die Leukippiden-Deutung. In der kleinen Mädchenfigur, die rechts im Bildfeld steht, ist sicher kein Kind oder halbwüchsiges Mädchen, wie noch von Krug angenommen wurde,[22] zu sehen, sondern eine Statue, wie sie auch auf Vasenbildern mit Frauenraubdarstellungen, auch der Leukippiden, wiedergegeben ist (Abb. 2–3).[23] Zwar ist die Haltung der auf den Vasen dargestellten Statuen nicht mit der auf dem Ilissosfries befindlichen Figur übereinstimmend, aber gerade die Vasenbilder zeigen deutlich, dass von dem Raub betroffene Frauen oder Mädchen dem Geschehen nicht unbeteiligt beiwohnen. Sie befinden sich entweder auf der Flucht oder suchen Schutz an einem Altar. Eine unbewegte, statuarische Haltung wie bei der Mädchenfigur auf dem Ilissosfries

Abb. 2. Hydria des Meidias-Malers, London Brit. Mus. E 224, Photo Brit. Mus., Neg. Nr. PS 117363.

Abb. 3. Hydria des Meidias-Malers, London Brit. Mus. E 224, Photo Brit. Mus., Neg. Nr. PS 117361.

Abb. 4. Apul. rf. Volutenkrater, Ruvo, Mus. Jatta, Inv. Nr. 1096, Photo DAI Rom, Neg. Nr. 64.1142.

Abb. 5. Platte E des Ilissos-Frieses, Wien Kunsthist. Mus. Antikensammlung, Inv. Nr. I 1093, Museumsphoto.

lässt sich in solchem Zusammenhang jedenfalls nicht feststellen. Auch auf den Vasenbildern lässt sich beobachten, dass Statuen erkennbar kleiner dargestellt sind als die am Geschehen beteiligten Personen. Ein ähnlicher Statuentypus findet sich auf einem Relief (Abb. 6) aus dem Dionysostheater in Athen aus dem Anfang des 4. Jh.v.Chr.[24] So kann diese Gestalt nur als Statue verstanden werden.

Abb. 6. Relief aus dem Dionysos-Theater in Athen, Nat. Mus. 1489. Photo DAI Athen 93/403.

Für die Deutung als Dioskuren sprechen aber noch weitere Indizien.

Die Dioskuren

Die Dioskuren besassen in Athen ein Heiligtum, das Anakeion,[25] das unter Kimon erneuert und von Polygnot und Mikon mit dem Raub der Leukippiden ausgemalt wurde.[26] Als Reiter "par excellence" verkörperten sie das aristokratische Ethos; dies erklärt auch die Popularität des Dioskuren-Kultes im peisistratidischen Athen.[27] Die Heimat der Dioskuren war Sparta.[28] Ihr Name "Anakes", unter dem sie in Athen verehrt wurden, ist altertümlich und lässt sich bis in mykenische Zeit zurückverfolgen.[29]

A. Hermary stellt für den Zeitraum 460–430 v. Chr. in Athen ein neues Aufblühen des "Dioskuren-Themas" fest und begründet dies mit der pro-lakedaimonischen Politik des Aristokraten Kimon.[30]

Von einer Altarinschrift wissen wir zudem, dass die Dioskuren in Athen auch den Beinamen Soteres besassen.[31]

Der Tempel

In der Forschung diskutiert aber nicht endgültig gelöst ist die Frage, welcher Gottheit der Tempel am Ilissos geweiht war. Insgesamt hat die Zuweisung an Artemis Agrotera wohl weitgehend Zustimmung erfahren.[32]

Die Verehrung der Artemis Agrotera in Athen ist durch Quellen belegt.[33] Nach der Schlacht von Marathon wurde der Artemis Agrotera alljährlich ein Ziegenopfer vom Polemarchen zum Gedächtnis der in Marathon Gefallenen dargebracht.[34]

Zusammenhang Artemis-Dioskuren/Leukippiden

Wie Felten ausgeführt hat, zeigen die Tempelfriese des 5. Jh. — mit Ausnahme der Akropolisfriese — keine Darstellungen, die sich unmittelbar auf die Tempelgottheit beziehen. Sie weisen nur einen indirekten Bezug zu dieser auf.[35] Gleichwohl lässt sich aber eine Verbindung zwischen Frauenraub und Artemis herstellen. So wird im 16. Gesang der *Ilias* davon berichtet, wie Hermes ein Mädchen aus dem Kreis des Chores der Artemis entführt.[36] Dass der Chor der Artemis die prädestinierte Gelegenheit für Mädchenraub darstellte, wurde bereits von Burkert hervorgehoben.[37]

Datierung

Zwischen dem Niketempel und dem Ilissos-Tempel wurde eine enge architektonische Verwandtschaft beobachtet, die in der Forschung zu einer vom Niketempel abhängigen Datierung des Ilissos-Tempels führte.[38] I.M. Shear vertrat sogar die Auffassung, beide Tempel seien von demselben Architekten, nämlich Kallikrates, errichtet worden.[39]

In der Darstellung eines Kriegers auf einem Fragment vom Ilissos-Fries im Athener Nationalmuseum[40] sah Krug Ähnlichkeiten zu den Kampfszenen auf den Nikefriesen; sie hielt aber die Szenen des Nikefrieses motivisch für die "primäre Erfindung."[41] Der Nike-Tempel wird nur aufgrund des Skulpturenstils in die zwanziger Jahre d. 5. Jh.v.Chr. datiert.[42] Gesichert ist allerdings, dass der Pyrgos und die Tempelfundamente in den späten dreissiger Jahren errichtet wurden. Childs hält demgegenüber die Schlüsse, die aus der architektonischen Übereinstimmung zwischen den beiden Tempeln gezogen wurden, für überzogen, zumal der Ilissos- und der Nike-Tempel die ersten ionischen Tempel sind, die wir in Athen kennen, eine Tatsache, die seiner Ansicht nach sicher zu ihrer grossen Ähnlichkeit mit beiträgt.[43] So datiert er den Ilissos-Fries plausibel aus stilistischen und historischen Gründen in die Zeit zwischen 445 und 440 v.Chr. und folgt damit im wesentlichen der Datierung von Studnizka.[44]

Schlussfolgerungen

Das Ilissosgebiet war bereits in der Zeit der Tyrannis durch die Peisistratiden für mehrere Heiligtümer in Anspruch genommen worden, so für den Bau des Olympieions, des Apollon-Pythios Heiligtums[45] und, etwas weiter entfernt, in Agrai für das Heiligtum des Poseidon, des Stammvaters der Peisistratiden.[46] In der Mitte des 5. Jh. wird im Ilissos-Gebiet, in unmittelbarer Nachbarschaft zum Olympieion und Apollon-Pythios Heiligtum, ein Tempel der Artemis Agrotera erbaut. Der Kult der Artemis Agrotera steht durch das alljährliche Opfer des Polemarchen unmittelbar mit Marathon in Verbindung, d.h. mit der Schlacht, in der die Athener allein gegen die Perser kämpften.[47] Erst die Schlachten von Salamis und Plataiai waren Siege der allierten Kräfte.[48]

Es stellt sich die Frage, ob in der Themenwahl der Leukippidenraubszene eine Anspielung auf Sparta und somit auf die gesamtgriechische Allianz zu sehen ist. Der Versuch, den Bogen von Marathon bis Plataiai zu einem gesamtgriechischen Konflikt Griechen — Perser zu spannen, wird verständlich, wenn dies der Ausdruck einer prolakedaimonischen Haltung ist, wie sie von der konservativen Partei, insbesondere schon von Kimon, gezeigt worden war.[49] So könnte sich in dem Bau des Ilissos-Tempels in einer Zeit der perikleischen Demokratie ein baupolitisches Wirken der konservativen Parteien im kultischen Bereich zeigen, das sich selbst auf der Akropolis in einem durch Kompromisse geänderten Bauprogramm hat nachweisen lassen.[50]

Anmerkungen

1. Geisonfragmente befanden sich noch am Beule'schen Tor. W.B. Dinsmoor, *The Architecture of Ancient Greece*[3] (London 1950) 185 Anm. 3; zwei Säulenbasen am Turm der Winde wurden von A. Rumpf — A. Mallwitz, "Zwei Säulenbasen," *AM* 76 (1961) 15ff. dem Ilissos-Tempel zugewiesen.
2. F. Studniczka, "Zu den Friesplatten vom ionischen Tempel am Ilissos," *JdI* 31 (1916) 167ff.
3. Vor Studnizcka beschäftigten sich mit den Friesplatten A. Brückner, "Ein Athenischer Theseus-Fries in Berlin und Wien," *ÖJh* 13 (1910) 50ff., der in den Platten B-E die Sage von Theseus, Helena und den Dioskuren sah, sowie R. v. Schneider, "Marmorreliefs in Berlin," *JdI* (1903) 91ff., der die Darstellung auf Platte D mit dem Raub der Leukippiden durch die Dioskuren erklärte. Studnizcka sah in den Platten eine fortlaufende Erzählung, die er für die Sage vom attischen Mädchenraub durch die Pelasger hielt. Widerspruch folgte von H. Möbius, "Das Metroon in Agrai und sein Fries," *AM* 60/61 (1935/36) 234ff., der in der Darstellung ein Initiationsfest im Metroon von Agrai erkannte. K. Kerènyi, "Zum Fries des Ilissostempels," *AM* 76 (1961) 22ff. lehnte diese Deutung mit der Begründung ab, die von Möbius herangezogene Sage sei nicht belegt, und schlug selbst eine Deutung auf den Hyakinthos-Mythos vor.
4. In der jüngeren Forschung wurde die Frage der Deutung des Frieses zurückgestellt, da die wenigen erhaltenen Platten eine sichere Deutung des Frieses kaum zuliessen, so A. Krug, "Der Fries des Tempels am Ilissos," *AntP* 18 (1979) 7ff., bes. 17f., Taf. 1-9.; C.A. Picón, "The Ilissos Temple Reconsidered," *AJA* 82 (1978) 47ff.; M.M. Miles, "The Date of the Temple on the Ilissos River," *Hesperia* 49 (1980) 309ff.; F. Felten, *Griechische tektonische Friese archaischer und klassischer Zeit* (Waldsassen 1984) 74; W.A.P. Childs, "The Frieze of the Temple on the Ilissos," *AM* 100 (1985) 207ff.
5. Brückner versuchte, alle Platten in den Theseus-Helena Mythos einzugliedern, Studnizcka hingegen sah eine fortlaufende Erzählung der Pelasgersage. Felten (supra Amm. 4) 75 wies darauf hin, dass den Friesen der archaischen und klassischen Zeit, mit Ausnahme des Parthenon, kein einheitliches Thema zugrunde liegt, vielmehr die Friese aus unterschiedlichen Szenen zusammengesetzt sind.
6. F. Robert, "ΚΥΝΗΤΙΝΔΑ," *Studien zur Kunst des Ostens, Festschrift J. Strzygowski* (Hellerau 1923) 58ff. deutete die Platten auf eine Artemisfestdarstellung und stellte damit, ebenso wie Möbius, einen direkten Bezug auf die Tempelgottheit her, die er, anders als Möbius, für Artemis Agrotera hielt. Felten ebenda: "Nicht einer der deutbaren Friese des 7./6. Jhs. bringt eindeutig die Tempelgottheit und ausschliesslich auf diese zu beziehende Darstellungen. Und eben dasselbe gilt für die Tempelfriese des 5. Jhs., wobei wiederum nur die Akropolisfriese die Ausnahme zu machen scheinen."
7. Der Zuweisung an Artemis Agrotera kommt die grösste Wahrscheinlichkeit zu, doch hat sich durch Grabungen der

schlüssige Beweis bislang nicht erbingen lassen, dazu J. Travlos, *Bildlexikon zur Topographie des antiken Athen* (Tübingen 1971) 112f. Abb. 156.157. Felten (supra Anm. 4) 70. Studnizcka (supra Anm. 2) 171 sah in dem Bau das Heiligtum der Athena *epi palladio*; diese Deutung wurde jüngst von M. Krumme, "Das Heiligtum der 'Athena beim Palladion' in Athen," *AA* (1993), 213ff. erneut aufgegriffen. Möbius (supra Anm. 3) 234ff. hielt den Tempel noch für das Metroon in Agrai; ebenso J.S. Boersma, *Athenian Building Policy from 561/0 to 405/4 B.C.* (Groningen 1970) 192f.

8. Felten (supra Anm. 4) 75.
9. Berlin, Pergamonmuseum SK. 1483 = K. 14. Krug (supra Anm. 4) 11ff. Dass sich die Platten D und E (Wien, Kunsthist. Museum Inv. I 1093) kaum voneinander trennen lassen, wie Felten (supra Anm. 4) 74 vertrat, müsste erst durch eine Anpassung nachgewiesen werden. Kompositorisch wie thematisch ist ein unmittelbarer Zusammenhang nicht zwingend. Die Auffassung, dass die Platten thematisch zusammengehören, müsste dann auch durch die Deutung begründet werden können. Eine mögliche Zusammengehörigkeit der Platten wurde auch von Krug (supra Anm. 4) 8 angenommen.
10. Das Motiv der linken Gruppe findet sich z.B. beim Raub der Oreithyia, auf einer apul. rf. Amphora, Neapel Mus. Naz. 81591, *LIMC* III (1986) 138 Nr. 65, Taf. 120, s.v. Boreas (S. Kaempf-Dimitriadou) oder die Akrotergruppe vom Ostgiebel des Tempels der Athener auf Delos mit der Entführung der Oreithyia durch Boreas, Delos, Mus. A 4283. A 4284, S. Kaempf-Dimitriadou, *Die Liebe der Götter in der att. Kunst des 5. Jh.v.Chr.*, *AntK-BH* 11 (1979) Nr. 395, Taf. 32.1–2, ähnlich ist auch die Darstellung bei der Entführung der Antiope durch Theseus im Giebel des Apollon-Tempels von Eretria, *LIMC* I (1981) 858, Nr. 2, Taf. 682, s.v. Antiope II (A. Kauffmann-Samaras), allerdings zeigt Antiope eine etwas andere Haltung. Motivische Entsprechungen der rechten Gruppe sind in zahlreichen Verfolgungsszenen, so z.B. auf einer Hydria in Athen, NM 13119, Kaempf-Dimitriadou ebenda Nr. 343, Taf. 30.1; auf einer Hydria des Coghill-M. in London, Brit. Mus. E 170, Kaempf-Dimitriadou ebenda Nr. 319, Taf. 25.2; auf einem Kolonettenkrater des Agrigent-M. in Oxford, Ashm. Mus. 1927.1, Kaempf-Dimitriadou ebenda Nr. 216, Taf. 14.3; auf einer Hydria des Berliner M. in Paris, Cab. des Méd. 439, Kaempf-Dimitriadou ebenda Nr. 207, Taf. 12.3; auf einem Kantharos des Brygos-M. in Boston, Mus. of Fine Arts 95.36, Kaempf-Dimitriadou ebenda Nr. 204, Taf. 1.2. Zu Verfolgungsdarstellungen s.a. M. Prange, *Der Niobidenmaler* (Frankfurt 1989) 59ff.
11. So z.B. Theseus — Antiope, Theseus — Helena, Boreas — Oreithyia, Hades — Persephone und Dioskuren — Leukippiden, s. Kaempf-Dimitriadou *passim*, R. Lindner, *Der Raub der Persephone* (Würzburg 1984); M. Prange, "Der Raub der Leukippiden auf einer Vase des Achillesmalers," *AntK* 35 (1992) 3ff.
12. K. Schefold, "Chronik," *AntK* 23 (1980) 104 deutete zuletzt noch den Frauenraub auf dem Fries als Überfall auf wasserholende Mädchen, doch ist ein Thema ohne direkten mythologischen Bezug auf einem Tempelfries schwer vorstellbar. Das Fehlen von Attributen oder spezieller Kleidung kennzeichnet auch die Figuren auf dem Westfries des Nike-Tempels, Felten (supra Anm. 4) 118.
13. Abgesehen davon, dass in den genannten Beispielen nur **eine** Frau geraubt wird, fehlen der männlichen Gestalt für eine Identifizierung als Boreas das wilde, zerzauste Aussehen und die Flügel. Eine Deutung auf Antiope ist aufgrund fehlender Charakterisierung als Amazone auszuschliessen. Hades raubt Persephone immer mit dem Wagen, Lindner (supra Anm. 11) 14ff. doch kommt dieser Mythos in der bildenden Kunst der archaischen und klassischen Zeit kaum vor, so Prange (supra Anm. 11) 5.
14. v. Schneider (supra Anm. 3) 91, Taf. 6.
15. Picón (supra Anm. 4) 64 ist der Auffassung, dass eine Deutung auf die Leukippiden die grösste Zustimmung erfährt.
16. Studnizcka (supra Anm. 2) 191.
17. Felten (supra Anm. 4) 74.
18. Die Deutung des Leukippidenraubes auf dem Südfries am Siphnierschatzhaus in Delphi, so *LIMC* III (1986) 585, Nr. 207, Taf. 474, s.v. Dioskuroi (A. Hermary) ist fraglich, Prange (supra Anm. 11) 16 schliesst diese Deutung aus. Gesichert ist die Darstellung auf dem Fries am Heroon in Gjölbaschi-Trysa, *LIMC* III ebenda 585, Nr. 208 m.d. ält. Lit.; die weitaus meisten Beispiele finden sich jedoch in der Vasenmalerei, s. *LIMC* III ebenda 583 ff.
19. So z.B. am Heroon in Gjölbaschi-Trysa; auf der Hydria E 224 in London, L. Burn, *The Meidias-Painter* (Oxford 1987) M5, 15ff. Taf. 3; auf dem apul. rf. Volutenkrater, Ruvo, Mus. Jatta 1096, H. Sichtermann, *Griechische Vasen in Unteritalien* (Tübingen 1966) 35, Nr. 39, Taf. 61; *LIMC* III 584, Nr. 202, s.v. Dioskuroi (A. Hermary).
20. Prange (supra Anm. 11) bemerkt: "Nicht mit letzter Sicherheit schlüssig zu erklären ist, warum in frühklassischer Zeit neben dem Wagenraubschema die Verfolgung zu Fuss als ikonographisches Schema eingeführt wurde. Vielleicht ist hierin ein Versuch zu sehen, die Darstellungen in ihrer Ikonographie an andere Liebesverfolgungen anzugleichen. Vielleicht drückt sich hierin auch eine gewisse Aversion gegen den 'adligen' Wagenraub aus, dem man mit einer 'Verbürgerlichung' der Heroen begegnen wollte. Dies ging allerdings auf Kosten der ikonographischen Prägnanz."
21. Felten (supra Anm. 4) 75 widerspricht einheitlichen Themen auf den Tempelfriesen des 5. Jh.v.Chr.; eine neue Deutung liefert auch er nicht, s. dazu auch supra Anm. 9.
22. Krug (supra Anm. 4) 13.
23. So z.B. auf der Hydria in London, Brit. Mus. E 224 (supra Anm. 20).
24. J.N. Svoronos, *Das Athener Nationalmuseum* II (Athen 1911) Nr. 1489, Taf. 114; Ders., *Das Athener Nationalmuseum* III (Athen 1937) S. 620, 261. Nr. 1489; *LIMC* III (1986) 494, Nr. 853, Taf. 403 s.v. Dionysos (C. Gasparri). In diesem Zusammenhang verdanke ich O. Palagia den Hinweis, dass sich auf der Platte 18 der Südmetopen des Parthenon eine kindliche Gestalt befand, bei der es sich ebenfalls um eine Statue gehandelt haben könnte; s. dazu F. Brommer, *Die Metopen des Parthenon* (Mainz 1967) 105, Taf. 151, 1 mit der älteren Literatur.
25. Paus. 1.18.2; W. Judeich, *Topographie von Athen*[2] (München 1931) 304; A. Hermary, "L'image de l'apotheose des Dioscoures," *BCH* 102 (1978) 72; G.S. Dontas, "The True Aglaurion," *Hesperia* 52 (1983) 47ff., bes. 60ff.; H.W. Parke, *Athenische Feste* (Mainz 1987) 263f.
26. K. Schefold — F. Jung, *Die Urkönige Perseus, Bellerophon, Herakles und Theseus in der klassischen u. hellenistischen Kunst* (München 1988) 303.
27. H.A. Shapiro, *Art and Cult Under the Tyrants in Athens* (Mainz 1989) 154. O. Palagia machte mich darauf aufmerksam, dass B.S. Ridgway, *The Archaic Style in Greek Sculpture* (Princeton 1977) 141 die Auffassung vertrat, dass der sog. Reiter Rampin auf der Akropolis zu einer Dioskuren-Gruppe gehört haben könnte, in der sich möglicherweise die Peisistratidensöhne darstellen liessen.
28. Plut. *Thes.* 31ff.; Shapiro (supra Anm. 27) 150.
29. Der Name "wanax" kennzeichnet üblicherweise im dorischen die "*Διόσκουροι σωτῆρες*," das Wort selbst findet sich bereits auf Linear B Täfelchen aus Pylos, P. Chantraine, *Dictionnaire étymologique de la langue grecque* (Paris 1968) 84 s.v. *ἄναξ*.
30. Hermary (supra Anm. 25) 72: "Nous voulons parler des années 460–430 qui voient, après l' effacement des cinquante années précédentes, une nouvelle floration de thèmes 'dioscouréens', et, cette fois, les origines en sont assez claires: d' une part, l' esprit pro-lacedaimonien de Cimon, qui dirige la politique athénienne ...". Kimon gehörte zum Geschlecht der Philaidai, *RE* XIX 1 (1938) 2113ff., s.v. Philaidai (F. Schachermayr), war Sohn des Miltiades und mit Isodike, einer Alkmeonidin verheiratet, *RE* XI 1 (1921) 437ff., s.v. Kimon (Swoboda); zur pro-lakedaimonischen Politik des Kimon s. auch Swoboda ebenda 441.
31. Shapiro (supra Anm. 27) 150: "In Athens the Dioskuroi did have

the epithet σωτῆρες (*IG* II[2], 4796), which may go back to a specific occasion of which we have no record." Zu der Retterfunktion der Dioskuren äussert sich Th. Lorenz, "Die Epiphanie der Dioskuren," *Kotinos, Festschrift für E. Simon* (Mainz 1992) 114ff.

32. Supra Anm. 7.
33. *CIA* I 210.223.270f11; *Schol.* Ar. *Eq.* 661; *Schol.* T zu *Il.* 21. 471.
34. *RE* I 1 (1894) 907, s.v. Agrotera (Wentzel); *RE* II 1 (1895) 1349 s.v. Artemis (Wernicke). Ein Ziegenopfer an Artemis Agrotera vor der Schlacht bezeugt auch Xen. *Hell.* 4.2.20 für die Spartaner, Wernicke ebenda; zur Verehrung der Artemis Agrotera in Athen nach Marathon auch Parke (supra Anm. 25) 77ff.
35. Felten (supra Anm. 4) 75.
36. *Il.* 16.183; dazu auch Wernicke (supra Anm. 34) 1353.
37. W. Burkert, *Griechische Religion der archaischen und klassischen Epoche* (Stuttgart 1977) 235: "Denn die Jungfräulichkeit der Artemis ist nicht Asexualität wie Athenas praktisch-organisatorische Klugheit, sondern ein eigentümlich erotisches, herausforderndes Ideal. In der *Ilias* wird der 'Chor der Artemis' nur einmal erwähnt (*Il.* 16.183), um zu berichten, wie Hermes für eine Teilnehmerin in Liebe entbrannte und sie alsbald zur Mutter machte. Auch sonst ist der 'Chor der Artemis' die prädestinierte Gelegenheit für Mädchenraub, ob nun die Dioskuren sich die Leukippiden greifen oder Theseus die Helena (Vase d. Meidias-M., *ARV*[2] 1313, Arias-Hirmer Taf. 214.; Plut. *Thes.* 31)".
38. Dazu Krug (supra Anm. 4) 19ff.; A. Kalpaxis, *Hemiteles* (Mainz 1986) 145ff.
39. I.M. Shear, "Kallikrates," *Hesperia* 32 (1963) 88ff.; der These Shears widersprach aber B. Wesenberg, "Zur Baugeschichte des Niketempels," *JdI* 96 (1981) 43. Wesenberg datiert aufgrund stilistischer Vergleiche mit den Propyläenbasen den Baubeginn sowohl des Ilissos-Tempels als auch des Niketempels in die mittleren dreissiger Jahre des 5. Jh., kommt aber zu dem Schluss, dass der Ilissos-Tempel, wie auch der Nike-Tempel und die anderen Sakralbauten Athens perikleischer Zeit, nach einem durch den peloponnesischen Krieg bedingten Baustopp erst in den zwanziger Jahren des 5. Jh. fertigstellt wurde. Wesenbergs Datierungseingrenzung aufgrund architektonischer Kriterien auf einen Zeitraum von knapp fünf Jahren erscheint allerdings zu eng gefasst. Dass die Ähnlichkeiten zwischen dem Ilissos-Tempel und dem Nike-Tempel keineswegs so gross sind, wie bisher in der Forschung häufig postuliert wurde, im Gegenteil die Fassaden durchaus voneinander unterschiedlich waren, beobachtete H. Büsing, "Zur Bauplanung ionisch-attischer Säulenfronten," *AM* 100 (1985) 188ff.; wobei er die Frage des Architekten offen lässt; zur Entwicklung der ionischen Architektur in Athen im 5. Jh. s. zuletzt U. Schädler, "Ionisches und Attisches am sog. Erechtheion," *AA* (1990) 361ff., der auch der Datierung des Niketempels in die 30iger Jahre des 5. Jh.v. Chr. und einer Entstehung des Ilissos-Tempels vor dem Nike-Tempel folgt.
40. Athen, NM Inv. Nr. 3941.
41. Krug (supra Anm. 4) 16: "Da jedoch in der attischen Reliefkunst von einer nur schrittweisen Entfaltung der Bewegungsmöglichkeiten nicht die Rede sein kann, muss man hier die Umformung eines bereits vorhandenen Motivs sehen," B.S. Ridgway, *Fifth Century Styles in Greek Sculpture* (Princeton 1981) 89, Abb. 53.54 datiert den Ilissos-Fries ebenfalls um 420 v.Chr.
42. Zuletzt Felten (supra Anm. 4) 121.
43. Childs (supra Anm. 4) 208; ebenso Büsing (supra Anm. 39) 188.
44. Childs (supra Anm. 4) 210.250f., so z.B. der Vergleich zwischen der stehenden Figur auf Block B des Ilissos-Frieses in Berlin und dem stehenden Mann W I auf dem Westfries des Parthenon, F. Brommer, *Der Parthenonfries* (Mainz 1977) Taf. 8. Dieser Vergleich hat insofern besondere chronologische Bedeutung für den Ilissos-Fries, als die Platte W I des Parthenonfrieses einer älteren Stilrichtung anzugehören scheint als der Parthenonfries im allgemeinen, so Childs (supra Anm. 4) 211. Auch für die Platte D finden sich Vergleiche am Parthenon, so an den Metopen W 1, O 6, N 24, die ebenfalls noch nicht zu den stilistisch weiter entwickelten Beispielen gehören, so Childs (supra Anm. 4) 213, vgl. Brommer (supra Anm. 24) Taf. 4.53.101.
45. Shapiro (supra Anm. 27) 13.50.60; E. Simon, *Gnomon* 64 (1992) 157; R.E. Wycherley, *The Stones of Athens* (Princeton 1978) 155f. weist allerdings auf eine vorpeisistratidische Phase im Bau des Olympieion hin.
46. Shapiro (supra Anm. 27) 102f.; Simon (supra Anm. 45) 159.
47. Thuk. 1.73.4f.; A. Powell, *Athens and Sparta. Constructing Greek Political and Social History from 478 B.C.* (London 1988) 60.
48. Hdt. 6.108.111.113.; Powell ebenda (supra Anm. 47)..
49. Prange (supra Anm. 11) 14 lehnt eine politisch-historische Deutung des Leukippidenraubes auf den Vasenbildern ab, aber die Themenwahl auf Friesen öffentlicher oder kultischer Bauten kann ohne Zweifel völlig anders motiviert sein als auf Vasenbildern, deren Adressaten zunächst allein im privaten Raum zu suchen sind. — Zur politischen Bedeutung Kimons äussert sich M.T.W. Arnheim, *Aristocracy in Greek Society* (London 1977) 140.155. Zweifellos kann Kimon, gestorben 450 v. Chr., nicht als Bauherr des Ilissos-Tempels angesehen werden. Die pro-lakedaimonische Haltung Kimons ist verschiedentlich in Frage gestellt worden, da er, um dem Verdacht des Lakonismus zu begegnen, seine Hetairen zum Kampf gegen Sparta aufforderte, H.J. Gehrke, *Stasis* (München 1985) 335 Anm. 31, und beim Bau der gegen Sparta gerichteten Langen Mauern mithalf, T. Hölscher, *Griechische Historienbilder* (Würzburg 1973) 76. Es ist dabei aber zu berücksichtigen, dass dieses Verhalten Kimons in die Zeit nach seiner Ostrakisierung, in jedem Fall aber in die Zeit seiner schwindenden politischen Bedeutung fällt. Die gegen die Demokratie gerichteten politischen Bestrebungen Kimons als auch seiner Nachfolger wurden von G. Prestel, *Die antidemokratische Strömung im Athen des 5. Jh. bis zum Tod des Perikles* (Breslau 1939) 32ff. 38ff. 43ff. untersucht. Die spartanische Verfassung war nach ihrer Struktur keine Aristokratie oder Oligarchie, erhielt aber durch ihren starken Bezug zur Tradition und spartiatischen Lebensweise den Charakter einer Oligarchie, wobei das Bild Spartas als Gegenpol zur Demokratie eine Schöpfung der Kritiker der Athener Demokratie war, so J. Bleicken, *Die Athenische Demokratie*[5] (Paderborn 1988) 344.
50. Zu der durch Parteienstreit bedingten Bauplanänderung der mnesikleischen Propyläen äussert sich P. Hellström, "The Planned Function of the Mnesiclean Propylaia," *OpAth* 17 (1988) 107ff. Der Areiopag wurde durch die Verfassungsreform des Ephialtes seiner Rechte entkleidet, behielt Aufsichtsrechte nur in sakralen Angelegenheiten, H. Bengtson, *Griechische Geschichte*[5] (München 1977) 188.199f; F. Gschnitzer, *Griechische Sozialgeschichte* (Wiesbaden 1981) 104; D. Stockton, *The Classical Athenian Democracy* (Oxford 1990) 41ff. In den vierziger Jahren des 5. Jh. waren die Aristokraten in der Volksversammlung zwar in der Minderheit, übten aber über den Areopag, den alten Adelsrat, in kultisch-religiösen Fragen einen entscheidenden Einfluss aus, so L. Schneider — C. Höcker, *Die Akropolis von Athen* (Köln 1990) 200f. Boersma (supra Anm. 7) 75 zählt den Ilissos-Tempel zu der Gruppe der Bauten, für die ein Bezug zur perikleischen Baupolitik nicht nachweisbar ist.

No Demokratia

Olga Palagia

To W.D.E.C.

This paper seeks to reopen the question of the original location and identity of the female torso Athenian Agora S 2370 (Fig. 1). The torso wears a transparent, high-girt chiton with a shoulder cord and a large himation. It was found in 1970, embedded in a Byzantine wall one metre east of the conglomerate foundation in front of the Royal Stoa (Fig. 2). It survives to a height of 1.54 m and is dated by general consensus to 330-320 B.C.[1] It is clearly an important original which served as the prototype of later works on a variety of subjects. The excavation report, by T.L.Shear, Jr., appeared in 1971[2]

Fig. 1. Athens, Agora S 2370. Photo American School of Classical Studies at Athens: Agora Excavations.

and the statue was published by the author in 1982.[3] Ten years later, however, its position and identity are still under discussion. The lack of attributes renders the identification of the Agora torso particularly problematic. The difficulty lies with the sculptural type, liberally employed for any number of major and minor deities and personifications in the period 330–280 B.C. A random glance at Attic reliefs of the late fourth century B.C. shows her as Artemis, Demeter, Kore, Hygieia, Boule, Demokratia, Eutaxia or a nymph.[4] In 1982 I used the iconographic type as a starting point and failed to reach a conclusion. This new attempt approaches the problem from a different angle, concentrating on the evidence of the two statue bases with which the torso has been associated.

We begin with the conglomerate foundation, measuring 2.75 × 2.03 m, aligned with the axis of the Royal Stoa (Fig. 2).[5] It supported the base of a massive monument. Its bottom courses are higher than the stylobate of the earlier Stoa behind it; a few sherds associated with it suggest a date in the second half of the fourth century B.C. Because it was excavated so close to the base, the torso S 2370 was placed on it by the excavator (Fig. 3),[6] and its identity became dependent on the function of the Royal Stoa. Three possibilities suggested themselves: Agathe Tyche, Themis, and Demokratia. Agathe Tyche was proposed by Leslie Shear,[7] and endorsed by Licia Guerrini who was the first to discuss the Agora torso in relation to her Roman copy, the Tyche of Leptis Magna (Fig. 4).[8] Homer Thompson[9] and Evelyn Harrison[10] recognised it as Themis on account of its similarity with the early Hellenistic "Themis" of Rhamnous (Fig. 5),[11] while in 1982 I tried to make a case for Demokratia by associating it with the base dedicated by the Boule of 333/2 B.C.[12]

The torso was assigned to the conglomerate foundation on the assumption that it was too heavy to be moved far from its original site.[13] It need not be so, however. Single statues and occasionally larger monuments are known to have been moved in antiquity. We need look no further than the Kerameikos and the Agora itself. The rectangular base at the entrance of the

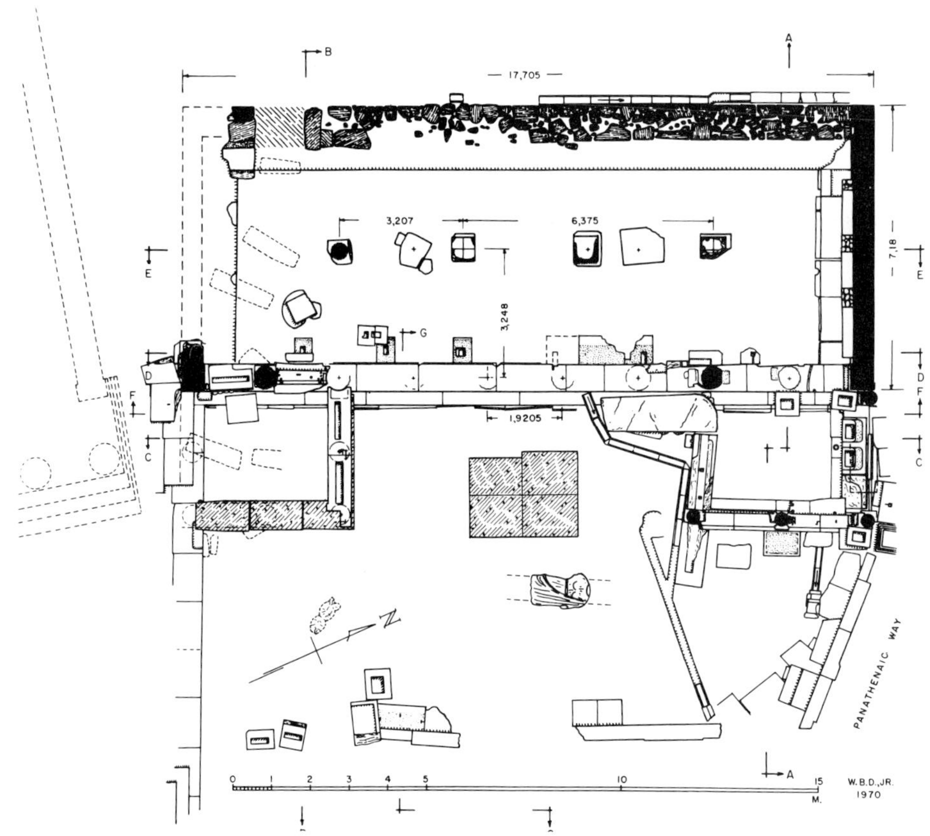

Fig. 2. State plan of Royal Stoa and its courtyard. Photo American School of Classical Studies at Athens: Agora Excavations.

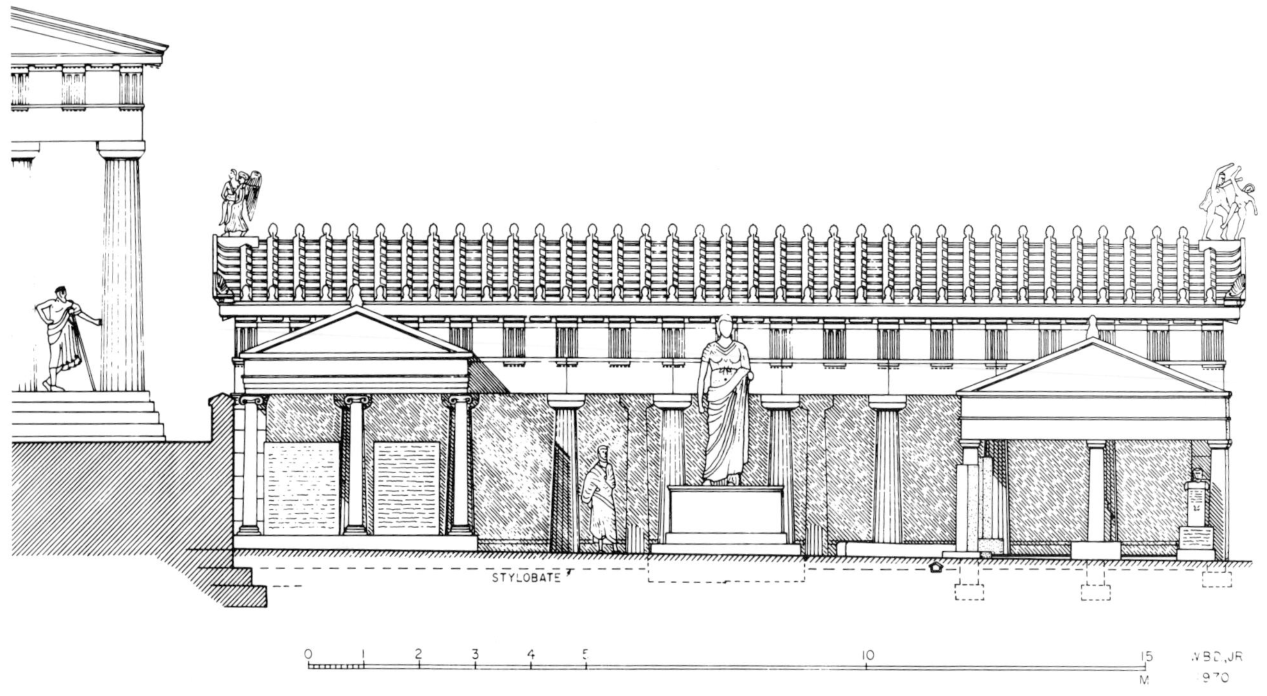

Fig. 3. The Royal Stoa at the end of the fourth century B.C.
Photo American School of Classical Studies at Athens: Agora Excavations.

Dipylon Gate was recently shown to have held a tall pedestal for a Hellenistic quadriga, similar to the "Agrippa Monument" on the Athenian Acropolis and to the quadriga monument of Attalos II in the Agora.[14] The poros foundation of the Kerameikos pedestal is dated by a coin to A.D. 139, the implication being that the monument was moved to this site in the Roman period. In the Agora itself, a good example of an over life-size torso excavated far from its original location is the Hellenistic Aphrodite Agora S 378, incorporated in the post-Herulian wall near the Library of Pantainos.[15] As she was found along with the fifth-century statue of Aphrodite S 1882 and with fragments of the ceiling of the temple of Ares, both statues were associated with those seen by Pausanias (1.8.4) near the temple of Ares.[16] The original location of the statue Agora S 378, however, is thought by Evelyn Harrison to be the open-air shrine of Aphrodite Hegemone, Demos and the Graces outside the northwest corner of the Agora.[17]

Let us now consider the relation of the statue's height to the width of the conglomerate base. In order to place the Agora statue, which was originally about 2.90 m high, on the conglomerate base which is 2.75 m wide, we should need a stepped pedestal of generous proportions (Fig. 3). Even so, the statue is too small for the base. The relation of its height to the width of this base is in fact closer to fifth-century practice, especially as regards cult statues placed on decorated bases. Parallels can readily be found among the cult statues by Pheidias and his school, whose monumental bases were decorated with reliefs of great complexity. The gold and ivory Athena Parthenos, about 10.107 m high, stood on a base 8.065 m wide.[18] The Nemesis of Agorakritos was about 3.55 m high, set on a base 2.43 m wide.[19] Plain bases of bronzes in the first half of the fifth century seem to have had more modest proportions, witness the base of the Tyrannicides in the Agora, with a restored width of about 1.60 m, each statue being 1.85 m high (p. 79, Fig. 9).[20]

When we begin to look at examples from the period of the Agora torso, however, we see that the relation of statue to base is more economical. On average, the width of the base tends to be about half the height of the statue. For example, the average height of the statues of the Daochos dedication at Delphi is 2.00 m, each requiring a base about 1.10–1.30 m wide.[21] The original height of Asklepios, Eleusis Museum 50, was 1.95 m, the width of his base 0.76 m.[22] The estimated height of the archaistic perirrhanterion, Eleusis Museum 57, is about 1.50 m, standing on a base 0.92 m wide.[23] The left-hand block of the base of a group dedicated by Atarbos, Acropolis Museum 1338 (Fig. 6), carries footprints 0.25 m long, which must have belonged to a bronze statue about 1.80 m high. The width of the base is 0.93 m.[24] At the beginning of the third century we observe a similar ratio: the so-called Themis, Athens National Museum 231 (Fig.5) is 2.022 m high, the width of her base 0.95 m.[25] The priestess Nikeso of Priene, Berlin, Pergamon-museum 1928, is 1.73 m high, her base 0.94 m wide.[26] But the clearest indication of the width of the original base of the Agora torso is provided by its copy from Leptis Magna (Fig. 4). The statue as extant is 2.40 m high, the width of its base 1.25 m.[27]

Fig. 4. Tyche of Leptis Magna. From the Forum of Septimius Severus. Tripoli Museum, Libya. Photo after L. Guerrini, StMisc *22 (1974–75) pl. 25.*

If the conglomerate foundation is far too large for the Agora torso, what sort of monument can be restored on it ? A single statue is ruled out unless it was over 5.00 m high. The group of Timotheos, Conon and King Euagoras of Salamis mentioned by Pausanias (1.3.2) as standing near the Royal Stoa probably belonged to the first half of the fourth century. In addition, Isocrates explicitly states that they were set up next to the statue of Zeus Eleutherios outside the Stoa of Zeus. Besides, the squarish shape of the foundation is not appropriate for a statuary group. Neither could it belong to a horseman. Its proportions are echoed more closely by the foundations of four-horse chariot groups from the late archaic period onward, except that these tend to be on a grander scale. We begin with chariot groups on lower foundations of two or three courses. The bronze quadriga dedicated on the Athenian Acropolis from the spoils of the Boeotians and Chalcidians on Euboea (c. 507/6 B.C.) rested on a

Fig. 5. Athens National Museum 231. From Rhamnous. Photo German Archaeological Institute, Athens, NM 311.

top course of 2.95 × 3.20 m, its foundation measuring 3.40 × 3.60 m.[28] The poros foundation of a fourth-century quadriga in Corinth measures 4.157 × 2.945 m (Fig. 7).[29] The golden chariot of the Rhodians at Delphi rested on a foundation of 3.70 × 2.55 m.[30] In the Hellenistic period chariot groups were often set on tall pillars, in which case the bottom course became considerably wider. The rock cuttings for a pillar outside the northeast corner of the Parthenon measure 4.43 × 4.91 m.[31] The plinth of the chariot on the Attalid monument usurped by Agrippa is 3.10 × 3.60 m, whereas the lower course is 3.31 × 3.80 m.[32] The top course of the stepped base of the chariot group in the Kerameikos measures 2.94 × 2.94 m, while the foundation course is 4.00 × 4.50 m.[33] The foundation course for the pillar carrying the chariot of Attalos II outside his Stoa in the Agora was 4.12 × 3.60 m.[34] The shape and size of the conglomerate base outside the Royal Stoa may indicate that it was meant for a chariot group, albeit a reduced one. If life-size quadrigas require a base of about 3.50 × 3.00 m, might not the Agora foundation have held a life-size biga ? The fact that it was not described by Pausanias may simply indicate that it did not attract his interest. He failed to mention the Stoa of Attalos II, for example. Alternatively, it could mean that the monument was no longer standing in his day and presumably the conglomerate base was covered over. A good case in point is the destruction of the portraits of Demetrius of Phaleron (318/7–308/7 B.C.), erected in Athens by himself. He is said to have set up 300 bronze portraits within 300 days, on horseback or riding quadrigas or bigas. They were not destined to suffer the ravages of time, however, for they were pulled down in his own lifetime.[35]

Still on the matter of statue bases, there is a final matter to be considered. In 1982 I first questioned the association of the Agora torso with the conglomerate base and suggested that it be placed instead on the base of the statue of Demokratia, dedicated by the Boule of 333/2 B.C., a fragment of which is in Athens, Epigraphical Museum 3913.[36] There was enough circumstantial evidence to suggest that the cult of Demokratia, first attested in the late 330s, was situated in the northwest side of the Agora.[37] The inscription on the base of

Fig. 6. Left-hand block of group dedicated by Atarbos. Acropolis Museum 1338. From the Acropolis. Photo Museum.

Fig. 7. Corinth Forum, south side. Poros base for bronze quadriga of the fourth century B.C. Photo American School of Classical Studies at Athens: Corinth Excavations.

Demokratia was first published in 1828 after Fourmont as being near the now demolished church of St. Nicolas to the north of the Royal Stoa.[38] The fragment in the Epigraphical Museum was identified and republished by Raubitschek.[39] It reads, as restored, "[Δη]μοκρατ[ί]α. /[Ἡ Βουλὴ ἡ] ἐπὶ Νικοκράτους ἄ[ρ]χοντος /[ἀνέθηκ]εν στεφανωθεῖσα ὑπ[ὸ] τοῦ δήμου/[ἀρετ]ῆς ἕνεκα καὶ δικ[αι]οσύνη[ς]". The remnants of the base are broken at the left. The smooth top, bottom and right-hand side are intact. No dimensions of the base have been published before. Its original height is 0.342 m, original depth 0.351 m, surviving width 0.26 m. Its estimated original width is between 0.75 and 0.82 m, which renders it far too small for the Agora torso. Although there are no iconographical grounds for ruling out the association of the Agora torso with Demokratia, the dedication of two contemporary statues certainly seems excessive.

Do the copies and variants of the Agora torso have any bearing on the identity of the original ? Two Roman copies and two early Hellenistic variants are important in this respect. Both Roman copies are to scale. The Tyche of Leptis Magna (Fig. 4) is of Pentelic marble, with a rudder in the right hand, resting on a globe at her feet. A specially dressed surface in the crook of her left arm was prepared for the attachment of a marble cornucopia. Unlike the Agora torso, she has long hair falling on her shoulders. A second copy to scale, more fragmentary and as yet unpublished, was found recently in Pamphylia and is now in the Antalya Museum (Fig. 8). She differs from the original in having the back of her himation drawn up over her head. This motif may have been borrowed from the prototype of the Roman Bona Fortuna in the Vatican (Fig. 9). In the absence of other evidence, it might be taken as an indication of the identity of the Antalya copy. The statue of Bona Fortuna (Fig. 9) was the primary comparandum cited by Leslie Shear for the identification of the Agora torso with Agathe Tyche.[40] He rightly recognised the Agora figure as the original source of inspiration for the Bona Fortuna, which differs from it in the long hair and the pointed overfold. The Fortuna had long been thought to reflect a fourth-century prototype; Cornelia Nippe has recently argued that this version with cornucopia is a retrospective creation of the late Hellenistic period.[41] In any case, Shear's argument in favour of Tyche was additionally sustained by two small

Fig. 8. Antalya Museum 3.18.87. Photo author.

Fig. 9. Bona Fortuna. From Ostia. Vatican Museum, Braccio Nuovo 86 (inv. no. 2244). Photo Alinari 6576.

holes in the Agora torso, one in the left shoulder, another in the left forearm, for the addition of a metallic attribute, which he restored as a cornucopia. Although the cornucopia was eventually accepted by a number of scholars, I was initially sceptical because it would have obscured the fine workmanship of the left arm.[42] The association with Agathe Tyche, however, was soon questioned in favour of what seemed at the time a more attractive candidate.

We now come to the first Hellenistic variant. The obvious debt of the so-called Themis by Chairestratos (Fig. 5) to Agora S 2370 prompted the latter's identification with Themis. Homer Thompson argued that the goddess of law was an appropriate ornament for the Royal Stoa as a seat of justice, and Evelyn Harrison interpreted her shoulder cord as a symbol of restraint, exercised by Themis.[43] Although statues of Themis are documented by the ancient sources, apart from the one of Rhamnous, no statue of Themis has ever been recognised.[44] The tentative identification of the Agora figure with Themis doubled their number overnight.

The identity of the Rhamnous statue, however, is by no means certain. It is based on the dedication by Megakles which names Themis as the sole recipient. The omission of Nemesis, main goddess of the sanctuary, is surprising. The dedicatory inscription was inexpertly carved, possibly when the statue was already *in situ*: "Μεγακλῆς Μεγακλ[έου]ς Ραμνούσ[ι]ος *ἀνέθηκε* Θέ*μιδι στεφανωθεὶς ὑπὸ τῶν δημοτῶν δικαι / οσύνης ἕνεκα ἐ[πὶ ἱ]ερείας* Καλλ*ιστοῦς καὶ νικήσας παισὶ καὶ ἀνδράσι γυμνασιαρχῶν*." It contains two additions below the inscription which were clearly an afterthought: "*καὶ* Φ*ειδοστράτης* Ν*εμέσει ἱερείας*"[45] and "*καὶ κωμωιδοῖς χορηγῶν*". There is no doubt that the statue signed by Chairestratos was no cult statue. It was excavated near the corner of the cella of the small temple in the sanctuary of Nemesis, in line with two other votive statues. The first, possibly showing a local hero, dates from the late fifth century B.C., the other, a portrait of Aristonoe, priestess of Nemesis, is Hellenistic.[46] Further fragments of statuary of archaic and later times were excavated inside the temple.[47] The identification of Athens National Museum 231 with Themis was first questioned by T.B.L. Webster, who suggested that her praying gesture indicated a simple worshipper by analogy with the archaic Korai on the Acropolis.[48] The great size of the figure, however, betrays a deity. Themis' identity was also challenged by B. Petrakos, who did not offer an alternative identification.[49] In a more systematic fashion, Alexandros Mantis suggested a new reading of the inscription, so that it carries a double dedication to Themis and Nemesis. He consequently recognised in the statue of Chairestratos both goddesses combined, implying that their shared cult actually reflected the dual nature of a single deity.[50] His reading of "καὶ Φειδοστράτης Νεμέσει ἱερείας" as implying a dedication to Nemesis (rather than defining Pheidostrate as priestess of Nemesis) is impossible. But the dedication should not, perhaps, be taken as an indication of the identity of the figure. It is not unthinkable that a statue of Nemesis should have been dedicated to Themis. Indicative of this mentality are the votive inscriptions on the two thrones from the small temple of Rhamnous, dedicated to Nemesis and Themis under the priesthoods of Kallisto and Pheidostrate.[51] The dedication to Themis is written under the name of Pheidostrate, priestess of Nemesis, while that to Nemesis appears under Kallisto's name.

No fourth-century statue of either Themis or Nemesis have come down to us for comparison[52] and we have already seen that the sculptural type in high-girt chiton and himation served various goddesses in that period. Supposing for the sake of argument that the statue by Chairestratos is in fact Nemesis, could the sculptor have had a special reason for using the Agora torso as a source of inspiration?

Nemesis is the daughter of Okeanos and therefore Tyche's sister.[53] The two may in fact act together on an Attic red-figure amphoriskos of the 430s in Berlin, where they witness Helen's seduction by Paris.[54] Nemesis is named, but of Tyche's name only the Y survives. The symbolism is obvious: Paris' great good fortune attracts divine retribution. In the period 300–280 B.C. the statuary type of Agora S 2370 served as a prototype for the cult statues of the twin Nemeseis of the new city of Smyrna, said to have been founded by Alexander the Great.[55] The Nemeseis of Smyrna are reproduced on Roman imperial coin types from the time of Domitian onward. The Smyrna type holds a cubit and dispenses with the stiff pose of the Agora figure by acquiring swinging hips. Several sculptured variants are known. Winged variants appear on Thasos in the second century A.D. (Fig. 10).[56] A statuette of the Smyrna type of the third century A.D. found in the theatre at Ephesos, shows Nemesis assimilated to Tyche, accompanied by Nemesis' beast, the griffin, and holding the cubit, symbol of Nemesis, and Tyche's rudder and cornucopia (Fig.11).[57] In the Roman period Nemesis and Tyche share attributes.[58] They are already assimilated in a Hellenistic inscription on a round altar from the sanctuary of Asklepios at Epidauros.[59] Hesychios

Fig. 10. Winged Nemesis. Thasos Museum 58. Photo École Française d'Athènes.

Fig. 11. Nemesis-Tyche. From the theatre at Ephesos. Vienna, Kunsthistorisches Museum I 931. Photo Museum.

assimilates Agathe Tyche with Nemesis and Themis.[60] In the second century A.D twin statuettes of Nemesis-Tyche holding cubit, rudder and wheel, flanked the entrance to the stadium at Olympia.[61]

The cult of Agathe Tyche is first attested in sixth-century Smyrna, also home to an archaic cult of Nemesis: the sculptor Boupalos of Chios was credited with the first statue of Tyche, wearing a polos and holding a cornucopia.[62] Tyche becomes a major goddess in the fourth century, and several fourth-century statues of her are mentioned by Pausanias throughout Greece.[63] A cult and sanctuary of Agathe Tyche in Athens are documented by the decree of religious reforms proposed by Lycurgus in 335/4 B.C.[64] The location of the sanctuary is not stated. Agathe Tyche was worshipped in the Agora in the first half of the fourth century as attested by a dedication by Philippos, son of Iasidemos of Kolonos, to the Twelve Gods and Agathe Tyche.[65] The findspot of this inscription is unknown. The only documented Athenian statue of Agathe Tyche, also associated with a cult, was reported by Aelian to be standing outside the Athenian Prytaneion in the second half of the second century A.D.[66] Since it was still *in situ* then, it cannot be identified with the Tyche by Praxiteles seen earlier by Pliny on the Capitoline in Rome.[67] Aelian's story of the Prytaneion Tyche belongs to a tradition of curious love affairs. The statue allegedly inspired a well-to-do Athenian adolescent with such passion that he killed himself because the city council would not sell it to him. His fervour was presumably of a religious nature since he was said to have offered sacrifice to the goddess before dying. Because the Tholos served as a dining hall to the prytaneis, its precinct was named the Prytanikon in Hellenistic inscriptions.[68] The Tholos came eventually to be confused with the Prytaneion in the late Roman period.[69] Aelian had probably no first-hand knowledge of the Agora and it is conceivable that he or his source fell victim to the confusion.[70] There is no shortage of vestiges of foundations for monumental statues and/or altars in the Tholos precinct though at the present state of the evidence it is impossible to attempt specific attributions.[71] We have seen that the over life-size Aphrodite Agora S 378 is thought to have been moved from one end of the Agora to the other or at least halfway across. There is no reason why Agora S 2370 could not have travelled from the Tholos to the Royal Stoa.

If the torso (Fig. 1) is recognised as Agathe Tyche, her identity may help explain the glossy surface of the stump of her left arm. It may be attributed to frequent handling.[72] The statue could perhaps have lost its left forearm but was left standing in a mutilated condition for hundreds of years. Touching statues for luck is a superstition that survives to this day; witness the bronze statue of St. Peter in St. Peter's Basilica in Rome.[73] What can be more effective than touching a statue of Tyche ?[74] At any rate, Aelian's account suggests that the Prytaneion Tyche stood at an accessible height since she was embraced and wreathed by her human suitor. In conclusion, we may think of her as a civic personification, bestowing her gifts of abundance and good guidance on the Athenians and comforting them in times of anxiety.

Acknowledgements

I am grateful to T.L. Shear, Jr. and John McK. Camp, II for their kindness in facilitating the study of the Agora material and to Dina Peppas-Delmouzou for providing all possible help at the Epigraphical Museum. Kevin Clinton estimated the original width of the Demokratia base *IG* II^2, 2791 (Epigraphical Museum 3913). I am indebted to Ismene Trianti for the photo Fig. 6 and to David M. Lewis and John S. Traill for epigraphical advice. This paper would not have been written but for the help and encouragement of William D.E. Coulson. I bear sole responsibility for the views expressed here.

Abbreviations

The following will be cited by author's name:

J.M. Camp, *The Athenian Agora* (London 1986)

H.R. Goette, "Eine grosse Basis vor dem Dipylon in Athen," *AM* 105 (1990) 269–278, pls. 55–58

L. Guerrini, "Problemi statuari: originali e copie", *StMisc* 22 (1974/75) 109–116, pls. 24–29

F.W. Hamdorf, *Griechische Kultpersonifikationen der vorhellenistischen Zeit* (Mainz 1964)

M.B. Hornum, *Nemesis, the Roman State, and the Games* (Leiden 1993)

M. Jacob-Felsch, *Die Entwicklung griechischen Statuenbasen und die Aufstellung der Statuen* (Waldsassen 1969)

A. Μάντης, *Προβλήματα της εικονογραφίας των ιερειών και των ιερέων στην αρχαία ελληνική τέχνη* (Athens 1990)

C. Nippe, *Die Fortuna Braccio Nuovo* (Berlin 1989)

O. Palagia, "A Colossal Statue of a Personification from the Agora of Athens," *Hesperia* 51 (1982) 99–113, pls. 29–36

H.A. Shapiro, *Personifications in Greek Art* (Zurich 1993)

T.L. Shear, Jr., "The Athenian Agora: Excavations of 1970," *Hesperia* 40 (1971) 241–279, pls. 45–59

H.A. Thompson and R.E. Wycherley, *Agora* XIV, *The Agora of Athens* (Princeton 1972)

R.E. Wycherley, *Agora* III, *Literary and Epigraphical Testimonia* (Princeton 1957)

Notes

1. This date was suggested on stylistic grounds by comparison with reliefs of the 330s and 320s. Palagia 101–103. See also Shear 271; E.B. Harrison, "The Shoulder-Cord of Themis," *Festschrift für F. Brommer* (Mainz 1977) 157, pl. 43,2 and 3; Camp fig. 78; B.S. Ridgway, *Hellenistic Sculpture* I (Bristol 1990) 55–56, pl. 29; A. Stewart, *Greek Sculpture. An Exploration* (New Haven 1990) 192, 198, fig. 575. A discordant note was struck by W. Geominy, *Die Florentiner Niobiden* (diss. Bonn 1984) 273–274, who suggested a date c. 310 B.C., followed by E. Voutiras, "Ηφαιστίων ήρως," *Εγνατία* 2 (1990) 130 n. 23, fig. 5; L. Todisco, *Scultura greca del IV secolo* (Milan 1993) 136, pl. 304.
2. Shear 270–271, pl. 56.
3. Palagia 99–113, pls. 29–30; pl. 31b for the statue as found. The reader is referred to this publication for detailed analysis of the sculpture and its relation to contemporary and other comparanda.
4. Palagia 106–109.
5. Shear 270, fig. 1, pl. 47. Thompson and Wycherley 84.

6. Shear 270; H.A. Thompson, *The Athenian Agora Guide*^{3} (Athens 1976) 85, fig. 36.
7. Shear 271.
8. Guerrini 109–110, pls. 24; 26–28. The identification with Agathe Tyche holding a cornucopia also followed by Mantis 105 n. 454; Nippe 58. A local variant of the same type of Agathe Tyche of the second century A.D. was found, along with a statue of Nemesis, in the Basilica of Cyrene: M. Luni, "Il Ginnasio-"Caesareum" di Cirene nel contesto del rinovamento urbanistico della media età ellenistica e della prima età imperiale," *Archeologia Cirenaica, AccNazLincei* (Rome 1990) 106–111, figs. 13b-14.
9. Thompson (supra n.6) 204–205, fig. 37; Thompson and Wycherley 84.
10. Supra n. 1.
11. Athens, National Museum 231. About 300–280 B.C. Signed by Chairestratos, son of Chairedemos, of Rhamnous. B. Στάης, "'Αγάλματα ἐκ Ραμνοῦντος,"*ArchEph* (1891) 48, pl. 4; J. Frel, "Le Sculpteur des Danseuses," *GettyMusJ* 6–7 (1978–79) 75–82; id., "Addenda et Corrigenda," *GettyMusJ* 8 (1980) 206; Palagia 105–106, pl. 33d-e; Mantis 104–115, pl. 46a; Ridgway (supra n. 1) 55–57, pl.31. O. Palagia and D. Lewis, "The Ephebes of Erechtheis 333/2 B.C. and their Dedication," *BSA* 84 (1989) 343; Todisco (supra n. 1) 138–139, pl. 306 with earlier bibliography. Inscribed base: *IG* II^{2}, 3109; A. Wilhelm, "Themis und Nemesis in Rhamnus," *ÖJh* 32 (1940) 200–209; J. Marcadé, *Receuil des signatures de sculpteurs grecs* I (Paris 1953) 12; J. Pouilloux, *La Forteresse de Rhamnonte* (Paris 1954) 152, no. 39.
12. Palagia 111–113, pl. 36f.
13. Shear 270; Thompson and Wycherley 84; Thompson (supra n. 6); Camp 105.
14. Goette 269–278, pls. 55–58.
15. J. McK. Camp II, *The Athenian Agora Guide*^{4} (Athens 1990) 195–196.
16. Camp (supra n. 15) 198.
17. E.B. Harrison, "Aphrodite Hegemone in the Athenian Agora," *Akten des XII. Internationalen Kongresses für klassische Archäologie. Berlin 1988* (Mainz 1990) 346, pl. 50,1: "Since it appears likely that the monuments outside the northwest corner of the Agora were damaged at the time of Sulla's sack, the statue of Aphrodite Hegemone might have been rehabilitated by bringing it into the Temple of Ares in the Augustan period." For the sanctuary of Aphrodite Hegemone, Demos and the Graces: *IG* II^{2}, 2798 (Athens National Museum 1495); Travlos, *PDA* 79–81; Thompson and Wycherley 160; Camp fig. 139.
18. N. Leipen, *Athena Parthenos* (Toronto 1971) 23–24.
19. Height of Nemesis: Γ. *Δεσπίνης*, *Συμβολή στη μελέτη του έργου του Αγορακρίτου* (Athens 1971) 62. Width of base: B. *Πετράκος*, "*Προβλήματα της βάσης του αγάλματος της* Νεμέσεως," in H. Kyrieleis, (ed.), *Archaische und klassische griechische Plastik* II (Mainz 1986) 93 n. 13.
20. S. Brunnsåker, *The Tyrant-Slayers of Kritios and Nesiotes*^{2} (Stockholm 1971) 77; 90; L.M. Gadbery, *Three Fifth Century B.C. Statue Bases from the Athenian Agora* (diss. New York 1988) 92–93.
21. Heights of statues: T. Dohrn, "Die Marmorstandbilder des Daochos-Weihgeschenks in Delphi," *AntP* 8 (1968) 33–52. Bases: J. Pouilloux, *La Région Nord du Sanctuaire*, *FdD* II (Paris 1960) 76–77.
22. Jacob-Felsch 141–142.
23. Jacob-Felsch 142–143.
24. *IG* II^{2}, 3025; M.Σ. Μπρούσκαρη, *Μουσείον Ακροπόλεως. Περιγραφικός κατάλογος* (Athens 1974) 20; *Το Πνεύμα και το σώμα* (Athens 1990) no. 101; here p. 152.
25. Jacob-Felsch 143–144. For the statue see supra n. 11.
26. Jacob-Felsch 145–146.
27. Guerrini 111, pl. 25.
28. Hdt. 5.77; Paus. 1.28.2. G.P. Stevens, "The Periclean Entrance Court," *Hesperia* 5 (1936) 504–6, fig. 54 ; A.E. Raubitschek, *Dedications from the Athenian Akropolis* (Cambridge, Mass. 1949) nos. 168 and 173.
29. Ch.K. Williams, II, "Corinth 1969: Forum Area," *Hesperia* 39 (1970) 6–9, pl. 2. I am grateful to Charles K. Williams, II for drawing my attention to this base.
30. J.F. Crome, "Die goldene Pferde von San Marco und der goldene Wagen der Rhodier," *BCH* 87 (1963) 221–228; Jacob-Felsch 167–168.
31. *IG* II^{2}, 3272; *BCH* 110 (1986) 674–5, fig. 8; Goette 274, no. 3.
32. G.P. Stevens, "Architectural Studies," *Hesperia* 15 (1946) 89–92; Jacob-Felsch 100; 198, no. II 177; Goette 274, no. 2.
33. Goette 270.
34. Thompson and Wycherley 107; Goette 273, no. 1; Camp (supra n. 15) 130. For other chariot groups in the Athenian Agora see H.A. Thompson, "The Odeion in the Athenian Agora," *Hesperia* 19 (1950) 71 and 72 n. 1, pls. 17 and 28a.
35. Strab. 9.1.20; Diog.Laert. *Vita Dem.* 75; Plut. *Praec.ger.reip.* 27; Dio Chrys. *Or.* 37.41. G. Hafner, *Viergespanne in vorderansicht* (Berlin 1938) 95–96.
36. *IG* II^{2}, 2791; *SEG* 21, 679. Palagia 111–113, pl. 36f. See also infra n. 39 and here p. 56.
37. The evidence is reviewed in Palagia 111–112.
38. *CIG* I, 95. The foundations of St. Nicolas came to light at the excavations of the northwest side of the Agora in 1992. On the church see also Palagia 111 n. 76.
39. A.E. Raubitschek,"Demokratia," *Hesperia* 31 (1962) 238–243, pl. 86d.
40. Shear 271. For the Bona Fortuna in the Vatican see also Palagia 102; 107, pl. 32a-b (the captions are reversed); Nippe 6–8, pls. 1–2.
41. Nippe 53–55.
42. Cornucopia proposed by Shear 270–271; accepted by Harrison (supra n.1) 157 n. 18; Guerrini 110; Mantis 105 n. 454; Nippe 58. Questioned by Thompson (supra n. 6) 205; followed by Palagia 109. The attribute in the right hand of S 2370 was very likely a phiale: Guerrini 112; Palagia 113.
43. Thompson (supra n. 6); Harrison (supra n. 1).
44. Statues of Themis listed in Hamdorf 109; Shapiro cat. nos. 142 and 144. In archaic relief sculpture Themis is named in the north frieze of the Siphnian treasury at Delphi, V. Brinkmann, "Die aufgemalten Namenbeinschriften an Nord- und Ostfries des Siphnierschatzhauses," *BCH* 109 (1985) 101; 123, fig. 93; J. Boardman, *Greek Sculpture. The Archaic Period*^{2} (1991) fig. 212.1. In fifth-century sculpture Themis may appear beside Nemesis on the statue base of Agorakritos' Nemesis at Rhamnous (430–420 B.C.). Pausanias (1.33.7–8) describes the scene as Leda leading Helen to her true mother Nemesis but does not name the fourth woman next to Nemesis: *Πετράκος* (supra n. 19) 97, fig. 4, pl. 112,4. This figure has been tentatively identified with Hermione (B. Petracos, "La Base de la Némésis d'Agoracrite," *BCH* 105 [1981] 240), Oinoe (A. *Δεληβορριάς*, "Α*μφισημίες και παραναγνώσεις*," *HOROS* 2 [1984] 99 *σημ*. 35; *Πετράκος* [supra n. 19] 95; 97; 102) and Clytemnaestra (K.D. Shapiro Lapatin, "A Family Gathering at Rhamnous ?"*Hesperia* 61 [1992] 111–113, pl.27d). The identification of the unknown goddess with Themis is supported by Nemesis' constant pairing with Themis in the Rhamnous sanctuary and by Themis' seminal role in the origins of the Trojan War which are indeed the main theme of Agorakritos' base. This identification was also suggested by P. Karanastassi in *LIMC* VI (1992) s.v. Nemesis p. 756. For Themis instigating the Trojan War see Shapiro 216.
45. Pheidostrate was probably buried in the grave peribolos of Diogeiton in the third century: B. *Πετράκος*, *Ραμνούς* (Athens 1991) 39, fig. 22.
46. B. *Πετράκος*, "Α*νασκαφή* Ρ*αμνούντος*," *Prakt* (1976) 51, no. 3, votive statuette of Lysikleides, Athens National Museum 199, late fifth century B.C.; no. 5, portrait statue of the priestess Aristonoe, Athens National Museum 232, third or second century B.C. See also *Πετράκος*, *Ραμνούς* 23–24, figs. 14–15.
47. *Πετράκος* 1976 (supra n. 46) 52, no. 12: peplos figure Athens National Museum 1848 (early classical); 54, no. 16: Athens National Museum 2569 (archaic); 55 no. 24: two herm heads; 56, no. 27: British Museum 154 (archaistic).

48. T.B.L. Webster, *Hellenistic Art* (London 1967) 64.
49. B. Πετρᾶκος, "Τὸ Νεμέσιον τοῦ Ραμνοῦντος," *Φίλια Ἔπη εἰς Γεώργιον Μυλωνᾶν* 2 (Athens 1987) 322; id., *Ραμνούς* 22–24, fig. 13.
50. Mantis 104–113.
51. *IG* II^2, 4638, Athens National Museum 2672 and 2673. Wilhelm (supra n. 11) 205–207, fig. 106; Pouilloux (supra n. 11) 152, no. 40; Mantis 108–109, pl. 48a-b. Because of the uncertain reading of Pheidostrate's name on the throne, Wilhelm rejected the obvious association of the priestesses in *IG* II^2, 4638 with those in *IG* II^2, 3109.
52. See supra n. 44. In the fourth century B.C. Themis and Nemesis are probably shown on the votive relief British Museum 1953. 5-30.1 + Rhamnous 530. Neither goddess resembles Athens National Museum 231 (Fig. 5). The relief was republished and discussed extensively in Palagia and Lewis (supra n. 11) 340–44, pl. 49a-b. On Demeter and Kore in Rhamnous (Palagia and Lewis 341) see now the votive inscription by the strategos of the paralia, Euxitheos of Kephisia, on the east gate of the citadel, *Ergon* (1989) 6, *Ergon* (1990) 4 and 7 and *Prakt* (1989) 21–22. On the Nemesia (Palagia and Lewis 344) see now the decree honouring Antigonos Gonatas, *Ergon* (1989) 8 and *Prakt* (1989) 31–34, which dates it to the 19th of Hekatombaion and provides it with a *γυμνικὸς ἀγών*.
53. Hesiod, *Theogony* 360; *Homeric Hymn to Demeter* 420; Paus. 1.33.3; 4.30.4; 7.5.3.
54. Antikensammlung Charlottenburg 30036; *ARV*^{2} 1173,1; *Addenda*^{2} 339; A. Shapiro, "The Origins of Allegory in Greek Art," *Boreas* 9 (1986) 11–14, pl. 1,3; Shapiro 227-8, cat. no. 129, figs. 151–154, 186: Nemesis (named) is paired with Tyche, Themis (?) with Heimarmene (named); *LIMC* VI (1992) s.v. Nemesis no. 211 (where I am misquoted as confusing Themis [?] with Tyche).
55. Pausanias 1.33.7; 7.5.2. B. Schweitzer, "Dea Nemesis Regina," *JdI* 46 (1931) 203–205; D.O.A. Klose, *Die Münzprägung von Smyrna in der römischen Kaiserzeit* (Berlin 1987) 28–30, pls. 42, R 2–3; 43, R 4; *LIMC* VI s.v. Nemesis nos. 3–29 and pp. 734; 756; Shapiro 173; Hornum 328–329, pl. I,5.
56. Thasos Museum 58 and 2106, second century A.D. Cl. Rolley, "Sculptures nouvelles à l'Agora de Thasos," *BCH* 88 (1964) 496–505; *LIMC* VI s.v. Nemesis nos. 29a-b.
57. Vienna, Kunsthistorisches Museum I 931, third century A.D. Schweitzer (supra n. 55) 208–209, fig. 9; W. Oberleitner et al., *Funde aus Ephesos und Samothrake* (Vienna 1978) 109–110 no. 146; Nippe 60–61; 100–101; *LIMC* VI s.v. Nemesis no. 181; Hornum pl. 17.
58. C.M. Edwards, "Tyche at Corinth," *Hesperia* 59 (1990) 533; *LIMC* VI p. 735; Hornum 20 n. 2.
59. *IG* IV.2, 311. Hornum 196, no. 79.
60. Hsch. s.v. 'Ἀγαθὴ Τύχη. Nemesis and Tyche assimilated in the Roman period: *LIMC* VI s.v. Nemesis p. 735.
61. Olympia Museum 963 and 1336, second century A.D. G. Treu, *Olympia* III (Berlin 1897) 237–239, pl. 59, 2–3; *LIMC* VI s.v. Nemesis nos. 180a-b.
62. Tyche by Boupalos: Pausanias 4.30.6. A. Rumpf, "Zu Bupalos und Athenis," *AA* (1936) 52–64; Klose (supra n.55) 34; Shapiro 227. Archaic cult and statue of Nemesis in Smyrna: Paus. 1.33.7; 9.35.6; Shapiro cat. no 113; Hornum 11. Boupalos was also responsible for the golden Charites in the temple of Nemesis in Smyrna: Paus. 9.35.6; Shapiro 173. It has also been suggested that Boupalos was a Hellenistic sculptor working in an archaistic style: R. Heidenreich, "Bupalos und Pergamon," *AA* (1935) 668–701; Guerrini 113 n. 30.
63. Pausanias 1.43.6; 9.16.2. On Tyche's cult and representations see Hamdorf 97–100; Shapiro 227–228; 264.
64. *IG* II^2, 333. C.J. Schwenk, *Athens in the Age of Alexander* (Chicago 1985) no. 21.
65. *IG* II^2, 4564. Athens, Epigraphical Museum 10380. Wycherley no. 376.
66. Aelian, *VH* 9.39: "*νεανίσκος δὲ 'Ἀθήνησι τῶν εὖ γεγονότων πρὸς τῶι πρυτανείωι ἀνδριάντος ἑστῶτος τῆς 'Ἀγαθῆς Τύχης θερμότατα ἠράσθη. κατεφίλει γοῦν τὸν ἀνδριάντα περιβάλλων, εἶτα ἐκμανεὶς καὶ οἰστρηθεὶς ὑπὸ τοῦ πόθου, παρελθὼν εἰς τὴν βουλὴν καὶ λιτανεύσας ἕτοιμος ἦν πλείστων χρημάτων τὸ ἄγαλμα πρίασθαι. ἐπεὶ δὲ οὐκ ἔπειθεν, ἀναδήσας πολλαῖς ταινίαις καὶ στεφανώσας τὸ ἄγαλμα, καὶ θύσας καὶ κόσμον αὐτῶι περιβαλλὼν πολυτελῆ εἶτα ἑαυτὸν ἀπέκτεινε, μυρία προσκλαύσας.*" Wycherley no. 542. On the location of the Prytaneion near the north slope of the Acropolis see Wycherley 166–174; S.G. Miller, *The Prytaneion* (Berkeley 1978) 42–49. See also T.L. Shear, Jr. in this volume, pp. 227–228.
67. Pliny *NH* 36.23. The two were associated by R. Kabus-Jahn, *Studien zu Frauenfiguren des vierten Jahrhunderts vor Christus* (Darmstadt 1963) 38; Hamdorf 99, no. 315; A. Corso, *Prassitele: Fonti epigrafiche e letterarie* 1 (Rome 1988) 96–97.
68. Wycherley 184.
69. Wycherley 166; 179. Schol. Ar.*Pax* 1183; Schol. Hdt. 1.46.2; Timaeus, *Lexicon Platonicum* 402; Hsch. s.v. *σκιάς*; Suda s.v. *πρυτανεῖον* and *θόλος*. See also T.L. Shear, Jr. in this volume, p. 241.
70. That Aelian may have confused the Tholos with the Prytaneion was first suggested by B. Veirneisel-Schlörb, "Nochmals zum Datum der Bauplastik des Asklepiostempels von Epidauros," *Festschrift für G. Kleiner* (Tübingen 1976) 75 n. 52, pl. 12,1. Her main object was to identify the Prytaneion Tyche with Agora S 37, found in a late foundation at the southeast corner of the Metroon close to the Tholos.
71. For the foundations see H.A. Thompson, *The Tholos of Athens and its Predecessors*, *Hesperia* Suppl. 4 (1940) 92–5.
72. Palagia 100.
73. M. Guarducci, "Riflessioni sulla statua bronzea di San Pietro," *Xenia* 16 (1988) 60, fig. 2. I owe this reference to Erika Simon.
74. *Cf.* J.J. Pollitt, *Art in the Hellenistic Age* (Cambridge 1986) 3: "In fact, far from being purely learned creations, figures of Tyche may have taken on a kind of magical quality, like good luck charms."

Religion and Politics in Democratic Athens

H. Alan Shapiro

My purpose in this brief paper is to explore some of the ways in which the Athenian state used public religion as a vehicle for defining itself in the fifth century.

It is a commonplace to observe that religion permeated every aspect of life in an ancient Greek *polis*.[1] To see how true this is, we need only consider some of the events that comprised the founding of the democracy in Athens. The murder of the tyrant Hipparchos (Fig. 1), which later Athenians would regard — whether rightly or wrongly — as the first blow for democracy, took place at the great festival of Athena, the Panathenaia of 514 B.C., and he was cut down at a hero-shrine, the Leokoreion.[2] (We might contrast an obvious Roman parallel, the murder of Julius Caesar. This took place in a theatre, in front of a statue of his old political rival, Pompey, on a purely political occasion, a meeting of the Senate.)

The actual fall of the tyranny, four years later, was precipitated in large part by the oracle of Apollo, goading the Spartans to free Athens.[3] Hippias tried at first to seek the protection of Athena's sanctuary on the Acropolis, until a threat to his children induced him to leave (Hdt. 5.65). When Kleisthenes had carried out his political reforms and the reorganization of the demes, this too required the seal of approval of Apollo at Delphi, and so the oracle selected the ten heroes for whom the new tribes would be named, the *Eponymoi*, from a list of one hundred submitted to it.[4]

At every step of the way, then, it seems the Athenians had to believe that the new political order was sanctioned by the gods, and most of all by two in particular: Apollo, the god of *nomos*, and Athena, the tutelary goddess of the city. The new democracy expressed its thanks to Athena by putting up a great new temple to her on the Acropolis, whose splendid marble pediment showing Athena victorious over the Giants could be read as a metaphor for the driving out of the tyrants from her city.[5]

Greek religion always operated on two levels, divine and heroic. In addition to divine sanction, the young democracy would also need its own hero-cults, like the patron saints of a Christian town. The best candidates for this role were none other than the Tyrannicides,

Fig. 1. The Murder of Hipparchos by Harmodios and Aristogeiton. Attic red-figure stamnos, Würzburg, Martin von Wagner-Museum der Universität, L515. Ca. 470 B.C. Museum photo.

Harmodios and Aristogeiton, who had paved the way (as was believed) for the democracy; who were perfect exemplars of the finest Athenian virtues: courage, loyalty, in short, *kalokagathia*; and who, best of all, were dead (for a Greek hero could never achieve that status while alive), having died particularly heroic deaths.[6]

Michael Taylor argues that the cult worship of Harmodios and Aristogeiton was instituted within a few years of the expulsion of Hippias, by about 507 B.C., or even earlier.[7] This included a yearly sacrifice conducted by the *Polemarch* and the marking out of a shrine at the site of their graves, on the road to the Academy. The founding of the democracy was tantamount to a *re*-foundation of the *polis*, and this had to be legitimated in the cult of a founding hero (or two heroes, in this case).

For Taylor, another aspect of the Tyrannicides cult was the setting up of the first statue group, made by Antenor, for which he inclines toward the traditional early dating of circa 510 to 507 B.C.[8] This date derives in turn from a comment of the Elder Pliny, who synchronizes the first Tyrannicides monument with the expulsion of the kings from Rome. The first major challenge to this dating in modern scholarship came from A.E. Raubitschek.[9] His grounds for a dating of the first Tyrannicides group after the Battle of Marathon were partly epigraphical — the lettering of the statue base found in the Agora Excavations in 1936[10] — and partly historical, that is, his belief that, so long as there were influential members of the Peisistratid family living in Athens, it would have been unthinkable to erect a public monument to the murderers of Hipparchos.[11] Only with the removal of Hipparchos, son of Charmos, ostracized in the first such procedure, in 487 B.C., could the statues be put up.[12] In recent years, archaeology has come to the aid of Raubitschek's historical argument, particularly the discovery at Baiae, on the Bay of Naples, of fragments of Roman plaster casts of the Tyrannicides statues.[13] These have led to a re-evaluation of other Roman copies, in marble, and the conclusion that some, at least, reflect the earlier, Antenor group. That is, the first group was made in the early 480's, stood less than ten years in the Agora before being carried off by Xerxes, and was replaced by more or less exact replicas by Kritios and Nesiotes in 477/6 B.C. (p. 79, Fig. 9). Since, however, the first group was back in Athens by the Early Hellenistic period (returned there by Alexander or one of his successors), standing alongside the replacements, it was available to be cast or copied by the Romans, who might well have preferred to copy this first, more "authentic" group.[14]

The downdating of the first Tyrannicides to the 480's does not vitiate Taylor's argument for the early foundation of the hero cult, but it does require us to reconsider the meaning of the statue group and the historical context of its erection. In a recent paper, Tonio Hölscher rightly pointed out the unique status of the Tyrannicides statues as the first political monuments in Athens and their primary role as a paradigm (a *Leitbild*) for all Athenian citizens.[15] I think, however, this view may underestimate the religious importance of the monument in light of the hero cult.

It is true, of course, that the statues did not stand at the tomb of the tyrant-slayers, where their cult would have been centered,[16] but in the Agora, the civic center of the city, probably at the very spot where the deed took place, and just alongside the Panathenaic Way. They are not a funerary monument, nor a dedication to a god, but a political monument, given a religious coloring by the prior existence of the hero cult.[17] The location was sacred to the Daughters of Leos, who had given *their* lives to save Athens from plague or famine in primitive times, just as Harmodios and Aristogeiton sacrified themselves to save the city from tyranny. Still others who died to save their city were the 192 Athenians who fell at Marathon in 490 B.C., and if indeed the first Tyrannicides were set up just a few years after that battle, a close and deliberate association cannot have escaped anyone who entered the Agora.

On the eve of the battle, according to Herodotos (6.109), Miltiades inspired his colleague Kallimachos, the *Polemarch*, with the thought of liberating Greece and thereby winning a "monument" or "memorial" (*mnemosyne*) to rival that of Harmodios and Aristogeiton. For Kallimachos, who was a fellow demesman of Harmodios and Aristogeiton, invoking their memory was particularly apt. The next day, at Marathon, Kallimachos did indeed emulate the Tyrannicides, for he died a hero's death and Athens was saved.[18] Had the Persians won that day, Hippias, who was with them, would presumably have been reinstated in power, effectively making a mockery of the Tyrant-slayers' deed. When the Antenor statues went up a few years later, it is not hard to see how they might be perceived as a monument to the victory over the Persians, the first victory of the democracy they had "founded" over a foreign enemy. It seems likely that Xerxes knew this too, for all the other free-standing statuary in Athens he merely damaged, but these he removed altogether. The ancient cult image of Athena was beyond his reach, for she had been rescued in the evacuation of the city (Plut., *Themistokles* 10.4), but the Tyrannicides, from whom the Athenians had drawn strength and inspiration to triumph over tremendous odds at Marathon, were the next best thing.[19]

But the Tyrannicides were not the only heroes who inspired the Marathonomachoi, for none other than Theseus appeared to them during the battle, to lead the charge (Plut., *Theseus* 35.5). His cult was, of course, much older, but must have taken on new meaning two decades earlier, with the founding of the democracy. The political reorganization carried out by Kleisthenes, in which all the citizens of Attica would henceforth be joined together in the complex network of demes, *trittyes*, and tribes, recalled Theseus' earlier act of unification, the *synoikismos*.[20] Plutarch (*Theseus* 25.1) would later go so far as to claim that Theseus had instituted a *demokratia* (while somehow still retaining his kingship),

Fig. 2. Theseus, accompanied by Athena, received by Amphitrite at the bottom of the sea. Attic red-figure cup, Louvre G 104. Ca. 500 B.C. Museum photo.

though it seems doubtful that Kleisthenes himself would have invoked the name of Theseus as a role-model for the kind of government he was trying to establish.

Rather, what caused the sudden Theseus revival in the first decades of the democracy, apart from the memory of the *synoikismos*, was a combination of other elements:

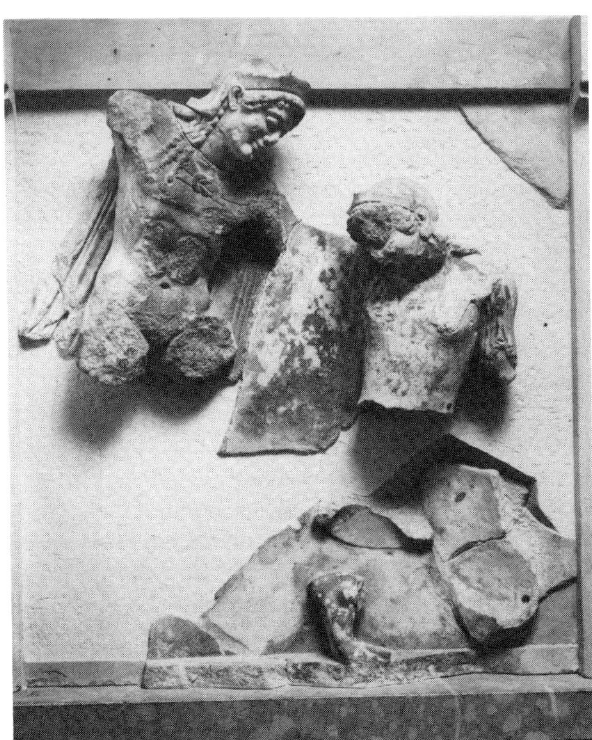

Fig. 3. Theseus fights the Amazon Queen Antiope. Metope from the Athenian Treasury at Delphi. After 490 B.C. Photo DAI Athens.

his role as the special protégé of Athena (Fig. 2); his campaign against an Eastern enemy, the Amazons (Fig. 3); and his embodiment of the finest qualities of the ideal Athenian ephebe: courage, daring, discipline, and grace. All these aspects are particularly emphasized in the burgeoning visual imagery of Theseus in Athenian art of the last decade of the sixth century and the first few decades of the fifth.[21] If Theseus was credited with sharing the Athenian victory in the first Persian invasion, he was no less helpful in the second. His native city of Troizen provided refuge for the Athenian women and children evacuated before Salamis, and his divine father, Poseidon, was instrumental in the naval victories — both Salamis and Mykale — that ended the Persian threat.[22]

But this was only the prelude to events of the 470's and later, when Theseus was pressed into service as both hero and symbol of the Athenian state. Kimon's great coup in 475 B.C., the bringing back to Athens of Theseus' bones, was the turning point.[23] Only one year earlier, the replacement Tyrannicides had been set up in the Agora.[24] The happy coexistence of Theseus and the Tyrannicides as joint heroes of the Athenian democracy — indeed the intermingling of their iconographies which many scholars have observed (Fig. 4)[25] — may reflect the mutual relationship of internal and external affairs under the democracy.

The Tyrant-slayers, as the slogan went, brought Athens *isonomia*, a fair and open society in which every citizen had his share of the democratic pie.[26] Even if the historical Harmodios and Aristogeiton did no such thing, the important point here is that they became the symbols of the new order, one in which (despite ongoing partisan

Fig. 4. Theseus in the pose of Harmodios, fighting Prokrustes. Attic black-figure lekythos, Athens NM 515. Ca. 490–80 B.C. Photo DAI Athens.

struggles) all Athenians genuinely took pride. Whatever the realities of the military situation, it really did look as if this democratic system had enabled Athens twice in the space of a decade to mount a successful defence against massive Persian forces.

After the Persian Wars, however, things started to change rapidly. The Delian League was soon founded, to protect Greek freedom against a future Persian threat, with Athens thrust into a position of leadership. Within a year of the League's founding, the Tyrannicides of Kritios and Nesiotes went up in the Agora, now carrying the added symbolism of panhellenic freedom in the face of Persian tyranny.[27] It is true that already in the time of Peisistratos, Athens claimed a leading role among Ionian Greeks, and even before that Solon had boasted of Athens as *presbytate gaia Iaonias* (the eldest land of Ionia).[28] But this had never before been expressed in terms of military aggression or expansionist foreign policy. Indeed, in the entire fifty years of the tyranny, we do not hear of Athens' involvement in a military campaign anywhere in the Aegean. By contrast, the democracy was no sooner established than Athens became embroiled in a war against Boeotia and Chalkis, her first great success (Hdt. 5.77). Then came the multiple victories over Persia, and by the mid-470's Kimon was commanding the League's forces in a series of surgical strikes on Persian strongholds in the North Aegean (Thuc. 1.98). In about 467 B.C, he would win his greatest, double victory, deep inside Persian territory at the River Eurymedon.[29]

This was the new face of the Athenian democracy: outward-looking, ambitious, self-confident, and its hero was Theseus.[30] The hero who in the sixth century had been a rather colorless, Archaic monster-slayer now acquires, in art and poetry, a whole career, replete with the very qualities that embody the outlook of the young democracy. His far-flung exploits take him overseas, to Crete, to face down an oppressive despot (Fig. 5). On his first journey to Athens, clearing the Saronic Gulf of various brigands and thugs (Fig. 6), he foreshadows Athens' new role as policeman of the Aegean. By asserting his descent from Poseidon (Fig. 2), he proclaims the naval supremacy that Athens now takes for granted as her god-given right.

How, we might ask, did democratic Athens propagate the image of Theseus as her national hero *par excellence*? Not, apparently, in a great sculptural monument, like the Tyrannicides (unless the Kritios Boy represents Theseus, as has recently been suggested, though even he is hardly monumental).[31] One means was wall-paintings by the leading masters of the day, Polygnotos and Mikon, those in the Theseion itself,[32] as well as the great Marathon Painting in the Stoa Poikile, in which Theseus' epiphany was surely prominent.[33] Another means was architectural sculpture, especially the late Kimonian temple above the Agora, whose sculptural decoration features Theseus so conspicuously that it was once called a Theseion, now usually identified as the Temple of Hephaistos (Fig. 7).[34] By contrast, Theseus is curiously absent from the Periclean Parthenon, apart from the scenes on the west metopes and the shield of the Athena Parthenos, in which he leads the defence of the Acropolis against Amazon attack (Fig. 8).[35]

Public artistic monuments are one way of celebrating a hero and keeping his image continually before the *demos*. Another is in the yearly celebration and re-enactment of his deeds at public festivals. For Theseus this meant not only the festival of the hero himself, the Theseia, but also several festivals of the principal gods of the city which, in the fifth century, found their aetiology in the Theseus myth. Thus, for example, the Oschophoria, a fertility rite in honor of Dionysos, featured a procession from the city down to the port of Phaleron that re-enacted the departure of Theseus and the fourteen Athenian youths and maidens for Crete and their triumphal return.[36] The Pyanopsia, a festival of Apollo, similarly commemorated events surrounding Theseus' Cretan adventure, and on Delos, the hub of the Delian League, the festival of Apollo re-created the victory dance (the Geranos) performed by Theseus and the young

Fig. 5. Theseus killing the Minotaur in the presence of Minos and Ariadne. Attic red-figure stamnos, formerly in a Swiss private Collection. Ca. 470–60 B.C. Photo courtesy Archäologisches Institut, Universität Zurich.

Fig. 6. Deeds of Theseus, left to right: Skiron, Prokrustes, Marathonian Bull. Attic red-figure cup, Florence, Museo Archeologico 70800. Ca. 470–60 B.C. Photo Soprintendenza delle Antichità dell' Etruria.

Fig. 7. Theseus fighting the Pallantidai (?). East Frieze of the so-called Theseum. Ca. 430 B.C. Photo DAI Athens.

Fig. 8. Battle of Athenians and Amazons. Roman copy of the shield of Athena Parthenos. Patras, Archaeological Museum. Photo DAI Athens.

Athenians on the journey home.[37] Such festivals provided the occasion for the performance of poetry and song celebrating the hero — both of Bacchylides' beautiful odes on Theseus were evidently composed for festivals, one in Athens, one on Delos[38] — as well as a visual re-enactment of his deeds. I believe that most of this activity originated in the circle of Kimon, chief architect of Athens' expansionist policies.

Yet another festival that may be seen, at least in part, as a celebration of Theseus is the Panathenaia. He was said to have founded the festival after he had accomplished the *synoikismos* (Plut., *Theseus* 24.1), though this is, admittedly, not the only ancient aetiology of the Panathenaia.[39] The festival actually commemorated many events of the distant past associated with Athena: the unification of Attica by her protégé Theseus; the kingship of her step-child Erechtheus; her victory, together with the other Olympians, over the Giants,[40] and her birth from the head of Zeus. Similarly, by the Early Classical period, I believe the Panathenaia had evolved into a kind of recapitulation of the history of democratic Athens. The Tyrannicides' deed, as we noticed, took place at the very festival. After that, the Athenians were surely aware that the expulsion of Hippias in 510 B.C., the victory over Boeotia and Chalkis in 506 B.C., and the Battle of Marathon in 490 B.C. all happened in years when the Greater Panathenaia were celebrated, the latter only a matter of weeks after the festival. Though I do not myself subscribe to any of the arguments that see the Parthenon frieze as representing one specific Panathenaia, whether in the distant or the recent past,[41] I would suggest that by the Periclean period (if not sooner), each Panathenaia was regarded as the birthday party of Athenian democracy, as well as of Athena herself.

Notes

1. See, for example, the various contributions in P.E. Easterling and J.V. Muir (eds.), *Greek Religion and Society* (Cambridge 1985).
2. Thuc. 1.20.2. For the ancient testimony on the Leokoreion see R.E. Wycherley, *Agora* III: *Literary and Epigraphic Testimonia* (Princeton 1957) 108–113. Cf. U. Kron, *Die zehn attischen Phylenheroen*, *AM-BH* 5 (1976) 195–200; H.A. Thompson, "Some Hero Shrines in Early Athens," in W.A.P. Childs (ed.), *Athens Comes of Age* (Princeton 1978) 101–102.
3. Hdt. 5.63.1; 6.123.2. See J. Fontenrose, *The Delphic Oracle* (Berkeley 1978) 309–310.
4. On this procedure see Kron (supra n. 2) 29–31. See also C.C. Mattusch in this volume, pp. 73–81.
5. K. Stähler, "Zur Rekonstruktion und Datierung des Gigantomachiegiebels von der Akropolis" in *Antike und Universalgeschichte*, Festschrift H.E. Stier (Münster 1972) 88–112. See also W.A.P. Childs in this volume, pp. 1–6.
6. For the suggestion that their deed and their death elevated the Tyrannicides to the level of Homeric heroes see J.W. Day, "Epigrams and History: the Athenian Tyrannicides, a Case in Point," in *The Greek Historians*, Festschrift A.E. Raubitschek (Stanford 1985) 29.
7. M.W. Taylor, *The Tyrant Slayers*[2] (Salem, New Hampshire 1991) 6.
8. *Ibid.* (supra n. 7) 13–14. The early date is argued, more strongly, by, among others, C.W. Fornara, "The Cult of Harmodios and Aristogeiton," *Philologus* 114 (1970) 157.
9. A.E. Raubitschek, "Two Monuments Erected after the Victory of Marathon," *AJA* 44 (1940) 58 n. 2.
10. B.D. Meritt, "Greek Inscriptions," *Hesperia* 5 (1936) 355–58.
11. On the tyrant family in Athens after 510 B.C. see M.F. McGregor, "The Pro-Persian Party at Athens from 510 to 480 B.C.," *HSCP* Suppl. 1 (1941) 71–95.
12. Aristotle, *Ath.Pol.* 22.3–4; see J.K. Davies, *Athenian Propertied Families* (Oxford 1971) 451.
13. C. Landwehr, *Die antiken Gipsabgüsse aus Baiae* (Berlin 1985) 27–47.
14. *Ibid.* (supra n. 13) 47. On the statues of the Tyrannicides see also C.C. Mattusch in this volume, pp. 73–81.
15. "Politik und öffentlichkeit im demokratischen Athen: Raüme, Denkmäler, Mythen," paper delivered at the Academy of Athens, November, 1992. Cf. Hölscher, "The City of Athens: Space, Symbol, Structure," in A. Molho, K. Raaflaub, and J. Emler (eds.), *City States in Classical Antiquity and Medieval Italy* (Stuttgart 1991) 371. The political nature of the Tyrannicides monuments is also a primary concern of B. Fehr, *Die Tyrannentöter* (Frankfurt 1984). He is entirely concerned, however, with the replacement statues of Kritias and Nesiotes and takes no position on the dating or appearance of the Antenor group (p. 77).
16. Pausanias 1.29.4 says that the tomb was located on the road to the Academy.
17. See Taylor (supra n. 7) 9, on the special regulations governing the vicinity of the Tyrannicides statues in the Agora.
18. On Kallimachos, and the monument he dedicated on the Acropolis, see A.E. Raubitschek, *Dedications from the Athenian Akropolis* (Cambridge, Mass 1949) no. 13; E.B. Harrison, "The Victory of Kallimachos," *GRBS* 12 (1971) 5–24. For other examples of the close association of Harmodios and Aristogeiton with the heroes of Marathon see Taylor (supra n. 7) 7.
19. On the Near Eastern custom of damaging or stealing statues of the enemy see Landwehr (supra n. 13) 27 n. 112. Cf. Pausanias' comment at 8.46.3 on Xerxes' taste for cult statues.
20. For the fullest statement of this parallel see K. Schefold, "Kleisthenes," *MusHelv* 3 (1946) 59–93.

21. I have discussed some of this imagery in "Theseus: Aspects of the Hero in Archaic Greece," in D. Buitron-Oliver (ed.), *New Perspectives in Early Greek Art* (Washington, D.C. 1991) 123–139. For more general treatments see F. Brommer, *Theseus* (Darmstadt 1982); J. Neils, *The Youthful Deeds of Theseus* (Rome 1987).
22. See A. Shapiro, "Theseus, Athens and Troizen," *AA* (1982), 291–97; J.J. Pollitt, "Pots, Politics, and Personifications," *YaleBull* (Spring 1987) 8–15.
23. Plut. *Theseus* 36.1–2; *Kimon* 8.5–6. See the recent discussion by R. Garland, *Introducing New Gods* (Ithaca 1992) 82–98.
24. Fehr (supra n. 15) 70, remarks, "Die Tyranentöter stehen am Beginn einer noch zu schreibenden Kunstgeschichte der Demokratie."
25. See Taylor (supra n. 7) ch. 4; E. Hudeczek, "Theseus und die Tyrannenmörder," *öJh* 50 (1972–75) 134–149.
26. On *isonomia* and the Tyrannicides *skolia* see M. Ostwald, *Nomos and the Beginnings of Athenian Democracy* (Oxford 1969) 121–130.
27. See the discussion of Fehr (supra n. 15) 53–54, who makes the additional suggestion that the Tyrannicides' victim, Hipparchos, was deliberately not included in the monument in order to make its message more relevant to all Greece (freedom vs. tyranny), and not pertinent only to Athens.
28. On the claims of Solon and Peisistratos see my discussion, in *Art and Cult under the Tyrants in Athens* (Mainz 1989) 48–49.
29. On the dating see most recently E. Badian, "The Peace of Kallias," *JHS* 107 (1987) 3–6.
30. See K. Tausend, "Theseus und der Delisch-attische Seebund," *RhM* 132 (1989) 225–235.
31. J. Hurwit, "The Kritios Boy: Discovery, Reconstruction and Date," *AJA* 93 (1989) 77; J. Neils, "The Quest for Theseus in Classical Sculpture," *Πρακτικά XII διεθνούς συνεδρίου κλασικής αρχαιολογίας* 2 (Athens 1988) 155–57.
32. Pausanias 1.17; J.P. Barron, "New Light on Old Walls," *JHS* 92 (1972) 20–45.
33. E.B. Harrison, "The South Frieze of the Nike Temple and the Marathon Painting in the Painted Stoa," *AJA* 76 (1972) 366–67.
34. H. Knell, *Mythos und Polis* (Darmstadt 1990) 127–139, on the sculptural program of the Hephaisteion.
35. See T. Stephanidou-Tiveriou, "Η *σύνθεση της φειδιακής αμαζονομαχίας και οι ήρωες Θησέας και* Κέκροπας," *Amytos*, Festschrift M. Andronikos (Thessaloniki 1987) 839–857.
36. L. Deubner, *Attische Feste* (Berlin 1932) 142–47. Plut., *Theseus* 23.2–3 gives the aitiology of the festival.
37. Plut., *Theseus* 22.4 (Pyanopsia); 21.2 (Geranos). On the latter see K. Friis Johansen, *Thésée et la danse à Délos* (Copenhagen 1945). I have collected some visual evidence related to these festivals, in "Theseus in Kimonian Athens: the Iconography of Empire," *Mediterranean Historical Review* 7 (1992) 29–49.
38. A.P. Burnett, *The Art of Bacchylides* (Cambridge, Mass. 1985) 15 (Ode 17); 117 (Ode 18).
39. N. Robertson, "The Origin of the Panathenaea," *RhM* 128 (1985) 231–295 and, most recently, J. Neils (ed.), *Goddess and Polis: the Panathenaic Festival in Ancient Athens* (Hanover/ Princeton 1992) 20–22. On the Panathenaia see also J. Neils in this volume, pp. 151–160.
40. G.F. Pinney, "Pallas and Panathenaea," *Ancient Greek and Related Pottery* (Copenhagen 1988) 465–477.
41. For a recent review of interpretations of the frieze see J. Boardman, "The Parthenon Frieze," in E. Berger (ed.), *Parthenon-Kongress Basel* (Basel 1984) 210–215.

Θησεύς καί Παναθήναια

Μιχάλης Α. Τιβέριος

Κατά τις ανασκαφές που διεξήγαγε η Αρχαιολογική Εταιρεία το 1907 και 1908, κάτω από τη διεύθυνση του Π. Καββαδία, ανατολικά του ναού του Ηφαίστου και της Αθηνάς στην αρχαία Αγορά των Αθηνών και σε περιοχή όπου ήδη ο W. Dörpfeld, το 1895 και 1896, είχε πραγματοποιήσει ορισμένες ανασκαφικές εργασίες, βρέθηκε ένα μελανόμορφο όστρακο από κλειστό αγγείο (εικ. 1). Το ότι το όστρακο αυτό εντοπίστηκε στα κατάλοιπα του Γ. Οικονόμου, που φυλάσσονται στην Αθήνα, στην Αρχαιολογική Εταιρεία, κάνει αρκετά πιθανόν να βρέθηκε κατά τις έρευνες του 1908, γιατί αυτές ουσιαστικά διεξήχθηκαν κάτω από την άμεση εποπτεία του τελευταίου.[1]

Εικ 1. Όστρακο παναθηναϊκού αμφορέα. Αθήνα, Αρχαιολογική Εταιρεία.

Ως γνωστόν κατά τις ανασκαφές του Dörpfeld είχε αποκαλυφτεί το μεγαλύτερο μέρος του ναού του Απόλλωνος Πατρώου και του ναόσχημου χώρου του ελληνιστικού Μητρώου, την αποκάλυψη του οποίου συνέχισε η Αρχαιολογική Εταιρεία. Η θέση ανεύρεσης του οστράκου δεν μπορεί να προσδιοριστεί με ακρίβεια. Σημειώνω πάντως ότι κατά τις έρευνες του 1908 ανασκάφηκε μέχρι του φυσικού βράχου ο χώρος του Ηφαιστείου, προκειμένου να μελετηθεί ο τρόπος κατασκευής του κρηπιδώματός του, όλος ο χώρος που βρίσκεται ανατολικά και βόρεια του ναού,[2] όπως και η περιοχή του Μητρώου. Επομένως, καλώς εχόντων των πραγμάτων, σε μια από τις παραπάνω περιοχές, πρέπει να βρέθηκε το όστρακό μας, που έχει μέγ. σωζ. διαστάσεις 0,075 μ. × 0,065 μ. και εικονίζει το κάτω μέρος ενδύματος, πιθανόν πέπλου, μιας μορφής. Το κυματοειδές κόσμημα που διακρίνεται εδώ, χωρίς αμφιβολία, πρέπει να κοσμούσε το κάτω μέρος του, ενώ οι διακρινόμενες χαρακτές, "διαγώνιες" και συγκλίνουσες προς τα πάνω πτυχές, μας βεβαιώνουν ότι το ένδυμα ήταν ζωσμένο στη μέση της μορφής που το έφερε.

Ασφαλώς το όστρακο δεν θα αποσπούσε την προσοχή μας, αν δεν συνέβαινε το απεικονιζόμενο σ' αυτό ένδυμα να διακοσμείται με μορφές και μάλιστα μ' έναν τρόπο, που θα τον χαρακτήριζα μάλλον απρόσμενο, αφού αυτές δεν καταλαμβάνουν τον χώρο μιας κάθετης ή οριζόντιας ταινίας, όπως συμβαίνει συνήθως σε ανάλογες παραστάσεις (εικ. 4,6,7),[3] αλλά φαίνεται ότι ήταν "διασκορπισμένες" ή σ' όλη την επιφάνεια του πέπλου ή μόνο στο τμήμα του εκείνο, από το ύψος του αποπτύγματος και κάτω.[4] Χωρίς ιδιαίτερες δυσκολίες μπορούμε να υποστηρίξουμε ότι ο πέπλος του οστράκου μας διακοσμείτο με μια παράσταση Αμαζονομαχίας. Αυτό μας το επιβεβαιώνει η έφιππη γυναικεία μορφή που διακρίνεται, πάνω δεξιά, να κινείται προς τ' αριστερά, επιτιθέμενη με δόρυ σ' έναν Έλληνα. Ο τελευταίος, ενώ κατευθύνεται και αυτός προς τ' αριστερά, στρέφεται προς τα πίσω, στην προσπάθειά του να αποκρούσει, με τη στρογγυλή του ασπίδα, το δόρυ της αντιπάλου του. Δόρυ κρατά και ο ίδιος με το δεξί χέρι, ενώ από την ασπίδα του, που κρατά με το κάπως εκτεταμένο αριστερό χέρι του και αποδίδεται από το εσωτερικό της, διακρίνεται καθαρά τόσο το όχανο όσο και η αντιλαβή της. Πολύ βοηθητική για την αναγνώριση της παράστασης ως Αμαζονομαχίας είναι και η πέλτη που κρατά με το εκτεταμένο αριστερό της χέρι μία, προφανώς Αμαζόνα, που γονατισμένη και βρισκόμενη σε αμυντική θέση, στο κάτω μέρος της παράστασης, προσπαθεί να αποφύγει το κτύπημα από το δόρυ, που ετοιμάζεται να της καταφέρει ο αντίπαλός της, από τον οποίο ελάχιστα ίχνη διασώζονται, όπως το δεξί του χέρι και μέρος πιθανότατα του κράνους του. Από μια πέμπτη έφιππη μορφή, προφανώς Αμαζόνα, στο πάνω μέρος του οστράκου, σώζονται μόνο μικρά τμήματα από το άλογό της, που είχε κατεύθυνση προς

Εικ 2. Σχεδιαστική απόδοση από την παράσταση της αρυβαλλοειδούς ληκύθου του Ζ. της Ερέτριας στη Βοστώνη, Museum of Fine Arts αρ. 95.48.(Φωτ. από LIMC *I 2, σ. 471, εικ. 240).*

τα δεξιά, όπως μας δείχνει το ισχυρά κεκαμένο πίσω σκέλος του ζώου. Η λεπτομέρεια αυτή μας επιτρέπει να φανταστούμε το άλογο αυτό κάπως ανορθωμένο, στηριζόμενο στα πίσω πόδια του. Οι μορφές της Αμαζονομαχίας αυτής έχουν αποδοθεί με ελαφριές χαράξεις και με τη χρησιμοποίηση δύο επίθετων χρωμάτων, του λευκού και του κροκωτού.[5]

Οι σωζόμενες λεπτομέρειες στο όστρακο, δεν επιτρέπουν μια στενή χρονολόγησή του. Ωστόσο τα μοτίβα των μορφών της Αμαζονομαχίας του, μας οδηγούν σε μια χρονολόγηση στην κλασική εποχή, αφού συγκρίνονται καλά με ανάλογα μοτίβα, που συναντούμε σε Αμαζονομαχίες, κυρίως του τρίτου τέταρτου του 5ου αι. π.Χ. (εικ. 3).[6] ῎Αλλωστε σε αττικές Αμαζονομαχίες, "εὐίππους ᾿Αμαζόνας" συναντούμε κυρίως μετά τα μέσα του αιώνα αυτού, πιθανόν κάτω από την επίδραση των δημιουργιών μεγάλων ζωγράφων της εποχής και κυρίως του Μίκωνα.[7] ῞Ενα όμως αττικό μελανόμορφο όστρακο, που χρονολογείται στο δεύτερο μισό του 5ου αι. π.Χ., μόνον από έναν παναθηναϊκό αμφορέα είναι δυνατόν να προέρχεται. Και πράγματι με μια τέτοια αναγνώριση συμφωνεί τόσο το πάχος του οστράκου μας (περίπου 0,0047 μ.) όσο και το υποτιθέμενο ύψος της εικονιζόμενης μορφής, όταν νοηθεί συμπληρωμένη. Γιατί δεν πρέπει να έχουμε καμιά αμφιβολία ότι εδώ μας έχει σωθεί το κάτω μέρος από τον πέπλο μιας Αθηνάς στραμμένης προς τ' αριστερά, που διακοσμούσε την κύρια όψη ενός παναθηναϊκού αμφορέα. Σημειώνουμε ότι όσους παναθηναϊκούς αμφορείς γνωρίζουμε, στους οποίους συμβαίνει το ένδυμα της εικονιζόμενης Αθηνάς να είναι διακοσμημένο με εικονιστικές παραστάσεις, χρονολογούνται όλοι τους προς τα τέλη του 5ου αι. π.Χ.[8] ῎Αλλωστε στις τελευταίες δεκαετίες του 5ου αι. π.Χ. βλέπουμε συχνά σε αττικά ερυθρόμορφα αγγεία, να διακοσμούνται τα ενδύματα των μορφών τους με εικονιστικές παραστάσεις.[9] Στο δεύτερο μισό του 5ου αι. π.Χ., γύρω στα 430 π.Χ., πιστεύω ότι θα πρέπει να χρονολογείται λοιπόν και το όστρακό μας, όπως μας βεβαιώνουν συγκρίσεις των μορφών της Αμαζονομαχίας του με ανάλογες πάνω σε αττικά αγγεία της εποχής αυτής,[10] ενώ και το κυματοειδές μοτίβο, που διακοσμεί την παρυφή του πέπλου της Αθηνάς σ' αυτό, το συναντούμε σε παρόμοια θέση και σ' άλλα σύγχρονα ή περίπου σύγχρονα αττικά αγγεία, όπως π.χ. σ'έναν καλυκωτό κρατήρα στη Μπολώνια του Ζ. του Κάδμου.[11]

Είναι γνωστόν ότι η απεικόνιση της αττικής Αμαζονομαχίας, δηλαδή αυτής με πρωταγωνιστή τον

Εικ 3. Σχεδιαστικό ανάπτυγμα της παράστασης της αρυβαλλοειδούς ληκύθου του Αίσωνα στη Νεάπολη, Museo Archeologico Nazionale αρ. RC 239. (Φωτ.από E.Löwy, Polygnot *[Βιέννη 1929] πίν.35).*

Θησέα, γνωρίζει στην Αθήνα ιδιαίτερη έξαρση μετά τα Περσικά. Όπως ήδη έχει επισημανθεί από την έρευνα, η συχνή απεικόνισή της οφείλεται στο ότι οι δημιουργοί της μ' αυτήν αποθανατίζουν ή καλύτερα διαιωνίζουν τις λαμπρές νίκες των Ελλήνων εναντίον των Περσών, στις οποίες οι ίδιοι οι Αθηναίοι είχαν παίξει έναν ιδιαίτερα σημαντικό ρόλο.[12] Ωστόσο η συχνή παρουσία σκηνών Αμαζονομαχίας για μεγάλο χρονικό διάστημα και μετά τα Περσικά, μέχρι τις τελευταίες δεκαετίες του 5ου αι. π.Χ. και στον 4ο αι., μια παρουσία που πρέπει να σημειωθεί ότι γνωρίζει ιδιαίτερη έξαρση στο τρίτο τέταρτο του 5ου αι. π.Χ., μας κάνουν να υποψιαζόμαστε μήπως υπάρχουν και άλλοι λόγοι, που έκαναν το θέμα της αττικής Αμαζονομαχίας ιδιαίτερα αγαπητό τα χρόνια αυτά. Και ασφαλώς μέσα στο ίδιο πνεύμα εντάσσονται και οι περίφημες Αμαζονομαχίες του 5ου αι. π.Χ., που διακοσμούσαν δημόσια κτήρια της Αθήνας και γενικότερα της Αττικής, έργα μεγάλων καλλιτεχνών της εποχής.[13]

Είναι γνωστό ότι στην αττική Αμαζονομαχία βασικός πρωταγωνιστής είναι ο Θησέας. Από την άλλη μεριά η φιλολογική έρευνα έχει καταλήξει στο συμπέρασμα, με βάση τις σχετικές σωζόμενες πηγές, ότι πιθανόν στον 5ο αι. π.Χ., πρέπει να αναχθεί μια προσπάθεια των Αθηναίων να αποδώσουν την ίδρυση των Παναθηναίων, της μεγαλύτερης γιορτής τους, στον ίδιο τον Θησέα, τον εθνικό τους ήρωα, που, ως έναν δεύτερον Ηρακλή (Πλούτ. *Θησεὺς* 29.3), επεδίωκαν να τον κάνουν γνωστό και εκτός των συνόρων τους, ενώ μέχρι τότε ως μυθικός ιδρυτής της παναθηναϊκής γιορτής εφέρετο ο Εριχθόνιος.[14] Χαρακτηριστικές γι' αυτό το θέμα είναι ορισμένες γραπτές πηγές που τις μνημονεύω αμέσως παρακάτω. "Παναθήναια ἀθήνησιν ἑορτὴ ἐπὶ τῶι ὑπὸ Θησέως γενομένωι συνοικισμῶι. Πρῶτον ὑπὸ Ἐριχθονίου τοῦ Ἡφαίστου καὶ τῆς Ἀθηνᾶς, ὕστερον δὲ ὑπὸ Θησέως συναγαγόντες τοὺς δήμους εἰς ἄστυ. Ἄγεται δὲ ὁ ἀγὼν διὰ πέντε ἐτῶν" μας πληροφορεί ανάμεσα σε άλλους και ο σχολιαστής του Πλάτωνα, ενώ ο Παυσανίας μας λέει: "οὐκέτι δὲ τὰ παρ' Ἀθηναίοις Παναθήναια τεθῆναι, πρότερα ἀποφαίνομαι. τούτωι γὰρ τῶι ἀγῶνι Ἀθήναια ὄνομα ἦν, Παναθήναια δὲ κληθῆναί φασιν ἐπὶ Θησέως, ὅτι ὑπὸ Ἀθηναίων ἐτέθη συνειλεγμένων ἐς μίαν ἁπάντων πόλιν." Τέλος από τον Πλούταρχο έχουμε την πληροφορία ότι ο Θησέας "ἓν δὲ ποιήσας ἅπασι κοινὸν ἐνταῦθα πρυτανεῖον καὶ βουλευτήριον ὅπου νῦν ἵδρυται τὸ ἄστυ, τὴν τε πόλιν Ἀθήνας προσηγόρευσε καὶ Παναθήναια θυσίαν ἐποίησε κοινήν."[15] Αλλά εκτός από τις άμεσες αυτές πληροφορίες υπάρχουν και άλλες έμμεσες, που θα μπορούσαν να συσχετίσουν τον Θησέα με τα Παναθήναια. Πολύ χαρακτηριστική για το θέμα που μας απασχολεί, είναι η πληροφορία των σχολιαστών του Αίλειου Αριστείδη: "ὁ τῶν Παναθηναίων ἀγών] τῶν μικρῶν. ταῦτα γὰρ ἀρχαιότερα, ἐπὶ Ἐριχθονίου τοῦ Ἀμφικτύονος γενόμενα ἐπὶ τῶι φόνωι Ἀστερίου τοῦ Γίγαντος".[16] Είναι πολύ πιθανόν ότι η ιστορία η σχετική με το φόνο του Γίγαντα Αστερίου, κατόρθωμα που έγινε η αιτία, σύμφωνα με την παραπάνω γραπτή μαρτυρία, να ιδρυθούν τα Παναθήναια, να μην είναι άλλη από την πολύ γνωστή ιστορία τη σχετική με την εξόντωση του Μινώταυρου από τον Θησέα. Ο Διόδωρος (4.60.2) γνωρίζει έναν Αστέριο γιο του Μίνωα και της Πασιφάης, ενώ ο Απολλόδωρος (3.1.4), για τον οποίο γνωρίζουμε ότι συχνά οι πηγές του είναι έγκυρες και παλιές, ρητά μας πληροφορεί ότι η Πασιφάη "Ἀστέριον ἐγέννησε τὸν κληθέντα Μινώταυρον."

Αλλά υπάρχουν και άλλοι λόγοι, που θα μπορούσαν να δικαιολογήσουν τις προσπάθειες του αθηναϊκού κράτους να συσχετίσει τον Θησέα με τα Παναθήναια. Είναι γνωστό ότι ο Ιπποκλείδης "ἐφ' οὗ ἄρχοντος <ἐν Ἀθήναις> Παναθήναια (το 566/5 π.Χ.) ἐτέθη" ήταν, σύμφωνα με τους Φερεκύδη και Ελλάνικο, Φιλαΐδης.[17] Γενάρχης των Φιλαϊδών, όπως μας πληροφορούν αρχαίες γραπτές μαρτυρίες, ήταν ο Φίλαιος (ή Φιλαίας ή Φιλαίος), που μαζί με τον Ευρυσάκη, ήταν γιοί του Αίαντα. Αλλες πηγές θεωρούν τον Φίλαιο γιο του Ευρυσάκη και επομένως εγγονό του Αίαντα.[18] Είτε ήταν ο Φίλαιος εγγονός είτε γιος του Αίαντα, γεγονός είναι ότι η Ερίβοια, η μητέρα του Αίαντα, φέρεται ως μία από τις νόμιμες γυναίκες του Θησέα.[19] Υπενθυμίζω ότι το Ευρυσάκειο, το αττικό ιερό προς τιμή των Αιαντιδών, βρισκόταν στον Αγοραίο Κολωνό, πιθανότατα Ν. και ΝΔ. του Ηφαιστείου,[20] κοντά δηλαδή στην περιοχή όπου, κατά πάσα πιθανότητα, έχει βρεθεί και το όστρακο των καταλοίπων του Οικονόμου. Είχαν λοιπόν λόγο οι Φιλαΐδες, οι οποίοι με τον Κίμωνα ηγέτη, εδέσποσαν στην πολιτική ζωή της Αθήνας σχεδόν αμέσως μετά τα Περσικά, να θέλουν να αποδώσουν την ίδρυση της πιό παλιάς και πιό μεγάλης γιορτής της Αθήνας, στον Θησέα. Αποδίδοντας την ίδρυση των Παναθηναίων στον Θησέα, με τον οποίο, όπως είδαμε, τόσο στενά σχετιζόταν ο γενάρχης τους, εύλογο είναι να υποθέσουμε ότι μ' αυτό επεδίωκαν να δώσουν στο γένος τους πρόσθετο κύρος και αίγλη. Και ασφαλώς γόητρο τους προσέδωσε και η ενέργεια του Κίμωνα να μεταφέρει το 475 π.Χ. από τη Σκύρο τα υποτιθέμενα οστά του Θησέα στην Αθήνα (εφαρμογή του "πάτριου νόμου") με μεγαλόπρεπη τελετή, τα οποία και εναπόθεσε στο ιερό του, στο λεγόμενο Θησείο, το οποίο είτε τότε το έκτισε για πρώτη φορά είτε αυτό προϋπήρχε και απλώς ο Κίμων το εξωράισε και το ελάμπρυνε.[21] Άλλωστε, όπως ήδη έχει παρατηρηθεί, στην Αθήνα των ιστορικών χρόνων, δεν υπήρχε κανένα αττικό γένος που να ανήγε απευθείας την καταγωγή του στον Θησέα και στους δύο γιους του, στους Δημοφώντα και Ακάμαντα.[22] Είναι μάλιστα πολύ πιθανόν ότι τη σχέση τους με τον Θησέα οι Φιλαΐδες θα την προπαγάνδιζαν τουλάχιστον από τον 6ο αι. π.Χ., αφού δεν μπορεί να είναι τυχαίο το γεγονός ότι στο γνωστό αγγείο François, στην παράσταση όπου εικονίζονται οι νέοι και οι νέες της Αθήνας που στάλθηκαν στην Κρήτη, μαζί με τον Θησέα, ως "βορά" του Μινώταυρου, πίσω ακριβώς από τον γιο της Αίθρας, που φορά επίσημη ενδυμασία, είναι η σύζυγός του Ερίβοια (ΕΠΙΒΟΙΑ), η μάνα του Αίαντα, ενώ η αμέσως επόμενη νέα είναι η Λυσιδίκη, η σύζυγος πιθανόν του τελευταίου και μητέρα του Φιλαίου, του γενάρχη τους.[23] Το ότι σ' ένα τόσο σημαντικό για το Θησέα κατώρθωμα φέρονται να πήραν μέρος πρόσωπα πολύ στενά συνδεδεμένα με τους Φιλαΐδες, τα οποία μάλιστα εικονίζονται και πίσω ακριβώς από τον παναττικό ήρωα, δύσκολα μπορεί να θεωρηθεί απλώς ως σύμπτωση. Και κατά τον 6ο αι. π.χ. οι Φιλαΐδες πιθανότατα είχαν και άλλους λόγους που θα ήθελαν να προβάλλουν τις σχέσεις τους με τους Θησείδες, τότε που ο Φιλαΐδης Μιλτιάδης, πιθανόν λίγο πριν από τα μέσα του 6ου αι. π.Χ., ήλθε και εγκαταστάθηκε στην περιοχή της Θράκης.[24] Προσπαθώντας να βρουν ερείσματα για να νομιμοποιήσουν το εγχείρημά τους αυτό δεν αποκλείεται να επρόβαλαν και το επιχείρημα ότι με τα μέρη αυτά είχαν από παλιά σχέσεις, αφού ο θησείδης Ακάμας (και κατ' άλλους ο Δημοφών), αμέσως μετά τα Τρωικά, είχε έλθει και εγκατασταθεί εδώ. Απλώς σημειώνω ότι ο βασιλιάς της Βισαλτίας, που φιλοξένησε τον Ακάμαντα, ονομαζόταν Φυλέας και η κόρη του Φυλλίδα.[25]

Αλλά και οι δημοκρατικοί Αλκμεωνίδες φαίνεται ότι είχαν λόγους να προβάλλουν τον Θησέα. Ο Θησέας ήταν αυτός που πρώτος στράφηκε στις λαϊκές μάζες, "συγκέντρωσε τους κατοίκους της Αττικής σ' έναν τόπο και τους οργάνωσε, σαν ένα ενιαίο λαό, σε μια πόλη," "καθιέρωσε ένα αβασίλευτο πολίτευμα και δημοκρατία, που είχε αυτόν τον ίδιο για αρχηγό, στον πόλεμο μόνο, και φύλακα των νόμων της, ενώ ως προς τα άλλα έδωσε σε όλους ισομοιρία." Ακόμη ίδρυσε "ένα κοινό για όλους Πρυτανείο και Βουλευτήριο" στην Αθήνα και επομένως δικαιωματικά επροβάλλετο ως ο μυθικός ιδρυτής του δημοκρατικού πολιτεύματος, που αυτοί εγκαθίδρυσαν στην Αθήνα, με άλλα λόγια ως το μυθικό πρότυπο του Κλεισθένη.[26] Αναφέρω εδώ και τη γνώμη ορισμένων μελετητών που πιστεύουν ότι το επικό ποίημα "Θησηΐς" πρέπει να δημιουργήθηκε στις τελευταίες δεκαετίες του 6ου αι. π.Χ. κατά προτροπή των Αλκμεωνιδών ή έστω με την υποστήριξή τους.[27] Έχοντας όλα αυτά κατά νου, καταλαβαίνουμε ίσως καλύτερα ορισμένα έργα, όπως π.χ. τη ζωγραφική σύνθεση του Ευφράνορα, που διακοσμούσε τη Στοά του Δία στην αθηναϊκή Αγορά και στην οποία είχαμε τον Θησέα με τις προσωποποιήσεις της Δημοκρατίας και του Δήμου. Χαρακτηριστικά είναι τα λόγια του Παυσανία, που αναφέρονται σ' αυτήν ακριβώς τη σύνθεση. "Η ζωγραφιά αυτή έχει το νόημα πως ο Θησέας έφερε στους Αθηναίους την πολιτική ισότητα. Στους πολλούς είναι διαδεδομένη και μια άλλη ερμηνεία, πως ο Θησέας είχε παραδώσει την εξουσία στο Δήμο και πως από τότε οι Αθηναίοι δημοκρατούνταν..."[28] Και δεν πρέπει βέβαια να ξεχνούμε και τους μεγάλους τραγικούς του 5ου αι. π.Χ., που ρητά, μαζί και με άλλους συγγραφείς, μνημονεύουν τον Θησέα ως τον πραγματικό ιδρυτή της αθηναϊκής Δημοκρατίας.[29]

Αλλά και οι οπαδοί της τυραννίας δεν φαίνεται να ήσαν αντίθετοι σε μια προβολή του Θησέα και στην αναγωγή του σε εθνικό ήρωα της Αθήνας, κάτι που, σύμφωνα και με τον A. Shapiro, επεδίωκαν οι Αθηναίοι ήδη από την εποχή του Σόλωνα.[30] Ορισμένες

Εικ 4. Σχεδιαστική απόδοση της κύριας παράστασης του παναθηναϊκού αμφορέα στο Λονδίνο, Βρετανικό Μουσείο αρ. 1866.4-15.249 (Β 606).(Φωτ. από E. Pfuhl, Malerei und Zeichnung der Griechen *[Ρώμη 1969] πίν.83, εικ. 306).*

Εικ 5. Παναθηναϊκός αμφορέας στο Αρχαιολογικό Μουσείο του Πολυγύρου από την Όλυνθο αρ. 8.29 (R 100).

παραδόσεις σχετικές με τη ζωή του Θησέα βοηθούσαν τον Πεισίστρατο στην επιτυχία της πολιτικής του, που απέβλεπε στο να ηγηθεί η Αθήνα του ιωνικού κόσμου,[31] πολιτική που συνεχίστηκε βέβαια και αργότερα. Είναι γνωστή η παρουσία του Θησέα στην ιωνική Νάξο, όπου και εγκατέλειψε την Αριάδνη,[32] ενώ οι δεσμοί του με τη Δήλο, το θρησκευτικό κέντρο των Ιώνων, ήταν ιδιαίτερα στενοί. Γυρίζοντας από την Κρήτη, έχοντας εξοντώσει τον Μινώταυρο, προσέγγισε στη Δήλο, θυσίασε στον Απόλλωνα, αφιέρωσε ένα άγαλμα στην Αφροδίτη και χόρεψε μαζί με τους αθηναίους νέους το γέρανο, γύρω από τον Κερατώνα βωμό.[33] Πολύ χαρακτηριστικό είναι και το εξής γεγονός. Στην περίφημη στήλη, που είχε στήσει στον Ισθμό της Κορίνθου, στη μια πλευρά της έγραψε "τάδ' οὐχὶ Πελοπόννησος, ἀλλ' Ἰωνία," ενώ στην άλλη "τάδ' ἐστὶ Πελοπόννησος, οὐκ Ἰωνία."[34] Τέλος, στο ίδιο κλίμα εντάσσονται και ορισμένες παραδόσεις, που ήθελαν διαφόρους Θησείδες, όπως π.χ. τον Οινοπίωνα ή τον Ίωξο, να είναι οικιστές της Χίου ή της Καρίας.[35] Έτσι καταλαβαίνουμε καλύτερα και την πληροφορία του Πλουτάρχου (*Θησεὺς* 20.2), σύμφωνα με την οποία ο στίχος 631 της ραψωδίας λ της *Οδύσσειας*, όπου ο Θησέας με τον Πειρίθου αναφέρονται ως "ἔνδοξα τῶν θεῶν τέκνα," είναι προσθήκη του Πεισίστρατου.

Επομένως όλες οι πολιτικές παρατάξεις στην Αθήνα του 6ου και 5ου αι. π.Χ. συμφωνούσαν (ή τουλάχιστον δεν αντιτίθενταν) στη διάδοση και επικράτηση μιας παράδοσης, σύμφωνα με την οποία σημαντικοί πολιτικοί και θρησκευτικοί θεσμοί της πόλης τους, όπως και σπουδαία ανδραγαθήματά της, σχετίζονταν με τον Θησέα.[36] Έχοντας αυτό υπόψη θεωρώ ως πιθανόν ότι και με την Αμαζονομαχία, που διακοσμεί τον πέπλο της Αθηνάς στο όστρακο του παναθηναϊκού αμφορέα μας, προβάλλεται ο ίδιος ο Θησέας, ο πρωταγωνιστής της, ενώ συγχρόνως δεν αποκλείεται, με τον τρόπο αυτόν, να υποδηλώνεται και η σχέση του τελευταίου με την καθιέρωση των Παναθηναίων, για την οποία ήδη έχω μιλήσει παραπάνω.

Με τα Παναθήναια είναι γνωστόν ότι δεν σχετίζεται η Αμαζονομαχία αλλά μία άλλη μάχη. Αυτή ανάμεσα στους θεούς του Ολύμπου και στους Γίγαντες. Ο παναθηναϊκός πέπλος που πρόσφεραν οι Αθηναίοι κάθε χρόνο και με ιδιαίτερη λαμπρότητα κάθε τέσσερα χρόνια στην πολιούχο θεά τους, ήταν διακοσμημένος με τη μάχη αυτή.[37] Επομένως μία απεικόνιση Γιγαντομαχίας, πάνω σε πέπλο Αθηνάς παναθηναϊκού αμφορέα, θα ήταν κάτι μάλλον αναμενόμενο και συνάμα εύκολα θα εύρισκε την εξήγησή του. Αν και τα γνωστά σε μένα παναθηναϊκά αγγεία, που ο πέπλος της Αθηνάς διακοσμείται με εικονιστικές παραστάσεις είναι πολύ λίγα, μόλις τρία,[38] στο ένα απ' αυτά, έχουμε πράγματι μία απεικόνιση Γιγαντομαχίας (εικ.5–7). Πρόκειται γιά έναν παναθηναϊκό αμφορέα από την Όλυνθο, σήμερα στο Αρχαιολογικό Μουσείο του Πολυγύρου στη Χαλκιδική, ο οποίος, από τον Π.Βαλαβάνη, χρονολογείται ανάμεσα στο 401 και 399 π.Χ.[39] Αν και το αγγείο αυτό είναι από παλιά γνωστό, εντούτοις είχαν σχεδόν μείνει απαρατήρητες οι ανθρώπινες μορφές που διακοσμούν μία ζώνη, στο κάτω μέρος του πέπλου της θεάς. Η ξαναεπισήμανση αυτής τη ζωφόρου από τον Π. Βαλαβάνη, με οδήγησε να εξετάσω προσεκτικά την παράσταση αυτή. Καθώς είχε αποδοθεί με λευκό επίθετο χρώμα, το οποίο έχει παντελώς απολεπιστεί αφήνοντας μόνον πολύ αχνά ίχνη, είναι σήμερα εξαιρετικά δυσδιάκριτη. Με κατάλληλο φωτισμό μπόρεσα να βεβαιωθώ ότι στον πέπλο της θεάς, στο παναθηναϊκό αυτό έπαθλο, είχαμε μια απεικόνιση Γιγαντομαχίας, την οποία και επιχείρησα να αποδώσω σχεδιαστικά με τη βοήθεια της μεταπτυχιακής φοιτήτριας Τριανταφυλλιάς Μήττα (εικ. 7). Στα άκρα της ζωφόρου είχαμε δύο μορφές Γιγάντων, που κατευθύνονταν προς τ' αριστερά

Εικ 6. Λεπτομέρεια παναθηναϊκού αμφορέα στο Αρχαιολογικό Μουσείο του Πολυγύρου από την Όλυνθο αρ. 8.29 (R 100).

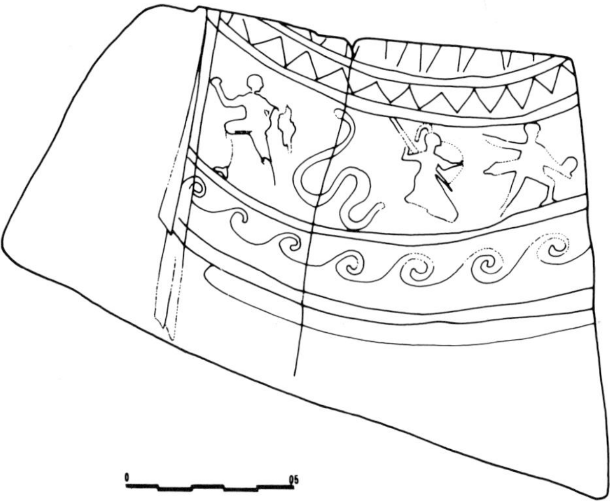

Εικ 7. Σχεδιαστική απόδοση λεπτομέρειας από τη διακόσμηση παναθηναϊκού αμφορέα στο Αρχαιολογικό Μουσείο του Πολυγύρου από την Όλυνθο αρ. 8.29 (R 100).

και δεξιά αντίστοιχα, καταδιωκόμενοι ή καλύτερα προσπαθώντας να αποφύγουν τα κτυπήματα των αντιπάλων τους, κρατώντας στα χέρια πιθανότατα λίθους. Ο Γίγαντας δεξιά έχει για αντίπαλο την ίδια τη θεά Αθηνά, που μάχεται κρατώντας στο δεξί της χέρι δόρυ, στο αριστερό ασπίδα, ενώ φέρει στο κεφάλι της κράνος. Ο αντίπαλος του αριστερού Γίγαντα είναι ένα πελώριο φίδι, χωρίς αμφιβολία "ὁ τῆς Πολιάδος φύλαξ δράκων" ή ο "μέγας ὄφις τῆς ἀκροπόλιος" των αρχαίων πηγών.[40] Το πόσο στενά ήταν συνδεδεμένος ο όφις αυτός με την Αθηνά, μας το επιβεβαιώνει ο ίδιος ο Ηρόδοτος (8. 41) με πολύ παραστατικό τρόπο. ῞Οταν οι Πέρσες πλησίαζαν στην Αθήνα, η τροφή, που κάθε μήνα προόριζαν οι Αθηναίοι για τον πελώριο οικουρό όφι της Ακρόπολης, έμεινε ανέπαφη και αυτό θεωρήθηκε από τους ίδιους τους Αθηναίους ως ένδειξη ότι η θεά εγκατέλειψε την πόλη τους.

Στην αττική εικονογραφία, η παλιότερη βεβαιωμένη αττική απεικόνιση της θεάς με τον όφι που γνωρίζω, διακοσμεί τον ώμο μιας μελανόμορφης υδρίας του Ζ. του Νικόξενου, που κάποτε βρισκόταν στο εμπόριο αρχαιοτήτων της Ρώμης και σήμερα θεωρείται χαμένη.[41] Σε παραστάσεις Γιγαντομαχίας, όπως είναι γνωστό, συναντούμε την Αθηνά να μάχεται έχοντας δίπλα της για συμπαραστάτη και βοηθό τον οικουρό της όφι, όπως π.χ. σε αγγεία του εργαστηρίου του Ζ. των Νιοβιδών (βλ. π.χ. εικ. 8).[42] Στον πέπλο λοιπόν της Αθηνάς του παναθηναϊκού αμφορέα από την ῞Ολυνθο, έχει απεικονιστεί το κύριο επεισόδιο μιας αθηναϊκής, θα τη χαρακτήριζα, Γιγαντομαχίας, μιας Γιγαντομαχίας πιθανότατα σχετικής με τα Παναθήναια, όπου κύριος πρωταγωνιστής είναι η πολιούχος θεά της πόλης, η Αθηνά. Και άλλες φορές πάνω σε αττικά αγγεία, που διακοσμούνται με παράσταση Γιγαντομαχίας, έχουμε την Αθηνά να κατέχει το κεντρικό σημείο της σύνθεσης, με τον Δία να βρίσκεται στην άκρη (εικ.8).[43] Τελειώνοντας με τον παναθηναϊκό αμφορέα από την ῞Ολυνθο, πιστεύω ότι και αυτός ενισχύει την άποψη, σύμφωνα με την οποία η πάνοπλη Αθηνά των παναθηναϊκών αμφορέων δεν είναι άλλη από την Αθηνά της Γιγαντομαχίας.[44] Αν θελήσουμε δε να ονοματίσουμε τους δύο Γίγαντες στο παναθηναϊκό αγγείο της Ολύνθου, θα πρότεινα για τον δεξιό το όνομα του Εγκέλαδου, ενώ για τον αριστερό αυτό του Πάλλαντα, του Ευβοίου, του Λαέρτα ή του Περιχθονίου. Πρόκειται για Γίγαντες που, από πηγές ή σχετικές παραστάσεις, αναφέρονται ως αντίπαλοι της Αθηνάς.[45] Και κάτι άλλο ακόμη. Ενώ οι μέχρι σήμερα σωζόμενες σχετικές ενδείξεις από την εικονογραφία, ενίσχυαν την υπόθεση ότι η Γιγαντομαχία στον παναθηναϊκό πέπλο πρέπει να βρισκόταν μέσα σε μία, ή έστω περισσότερες οριζόντιες, πιθανότατα, ζώνες (εικ. 4-7), όπως δηλαδή βλέπουμε και στον παναθηναϊκό αμφορέα της Ολύνθου και σε πολλά άλλα αττικά αγγεία,[46] το όστρακο των καταλοίπων Οικονόμου (εικ.1) μας δείχνει και μια άλλη δυνατότητα, που τουλάχιστον δεν μπορούμε να αγνοήσουμε παντελώς: δηλαδή οι μορφές της Γιγαντομαχίας να κάλυπταν ολόκληρη την προσφερόμενη έκταση του πέπλου ή τουλάχιστον ένα μεγάλο τμήμα του, τοποθετημένες ελεύθερα και σε διαφορετικά ύψη, χωρίς να είναι ενταγμένες σε μία ή περισσότερες μικρότερες ζώνες.[47]

Είναι γνωστόν ότι οι απεικονίσεις της Γιγαντομαχίας συμβολίζουν τη νίκη των θεών του Ολύμπου εναντίον της αταξίας, της ασέβειας, της αλλαζονείας, της βαρβαρότητας και του παραλογισμού. Ειδικότερα η νίκη της Αθηνάς εναντίον του Εγκέλαδου, το κύριο επεισόδιο της παναθηναϊκής Γιγαντομαχίας, υπενθύμιζε στους Αθηναίους τη συμβολή της πόλης τους στην επικράτηση του ορθού λόγου, της λογικής και εν γένει του πολιτισμού.[48] Και χωρίς αμφιβολία συμβολισμό υποκρύπτουν και οι παραστάσεις της Αμαζονομαχίας. ῞Οπως είπαμε και παραπάνω, στην περίοδο των πρώτων δεκαετιών του 5ου αι. π.Χ. και μέχρι περίπου τα μέσα του αιώνα αυτού, οι παραστάσεις της Αμαζονομαχίας συμβολίζουν τη νίκη των Ελλήνων εναντίον των Περσών. Σιγά-σιγά όμως οι Αθηναίοι προσπαθούν να οικειοποιηθούν το θέμα, θέλοντας να προβάλλουν και να εξάρουν, αποκλειστικά σχεδόν, τη δική τους συμμετοχή στην εξουδετέρωση του περσικού κινδύνου. Αυτό μας το δείχνει πολύ καθαρά και το γεγονός ότι από τα μέσα του 5ου αι. π.Χ. και καθόλη τη διάρκεια του τρίτου τέταρτου του αιώνα, συχνά οι πρωταγωνιστές της Αμαζονομαχίας πάνω στα αττικά αγγεία, παύουν να είναι ανώνυμοι. Τις μορφές των Ελλήνων συνοδεύουν ονόματα (βλ. π.χ. εικ.2-3) όπως Θησέας, Ακάμας, Πειρίθους, Φάληρος, Μεγαρεύς, Μούνυχος, Αστύοχος, Φύλακος, Φόρβας, που όλοι τους σχεδόν είναι γνωστοί Αθηναίοι ήρωες, με πρώτον φυσικά ανάμεσά τους τον Θησέα.[49]

Είναι πιθανόν ο πρωταγωνιστικός ρόλος του Θησέα στην Αμαζονομαχία να συνετέλεσε ώστε το θέμα αυτό να σχετιστεί πιο στενά με τους περσικούς πολέμους, αφού και σ'αυτούς φέρεται ότι ανδραγάθησε ο γιός της Αίθρας. Σύμφωνα με την παράδοση, πολλοί ήταν εκείνοι που υποστήριζαν ότι στη μάχη του Μαραθώνα τον είδαν να πολεμά πάνοπλος εναντίον των εχθρών.[50] Και γι' αυτό βέβαια ανάμεσα στους πρωταγωνιστές της μάχης του Μαραθώνα, που διακοσμούσε την Ποικίλη Στοά, είχαμε και τον Θησέα "ἀνιόντι ἐκ γῆς."[51] Και ασφαλώς στην ευρεία διάδοση των σκηνών της Αμαζονομαχίας, αμέσως μετά τα Περσικά και καθόλη τη διάρκεια του 5ου αι. π.Χ., συνετέλεσε και το γεγονός ότι ο Θησέας είχε έναν πρωταγωνιστικό ρόλο στη μυθική αυτή μάχη. ῞Εναν ρόλο που βοήθησε τους Αθηναίους να καταστήσουν το θέμα αυτό όχι μόνο σύμβολο της δικής τους συμμετοχής στην εξουδετέρωση του περσικού κινδύνου αλλά συγχρόνως και μυθικό τους πρότυπο και αποδεικτικό στοιχείο της δικής τους υπεροχής και δύναμης, στοιχεία που δικαιολογούσαν εν κατακλείδι τη δημιουργία της αθηναϊκής αυτοκρατορίας στα χρόνια αμέσως μετά τα Περσικά. Ορισμένα μέρη που προσδέθηκαν στο ζυγό της αθηναϊκής κυριαρχίας σχετίζονταν στενά με τον Θησέα, τον εθνικό τους ήρωα και επομένως, κατά κάποιο τρόπο, νομιμοποιούταν η εξάρτησή τους αυτή,[52] ενώ πολλές ενέργειες του τελευταίου, όπως η προσάρτηση της Μεγαρίδας, η συμμετοχή του στην εκστρατεία του Εύξεινου Πόντου εναντίον των Αμαζόνων, στην αργοναυτική εκστρατεία, στο κυνήγι του καλυδώνιου κάπρου, στην Κενταυρομαχία[53] ή οι αποικιακές δραστηριότητες των παιδιών του[54] κ.ά., συμφωνούσαν και συμβάδιζαν με τα επεκτατικά σχέδια της Αθήνας της εποχής του Κίμωνα και του Περικλή.

Με τις παραστάσεις λοιπόν της Αμαζονομαχίας οι Αθηναίοι του 5ου αι. π.Χ. προπαγάνδιζαν για τους ένδοξους προγόνους τους, οι οποίοι είχαν κάνει τόσο λαμπρά κατωρθώματα και εύρισκαν ερείσματα για να δικαιολογήσουν την αυτοκρατορία τους και την επιδιωκόμενη παντοδυναμία τους. Είναι χαρακτηριστικό ότι στην κλασική εποχή, όταν οι Αθηναίοι ήθελαν να υπενθυμίσουν στους άλλους ΄Ελληνες πόσων σπουδαίων προγόνων παιδιά είναι, από τα κατωρθώματα των τελευταίων πρώτο ανέφεραν συχνά αυτό της Αμαζονομαχίας, που σύμφωνα και με τον Παυσανία (5.11.7) ήταν το πρώτο ανδραγάθημα των Αθηναίων εναντίον "άλλοφύλλων." Σχετικά με το θέμα αυτό θα περιοριστώ μόνο στον Ισοκράτη, σ' έναν Αθηναίο της κλασικής εποχής, ο οποίος, γύρω στο 380 π.Χ., διακήρυττε στον *Πανηγυρικό* του, με πολύ χαρακτηριστικά λόγια:[55] "Ο επιφανέστερος βέβαια από τους πολέμους υπήρξε ο περσικός, δεν αποτελούν όμως μικρότερης σημασίας επιχειρήματα, γι' όσους αμφισβητούν την ανδρεία των προγόνων μας, τα παλιά κατορθώματα. ΄Οταν λοιπόν η Ελλάδα ήταν ακόμη αδύνατη, εισέβαλαν στη χώρα μας Θράκες ... και Σκύθες μαζί με τις Αμαζόνες, τις κόρες του ΄Αρη ... Και ενώ όλοι αυτοί μισούσαν όλους τους ΄Ελληνες, επετέθηκαν μόνο εναντίον μας ... γιατί θεωρούσαν ότι, αν θα μας κατέβαλαν, θα κυριαρχούσαν σ' όλες τις ελληνικές πόλεις. Δεν πέτυχαν όμως του σκοπού τους. Αν και συγκρούσθηκαν μόνο με τους προγόνους μας, υπέστησαν τέτοια καταστροφή, που ήταν σαν να πολέμησαν μ' όλους μαζί τους ανθρώπους ... Οι παραδόσεις," συνεχίζει ο Ισοκράτης, "οι σχετικές με τους πολέμους αυτούς δεν θα ήταν δυνατόν να διατηρηθούν για τόσο μεγάλο χρονικό διάστημα, αν και τα αποτελέσματά τους δεν είχαν τόσο μεγάλη διαφορά από τα άλλα. Για τις Αμαζόνες λοιπόν λέει η παράδοση ότι από όσες ήλθαν εναντίον της πόλης μας καμιά δεν επέστρεψε στην πατρίδα της ..." Και θα τελειώσω με τον Ισοκράτη αναφέροντας δύο ακόμη φράσεις του, πολύ διαφωτιστικές για το θέμα που μας απασχολεί: "Και αυτά λοιπόν τα κατωρθώματα και ωραία είναι και ταιριαστά για όσους διεκδικούν την ελληνική ηγεμονία. Και ισάξια μ' αυτά είναι και όσα κατώρθωσαν οι απόγονοι των ηρώων εκείνων, πολεμώντας εναντίον του Δαρείου και του Ξέρξη."

Αλλά ο Θησέας, ως νικητής των Αμαζόνων και υπερασπιστής της ελευθερίας της Αθήνας, χρησίμευε συγχρόνως, όπως ήδη πολύ εύστοχα έχει παρατηρηθεί, και ως μυθικό πρότυπο των Αθηναίων στην προσπάθειά τους να εγκαθιδρύσουν δημοκρατικό πολίτευμα.[56] Και φυσικά η σχέση αυτή του Θησέα με τη Δημοκρατία, για την οποία ήδη μιλήσαμε, τον καθιστούσε συγχρόνως και ως σύμβολο εναντίον της Τυραννίας. Δεν μπορεί να είναι τυχαίο το γεγονός ότι στην αττική εικονογραφία, όπως ήδη έχει παρατηρηθεί, π.χ. σε σκηνές θεσσαλικής Κενταυρομαχίας, που επίσης στον 5ο αι. είναι ιδιαίτερα συχνές, ασφαλώς εξαιτίας της καίριας συμμετοχής του Θησέα και σ' αυτήν, ή σε σκηνές που εικονίζουν άθλους του, ο ήρωας παριστάνεται με το μοτίβο των Τυραννοκτόνων, ιδιαίτερα μάλιστα μ' αυτό του Αρμόδιου.[57] Τη σχέση αυτή του Θησέα, ως εξολοθρευτή των Αμαζόνων, με την τυραννοκτονία, μας τη δείχνει ίσως πολύ παραστατικά και ο λεγόμενος θρόνος Elgin, σήμερα στο J. Paul Getty Museum, που στο ένα του ερεισίχειρο εικονίζει τους Τυραννοκτόνους, Αρμόδιο και Αριστογείτονα και στο άλλο, πιθανότατα τον ίδιο τον Θησέα, να εξοντώνει μια Αμαζόνα.[58] Υπενθυμίζω απλώς εδώ ότι τόσο το σύνταγμα των Τυραννοκτόνων

Εικ 8. Λεπτομέρεια από τη διακόσμηση καλυκωτού κρατήρα του "τρόπου" του Ζ. των Νιοβιδών στη Βασιλεία, Antikenmuseum und Sammlung Ludwig αρ. Lu 51. (Φωτ. από LIMC *IV 2, σ. 140, εικ. 312).*

όσο και το σύμπλεγμα του Θησέα με την Αμαζόνα, τα συναντούμε και πάνω σε παναθηναϊκούς αμφορείς,[59] στα έπαθλα των Παναθηναίων που, όπως είπαμε και παραπάνω, στον 5ο αι. π.Χ., οι Αθηναίοι πίστευαν ότι είχαν ιδρυθεί από τον εθνικό τους ήρωα. Αλλά τη σχέση του Θησέα με την ελευθερία της Αθήνας, τη διάλυση της Τυραννίας και την εγκαθίδρυση της Δημοκρατίας, μας την υποδηλώνει ίσως και κάτι άλλο. Όπως ήδη έχουμε πει, τη Στοά στην αθηναϊκή Αγορά που ήταν αφιερωμένη στο Δία Ελευθέριο, στο Δία δηλαδή που τιμούσαν όλοι οι Έλληνες για τη βοήθεια που τους προσέφερε στο να απαλλαγούν από την περσική τυραννία, οι Αθηναίοι του 4ου αι. π.Χ., τη διακόσμησαν με τη σύνθεση του Θησέα, του Δήμου και της Δημοκρατίας.[60]

Έχοντας υπόψη όλα τα παραπάνω, καταλαβαίνουμε ίσως καλύτερα το γιατί ένας σημαντικός αριθμός από δημόσια οικοδομήματα της αθηναϊκής Δημοκρατίας του 5ου αι. π.Χ., διακοσμήθηκε με πλαστικές ή ζωγραφικές συνθέσεις Αμαζονομαχίας, όπως π.χ. το Θησείο, η Ποικίλη Στοά, ο Παρθενώνας κ.ά.[61] Έτσι μπορούμε να πούμε ότι η αττική Αμαζονομαχία, κατά τον 5ο αι., όχι μόνο συναγωνίζεται αλλά και υπερτερεί σε συχνότητα και σπουδαιότητα των παραστάσεων της Γιγαντομαχίας, που λόγω της συμμετοχής σ' αυτήν των ίδιων των θεών, ταίριαζε καλύτερα στο έντονο θρησκευτικό σέβας της αρχαϊκής εποχής και γι' αυτό και κυριαρχούσε στην τέχνη της εποχής αυτής. Η αττική Αμαζονομαχία με συμμετοχή σ' αυτήν ηρώων και όχι θεών, παίζει σημαντικό ρόλο στη λιγότερο θρησκευτική αττική τέχνη του 5ου αι. επειδή, όπως ήδη τονίστηκε και παραπάνω, σ' αυτήν κεντρικό πρόσωπο είναι ο Θησέας. Ο μυθικός ηγέτης των Αθηναίων εναντίον των αλλοφύλων, ο μυθικός ιδρυτής του δημοκρατικού πολιτεύματός τους και καταλυτής της τυραννίας, το μυθικό τους πρότυπο που ενέπνεε σεβασμό σε όλους, επιβεβαίωνε τη δύναμη και την υπεροχή τους στον αρχαίο ελληνικό κόσμο και δικαιολογούσε την κυριαρχία τους.

Με αναβαθισμένο το ρόλο του Θησέα στα δημόσια πράγματα της Αθήνας κατά τον 5ο αι. π.Χ., και με δεδηλωμένη την τάση των Αθηναίων να θέλουν να συσχετίσουν με τον εθνικό τους ήρωα σημαντικά και σπουδαία πράγματα της πόλης τους, ας θυμηθούμε και τη φράση "ούκ ἄνευ Θησέως" (Πλούτ. *Θησεὺς* 29.3), φυσικό ήταν να επιχειρήσουν να αποδώσουν σ' αυτόν και την ίδρυση της πιο μεγάλης γιορτής τους, των Παναθηναίων. Άλλωστε ο ίδιος ο Θησέας είχε οργανώσει ανάλογους αγώνες στη Δήλο, για να ευχαριστήσει τους θεούς για τη σωτηρία των Αθηναίων από τον Μινώταυρο και έδωσε στους νικητές, ως βραβεία, κλαδιά φοίνικα.[62] Στον Ισθμό φέρεται να οργάνωσε επίσης αγώνες προς τιμή του πατέρα του Ποσειδώνα.[63] Σημειώνω ακόμη εδώ και τις πληροφορίες που μας δίνουν ορισμένες γραπτές πηγές και σύμφωνα με τις οποίες ο ίδιος ήταν ο ευρετής της έντεχνης πάλης και ενός είδους παγκρατίου, ενώ γι' αυτόν για πρώτη φορά καθιερώθηκε και η φυλλοβολεία.[64] Επομένως δεν πρέπει να μας ξαφνιάζει το γεγονός ότι πάνω σ' ένα παναθηναϊκό έπαθλο, όπως ήταν ο παναθηναϊκός αμφορέας από τον οποίο προέρχεται το όστρακο των καταλοίπων Οικονόμου (εικ.1), είχε απεικονιστεί Αμαζονομαχία, ένα θέμα με το οποίο τόσο στενά ήταν συνδεδεμένος ο ίδιος ο Θησέας.

Έχουμε επανειλημμένα μιλήσει για τη σημασία που απόκτησε το θέμα της Αμαζονομαχίας στην αττική τέχνη του 5ου αι. π.Χ., μια σημασία ισάξια, αν όχι και μεγαλύτερη, απ' αυτή του θέματος της Γιγαντομαχίας. Στην παναθηναϊκή Γιγαντομαχία, κύριος πρωταγωνιστής, όπως μας δείχνει και ο παναθηναϊκός αμφορέας της Ολύνθου (εικ. 5–7), ήταν η πολιούχος θεά της πόλης μαζί με τον οικουρό της όφι, ενώ στην αθηναϊκή Αμαζονομαχία, ο εθνικός ήρωας της πόλης, ο Θησέας. Η Αμαζονομαχία και η Γιγαντομαχία την εποχή αυτή στην Αθήνα, εμφανίζονται να σχετίζονται μεταξύ τους. Εκτός του ότι στο όστρακο του παναθηναϊκού αμφορέα των καταλοίπων του Οικονόμου έχουμε στον πέπλο της θεάς Αθηνάς Αμαζονομαχία (εικ.1), ενώ πιό λογικό θα ήταν να είχαμε παράσταση Γιγαντομαχίας, τα δύο αυτά θέματα τα βρίσκουμε να συνυπάρχουν και σε μνημεία ή στη διακόσμηση κτηρίων, όπως π.χ. στην ασπίδα της Αθηνάς Παρθένου του Φειδία ή στον Παρθενώνα αντίστοιχα.[65] Αλλά γιά μία σχέση ανάμεσα στα δύο αυτά επεισόδια γίνεται λόγος τόσο από τη γραπτή παράδοση όσο πιθανότατα και από την εικονογραφική. Σύμφωνα με ορισμένες, αν και κάπως μεταγενέστερες πηγές, σε μια διαμάχη ανάμεσα στο Διόνυσο και στους Τιτάνες πήραν μέρος, ως σύμμαχοι του πρώτου, οι Αμαζόνες, που ξεχώριζαν για την ανδρεία τους. Ηταν αυτές μάλιστα που παρακίνησαν και την Αθηνά να πάρει μέρος στη σύγκρουση με το πλευρό τους. Τη διοίκηση του στρατεύματος των ανδρών ανέλαβε ο Διόνυσος, ενώ των γυναικών η ίδια η Αθηνά.[66] Το ότι στην παραπάνω αναφερόμενη μάχη οι αντίπαλοι της Αθηνάς και του Διονύσου δεν είναι Γίγαντες αλλά Τιτάνες, αυτό δεν πρέπει να μας προβληματίζει. Μια σύγχυση ανάμεσα σε Γίγαντες και Τιτάνες είναι από παλιά γνωστή, όπως μας βεβαιώνουν σχετικές γραπτές μαρτυρίες. Π.χ. ο Ευριπίδης ρητά αναφέρει ότι στον πέπλο της Αθηνάς δεν είχαμε απεικόνιση Γιγαντομαχίας, όπως είναι γνωστό από άλλες πηγές, αλλά Τιτανομαχίας.[67]

Αξίζει εδώ να υπενθυμίσουμε ότι την Αθηνά με τον Διόνυσο τους ξαναβρίσκουμε συμμάχους, πολεμώντας ο ένας πλάι στον άλλο, και στη γνωστή διαμάχη που ξέσπασε ανάμεσα στην Αθηνά και τον Ποσειδώνα για την κατοχή της Αθήνας, όπως μας δείχνει π.χ. μία γνωστή από παλιά αττική υδρία στην Αγία Πετρούπολη, του Ζ. της Γαμήλιας Πομπής, γύρω στα μέσα του 4ου αι. π.Χ. (εικ. 9)[68] και ένα σχετικά πρόσφατο εύρημα από την Πέλλα, μια αττική υδρία, που χρονολογείται γύρω στο 400 π.Χ. ή μόλις μετά.[69]

Αλλά σχέση Αμαζόνων και Γιγάντων μας δείχνει

Εικ 9. Σχεδιαστική απόδοση της παράστασης της υδρίας του Ζ. της Γαμήλιας Πομπής στην Αγία Πετρούπολη, Μουσείο Ερμιτάζ αρ.1872.130. (Φωτ. από Pfuhl [ό.π. εικ.4] πίν.246, εικ. 604).

ίσως και ο γνωστός αμφορέας με λαιμό του Ζ. της Suessula στο Μουσείο του Λούβρου αρ. S 1677[70] ο οποίος πιθανότατα προέρχεται από την Ιταλία και όχι από τη Μήλο, όπως συχνά αναφέρεται.[71] Στην κύρια όψη του αγγείου αυτού, ανάμεσα στις μορφές που βρίσκονται στο κάτω μέρος της εικονιζόμενης εδώ Γιγαντομαχίας (εικ. 10), συναντούμε και μια γυναικεία που φέρει στο λαιμό της περιδέραιο, φορά ψηλές εμβάδες, χιτωνίσκο και ιματίδιο, ενώ με το δεξί της χέρι κρατά ένα δόρυ. Από το αριστερό χέρι φαίνεται να της έχει ξεφύγει ένα αντικείμενο, που μοιάζει με πέλτη, πράγμα που κάνει ορισμένους ερευνητές να τη θεωρούν Αμαζόνα. Η γυναικεία αυτή μορφή έχει προκαλέσει πολλές συζητήσεις ανάμεσα στους ερευνητές. Ο Devambez υποστήριξε ότι εδώ κανονικά θα έπρεπε να είχαμε την Ήρα. Αλλά ο αγγειογράφος επηρεασμένος καθώς ήταν, όπως πίστευε, από τη σύνθεση της ζωγραφιστής, πιθανότατα, Γιγαντο-

Εικ 10. Σχεδιαστική απόδοση της κύριας παράστασης του αμφορέα του Ζ. της Suessula στο Παρίσι, Μουσείο του Λούβρου αρ. S1677. (Φωτ. από W.Kraiker, Die Malerei der Griechen *[Stuttgart 1958]* πίν. 56).

μαχίας, που διακοσμούσε το εσωτερικό της ασπίδας της Αθηνάς Παρθένου, μπέρδεψε τα πρότυπά του και αντί να ζωγραφίσει τη μορφή της Ήρας, έβαλε εδώ τη μορφή μίας Αμαζόνας, που πήρε από την ανάγλυφη Αμαζονομαχία της εξωτερικής πλευράς της φειδιακής αυτής ασπίδας.

Ωστόσο δεν αποκλείεται, ο Ζ. της Suessula, κάνοντας μια τέτοια σύνθεση, να είχε υπόψη του μια παράδοση, ανάλογη μ' αυτή που μας διασώζει ο Απολλόδωρος (*Βιβλιοθ.* 2.5.9) και σύμφωνα με την οποία, κατά το επεισόδιο το σχετικό με τον Ηρακλή και την Αμαζόνα Ιππολύτη, η Ήρα μεταμορφώθηκε σε Αμαζόνα. Η δυσερμήνευτη μορφή στον αμφορέα του Λούβρου είναι φανερό ότι βρίσκεται σε δυσχερή θέση και αυτό, σε συνδυασμό με την παραπάνω μεταμόρφωση της Ήρας σε Αμαζόνα, μας κάνει να θυμηθούμε και πάλι τον Απολλόδωρο (*Βιβλιοθ.* 1.6.2), που περιγράφοντας τη μάχη των θεών εναντίον των Γιγάντων, λέει:"Ζεὺς δὲ (Πορφυρίωνι) πόθον Ἥρας ἐνέβαλεν, ἥτις καὶ καταρρηγνῦντος αὐτοῦ τοὺς πέπλους καὶ βιάζεσθαι θέλοντος βοηθοὺς ἐπεκαλεῖτο καὶ Διὸς κεραυνώσαντος αὐτὸν Ἡρακλῆς τοξεύσας ἀπέκτεινε." Με το να έχουμε εδώ την Ήρα ως Αμαζόνα, ο Ζ. της Suessula παρουσιάζεται να εικονογραφεί, με πολύ μεγάλη ακρίβεια, το παραπάνω κείμενο του Απολλόδωρου, ενώ συγχρόνως, για μια ακόμη φορά, οι πηγές του τελευταίου αποδεικνύονται και παλιές και έγκυρες. Πρέπει δηλαδή να έχουμε, στο κεντρικό μέρος της Γιγαντομαχίας αυτής (εικ.10), τον γίγαντα Πορφυρίωνα, που έχοντας προσπαθήσει να βιάσει την "μιᾶι τῶν Ἀμαζόνων εἰκασθεῖσα" Ήρα, δέχεται τον κεραυνό του Δία και το θανατηφόρο βέλος από το τόξο του Ηρακλή.

Θα ήθελα να εκφράσω τις θερμές μου ευχαριστίες προς τον Γενικό Γραμματέα της Αρχαιολογικής Εταιρείας κον Β. Πετράκο, που μου επέτρεψε να μελετήσω και να δημοσιεύσω το όστρακο (εικ. 1) από τα κατάλοιπα του Γ. Οικονόμου που φυλάσσονται στην Αρχαιολογική Εταιρεία. Επίσης ευχαριστώ και την κα Α. Μπικάκη η οποία μου υπέδειξε το όστρακο αυτό και μου έδωσε χρήσιμες πληροφορίες για το αρχείο Οικονόμου που η ίδια έχει ταξινομήσει. Τέλος για διάφορες εξυπηρετήσεις ευχαριστίες οφείλω στους Ι. Ακαμάτη, Π. Βαλαβάνη, Ι. Βοκοτοπούλου και Ε. Μανακίδου. Τις φωτογραφίες των εικ. 5 και 6 τις οφείλω στον Κ. Τουτουντζίδη, ενώ αυτήν της εικ. 1 στον Π. Βαλαβάνη, τις υπόλοιπες στον Μ. Στεφανίδη, και το σχέδιο της εικ. 7 στην Τριανταφυλλιά Μήττα.

Σημειώσεις

1. Για τις ανασκαφές αυτές βλ. *AM*21 (1896) 107 κε. 460. *AM*22 (1897) 225. 478. *Πρακτ* (1907) 54 κε. *Πρακτ* (1908) 59 κε. Βλ. και Γ.Οικονόμος, "Ἐπιγραφαὶ ἐκ τῆς ἐν Ἀθήναις ἀγορᾶς," *ΑρχΕφ* (1910) 1 κε. 175/6 401 κε. και *ΑρχΕφ* (1911) 222 κε., όπου δημοσιεύονται οι επιγραφές που βρέθηκαν κατά τη διάρκεια των ανασκαφών αυτών της Αρχαιολογικής Εταιρείας.
2. *Πρακτ* (1908) 59 κε.
3. Βλ. σχετικά E. Barber, "The Peplos of Athena," στο J. Neils (εκδ.), *Goddess and Polis* (Princeton 1992) κυρίως 114 κε.
4. Βλ. σχετικά παρακάτω σημ. 47.
5. Λευκό διασώζεται στα άλογα και στο πρόσωπο και στην ενδυμασία της έφιππης Αμαζόνας, ενώ κροκωτό στην αλωπεκίδα και το δόρυ της. Κροκωτό χρώμα διασώζεται επίσης στην πέλτη της πεσμένης Αμαζόνας, στο κράνος του επιτιθέμενου Ελληνα, στο δόρυ, στο όχανο και στην αντιλαβή της ασπίδας και στο ιματίδιο που έπεφτε από το αριστερό χέρι του αμυνόμενου.
6. Σύγκρινε τις μορφές του οστράκου μας π.χ. με μορφές από την Αμαζονομαχία του ελικ. κρατήρα της Νέας Υόρκης, Μητροπολιτικό Μουσείο αρ. 07.286.84 του Ζ. των Μαλλιαρών Σειληνών (J. Boardman, *Athenian Red Figure Vases: The Classical Period* [London 1989] 22, εικ. 12) ή της αρυβαλλοειδούς ληκύθου στη Βοστώνη, Museum of Fine Arts αρ. 95.48 του Ζ. της Ερέτριας (εικ.2).
7. Βλ. π.χ. D. von Bothmer, *Amazons in Greek Art* (Oxford 1957) 163 175 κε. 229. J. Barron, "New Light on Old Walls,"*JHS* 92 (1972) 33 κε. J. Boardman, "Herakles, Theseus and Amazons," στο D.C. Kurtz-B.S. Sparkes (εκδ.), *The Eye of Greece, Studies in the Art of Athens* (Cambridge 1982) 11.
8. Βλ. π.χ. Μ. Τιβέριος, "Saltantes Lacaenae," *ΑρχΕφ* (1981) 25 κε., πίν. 4α (εικ. 4) και παρακάτω σημ. 38.
9. Π.χ. σε έργα του Ζ. του Τάλω ή του Ζ. του Προνόμου.
10. Σύγκρινε π.χ. μορφές του οστράκου μας με αντίστοιχες πάνω στη γνωστή αρυβαλλοειδή λήκυθο του Αίσωνα στη Νεάπολη, Museo Nazionale Archeologico αρ. RC 239 (εικ. 3), που πρέπει να χρονολογείται γύρω στα 435-430 π.Χ. Βλ. U. Knigge, "Aison, der Meidiasmaler?" *AM* 90 (1975) 140 και σημ. 53.
11. Βλ. π.χ. E. Pfuhl, *Malerei und Zeichnung der Griechen* 3 (Roma 1969) πίν. 237, εικ. 590 (*ARV*[2] 1184-1185,6).
12. Από τη μεγάλη σχετική βιβλιογραφία βλ. T. Hölscher, *Griechische Historienbilder des 5. und 4. Jhs v. Chr.* (Würzburg 1973) 71 κε. W. Gauer, *Weihgeschenke aus den Perserkriegen* (*Ist Mitt-BH* 2, Tübingen 1968) 18 κε. E. Thomas, *Mythos und Geschichte* (Köln 1976) 35 κε. και κυρίως 39 κε. Boardman (σημ. 7) 5 κε. S. Morris, *Daidalos and the Origins of Greek Art* (Princeton 1992) κυρίως 285 κε. 343 κε. Βλ. και τις ενδιαφέρουσες παρατηρήσεις της L. Hardwick, "Ancient Amazons-Heroes, Outsiders or Women?" *GaR* 37 (1990) κυρίως 31 κε.
13. Γι' αυτές βλ. Boardman (σημ. 7) 16 κε.
14. Βλ. *FGrHist* III b I, 629 κε., αρ. 334, F 4. Οι W.B. Tyrrell - F.S. Brown, *Athenian Myths and Istitutions* (New York - Oxford 1991) 165 πιστεύουν ότι τα Παναθήναια σχετίστηκαν με τον Θησέα ήδη από την εποχή του Πεισίστρατου.
15. *FGrHist* III b I, 629 κε., αρ. 334, F 4.
16. J.K. Davison, "Notes on the Panathenaea," *JHS* 78 (1958) 24.
17. J.K. Davies, *Athenian Propertied Families 600-300 B.C.* (Oxford 1971) 293 κε. (αρ. 8429).
18. U. Kron, *Die zehn attischen Phylenheroen* (*AM-BH* 5, Berlin 1976) 172, όπου και σχετική βιβλιογραφία.
19. Kron (σημ. 18) όπου και σχετική βιβλιογραφία. Πρβλ. και *FGrHist* III B, αρ. 334 F 10 (Ίστρος). Πρόσφατα έχει υποστηριχτεί ότι την παράδοση σύμφωνα με την οποία ο Αίας ήταν γιος του Θησέα και της Ερίβοιας, τη δημιούργησε ο Φερεκύδης. Βλ. J. Barron, "Bakchylides, Theseus and a Woolly Cloak," *BICS* 27 (1980) 2-3 και σημ. 30. Ωστόσο το αγγείο François παρέχει ενδείξεις ότι η παράδοση αυτή είναι τουλάχιστον έναν αιώνα παλιότερη. Βλ. παρακάτω σημ. 23.
20. Kron (*σημ.* 18) 173 κε., όπου και σχετική βιβλιογραφία.
21. H.A. Thompson - R.E. Wycherley, *Agora* XIV, *The Agora of Athens* (Princeton 1972) 124 κε. Σ. Κουμανούδης, "Θησέως Σηκός," *ΑρχΕφ* (1976) 194 κε. Για τις ενέργειες του Κίμωνα σε σχέση με τον Θησέα και γενικά για τις πολιτικές τους επεκτάσεις βλ. C. Sourvinou-Inwood, *Theseus as Son and Stepson* (*BICS* Suppl. 40, London 1979) 48 και 54 κε. Tyrrell - Brown (σημ. 14) 167 κε. E.D. Francis, *Image and Idea in Fifth-Century Greece: Art and Literature after the Persian Wars* (London 1990) κυρίως 43 κε. Morris (σημ. 12) 348 κε. 357.

H.A. Shapiro, "Theseus in Kimonian Athens: The Iconography of Empire," *Mediterranean Historical Review* 7 (1992) 30 κε.

22. H.A. Shapiro, "Theseus: Aspects of the Hero in Archaic Greece," στο D. Buitron-Oliver (εκδ.), *New Perspectives in Early Greek Art* (Washington 1991) 130.
23. E. Simon, *Die griechischen Vasen* (München 1981) 73–74.
24. Davies (σημ. 17) 299 κε. 300 κε. 302. J. Kleine, *Untersuchungen zur Chronologie der attischen Kunst von Peisistratos bis Themistokles* (*IstMitt-BH* 8, Tübingen 1973) 24 κε.
25. Kron (σημ. 18) 143 κε., όπου και σχετική βιβλιογραφία.
26. Πλούταρχος, *Θησεὺς* 24 (μτφρ. Μ. Μερακλή-Εκδ. Γαλαξία). Βλ. K. Schefold, "Kleisthenes," *MusHelv* 3 (1946) 65 κε. Πρβλ. K. Schefold, *Götter- und Heldensagen der Griechen in der spätarchaischen Kunst* (München 1978) 158. 166–167. Morris (σημ. 12) 338 κε. Για σχέσεις των Αλκμεωνιδών με τον Θησέα βλ. και Tyrrell - Brown (σημ. 14) 165 κε. Για τον Συνοικισμό και τις άλλες πολιτικές δραστηριότητες του Θησέα βλ. και *RE* Suppl. XIII, λ. Theseus, 1212 κε. (H. Herter).
27. Schefold, *MusHelv* 3 (1946) 65 κε. και *Götter- und Heldensagen der Griechen in der spätarchaischen Kunst* 161 κε. F. Brommer, *Theseus* (Darmstadt 1982) 74 και σημ. 19 με βιβλιογραφία. *FGrHist* III b I, 604–605 και III b II, 344, 20. M.W. Taylor, *The Tyrant Slayers: The Heroic Image in Fifth-Century B.C. Athenian Art and Politics* (New York 1981) 85 κε. 141 σημ. 15. *The Tyrant Slayers*^{2} (Salem 1991) 39 και σημ. 15. Σκεπτικοί ή αντίθετοι με την ύπαρξη μιας "Θησηΐδος" στα τέλη του 6ου αι.π.Χ. είναι ανάμεσα σε άλλους και οι: J. Neils, *The Youthful Deeds of Theseus* (Rome 1987) 11–12. Morris (σημ. 12) 341–342 και σημ. 104. Francis (σημ. 21) 43 κε. H. J. Blok, "Patronage and the Pisistratidae," *BABesch* 65 (1990) 21 κε., αμφιβάλλει για την παρουσία κάποιας ιδιαίτερης σχέσης ανάμεσα στους Αλκμεωνίδες και στον Θησέα.
28. Παυσανίας 1.3.3–4 (μτφρ. Ν. Παπαχατζή, Αθήνα 1974).
29. Βλ. π.χ. Ευριπίδης, *Ἱκέτ.* 353, 404–408, 433–441 ή Σοφοκλής, *Οἰδ. ἐπὶ Κολ.* 911 κε.
30. H.A. Shapiro, *Art and Cult under the Tyrants in Athens* (Mainz am Rhein 1989) 145. Οι Tyrrell - Brown (σημ. 14) 161 και 163 κε. πιστεύουν ότι ο Πεισίστρατος ήταν αυτός που πρώτος προσπάθησε να κάνει τον Θησέα παναθηναϊκό ήρωα. Πρβλ. Taylor (σημ. 27) 81 κε. και Morris (σημ. 12) 336 κε. 356–357.
31. Βλ. M.P. Nilsson, *Cults, Myths, Oracles, and Politics in Ancient Greece* (Lund 1951) 59 κε. Shapiro (σημ. 30) 48–49. 103–104. 148.
32. Brommer (σημ. 27) 86 κε.
33. Για τον Θησέα στη Δήλο, βλ. *RE* Suppl. XIII, λ. Theseus, 1141 κε. και Shapiro (σημ. 21) 38. Πρβλ. Πλούταρχος, *Θησεὺς* 21.
34. Πλούταρχος, *Θησεὺς* 25. 3.
35. Πλούταρχος, *Θησεὺς* 8 και 20. Βλ. και Shapiro (σημ. 21) 46 και (σημ. 22) 131.
36. Πρβλ. Shapiro (σημ. 30) 149. Αλλωστε ο τρόπος διακυβέρνησης του Θησέα φαίνεται ότι είχε στοιχεία τόσο της βασιλείας και τυραννίας όσο και της δημοκρατίας. Βλ. J.K. Davies, "Theseus the King in Fifth-Century Athens," *GaR* 29–30 (1982–1983) κυρίως 28 κε. Για μία βιβλιογραφία βλ. και παρακάτω σημ. 56.
37. Για τον πέπλο της Αθηνάς, βλ. Barber (σημ. 3) 103 κε. και κυρίως 112 κε. Μ. Τιβέριος, *Ο Λυδός και το έργο του* (Αθήνα 1976) 59 κε.
38. Πρόκειται για τον παναθηναϊκό αμφορέα στο Λονδίνο, Βρετανικό Μουσείο αρ. 1866.4–15.249 (B 606) (εικ. 4), για το όστρακο από τα κατάλοιπα Οικονόμου (εικ. 1) και για έναν παναθηναϊκό αμφορέα από την Όλυνθο, σήμερα στο Αρχαιολογικό Μουσείο του Πολυγύρου (εικ. 5–7). Για τον τελευταίο βλ. *ABV* 412 και P. Valavanis, "Säulen, Hähne, Niken und Archonten auf panathenäischen Preisamphoren," *AA* (1987), 470 κε. σημ. 14 και εικ. 3–5.
39. Valavanis (σημ. 38).
40. Βλ. Ν.Μ. Κοντολέων, *Τὸ Ἐρέχθειον ὡς οἰκοδόμημα χθονίας λατρείας* (Ἀθῆναι 1949) 18 κε.
41. *ABV* 393,20. Pfuhl (σημ. 11) πίν. 80, εικ. 297. Shapiro (σημ. 30) 30–31 και πίν. 10c. Ακόμη παλιότερη είναι η παράσταση που διακοσμεί μια βοιωτική λεκάνη στο Λονδίνο, Βρετανικό Μουσείο αρ. B 80. Εδώ έχουμε μια πομπή θυσίας και πίσω από ένα άγαλμα της Αθηνάς εικονίζεται ένα φίδι. Βλ. Pfuhl (σημ. 11) πίν. 39, εικ. 169. Για τη χρονολόγηση του αγγείου αυτού βλ. P.N. Ure (εκδ.), *Sixth and Fifth Century Pottery from Rhitsona* (Oxford 1927) κυρίως 32 και 57. Βλ. και K. Kilinski II, *Boeotian Black-Figure Vase-Painting of the Archaic Period* (diss. University of Missouri 1974) 141, αρ.28.
42. Βλ. π.χ. N.Alfieri - P.Arias - M.Hirmer, *Spina* (München 1958) πίν. 35 και E.Berger - R.Lullies (εκδ.), *Antike Kunstwerke aus der Sammlung Ludwig* I (Basel 1979) 140, εικ. 51A (εικ.8).
43. Βλ. π.χ. Alfieri-Arias-Hirmer (σημ. 42) πίν. 69–73 και εδώ εικ.8. Πρβλ. και F.Vian, *Répertoire des gigantomachies figurées dans l' art grec et romain* (Paris 1951) πίν. XXIX, αρ.150 (αριστερά). XXXI, αρ. 161. 169. 222 XXXII, αρ. 298. XXXVIII, αρ. 339.
44. Βλ. Τιβέριος (σημ. 37) 60 και 111 σημ. 272. Πρβλ. και G. Ferrari Pinney, "Pallas and Panathenaea," στο J.Christiansen - T. Melander (εκδ.), *Proceedings of the 3rd Symposium on Ancient Greek and Related Pottery*, Copenhagen, August 31–September 4 1987 (Copenhagen 1988) 465 κε. και κυρίως 471 κε. Για την Αθηνά των παναθηναϊκών αμφορέων βλ. και Shapiro (σημ. 30) 27 κε.
45. Απολλοδ. 1.6.1–2 και *LIMC* IV 1, λ. Gigantes, 268–269 (F. Vian με συνεργασία M.Moore).
46. Βλ. και παραπάνω σημ. 3.
47. Για κάτι ανάλογο βλ. *Greek Vases in the J.Paul Getty Museum, Occasional Papers on Antiquities* 3, 2 (1985) 98, εικ.3 (J.R. Green).
48. Thomas (σημ. 12) 23. 25 κε. 28. Πρβλ. Πλάτων, *Σοφιστὴς* 246 α-β.
49. Βλ. Bothmer (σημ. 7) 234. Boardman (σημ. 7) 21 κε. Πρβλ. και K.Schefold - F.Jung, *Die Urkönige, Perseus, Bellerophon, Herakles und Theseus in der klassischen und hellenistischen Kunst* (München 1988) 283–284.
50. Πλούταρχος, *Θησεὺς* 35.
51. Παυσανίας 1.15.3.
52. Έχουμε ήδη αναφέρει τις σχέσεις του Θησέα με τη Δήλο και τη Νάξο.
53. Βλ. Brommer (σημ. 27) 104 κε. 115 κε. 133 κε. 135 κε. *RE* Suppl. XIII , λ. Theseus, 1149 κε. 1157. 1205 κε. 1206 κε. Για τη Μεγαρίδα βλ. και Nilsson (σημ. 31) 56 κε. Πρβλ. και Πλούταρχος, *Θησεὺς* 25.26.29.
54. Βλ. παραπάνω σημ. 35.
55. Ισοκράτης, *Πανηγυρικὸς* 68–71 (μτφρ.βασισμένη σ' αυτήν του Χρ. Θεοδωράτου, Εκδ. Ελληνικός Εκδοτικός Οργανισμός). Πρβλ. Ισοκράτης, *Ἀρχίδαμος* 42, *Ἀρεοπαγιτικὸς* 75, *Παναθηναϊκὸς* 191–193 και Λυσίας, *Ἐπιτάφιος* 3–6.
56. Πρβλ. Sourvinou-Inwood (σημ. 21) 48 κε. 53 κε. A.Shapiro, "Theseus, Athens and Troizen," *AA* (1982), 291 κε. J.Binder, "The West Pediment of the Parthenon: Poseidon," στο A. L. Boegehold κ.ά. (εκδ.), *Studies Presented to Sterling Dow* (*GRBM* 40, Durham, N.C. 1984) 21 κε. Schefold, *Götter- und Heldensagen der Griechen* 158. Για τον Θησέα βλ. και Morris (σημ. 12) κυρίως 332 κε. και 336 κε. και Nilsson (σημ. 31) 51 κε.
57. Βλ. π.χ Taylor (σημ. 27) κυρίως 79 κε. Sourvinou-Inwood (σημ. 21) 71 σημ. 155. Morris (σημ. 12) 349 κε.
58. Βλ. N.Eschbach, *Statuen auf panathenäischen Preisamphoren des 4.Jhs v.Chr.* (Mainz am Rhein 1986) 86 κε. σημ. 329 (με βιβλιογραφία) και πίν. 24.
59. Βλ. π.χ. Eschbach (σημ. 58) 83 κε. και πίν. 23, εικ. 1 και 2 (για την Αμαζονομαχία) και Valavanis (σημ. 38) 470 και σημ. 12 και 471, εικ. 1–2 (για τους Τυραννοκτόνους).
60. Morris (σημ. 12) 350 κε. Για τη Στοά του Ελευθερίου Διός βλ. Thompson - Wycherley (σημ. 21) κυρίως 96 κε.
61. Βλ. Boardman (σημ. 7) 16 κε.
62. Πλούταρχος, *Θησεὺς* 21. Βλ. και Shapiro (σημ. 21) 46.
63. Πλούταρχος, *Θησεὺς* 25. Βλ. και E.Gebhard," The Early Stadium at Isthmia and the Founding of the Isthmian Games," στο W. Coulson - H.Kyrieleis (εκδ.), *Proceedings of an International Symposium on the Olympic Games, 5–9 September 1988* (Αθήνα 1992) 73 κε.

64. *RE* Suppl. XIII, λ. Theseus, 1219. Πρβλ. Nilsson (σημ. 31) 55-56.
65. Πρβλ. Γ. Δεσπίνης, " Τα γλυπτά των αετωμάτων του ναού της Αθηνάς Νίκης," *ΑρχΔελτ* 29 (1974) Μελέται, 22 κε.
66. Διοδ. 3.71. Πρβλ. J. Dörig - O. Gigon, *Der Kampf der Götter und Titanen* (Olten-Lausanne 1961) 49 κε.
67. Ευριπίδης, *Ἰφιγέν. ἐν Ταύρ.* 224 και *Ἑκάβη* 472-474.
68. Π. Βαλαβάνης, *Παναθηναϊκοί αμφορείς από την Ερέτρια* (Αθήνα 1991) 293, αρ. 1 και πίν. 142. 143.
69. ΙΖ' Εφορεία Αρχαιοτήτων (εκδ.), *Πέλλα, πρωτεύουσα των αρχαίων Μακεδόνων*, ΔΕΘ:περίπτερο 7, 27 Οκτωβρίου-31 Δεκεμβρίου 1987 (Θεσσαλονίκη 1987) πίν. 21. A. Delivorrias (εκδ.), *Greece and the Sea*, Amsterdam 29 October-10 December 1987 (Amsterdam 1987) 202 κε. αρ. 104 και εικ. σ. 204-205 (S. Drougou). *LIMC* VI,I λ. Kekrops, 1087, αρ. 24 (I. Kasper-Butz, I. Krauskopf, B. Knittlmayer). O. Palagia, *The Pediments of the Parthenon* (Leiden 1993) εικ. 11.
70. *ARV*^{2} 1344,1. T.H. Carpenter, *Beazley Addenda*^{2} (Oxford 1989) 367 (1344,1).
71. P. Devambez, "L' Amazone de l'amphore de la Gigantomachie au Louvre et le bouclier de la Parthenos" στο *Χαριστήριον εἰς Ἀναστάσιον Κ. Ὀρλάνδον* 3 (Ἀθῆναι 1966) 102 κε., όπου και η σημαντικότερη βιβλιογραφία.

Democracy and Imperialism in the Panathenaic Procession: The Parthenon Frieze in its Context

Robin Osborne

In asking what is the significance of putting the Panathenaia on the frieze of the Parthenon, I am going to concentrate not on the old issues of whether this is a past or a present Panathenaia or of what, if this is a present Panathenaia, the religious impact of putting contemporaries on a temple was. Rather I am going to concentrate on what the significance of juxtaposing the Panathenaia of the frieze to the sculptures of the metopes and pediments might be. And in asking about the significance of putting the Panathenaic frieze on the Parthenon in the time of Perikles, I am not going to be hunting for precise allusions to personal policies but rather looking at the implications of the juxtapositions of the sculptures for an imperial power that regarded itself as a democracy.[1]

I cannot prove that the sculptures of the Parthenon form a programme. I cannot prove that any Athenian looked at the sculptures against one another, rather than looking first at the metopes, then at the frieze and then at the pediments (as modern scholars almost universally do), or looking at none at all, or only some, of the sculptures. But I suggest that the arrangement of the sculptures on the building made possible the viewing of the sculptures 'side by side' in the way that I am going to view them, and arguably encouraged such viewing - even if it did not encourage such viewing in Pausanias, our only preserved ancient view. I have argued that case as best I can elsewhere for the frieze (see infra n. 9): those who find that argument improbable or unpalatable will probably be rendered apoplectic by the extension of that view which follows.

Any individual viewer of the Parthenon in the fifth century, as any viewer now, will have come to the monument with his or her own concerns, his or her own view. We can hardly begin to enter into any fifth-century mind, but we may perhaps suppose three things about Athenian viewers of the Parthenon sculptures in the 430s: that they were conscious of living in a democracy, that they were conscious that Athens was a city which exercised power over other cities, some of which did not welcome their subjection to Athens, and that they were aware that the part which an individual played in Athenian life, both public and private, was determined in crucial ways by their gender.

What happens, then, when we look at the Parthenon sculptures as a group through the eyes of a gendered viewer conscious that both democratic equality and imperialist behaviour are issues? We have a model of just such a viewer in Lysistrata: both the fictional character and the real woman most probably behind the fiction spent much time on the Acropolis, and the fictional character, at least, was very conscious of issues of democracy and of gender.[2]

The sculptures of the west pediment will have been the most that the visitor exiting from the Propylaia could see clearly.[3] The counterposed horses framing the two central protagonists will have stood out even for the viewer from afar; while she might be able to make out little more in the way of detail, she will have realised that a mighty conflict dominated the western gable. Little more will have come clear until the visitor stood at the foot of the steps of its terrace. From there the whole composition of the pediment will have been visible in detail (Fig. 1).[4]

The two deities were the central figures, Athene to the left, Poseidon to the right, in mirror poses. Behind them came rampant horses with their charioteers and an

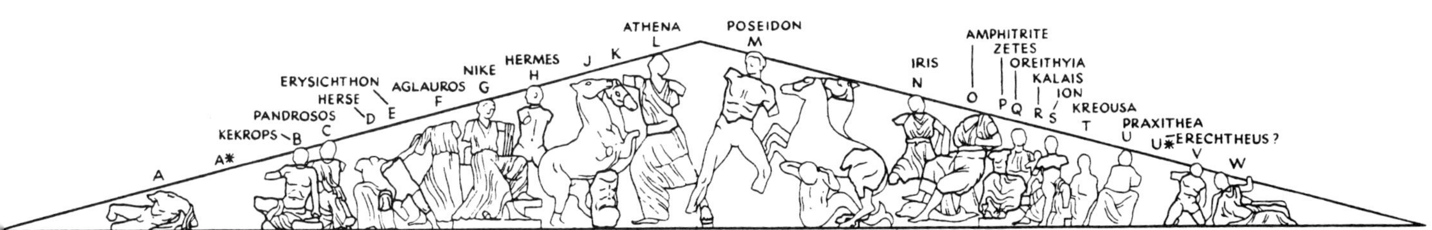

Fig. 1. Parthenon West Pediment, drawing by M. Cox. After O. Palagia, The Pediments of the Parthenon *(Leiden 1993) fig. 22.*

attendant deity (Iris for Poseidon, Hermes for Athene), and the corners of the gable were then probably taken up with figures from the mythical early history of Attica (probably including King Kekrops and his daughters).

What sort of agenda does this pediment set? Here is a conflict with ramifications for all who look on it, a contest which determines the subsequent history of Athens. Athene's victory not only leaves Athens with the olive (an olive tree may have been carved centrally behind Athene and Poseidon), it rids Athens of the monsters of the sea who cluster behind Poseidon and under his chariot. The figures towards the corners look variously towards the contest or out towards the viewer, and by doing so they join the world of the viewer so that the distant descendant of Kekrops belongs with Kekrops' immediate family, linking historic present and mythical past as powerfully as does the chorus of an Athenian tragedy. There are nice human touches here - a small boy (perhaps Erysikhthon?) pulls at his sister's hand, trying to drag her away; a younger woman (a daughter?) whose garment has slipped off her shoulder in her distraction to reveal her left breast puts her arm round an older man (Kekrops?). The fundamental contest which will determine Athens' patron deity takes place in the midst of a quite normal community, a community dominated by love, motherhood and family life, eager to see whether this contest will disrupt or reinforce its daily routines.

The decision to show Athene's contest with Poseidon on this pediment was an important one. We first hear the story from Herodotos (8.55) in the context of the Persian destruction of the olive tree on the Acropolis and its miraculous growing up again; just how ancient the story was it is difficult to tell, but it seems rarely to have been represented in art - unlike the story of the birth of Athene. Representing this story in this position makes clear that this monument, built with allies' money, was a celebration of Athens and not simply a celebration of generalised Greek traditions. This story proclaims Athens' superiority. The city whose political influence rested on her navy, on her control of the whole Aegean sea, and beyond, chooses to display the victory of Athene over Poseidon, to claim that Athens has gifts from the gods still greater than the gift of power over the sea. What Athene brings to her people is not just freedom from the monstrous but a guarantee of civilised life. To be Athenian, this pediment seems to suggest, is not simply to have acquired unprecedented power over the sea and so over other Greeks, it is also to be part of a city which values women and children and recognises their central role in the city.

More difficult to assess is the extent to which this pediment also carries a class message for Athenians. Poseidon was associated with the sea, but he was also associated with horses, and not far outside the town wall was the sanctuary of Poseidon Hippios which seems to have been a gathering place for young men of wealth. In 411 B.C. it was to be at an Assembly uniquely called to meet close to this sanctuary that the Athenians were persuaded to vote democracy out of existence and to replace it with a rather more limited franchise restricted to the wealthier classes (Thuc. 8.67). As a result of their activities in 411 and 404 B.C. the cavalry in Athens acquired a bad reputation – after the Peloponnesian War their pay was cut and the Athenians took advantage of an opportunity to ship 300 cavalry off to help the Spartans fighting in Asia Minor.[5] Prior to 411 there is no doubt that the cavalry had an association with extravagant and undisciplined young men and with men critical of democracy. It is such critics of democracy that Aristophanes makes the chorus of his *Knights*, of 424 B.C. In that play the chorus invokes Poseidon immediately prior to launching into praise of the past and criticism of the present, but Poseidon is invoked there as 'lord of horsemen who loves the din of bronze-footed horses' (551–5), and the Knights invoke Pallas Athene too (581ff.). Athenians would perhaps associate Athene's victory over Poseidon with the displacement of the wealthy from the reins of power in Athens, but in the 430s at least no stronger a put-down than that should probably be read into this subject.

The viewer who has come close enough to survey all this soon comes to realise that there is a sculptural commentary on the pediment provided in the further sculptures just below on the metopes. That the metopes show scenes of mounted combat and combat on foot is clear, what is less clear is between whom the combat takes place. The impossibility of determining the identity of the combatants means that scholars hold very fixed views; I regard it as marginally more probable that the mounted figures are Amazons, and will treat them as such in what follows, but I have no particular confidence in this view.[6]

The strong Athenian tradition of past encounters with Amazons centred on Theseus carrying off Antiope and the Amazons launching a revenge raid on Athens.[7] Read against the pediment, therefore, there can be little or no doubt that Athenians would have seen a combat with Amazons on the metopes as Theseus' combat with Amazons on this very site. The positive triumph of Athene in winning Attica in contest with Poseidon is thus juxtaposed with the negative triumph of Theseus in managing to keep Attica safe from outside threat. Yet while Athene is unquestionably the central actor in the pedimental scene, the metopes allow of no prominent individual. The square space which a metope provides will accommodate combat between two figures but it will not establish the priority of any particular combat or any particular triumphant figure over any other. So, while the juxtaposition with the pediment hints very strongly that this is Theseus' combat, the metopes effectively remove Theseus himself from the scene. What we see is Athenians defending themselves against the Amazons.

The battle with the Amazons raises further questions of gender. The Athens whose patron Athene contests to become in the pediment is an Athens where women and men both have a role. The Athens defended in the metopes is an Athens attacked by women and defended by men. But how unproblematic is this to be seen to be?

The literary tradition on Theseus' exploits and on his relations with Antiope the Amazon queen was ambivalent about his behaviour.[8] Some traditions made Antiope Theseus' share of the booty from a successful military expedition, and debated whether she liked him or not; other traditions had Theseus abduct Antiope. Similarly her final fate was contested - did she die fighting valiantly at Theseus' side against the Amazons? Or did Theseus kill her to prevent her making a nuisance of herself (Medea-style) when he wanted to marry another woman? Only on a very selective understanding of the tradition could the battle against the Amazons be taken as a model of the just war.

The result of the war with the Amazons would not be in question for any viewer, but in the metopes the battle honours are even: Amazons get the better of men, as well as men of Amazons. The combat, not the result, is the focus of attention. The disjunction that is a fundamental feature of metopal sculptures, as well as removing any sense of climax, must have given this combat a certain timelessness, so that the viewer had space to project her questions about the role of women in warfare and in the life of the city, and about the nature of combat between men and women, onto this combat between men and Amazons. Where is the place of war in the civilised world Athene promises in the pediment?

The viewer whose eyes have drifted down from the pediment to the metopes would in due course become aware that there was yet a third tier of sculpture on display, as she got shadowy glimpses of the sculpted frieze. At first glance the frieze might seem to be already familiar: here were more rampant horses and more mounted warriors. But closer observation would reveal that for all the iconographical parallels this was a very different sort of scene, for here was no combat and no contest, but a cavalcade.

The visitor who has gazed upon the pediments and metopes which parade before her the mythical past of Athens, raising questions about the present city and its relations with the gods through the structures and gaps in past stories, is turned into an active participant in a present parade by the frieze, is made to join in a religious ritual. Any attempt to distance the problems which the metopes and pediments raise by invoking the otherness of the past has to collapse in the face of these sculpted figures of the frieze which insist on being present. The shock of this novel trope, for which there is no parallel in earlier architectural sculpture, forces a reassessment of the scenes already assimilated, turning the questions of the role of women and children in current Athens, of the propriety of Athenian wars, of ethical standards in men's dealings with women, into current questions. It also makes a presumption of sympathy which means that the frieze is taken on board as current without its own subject matter being fully analysed - an effect partly achieved because it is impossible ever to gain a complete view of the frieze, because of the constant deferment of any possibility of closure.[9]

In fact the frieze, and particularly this western side, is exceedingly odd as a view of current Athenian life.[10] All the figures are men, all are involved with horses. The men are a motley crew, some naked or wearing just a cloak, others not only fully clothed but also helmeted, others wearing no helmet but a broad-brimmed hat. The horses are unduly small by comparison with the men and are also unduly lively. Athenian cavalry were notorious for their undiscipline, but hardly to this extent. There never was nor could be a procession like this, even in Athens. So why does the frieze choose to portray such a group? Part of the answer may be purely practical, but practical considerations cannot account for the full range of oddities listed above.

To explain the strange subject-matter of the frieze it is essential to see the frieze in its full context. The lively horses of the frieze not only make a long procession more visually interesting, they also mean that, whatever intercolumniation the viewer peers through, the frieze always provides a parallel for the rampant horses of the pediment and for the only slightly less lively horses which feature in every other metope (1,3,5 etc.). The hint that the frieze has a relationship with the metopes and the pediment is hard to miss. The horses of the pediment belong to deities, the horses of the metopes to Amazons: what are we to make from the comparison of Athenian horses and horsemen with these horses and those in charge of them? Our question about how far there was a class-political message in advertising the defeat of Poseidon by Athene becomes a much more insistent question in the face of the frieze. What is implied by making this the most prominent sculpted face of contemporary Athens? We are not faced here with the grimly uniform appearance of the highly regimented military force where uniformity has become a cult which renders all individual differences irrelevant. Rather we are faced with an insistence that the men who master these horses are young men of all sorts, all doing their own thing but all attempting at least to work towards the same end as they pull their horses about to get them to move off in the same direction. It is the capaciousness of this frieze to accommodate all-comers that makes it so easy for the viewer to join in its activity: even though these are all horsemen, nevertheless the message given is that there is a space for every citizen here, that this is a community which is inclusive and not exclusive. The irony of making cavalry, the very people whose value might seem to be most undermined by Poseidon's defeat at the hands of Athene, into the model of Athens as the city which is all-inclusive, serves to underline the demand that the spectator respond to these sculptures with questions rather than with answers, that she adopt them as a lens through which critically to view the realities of contemporary Athens. At the same time, we might note in anticipation, that as the viewer moves from west to east the horses become fewer until they are entirely absent from the east façade; the viewer moves from a world in which Poseidon still contests to a world in which Athene reigns unchallenged, from the world of aristocratic combat to the world of democratic ritual.

Whichever way the viewer turns she is in for a surprise. At the west end of both north and south sides the frieze continues to show horsemen, increasingly well ordered and ever more steadily on the move. But the scenes juxtaposed to these in the metopes are no longer scenes of Amazons.

The last metope on the north side (Metope 32) is the best preserved (Fig. 2). It presents the viewer with two female figures. The seated figure seems very likely to be Athene, her companion another goddess. The treatment of the two figures is markedly contrasting making Athene the main focus of the metope and the standing figure melt before her and not interrupt her eastward gaze. The metope urges the viewer on eastward. But making Athene the pointer ensures that the viewer continues to ask what difference it makes having Athene as patron goddess, and it prepares us for scenes in which Athene will have an intimate concern and which promise some contribution towards an answer to that question.

The next metopes increase the anticipation of what is to come. In 31 we have Iris perhaps and Zeus. In 30 perhaps Poseidon and Hermes. What is to come is evidently of interest to all the gods. Metope 28 presents four figures, a woman standing to left, a man in the centre, a man with a shield striding out to meet us to the right, and a smaller figure in front of him (Fig. 3). For the viewer coming to this metope from the west precise identification of the figures can never have been easy. The chief clues will have been the combination of an armed warrior preceded by a juvenile with two civilian figures. The action from which the warrior departs can hardly be the field of battle, for there would be no civilians or children to take from the field of battle, but nor, given that he is armed, can it be some purely domestic scene. The clues demand that the action must be fighting in a city - and the fought-in city *par excellence* is Troy, the family whose flight from Troy is most famed that of Aineias. The iconography of this metope is not in fact identical to the iconography used on painted pottery to show Aineias departing from Troy. The designer of the metope has deliberately chosen to make this a full family group, combining not only all three generations but both sexes. The place of women within the city is being kept on the agenda.

Metope 25 on the north side introduces two new elements into the story (Fig. 5). It has two standing female figures. On or just behind the shoulder of the left hand figure is a small, naked, winged figure moving off to the left. At the right hand side of the metope is a figure wearing a peplos, standing on a stone base; this is the statue of a female goddess, perhaps the famous statue of Athene at Troy, the Palladion, which in some stories was stolen by Odysseus and Diomedes, but in others was rescued by Aineias. The right-hand female figure has her hand on the shoulder of this statue: she is seeking sanctuary. We have penetrated into the city which

Fig. 2. Parthenon Metope N.32. Photo DAI Athens.

Fig. 3. Parthenon Metope N.28. Photo DAI Athens.

Fig. 4. Parthenon Metope N.24. Photo DAI Athens.

Fig. 5. Parthenon Metope N.25. Photo DAI Athens.

Aineias and his family are leaving and are at the heart of the city which is being sacked. The winged figure of Eros makes it highly likely that the female figure is Aphrodite and that the woman seeking sanctuary is that most desirable of women, Helen. We are not simply at the heart of Troy, we are at the heart of the Trojan expedition launched on behalf of Menelaos from whom Paris had snatched, or seduced, Helen.

There in the next metope is Menelaos (Fig. 4). It is from Menelaos in particular that Helen is taking refuge. It is from Aphrodite towards Menelaos that Eros is leaping. In metope 24 Helen's cuckolded husband advances. Like Aineias he is naked and his shield is extended behind him, but Menelaos is armed for attack and not for defence. He heads for Helen with drawn sword. This is the first detail we have of what Aineias is taking his family to safety from: from a husband attacking a wife, and from warfare penetrating even into the sanctuaries of the gods.

The visitor whom the west pediment has made question the value of Athene's patronage is here confronted with the sack of another city of which Athene was patron. If Amazons enjoy some success against the Athenians, in the end the Athenians will win through. But here is a city of Athene's which was sacked. There could be no more stark way of reminding the viewer that the city Aineias and his family fled was Athene's city than this of presenting the statue of the goddess before our eyes. The viewer has been encouraged to join a procession which at this very moment is gathering momentum in the mass of hooves pounding away on the frieze beneath, a procession already evocative of the procession to Athene at the Panathenaia, and here she finds herself confronted with an image of Athene evocative of the old statue of Athene Polias to which that Panathenaic procession was directed, but a statue which has become not a focus for self-glorification and self-confidence but a last refuge from danger.

Helen's quest for sanctuary at the statue of Athene puts women at the centre of Athene's city. To the question 'Are all wars really wars against women?' Helen offers a particular answer. Helen's answer is one in which her sex is an essential and not simply an accidental element, for this was a war fought in defence of her husband's 'rights' with total disregard for her own wishes. This was a war which put the integrity of the household above the security of the city, making a whole city suffer for the sake of one particular sexual conquest. That sexual desire is on the agenda here the presence of Eros and Aphrodite puts beyond doubt. While Antiope remained invisible, in all probability, in the western metopes and the viewer was left to puzzle over her place in this struggle on her own, Helen is not just visible here but visible as the sexually desirable object. The Aineias metope had deliberately shocked the connoisseur of painted pottery by its inclusion of a woman in the group, and so had given emphasis to its introduction of woman the suffering victim of war. This metope gives prominence to another face of woman and war, the woman who is fought for and over in war, the woman who causes men to do and suffer in the battlefield.

We do not know how the sculptors developed these

questions. Little other than the three easternmost metopes survive, but these make it clear that the viewer who moves from west to east is made to see the episodes of the taking of Troy in a reverse chronological order, just as she is also made to view Athene's combat with Poseidon, before viewing her birth. In these metopes this has striking effects, for the viewer begins by seeing the victims, not by following the progress of the Greek invaders, and the Greeks are traced back from the scene of atrocities to their initial invasion. The viewer is thus encouraged to view the Greek attack on Troy teleologically, and to ask whether the means employed justified the ends. The question raised in the west of whether the heroic deeds of the past provide a model for straightforward emulation is not given any firm affirmative answer here.

While the viewer is establishing that it is the sack of Troy on the metopes, the frieze continues with its lines of overlapping horsemen clattering forward on spirited beasts whose forefeet never touch the ground. Just before we are half way along the cavalry give way to men armed as hoplites engaged in jumping onto moving chariots. As the metopes have moved into scenes of open warfare of one city against another, the frieze confirms that these cavalry are not headed for battle but are participants in a ritual procession. On the metopes we see soldiers threatening Athene's statue, on the frieze we see soldiers displaying their paramilitary skills to the glory of a deity.

In the last quarter of the north side the character of the frieze changes again. While the metopes above showed scenes of the destruction of a city and its life, the frieze displays before us the city engaged in the worship of its patron deity. The spectator who is presented by the metopes with ugly scenes of exclusion and destruction which she can do nothing to control, is able to create an even larger and more catholic community as she opens up new vistas among the columns.

The metopes and frieze on the south side develop the agenda of the west sculptures by exploring the way in which we create the image of our enemy and giving the viewer the chance to see through the mask of the centaur, as well, probably, as contrasting male destruction and female creation.[11] But whichever route the viewer takes and however her view is developed, on the east the viewer's attention is perforce turned, or turned back, to the relations between men and women and gods and goddesses.

The scene of the birth of Athene on the pediment dominated the view from the east.[12] It seems most likely that Athene appeared in full stature beside Zeus her father from whose head she had sprung, admired by an audience of amazed gods and goddesses. On the west pediment the viewer took a line of view from the ancestral Athenian spectators watching the crucial victory of Athene over Poseidon. Here, within this cosmic setting it is less a matter of action to follow than of awe to become enthralled in, as the viewer takes up the gaze of the spectating figures.

The surviving spectating deities introduce the viewer to the variousness of the Olympians. At the south end Dionysos is totally relaxed consciously ignoring the great epiphany at the centre. Behind him come Demeter and Kore, physically close. A standing female figure moves away from the central epiphany, perhaps Artemis, an agitated figure with a timidity quite different from the relaxed curiosity of Demeter and Kore or the nonchalance of Dionysos. On the right hand side of the pediment we have a different view of the gods again: one, perhaps Hestia, sitting pertly upright; her two northern neighbours, a distinctly languorous Aphrodite resting in the lap of either her mother Dione or of Themis.

Like the centaurs of the south metopes, the gods and goddesses in the pediment abound in variety, as lacking in homogeneity as the citizen body itself. They offer a model not of pious uniformity but of the variety of ways in which the divine presence can be assimilated. Whatever the viewer's attitude as she approaches the east front of the Parthenon she can find a model for it among the deities here displayed to her.

At first sight the metopes make a curious sort of commentary on the scene in the pediment. What place do battles between gods and giants have in the context of contemplation of the divine which the pediment has created? The figures seen in calm contemplation and characterised so individually in the pediment are each in turn thrust into single combat with the giants in the metopes. Even for the gods there are demands which preclude life being simply the pursuit of what each individual most enjoys; even for the gods there are community interests that have to be met. Athene appears not simply to be contemplated but to fight. It is a fair bet that most of the figures in the pediment are in the metopes too: certainly scholars have thought to find Dionysos, Hephaistos, Poseidon, Zeus, Athene, Artemis, Aphrodite and Helios in both places.

The arrangement of the metopes promotes the comparison with the pediment - a deliberate parallelism challenges the viewer to compare and contrast. The gods who are quietly absorbed in self-congratulatory contemplation on the pediment are gods who get closely involved in struggles against those that threaten them.[13] War is not some human activity which the gods simply delight to interfere in, but an activity ineradicable even from the world of the gods. For all the pain of war to which the viewer has been introduced in the north metopes, for all the questioning of the way in which enemies are typecast as beasts which the viewer has been encouraged to undertake in the south metopes, war remains present and necessary.

Once the metopes have destroyed any illusion that the pediment might have given that the worship of the gods is simply a matter of passive contemplation, we join the women carrying bowls for the libations, an incense burner. The viewer might reasonably expect an altar and the accountrements of sacrifice. Instead some of the women at the south end carry heavy objects that may be loom stands; in front of the women come more old men who loiter, then beyond the old men come slightly larger seated figures, who contemplate that procession rather as the gods of the pediment contemplate newly-born Athene. The seated figures include men and women, and one smaller naked male figure, and some are carrying things. A moment's contemplation reveals that these are gods and goddesses. This procession, which has become ever more familiar as a procession including many of the features found in the Panathenaic procession, and which the viewer has been encouraged to join in, has brought the viewer face to face not with a sacrificial communication with the divine but with the deities themselves.

The gods of the frieze are characterised in the same lively way as those of the pediment. This is as natural a group of mildly interested spectators as one could wish for. But the realism of these figures, which has so often been remarked upon, has a distinct theological, and a distinct political, charge to it, for in destroying the distance between the viewer and the sculpted figures it destroys the distance between the viewer and the gods. In putting the gods and goddesses on public display in the midst of an Athenian world in this way, and especially by putting them next to the entirely male collection of eponymous heroes of the Athenian tribes, the sculptor also raises questions about equality of gender on Olympos and about the engendering of activities in Athens.

But if the gods and goddesses were unexpected, more unexpected still is the fact that they do not form the climax. For between Zeus and Athene comes a further scene upon which their backs are turned, and it is the scene that the viewer gazes at as she looks up from the centre of the east façade, standing in front of the door to the cella. Just five figures compose this scene: to the left are two girls with padded stools on their heads; in the centre is a woman who is turned to face them; to the right a man receives a piece of folded cloth from, or perhaps gives a piece of folded cloth to, a small child, whose sex has been much disputed by scholars. And that is all. The centre of this scene comes between the backs of the woman and the man. The reference of the scene is not difficult to work out: the culmination of the annual Panathenaic procession consisted in giving a new peplos to the statue of Athene Polias, a peplos woven during the year by young girls chosen from noble Athenian families especially for this ritual and who lived on the Acropolis. But what is this scene doing here: for we have the peplos but no image of Athene for it? And why is the climax of the Panathenaic procession of no interest to the gods and goddesses? What have they gathered for if not for this? The frieze which has resisted closure throughout its length remains resistant to closure to the very end.

The answer to all these questions rests with the viewer. The viewer who has picked up the clues offered by the frieze, has joined the procession and moved round the temple, finds on moving across the east façade that it is her procession that the gods and goddesses are watching. It is the people of Athens in whom the gods and goddesses are taking an interest, just as it was the possession of Attica for which Athene and Poseidon contested on the west pediment. All the people of Athens. Divine attention is not limited to the Athens of old, to some primeval time, but is brought into the very present moment: the gods and goddesses are here, waiting and watching the procession of which the viewer is part. The attention of the deities is not simply focused on one bit of ritual, what they are interested in is the fact of the procession and that procession as a sign of proper attitudes towards the gods on the part of the Athenian people as a whole. They have gathered for to see the whole Athenian people.[14]

But if it is the procession that the gods and goddesses are interested in, why do we have the scene of the peplos at all? The scene of the peplos has a special relationship to the viewer. By the time the viewer sees the scene of the peplos she is standing right in front of the middle of the east façade, in front of the main entrance to the cult chamber. The peplos that is being brought (or taken away) has no object in the frieze; it seems to be redundant. The procession has come this far and now its central ceremony seems aborted. But the procession that the viewer has made is not aborted, the viewer has indeed come to the climax and the climax is not absent, it is there. As soon as her eyes descend from the frieze she has before them the new cult statue of Athene, resplendently arrayed in gold and ivory.[15] Athene is present in quite untold glory. The once yearly procession to take a new peplos to Athene has become a procession that can be repeated as often as any Athenian wishes to repeat it, and always there at the end will be an Athene clothed in greater glory than any newly woven peplos could ever give her. This new Athene does not render the old Athene obsolete, nor does this new procession put an end to the performance of the Panathenaia; but the frieze establishes a new procession for the new goddess in her new temple, the procession of every viewer, requiring no particular occasion and no particular organisation, a procession which, whenever and in whatever circumstances it is undertaken, will bring the viewer face-to-face with an Athene such as no Greek had ever before witnessed. An Athene financed by the spoils of war, the sacking of cities, the enslavement of women, and an empire crucially founded upon the barbarising of the enemy. The monument built to house this statue does not conceal such issues, it, like the tragedies, and above all the tragedies of Euripides, and like the works of Herodotus and Thucydides, keeps them on the agenda.

Notes

1. This paper is a very abbreviated version of chapter 3 of R.G. Osborne, *The Parthenon* (London and Turin forthcoming), and is presented here substantially as delivered. I am grateful to Alan Shapiro for inviting me to take part in the conference and for subsequent discussion of the issues raised here. I have added a few skeletal footnotes which are not intended to provide an exhaustive survey of relevant modern literature.
2. On the question of the 'real' Lysistrata see D.M. Lewis, "Who was Lysistrata?" *BSA* 50 (1955) 1–2.

3. Although it is increasingly clear that Stevens was in some important respects mistaken over the date of relevant structures, the basic account of the fifth century approach to the Parthenon remains G.P. Stevens, "The Periklean Entrance Court of the Acropolis of Athens," *Hesperia* 5 (1936) 443–520. For some very useful reconstruction sketches and a sensitive account (which is partly out-dated by Stevens) see A. Choisy, *Histoire de l' architecture* 1 (Paris 1899) 412–417. Note also the remarks of D. Preziosi, *Rethinking Art History. Meditations on a Coy Science* (New Haven 1989) 168–178.
4. For the pedimental sculptures see F. Brommer, *Die Skulpturen der Parthenon-Giebel* (Mainz 1963); O. Palagia, *The Pediments of the Parthenon* (Leiden 1993). On the interpretation of the west pediment see J. Binder, "The West Pediment of the Parthenon: Poseidon," in A.L. Boegehold et al. (eds), *Studies Presented to Sterling Dow on his Eightieth Birthday, GRBM* 10 (Durham 1984). For a recent attempt to see distinct Athenian and Eleusinian presence among the spectators see B.S. Spaeth, "Athenians and Eleusinians in the West Pediment of the Parthenon," *Hesperia* 60 (1991) 331–62.
5. Lysias, *Against Theozotides* frg. VI 3.II (Gernet/Bizos); Xenophon, *Hellenika* 3.1.4.
6. For the Parthenon metopes F. Brommer, *Die Metopen des Parthenon* (Mainz 1967) is now supplemented in important ways by E. Berger, *Der Parthenon in Basel. Dokumentation zu den Metopen* (Mainz 1986). On the subject of the west metopes see B. Wesenberg, "Perser oder Amazonen? Zu den Westmetopen des Parthenon," *AA* (1983) 203–8.
7. On Amazons see L. Hardwick, "Ancient Amazons - Heroes, Outsiders or Women?" *GaR* 38 (1990) 14–35.
8. Pausanias 1.2.1, 1.41.7; Plutarch, *Theseus* 26–7.
9. On the conditions of viewing the frieze see R. Stillwell, "The Panathenaic Frieze: Optical Relations," *Hesperia* 38 (1969) 231–41 and R.G. Osborne, "The Viewing and Obscuring of the Parthenon Frieze," *JHS* 107 (1987) 98–105.
10. Basic introductions to the Parthenon frieze are provided by F. Brommer, *Der Parthenonfries* (Mainz 1977), and by C.M. Robertson and A. Frantz, *The Parthenon Frieze* (London 1975).
11. On the subject matter of the south metopes see C.M. Robertson, "The South Metopes: Theseus and Daidalos," in E. Berger (ed.), *Parthenon-Kongress Basel* (Mainz 1984) 206–9. Other scholars hold that these metopes show Ixion, Phaidra and Alcestis, or local Attic stories.
12. E. Berger, *Die Geburt der Athena im Ostgiebel des Parthenon* (Basel 1974).
13. On the identification of the gods in the metopes see M.A. Tiverios, "Observations on the East Metopes of the Parthenon," *AJA* 86 (1982) 227–9.
14. The view offered here in many ways complements that offered by I.S. Mark, "The Gods of the East Frieze of the Parthenon," *Hesperia* 53 (1984) 289–342, who gives a Protagorean reading of the east frieze.
15. On the statue of Athena Parthenos see N. Leipen, *The Athena Parthenos. A Reconstruction* (Toronto 1971) and G. Becatti, *Problemi fidiaci* (Milan 1951) 109–124. For the shield see E.B. Harrison, "Motifs of the City-Siege on the Shield of the Athena Parthenos," *AJA* 85 (1981) 281–317.

The Panathenaia and Kleisthenic Ideology

Jenifer Neils

Although today we commemorate the year 508 B.C. as the founding of Athenian democracy, in ancient Athens the *demos* may have reckoned it at 514 B.C. Just as the French elevated the dramatic and violent storming of the Bastille to a national holiday, so the Athenians celebrated the slaying of Hipparchos as the end of their years of tyranny. Harmodios and Aristogeiton were lionized with drinking songs and statuary as tyrannicides, whereas Kleisthenes enjoyed no such fame and was almost forgotten by later generations. While the murder of Peisistratos' younger son was no more an end to tyranny than the fall of the Bastille, nevertheless both events reverberated in the popular imagination much more than constitutional reforms, and so became respectively the touchstones of democracy. It is just such popular responses to change that are the topic of my paper.

Not coincidentally the slaying of Hipparchos came about during the quadrennial celebration of the city's most important festival, the Greater Panathenaia. The ostensible reason for the revenge was an insult to Harmodios' sister inflicted by the tyrant Hippias; she was first invited, then disqualified, to march in the Panathenaic procession as a *kanephoros* (Thuc. 6.54–57). This role was clearly a distinguished one in a festival where women were prominent; in vase-painting depictions of sacrificial processions, the *kanephoros* nearly always comes first. Whether this grave insult was of a political or sexual nature, we may never be sure, but certainly the timing, near the celebration of an important civic festival when patriotic fervor would have been at an all-time high, only fanned the flames of vengeance.[1]

A pattern of convergence between religious festivals and political disturbances has been noted by scholars of Athenian history,[2] but its corollary — how such rituals served to resolve social conflict and promote political change — has not been fully investigated. I propose to examine here one of the most distinctive aspects of the Panathenaia as opposed to other festivals, namely its tribal contests, in order to demonstrate how they might have helped to consolidate Kleisthenes' sudden and far reaching reforms, and in so doing, have contributed in no small way to the success of the city's democracy.

In order to override the old class distinctions based on wealth, Kleisthenes divided the population of Attica into ten new tribes. The make-up of each tribe was not only economically heterogenous, but socially and geographically as well. Each tribe was represented in the new Council of Five Hundred by fifty citizens chosen by lot, and since there were "term limits" a large proportion of the citizen body, about one-third, would take a turn on the Boule. It was also the obligation of each tribe to provide a regiment of infantry to the Athenian army. It is at this time as well that the practice of state burial, as described by Thucydides (2.34) begins; the war dead are borne to the cemetery in ten wooden coffins, one for each tribe, and the grave stelai listed casualties by tribe.[3]

Besides these political and military obligations, the new tribesmen were bound together by communal cult. Each tribe as a namesake was assigned a traditional hero, sanctioned by the oracle at Delphi, and bronze statues of these *Eponymoi* (Hippothoon, Antiochos, Ajax, Leos, Erechtheus, Aigeus, Oineus, Akamas, Kekrops, and Pandion) were set up in the Agora before the end of the fifth century.[4] These heroes seem to have been worshipped both collectively, as suggested by the dedication of ten silver *kylikes* to the *Eponymoi* by the Boule in 328/7 B.C.,[5] and individually with their own *heroa*, priesthoods, festivals and rituals.[6] Although the cults of these eponymous heroes existed before Kleisthenes' reforms, they took on a new and more significant role in the democratic reorganization of the Athenian citizenry.

Likewise the great festival of the patron deity of Athens, the Panathenaia, was not unaffected by the new democracy. The most obvious enhancement was the addition of competitions amongst the tribes. These were naturally limited to Athenian citizens, unlike the other athletic, equestrian and musical contests which were open to all Greeks, regardless of origin. Our main source of information about these events, and others at the Panathenaia, is the inscription *IG* II^2, 2311, dated to ca. 370 B.C. It lists as tribal competitions the following: *pyrrhike* or dance in armor for boys, youths and men; a contest in *euandria*, a vague term often translated as manly excellence; a torch race; and a contest of ships. In the dance, *euandria* and torch race contests the prizes recorded are 100 drachmas and a bull, presumably money and meat for a tribal victory banquet. The boat racers are more amply rewarded: 300 drachmas, 3 bulls and 200 free meals for the first prize, and 200 drachmas and 2 bulls for the second. It is at this point that the stone breaks off, and there may well have been other tribal contests listed below. A third-century inscription adds the *anthippasia* to the tribal events held at the Panathenaia; according to Xenophon (*Hipparch.* 3.10–13) it was a mock cavalry battle in which two squads of five tribal units charged each other three times in the hippodrome.[7] This event may have been added at the end of the fifth century when the Athenian cavalry was developed.

This late inscriptional evidence is augmented by commemorative monuments set up in the Athenian Agora by victorious tribes. The *anthippasia* for instance is represented on the well-known relief base signed by Bryaxis, which depicts three phylarchs riding toward the victory tripod.[8] Another hippic event is commemorated in a relief found in the Agora in 1970.[9] In addition to the cavalry on one side, there is a figure of a lion, partially preserved on the other. It is a canting device referring to the name of the winning tribe Leontis. The tribal pyrrhic is shown on the relief dedicated by Atarbos which was found built into a bastion near the Beulé Gate.[10] The left-hand section of the relief shows a cyclic chorus, an event not otherwise documented at the Panathenaia (p. 116, Fig. 6).[11] Alan Boegehold has recently suggested that this latter group may represent the *euandria* contestants, wherein manliness would consist of stately synchronized movement and singing by elderly draped men.[12] I will return to this event shortly.

The reliefs just mentioned are all of the fourth century, but what evidence is there for these events occurring in the fifth century following the reforms of Kleisthenes? Since the prizes were not Panathenaic prize amphorae, we cannot turn to this obvious source for representations. However, the pyrrhic dance, for instance, is abundantly depicted on Attic black- and red-figure vases of other shapes.[13] This series begins just around 510 B.C. and is especially popular in the first quarter of the fifth century. The majority of the vases show armed warriors practising their dancing to the accompaniment of an aulete in the palaestra, indicated by a stool with drapery. However, one early red-figure example produced in the workshop of Nikosthenes and found on Thasos (Fig. 1) may represent an actual contest, since it is one of the few vases that shows a team of dancers.[14] It is also very clearly set in Athens, as indicated by the multiple herm at the far left. Thus, we have good evidence for competitive pyrrhic dancing in the late sixth century.

Depictions of the torch race are somewhat more problematic in that this contest was part of a number of Attic festivals besides the Panathenaia. We know from the Panathenaic prize inscription that it was a tribal contest, and the extant vase depictions make this especially clear.[15] On a late fifth-century krater by the Nikias Painter in London (Fig. 2),[16] the runners wear the distinctive spiked crown of torch racers, but here their bands are inscribed. That of the victor crowned by Nike reads ANTIOX for the tribe Antiochis. This vase is also exceptional in that it was signed by the potter Nikias with his father's name and his deme "Nikias, son of Hermo-

Fig. 1. Attic black-figure skyphos by Nikosthenes, from Thasos. Photo after BCH *92 (1968) 554.*

Fig. 2. Attic red-figure krater by the Nikias Painter. London, British Museum 98.7–16.6. Photo after W. Fröhner, Collection Tyskiewicz *pl. II.*

kles, of Anaphlystos." Appropriately enough the deme of Anaphlystos belonged to the tribe Antiochis, and so the artist has evidently made this krater, which was found in Greece, for the victory celebration of his own tribe. While this particular vase has been said to depict the torch race for Prometheus, a krater in the manner of the Peleus Painter at Harvard definitely represents the Panathenaic torch race, as shown by the olive tree behind the altar of Athena Polias.[17] Before the altar is the prize for the winning runner as listed in *IG* II^2, 2311, a hydria. One should note that on this vase the two competitors wear different headgear, a distinction which probably served to differentiate the tribes.

Although scenes of ships are numerous in black-figure vase-painting and in late reliefs, none of them can be linked to the "contest of ships" that we know took place at the Panathenaia. Given the artistic challenge of representing ships on cylindrical vases,[18] perhaps fifth-century painters took a different approach to the depiction of the contest. A small group of vases and two terracotta votive shields from the Acropolis show an unidentified woman, winged Nike or Athena holding an aphlaston (Fig. 3).[19] Traditionally it has been said that this curving trireme stern with a standard in front of it, represents the capture of an enemy ship. Since these vases date within twenty years after the Persian Wars, they are interpreted as direct references to the naval victories of the Athenians, specifically at the Eurymedon River. It would constitute a rare instance in Athenian art in which a vase-painting so explicitly referred to a contemporary event. However, at precisely this time small vases with Nike carrying a musical instrument commemorate victories in musical competitions which took place at the Panathe-

Fig. 3. Attic red-figure lekythos by the Brygos Painter. New York, The Metropolitan Museum of Art, Purchase, 1925, Funds from Various Donors. (25.189.1). Photo: Museum.

naia.[20] Therefore I make the tentative suggestion that this group of vases may allude to the elusive contest of ships at the Panathenaia.[21]

But what of the *euandria*? The term has been translated as "an abundance of men, especially of good men and true; physical fitness as a subject of a contest; manliness."[22] As an abstract noun it does not conjure up an image of a contest. One ancient text, Athenaeus 13.565, discusses *euandria* in greater detail. He says "I myself praise beauty (*kallos*). In fact in the euandria they choose the most beautiful males (*kallistous*) and have them "*protophorein*". The passage then goes on to talk about an actual beauty contest conducted at Elis. The victor in this contest carried the vessels of the goddess, the runners-up led an ox and set out the sacrifice. There was a second competition at Elis, known as the *agon kallous*, which was held in honor of Athena. The winner of this contest received weapons as prizes, was decked out with ribbons by his friends, led the procession to the temple where he was given a crown of myrtles (Athen. 13.609f-610a). Back in Attica age seems to have been no impediment to beauty, since Athens had another beauty competition in conjunction with the Panathenaia, in which "beautiful" old men were chosen to be bearers of the olive branch in the procession of Athena. This group may be represented by the handsome older men on the Parthenon frieze (North IX-X), several of whom are thought to have been carrying a branch in their clenched fists.

Other sources provide snippets of information about this contest. The event, like the other tribal contests, was financed as a liturgy, by a wealthy individual who personally undertook the expenses pertaining to the contest. He undoubtedly paid for the prizes, an ox for a feast according to the fourth-century prize inscription, but shields according to Aristotle (*Ath.Pol.* 60.3). If both sources are correct, then the winning tribe received the ox and the individual victor the shield. An inscription that records the one known successful competitor (*IG* II^2, 3022) speaks of himself as the winner rather than his tribe, thus suggesting that it was an individual rather than a team event.

Given the vagueness of this term and the lack of detail in our sources, the *euandria* contest has been associated with a variety of imagery. In 1958 in a footnote in an important article on the Panathenaia, J.A. Davison suggested that the enigmatic scene on a Panathenaic-shaped amphora in the Cabinet des Médailles (Fig. 4) might represent this contest.[23] Here we see a man with two shields who appears to have leapt onto the rump of a horse to the accompaniment of the flute-player. At the far left is a stand full of cheering spectators, one of whom shouts *"kados toi kybisteistoi"* or "a jar for the tumbler."[24] The clue to this scene appears at the far right, a pair of inclined sticks, which is shown on other vases, such as a red-figure skyphos in Tampa,[25] to be a sort of spring board, off of which acrobats with two shields jump. On an Etruscan tomb painting in Chiusi, we see the jump, without shields, in progress.[26] Although Beazley suggested that this was simply a "side-show" at the Panathenaia, another shcolar more recently provided what to her was further evidence substantiating this identification, namely a unique Panathenaic prize amphora formerly in the collection of Nelson Bunker Hunt (Fig.

Fig. 4. Attic black-figure amphora of Panathenaic shape. Paris, Cabinet des Médailles 243. Photo after N. Yalouris, The Eternal Olympics *(Athens 1976) 187, fig. 90.*

Fig. 5. Attic black-figure Panathenaic prize amphora by the Kleophrades Painter. New York, private collection. Photo after Wealth of the Ancient World *(Fort Worth 1983) 66.*

5).[27] A closer look at the reverse shows an athlete juggling two shields, while a second figure, surely a servant as correctly identified by Tiverios on account of his dress, bends over to lift a third shield.[28] Von Bothmer has identified this scene as pyrrhic dancing,[29] but both the *pyrrhike* and the *euandria* were tribal contests for which amphoras of olive oil were definitively not the prize. Rather this vase must represent preparations for another well-known Panathenaic contest, the race in armor for hoplites. This identification is secured by the shield device of the running warrior, a motif that appears frequently in depictions of this event.[30]

Having now rejected all of the visual evidence brought to bear on this subject, we must fill the lacuna with an alternative. If one wants to insist that this contest must have an athletic dimension, since it is listed between the pyrrhic dance and the torch race, one might submit the unusual vase attributed to Euthymides, which shows a pair of synchronized jumpers performing to the sounds of the double pipes.[31] Although it recalls a prize vase, the well-known Middle Corinthian aryballos from Corinth,[32] featuring a solo jumper followed by teammates, it remains unique in the repertoire of Greek vase-painting, and has no obvious association with the Panathenaia.

I would like to suggest an alternative image. On a number of late sixth- and early fifth-century red-figure vases one sees a nude youth in the process of being crowned by a draped, bearded man.[33] Often the boy's hands are held forth in front of him filled with branches, a tradition known as *phyllobolia* (Fig. 6).[34] Sometimes

Fig. 6. Attic red-figure psykter by Oltos. New York, The Metropolitan Museum of Art, Rogers Fund 1910 (10.210.18). Photo: Museum.

Fig. 7. Attic red-figure hydria of the Pezzino Group. Munich, Antikensammlungen 2420. Photo: Museum.

these youths also wear prominent red sashes tied around their arms and thighs (Fig. 7).[35] They are traditionally identified as victorious athletes in the process of being crowned. There are two problems with this interpretation. First, they are smaller and hence younger than the robust athletes depicted on these and other vases. Young boys are occasionally shown as attendants at the palaestra in the sixth and early fifth centuries, but boy contestants are not depicted before the second half of the fifth century when they appear on red-figure vases and Panathenaic prize amphoras.[36] Secondly, there is no way to tell in what sport these boy victors competed since they are not shown in the midst of a specific action, like the other athletes on these vases. On some later examples the victory is even more ambiguous, as when an older man is depicted in the process of tying a ribbon around a boy's arm,[37] or when two Nikai flutter in with fillets for a boy standing at an altar.[38] It is not like Attic vase-painters to leave the nature of the athlete's victory in question. Certainly the loveliest example of this genre is the white-ground "bobbin" in New York which shows Nike about to tie a fillet onto a beautiful boy who carries a small branch in his left hand (Fig. 8).[39] This child with his long flowing hair is surely not an athlete. The prominent inscription here, as on most of these vases, draws the viewer's attention to the beauty of the boy.

Might not these fillets, wreaths and branches in association with young boys represent a cluster of symbols connoting a specific contest, namely the *euandria*? An amphora by Douris in St. Petersburg shows Nike on one side and the victor on the other (Fig. 9).[40]

Fig. 8. Attic white-ground "bobbin" by the Penthesilea Painter. New York, The Metropolitan Museum of Art, Fletcher Fund 1928 (28.267). Photo: Museum.

Fig. 9. Attic red-figure amphora by Douris. St. Petersburg, Hermitage 5576. Photo after D. Sansone, Greek Athletics and the Genesis of Sport *(Berkeley 1988) fig. 1.*

Fig. 10. Attic red-figure cup by Douris: exterior. Dresden, Staatliche Kunstsammlungen (lost since 1945). Photo: Museum.

Not only does he carry branches and wear two body ribbons, but he sports a distinctive helmet-like cap with a long peak. A third ribbon fluttering from the tip is inscribed with the words HO PAIS KALOS.[41] If one were looking for the winner of a beauty contest, what more obvious candidate? Since it is clear that in Greek art attributes such as dress, hairstyle and headgear are very specific signs to the viewer by which he is immediately informed of the identity of the figures represented, I think that this distinctive cap must be more than a flight of fancy by the artist.[42] He shows it again on a cup in Dresden where the youth is flanked by older bearded men who are clearly admiring him (Fig. 10).[43] On the interior of this cup we encounter an older man holding forth his money pouch (Fig. 11). Perhaps he is the *leitourgos* who will finance the beautiful youth of his tribe in the *euandria*?[44] This distinctive cap occurs in the tondo of a third vase, a kylix in Paris by the Ashby Painter, where an older draped man is in the process of tying a red fillet to it.[45] The nude youth who wears the cap holds a wreath and branches in his outstretched hands, and has more red fillets fluttering from his arms. Again the words HO PAIS KALOS fill the background. This cap is more elaborate in that the peak terminates in a griffin's head.[46]

Nike also appears in conjunction with this spike-capped youth. She is crowning him on a red-figure pelike attributed to the Geras Painter.[47] At least two red-figure lekythoi feature Nike alone, in flight to the right, holding just such a spiked cap.[48] Not unlike the kithara-bearing Nikai who commemorate victories in musical contests, these goddesses of victory must also refer to some athletic contest in which the competitors wore these distinctive spiked helmets.

Although these vases display a very distinct attribute of the beautiful youth, other examples which I believe could represent this contest are not as obvious. For instance a red-figure lekythos by Douris in Bologna shows Nike before a youth crowned with an olive wreath (Figs. 12–13).[49] She is about to make a libation in his honor. That he might be a tribal victor is indicated by the shoulder motif, the lion. This red-figure decoration on the shoulder of a lekythos is very unusual in the work of Douris.[50] Perhaps, like the lion on the Agora relief, it is meant to refer to the tribe of Leontis? We may never know, but astute scholars like Evelyn Harrison have

Fig. 11. Attic red-figure cup by Douris: interior. Dresden, Staatliche Kunstsammlungen (lost since 1945). Photo: Museum.

Fig. 12. Attic red-figure lekythos by Douris: body. Bologna, Museo Civico Archeologico G 80. Photo: Museum.

Fig. 13. Attic red-figure lekythos by Douris: shoulder. Bologna, Museo Civico Archeologico G 80. Photo: Museum.

shown us to look for such clues in the dress of the horsemen of the Parthenon frieze,[51] and in other equally subtle ways the tribes of Athens may have been alluded to in contemporary art.

Finally I end with a stunning vase by the Kleophrades Painter (Fig. 14).[52] Here is what I take to be the exemplar of *euandria*, a handsome youth, his muscular body adorned with fillets, bearing love-gifts, a live hare and a walking stick, about to be crowned by a draped man on the other side of the vase. Although not a prize vase, in shape it is a Panathenaic, and so, like many other red-figure Panathenaics, might well allude to the contest for which the youth is being rewarded. That he bears love gifts from his admirers is appropriate for a *pais kalos*, who has won the local beauty contest.

Whether or not we can find definite visual evidence for these tribal contests, they must have played a significant role in the budding Athenian democracy. Just as team sports today bring out patriotic feelings and strong civic identification, so these contests among the newly created Athenian tribes must have promoted group solidarity and tribal loyalty. Kleisthenes, the statesman astute enough to devise the safeguard of ostracism, might well have exploited competitive athletics to consolidate his daring reforms.

Whether or not we can associate the peculiar spiked cap of Douris' athlete with the *euandria*, another pointed cap came to play a prominent role in the French fight for liberty. How ironic that in fact it was the "Phrygian bonnet" of Athens' enemies, who were once considered the greatest threat to democracy.

Notes

1. For the suggestion that the insult was sexual in nature, i.e. that the sister was not a virgin, see B.M. Lavelle, "The Nature of Hipparchos' Insult to Harmodios," *AJP* 107 (1986) 318–31.
2. W.R. Connor, "Tribes, Festivals and Processions; Civic Ceremonial and Political Manipulation in Archaic Greece," *JHS* 107 (1987) 40–50; T. Figueira, "The Ten *Archontes* of 579/8 at Athens," *Hesperia* 53 (1984) 466–69.
3. C. Clairmont, *Patrios Nomos: Public Burial in Athens During the Fifth and Fourth Centuries B.C.* (Oxford 1983). See also R. Stupperich in this volume, pp. 93–104.
4. T.L. Shear, Jr., "The Monument of the Eponymous Heroes in the Athenian Agora," *Hesperia* 39 (1970) 145–222; H.A. Thompson and R.E. Wycherley, *Agora* XIV, *The Agora of Athens* (Princeton 1972) 38–41; E.B. Harrison, "The Iconography of the Eponymous Heroes on the Parthenon and in the Agora," *Greek Numismatics and Archaeology, Essays in Honor of Margaret Thompson*, (Wetteren 1979) 71–85. See also C.C. Mattusch in this volume, pp. 73–82.
5. S. Rotroff, "An Anonymous Hero in the Athenian Agora," *Hesperia* 47 (1978) 196–209.
6. On the ten eponymous heroes, see U. Kron, *Die zehn attischen Phylenheroen*, *AM - BH* 5 (Berlin 1976); E. Kearns, *The Heroes of Attica*, *BICS* Suppl. 57 (London 1989).
7. On cavalry display in general and the *anthippasia* in particular, see G.R. Bugh, *The Horsemen of Athens* (Princeton 1988) 59–60.
8. Athens, National Archaeological Museum 1733. See. O. Tzachou-Alexandri (ed.), *Mind and Body* (Athens 1989) 320–321, no. 105. (Hereafter *Mind and Body*).
9. Agora I 7167. See *Hesperia* 40 (1971) 271–72, pl. 57c. For a reconstruction, see J.M. Camp, *The Athenian Agora* (London 1986) 121, fig. 96.
10. Acropolis 1338. See *Mind and Body*, 208–210, no. 101; here p. 115. The draped figure at the far left is often incorrectly identified as male. She is clearly female as is the figure leading the cyclic chorus on the other portion of the relief.
11. This portion of the relief is also illustrated in J.E. Harrison, *Mythology and Monuments of Ancient Athens* (London 1890) 347, fig. 2b.
12. In a paper entitled "Group and Single Competitions at the Panathenaia," presented at the symposium "Athens and Beyond" held at Dartmouth College, Hanover, New Hampshire on October 24, 1992.
13. See J.-C. Poursat, "Les Représentations de danse armée dans la céramique attique," *BCH* 92 (1968) 550–615.
14. Poursat (supra n. 13) 554–559, figs. 1–4.
15. C.Q. Giglioli, "La corsa della fiaccola ad Atene," *RendLinc* 31 (1922) 315–335.

Fig. 14. Attic red-figure amphora of Panathenaic shape by the Kleophrades Painter. Boston, Museum of Fine Arts 10.178. Photo: Museum.

16. British Museum 98.7-16.6. *ARV*^{2} 1133, no. 1. This vase is discussed as a special commission by T.B.L. Webster, *Potter and Patron in Classical Athens* (London 1972) 44.
17. Harvard University Art Museum 1960.344. *ARV*^{2} 1041, no. 10. See J. Neils (ed.), *Goddess and Polis: The Panathenaic Festival in Ancient Athens* (Hanover and Princeton 1992) 179, no. 50. (Hereafter *Goddess and Polis*).
18. A case in point is the white-ground oinochoe from Rhitsona (Thebes R 46.83) by the Athena Painter that depicts the prow of a ship sailing to right preceded by Nike flying over the sea. See *ABL* 259, no. 115; *ABV* 530, no. 70; *ArchEph* (1912) 102 fig. 1, pl. 6,1.
19. These are listed in Webster (supra n. 16) 76. See also H.T. Wade-Gery, *JHS* 53 (1933) 100–101, and J.D. Beazley, *Der Panmaler* (Berlin 1931) 20. U. Hausmann discusses the sherds from the Acropolis in "Akropolisscherben und Eurymedonkämpfe," in K. Schauenburg (ed.), *Charites Langlotz*, (Bonn 1957) 144–151, pl. 20.
20. On Nike and musical contests see H.A. Shapiro, "Mousikoi Agones: Music and Poetry at the Panathenaia," in *Goddess and Polis* 69, and D. Shafter, "Musical Victories in Early Classical Vase Paintings," (abstract of paper) *AJA* 95 (1991) 333–34.
21. In reference to these vases with Nike, Webster (supra n. 16) 76, notes "Nike can be victory against the enemy but could also be victory in some naval competition like a race. Probably all the vases, except the votive-shields, were commissioned for a party to celebrate a trierarch's success whether in war or peace..." In this context one might also mention the Nike holding an aphlaston which appears on the columns of a Panathenaic prize amphora (Oxford 572) dated 373/2 B.C. See. N. Eschbach, *Statuen auf panathenäischen Preisamphoren des 4.Jhs.v.Chr.* (Mainz 1986) 27–29, pl. 7,3.4.
22. Liddell and Scott, s.v. εὐανδρία.
23. J.A. Davison, "Notes on the Panathenaea," *JHS* 78 (1958) 26, n. 4. The vase, Cab. Méd. 243, is illustrated in N. Yalouris (ed.), *The Eternal Olympics* (Athens 1976) 187, fig. 90; *Goddess and Polis*, fig. 23.
24. This inscription has often been misread as "kalos", although it is correct in *CVA* Vienna 2, pls. 88–89. *Kados* as the name of a vessel is discussed in M.L. Lazzarini, "I Nomi dei vasi greci nelle iscrizioni dei vasi stessi," *ArchCl* 25-26 (1973–74) 363–365.
25. Tampa 86.93 (ex-Noble). See *Goddess and Polis*, 176, no. 47, and illus. p. 96.
26. Chiusi, Tomba di Poggio al Moro (now lost). See J. Jüthner, *Die athletischen Leibesubungen der Griechen* I (Vienna 1965) pl. 19.
27. N.B. Reed, "The *euandria* Contest at the Panathenaia Reconsidered," *AncW* 15 (1987) 59–64. See also *Goddess and Polis* 35–36 and 175, no. 46.
28. M. Τιβέριος, "Παναθηναϊκή εικονογραφία," *Θρακική Επετηρίδα* 7 (1987–1990) 288–91, 295, fig. 3.
29. D. von Bothmer in *Wealth of the Ancient World* (Fort Worth 1983) 66–67, no. 9.
30. E.g. Berlin inv. 1960.2; *ARV*^{2} 861, no. 12, kylix by the Pistoxenos Painter. See J.D. Beazley, "A Hoplitodromos Cup," *BSA* 46 (1951) 7–15, pls. 5–7.
31. Published by M. Robertson, "Jumpers," *BurlMag* 119 (1977) 79–86.
32. Corinth C-54-1. D.A. Amyx, *Corinthian Vase-Painting of the Archaic Period* (Berkeley 1988) 165; M.C. and C.A. Roebuck, "A Prize Aryballos," *Hesperia* 24 (1955) 158–163, pl. 63.
33. These are listed in Webster (supra n. 16) 154–156.
34. G.Q. Giglioli, "Phyllobolia," *ArchCl* 2 (1950) 31–45.
35. See J. Jüthner, "Siegerkranz und Siegerbinde," *ÖJh* 1 (1898) 42–48; A. Krug, *Binden in der griechischen Kunst* (Diss. Mainz 1968); M. Blech, *Studien zum Kranz bei den Griechen* (Berlin 1982).
36. Cf. for instance the calyx-krater attributed to the Painter of Munich 2335 in Larisa; see M. Tiverios, *Περίκλεια Παναθήναια* (Athens 1989). For late fifth-century Panathenaics with young athletes being proclaimed victors, see P. Valavanis, "La proclamation des vainquers au Panathénées," *BCH* 114 (1990) 325–359.
37. E.g. pelike Florence 4021; *ARV*^{2} 873, no. 1; *CVA* pl. 31, 5 and pl. 35, 1–2.
38. Louvre G 278, kylix by the Briseis Painter; *ARV*^{2} 824, 23. See C. Bérard et al., *A City of Images*, trans. D. Lyons (Princeton 1989) 38, fig. 48.
39. New York 28.167, attributed to the Penthesilea Painter; *ARV*^{2} 890, no. 175.
40. St. Petersburg 5576; *ARV*^{2} 446, no. 263. See Yalouris (supra n. 23) 135, fig. 56.
41. A kylix signed by Apollodoros (Louvre G 139–140) shows a symposiast in the tondo wearing a taenia around his head inscribed HO PAIS KALOS. *ARV*^{2} 120, no. 1.
42. On headgear as a distinguishing attribute, see B.S. Ridgway, "Birds, 'Meniskoi', and Head Attributes in Archaic Greece," *AJA* 94 (1990) 583–612; E.R. Knauer, "Mitra and Kerykeion, Some Reflections on Symbolic Attributes in the Art of the Classical Period," *AA* (1992), 373–399.
43. Dresden, kylix by Douris; *ARV*^{2} 430, no. 33. See M. Wegner, *Duris* (Münster 1968) figs. 14, 16.
44. M. Meyer, "Männer mit Geld," *JdI* 103 (1988) 87–125.
45. Cab. Méd. 532, attributed to the Ashby Painter; *ARV*^{2} 455, no. 10. See D. Sansone, *Greek Athletics and the Genesis of Sport* (Berkeley 1988) fig. 4.
46. Cf. the bronze statuette of a victorious athlete in the collection of George Ortiz; here the pointed cap terminates in a swan's head. See *Hommes et Dieux de la Grèce antique* (Brussels 1982) 224, no. 140.
47. Vienna IV 905. See *CVA* Vienna (2) pl. 73, 3–5; *Alltag, Feste, Religion: Antikes Leben auf griechischen Vasen* (1991) 56, no. 6. The other side of the vase depicts an older athlete with his hair rolled up, throwing the discus in the palaestra.
48. One is illustrated in H. Moses, *Vases from the Collection of Sir Henry Englefield Bart.* (1848) suppl. pls. 4.3 and 7. The other, attributed to the Providence Painter and said to be from Sicily is currently on the art market. I thank Michael Padgett for bringing these vases to my attention.
49. Bologna G 80 (PU 321), attributed to Douris; *ARV*^{2} 446, no. 267. See L. Laurenzi, "La 'Lekythos Palagi' del Museo Civico di Bologna," *Arte antica e moderna* 1 (1958) 11–13.
50. The Berlin Painter decorated the shoulder of two of his black-bodied lekythoi with lions; *ARV*^{2} 211, nos. 199–200. See also D.C. Kurtz, *Athenian White Lekythoi* (Oxford 1975) 124–25.
51. E.B. Harrison, "Time in the Parthenon Frieze," *Parthenon Kongress, Basel* (Mainz 1984) 230–234.
52. Boston 10.178; *ARV*^{2} 183, no. 9.

The Eleusinian Mysteries and Panhellenism in Democratic Athens

Kevin Clinton

In 380 B.C. Isocrates argued in his *Panegyric* that Athens was pre-eminently qualified to lead a great Panhellenic alliance. One of his arguments had to do with Eleusis, and it is this Eleusinian aspect of Athens' Panhellenic qualifications that I wish to consider here.

It will be useful to quote Isocrates in full, as he provides the most convenient framework for our discussion:

> First of all, that which mankind first needed was provided by our city. For even if the story is mythic, nevertheless it is fitting for it to be told even now. When Demeter arrived in our land, having wandered about after Kore was abducted, and was well disposed to our ancestors because of their kindnesses (εὐεργεσίαι) which it is not possible for those who are not initiated to hear, and gave them double gifts (δωρεὰς διττάς), which happen to be the greatest — the fruits of the earth (τοὺς καρποὺς) which are reponsible for the fact that we do not live like animals, and the festival (τὴν τελετήν), the participants in which have sweeter hopes concerning the end of life and all time — our city behaved so reverently (θεοφιλῶς) and generously (φιλανθρώπως), when it was in possession of such great good things, that it did not begrudge them to others but let all share in the things which it received (28–29).

A short while later he added:

> Most cities, as a remembrance of our ancient kindness, send first-fruits (ἀπαρχαί) of grain to us every year, and those who fail to do so have often been commanded by the Pythia to remit their share of the harvest and perform the ancestral practice toward our city... (31).

This notion that most Greek cities were donating first-fruits by the year 380, has been met with scepticism by modern scholars.[1] But it would be surprising, I think, if Isocrates told an outright lie; the obvious falsehood would do him more harm than good. So we should not be too quick to call it untrue. There was no doubt some exaggeration. It was probably not a matter of "most" (or "very many") Greek cities — "most" (or "very many") was merely a congenial way of saying "many". As we shall see, there is reason to think it not incredible that "many" Greek cities sent donations of first-fruits around the year 380.

There are other points about Isocrates' message that are worth keeping in mind. Athens' claim to Panhellenic leadership here is not based on the mere *fact* that she gave grain and the Mysteries to the rest of the Greeks, with the implication that she deserves the leadership in return for this gift, as if it were some kind of business deal. What makes Athens worthy of special status, according to Isocrates, are the virtues she displayed in making these gifts — her reverence and generosity: she behaved θεοφιλῶς καὶ φιλανθρώπως. It is these *qualities* that make her deserving of Panhellenic respect.

A small point, but a significant one, is the order of Demeter's two gifts. They are, first, grain (καρποί), second, the Mysteries (ἡ τελετή). It was the grain, or more broadly agriculture, that was responsible for our abandoning a savage way of life. But the grain comes first, the Mysteries are in second position. The order is not insignificant, as we shall see later.

The grain and the Mysteries are two aspects of Eleusis. It is interesting, incidentally, that Isocrates makes no reference to "Eleusis" in this passage; for him these aspects simply belong to Athens. What I would like to explore in this paper is the process by which "Eleusis" became a special attribute of Athens, i.e. one of the qualities that won her respect among other states, and how this process was affected by the democracy. Unfortunately the available evidence will only allow me to sketch some of the stages in this development and to present a picture that is, of necessity, somewhat hypothetical. In keeping with the theme of the conference I shall concentrate mainly on the period immediately before and after the beginning of Athenian democracy; but it will be interesting, too, to take a brief look again at what resulted from this process quite a bit later, around the time of Isocrates' *Panegyric*, specifically in the second quarter of the fourth century, a particularly vibrant period in the history of the Eleusinian sanctuarv.

Let us step back a moment and consider the early relationship of Eleusis to Athens.

Some scholars still give credence to the rather surprising notion that Eleusis was independent of Athens as late as the end of the seventh century or the beginning of the sixth. Thucydides, however, attributed the political unification of Attica, which he called συνοικισμός, to the time of Theseus (2.15.1–2), i.e. before the Trojan War. It is therefore safe to say that he possessed no information that suggested to him that Eleusis was independent as late as the seventh century. Moreover, the fact that the administration of the festival of the Mysteries was in the hands of the *archon basileus* should indicate that it was under Athenian control from a very early date, conceivably as early as the beginning of the seventh century.[2]

Therefore the most important buildings at Eleusis in the Archaic period, namely the two successive Telesteria, were built when Eleusis was part of Athens. The second of these Telesteria, once thought to have been built in the reign of Peisistratos, is now being recognized as later, certainly after the third quarter of the sixth century,[3] possibly (as we shall see) even as late as the end of the century. At any rate, this new, late Archaic Telesterion, approximately twice the size of its predecessor, offers graphic proof of the growing popularity of the Mysteries.

Of course it would be interesting to know whether the new democracy was responsible for this building. In the present state of our knowledge the question cannot be answered definitively. But what is clear is that the necessity for the new building is not likely to have manifested itself suddenly: the popularity of the cult, which finally made this building inevitable, must have been steadily increasing over the course of decades. It seems only reasonable to attribute this rising popularity, in part, to the period of peace and prosperity that Athens enjoyed under Peisistratos. At any rate, whether the new Telesterion was built under the sons of Peisistratos or under the new democracy, it was surely the result of a development that had been in progress over an extended period of time.

There is a structure at Eleusis from the same period that is even more imposing than this Telesterion — the contemporary peribolos wall. It is not merely an enclosure wall for the sanctuary, modest in size like the one it replaced, but rather a massive fortification wall that surrounded not just the sanctuary but a large portion of the hill of Eleusis.[4] It measures approximately 850 meters in circumference.[5] This was an extraordinary undertaking, and it must have been carried out in response to a serious threat. It clearly was not built in haste. In fact, in those sections of the wall which were not affected by later expansion of the sanctuary, it served the fortification of Eleusis for virtually the rest of antiquity.

What might have impelled Athens to construct it? The long period of peace under Peisistratos and his sons does not seem to be a likely time. Hippias toward the end of his rule had reason to be worried about Sparta and the Alcmaeonidae, but the only fortifications attested for him are modest and were designed primarily for his own protection (Hdt. 5.64.2–65.1; Aristotle, *Ath.Pol.* 19.2).[6] It seems, therefore, we should look elsewhere for the cause.

In the year 511 B.C. approximately, the Spartans invaded Attica but were defeated (Hdt. 5.63). In 510 they invaded again and drove Hippias from power (5.64–65). In 507 Cleomenes invaded Attica in an attempt to install Isagoras as tyrant but was foiled by the Athenian people (5.70–72). In 506, however, he came back, at the head of a much larger force, this time gathered from the entire Peloponnese. They occupied Eleusis. The Athenians marched out to do battle, but were fortunate that the Peloponnesian army, for various reasons, withdrew before battle could be joined (5.74–76). Afterwards the Athenians let it be known that Cleomenes sacked the sanctuary of the Two Goddesses (6.75.3). It seems unlikely that the sanctuary would have been sacked if the hill of Eleusis had been fortified and garrisoned.[7] Thus a date after 506 for the fortification, under the new democracy, deserves serious consideration. In the first years of the democracy the Spartans posed a threat that was real, and it is easy to understand that after four invasions over a five-year span the Athenians would want to do everything possible to discourage them from making it a habit. This date seems to be in harmony with the archaeological evidence. The ram's head on the sima of the Telesterion (which must have been built at the same time or slightly later than this wall) is dated by T. Hayashi on stylistic grounds to the last decade of the century.[8] Less conclusive is a sacrificial pyre found on the outside of the (early Archaic) peribolos that may have been replaced by this new wall; it contained pottery that included very late black-figure as well as red-figure of the early fifth century.[9] It seems to me likely that the earlier peribolos was not replaced in this area (it became a retaining wall) and the pyre continued in use, but we lack a definitive determination.

Further light on the Mysteries and the interest that the democracy took in them is provided by a law passed in the 470's or 460's, now in the British Museum — *IG* I[3], 6. Originally inscribed on all four sides of a pillar, it was for its time apparently a fairly complete list of regulations governing the public part of the Mysteries, including finances, payments to priests, duties of the Eumolpidae and Kerykes, regulations concerning the Sacred Truce, and even the behaviour of other cities toward the sanctuary. The regulations concerning the Truce are of special interest. The Truce is to apply, it says, to "foreign initiates, *epoptai*, servants, and their baggage and to all Athenians." It is to be in effect "among the cities that make use of the sanctuary and among Athenians in the same cities." What is impressive is the universal validity of this Truce; it is to be in effect in all cities "which *use the sanctuary*" (χρῶνται τῶι ἱερῶι). Thus the law is not aimed just at individuals who come to the sanctuary but at entire cities all over Greece. This aim is even more striking on Side A, which unfortunately happens to be the most mutilated. Where the text on this side is somewhat better preserved, we see that it concerns disputes with cities. One of the penalties imposed on a city for improper conduct is exclusion from the sanctuary — μὴ χρώσθω τῶι ἱερῶι — i.e., all of its citizens will be denied entry. This is of considerable importance: here we see the democracy using access to the sanctuary as a tool in international relations. Moreover, the text does not suggest that this procedure is something new. It assumes that access to the sanctuary has become desirable to cities throughout Greece; that is, the sanctuary seems already to have achieved Panhellenic status. And the Athenian democracy is making good use of it.

What is happening here has a parallel with certain customs at the Olympic Games. In the year 420 B.C. when the Eleans accused the Spartans of violating the Olympic Truce (Ὀλυμπιακαὶ σπονδαί), the punishment they imposed on the Spartans was prohibition of access to the sanctuary — a privilege that the Spartans clearly were very desirous of, and which was expressed by the same technical term that we find in the Athenian law, χρῆσθαι τῶι ἱερῶι (Thuc. 5.49-50). Such prohibition was a standard punishment for violating the Olympic Truce. The Sacred Truce for the Mysteries was to apply in all Greek cities that use the sanctuary. Obviously, just as in the case of the Olympic Games, a city that did not honor the Truce would not have access to the sanctuary.[9] The Eleans sent heralds to many Greek cities to announce the Olympic Truce. The Athenians too, at the time of this law, must have likewise sent heralds to announce the Mysteries and the Truce. A truce, if not announced, would of course be ineffectual. In documents of about a century later we first learn that the Eleusinian heralds were called *spondophoroi*, and at this time and later their presence is attested in Aetolia, Phocis, Thessaly, the islands, Syria, and Alexandria.[10] The Olympic heralds may also have been called *spondophoroi* at an early date (Pindar once refers to them in this way, *Isthm.* 2.22). In any event, the situation at Eleusis, with its Sacred Truce and the penalty of denial of access to the sanctuary, follows the pattern of practice surrounding the Olympic Games. The fact that the democracy could pass a law proclaiming these penalties on Greek cities shows that Athens was dealing from a position of strength, as the home of a Panhellenic festival.

As I indicated earlier, it is unlikely that this process had taken just a short time. It would be no surprise if it was actively encouraged by Peisistratos. In any case it must have had broad support within the Polis. The sixth century saw, in addition to the Olympic Games, the ascendancy of festivals in other cities and regions to Panhellenic status: in Delphi (Pythia, 586 B.C.), Argos (Nemea, 573), and Corinth (Isthmia, 582).[11] It would be natural for Athens to promote a festival of its own. And the Mysteries were the obvious choice: a festival of respectable antiquity, they were already attracting international attention by the end of the seventh century, as the *Homeric Hymn to Demeter* implies. None of the Athenian agonistic festivals, like the Eleusinia or Panathenaia, could claim similar international status. Although athletes from other cities competed at the Eleusinia and Panathenaia, these festivals did not attract foreigners on the scale that the Mysteries did.[12]

That pilgrims from abroad were coming in increasing numbers in the early fifth century can be inferred with some probability just from what was happening to the Telesterion. T.L. Shear, Jr. has shown that the Telesterion that was built in the last quarter of the sixth century had been dismantled by 480 B.C.; and construction of a new Telesterion of *twice* the capacity was underway when the Persians invaded and brought the project to its demise.[13]

It was in this year, too, that the famous Iakchos procession took place as the Persians were in control of an abandoned Attica (Hdt. 8.65). From Eleusis came the sound of the Iakchos-song, and a dust-cloud arose as if from a crowd of about 30,000 initiates. When a Spartan asked what it was all about, he was told it was the festival that the Athenians celebrate every year to the Mother and the Daughter, a festival in which "any Athenian who wishes and any Hellene may be initiated." The dust-cloud carried in the direction of the ships on Salamis, signalling that the Persian fleet would be destroyed by the Two Goddesses. And so in this famous image the Two Goddesses and the Mysteries became inextricably linked with the salvation of the Hellenes.

The rise of the Mysteries is also reflected in Attic vase painting, especially in Triptolemos scenes. The last five years have seen two books published on these scenes, which now number about 170.[14] The development of the image seems to proceed along roughly similar lines to what we have assumed for the growth of the sanctuary's popularity. First occur scenes of Triptolemos in his local agrarian context; next scenes which celebrate his departure from Eleusis, and which serve also as an advertisement for the Mysteries; finally scenes in which his chariot sprouts wings.

With vase painting we leave legal documents and political policy and enter the world of myth and symbol. Let us step back for a moment and consider Eleusinian myth and festivals from a wider perspective. So far we have been speaking only of the Mysteries, but there were other important festivals of Demeter celebrated at Eleusis, viz. the Eleusinia, the Haloa, the Kalamaia, and — most famous of all — the Thesmophoria. Of these festivals the Thesmophoria were extremely ancient, and as I have argued recently, probably more ancient than the Mysteries.[15]

Although Triptolemos scenes predominate among Eleusinian imagery on vases, and he is otherwise clearly and abundantly associated with the Mysteries, it would be a mistake, I think, to jump to the conclusion that Triptolemos could not occur in representations that reflect other festivals of Demeter at Eleusis, in particular the Thesmophoria.[16] The ritual of the Thesmophoria has a much more fundamental relationship with agriculture and fertility than that of the Mysteries. The essential nature of Triptolemos is rooted in the agrarian sphere; it is not expressive of the *primary* sphere of the Mysteries, the underworld. In the Thesmophoria the women engage in specific ritual acts that aim at promoting the fertility of the fields; in particular, they fetch up from the underground pits, the so-called *megara*, rotten remains of piglets and place them on altars, so that people can take bits of this sacred compost and mix it with their grain-seed.[17] This compost is in effect the gift of Demeter to the farmers of Attica. It parallels the myth of the gift of grain, which also goes from the sanctuary to the world. According to the myth Triptolemos receives Demeter's seed at the sanctuary and spreads it abroad, originally no doubt just to the farmers around Eleusis and elsewhere in Attica;[18] so too fertility, through the sacred compost, was transferred from Demeter's sanctuary to the fields of Attica. The primary cults that promoted such fertility were the Thesmophoria and other Demetriac festivals at Eleusis.[19] The fact that there was a Threshing Floor of Triptolemos in the Rharian Field (Paus. 1.38.6) implies that at Eleusis a ritual took place at harvest time in which Triptolemos played a part. Therefore Triptolemos was associated with both beginning and end of the agrarian cycle at Eleusis. It would be surprising if this association, in some form or other, did not extend to festivals of Demeter that celebrated other moments of that cycle.[20]

Furthermore, as I recently pointed out, the main aetiological elements in the *Homeric Hymn to Demeter* — the Iambe episode, the nursing of Demophon — are explanatory of ritual that took place not in the Mysteries but in the Thesmophoria.[21] In the *Hymn* the Mysteries represent a new element, added at the end, as a gift from Demeter for the return of Kore: the poet has used an older traditional story, which reflects a much older cult, to honor in the end a relatively recent institution, the Mysteries. Thus the *Homeric Hymn to Demeter* is a kind of hybrid story, in which the episode of Triptolemos and the grain has been replaced by the gift of the Mysteries, and this new ending serves to recommend the Mysteries to a broader Hellenic audience.[22] As it happens, the position of the Mysteries in the *Hymn* actually reflects the order in which the festivals came into existence: first the Thesmophoria, then the Mysteries. This happens also to be the very order that Isocrates gives for the two gifts of Demeter: he mentions first the grain, then the Mysteries. And it is the same order that we see in the chronicle of the *Parian Marble*: Demeter arrives with the grain and gives it to Triptolemos, who sows it in the Rharian Field, several years before the Mysteries were established.[23] In very rough terms, we see a somewhat similar order in vase painting, first a focus on Triptolemos in an agrarian setting in which grain is the important element, but finally, in the fourth century, a focus that is directed predominantly on the Mysteries.

At any rate, Triptolemos must be a fairly old farmer-god.[24] Before the Mysteries came to be, he was, I suspect, associated with the Thesmophoria and other Eleusinian festivals, at least in myth but sometimes also in ritual. The Mysteries also promoted agrarian prosperity (Ploutos), but the cult did this more through image and symbol than the sort of ritual act that was performed at the Thesmophoria.[25] And Triptolemos would seem to fit the overall pattern by which features of the Thesmophoria (e.g. *aischrologia*) were incorporated in the Mysteries, now somewhat transformed or given different emphasis.[26] Within the original (mythic) context of the Thesmophoria Triptolemos would be merely a local god of fertility, but in the Mysteries he became, like Ploutos, an image of what was promised (though he played of course, as *spondophoros*, a much greater role than Ploutos); and as the Mysteries began to receive international recognition and were used by Athens to further her international reputation, it seems only natural to suppose that it was in the service of the Mysteries that he gradually extended his mythic travels, eventually beyond the borders of Attica. At the same time, however, he did not lose his original association with other local festivals of Demeter at Eleusis.

This, I think, is reflected in vase painting, though it can only be seen to some extent, since the evidence starts at a relatively late stage within the process. We see the development of Triptolemos from a (more or less) local figure to one of Panhellenic dimensions, reflecting his final status as a major god in the Mysteries.

In the earliest black-figure scene (Figs. 1–2), on an amphora by the Swing Painter in Göttingen, he sits on a stool in a cart that hovers in the air between two pairs of figures, each pair consisting of a male in the foreground, a female in the background.[27] These figures have been understood to be country folk, receiving instruction and the gift of the grain from the god. This interpretation seems to be reasonable, except that the figures may well be Eleusinians, and I doubt that women would be shown receiving instruction in agriculture. In fact we should not expect instruction in agriculture at all: the gift of agriculture is a later embellishment. Isocrates said that Demeter gave the Athenians grain (not agriculture), and the grain is what the Athenians passed on. The Eleusinian *dadouchos* Kallias once told the Spartans: "It is said that the first foreigners to whom our ancestor Triptolemos caused the secret rites of Demeter and Kore to be shown were Herakles, your *Archegetes*, and the Dioskouri, your fellow citizens, and the Peloponnese was the first country to which he gave the *seed* of Demeter's fruit, *σπέρμα ... τοῦ Δήμητρος καρποῦ*."[28] Triptolemos distributed seeds — he did not teach agriculture, at least not in the early days; his elevation to instructor in agriculture came later.[29] In the scene on the amphora Fig. 2 the woman on the left has a small round object in her hand, pressed between her thumb and fingers; the woman on the right is looking at her hand, as if anticipating something she is about to receive (there is evidently nothing yet in her hand). The round object has been called an apple,[30] but that cannot be right; Triptolemos was not a distributor of apples. It looks like a significant element of the scene; we may assume therefore it is a small part of an ear of wheat, containing a few seeds. A somewhat similar scene occurs on an unattributed black-figure amphora in Würzburg (Fig. 3).[31] Here too the woman on the left is holding something very small (smaller than the object in Fig. 2) with the tips of her fingers; the woman on the

Figs. 1 & 2. Göttingen, Archäologisches Institut der Universität J 14 (Photo: S. Eckardt). Black-figure amphora by the Swing Painter, with a Triptolemos scene.

right is looking at her own hand, again perhaps in anticipation of something that she is about to hold.[32] Triptolemos is facing the woman on the right, while on the amphora in Göttingen he looks back at the woman on the left. In each case he seems to have finished with the woman on the left and has turned (or is about to turn) his attention to the figure on the right. On the Würzburg amphora it is, I suspect, significant that one of the ears of wheat held by Triptolemos is situated right next to the hand of the woman on the right. She is apparently about to pluck some kernels from the ear, as the woman on the left has already done. The gestures of these women are much more comprehensible than on the amphora in Göttingen, where their gestures are not so well related to Triptolemos.[33]

An amphora in Brussels by the Swing Painter shows Triptolemos hovering not quite so high, this time between a pair of male figures, again probably country folk.[34] The other side of the vase depicts a black African and two Amazons, and Alan Shapiro has suggested that this pairing, like the pairing of Scythians and Ethiopians on other vases, may be "a shorthand reference to the whole of the inhabited earth, the *oikoumene*," which will receive the seeds from Triptolemos.[35] He also points out

Fig. 3. Würzburg, Martin v. Wagner - Museum der Universität L 197. Black-figure amphora, with a Triptolemos scene.

that the magical quality of Triptolemos' cart, hovering as it is in mid air, may also allude to his world-wide mission. Hayashi in his recent book has emphasized that the wheels of his vehicle are not the type found on a typical, slow-moving country cart: they are the wheels of an aristocratic racing chariot, made for speed.[36]

The two amphoras by the Swing Painter date from ca. 540 and 530 B.C. respectively, so are from the time of Peisistratos, and if Shapiro's suggestions are correct, we may conclude that the mission of Triptolemos had already been expanded beyond the borders of Attica during the reign of the tyrant. This seems consistent with everything else we know.

Other black-figure vases show Triptolemos in the presence of Demeter and Kore, evidently at his departure.[38] On red-figure vases the departure of Triptolemos from Eleusis was of course to become canonical, and a frequent motif in the departure scene was the pouring of a libation, a σπονδή. It first occurs on a hydria by the Berlin Painter ca. 480 B.C.[39] Now according to myth Triptolemos not only distributed seed on his mission, but as the *dadouchos* Callias told the Spartans, he also announced the Mysteries. In the human world the announcement was made by the *spondophoroi*, who travelled far and wide heralding the Mysteries and the Sacred Truce.[40] The law that we discussed above reveals that the Sacred Truce was a well-established institution by the 460's. So it seems justified to see in the new motif, the pouring of the libation by Triptolemos, an allusion to Triptolemos as *spondophoros*.[41] Although it is conceivable that the *spondophoria* was first instituted under the democracy, it is much more likely, in view of the success of the Mysteries, that it existed at least as far back as the reign of Peisistratos. It seems reasonable to assume that some time elapsed before the *spondophoria* found expression in art, though I think we see a hint of it already around 540 B.C. in the racing wheels on Triptolemos' vehicle. At any rate, the paintings and the law indicate that the Eleusinian *Spondai* were certainly an important aspect of the Mysteries in the early years of the democracy. The range of these missions, both in myth and life, was evidently becoming more and more impressive. Details of the myth are given by Sophocles. From fragments of his *Triptolemos*, produced in the 460's, perhaps in 468--therefore right around the time of the law — we learn that Triptolemos went at least as far afield as Italy, Liguria, and Carthage, and in the north to the Illyrians and Scythians.[42]

The wings which first appear on Triptolemos' wagon were not necessarily inspired by the rigors of this journey.[43] They appear for the first time on a red-figure vase of the late sixth century,[44] but right around the same time (510 B.C.) they also happen to appear on a wagon carrying Dionysos (in a black-figure scene)[45] as well as on a wagon carrying Hephaistos (in two red-figure scenes).[46] (The same vase that exhibits the Dionysos scene has a similar scene on the other side, featuring Triptolemos, but here, just where you would most expect Triptolemos to have wings, he has none.) The wings perhaps have more to do with the marvelous quality of these gods as civilizers:[47] Dionysos, donor of wine; Hephaistos, inventor of ingenious technology; Triptolemos, distributor of grain.[48] In the case of Dionysos and Hephaistos the wings quickly disappeared; in the case of Triptolemos they stuck — they were, obviously, happy symbols. So, in the end, they did serve to emphasize the far-reaching sweep of his mission and of course that of his human counterparts, the *spondophoroi*.

The Berlin Painter was fond of Eleusinian scenes, and some of his scenes with Triptolemos allude to a broader Eleusinian context than just the Mysteries. This type of scene, which draws upon more than the Mysteries, has, as I mentioned earlier, precedents in our earliest Triptolemos scenes, and it continues into the third quarter of the fifth century. Several scenes of this type are extremely difficult to interpret.[49] In the space available here I would like to touch on three examples of those that are a bit less difficult. First, just to mention it briefly, the famous skyphos by Makron in the British Museum, which reflects the rich cultic life of Eleusis: Dionysos and his father Zeus (Dionysos had a sanctuary there, with a theater), Eumolpos and his father Poseidon, the departure of Triptolemos flanked by Demeter and Kore and Eleusis herself.[50] A very different scene appears on the name vase of the Painter of London E 183 (Figs. 4–6); the figures from left to right are: Plouton, a woman handing torches to Kore, Kore, Triptolemos, Demeter (inscribed), Hekate (inscribed), a woman running up with a basket.[51] Plouton, the preponderance of women, the basket (perhaps containing sacred compost), and Hekate do not evoke the Mysteries but seem to suggest, with the help of a passage in Nonnus, the Thesmophoria.[52] My third example (Figs. 7–9, and Fig. 7 on p. 78) is a new scene, on a footed dinos in the Getty Museum, by a contemporary of the Berlin Painter, the Syleus Painter (according to the attribution of J.R. Guy, who kindly provided inscriptions).[53] The main scene (Fig. 7) shows Triptolemos in a chariot equipped with a magnificent pair of wings; Demeter is on the left, and Kore on the right is handing him his phiale; at her feet, a wonderful spotted, bearded snake, unattached to the chariot, is advancing upon her. Standing behind Demeter (Fig. 8; Fig. 7 on p. 78) are Hippothon (with inscription), the eponymous hero of the tribe Hippothontis, of which Eleusis was a part, and Eleusis herself (with inscription), pouring a libation; the male figure behind Eleusis, bundled up in his himation, is unfortunately uninscribed. Standing behind Kore, on the right (Fig. 9), is Kalamites, the eponymous hero of the Kalamaia, an Eleusinian festival held in the spring for the benefit of the rising grainstalks.[54] Opposite the Triptolemos scene, on the other side as it were, a rather regal couple face each other (Figs. 8–9): they are Theos and Thea, the special gods of the Mysteries who are the equivalent of Hades and Persephone.[55] It is our first inscribed example of Theos in Attic vase painting; though the name of Thea is

4.

5.

6.

Figs. 4–6. London, British Museum E 183. Red-figure hydria by the Painter of London E 183, depicting Plouton, woman, Kore, Triptolemos, Demeter, Hekate, woman.

not inscribed, there can be no doubt that it is she; a very similar pair appears on a crater by the Berlin Painter, again opposite a Triptolemos scene.[56] This painting gives us our first known depiction of Kalamites, a little-known hero who had a shrine next to the Agora. The scene presents a range of Eleusinian images. The figure of Eleusis herself emphasizes that the focus on Eleusis is a rather broad one. Theos and Thea of course illustrate the principal cult, the Mysteries, but Kalamites alludes to the Kalamaia, the more agrarian festival. It is from this agrarian sphere that the great snake is drawn, as is the snake that is more commonly attached to Triptolemos' wagon. The snake is not a symbol of the Mysteries.[57] The women at the Thesmophoria believed that snakes

Fig. 7. Malibu, The J. Paul Getty Museum 89.AE.73. Red-figure footed dinos attributed to the Syleus Painter, depicting Demeter, Triptolemos, Kore.

Fig. 8. Malibu, The J. Paul Getty Museum 89.AE.73. Red-figure footed dinos attributed to the Syleus Painter, depicting Theos, Thea, man, Eleusis, Hippothon.

Fig. 9. Malibu, The J. Paul Getty Museum 89.AE.73. Red-figure footed dinos attributed to the Syleus Painter, depicting Kore, Kalamites, Theos, Thea.

dwelled amidst the rotting pigflesh in the great pits that were called *megara*; it is in the context of this festival (and similar ones) that we should expect to see the snake.[58] In the figure of Hippothon the painting also presents a political dimension — an allusion to the position of the deme of Eleusis in the Athenian Polis.

Scenes which give us these broader glimpses of Eleusis and her cults virtually disappear by the end of the third quarter of the fifth century.[59] In the fourth century when Triptolemos appears on vases in the company of other figures, the scenes nearly always depict just the Eleusinian Mysteries,[60] as in the scene on a relief hydria in St. Petersburg, the so-called Regina Vasorum (Fig. 10).[61] This scene presents an outline of the myth enacted in the Mysteries; it also shows the divine initiates (nos. 4 and 7) who attended the festival; and it does not

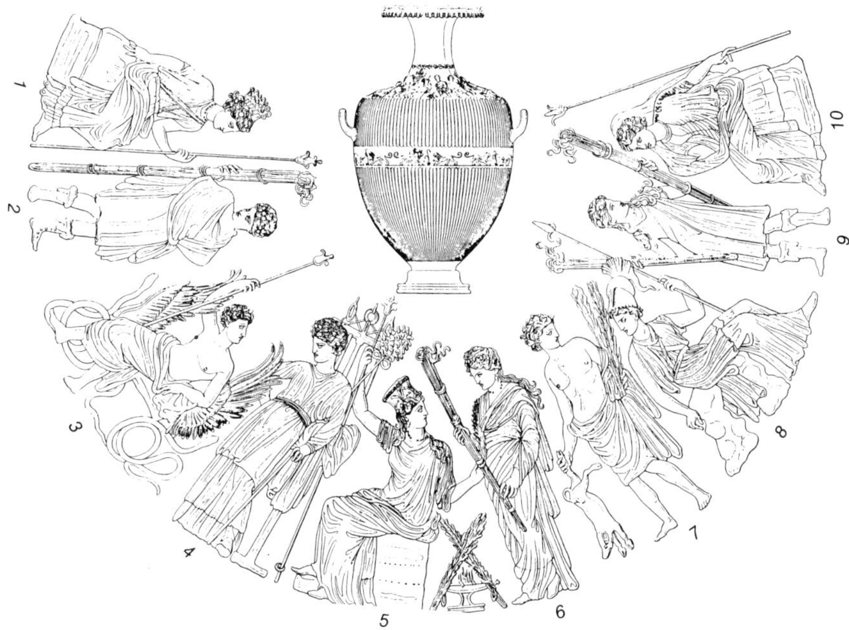

Fig. 10. St. Petersburg, Hermitage 525. Relief hydria from Cumae, depicting (1) Demeter on Mirthless Rock, (2) Iakchos, (3) Triptolemos, (4) Dionysos, (5) Demeter, (6) Kore, (7) Herakles, (8) Athena, (9) Eubouleus, (10) Thea. After A. Baumeister, Denkmäler des klassischen Altertums, *I (Munich and Leipzig 1885) 474, fig. 520.*

let us forget that it was Athens who invited them. Both Triptolemos (no. 3) and Athena (no. 8) are shown next to an initiate, and Triptolemos and Athena are specifically linked by their symmetrical positions with respect to the edges and the center of the scene. This close association of the goddess of Athens and the divine *spondophoros* of the Mysteries is also advertised on several fourth century Panathenaics, which show Triptolemos on top of columns flanking Athena.

The Panathenaics with Triptolemos start in the year 367/6 B.C., and are attested for two additional years, 364/3 and 336/5.[62] N. Eschbach has argued that the choice of the figure on the column was probably the result of a decision by the Athenian Boule. If he is correct, then at least some elements of Eleusinian iconography had entered the sphere of religious iconography that was carefully handled by the Polis.[63] It is precisely in this period that the Polis decided to issue a new bronze coinage, featuring symbols such as the piglet and the figure of Triptolemos, for use as a festival coinage at the Mysteries, "as another amenity to benefit the many foreign visitors attending the festival."[64] It is also at this time that the Polis published a new, comprehensive law governing the Mysteries.[65] Its many fragments found in the Eleusinion reveal that it was perhaps even more detailed than the law that was issued approximately one hundred years earlier (*IG* I^3, 6). Also at this time, the decade of the 360's, the Polis launched a major building project at the sanctuary in Eleusis, as the excavations of K. Kourouniotes and G. Mylonas revealed.[66] The sanctuary was extended to the south and west, which necessitated the construction of a new peribolos to surround this extension. Shortly afterwards a new foundation was laid around the Telesterion, and G. Mylonas and J. Travlos concluded that it was meant to support a major expansion of the hall of the Mysteries.[67] In the next decade work was begun on a building that stood next to the new peribolos wall in the south,[68] and thought was given to a stoa for the Telesterion.[69] For various reasons, mainly financial, the Telesterion was not expanded, and construction of the stoa was postponed.[70] Clearly the second quarter of the fourth century was a period in which the sanctuary reached a new height of prosperity and popularity, with the city offering every encouragement to initiates from all over Greece. I think it entirely credible, therefore, that *many* cities were contributing first-fruits to the sanctuary at this time, as Isocrates stated in his *Panegyric* of 380 B.C.[71] The response of Greeks at large, by the end of the second decade of the century, to the appeal of the Mysteries evidently encouraged Athens to tighten the association of the Polis and the Mysteries, and this development is reflected in the very striking change in scenes on vases. Now there is a strong interest in scenes which show initiates, i.e. the divine initiates, Dionysos, Herakles, and the Dioskouri. The presence of Herakles and the Dioskouri alludes of course to the respect held for the Mysteries by the Dorian states of the Peloponnese (or the respect that Athenians felt they should have).

What we miss in fourth-century painting is Triptolemos' original associations with the broader array of agrarian cults at Eleusis, associations which persisted from the very beginning of Triptolemos imagery in painting to the end of the third quarter of the fifth century. This change seems also to be tied together with the Athenian interest in advertising its Panhellenic festival. Other agrarian cults of Eleusis, like the Thesmophoria and Kalamaia, were of great local interest, but their images did nothing for the glory of Athens. And the painters followed the national interest.

In conclusion: Athens began to promote the Mysteries among other Greek cities at least as early as the first part of the sixth century; the pace of this process seems to accelerate under the early democracy; and it culminates in the fourth century in some of the images we have discussed, which express the same sentiment that Isocrates put forth in his *Panegyric*: in both speech and image the focus is fixed sharply on the Mysteries as gift and Athens as donor. In the speech Eleusis is not mentioned; in vase painting the figure of Eleusis no longer appears. The process of Panhellenization of the Mysteries, which was at work in the early democracy, but which in the last quarter of the fifth century must have suffered, regained its momentum in the fourth century and, certainly by the Hellenistic period, was crowned with success: the Mysteries had achieved a status equal to that of the Olympic Games, a status that lasted till the end of antiquity.[72] It is no great surprise, therefore, to see the festival so described, in the second century after Christ, by a famous tourist from Asia Minor — Pausanias: "Many are the sights to be seen in Greece, and many are the wonders to be heard; but on nothing do the gods bestow more care than on the Eleusinian rites and the Olympic Games."[73]

Abbreviations

Clinton, *Iconography* = K. Clinton, *Myth and Cult: the Iconography of the Eleusinian Mysteries* (*ActaAth*-8, 11, Stockholm 1992).

Deubner, *Feste* = L. Deubner, *Attische Feste* (Berlin 1932).

Eschbach = N. Eschbach, *Statuen auf panathenäischen Preisamphoren des 4. Jhs. v. Chr.* (Mainz/Rhein 1986).

Hayashi, *Bedeutung* = T. Hayashi, *Bedeutung und Wandel des Triptolemosbildes vom 6.-4. Jh. v. Chr.* (*Beiträge zur Archäologie* 20, Würzburg 1992).

Mylonas, *Eleusis* = G.E. Mylonas, *Eleusis and the Eleusinian Mysteries* (Princeton 1961).

Shapiro, *Art and Cult* = H.A. Shapiro, *Art and Cult under the Tyrants in Athens* (Mainz/Rhein 1989).

Schwarz, *Triptolemos* = G. Schwarz, *Triptolemos, Ikonographie einer Agrar- und Mysteriengottheit* (*Grazer Beiträge*, Suppl. 2, Horn-Graz 1987).

I am grateful to the J. Paul Getty Museum, the Martin von Wagner-Museum of the University of Würzburg, and the Archäologisches Institut of the University of Göttingen for providing photographs of vases in their collections.

Notes

1. They point to a document at Eleusis, *IG* II^2, 1672, of the year 329/8, which lists the donors of the first-fruits in that year; none of them are from outside Attica except for islands under Athenian control: Salamis, Skyros, Lemnos, and Imbros. But we must bear in mind that this is fifty years later; the position of Athens in 329/8 was far different from what it was when Isocrates wrote his *Panegyric*, and 329/8 was a year in which grain was scarce.
2. For a full discussion of the subject see my article, "The Sanctuary of Demeter and Kore at Eleusis," in R. Hägg and N. Marinatos (eds.), *Greek Sanctuaries: New Approaches* (London 1993) esp. 110–112.
3. T.L. Shear, Jr., "The Demolished Temple at Eleusis," *Hesperia Suppl.* 20 (1982) 131, noted that this Telesterion should not be assigned to Peisistratos but to his sons.
4. Mylonas, *Eleusis*, 91–96; Travlos, *Attika*, 93–94, figs. 136, 144–148.
5. As measured on Travlos' plan, *Attika*, fig. 136.
6. Cf. D.M. Lewis, *CAH* IV^2 300.
7. During the Peloponnesian War the Spartans evidently never attempted to occupy Eleusis, presumably because the fortress was garrisoned.
8. Ram's head: Mylonas, *Eleusis* 81, fig. 21. Hayashi, *Bedeutung* 20–23.
9. Pottery and other finds: K. Kourouniotes-G.E. Mylonas, "Excavations at Eleusis, 1932," *AJA* 37 (1933) 281–282; now K. Kokkou-Vyridi, *Πρώιμες πυρὲς θυσιῶν στὸ Τελεστήριο τῆς Ἐλευσίνας* (diss. Athens 1991) 92–141, 150–157, 185–241, who dates the finds to a period from the second quarter of the sixth century to the first quarter of the fifth (except for two terracotta figurines, which she assigns to the middle of the fifth century, although their provenience cannot be documented). (I am very grateful to Dr. Kokkou-Vyridi for allowing me to read her dissertation.) Discussion: Hayashi, *Bedeutung* 22–23 with further bibliography. Mylonas and Kourouniotes believed that the pyre continued to be used even after the new peribolos was built, but F. Noack, *Eleusis: die baugeschichtliche Entwicklung des Heiligtums* (Berlin and Leipzig 1927) 88, had reason to believe that the opposite was true.
10. The penalty for violating the truce is not preserved in *IG* I^3, 6; but if there is any doubt about it, the provision that the truce is to apply to "the cities who use the sanctuary" (B.27–32) implies of course that where the truce is not in effect, those cities do not use the sanctuary.

    On the truce for the Mysteries and the Olympic Games cf. M. Sakurai and A.E. Raubitschek, "The Eleusinian Spondai (*IG* I^3, 6, lines 8–47)," *Φίλια Ἔπη* 2 (Athens 1987) 263–265. I cannot accept the conclusions of G. Rougement, "La Hiéroménie des Pythia," *BCH* 97 (1973) 75–106, that the period designated for the spondai of *IG* I^3, 6 does not constitute an international truce but merely a local Attic "truce," i.e. a period of civil and judicial inactivity; see the commentary to my forthcoming edition of this document.
11. Aetolia: E. Schweigert, "Greek Inscriptions (1–13)," *Hesperia* 8 (1939) 5–12, no. 3, lines 8–14. Phocis: Aeschines 2.133–134. Thessaly: B. Helly, *Gonnoi* II (Amsterdam 1973) no. 109. Islands: *IG* II^2, 1672, line 4. Syria: *IG* II^2, 785; 1236; G.A. Stamires, "Greek Inscriptions," *Hesperia* 26 (1957) 47–51, no. 7 (= L. Robert, *Hellenica* 11–12 [1960] 92–111). Alexandria: Polybius 28.19.4, where the general Greek term *theoroi* is used in place of *spondophoroi*. It should be noted that the Athenians used the term *spondophoroi* for all their *theoroi* (announcers of festivals); consequently not every one of the above references need to be an announcement of the Mysteries.
12. For a recent survey of the early archaeological development of these sanctuaries see C.Morgan, "The Origins of Panhellenism," in Marinatos and Hägg (supra n. 2) 18–44 (with further bibliography); on the Isthmia, E.R.Gebhard, "The Evolution of a Panhellenic Sanctuary : From Archaeology Towards History at Isthmia," ibid. 154–177; on the foundation date of the Pythian Games, S.G.Miller, "The Date of the First Pythaid," *CSCA* 11 (1978) 127–158; A.A.Mosshammer, "The Date of the First Pythaid - Again," *GRBS* 23 (1982) 15–30.
13. The evidence of course is from later periods; for example, Aristides, *Panathenaic* 257 Oliver (= 311 D): "... but you alone of the Hellenes every year put on a festival inferior to no quadriennial festival and receive in the Eleusinion more than others receive in their whole city" (Oliver). On participation in the Panathenaia cf., for example, the discussion of victor lists by S.V. Tracy and C. Habicht, "New and Old Panathenaic Victor Lists," *Hesperia* 60 (1991) 189–236.
14. Supra n. 3.
15. Schwarz, *Triptolemos*, and Hayashi, *Bedeutung*.

16. Clinton, *Iconography* 30–37.
17. We have hardly any information about the sacrificial ritual of these cults, so it is impossible to know whether offerings to Triptolemos were included. But there are versions of the *myth* which end with the gift of the grain and the subsequent role of Triptolemos, but in which the establishment of the Mysteries is either not mentioned at all or plays at best a subordinate role: 1) the Orphic version represented by *Orph. Frag.* 49 (Kern), supplemented from other sources by N.J. Richardson, *The Homeric Hymn to Demeter* (Oxford 1974) 79–82 and F. Graf, *Eleusis und die orphische Dictung Athens in vorhellenistischer Zeit* (*RGVV* 33, Berlin and New York 1974) 165–168 (the Mysteries are apparently not mentioned); 2) the mythical events as described in the *Marmor Parium* 12–15 (Jacoby), which puts Demeter's arrival and giving of the grain to Triptolemos in one year, Triptolemos' sowing and harvesting of it in the following year, and Eumolpos' first showing of the Mysteries at least ten years later; 3) the poem of Musaeus referred to by Pausanias 1.14.2–3, in which Triptolemos appears as the first sower of grain, and it is not clear whether the Mysteries were mentioned; and 4) most interestingly, a version of the story given by Hyginus, *Fab.* 147 (Rose), in which after Triptolemos returns from distributing the grain, he establishes the Thesmophoria (cf. the very similar version in Servius and Lactantius Placidus, conveniently printed in H.J.Rose, *Hyginae Fabulae* [Leiden 1933] 183–184; discussion in Clinton, *Iconography* 32).

    Diodorus Siculus in telling the story of the Rape of Persephone (5.68) and the gift of grain to Triptolemos ends with a description of Demeter as Thesmophoros, lawgiver (by an etymology then popular but now known to be false; Deubner, *Feste* 44–45). This association with Demeter Thesmophoros probably led to the attribution of lawgiving to Triptolemos himself that we find in Porphyry, *Abst.* 4.22. And of course in literature there are numerous references to Triptolemos, the gift of grain, and his sowing without any reference to the Mysteries. Note that in the *Marmor Parium* Triptolemos harvests as well as sows; Callim. *Cer.* 21 implies that he is involved in the harvest; Diodorus 1.18 also assigns the harvest to Triptolemos. This must go back to Eleusinian ritual: Paus. 1.38.6 reports a Threshing Floor of Triptolemos. It is probably also relevant that some of the ritual in the Thesmophoria was regarded as imitating the "old way of life" before the discovery of grain (Diodorus 5.6.7; other references and discussion in Graf, *op. cit.* 178–179), and the gift of the piglets at the Thesmophoria was regarded as a thank-offering for Demeter's introduction of civilized life (*Schol.* Lucian 276, lines 21–22 Rabe). Triptolemos of course was the one who brought this new way of life to the whole world; Soph. frgs. 605–606 Radt; Plato, *Leg.* 782B; Aristides, *῾Ρώμης ἐγκώμιον* 225 (*τὸν νομιζόμενον πρὸ Τριπτολέμου βίον*); Philo, *De praemiis* 8. This notion of course is implicit in the frequent descriptions of Triptolemos as distributor of *καρπὸς ἥμερος* (e.g., Paus. 1.14.3). The Mysteries also became associated with this "new life"; cf. Cicero, *Leg.* 2.36.
18. Deubner, *Feste* 50–60; Clinton, "Sacrifice in the Eleusinian Mysteries," in *Early Greek Cult Practice, Proceedings of the Fifth International Symposium at the Swedish Institute in Athens, 26–29 June, 1986* (*ActaAth*-4 38, Stockholm 1988) 69–80.
19. First to the Rharian Field, where there was Triptolemos' Threshing Floor and his altar: Paus. 1.38.6; *Marm. Par.* 13; cf. Eur. *Supp.* 28–31; Richardson (supra n. 17) 297 *ad* line 450.
20. M.P. Nilsson, "Die eleusinische Gottheiten," *ArchRW* 32 (1935) 86, emphasized the importance of the agrarian aspect of Eleusinian religion and the fact that the story of Triptolemos and his mission is rooted in this aspect.
21. R.M. Simms, "The Eleusinia in the Sixth to Fourth Centuries B.C.," *GRBS* 16 (1975) 269–279, argues that Triptolemos was included in the mythic and ritual context of the Eleusinia. This is basically reasonable, but *IG* I^3, 5 cannot be used as evidence: see Clinton, "*IG* I^2, 5, the Eleusinia, and the Eleusinians," *AJP* 100 (1979) 1–12.
22. *Iconography* 28–37.
23. The form of the episode that has been replaced can only be conjectured. It presumably involved Triptolemos.
24. Supra n. 17.
25. Like Echetlaeus, on whom see M.H. Jameson, "The Hero Echetlaeus," *TAPA* 82 (1951) 49–61; cf. *LIMC* III (1986) s.v. Echetlos. (J.G. Szilágyi).
26. Cf. Clinton, *Iconography* 91–94.
27. Clinton, *Iconography* 63.
28. *ABV* 309.83; E. Böhr, *Der Schaukelmaler* (Mainz/Rhein 1982) 35, no. 103, pls. 104A, 105A; Shapiro, *Art and Cult* 76–77, pl. 33d.
29. Incidentally, Xenophon does not mean to say that Triptolemos showed the Mysteries — he is using the verb "show" in a causative sense. By announcing the Mysteries to the Peloponnesians Triptolemos caused them to be shown to Herakles and the Dioskouri. Only Eumolpos, the first hierophant, could perform the showing.
30. Certainly by the Hellenistic period: Diodorus 5.68.2 (from Timaeus).
31. Schwarz, *Triptolemos* 74.
32. Schwarz, *Triptolemos* 30 V 7; Shapiro, *Art and Cult* 77, pl. 35a; E. Simon, *Die Götter der Griechen* (Munich 1969) 109, fig. 101; eadem, *Führer durch die Antikenabteilung des Martin von Wagner Museums der Universität Würzburg* (Mainz/Rhein 1975) 116, L 197.
33. Each woman has a small black spot in the middle of her hand, probably not an object but an indication of the hollow of her palm.
34. The painter may not have been interested in this aspect of a scene which he took from a predecessor.
35. *ABV* 308.82; Böhr (supra n. 28) 35, pl. 123; Schwarz, *Triptolemos* 29 V 3.
36. Shapiro, *Art and Cult* 77.
37. Hayashi, *Bedeutung* 30–31, 59–61.
38. E.g., Schwarz, *Triptolemos* 29, V 4–5.
39. Copenhagen, Ny Carlsberg Glyptotek 2696; *ARV*^{2} 210.181; Schwarz, *Triptolemos*, 36, V 42; Hayashi, *Bedeutung* 136, no. 39.
40. Supra n.11.
41. This allusion is accepted by Hayashi, *Bedeutung* 84. Whether or not the heralds were called *spondophoroi* at this date (supra n. 11) is not important; what matters is that their activity parallels Triptolemos' mission. In *Iconography* 80–82 I noted this role in fourth-century scenes.
42. Frgs. 598, 601–602, 604 Radt. Nothing is said in these fragments or their contexts about the Mysteries.
43. On the wings see especially Hayashi, *Bedeutung* 56–57.
44. Athens, Acropolis 147; *ARV*^{2} 89.19; Schwarz, *Triptolemos* 34, V 32; Hayashi, *Bedeutung* 133, no. 27.
45. Neck amphora of the Priam Painter, Compiègne, Mus. Vivenel 975; *ARV*^{2} 331.13, *Add.*^{2} 90; Schwarz, *Triptolemos* 30, V 8; Hayashi, *Bedeutung* 130, no. 15B. Photograph: K. Schefold, *Götter- und Heldensagen der Griechen in der spätarchaischen Kunst* (Munich 1978) 35, fig. 29.
46. Hayashi, *Bedeutung* n. 186: 1) Kylix, Berlin, Staatliche Mus. F 2273; *ARV*^{2} 174.31; Schefold (supra n. 45) 35, fig. 30. 2) *CVA* Florence (4) pl. 118.2; Simon 1969, (supra n. 32) 223, fig. 209.
47. So also, it seems, Hayashi, *Bedeutung* 56–57 suggests.
48. The Athenians are civilizers like Hephaistos, Aesch. *Eum.* 13–14: "the highway-building sons of Hephaistos who made the untamed land civilized."
49. E.g. a kylix in Frankfurt, Liebieghaus STV 7 (near the Castelgiorgio Painter, *ARV*^{2} 386; Schwarz, *Triptolemos* 38, V 56, figs. 11a-b; Clinton, *Iconography* 139, no. 18); a volute crater in Paris, Louvre G 343 (by the Niobid Painter, *ARV*^{2} 600.17; Schwarz, *Triptolemos* 44, V 83; Clinton, *Iconography* 139, no. 8); a calyx crater in Ferrara, Nat. Mus. 2891 (by the Niobid Painter, *ARV*^{2} 602.24; Schwarz, *Triptolemos* 43, V 80; Clinton, *Iconography* 139, no. 9).
50. British Museum E 140; *ARV*^{2} 459.3. Discussion: Clinton, *Iconography* 124.

51. *ARV*^{2} 1191.1; Schwarz, *Triptolemos* 51, V 121; Hayashi, *Bedeutung* 158–159, no. 117.
52. See Clinton, *Iconography* 112–113, figs. 74–76. Nonnus: *Dionysiaca* 27.285–286.
53. Inv. No. 89.AE.73. See Clinton, *Iconography* 106–107, figs. 43–46. Preliminary notice: *GettyMusJ* 18 (1990) 167, no. 5. See also C.C. Mattusch in this volume, pp. 73–82.
54. Inscription: K<A>ΛΑΜΙΤΕ[Σ]. The first alpha was omitted; Clinton, *Iconography* 106, n. 6. Kalamites: Dem. *De Cor.* 129; Clinton, loc. cit. Kalamaia: Deubner, *Feste* 67–68; it was also celebrated in Piraeus, *IG* II^{2}, 1177, line 6.
55. On this pair see Clinton, *Iconography* 114–115.
56. Karlsruhe, Badisches Landesmus. 68.101; *Para.* 344.131bis, *Add.*^{2} 194; Clinton, *Iconography* 106–107, fig. 48.
57. For the view that the snake is a sign of the Mysteries, Hayashi, *Bedeutung* 57–58, cites E. Küster, *Die Schlange in der griechischen Kunst und Religion* (*RGVV* 13, Berlin 1913) esp. 146–149, but the only evidence that Küster can muster is 1) the snake that came to Eleusis from Salamis (see infra n.58), 2) a passage from Herrenius Philo of Byblos, *FGrHist* 790 F 4, which refers to the existence of snakes "in cults and mysteries," and 3) a snake crawling out of a *cista mystica* supposedly on Eleusinian reliefs. None of this is relevant to the Eleusinian Mysteries. Philo does not refer to this cult but to "mysteries" in general, and of course snakes did exist in other mystery cults. Of the two "Eleusinian" reliefs Küster cites neither is from Eleusis. Ny Carlsberg Glyptotek Cat. no. 144 (= F. Poulsen, *Catalogue of Ancient Sculpture in the Ny Carlsberg Glyptotek* [Copenhagen 1951] 116–117, no. 144) is a terracotta relief showing Demeter next to a basket with a snake winding around it; acquired in Rome, it is "stated to have come from Palermo"; Poulsen suggests a Sicilian prototype. The other is the so-called Lovatelli Urn, found in a tomb in Rome (F. Sinn, *Stadtrömischen Marmorurnen* [Mainz/Rhein 1987] 88–90); the relation of its iconography to Eleusinian is rather distant; cf. Clinton, *Iconography* 137, no. 6. What is in fact remarkable in Eleusinian imagery is the complete absence of snakes (except of course on Triptolemos' wagon) in scenes that reflect the Mysteries. If snakes were a significant aspect of the Mysteries, there seems to be no reason why they would not have appeared in these scenes. On snakes and the Mysteries see especially H. Möbius, *AbhMünch* 59 (1964) 36–39.
58. *Schol.* Lucian p. 276, lines 8–13. Cf. Nilsson, *GGR* I^{2}, 415. A story was told by Hesiod, frg. 226, about a snake that was driven from Salamis and accepted by Demeter at Eleusis as ἀμφίπολος — most likely in the context of the more agrarian cults at Eleusis, not Mysteries.
59. In the fourth quarter of the century Triptolemos scenes in general are quite scarce; Hayashi, *Bedeutung* 68–77 attributes the scarcity to the effects of the Peloponnesian War.
60. My interpretation of fourth-century scenes, *Iconography* esp. 64–94, differs considerably from Hayashi's, *Bedeutung* 77–87. A key point, on which we fundamentally disagree, is his reliance on E. Simon's interpretation of a torch-bearing figure as Eumolpos. Our only certain information about Eumolpos indicates that he was not a torch-bearer: see Clinton, *Iconography* 64, 75.

    An exception to the concentration on only the Mysteries is offered by some scenes which reflect both the Mysteries and the Dionysia at Eleusis, i.e. the two major cult spectacles there; Clinton, *Iconography* 121–125.
61. Hermitage St. 525; Clinton, *Iconography* 78–81, 134 no. 5 (with further bibliography).
62. Eschbach 158–159.
63. Eschbach 115–125. He also argues with some merit that the image of 364/3 imitates the cult statue of Triptolemos in the Eleusinion in Athens. On supervision of the design of Athena's Robe cf. Aristotle, *Ath.Pol.* 49.3.
64. J.H. Kroll, "Athenian Bronze Coinage and the Propagation of the Eleusinian Mysteries," *AJA* 96 (1992) 355–356 (abstract of paper delivered at the 93rd general meeting of the A.I.A.).
65. Clinton, "A Law in the City Eleusinion Concerning the Mysteries," *Hesperia* 49 (1980) 258–288.
66. Mylonas, *Eleusis* 130–133.
67. Mylonas and Travlos, *Prakt* (1983) 148–150; Travlos, *Attika* 95.
68. See my forthcoming edition of *IG* II^{2}, 1682.
69. *IG* II^{2}, 204; 1666.
70. Cf. Clinton, "Inscriptions from Eleusis," *ArchEph* (1971) 108–115.
71. Supra, p. 161. In keeping with the scope of this paper I pass over the history of the sanctuary in the second half of the fifth century, including of course the famous first-fruits decree (*IG* I^{3}, 78) and the problems caused by the war. These topics are treated to some extent by M.B. Cavanaugh, *Eleusis and Athens: Documents in Finance, Religion, and Politics in the Second Half of the Fifth Century* (Atlanta, forthcoming), and in two of my articles, "The Date of the Classical Telesterion at Eleusis," Φίλια Ἔπη 2 (Athens 1987) 254–262, and "The Epidauria and the Arrival of Asclepius in Athens" in *International Seminar: "Ancient Greek Cult Practice from the Epigraphical Evidence", Athens, 22–24 November 1991* (*ActaAth-8*, Stockholm 1994 forthcoming).
72. Cf. the status accorded Athens and the Mysteries by the Amphictiones at Delphi in 117 B.C., *IG* II^{2}, 1134, lines 16–23.
73. Pausanias 5.10.1.

The Rural Demes of Attica

Frank J. Frost

In a well known passage Thucydides attributed the *synoikismos* of Attica to Theseus (2.15.1–2): "In Attica from the time of Kekrops and the first kings until Theseus the inhabitants dwelt in individual poleis, having their own prytaneia and archons ... But when Theseus became king ... he reorganized the country and dissolved the other poleis and bouleuteria and magistrates into what is now the polis, creating one bouleuterion and prytaneion, and he united (*ξυνώικισε*) all the inhabitants and compelled them to use one single polis, although dwelling as before on their own lands."

It was the unanimous opinion of antiquity that Theseus had brought about the *synoikismos* of Athens, as can be seen in 28 other passages collected by Mauro Moggi in his *Sinecismi interstatali greci*.[1] When Thucydides called these individual communities "poleis" he was probably thinking of the legendary twelve poleis of Attica, the dodekapolis that was enumerated by the Atthidographer Philochoros: Κεκροπία, Τετράπολις, 'Επακρία, Δεκέλεια, 'Ελευσίς, Αφίδναι ..., Θορικός, Βραυρών, Κύθερος, Σφηττός, Κηφισιά. There is a problem of course with the text of Strabo, who preserved the citation of Philochoros. A simple count of the names will show that there are only eleven and so there must be a lacuna in the text.[2] Of these names Tetrapolis, Epakria, Eleusis, Thorikos, and Sphettos are known as trittyes after Kleisthenes[3] and the remainder are known as post-Kleisthenic demes, with the exception of Brauron, an ancient cult center, and Kekropia, often thought to represent the asty itself.[4]

Although Thucydides and Philochoros are almost universally agreed to be among our most intelligent and reliable historians and although most of these sites do in fact bear evidence of Bronze Age occupation,[5] the notion of a Mycenaean Theseus unifying all of Attica is today regarded as a quaint patriotic fiction.[6] It may be objected that the very wording of Thucydides is puzzling, because he certainly knew that even in his day the villages of the Attic countryside continued to elect local officials, to meet in council, to enact legislation, to regulate local cult calendars, and even to send their own delegations to Delphi and Delos.[7] What he seems to be referring to is not actually a *synoikismos* — a migration from the country into the city — but a *sympoliteia*, in which all inhabitants stayed in their towns but agreed to use the same laws. Another objection is that archaeology can now demonstrate that population movement in Attica during the Geometric period was the reverse of that implied by the tradition: instead of gathering into the city, the Athenians seem to have spent several centuries of the Geometric period moving *out* to colonize their *chora*.[8]

Although we have some testimony for the nature of deme government after Kleisthenes, consitutional historians are concerned over the complete lack of evidence for the manner in which these communities were governed at the time of Peisistratos or Solon. Another concern is the nature of the relationship between these communities, whether known as poleis, komai, or demoi, and the asty of Athens during the long centuries before Kleisthenes. Our literary sources were convinced that a *synoikismos* had taken place and therefore that one law had united many communities, some of them a two or three day journey from the Acropolis. But doubts linger. A grave inscription from the early sixth century on the road to Acharnai asks the passersby to grieve for Tetichos, "whether a man of the asty or a xenos."[9] This seems to show an ancient distinction between the city dwellers and those of the countryside, who may well have been thought of as xenoi by city folk. The homicide law of Drakon is the first document we know that referred to *Athenaioi*, meaning all inhabitants of Attica.[10] Such inhabitants may have felt themselves bound by Drakon's procedures for dealing with the pollution of homicide, for the resulting divine punishment could strike everyone in the land. All inhabitants may have agreed to celebrate the most important shared rituals, like the Apatouria, on the same day of the month. But collegiality may not have gone much further. Can we imagine that the villagers of Thorikos or Sphettos or Rhamnous believed for a moment that Solon's quainter laws had anything to do with them, even if we can find a Solonian law that we all agree is authentic?[11]

These are just a few of the problems raised by the literary testimonia — or rather, by their lack. It is doubtful that there will be any new texts to solve our problems, so we must turn to topographical and archaeological data for any significant improvement in our knowledge of the pre-Kleisthenic demes. Great progress in the identification of the Attic deme sites has been made since the last century. To realize that progress continues one need only consult the appendix in John Traill's *Demos and Trittys*, where one will find, among other data, that between 1973 and 1986 ten deme locations have been recovered; it is true that during the same time four have been lost, but this is also progress of a kind.[12]

Surface surveys and chance finds will undoubtedly continue to contribute to our map of the Attic demes. But real archaeological excavation shows the greatest promise for improving our knowledge of rural Attica. In a paper first presented in 1976 I was led in my frustration over the lack of evidence for the rural demes to say the "the great mass of the population might as well have lived in tents, for all we know of them."[13] One can be slightly more optimistic today. The limited data produced over the last two decades have already made valuable contributions. Although Aristotle, for instance, believed that there were economic differences in the three areas of Attica at the time of Peisistratos, archaeology can show from graves and dedications that all districts were inhabited by the mixture of all economic classes. Discovery of various cult calendars shows the rich variety of religious observation and the persistence of local cults.[14] Unfortunately, excavation has so far only scratched the surface and has led to an unbalanced picture in some areas. Demes that are almost unmentioned in our literary testimony are the location of cemeteries that have provided the bulk of our evidence from graves[15] while famous demes like Acharnai scarcely exist archaeologically.[16] If this picture is to change it will do so because of the present and continuing efforts of the Greek Archaeological Service and of those foreign Schools that have contributed to our knowledge.

Notes

1. (Pisa 1976) 44–62.
2. Strabo 9.1.20, *FGrHist* 328 F 94. Charax of Pergamon (*FGrHist* 103 F 43, ap. Steph. Byz. s.v. *Athenai*) further confused the issue by claiming that Theseus had unified the *eleven* cities of Attica. See Jacoby ad 328 F 94; J.S. Traill, *Demos and Trittys* (Toronto 1986) 47 n. 9.
3. Traill (supra n. 2) ch. V and summary on 110.
4. On Kyther(r)os, see Traill (supra n. 2) 47–51.
5. R. Hope Simpson, *Mycenaean Greece* (Park Ridge, NJ 1981) 41–45, although by no means up to date, collects the evidence for most of the sites listed by Philochoros.
6. See especially S. Diamant, "Theseus and the Unification of Attica," in *Studies Presented to Eugene Vanderpool*, *Hesperia* Suppl. 19 (1982) 38–45.
7. Deme legislation: *IG* I², 183, 186–189; *SEG* 10.210, etc. for the fifth century; many more from the fourth: *IG* II², 1177 sq. The Marathonian tetrapolis sent its own theoroi to Delos and Delphi according to Philochoros, *FGrHist* 328 F 75 (Schol. Soph. *OC* 1047).
8. David Whitehead, *The Demes of Attica* (Princeton 1986) 5–9.
9. *IG* I², 976. See my remarks in "Aspects of Early Athenian Citizenship," in Adele Scafuro, Alan Boegehold (eds.), *Athenian Identity and Civic Ideology* (Baltimore 1994) 51.
10. *ML* no. 26.28; cf. Demosth. 23.41.
11. E.g., the supposed law forbidding agricultural exports, Plut. *Solon* 24.1, which is widely held to be genuine; commentary by M. Manfredini, L. Piccirilli, *Plutarco, La vita di Solone* (Milan 1977) 249–51. Would such a "law" have prevented Marathonians from trading with the Euboian coastal towns?
12. Traill (supra n. 2) 148f.
13. In a paper originally presented at the 1976 annual meeting of the Association of Ancient Historians in Berkeley, later published as "Towards a History of Peisistratid Athens," in J. Eadie, J. Ober, (eds.), *The Craft of the Ancient Historian* (Lanham, MD 1985) 62.
14. Conveniently compiled by Jon D. Mikalson, *The Sacred and Civil Calendar of the Athenian Year* (Princeton 1975).
15. Merenda and Vari, just to name the most prominent burial grounds that come to mind.
16. I remember John Camp saying something like this while driving around Menidi in 1985; but see now Maria N. Platonos, "Είδη τάφων και τρόποι ταφής στα νεκροταφεία των Αχαρνών," and Alexandra Patrianakou-Iliaki, "Αρχαιολογικές έρευνες στο δήμο Αχαρνών," *Α΄ Συμπόσιο Ιστορίας-Λαογραφίας Βορείου Αττικής, Πρακτικά* (Αχαρνές 1989) 241–86.

Παρατηρήσεις στην οικιστική μορφή των αττικών δήμων

Γιώργος Σταϊνχάουερ

Η ανανέωση τα τελευταία χρόνια του ενδιαφέροντος για τους αττικούς δήμους[1] έχει κάνει αισθητή την ανάγκη της συμπλήρωσης της βασισμένης κυρίως στη φιλολογική παράδοση και το επιγραφικό υλικό, γνώσης της πολιτικής οργάνωσης και της θρησκευτικής ζωής του δήμου, με το πλήθος των πληροφοριών για την οικιστική μορφή του, οι οποίες εδώ και μερικές δεκάδες χρόνια συγκεντρώνονται χάρη στις ανασκαφές της Εφορείας Αρχαιοτήτων της Αττικής.[2] Η επισκόπηση που ακολουθεί δεν φιλοδοξεί να δώσει την περίληψη ή έστω ένα περίγραμμα των αποτελεσμάτων των ερευνών αυτών. Θα εκτεθούν εν συντομία ορισμένα προσωρινά συμπεράσματα που αναφέρονται στην οικιστική μορφή του αττικού δήμου. 'Οπως και αυτή της Ι. Ανδρέου που δίνει στον ίδιο τόμο την περιγραφή του εξαιρετικά ενδιαφέροντος και εκτενέστερα ερευνηθέντος δήμου των Αλών Αιξωνίδων, η παρούσα ανακοίνωση αποτελεί μια πρώτη αναφορά στην προετοιμαζόμενη από την Εφορεία Αρχαιοτήτων Αττικής δημοσίευση των αττικών δήμων. Εν προκειμένω θα βασισθώ στα αποτελέσματα της ανασκαφής του αεροδρομίου των Σπάτων,[3] μιας εκτεταμένης δοκιμαστικής τομής στο κατ' εξοχήν αττικό αγροτικό τοπίο των Μεσογείων και στη σύγκριση με εκείνα της έρευνας των άλλων αττικών δήμων, κατά κύριο λόγο των Αλών Αιξωνίδων.

Η ανασκαφή του αεροδρομίου των Σπάτων

Ο χώρος του αεροδρομίου των Σπάτων αποτελεί μία λωρίδα, πλάτους περίπου 2,5 και μήκους 5,5 χιλιομέτρων, που τέμνει διαγωνίως κατά τον ΒΑ./ΝΔ. άξονα, την περιοχή των Μεσογείων, ΝΑ. των Σπάτων. Σε αντίθεση με το πεδινό δυτικό, το ανατολικό ήμισυ της λωρίδας αυτής καταλαμβάνει σε όλο το μήκος της, ο χαμηλός λόφος του Καράμπαμπα, ο πρώτος μιας σειράς λόφων που φθάνουν έως την παραλία (εικ. 1). Γεωγραφική θέση, έκταση και μορφολογία του εδάφους υποδεικνύουν ότι η περιοχή περιελάμβανε τμήματα περισσοτέρων του ενός από τους μικρούς και ανώνυμους δήμους του Β. και ΒΑ. τμήματος της πεδιάδας των Μεσογείων.[4] Πράγματι αυτή καταλαμβάνει πάνω από το ήμισυ της ανατολικής πλευράς της πεδιάδας, δηλαδή μια έκταση που ξεπερνάει κατά πολύ τη συνηθισμένη των 4–5 τετρ. χιλιομέτρων ενός μεσαίου αττικού δήμου.[5] Τούτο επιβεβαιώνεται από την αρχαιολογική εικόνα του χώρου. Η ανασκαφική έρευνα περιορίστηκε στους χώρους με την πυκνότερη συγκέντρωση οστράκων, στο βόρειο και νότιο άκρο του λόφου Καράμπαμπα.[6] Αντίθετα διαπιστώθηκε ότι η κατοίκηση ήταν πολύ αραιότερη, και ως επί το πλείστον μεταγενέστερη, στο κεντρικό τμήμα του αεροδρομίου, τόσο στην πεδιάδα δυτικά του Καράμπαμπα, όσο και στη λοφώδη περιοχή ανατολικά του (εικ. 2).

Η πρώτη οικιστική ενότητα (εικ. 3) βρίσκεται πολύ κοντά στο δρόμο της Λούτσας, στο νότιο άκρο μιας κλειστής πεδιάδας 7,000 περίπου στρεμμάτων (εικ. 1) που επικοινωνούσε με τη θάλασσα μέσα από δύο περάσματα στα νότια (δημοσιά Λούτσας) και στα βόρεια του όρους Ζάγανι (200 μ.), που ελεγχόταν από ένα οχυρό.[7] Και τα δύο ή τρία κέντρα της πεδιάδας, συγκεκριμένα οι χώροι όπου (στο φύλλο VII των *Karten von Attika*) σημειώνονται συγκεντρώσεις αρχαίων ερειπίων, βρίσκονται έξω από το χώρο του αεροδρομίου: πλησιέστερη στον ερευνηθέντα χώρο είναι η θέση Λάπαρι ή 'Αγ. Κωνσταντίνος μεταξύ του αεροδρομίου και των Σπάτων. Το δεύτερο κέντρο του ίδιου προφανώς δήμου βρίσκεται βορειότερα στο κέντρο της πεδιάδας ('Αγ. Γεώργιος Βουρβά)˙ όσο για το τρίτο, που τοποθετείται ακόμα βορειότερα στη θέση μιας παλαιοχριστιανικής βασιλικής στον 'Αγιο Βασίλειο, ανήκει πιθανότατα σε κάποιον άλλο δήμο. Είναι άγνωστη η ταυτότητά του ή των αντιστοίχων δήμων, στους οποίους συμβατικά μόνο θα μπορούσαν να δοθούν τα ονόματα της *Μυρρινούτας* ή της *Κονθύλης*.[8]

Η φυσιογνωμία της βόρειας οικιστικής ενότητας προσδιοριζόταν από τη διασταύρωση των κυριωτέρων δρόμων της περιοχής δίπλα σε ένα πηγάδι (εικ.4), 200 μ. βορειότερα από το γνωστό από την αρχαιολογική βιβλιογραφία Βαθύ Πηγάδι, που είχε αποτελέσει και αυτό για αιώνες — έως το 1980 — το κέντρο της γύρω περιοχής. Την τοπική σημασία και του αρχαίου πηγαδιού αποδεικνύουν οι διαδοχικές επεμβάσεις στο

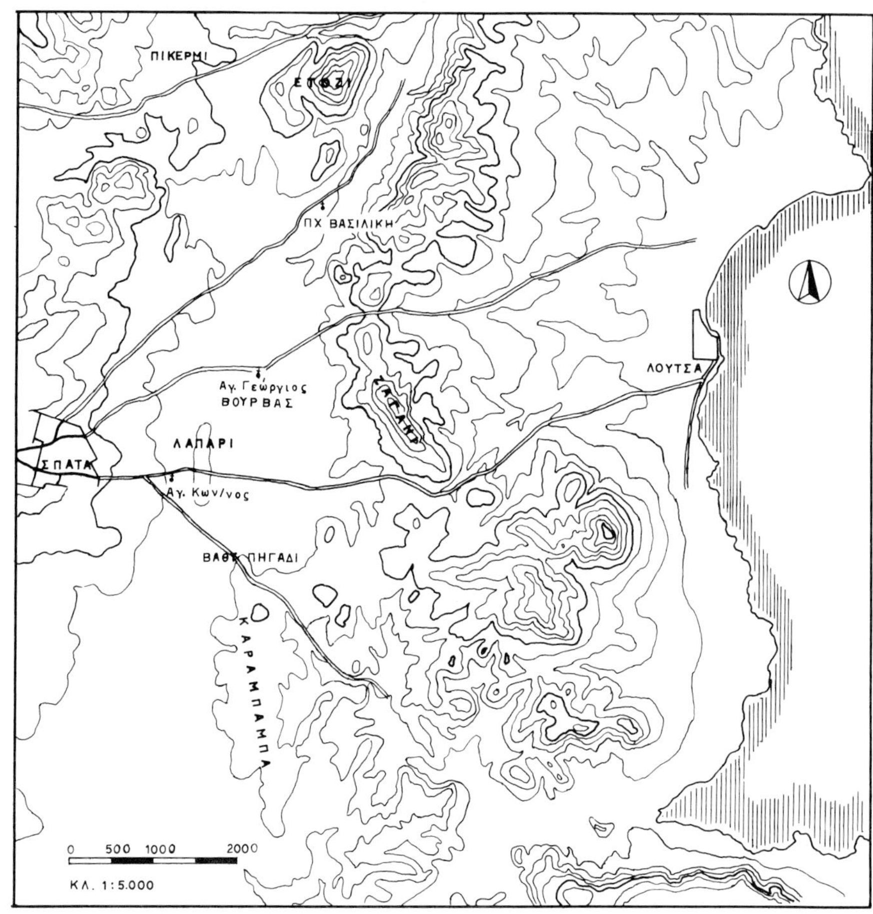

Εικ. 1. Τοπογραφικό του ΒΑ. τμήματος της περιοχής Μεσογείων.

χώρο γύρω από αυτό, ο οποίος κάποια στιγμή με την κατασκευή ενός οικίσκου (πιθανότατα να πρόκειται για κάποιο ναΐσκο) απέκτησε ένα σχετικά μνημειώδη χαρακτήρα. Το πηγάδι συνορεύει και πιθανώς συνδεόταν με ένα τέμενος (σώζεται ο περίβολος και τα ίχνη του βωμού), που κατελάμβανε τη μία από τις γωνίες του σταυροδρομίου. Μεγαλόπρεπα, για τα αγροτικά μέτρα της περιοχής, διαμορφωμένη ήταν η απέναντι γωνία, όπου σώζεται ο ημικυκλικός περίβολος και η βάση ενός κλασσικού ταφικού μνημείου. Από τους αγροτικούς δρόμους, που διασταυρώνονταν εδώ, στενούς δρόμους πλάτους 3,50 μ. στρωμένους με χαλίκι, που όριζαν οι μαντρότοιχοι των κτημάτων, ο πρώτος διαπιστώθηκε ότι αποτελούσε τον κύριο Β./Ν. άξονα του χώρου: ακολουθώντας το λόφο Καράμπαμπα σε όλο το μήκος του, από τα ΒΑ. στα ΝΔ., συνέδεε έτσι το βόρειο δήμο με τον δρόμο που ένωνε την Ερχιά με το δήμο των Φιλαϊδών και την περιοχή της Βραυρώνος. Ο δεύτερος ερχόταν από τα ΒΑ. (την περιοχή του Αγ. Κωνσταντίνου στο Λάπαρι που προαναφέραμε) με κατεύθυνση το εσωτερικό της λοφοσειράς που κλείνει τον ορίζοντα από την πλευρά της θάλασσας, είχε δηλαδή πορεία παράλληλη αυτής της σημερινής δημοσιάς της Λούτσας. 'Ολους τους παραπάνω δρόμους είναι δυνατόν να παρακολουθήσει κανείς και στις τέσσερις κατευθύνσεις σε αρκετή απόσταση από το σταυροδρόμι, διαπιστώνοντας ότι, με την εξαίρεση της κεντρικής Β./Ν. αρτηρίας, οι υπόλοιποι διασταυρώνονταν σε απόσταση περί τα 200 ή 240 μ. με άλλους του ίδιου πλάτους και κατασκευής, με αποτέλεσμα την κατάτμηση της πεδιάδας σε μεγάλα τριγωνικά διαμερίσματα περίπου 80 στρεμμάτων το καθένα, αξίας δηλαδή περίπου ενός ταλάντου ή και μεγαλύτερης, πράγμα που συμφωνεί με τις πληροφορίες για τη μεγάλη ιδιοκτησία στην περιοχή.[9] Η συγκέντρωση ιδιοκτησιών στον 4ο αι. αποδεικνύεται τουλάχιστον σε μία περίπτωση, όπου διαπιστώνεται η κατάργηση ενός δευτερεύοντος δρόμου με σκοπό τη συνένωση των εκατέρωθεν κτημάτων (εικ. 5).

Το κύριο ενδιαφέρον της ανασκαφής βρίσκεται στις πληροφορίες για την οικιστική φυσιογνωμία του αντίστοιχου δήμου: τον χαλαρό οικιστικό ιστό που χαρακτηρίζεται από τη συνυφασμένη με τη μεγάλη ιδιοκτησία αραιή διάταξη των σπιτιών, και τη θέση που έχει μέσα σ' αυτόν το πηγάδι στο σταυροδρόμι των κεντρικών δρόμων. Στο δείγμα που ερευνήθηκε, ο χώρος (μία έκταση 500 περίπου στρεμμάτων) είναι σπαρμένος με 4 ή 5 σπίτια, κτισμένα κατά μήκος των δρόμων, σε αποστάσεις 120 έως 250 μ. μεταξύ τους, σε αντιστοιχία προς τα κτήματα. Ως προς τη μορφή τους τα σπίτια αυτά ακολουθούν γνωστούς τύπους (εικ. 6–7): διακρίνεται η τυπική οικία με μικρή αυλή, που περιβάλλεται στις τρεις πλευρές από δωμάτια με πολλούς βοηθητικούς χώρους, όπως και το *οικίδιον*,[10] που αποτελείται από ένα δωμάτιο (διαστ. 4 × 5 μ.) στο βάθος της μικρής αυλής, δίπλα στο οποίο διακρίνεται η σκάλα για το υπνοδωμάτιο στο δώμα (εικ. 7). Είναι αξιοσημείωτη η απουσία εδώ, σε αντίθεση με τους περισσότερους από τους δήμους της παραλίας (Αλαί Αιξωνίδαι, Αναγυρούς, Ατήνη, Σούνιο, Θορικός, Ραμνούς) του τύπου του σπιτιού με πύργο για τη φύλαξη της σοδειάς και των δούλων. Το μικρό μέγεθος και η απλή κατασκευή αυτών των σπιτιών, καθώς και η φανερή απουσία πριν από τα

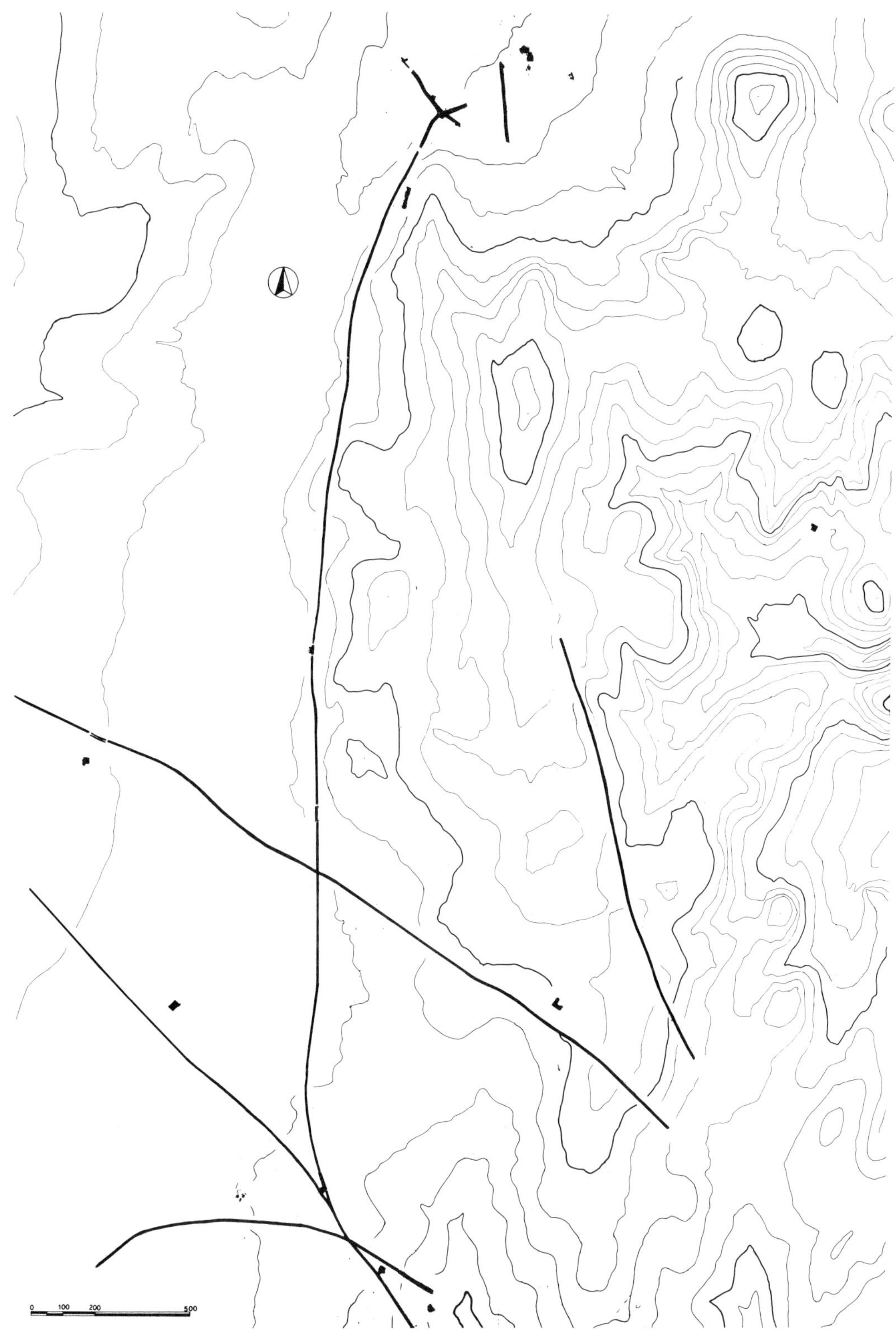

Εικ. 2. Τοπογραφικό σχέδιο αεροδρομίου Σπάτων: η θέση των ανασκαφών και το αρχαίο οδικό δίκτυο της περιοχής.

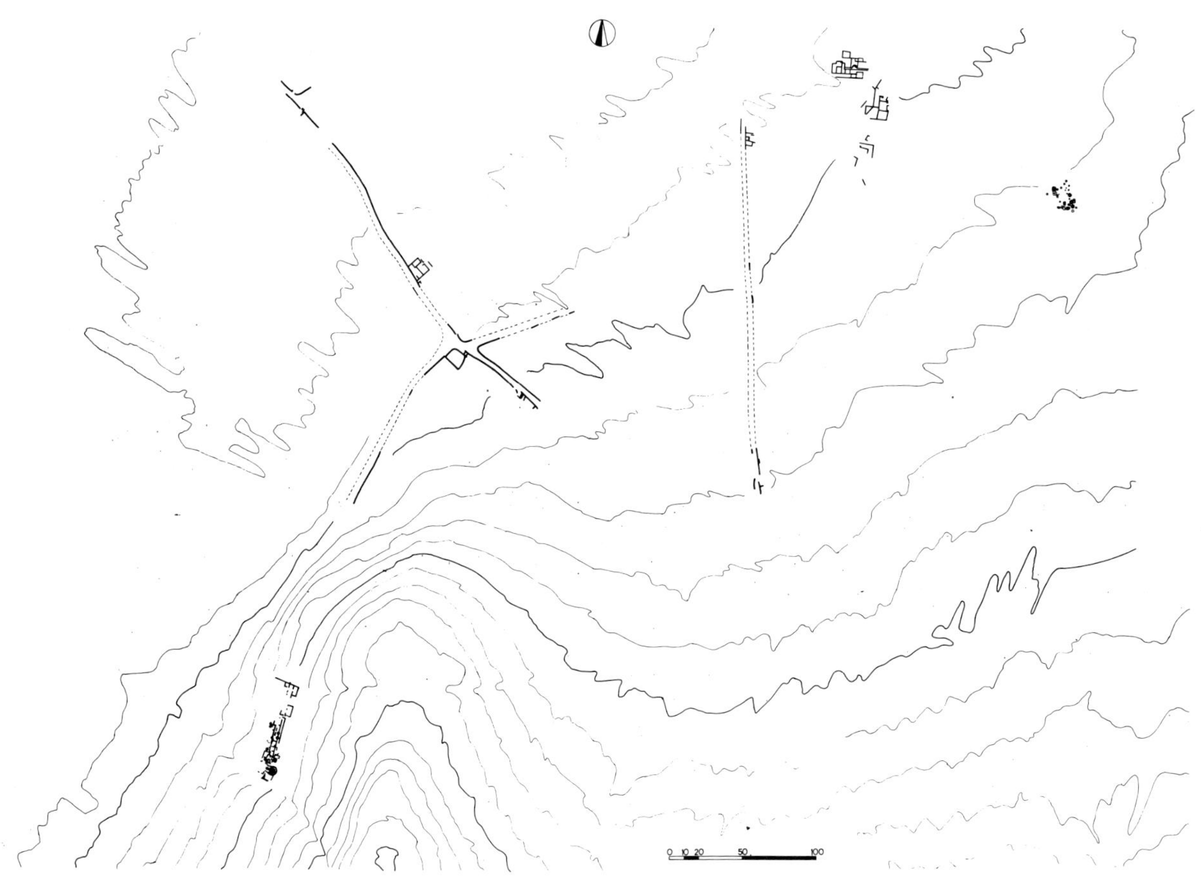

Εικ. 3. Η βόρεια οικιστική ενότητα: γενικό τοπογραφικό.

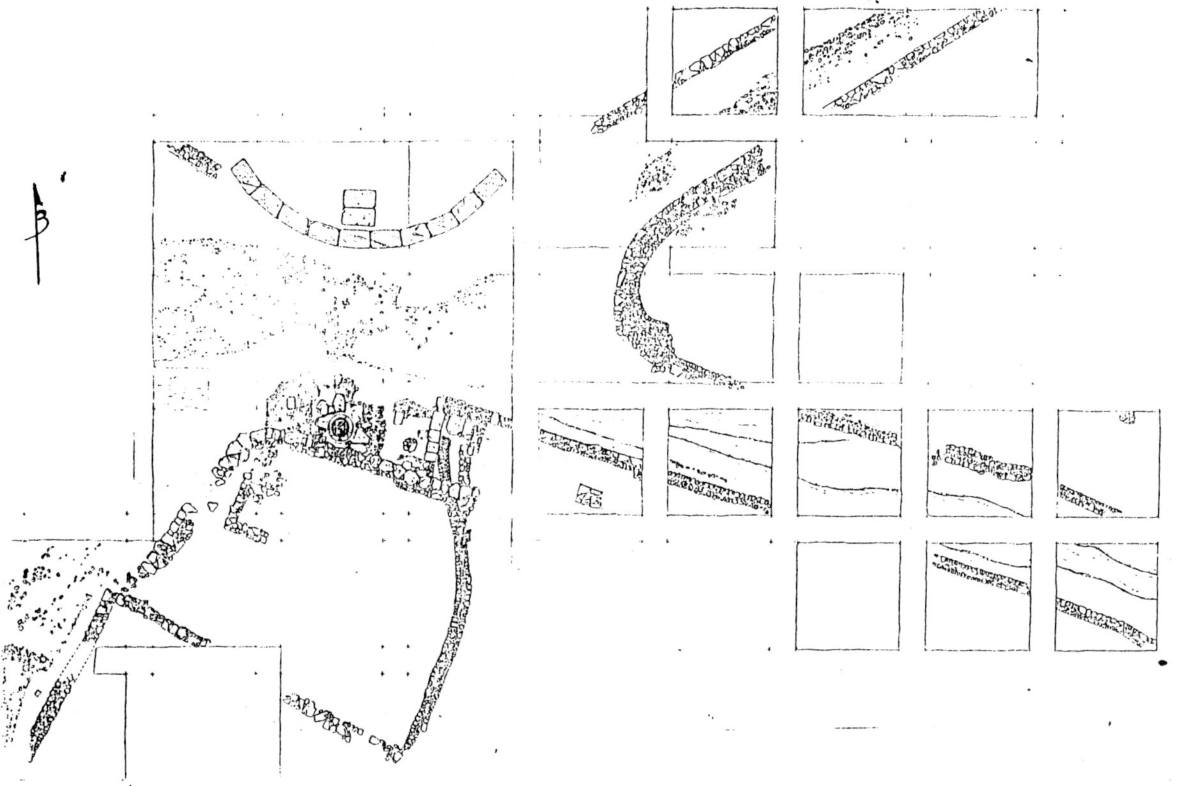

Εικ. 4. Η βόρεια οικιστική ενότητα: κεντρικό σταυροδρόμι.

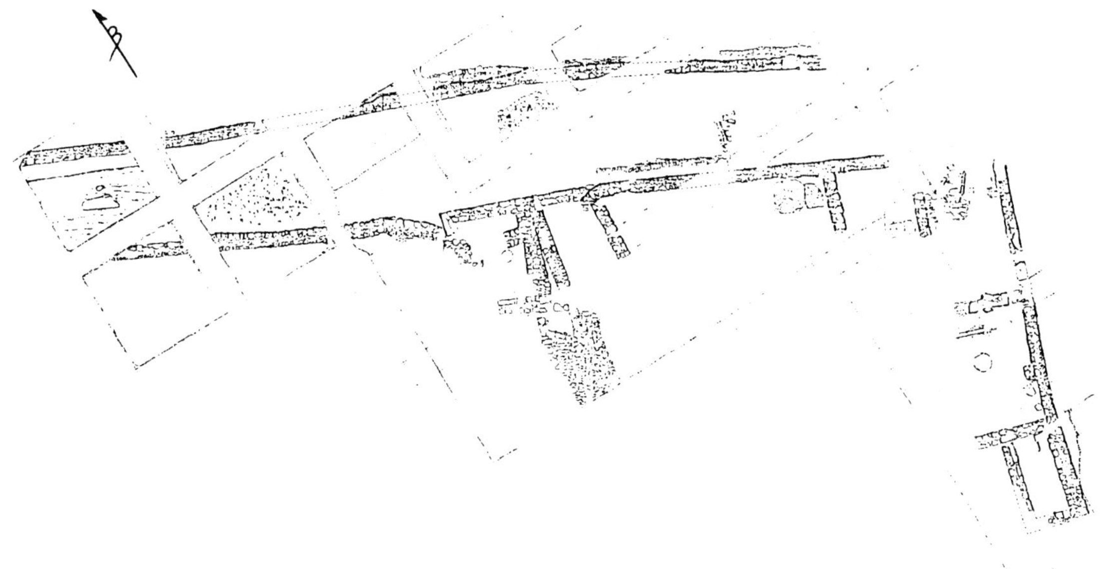

Εικ. 5. Η βόρεια οικιστική ενότητα: συνένωση ιδιοκτησιών.

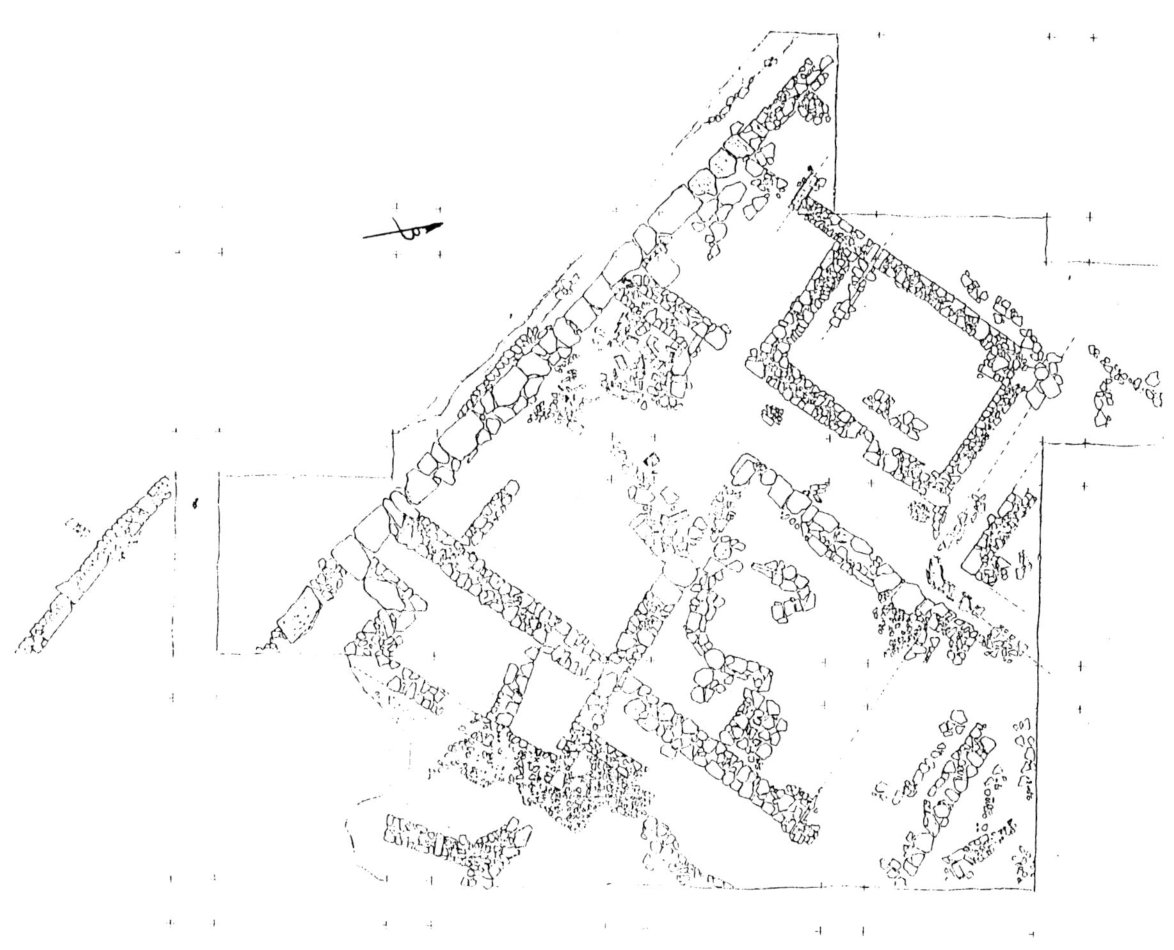

Εικ. 6. Η βόρεια οικιστική ενότητα: τύποι οικιών.

Εικ. 7. Η βόρεια οικιστική ενότητα: τύποι οικιών.

ρωμαϊκά χρόνια της αρχοντικής αγρέπαυλης, με τα υποστατικά, τους στάβλους και τις αποθήκες της, όχι μόνο δεν έρχεται σε αντίθεση με το σχήμα της μεγάλης ιδιοκτησίας, αλλά αντίθετα αποτελεί ένδειξη για τη (διαπιστωμένη επιγραφικά) κατάτμησή της, πιθανώς και για την απουσία μόνιμης εγκατάστασης των *άστικῶν* (Δημοσθ. 55.1274) ιδιοκτητών. Τα ανασκαφέντα σπίτια είναι πολύ πιθανό ότι χρησίμευαν απλώς ως κατοικίες επιστατών.[11] Τούτο θα έδινε ενδεχομένως μία εξήγηση και για την απουσία του πύργου που επισημάνθηκε προηγουμένως, η οποία δεν μπορεί να αποδοθεί απλώς στη μεγαλύτερη ασφάλεια που προσέφερε η απόσταση από την παραλία.[12] Την επιβεβαίωση γι' αυτό το οικιστικό σχήμα παρέχει, έμμεσα, η απουσία ενός συγκροτημένου νεκροταφείου. Από τους τέσσερις ταφικούς περιβόλους που εντοπίσθηκαν και ανασκάφηκαν, οι τρεις βρίσκονται διασκορπισμένοι κατά μήκος των δρόμων στα όρια του οικισμού ενώ εκείνος του σταυροδρομίου, ο μοναδικός που είχε μνημειώδη χαρακτήρα και κεντρική θέση, δεν φαίνεται να περιελάμβανε κάποια ταφή.

Στα ανατολικά και νοτιοανατολικά όρια του κάμπου απλώνεται η διπλή λοφοσειρά του *φελλέως*, που φθάνει έως την παραλία. Πρόκειται για χώρο βοσκής και υλοτομίας, μια άγονη έκταση καλυμμένη με θάμνους και πουρνάρια, όπως δείχνουν τα ίχνη μιας συστάδας κλιβάνων για ξυλοκάρβουνο στη ρίζα των λόφων στο ΒΔ. άκρο της πεδιάδας. Η περιοχή πρέπει να ήταν ως επί το πλείστον ακαλλιέργητη και ακατοίκητη, με εξαίρεση μεμονωμένα σημεία στο εσωτερικό της, όπως είναι μια κλασσική αγροικία *ἐσχατιὰ* του δήμου,[13] και – πράγμα που είναι εξαιρετικά ενδιαφέρον και για το λόγο αυτό αναφέρεται εδώ, έστω και αν ξεφεύγει από το χρονολογικό πλαίσιο της παρούσας – μία μικρή συνοικία (αμπελουργών όπως δείχνει η παρουσία ενός ληνού) της ύστατης αρχαιότητας. Παρόμοια εικόνα θα παρουσίαζε και η περιοχή στα νότια όρια του δήμου, που πρέπει να συνέπιπταν με τη μύτη που σχηματίζει ο λόφος 200 μ. από το σταυροδρόμι, στη θέση Βαθύ Πηγάδι που προαναφέρθηκε. Εκεί, στις πλαγιές του Καράμπαμπα, ήταν εγκατεστημένο γιά μία σειρά πολλών γενεών (από τον 4ο στον 2ο αι. π.Χ.) ένα αρκετά σημαντικό ως προς την έκταση και τη διάρκεια της λειτουργίας του, κεραμεικό εργαστήριο με τέσσερις κλιβάνους σε διαδοχική χρήση, τις αποθήκες και την οικία του τελευταίου ιδιοκτήτη, του οποίου χάρη σε ένα σφράγισμα γνωρίζουμε και το όνομα (*Ἔνβιος*).

Ανάλογη, αν και όχι ταυτόσημη με εκείνη του βορείου τμήματος του αεροδρομίου, είναι η οικιστική φυσιογνωμία της περιοχής που καταλαμβάνει το νοτιώτατο άκρο του λόφου Καράμπαμπα και τις πλαγιές των προς ανατολάς λόφων, που πλαισιώνουν ένα από τους παραπόταμους του Ερασίνου (εικ. 8). Η θέση της στην είσοδο ενός ακόμη σημαντικού περάσματος προς τη θάλασσα, συγκεκριμένα αυτού που οδηγεί στη Βραυρώνα, συνηγορεί με την υπόθεση ότι η περιοχή αποτελούσε τμήμα του δήμου των Φιλαϊδών, όπου ανήκε και το ιερό της Βραυρωνίας Αρτέμιδος. Στο κέντρο της βρίσκεται και εδώ ένα σταυροδρόμι. Στο βαθμό που είναι δυνατή η αποκατάσταση του οδικού δικτύου με τη βοήθεια των αεροφωτογραφιών διαπιστώνεται ότι στο σημείο αυτό ο κεντρικός οδικός άξονας που παρακολουθήσαμε κατά μήκος του λόφου Καράμπαμπα διασταυρώνεται με το δρόμο που έρχεται από τη Βραυρώνα, ο οποίος εν συνεχεία διακλαδώνεται προς τα βόρειο- και νοτιοδυτικά, δηλαδή αντίστοιχα προς Ερχιά – Παιανία και προς το Σφηττό. Από τις έξι αγροικίες του οικισμού που ανασκάφηκαν, οι τρεις βρίσκονται κατά μήκος του δρόμου προς την Ερχιά, σε απόσταση 200 έως 300 μ. μεταξύ τους και από το σταυροδρόμι. Οι υπόλοιπες σχηματίζουν μία τρόπον τινα εξωτερική ζώνη του οικισμού, σημειώνοντας περί τα 900 μ. και 1,500 μ. ΒΑ. και ΒΔ. από το σταυροδρόμι, την πορεία ενός βορειότερου παράλληλου του προαναφερθέντος δρόμου μέσα από τη λοφώδη περιοχή του Καράμπαμπα.

Η μορφή των οικιών (εικ. 9–10) είναι δυνατόν να αποκατασταθεί με κάποια βεβαιότητα, και τούτο παρά την πολύ κακή κατάσταση διατήρησης των ερειπίων, που οφείλεται στις καταστροφές από τη βαθειά άρωση για τη φύτευση και το ξερρίζωμα των αμπελιών. Ο τύπος που συναντάται εδώ, σε αντίθεση με τον βόρειο οικισμό του αεροδρομίου είναι ο γνωστός από τις δημοσιευμένες οικίες της Βάρης και του Δέματος,[14] με μια μεγάλη αυλή σε όλο το μήκος (12–15 μ.) της πρόσοψης, στο βάθος της οποίας, απέναντι στην είσοδο, βρίσκεται μια σειρά δωματίων. Ένα καλά διατηρημένο δείγμα προσφέρει η αγροικία ανατολικά από το σταυροδρόμι στο δρόμο της Βραυρώνας. Το σπίτι βρίσκεται στο βάθος του κήπου, σε απόσταση 30 μ. από το δρόμο. Σώζονται οι δύο συνεχόμενες πλευρές του: κατά μήκος της μακράς πλευράς υπήρχε πίσω από μία αβαθή στοά, μία σειρά έξι ή επτά ομοιόμορφων, πολύ μικρών (εσωτ. διαστάσεων 1,60 × 1,90 μ.) δωματίων, αποθηκών ή σταύλων και βοηθητικών χώρων. Τη στενή πλευρά καλύπτει αντίθετα ένας ενιαίος μακρόστενος (3 ×

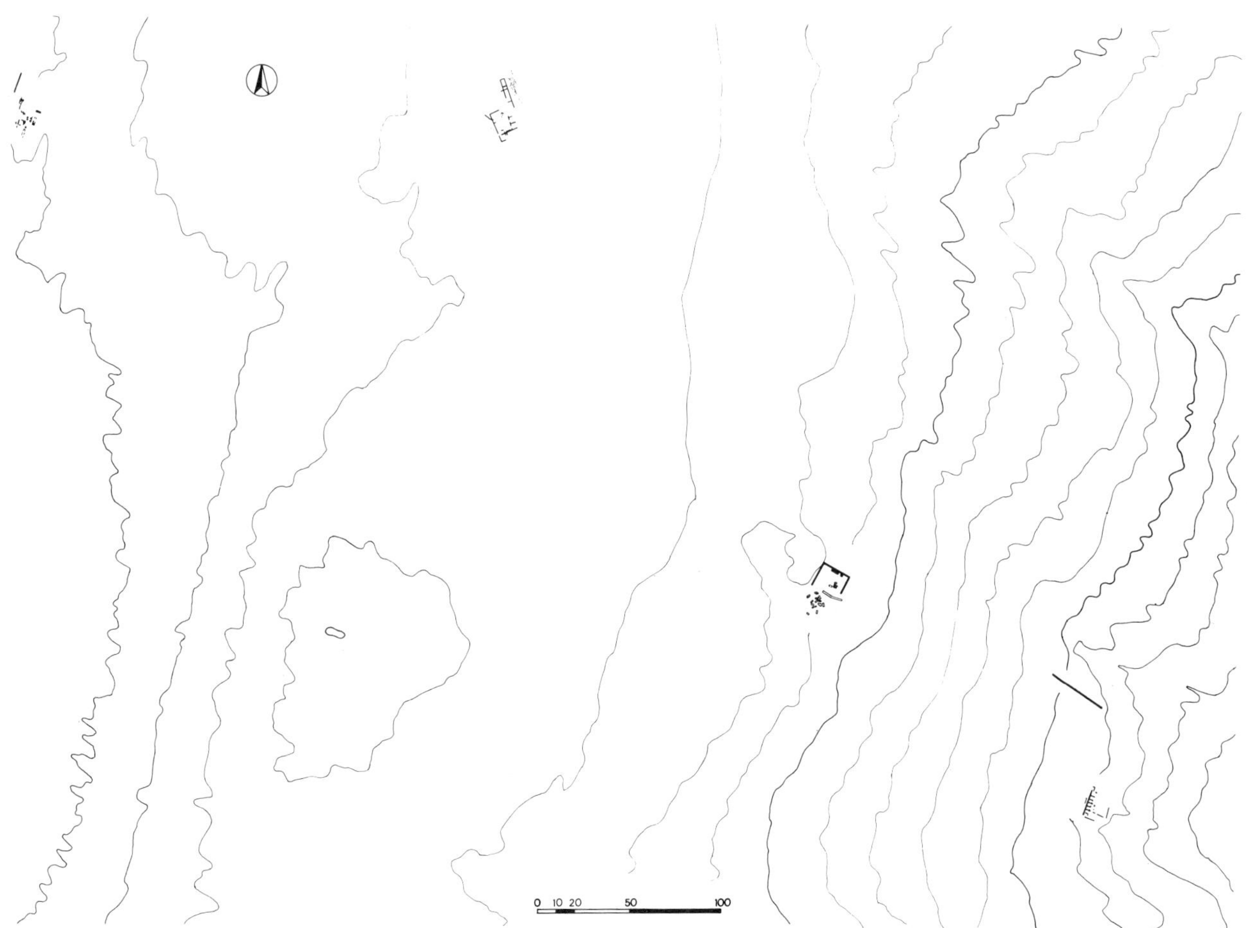

Εικ. 8. Η νότια οικιστική ενότητα: γενικό τοπογραφικό.

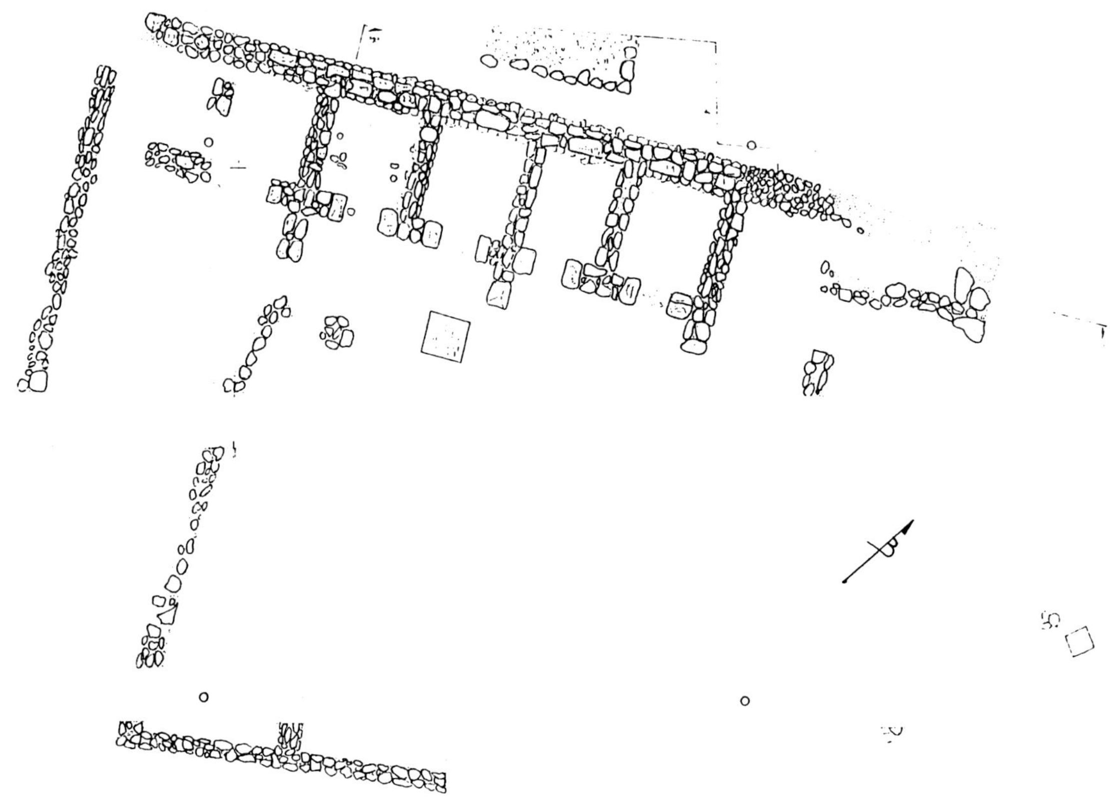

Εικ. 9. Η νότια οικιστική ενότητα: τύποι οικιών.

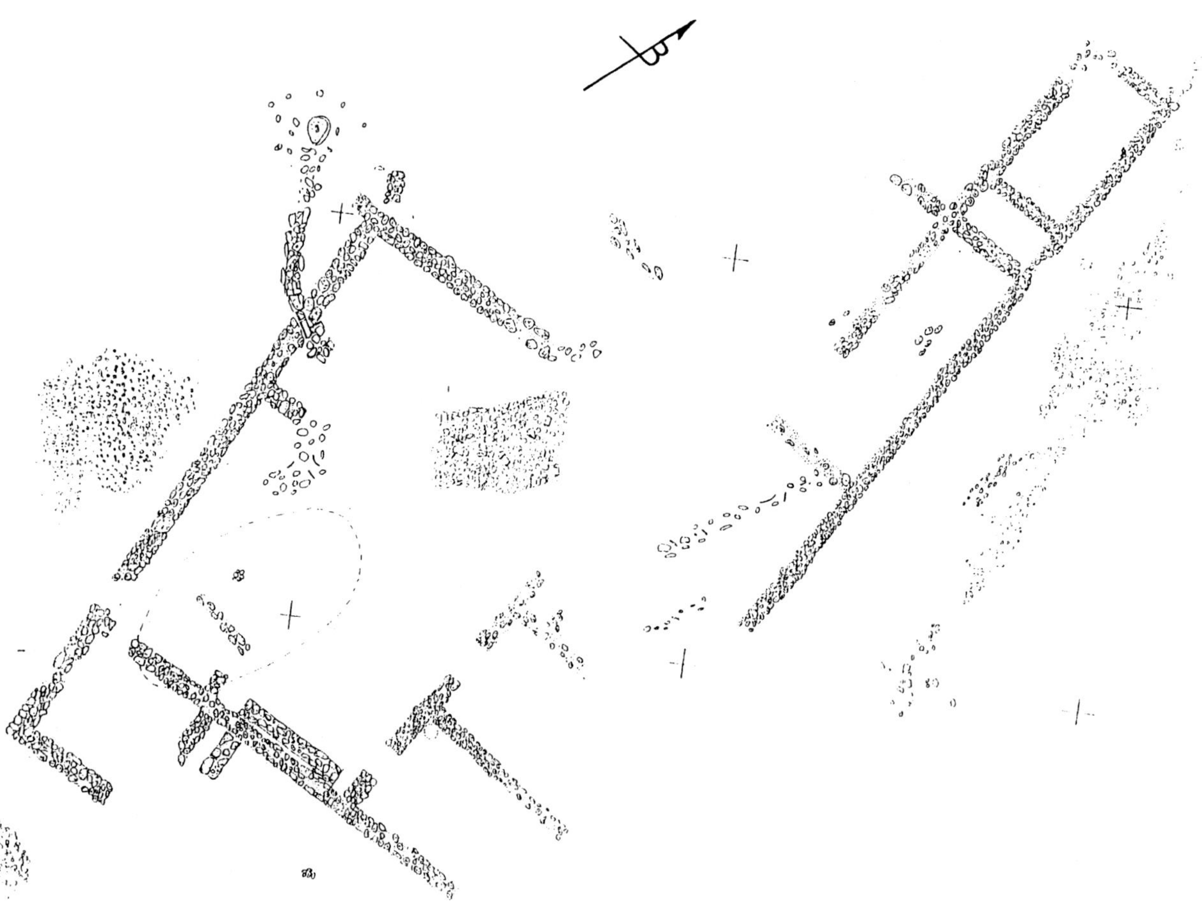

Εικ. 10. Η νότια οικιστική ενότητα: τύποι οικιών.

10 μ.) χώρος. Η αυλή πρέπει να είχε διαστάσεις 15 × 20 μ. περίπου. Ιδιαίτερα ενδιαφέρουσα είναι κατά τα άλλα η διαπίστωση ότι σε μία, πιθανόν δύο περιπτώσεις τα ερείπια ανήκουν σε συγκροτήματα δύο ομόρων οικιών. Μία μεγάλη αγροικία με κεντρική αυλή, διαστάσεων 9 × 9 μ., με πεσσοστοιχίες στις τέσσερις πλευρές και συμμετρική διάταξη των δωματίων, η δυτικώτερη (στην περιοχή των Αγίων Ασωμάτων) από τις δύο που επισημάνθηκαν στον περιφερειακό δρόμο προς την Ερχιά, ανήκει στην ελληνιστική εποχή.

'Ενα ακόμη στοιχείο που διαφοροποιεί τη μορφή του βορείου από το νότιο οικισμό του αεροδρομίου είναι η έλλειψη στον τελευταίο (τουλάχιστον στο δείγμα που ερευνήθηκε) των μεμονωμένων, αντιστοιχούντων στα κτήματα, ταφικών περιβόλων. Διαπιστώθηκε μία μόνο συγκέντρωση τάφων, κοντά στο κεντρικό σταυροδρόμι: τούτο κυριαρχείται από ένα μνημειώδη ταφικό περίβολο με πρόσοψη 16 μ., στο κέντρο του οποίου σώζεται η βάση του ταφικού μνημείου. Στα Ν. και ΝΔ. έξω από το περίβολο ανασκάφηκαν δέκα τάφοι και ταφικές πυρές του 5ου αι. π.Χ.

Ο χώρος στο ενδιάμεσο των δύο οικιστικών περιοχών δεν διατηρεί ίχνη κατοίκησης των κλασσικών χρόνων. Κατά μήκος της κεντρικής αρτηρίας που ενώνει τις δύο περιοχές, ανασκάφηκαν δύο ταφικοί περίβολοι με συνεχή χρήση από τον 5ο έως τον 4ο αι. π.Χ. Η προτεινόμενη δοκιμαστικά (σύμφωνα με το σχήμα του Traill) ταύτιση των δήμων στο χώρο του αεροδρομίου με τη Μυρρινούτα και τους Φιλαΐδες βρίσκει μια πρόσθετη απόδειξη στην κατεύθυνση των δρόμων που συνδέουν τους δύο ανασκαφέντες οικισμούς με την παραλία και τους δήμους της Μεσογαίας. Οι δρόμοι αυτοί εντάσσονται σε ένα γενικότερο σχήμα σύνδεσης, πιθανώς, όπως έχει προταθεί, για στρατιωτικούς λόγους, των παραλίων με τις μεσόγειες τριττύες των φυλών της ανατολικής Αττικής.[15] Τούτο διαπιστώνεται τόσο στην περίπτωση της Ακαμαντίδος, με το δρόμο που συνδέει το Θορικό και την Κεφαλή με το μεσόγειο Αγνούντα, τα Πρόσπαλτα και το Σφηττό, όσο και της Πανδιονίδος, με τη σύνδεση των παραλίων Πρασιών, της Στειρίας, της Αγγελής και του Μυρρινούντα με τους μεσόγειους δήμους της Παιανίας, Όας και Κονθύλης. Είναι προφανές συνεπώς, ότι τα δύο οικιστικά κέντρα του αεροδρομίου ανήκουν αντίστοιχα στον παράλιο (Φιλαΐδες) και σε ένα μικρό δήμο της μεσόγειας τριττύος της Αιγηίδος φυλής, ο οποίος εφόσον αποκλεισθεί η Ερχιά, που βρίσκεται ανατολικώτερα νοτίως των Σπάτων, δεν μπορεί να είναι άλλος από τη Μυρρινούτα.

Γενικά συμπεράσματα για την τυπική μορφή του αττικού δήμου

Είναι φανερό ότι οι δήμοι που εντοπίσθηκαν και εν μέρει ανασκάφηκαν στο χώρο του αεροδρομίου δεν είχαν τη μορφή ενός χωριού συγκροτημένου γύρω από ένα κεντρικό οικιστικό πυρήνα. Δίνεται περισσότερο η εντύπωση ενός διάσπαρτου οικισμού που αποτελείται από μεμονωμένες αγροικίες, του τύπου που είναι γνωστός από το δήμο της Ατήνης.[16] Στη γενίκευση αυτού του οικιστικού σχήματος, με ορισμένες εξαιρέσεις όπως αυτή των Αλών Αιξωνίδων ή του Θορικού, φαίνεται να συνηγορούν και τα συμπεράσματα από το μακροχρόνιο συστηματικό έλεγχο ενός μεγάλου αριθμού αττικών δήμων.[17] Θα αποτελούσε εν τούτοις μεθοδολογικό σφάλμα η εκ προοιμίου αποδοχή, βάση ενός *argumentum ex silentio*, της απόλυτης ομοιομορφίας των αττικών δήμων. Η δημιουργία τους πριν από 2,500 χρόνια δεν υπήρξε η ιδρυτική πράξη των αντίστοιχων οικισμών, πολύ δε λιγότερο επέβαλε σ' αυτούς κάποια οικιστική ή άλλη ομοιομορφία. Πέρα από την ύπαρξη ή όχι συνέχειας με κάποιο τοπικό προϊστορικό κέντρο, είναι φυσικό και αναμενόμενο ότι η μορφή τους προσδιορίστηκε απ' αρχής, αλλά και στην εξέλιξή της από γεωγραφικούς, ιστορικούς και οικονομικούς, όπως το μέγεθος του πληθυσμού και ο τρόπος παραγωγής, λόγους.

Θεωρώντας την πολεοδομική εξέλιξη — την αρχαία όπως και τη σύγχρονη — των Αθηνών, δεν μπορούμε να παραγνωρίσουμε το ρόλο που θα έπαιξε εν προκειμένω η απόσταση από τα αστικά κέντρα, την Αθήνα και τον Πειραιά, η δυνατότητα δηλαδή της αυθημερόν επιστροφής από τους αγρούς, τα απρόσμενα παρεπόμενα της οποίας είναι γνωστά από τον *κατὰ Ἐρατοσθένους* λόγο του Λυσία.[18] Τούτο εξηγεί κατ' αρχήν την ιδιομορφία της φυσιογνωμίας του συνόλου σχεδόν των δήμων των αστικών τριττύων: πρόκειται για την οικεία στους ανασκαφείς της Αττικής εικόνα ενός τοπίου που κυριαρχείται από οικογενειακούς ταφικούς περιβόλους ιδρυμένους κατά μήκος των δρόμων οι οποίοι προσδιορίζουν τον αγροτικό ιστό του λεκανοπεδίου.[19] Το γεγονός ότι — παρά την ανοικοδόμηση κατά τις τελευταίες δεκαετίες, όλων των αθηναϊκών προαστίων — ούτε μια αρχαία αγροικία δεν έγινε δυνατόν να εντοπισθεί με βεβαιότητα,[20] αποτελεί απόδειξη αν όχι για την απόλυτη απουσία τους, κάτι το οποίο διαψεύδεται από τις αρχαίες πηγές,[21] όμως τουλάχιστον για την εξαιρετικά αραιή κατοίκηση του χώρου. Ο προσδιοριστικός ρόλος της απόστασης από το άστυ εξηγεί και τις εξαιρέσεις που αποτελούν ανάμεσα στους αστικούς δήμους οι ακραίοι δήμοι του Ευωνύμου και του Αλιμούντος, όπου φαίνεται ότι κατοικούσε μόνιμα ένα μεγάλο μέρος των πρεσβυτέρων δημοτών.[22]

Διαφορετική από την προηγούμενη είναι η εικόνα που παρουσιάζουν οι πιο απομακρυσμένοι από το άστυ δήμοι της Αττικής για τους οποίους υπάρχουν ανασκαφικές πληροφορίες.[23] Χαρακτηριστικό πολεοδομικό στοιχείο είναι εν προκειμένω η αραιή οικοδόμηση γύρω από δύο ή — καμμιά φορά — τρεις πυρήνες, των οποίων ενίοτε παραδίδονται τα ονόματα όπως π.χ. στο Σούνιο και τις Αφίδνες.[24] Παραδείγματα τεκμηριωμένα αρχαιολογικά προσφέρουν ο δήμος των Αχαρνών και σχεδόν όλοι οι δήμοι της παραλίας.[25] Εκτενέστερος λόγος θα γίνει πιο κάτω για τις Αιξωνίδες Αλές και το Θορικό. 'Ενας οικιστικός πυρήνας αναπτύσσεται συνήθως κατά μήκος του κεντρικού δρόμου ή οργανώνεται γύρω από το σταυροδρόμι των πλέον σημαντικών δρόμων της περιοχής. Στο σημείο αυτό αναμένεται η ύπαρξη ενός δημοσίου φρέατος, το οποίο καμμιά φορά έμελλε όπως π.χ. το Βαθύ Πηγάδι των Σπάτων ή το Κίτσι Πηγάδι των Λαμπτρών, να έχει μακραίωνη ιστορία. Είναι πολύ πιθανό ότι η θέση του δημοσίου φρέατος έπαιξε, παράλληλα με τους άλλους, κοινωνικούς-ιστορικούς (π.χ. έδρα ενός γένους, ή συγγένειας) ή πρακτικούς λόγους, όπως είναι η γειτνίαση των αγρών, κάποιο σημαντικό ρόλο στο σχηματισμό των πολλαπλών αρχικών πυρήνων. Σύμφωνα με τη νομοθεσία του Σόλωνος, που έθεσε το νομικό πλαίσιο της αττικής αγροτικής οικονομίας (Πλουτ. *Σόλων* 23.6), η προβλεπόμενη ακτίνα για τη διάνοιξη φρέατος είναι τέσσερα στάδια από το πλησιέστερο δημόσιο φρέαρ, ακριβώς όση και η απόσταση που χωρίζει τους δύο οικισμούς, τόσο στις Αλές Αιξωνίδες, όσο και π.χ. στο δήμο που ανασκάφηκε στο Ντράφι.[26] Το κέντρο του δήμου προσδιορίζεται συχνά από τη γειτνίαση ενός παλαιότερου ιερού ή οικισμού που παίζει το ρόλο της ακροπόλεως, όπως δείχνουν τα παραδείγματα των Αλών Αιξωνίδων, του Αναγυρούντος(Λαθούρεζα),[27] των Λαμπτρών(Παναγιά Θίτι),[28] του Σφηττού (Χριστός Κορωπίου), της Ερχιάς (Πόλις, Πάγος).[29] Κοινό στοιχείο που χαρακτηρίζει πιθανόν το ένα από τα θρησκευτικά κέντρα πολλών, αν και όχι όλων των δήμων, είναι το θέατρο: από τα αρχαιότερα είναι αυτό του Θορικού, ένα από τα λαμπρότερα παραδείγματα το θέατρο που έσκαψε πρόσφατα η Όλγα Αλεξανδρή στο Ευώνυμο. Πολλά παραδίδονται επιγραφικώς.[30] 'Οσο για την κατοίκηση, αυτή εναλλάσσεται — κατά μήκος των μικρών δαιδαλωδών δρομίσκων που ορίζουν οι αιμασιές των κτημάτων — με ταφικούς περιβόλους και μικρά ιερά, τα οποία στις επιγραφές συχνά αναφέρονται ως όρια ιδιοκτησιών.[31] Το σπίτι βρίσκεται δίπλα στο δρόμο, στην άκρη του χωραφιού (όπως στο βόρειο οικισμό των Σπάτων) ή στο βάθος του κήπου. Ο τύπος αυτός της οικοδόμησης είναι σύμφωνος με τη λογική του αγροτικού οικισμού και επιβεβαιώνεται από την μαρτυρία των όρων υποθηκών: πράγματι η μεγάλη πλειοψηφία των *ὅρων χωρίου καὶ οἰκίας* όπως και των *ὅρων χωρίου* προέρχονται από τους δήμους, ενώ σχεδόν όλοι οι σωζόμενοι *ὅροι οἰκίας* από το άστυ, τον Πειραιά και την Ελευσίνα.[32] Παρόμοια και με τις μισθώσεις. Ενώ στα αστικά κέντρα είναι οι μισθώσεις οικιών (π.χ. *ἐν Κυδαθηναίων* ή *ἐν Σαλαμῖνι*) που κατ' εξοχήν συναντώνται, στον αγροτικό χώρο των δήμων επικρατούν οι μισθώσεις κήπων, χωρίων ή εσχατιών.[33] Η σταδιακή και τυχαία οικοδόμηση δίνει στον αγροτικό οικισμό μία όψη τελείως διαφορετική από εκείνη των δήμων με "ιπποδάμειο" σχεδιασμό που όπως ο Πειραιάς ή η Ελευσίνα προάχθηκαν σε αστικά κέντρα, ή εκείνη των κληρουχιών όπως η Σαλαμίνα.[34] Χαρακτηριστική της διαφοράς από το αστικό, ιπποδάμειο ή μή, σύστημα είναι συχνά η έκκεντρη θέση της εμπορικής αγοράς, όπως για παράδειγμα συμβαίνει με την (ελληνιστική) αγορά στο Πασά Λιμάνι του Σουνίου, ή συμπεραίνεται για τη Βήσσα, όπου η αγορά αναφέρεται ως όριο ενός ορυχείου.[35] Κατ' αυτόν τον τρόπο ο οικισμός εκτείνεται αν όχι ομοιόμορφα, ούτε σε ολόκληρο, πάντως σε μεγάλο μέρος του δήμου. Εννοείται ότι οι κατοικίες είναι αραιότερες ή λείπουν τελείως στις εσχατιές, το χώρο ενός Τίμωνος ή του Δύσκολου του Μενάνδρου.[36] Στη θέση τους βρίσκονται αλώνια και αποθήκες. 'Οπως εύκολα διαπιστώνεται στο χάρτη, η απόσταση ανάμεσα στα ακραία όρια ενός τέτοιου οικισμού δεν ξεπερνά τα 3–4 χιλιόμετρα, δηλαδή πορεία μίας ώρας. Η μεγαλύτερη απόσταση που θα είχε συνεπώς κάποιος να διανύσει ανάμεσα στο σπίτι του και το θρησκευτικό κέντρο του δήμου (αν υποθέσουμε ότι υπήρχε ένα και μοναδικό τέτοιο κέντρο) ή πιό συγκεκριμένα το θέατρο ή την αγορά, είναι ακόμα και στην ακραία περίπτωση του κατοίκου των εσχατιών το πολύ 20 έως 30 λεπτά.

Η αρχαιολογική εικόνα του αττικού δήμου που σκιαγραφήθηκε προηγουμένως αποκτά χρώμα και πνοή στα σωζόμενα κείμενα των κωμικών και των ρητόρων. Μέσα από αυτή την παράδοση αντλείται η αίσθηση της αμεσότητας που διαπνέει την απλή, αυτάρκη ζωή στους αγρούς, όπως χαρακτηριστικά ονομάζονται οι δήμοι. Διακρίνουμε τα σπίτια στο βάθος των κήπων ανάμεσα στις συκιές και τις ελιές ή στην άκρη του αμπελώνα.[37] Η κνίσσα και οι φωνές, όπως και το κέρασμα από τη γιορτή στο σπίτι του γείτονα δείχνουν ωστόσο ότι τα σπίτια αυτά δεν είναι μεμονωμένα αγροκτήματα.[38] Οι αποστάσεις δεν είναι τέτοιες που να καταστρέφουν το σπουδαιότερο στοιχείο της δημοτικής ζωής, την αίσθηση της γειτονείας με τα καλά και τα κακά της, την αλληλοβοήθεια και τη συμπαράσταση στον κίνδυνο[39] αλλά και τις ατέλειωτες προστριβές για τους φράχτες και τις αποχετεύσεις.[40] Ειδικά στα δικανικά κείμενα, όπου συχνά θίγεται η σχέση με το δήμο των εγκατεστημένων στο άστυ πλουσίων δημοτών, η γειτονιά ταυτίζεται με την εκλογική και πολιτική πελατεία, αλλά κυρίως με τη συλλογική μνήμη, η οποία προσφέρει την εγγύηση της γνησιότητος του γάμου, των παιδιών και της ιδιοκτησίας.[41]

Θα αναφερθώ σύντομα στις περιπτώσεις που απομακρύνονται περισσότερο από το οικιστικό σχήμα που σκιαγραφήθηκε προηγουμένως. Στα δύο άκρα βρίσκονται από τη μία πλευρά οι δήμοι με μικρό πληθυσμό, όπως αυτοί του αεροδρομίου των Σπάτων (για τους οποίους έγινε ήδη λόγος) ή η Ατήνη δυτικώς του Σουνίου, δήμοι όπου η διασπορά της κατοίκησης ήταν πλήρης και οι αποστάσεις ανάμεσα στα σπίτια καμμιά φορά ξεπερνούσαν τα 200 μ. Από την άλλη έχουμε δήμους, στους οποίους η πυκνότητα της κατοίκησης αλλά και ο τρόπος της δόμησης φαίνεται να προσδίδουν ένα σχεδόν αστικό χαρακτήρα. Τυπικά δείγματα θεωρούνται ο Θορικός και οι Αιξωνίδες Αλαί. Η παραδεδομένη εικόνα πρέπει ωστόσο και στις δύο αυτές περιπτώσεις να μετριασθεί. Τόσο ως προς το σχήμα της γενικής διάταξης, τον πολλαπλό δηλαδή πυρήνα, αλλά και τις αρχές που διέπουν την εξέλιξή τους, οι οικισμοί των δήμων αυτών δεν διαφέρουν ουσιαστικά από τους υπολοίπους δήμους της Παραλίας, της Λαυρεωτικής και της Μεσογαίας. Σε καμμιά περίπτωση ο οικισμός δεν περιορίζεται σε ένα πυκνά δομημένο κέντρο, το οποίο θα μπορούσε να μονοπωλήσει το όνομα του δήμου. Την απόδειξη, ως προς το Θορικό, παρέχει η συνεχιζόμενη έρευνα της ευρύτερης περιοχής του δήμου,[42] συγκεκριμένα η αποκάλυψη σε απόσταση περίπου 1,300 μ. νοτιώτερα από τον οικισμό στο λόφο Βελατούρι ενός δεύτερου οικιστικού κέντρου, χαρακτηριζόμενου από κανονικές ως προς τη μορφή και το μέγεθος οικίες του γνωστού από όλους τους αττικούς δήμους τύπου, ενώ ένας τρίτος πυρήνας υπήρχε ένα περίπου χιλιόμετρο ανατολικώς από τον ίδιο λόφο, στο λαιμό της χερσονήσου, όπου βρίσκεται το κλασσικό οχυρό του Αγ. Νικολάου. Το οικιστικό σχήμα συμπληρώνεται με μία στεφάνη έξι αγροικιών κτισμένων σε μία ακτίνα 1,5 και 2 χιλιομέτρων ΝΔ. από το Βελατούρι στις πλαγιές δηλαδή των λόφων (Στεφάνι κλπ) που πλαισιώνουν από την πλευρά αυτή την πεδιάδα του Θορικού και σε απόσταση 500–800 μ. μεταξύ των. Στις Αιξωνίδες Αλές, που αποτελεί το αντικείμενο της ανακοίνωσης της Ι. Ανδρέου στον παρόντα τόμο, ο δήμος εκτός από την ακρόπολη αποτελείται από δύο σε απόσταση 700 μ. μεταξύ των, ανεξάρτητους οικισμούς, εκτάσεως 90 έως 150 περίπου στρεμμάτων, με χωριστά νεκροταφεία. Ένας τρίτος, μικρότερος, οικισμός πρέπει να υποτεθεί περί τα 2,5 χιλιόμετρα νοτιώτερα, στην περιοχή του Ζωστήρος. Γύρω από τους δύο ή τρεις αυτούς πυρήνες εκτείνεται μια ευρύτερη ζώνη αραιής κατοίκησης διάσπαρτη από ταφικούς περιβόλους, έτσι ώστε το σύνολο του κατοικημένου χώρου να καταλαμβάνει δύο περίπου χιλιόμετρα.

Ο αστικός χαρακτήρας των εν λόγω δήμων οφείλεται όχι τόσο στην (υποθετική) ύπαρξη ενός συγκροτημένου χωριού, ούτε κάν στην πυκνότητα της κατοίκησης, η οποία αποτελεί συνάρτηση του μεγέθους των κλήρων, όσο στη νέα ορθολογική αρχή οργάνωσης των οικιστικών μονάδων, που εκδηλώνεται με την εφαρμογή πάνω στο χαλαρό πλέγμα των αγροτικών δρόμων, ενός συστήματος από ομοιόμορφα συγκροτήματα κατοικιών. Το σχήμα αναγνωρίζεται στο κτήμα Καλαμπόκα, συγκεκριμένα στο σύστημα πέντε κατοικιών γύρω από τον πύργο στο ΒΑ. άκρο του οικοπέδου, όπως και στο γειτονικό, σε απόσταση 150 μ. οικόπεδο Λογοθέτη.[43] Το ίδιο περίπου σχήμα επαναλαμβάνεται στο *Tower Compound* 1 του Θορικού.[44]

Σε προσεκτικώτερη εξέταση διαπιστώνεται εν τούτοις ότι αυτές οι *insulae* αποτελούν την τελευταία επέμβαση σε ένα παλαιότερο τυπικό αγροτικό

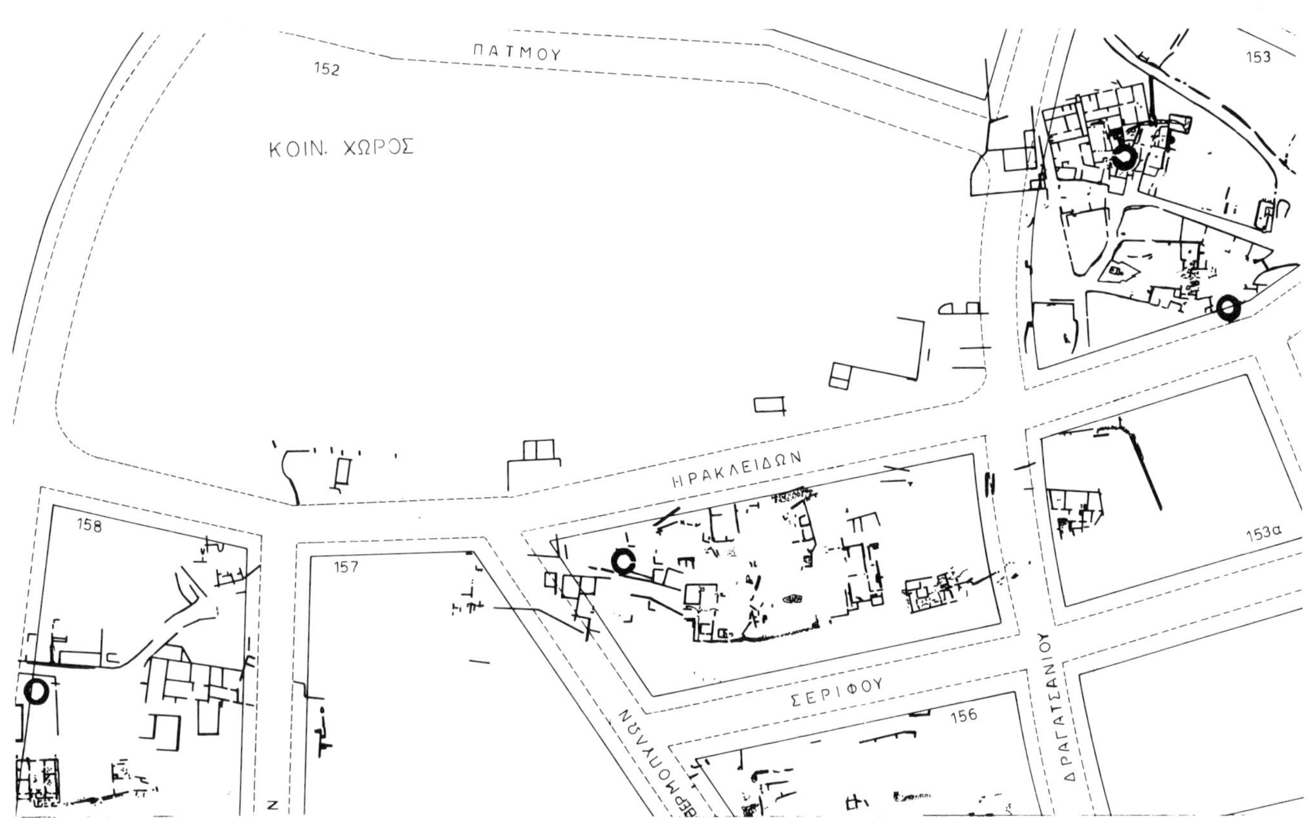

Εικ. 11. Οικισμός Αλών Αιξωνίδων: πύργοι και συγκροτήματα σπιτιών.

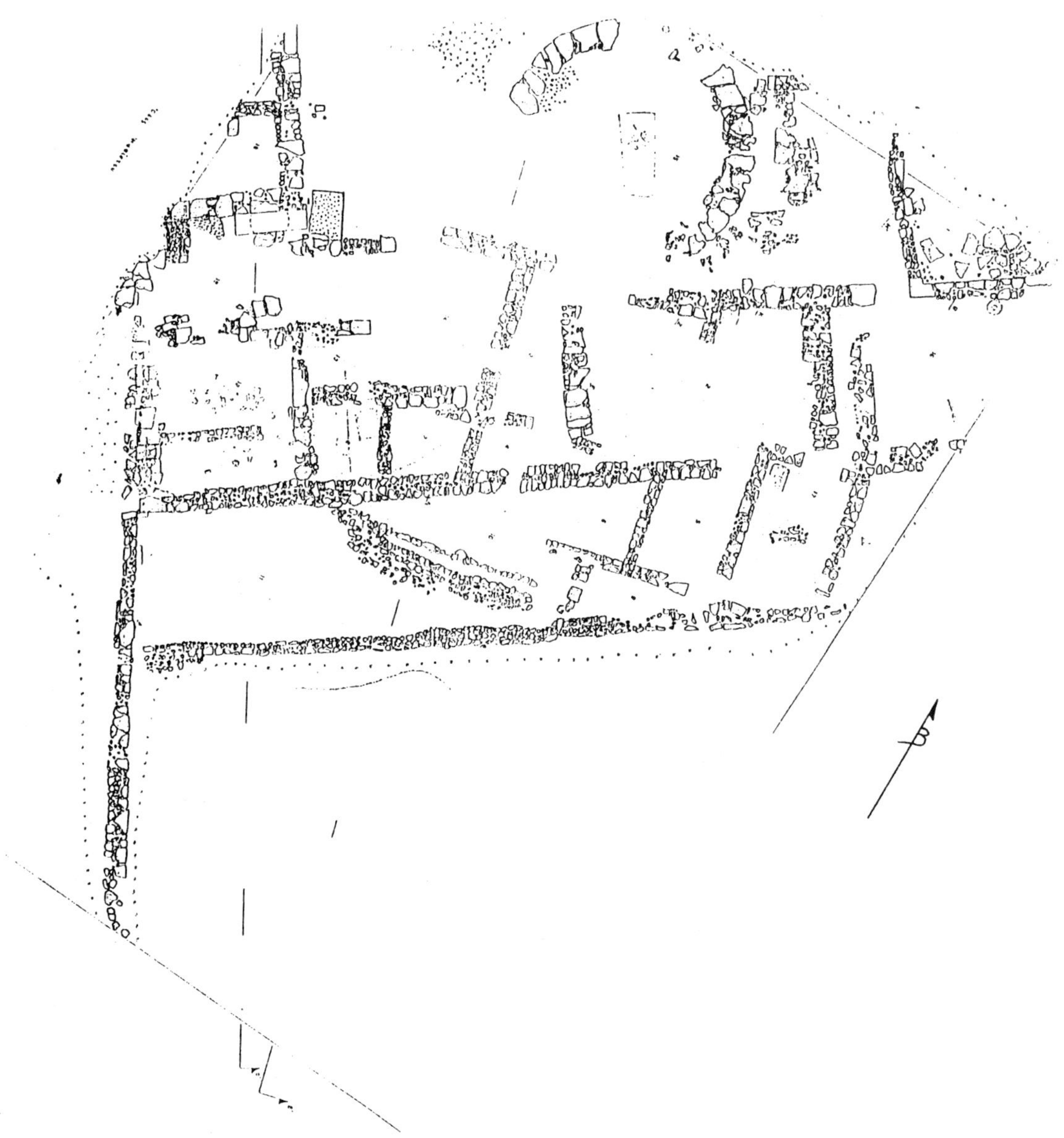

Εικ. 12. Αναγυρούς, insula *και πύργος (οικόπεδο Γυφτοπούλου).*

οικιστικό ιστό, που καθοριζόταν αρχικά από ένα ακανόνιστο πλέγμα περιφραγμένων αγροκτημάτων, *χωρίων* παρόμοιων με εκείνα των Σπάτων, αν και σαφώς μικρότερων, οι μαντρότοιχοι των οποίων ακολουθούσαν την ελικοειδή πορεία των αγροτικών δρόμων. Μικρά τεμένη με ή χωρίς ναΐσκο, που συναντώνται συχνά στα σταυροδρόμια, καθώς και η παρουσία εδώ και εκεί ανάμεσα στα σπίτια και τα ιερά ενός ταφικού περιβόλου, αποτελούν υπόμνηση του αρχικού αγροτικού χαρακτήρα του οικισμού.[45] Η πρώτη οικοδομική φάση του χώρου χαρακτηρίζεται από την εγκατάσταση σε αραιά διαστήματα 50–120 μ. στο ΒΑ. οικισμό των Αιξωνίδων Αλών μιας σειράς από πύργους, γύρω από τους οποίους οργανώνεται το αγρόκτημα. Η γενική εικόνα του πρώτου οικισμού των Αλών στα Πηγαδάκια της Βούλας (εικ. 11) όπως και αυτή του σύγχρονού του Θορικού στο Βελατούρι δεν πρέπει να διέφεραν αισθητά από εκείνη της Αθήνης[46] ή άλλων δήμων της παραλίας. Η εξέλιξη από τον 5ο στον 4ο αι., όπως αποδεικνύεται από τη μετατόπιση των *αιμασιών*, που συχνά συνοδεύεται από την κατάργηση των δρόμων ανάμεσα στα κτήματα (ένα παράδειγμα παρόμοιας συνένωσης ιδιοκτησιών διαπιστώθηκε και στα Σπάτα, βλ. παραπάνω), φαίνεται να συμπίπτει με τη (μαρτυρούμενη και από αλλού) συγκέντρωση της ιδιοκτησίας, δεν αποκλείεται μάλιστα να είναι αποτέλεσμά της: πράγματι η σύγχρονη οικοδόμηση των *insulae* είναι προφανώς αποτέλεσμα προγραμματισμένης επιχείρησης οικοπεδοποίησης, όπως δείχνει η κανονικότητα της διάταξης και η ομοιομορφία των οικιών.[47] Ενδείξεις για τη σύγχρονη έκταση της "αστικού τύπου" οργάνωσης του αγροτικού χώρου παρέχουν ανάλογες περιπτώσεις από άλλους δήμους, όπως η δημιουργία συνοικιών στη θέση ενός παλαιότερου πύργου σε δύο τουλάχιστον θέσεις στον

Αναγυρούντα (εικ. 12) και η σχεδίαση μιας *insula* στο δήμο της Ξυπετής στο Μοσχάτο.[48]

Εάν η συγκέντρωση της ιδιοκτησίας της γης υπήρξε η προϋπόθεση της, στην ιδιαίτερη, μέσα σ' αυτό το πλαίσιο, εξέλιξη του δήμου των Αλών Αιξωνίδων ή των άλλων προαναφερθέντων δήμων συνέβαλαν αναμφισβήτητα και άλλοι συγκεκριμένοι ιστορικοί παράγοντες. Η στροφή στη γεωργία που χαρακτηρίζει τον 4ο αι.[49] και η εντατικοποίηση της εκμετάλλευσης της γης, υποδειγματική ως γνωστόν στους δήμους της δυτικής παραλίας,[50] προϋπέθετε την αύξηση των καλλιεργητών ή τη μίσθωση των γαιών και συνεπώς την εγκατάσταση νέου και συχνά ξένου προς την περιοχή πληθυσμού.[51] Στην περίπτωση των Αλών Αιξωνίδων στην προσέλκυση ξένων συνέβαλε πιθανόν και η θέση του δήμου, η σχέση με το ιερό, αλλά κυρίως με το λιμάνι του Ζωστήρος, που είναι η αναγκαστική σκάλα στον πλούν προς το Σούνιο και τα νησιά, και η αφετηρία του εσωτερικού δρόμου προς τη Μεσογαία και την Αθήνα. Από την άλλη πλευρά, η ιδιαίτερη πυκνότητα του τύπου αυτού της κατοίκησης που σημειώνεται σε δήμους όπως ο Θορικός και ο Ραμνούς, αποδίδεται σε διαφορετικό σε κάθε περίπτωση λόγο. Στο Θορικό έχουμε να κάνουμε με ένα πληθυσμό μετοίκων και ετεροδημοτών εμπορευομένων, εργατών, τεχνιτών, επιστατών και άλλων βαναύσων που (όπως και οι καλλιεργητές των Αλών), επειδή είτε δεν μπορούν είτε δεν τους συμφέρει να την αγοράσουν, υποχρεώνονται να νοικιάσουν τη στέγη τους. Στο Ραμνούντα την εξήγηση δίνει η παρουσία της φρουράς και η στενότητα του χώρου μέσα στο οχυρό. Και στις δύο περιπτώσεις η μορφή του οικισμού χαρακτηρίζεται έτσι από την (άγνωστη στις συνοικίες του τύπου των Αλών Αιξωνίδων, του Αναγυρούντος και της Ξυπετής) άτακτη συσσώρευση μικρών χώρων, που δυσκολεύει εξαιρετικά την ερμηνεία τους, η οποία είναι πάντως τελείως ξένη στην έννοια του αγροτικού δήμου, που νοσταλγεί ο Δικαιόπολις (Αριστοφ. *Ἀχαρν.* 32), και εμείς μαζί του, μέσα από τα τείχη των Αθηνών.

Σημειώσεις

1. Τα σημαντικότερα βιβλία στα οποία γίνεται στη συνέχεια αναφορά μόνο με το όνομα του συγγραφέα είναι τα εξής: J.S. Traill, *The Political Organization of Attica: A Study of the Demes, Trittyes and Phylai, and their Representation in the Athenian Council*, *Hesperia* Suppl. 14 (Princeton 1975). R. Osborne, *Demos: the Discovery of Classical Attika* (Cambridge 1985). D. Whitehead, *The Demes of Attica 508/7 — ca. 250 B.C.* (Princeton 1986). Περιγραφή των δήμων και του τοπίου της Αττικής με βάση κυρίως τις φιλολογικές και επιγραφικές πηγές δίνει το άρθρο του E. Arrigoni, "Στοιχεῖα πρός ἀναπαράστασιν τοῦ τοπίου τῆς Ἀττικῆς κατά την κλασσικήν ἐποχήν" που δημοσιεύθηκε σε δύο συνέχειες στο περιοδικό *Ἀθηνᾶ* 71 (1969–1970) 332–386 και 74 (1971) 25–86.
2. Μια σύγχρονη αρχαιολογική περιγραφή των δήμων της Αττικής αποτελεί επείγον *desideratum* της έρευνας. Για ένα χρήσιμο τοπογραφικό ευρετήριο βλ. Μ. Πετροπουλάκου - Ε. Τσιμπίδης-Β. Πεντάζος, *Ἀττική-Οἰκιστικά στοιχεῖα, Ἀρχαῖες ἑλληνικές πόλεις* 21 (Αθήνα 1973). Χρησιμότατο ακόμη, αν και ξεπερασμένο από το πλήθος των νέων στοιχείων, είναι το περιορισμένο στη δυτική παραλία βιβλίο του C.W.J. Eliot, *The Coastal Demes of Attika: a Study in the Policy of Kleisthenes*, *Phoenix* Suppl. 5 (Toronto 1962). Αυτή την ανάγκη δεν έχει σκοπό να εξυπηρετήσει ούτε το (κατ' ανάγκην συνοπτικό) J. Travlos, *Bildlexikon zur Topographie des antiken Attika* (Tübingen 1988). Η συστηματική ανασκαφική έρευνα του Θορικού δημοσιεύεται στη σειρά *Thorikos* (ο πρώτος τόμος το 1968). Δές και την ανακοίνωση του H.F. Mussche στον παρόντα τόμο, σελ. 211–215. Ιδιαίτερο ενδιαφέρον έχουν οι έρευνες στην περιοχή του δήμου της Ατήνης που διεξάγονται από το Πανεπιστήμιο του Bochum, βλ. τελευταία H. Lohmann, "Zur Prosopographie und Demographie der attischen Landgemeinde Atene ('Ατήνη)," Eckh. Olshausen und H. Sonnabend (eds.), *Stuttgarter Kolloquium zur historischen Geographie des Altertums*, 2, 1984 und 3, 1987 (Bonn 1991) 203–258. Για μια πρώτη συγκέντρωση του υλικού από τις ανασκαφές της Αιξωνής βλ. Ε. Γιαννοπούλου-Κονσολάκη, *Γλυφάδα: Ἱστορικό Παρελθόν καί Μνημεία* (Αθήνα 1990).
3. Για μια πρώτη έκθεση των ανασκαφών στο χώρο του αεροδρομίου βλ. Γ. Σταϊνχάουερ, *Πρακτ* (1982) [1984] 124.
4. Για τα ονόματα των δήμων αυτών και τις δοκιμαστικές ταυτίσεις των βλ. Traill 35–55 και χάρτη 3.
5. Λαμβάνοντας υπόψη τους βασικούς συντελεστές υπολογισμού για τα μεγέθη των αττικών δήμων, δηλ. τον αριθμό των βουλευτών, αρχόντων ή εφήβων, τη μορφολογία και την ποιότητα του εδάφους (Osborne 37–46).
6. Ο εντοπισμός των περιοχών αρχαιολογικού ενδιαφέροντος έγινε από τη συνάδελφο Κλαίρη Ευστρατίου με εκτεταμένη επιφανειακή έρευνα του χώρου του αεροδρομίου, και συγκεκριμένα αυτών των περιοχών, όπου παλαιότερα (A. Milchhoefer, *Karten von Attika* [Berlin 1881–1900]) είχαν επισημανθεί αρχαιότητες. Στην ανασκαφική έρευνα του αεροδρομίου έλαβαν μέρος εκτός από την Κ. Ευστρατίου οι αρχαιολόγοι Ξ. Αραπογιάννη, Π. Παπαγγελή και Ε. Κουρίνου.
7. Ένα συνοπτικό σχέδιο του οχυρού βρίσκεται στο βιβλίο των Πετροπουλάκου-Πεντάζου (σημ. 2). Τα πρώτα ίχνη εγκατάστασης στην κορυφή του λόφου χρονολογούνται, όπως τώρα διαπιστώθηκε, στα νεολιθικά χρόνια. Το οχυρό που έδωσε ελάχιστα ανασκαφικά στοιχεία για χρονολόγηση, ανήκει στην ίδια κατηγορία με εκείνο του Έτοζι που ελέγχει τα βορειότερα περάσματα από το Πικέρμι (αρχ. Τειθράς) στη Ραφήνα (J.R. McCredie, *Fortified Military Camps in Attica*, *Hesperia* Suppl. 11 [Princeton 1966] 79–81).
8. Τα υπάρχοντα στοιχεία δεν επαρκούν για την ταύτισή του ή των δήμων. Η περιοχή κατανέμεται συνήθως (Traill, Travlos) ανάμεσα στους δύο αυτούς δήμους: το βόρειο τμήμα (Άγ. Γεώργιος Βουρβά, Άγ. Βασίλειος) ταυτίζεται με τη Μυρρινούτα (E. Vanderpool, "The Location of the Attic Deme Erchia," *BCH* 89 [1965] 24–26), το νότιο (Λάπαρι) με την Κονθύλη. Η ταύτιση με το δήμο της Κονθύλης βασίζεται στη στήλη της Καλλιστούς (*IG* II^2, 6533, A. Milchhoeffer, "Antikenbericht aus Attika," *AM* 12 [1887] 91) από τη θέση Μαζαρέϊκα, στα 2/3α του δρόμου ανάμεσα στο Βαθύ Πηγάδι και τα Σπάτα. Βλ. Milchhoefer, *Karten von Attika* VII, Text 5. Πιστεύω ότι η περιοχή Βουρβά-Λάπαρι-βορείου τομέα αεροδρομίου αποτελεί μια γεωγραφικά ενιαία περιοχή, που ανήκε σε ένα δήμο. Για τους λόγους προτιμήσεως του δήμου της Μυρρινούτης βλ. παρακάτω.
9. Για τη μεγάλη ιδιοκτησία στην περιοχή βλ. Arrigoni (σημ. 1) (1971) 80–81.
10. Βλ. Λυσίας, 1.9.
11. Οι πλούσιοι γαιοκτήμονες (σε αντίθεση με αυτούς του 5ου αι. βλ. Ισοκράτης, *Ἀρεοπαγ.* 52) είχαν την κυρία κατοικία τους στην Αθήνα,: π.χ. Ισαίος 11.42 "ἀγρὸν μὲν Θριᾶσι πένθ' ἡμιτάλαντα εὑρίσκοντα, οἰκίαν ἐν Μελίτῃ" κλπ και παρακάτω 44 "χωρίον ἐν Οἰνόῃ πεντακισχιλίων καὶ Προσπαλτοῖ τρισχιλίων, καὶ οἰκία ἐν ἄστει δισχιλίων" κλπ. Τη διαχείριση του κτήματος έχει ο επιστάτης, βλ. Θεοφρ. *Χαρ.* 30.16 "καὶ λογισμὸν λαμβάνειν παρὰ τοῦ εἰς ἀγρὸν ἐγχειρίζοντος." Η σοδειά όμως συγκεντρώνεται στην αστική

κατοικία του ιδιοκτήτη (βλ. R. Osborne, *Classical Landscape with Figures [London 1987] 23).*

12. Η αποδοχή του πειρατικού κινδύνου ως καθοριστικού παράγοντα για κατασκευές, όπως αυτές, που χρονολογούνται στον 5ο, αιώνα, είναι αδιανόητη. Για τη χρονολόγηση των αττικών πύργων στον 5ο αιώνα βλ. J. Young, "Studies in South Attica: Country Estates at Sounion," *Hesperia* 25 (1956) 112. Πρβλ. επίσης τα συμπεράσματα των βελγικών ανασκαφών για τη χρονολόγηση των οικοδομικών φάσεων στο Θορικό (*MIGRA* 1 [1975] 49–50). Τελείως διαφορετικές είναι βέβαια οι συνθήκες στην ελληνιστική εποχή. Βλ. L. Haselberger, *Befestigte Turmgehöfte im Hellenismus* (διδακτ. διατριβή του Πολυτεχνείου του Μονάχου, 1978).
13. Ἁρποκρ. Ἐσχατιά· "Τὰ πρὸς τοῖς τέρμασι τῶν χωρίων ἐσχατιὰς ἔλεγον, οἷς γειτνιᾷ εἴτε ὄρος εἴτε θάλασσα."
14. E. Jones — L.H. Sackett — A.J. Graham, "The Dema House in Attica," *BSA* 57 (1962) 75–114, ιδ., "An Attic Country House below the Cave of Pan at Vari," *BSA* 68 (1973) 355–452.
15. Σύμφωνα με την υπόθεση του P. Siewert, *Die Trittyen Attikas und die Heeresreform des Kleisthenes, Vestigia, Beiträge zur Alten Geschichte* 33 (München 1982) 136–141 και χάρτης 4.
16. Lohmann (σημ. 2) 215–216.
17. Τα συμπεράσματα από την αποδελτίωση των δημοσιευμένων στο *ΑρχΔελτ* από το 1960 κ.ε. ανασκαφών της Εφορείας συμπληρώνονται από τα αρνητικά στοιχεία από τον έλεγχο των εκσκαφών που πραγματοποιήθηκαν στο ίδιο διάστημα.
18. Λυσίας 1.11 "προϊόντος δὲ τοῦ χρόνου *ἧκον ἀπροσδοκήτως ἐξ ἀγροῦ*" (δηλ. αντίθετα προς τη συνηθισμένη κατά τη γεωργική περίοδο διανυκτέρευση στους αγρούς). Πρβλ. και 22 "Σώστρατος ἦν μοι ἐπιτήδειος καὶ φίλος. τούτῳ ἡλίου δεδυκότος ἰόντι ἐξ ἀγροῦ ἀπήντησα. *Εἰδὼς δ' ἐγὼ ὅτι τηνικαῦτα ἀφιγμένος οὐδὲν ἂν καταλήψοιτο οἴκοι τῶν ἐπιτηδείων, ἐκέλευον συνδειπνεῖν.*" Βλ. και παρακάτω σημ. 22.
19. R. Garland, "A First Catalogue of Attic Peribolos Tombs," *BSA* 77 (1982) 125–176.
20. Βλ. και *IG* II^2, 1598 όπου αναφέρεται μια σειρά χωρίων (καμμία όμως οικία) από το Φάληρο (σε αντίθεση βλ. μισθώσεις αποκλειστικά οικιών στον αστικό δήμο των Κυδαθηναίων *IG* II^2, 1590). Εξαίρεση αποτελεί ίσως το Μοσχάτο (αρχαίος δήμος Ξυπετής) βλ. Travlos (σημ. 2) 288, εικ. 365, σ. 292).
21. *IG* II^2, 2498. Μίσθωση από τους Πειραιείς της Παραλίας, της Αλμυρίδος, του Θησείου κλπ. όπου αναφέρεται (στ. 22/23) και "οἰκία [ἐν Ἁλμυρίδι] στέγουσα καὶ ὀρθή." Για μια οικία με πύργο πλησίον του Πειραιώς βλ. [Δημοσθ.] 47.1059 και 1157: "ἐπειδὴ τοίνυν μοι ἀπηγγέλθη εἰς Πειραιᾶ τα γεγενημένα ὑπὸ τῶν γειτόνων, ἐλθὼν εἰς ἀγρὸν" κλπ, πρβλ. 1162 ("γεωργῷ δὲ πρὸς τῷ ἱπποδρόμῳ, ὥστε οὐ πόρρω ἔδει αὐτὸν ἐλθεῖν"). Ότι η οικία δεν είναι απομονωμένη φαίνεται από την περιγραφή της βοηθείας που δίνουν οι θεράποντες των γειτόνων (τα αφεντικά τους πιθανόν εργάζονται στο άστυ ή στον Πειραιά, όπως και ο ενάγων), ο.π. 1157: "*ἀκούοντες* δὲ οἱ θεράποντες τῶν γειτόνων τῆς κραυγῆς *καὶ ὁρῶντες* τὴν οἰκίαν πορθουμένην τὴν ἐμήν, *οἱ μὲν ἀπὸ τῶν τεγῶν τῶν ἑαυτῶν ἐκαλίστρουν τοὺς παριόντας*, οἱ δὲ εἰς τὴν ἑτέραν ὁδὸν ἐλθόντες" κλπ.
22. Δημοσθ. 57.1302: "πέντε καὶ τριάκοντα στάδια τοῦ ἄστεως ἀπέχοντος καὶ τῶν πλείστων ἐκεῖ οἰκούντων, ἀπεληλύθεσαν οἱ πολλοί· οἱ δὲ κατάλοιποι ἦσαν οὐ πλείους ἢ τριάκοντα." Οι πρεσβύτεροι (και οι πτωχότεροι) αποτελούσαν το μεγαλύτερο μέρος του μόνιμου πληθυσμού των δήμων. Εκτός από τη γραφική περιγραφή των Αχαρνέων γερόντων που αποτελούν το χορό στην ομώνυμη κωμωδία του Αριστοφάνους (σ. 179–183, 211–213) βλ. και Λυσία 20.11–12 και 31.17 ("περιιὼν κατὰ τοὺς ἀγροὺς καὶ ἐντυγχάνων τῶν πολιτῶν τοῖς πρεσβυτάτοις, οἳ κατέμειναν ἐν τοῖς ἀγροῖς, ὀλίγα μὲν τῶν ἐπιτηδείων ἔχοντες"). Πρβλ. και Δημοσθ. 59.1239: "ἐπειδὴ ᾔσθετο ἀδυνάτως ἤδη ἔχοντα τὸν πατέρα καὶ μόγις εἰς ἄστυ ἀναβαίνοντα."
23. Πρόκειται κατά κύριο λόγο για την περιοχή των δήμων της Παραλίας, από την Αιξωνή (Γλυφάδα) έως τις Αλές Αραφηνίδες (Ραφήνα) και τους δήμους της Τετραπόλεως του Μαραθώνος, που γνώρισε κατά τις τελευταίες δεκαετίες και έως σήμερα τη μεγαλύτερη οικοδομική δραστηριότητα, τέλος το δήμο των Αχαρνέων.
24. Για τις Αφίδνες βλ. *IG* II^2, 1594: "Ἀφίδναις ἐν Ὑπωρείᾳ, ἐν Πεταλίδῳ ὑπὸ τῷ Φανερῷ." Πρβλ. Osborne 36, για τον οποίο το Σούνιο αποτελεί εξαίρεση στον κανόνα του *nucleated settlement*.
25. Στις Αχαρνές τα ευρήματα καλύπτουν μεγάλο μέρος των δύο συγχρόνων δήμων του Μενιδίου και των Λιοσίων. Πιθανά κέντρα είναι οι λόφοι των Αγ. Σαράντα και του Προφ. Ηλία (ελάχιστα κλασσικά οικοδομήματα έχουν έλθει στο φως, για τη θέση των νεκροταφείων βλ. τελευταία Αλ. Πατρινάκου-Ηλιάκη, "Αρχαιολογικές έρευνες στο δήμο Αχαρνών," *Α' Συμπόσιο Ἱστορίας-Λαογραφίας Βορείου Ἀττικῆς* [Αχαρνές 1989] 269–274). Για το δήμο του Πειραιώς χαρακτηριστική είναι η διαίρεση μεταξύ Μουνιχίας και Πειραιώς. Για την Αιξωνή βλ. το τοπογραφικό σχεδιάγραμμα (Κονσολάκη [σημ. 2] 200–201) όπου διακρίνονται τουλάχιστον δύο (χαλαρές) οικιστικές ενότητες. Τη διασπορά του οικισμού και των νεκροταφείων στον Αναγυρούντα δέχεται (παρά τη γενικά αντίθετη στη διατυπωμένη εδώ, θέση του για την οικιστική μορφή των δήμων), και ο Osborne 26–26. Για το Σούνιο βλ. J.H. Young, "Studies in South Attica," *Hesperia* 10 (1941) 163–191 και "Studies in South Attica," *Hesperia* 25 (1956) 122–146, Travlos (σημ. 2) 406. Πρβλ. Osborne 31–36 (ο οποίος προσπαθεί να εξηγήσει το φαινόμενο με την ιδιαιτερότητα του συγκεκριμένου δήμου). 3–4 οικιστικοί πυρήνες υποτίθενται βάσει επιφανειακών ευρημάτων και για τους δήμους των Φρεαρίων, της Αναφλύστου (Travlos 15–16) της Βήσσης και της Αμφιτροπής (Eliot [σημ. 2] 112–114).
26. Για τις Αλές Αιξωνίδες βλ. το άρθρο της Ι. Ανδρέου στον παρόντα τόμο, σελ. 191–209 και εδώ εικ. 11. Ο αρχαίος οικισμός που ανασκάφηκε από τον Παπαδημητρίου στο Ντράφι ταυτίζεται από τον Traill με το δήμο των Ιωνιδών (ταύτιση με Φηγαία *BCH* 81 [1956] 247). Αντίθετα ο Vanderpool ("News Letter from Greece," *AJA* 60 [1956] 269) προτείνει την ταύτιση με το δήμο των Κυδαντιδών. Σύντομη περιγραφή του οικισμού J.E. Jones, "Town and Country Houses of Attica in Classical Times," *MIGRA* 1 (1975) 102.
27. H. Lauter, *Lathuresa. Beiträge zur Architektur und Siedlungsgeschichte in spätgeometrischer Zeit* (Mainz am Rhein 1985).
28. D. Hagel, "The Fortifications of the Late Bronze Age on Kiapha Thiti, Attika," S. Van de Maele and J.M. Fossey (eds.), *Fortificationes Antiquae* (Amsterdam 1992) 45 και H. Lauter, "Some Remarks on Fortified Settlements in the Attic Countryside," ο.π. 77–91.
29. G. Daux, "La Grande Démachie: un nouveau calendrier sacrificiel d' Attique," *BCH* 87 (1963) 603–634, J.D. Mikalson "Religion in the Attic Demes," *AJP* 98 (1977) 424, Vanderpool (σημ. 8) 23.
30. Τούτο ισχύει βέβαια μόνο για τους μεγαλύτερους δήμους. Θέατρα έχουν ανασκαφεί σε πέντε δήμους: Ικάριον, Πειραιά, Ραμνούντα, Θορικό και Ευώνυμον. Μόνο επιγραφικώς αναφέρονται άλλα δύο (Αχαρνές, Αιξωνή), ενώ έμμεσα (από τη μνεία χορηγήσεως προεδρίας ή από την ύπαρξη χορηγικών μνημείων) συμπεραίνεται η ύπαρξη άλλων επτά.
31. Βλ. π.χ. *SEG* XXIV 151 στ. 9 ("χωρίον ᾧι γείτων ... καὶ τὸ ἡρῷον τὸ Ἐπιγόνου νοτόθεν δὲ τὸ Ἡράκλειον καὶ τὸ χωρίον ἥρωος Δακτύλου καὶ τὸ τοῦ Διὸς τέμενος") ή την περιγραφή της περιουσίας του Φιλοκράτους: B.D. Meritt, "Greek Inscriptions," *Hesperia* 5 (1936) 393 κ.ε., αρ. 10, στ. 10–73, πρβλ. Osborne 228 σημ. 26.
32. Βλ. τον πίνακα Osborne 60: όροι οικίας (32 από το άστυ, 5 εκτός άστεως), όροι χωρίου και οικίας (13 από το άστυ, 31 από τους δήμους), όροι χωρίου (17 από το άστυ, 27 από τους δήμους) και οικίας (13 από το άστυ, 31 από τους δήμους), όροι χωρίου (17 από το άστυ, 27 από τους δήμους).

33. *IG* II², 1590, 1591, 1598.
34. Βλ. π.χ. *ΑρχΔελτ* 42 (1987) Β1 (Χρονικά) 66, σχέδ. 3.
35. Eliot (σημ. 2) 120 σημ. 8-9.
36. Λουκιανός *Τίμων* 154, Μένανδρος *Δύσκολος* 161, 220, 226.
37. Αριστοφ. *Ἀχαρνῆς* 994-995.
38. Αριστοφ. *Ἀχαρνῆς* 1043-1046 ("Δικαιόπολις: Ὀπτᾶτε τἀγχέλεια./Χορός: Ἀποκτενεῖς λιμῷ ᾽με καὶ/τοὺς γείτονας κνίσῃ τε καὶ/φωνῇ, τοιαῦτα λάλκων"), 1048-1049 ("Ἔπεμψε τίς σοι νυμφίος ταυτί κρέα ἐκ τῶν γάμων").
39. Αλληλοβοήθεια: Δημοσθ. 53.1247.4 ("οὗτος τε αὖ μοι οὐκ ἄχρηστος ἦν πρὸς τὸ ἐπιμεληθῆναι καὶ διοικῆσαι, καὶ ὁπότε ἐγὼ ἀποδημοίην ἢ δημοσίᾳ τριηραρχῶν ἢ ἰδίᾳ κατ᾽ ἄλλο τι, κύριον τῶν ἐν ἀγρῷ κατέλιπον"). Θεοφρ. *Χαρ.* 14.14 ("καὶ εἰ τὸ ἄροτρον ἔχρησεν ἢ κόφινον ἢ δρέπανον ἢ θύλακον ταῦτα τῆς νυκτὸς κατὰ ἀγρυπνίαν ἀναμιμνησκόμενος ἀναστὰς ἀπαιτεῖν"). Συμπαράσταση στον κίνδυνο: Δημοσθ. 47.1157.
40. Βλ. π.χ. Δημοσθ. 53.1251. Τούτο αποτελεί το αντικείμενο του λόγου του Δημοσθένους 55 (*Πρός Καλλικλέα περί χωρίου βλάβης*, ιδ. 1275-1281). Οι έριδες κληρονομούνται από τον πατέρα στο γιο (ο.π. 1280).
41. Βλ. π.χ. Ισαίο 7.64 α-γ, 8.1518, 9.18-19. Δημοσθ. 43.1051 5, 1077, 44.1086.5, 1090, 1091, 1092, 57.1037, 1317. Για το λόγο αυτό η εγγραφή στους πολίτες αποτελούσε βασική λειτουργία του δήμου (Αριστ. *Ἀθ.Π.* 42.1-2. Πρβλ. Whitehead 97-109).
42. Σύμφωνα με προφορικές πληροφορίες της ανασκαφέως Μ. Οικονομάκου (*ΑρχΔελτ* 45 [1990] Χρονικά, υπό εκτύπωση).
43. Travlos (σημ. 2) 475, εικ. 597. *ΑρχΔελτ* 40 (1985) Χρον. 54-57.
44. Travlos (σημ. 2) 440-441, εικ. 555-557.
45. *ΑρχΔελτ* 39 (1984) Χρον. 36-39.
46. Βλ. π.χ. την ομάδα των αγροκτημάτων με πύργους στο Χάρακα, Lohmann (σημ. 2) εικ. 27.
47. Για την χρονολόγηση της εξέλιξης στο Θορικό βλ. H. Mussche, "Thorikos in Archaic and Classical Times," *MIGRA* 1 (1975) 49-50 (ριζική αναδιάρθρωση του πολεοδομικού συστήματος μέσα στο γ' τέταρτο του 4ου αι., ίδρυση του πύργου στο α' ήμισυ του 5ου αι., μετατροπή του σε ορθογώνια αίθουσα στον 4ο αι.).
48. Travlos (σημ. 2) 292, εικ. 365.
49. Η αύξηση της σημασίας της γεωργικής παραγωγής στον 4ο και 3ο αι. (που συμβαδίζει με την υποχώρηση της ναυτικής δύναμης των Αθηνών, φαίνεται στη διαμόρφωση της νέας (αμυντικής) στρατηγικής των Αθηνών (βλ. Y. Garlan, *"Recherches de poliorcétique grecque," BEFAR* 233 [Paris 1974] 19-86, J. Ober, *Fortress Attica: Defense of the Athenian Land Frontier 404-32 B.C.* [Leiden 1985] 50-86). Χαρακτηριστική του νέου πνεύματος είναι η αναφορά στον όρκο των αθηναίων εφήβων, G. Daux, "Deux stèles d' Acharnes," *Χαριστήριον είς Ἀ. Ὀρλάνδον* 1 (Ἀθῆναι 1965) 80-81 (στ. 19" ὅροι τῆς πατρίδος, πυροί, κριθαί, ἄμπελοι, ἐλαῖαι, συκαῖ.")
50. Ολόκληρη η δυτική πλαγιά του Υμηττού καλύπτεται από αναλημματικά τοιχία (πεζούλες). Τούτο είχε επισημανθεί ήδη κατά την αεροφωτογράφηση της περιοχής στον Β' Παγκόσμιο Πόλεμο: J. Bradford, "Fieldwork on Aerial Discoveries in Attica and Rhodes, Part 2. Ancient Field Systems on Mt. Hymettos near Athens," *AntJ* 36 (1956) 172-180. Στη διάρκεια των τελευταίων ετών έχουν έρθει στο φως εκτεταμένα έργα διευθέτησης των χειμάρων και αξιοποίησης των υδατίνων πόρων για την άρδευση κλπ. Η ίδια εικόνα επαναλαμβάνεται και στο μικρό δήμο της Ατήνης κοντά στο Σούνιο (Lohmann [σημ. 2] 232-33, 237). Τη φροντίδα για την καλλιέργεια δείχνει μια περιγραφή της Αττικής στο τέλος του 4ου αι. *FHG* II 254: "Ἐντεῦθεν εἰς τὸ Ἀθηναίων ἔπεισιν ἄστυ˙ ὁδὸς δὲ ἡδεῖα, γεωργουμένη πᾶσα, ἔχουσα τι τῇ ὄψει φιλάνθρωπον."
51. Για παράδειγμα μίσθωσης χωρίων σε απελεύθερο βλ. Λυσία 7.5-10, 18. Για την εγκατάσταση μετοίκων στους δήμους βλ. Whitehead 81-85 (πρβλ. του ιδίου, "The Ideology of the Athenian Metic," *PCPS* Suppl. 4 [Cambridge 1977] 140-147). Ως ο κατεξοχήν τόπος εγκαταστάσεως των μετοίκων συμπεραίνεται (επιγραφικώς) ότι ήταν το άστυ με τα προάστεια (61%) και ο Πειραιάς (19%). Από τον Whitehead δεν αναφέρονται στήλες μετοίκων από τις Αλές Αιξωνίδες ή τον Αναγυρούντα, εν τούτοις σε πρόχειρη έρευνα διαπίστωσα την ύπαρξη στο Μουσείο Πειραιώς δύο στηλών μετοίκων ή ξένων: μιας Μιλησίας από τη Βάρη (αρ. Μ. Πειραιώς 3524) και ενός Ροδίου από τις Αλές Αιξωνίδες (αρ. Μ. Πειραιώς 3569).

Ο δήμος των Αιξωνίδων Αλών

Ιωάννα Ανδρέου

Γενικά

Ο εντοπισμός, η αποκάλυψη και η ταύτιση των εκτεταμένων λειψάνων του δήμου των Αιξωνίδων Αλών,[1] όπως άλλωστε και ο οριστικός μάλλον ενταφιασμός τους, οφείλεται στην οικιστική ανάπτυξη των σημερινών δήμων Βούλας και Βουλιαγμένης. 'Ηδη στο τέλος του περασμένου αιώνα και στις αρχές του 20ού, προϊόντα αρχαιοκαπηλικής δράσης στην περιοχή είχαν διοχετευτεί σε μουσεία του εξωτερικού και σε ιδιωτικές συλλογές, δίνοντας αφορμή για τον εντοπισμό του μυκηναϊκού νεκροταφείου στα σύνορα Γλυφάδας-Βούλας[2] αλλά και του εκτεταμένου νεκροταφείου των κλασσικών χρόνων στην περιοχή του Αγίου Νικολάου Πάλων, τα σημερινά Πηγαδάκια.[3] Οι επιγραφές των επιτυμβίων στηλών και μαρμάρινων ληκύθων του νεκροταφείου οδήγησαν στην ταύτιση της περιοχής με τον δήμο των Αιξωνίδων Αλών, ο οποίος σύμφωνα με τις πηγές τοποθετείται μεταξύ της Αιξωνής και του Αναγυρούντος.[4] Η πρώτη συστηματική έρευνα που πραγματοποιήθηκε το 1927 στο Λαιμό της Βουλιαγμένης αποκάλυψε το ιερό του Απόλλωνος Ζωστήρος[5] και επιβεβαίωσε την απόδοση του χώρου στο δήμο των Αλαιέων.

Η αρκετά εκτεταμένη περιοχή των Αλαιέων ήταν κατοικημένη ήδη από τους προϊστορικούς χρόνους. Επιφανειακές ενδείξεις σε διάφορα σημεία, κατά μήκος κυρίως της ακτής (ακρωτήριο Πούντα,[6] νησίδα Κατραμονήσι ή Υδρούσσα,[7] χώρος νότια Αγ. Νικολάου Πάλων,[8] λόφος στη χερσόνησο Καβούρι[9]), υποδηλώνουν ότι ο χώρος κατοικήθηκε τουλάχιστον από την ύστερη νεολιθική εποχή. Εξάλλου, η αποκάλυψη και έρευνα πολλών θαλαμοειδών μυκηναϊκών τάφων της ΥΕ ΙΙΙβ-γ εποχής στο δυτικό άκρο της σημερινής λεωφόρου Πρίγκηπος Πέτρου, προϋποθέτει την ύπαρξη σύγχρονου ακμαίου συνοικισμού στην περιοχή.[10]

Ευρήματα που έφεραν στο φώς οι ανασκαφικές έρευνες φανερώνουν ότι υπήρχαν μόνιμες εγκαταστάσεις και κατά τους γεωμετρικούς χρόνους (τάφοι στα νεκροταφεία των Αλαιέων,[11] όστρακα και θεμέλια κτισμάτων στον ΒΔ. συνοικισμό,[12] γεωμετρικά αγγεία, προφανώς από τάφους, στο χώρο του μυκηναϊκού νεκροταφείου[13]). Για την πρώιμη και μέση αρχαϊκή εποχή υπάρχουν επίσης ενδεικτικά στοιχεία,[14] ανάλογα με αυτά της γεωμετρικής, ενώ στους ύστερους αρχαϊκούς χρόνους τα στοιχεία πολλαπλασιάζονται. Συγκεκριμένα, στο τέλος τους 6ου αι. ανάγεται η πρώτη οικοδομική φάση του ιερού του Απόλλωνος Ζωστήρος και της ιερατικής οικίας,[15] τότε χρονολογούνται αρκετοί τάφοι ενταγμένοι στο κύριο και στα μικρότερα νεκροταφεία των Αλαιέων[16] και την ίδια εποχή αρχίζει η αφιέρωση ειδωλίων στα ιερά του δήμου, όπως μαρτυρούν οι αποθέτες.[17] Τέλος, θεμέλια σπιτιών και όστρακα από το χώρο των συνοικισμών,[18] τοποθετούν την αρχή της οικιστικής οργάνωσης του δήμων των Αιξωνίδων Αλών στο τέλος του 6ου αι. π.Χ., στην εποχή δηλαδή της μεταρρυθμίσεως του Κλεισθένους.

Σύμφωνα με την Κλεισθένεια οργάνωση, ο δήμος των Αλαιέων μαζί με την γειτονική Αιξωνή απαρτίζουν την παραλιακή τριττύ της Κεκροπίδος φυλής, η οποία περιελάμβανε επίσης τέσσερις δήμους του άστεος και πέντε της μεσογαίας, συνολικά έντεκα. Οι Αλαιείς εξέλεγαν έξι βουλευτές, ανήκαν δηλ. από πλευράς πληθυσμού στους μεσαίους δήμους της Κεκροπίδος φυλής, δεδομένου ότι οι Αιξωνείς εξέλεγαν οκτώ, οι Μελιτείς, Ξυπεταίοι και Φλυείς ανά επτά και οι υπόλοιποι από ένα έως τρείς βουλευτές.[19] Ο αριθμός των έξι βουλευτών θεωρητικά και χονδρικά υπολογίζεται ότι αντιστοιχεί σε 200 άνδρες με πλήρη πολιτικά δικαιώματα και σε συνολικό πληθυσμό 800 περίπου ελεύθερων ατόμων.[20] Επισημαίνεται εδώ το γεγονός ότι από τον πολυανθρωπότερο και, όπως θα αναμενόταν, οικιστικά περισσότερο ανεπτυγμένο δήμο της Αιξωνής, ελάχιστα οικοδομικά σύνολα έχουν αποκαλυφθεί,[21] διαπίστωση που ισχύει άλλωστε για την πλειονότητα των μεγάλων δήμων της Αττικής. Να αποδώσουμε άραγε το γεγονός στην αστυφιλία των Αιξωνέων ή μήπως στον διαφορετικό τρόπο οργάνωσης του δήμου τους;

Η ονομασία του δήμου των Αιξωνίδων Αλών προφανώς οφείλεται στην γεωγραφική του θέση και στην φυσική διαμόρφωση της περιοχής, δηλαδή αφ' ενός στην γειτνίασή του με την Αιξωνή και αφ' ετέρου στην ύπαρξη αλυκών κατά μήκος της ακτής. Οι αλυκές ήσαν εμφανείς μέχρι πριν μερικές δεκαετίες στην θέση των σημερινών εγκαταστάσεων του ΕΟΤ, ενώ η ΒΔ. περιοχή της Βούλας ήταν γνωστή ως Αλυκή Γλυφάδας, υπήρχε δηλαδή

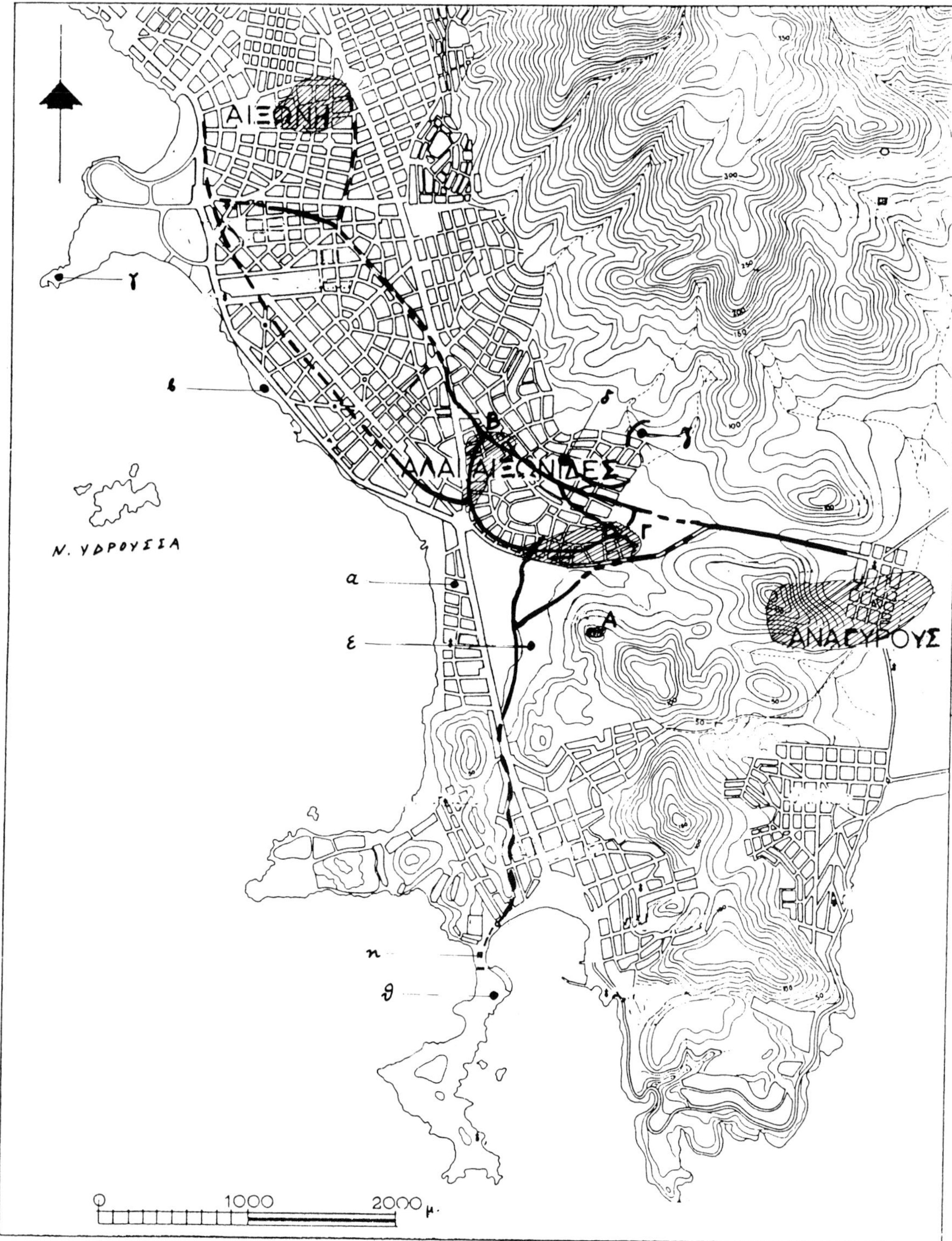

Εικ. 1.Γενικό τοπογραφικό περιοχής δήμων Αιξωνής, Αλών Αιξωνίδων και Αναγυρούντος.

πλήρης αντιστοιχία με την αρχαία ονομασία.[22] Η συνεχής κατοίκηση και χρήση του χώρου του δήμου των Αλαιέων από τους αρχαϊκούς μέχρι και τους ύστερους κλασσικούς χρόνους, όπως τεκμηριώνεται από τα ανασκαφικά δεδομένα, δικαιολογεί την πληρέστερη διατήρηση των οικοδομικών λειψάνων του 4ου κυρίως αι. σε βάρος των προγενέστερων. Η ελληνιστική και ρωμαϊκή εποχή αντιπροσωπεύονται από ελάχιστα οικοδομικά λείψανα και μερικούς τάφους,[23] οι βασικοί όμως οδικοί άξονες παρέμειναν σε χρήση κατά την ύστερη αρχαιότητα και τους πρώιμους βυζαντινούς χρόνους, όπως αποδεικνύουν τα ευρήματα των ανασκαφών.[24]

Οικιστική Οργάνωση

Η οικιστική ανάπτυξη του δήμου των Αιξωνίδων Αλών στηρίχθηκε στους άξονες κυκλοφορίας και επικοινωνίας που προϋπήρχαν στο χώρο και εξυπηρετούσαν τις

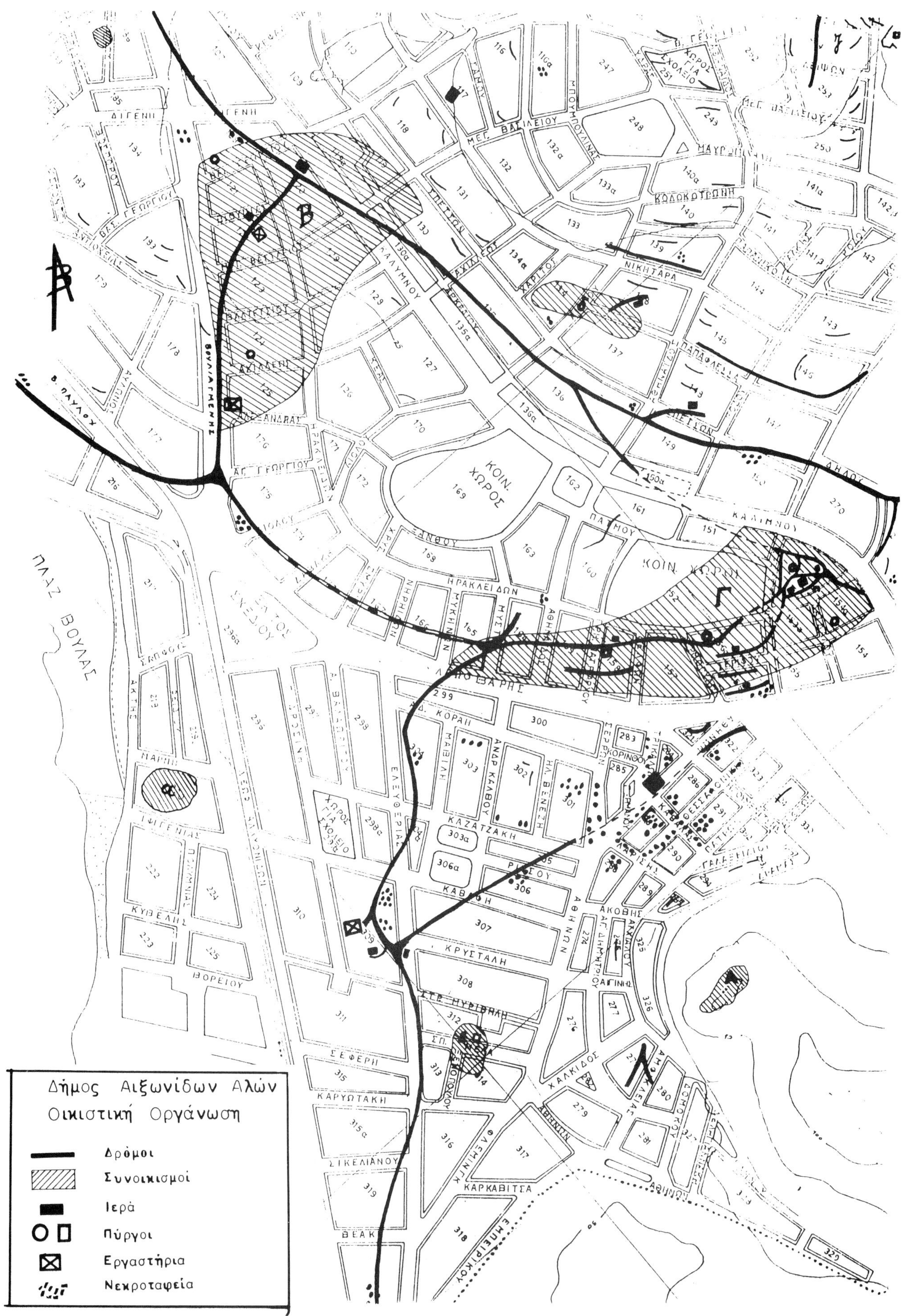

Εικ. 2. Τοπογραφικό οικιστικής περιοχής δήμου Αιξωνίδων Αλών.

εσωτερικές ανάγκες των Αλαιέων, ενώ παράλληλα τους συνέδεαν με τους γειτονικούς δήμους. Είναι χαρακτηριστικό ότι τέσσερις βασικές αρχαίες αρτηρίες ταυτίζονται σχεδόν με αντίστοιχες σημερινές, τις λεωφόρους Βουλιαγμένης, Βάρης, Καλύμνου και Β. Παύλου (εικ. 1 και 2). Η πρώτη αρτηρία συνέδεε τους Αιξωνείς με τους Αλαιείς ακολουθώντας τις υπώρειες του Υμηττού, περίπου κατά μήκος των σημερινών οδών Αγ. Νικολάου Γλυφάδας και Παπάγου-Βουλιαγμένης της Βούλας.[25] Στα Πηγαδάκια, ακριβώς στη θέση του σημερινού συγκοινωνιακού κόμβου, ενώνονταν με τον προηγούμενο δύο ακόμα σημαντικοί δρόμοι.[26] Ο ένας συνέδεε τους Αλαιείς με τον δήμο του Αναγυρούντος και ταυτίζεται με την σημερινή λεωφόρο Βάρης,[27] ενώ ο δεύτερος ακολουθούσε την πορεία της οδού Β. Παύλου της Βούλας και παραλιακά προεκτεινόταν μέχρι την Αιξωνή.[28] Η τέταρτη αρχαία αρτηρία προδιέγραψε την χάραξη της σημερινής λεωφόρου Καλύμνου, σχηματίζοντας τρίγωνο με τις δύο πρώτες.[29] Στους σημαντικούς οδικούς άξονες του δήμου των Αλαιέων πρέπει να ενταχθεί και ο δρόμος που συνέδεε τον οικισμό με το ιερό του Απόλλωνος Ζωστήρος, διασχίζοντας το κύριο νεκροταφείο του δήμου. Ταυτίζεται σχεδόν ακριβώς με την σημερινή οδό Ελευθερίας και έχει αποκαλυφθεί σε όλο το μήκος της.[30]

Η κατασκευή των δρόμων είναι απλή. Στις υπώρειες του Υμηττού και των λόφων χρησιμοποιήθηκε ως οδόστρωμα η επιφάνεια του φυσικού βράχου, πάνω στον οποίο οι ρόδες των αμαξών χάραξαν ζεύγος αυλακώσεων με μεταξόνιο 1.40–1.50 μ. (εικ. 3).[31] 'Οπου η κλίση το επέβαλε ή το υπόστρωμα δεν ήταν αρκετά σταθερό, κατασκευάστηκαν αναλημματικοί τοίχοι στην μία ή και στις δύο πλευρές του δρόμου και το κατάστρωμα διαμορφώθηκε με χώμα και μικρές πέτρες. Στις πεδινές περιοχές κρίθηκε απαραίτητη η κατασκευή δύο ισχυρών αναλημμάτων και η δημιουργία οδοστρώματος με χώμα, πέτρες, άμμο, θηραϊκή γή, χαλίκια και στάχτη.[32] Το μέσο πλάτος των δρόμων είναι 2.50–3.00 μ., αποκαλύφθηκαν όμως και τμήματα πλάτους μέχρι 5.00 μ.[33]

Η αρχαιολογική έρευνα απέδειξε ότι οι οικιστικές μονάδες των Αλαιέων αναπτύχθηκαν στον κεντρικό χώρο της αρκετά εκτεταμένης περιοχής του δήμου, δίπλα στις αρτηρίες που τον συνέδεαν με τους γειτονικούς δήμους (εικ. 2). Οι χαμηλοί λόφοι (ύψους 25–30 μ.), πάνω στους οποίους ιδρύθηκαν οι συνοικισμοί, παρεμβάλλονται μεταξύ των ΝΔ. υπωρειών του Υμηττού και της παρα-

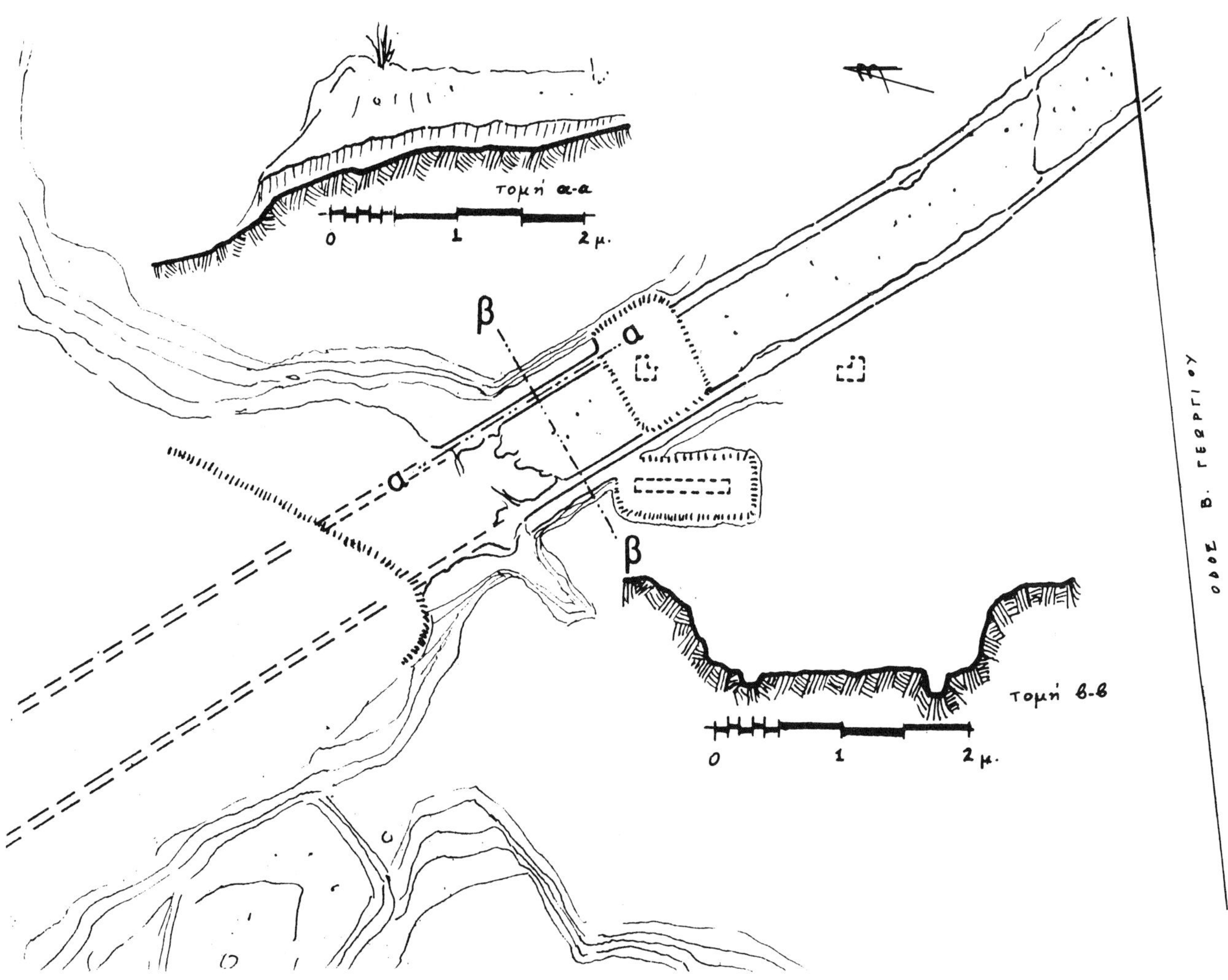

Εικ. 3. Κάτοψη και τομή τμήματος δρόμου στον ΒΔ. συνοικισμό των Αλαιέων.

θαλάσσιας ζώνης και ισαπέχουν περίπου τόσο από το κέντρο της Αιξωνής και του Αναγυρούντος, όσο και από το ιερό του Απόλλωνος Ζωστήρος. Βρίσκονται σε μικρή απόσταση από την παραλία, σε τρόπο ώστε να έχουν άμεση σχεδόν πρόσβαση στη θάλασσα, χωρίς όμως να υφίστανται τις επιπτώσεις της άμεσης γειτονίας με τις αλυκές και τις ελώδεις εκτάσεις της ακτής. Στον υπόλοιπο χώρο του δήμου είχαν διασπαρεί μικρότερες οικιστικές μονάδες, αγροτικού και οικογενειακού χαρακτήρα.

Η σύνθεση των επί μέρους οικοδομικών λειψάνων που αποκάλυψαν οι σωστικές ανασκαφές στην περιοχή της Βούλας έδωσε εξαιρετικά ενδιαφέροντα αποτελέσματα. Κυρίως κατέδειξε ότι ο δήμος των Αιξωνίδων Αλών περιελάμβανε ανεπτυγμένα οικιστικά σύνολα σε αντίθεση με ό,τι είναι γνωστό, μέχρι τώρα τουλάχιστον, για τους εκτός άστεος δήμους. Στους αγροτικούς δήμους της Αττικής συνήθως συναντώνται μεμονωμένες μονάδες αγροτικού-οικογενειακού χαρακτήρα, περιωρισμένης εκτάσεως.[34] Από τον δήμο των Αλαιέων δεν λείπουν μεμονωμένα συγκροτήματα σπιτιών, διεσπαρμένα κατά μήκος των βασικών αξόνων επικοινωνίας, το οικιστικό όμως βάρος φέρουν κυρίως οι δύο εκτεταμένοι συνοικισμοί και η ακρόπολη.

Η ακρόπολη βρίσκεται στην κορυφή του λόφου Καστράκι,[35] σε υψόμετρο 100 μ., ακριβώς στα σύνορα των σημερινών δήμων Βούλας, Βουλιαγμένης και Βάρης (εικ. 1 και 2, θέση Α). Το πλάτωμα που καταλαμβάνει έχει μικρές σχετικά διαστάσεις (100 x 40 μ.) αλλά εξαιρετικά επίκαιρη θέση. Από εκεί είναι πανοραμική η θέα ολόκληρου του γεωγραφικού χώρου του δήμου των Αλαιέων, τμήματος του γειτονικού δήμου του Αναγυρούντος, μεγάλο μέρος της δυτικής Αττικής και όλης της έκτασης του κεντρικού Σαρωνικού. Επομένως, η θέση εξασφάλιζε δυνατότητα πλήρους ελέγχου της θαλάσσιας οδού προς την Αθήνα και της οδού που συνέδεε τους παραλιακούς δήμους με τα Μεσόγεια μέσω του Αναγυρούντος. Παράλληλα, οι Αλαιείς μπορούσαν να παρακολουθούν από την ακρόπολη την κίνηση σε όλες τις αρτηρίες που διέσχιζαν τον χώρο του δήμου τους και να εποπτεύουν τους δύο συνοικισμούς και το ιερό του Ζωστήρος.

Το τείχος της ακροπόλεως είναι κατασκευασμένο από αδρά επεξεργασμένους ογκόλιθους εξωτερικά και μικρότερους λίθους εσωτερικά. Μεγάλα τμήματά του έχουν κατακρημνιστεί στην πλαγιά του λόφου, παρακολουθείται όμως στο μεγαλύτερο μήκος του η θεμελίωση. Ανατολικά και δυτικά ο χώρος της ακροπόλεως προστατεύεται εν μέρει και από την κρημνώδη διαμόρφωση του εδάφους ενώ στα νοτιοανατολικά η οχύρωση ενισχύεται με ισχυρό πύργο (εικ. 4). Η ακρόπολη ως οικιστική μονάδα απαρτίζεται

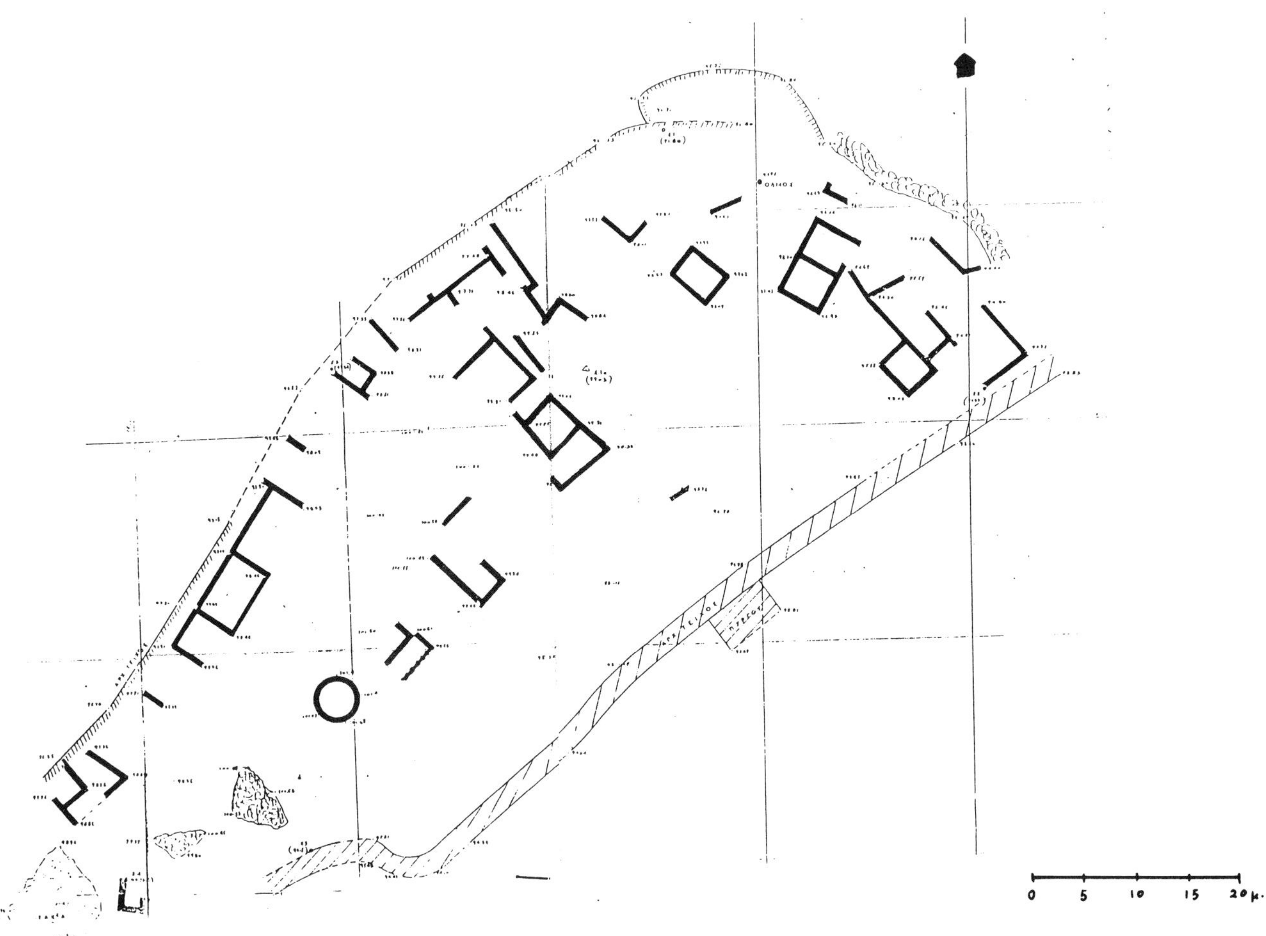

Εικ. 4. Κάτοψη της ακροπόλεως των Αιξωνίδων Αλών.

Εικ. 5. Θεμέλια κτιρίων στην ακρόπολη των Αιξωνίδων Αλών.

από κτίσματα σε πυκνή διάταξη, τα θεμέλια των οποίων διακρίνονται επιφανειακά σε όλη την έκταση του πλατώματος (εικ. 5). Μεταξύ των κτιρίων δύο παρουσιάζουν ναϊσκόμορφη κατασκευή ενώ τρίτο έχει κυκλική κάτοψη, όμοια με αυτές που αποδίδονται σε πύργους. Ο χώρος της ακροπόλεως δεν έχει ερευνηθεί ανασκαφικά, επιφανειακά όμως όστρακα και κομμάτια κεραμιδιών στέγης αποδεικνύουν χρήση τουλάχιστον από τις αρχές του 5ου αι. π.Χ.

Ο ΒΔ. συνοικισμός των Αλαιέων (εικ. 1 και 2, θέση Β) καταλαμβάνει έκταση περίπου 60.000 τ.μ., έχει χονδρικά τριγωνικό σχήμα και αναπτύχθηκε γύρω από αρχαίο ναό, θεμέλια του οποίου έχουν αποκαλυφθεί στην οδό Καλύμνου (Ο.Τ. 120 Βούλας). Ο ναός βρίσκεται δίπλα στην συμβολή των δύο αρχαίων οδικών αρτηριών που αντιστοιχούν στις λεωφόρους Βουλιαγμένης και Καλύμνου και μπορεί να θεωρηθεί από τους σημαντικότερους του δήμου, μετά το ιερό του Ζωστήρος. Έχει εξωτερικές διαστάσεις 8.50 × 5.75 μ. και αποτελείται από πρόδομο και σηκό, των οποίων σώζεται μόνο η ευθυντηρία κατασκευασμένη από αδρά δουλεμένες πωροπλίνθους. Η αρχαιοκαπηλική δράση έχει καταστρέψει το μεγαλύτερο μέρος του χαλικόστρωτου δαπέδου του ναού και σημαντικά για την έρευνα στοιχεία.[36] Στον ίδιο συνοικισμό, στις δύο πλευρές των βασικών δρόμων και άλλων δευτερεύουσας σημασίας, έχουν αποκαλυφθεί μικρότερα ιερά,[37] αρκετές κατοικίες[38] (εικ. 6) και δύο τουλάχιστον εργαστήρια κεραμεικής (το ένα εικ. 6), οργανωμένα με συστήματα υδρεύσεως και αποχετεύσεως, δεξαμενές και αγωγούς.[39] Εντοπίστηκαν επίσης θεμέλια κυκλικών κτισμάτων, πολυσυζητημένης αλλά ανεπιβεβαίωτης χρήσεως,[40] σε ένα μάλιστα αποδίδεται πιθανή λατρευτική σημασία.[41]

Ο ΝΑ. οικισμός (εικ. 1-2, θέση Γ) έχει επιμηκυσμένο τριγωνικό σχήμα και καταλαμβάνει την ΝΑ. γωνία του τριγώνου που σχηματίζουν οι τρείς αρχαίοι οδικοί άξονες, οριοθετείται δηλαδή από τις σημερινές λεωφόρους Καλύμνου (ανατολικά) και Βάρης (νότια). Διασχίζεται από δευτερεύοντες δρόμους περίπου παράλληλους προς τη λεωφόρο Βάρης, μεταξύ των οποίων παρεμβάλλονται μικρότεροι εγκάρσιοι, ιδιωτικοί ή κοινόχρηστοι. Τα σπίτια είναι χτισμένα μεταξύ των δρόμων, όπως και μικρά ιερά ενταγμένα σε ιδιαίτερους περιβόλους. Ιδιομορφία παρουσιάζει το βόρειο άκρο του συνοικισμού Γ, το οποίο ερευνήθηκε ενιαίο στο Ο.Τ. 153 της Βούλας (οικόπεδο Καλαμπόκα, εικ. 7). Περιλαμβάνει ένα οικιστικό σύνολο 6-7 σπιτιών, αρκετά κανονικού σχήματος, τα οποία περιβάλλονται από δρόμους. Μεταξύ των σπιτιών δεσπόζει μονόχωρο κτίσμα ισχυρής κατασκευής και κυκλικής κατόψεως, διαμ. 6.00 μ., με είσοδο στην αυλή ενός από τα σπίτια. Ανατολικά του συγκροτήματος αποκαλύφθηκε σύστημα δεξαμενών υδρεύσεως ενώ, σε μερικές κατοικίες, υπήρχαν δίκτυα αποχετευτικά, εγκαταστάσεις λουτρών και οικιακά εργαστήρια.[42]

Νότια και ανατολικά του προηγούμενου οικιστικού συνόλου έχουν διαμορφωθεί ελεύθεροι χώροι σε επάλληλα άνδηρα που ορίζονται από περιβόλους, οι οποίοι παράλληλα χρησιμοποιήθηκαν ως αναλήμματα των διαφορετικών επιπέδων και των μεταξύ τους

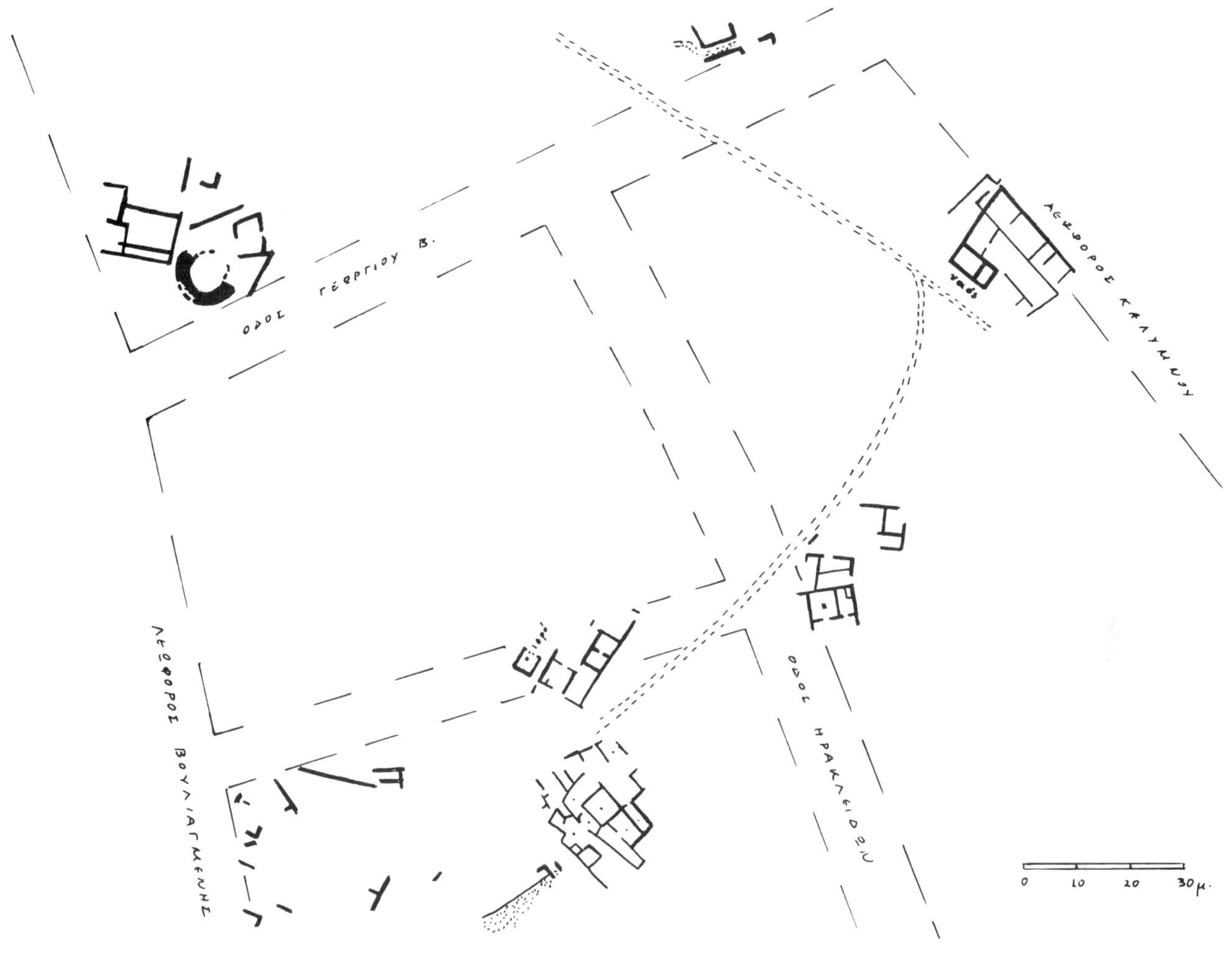

Εικ. 6. Κάτοψη τμήματος του ΒΔ. συνοικισμού των Αλαιέων.

δρόμων. Μέσα στους ευρύτερους περιβόλους εντάσσονται ιερά σε ιδιαίτερα περιτειχισμένους χώρους, ενώ σε άλλα σημεία σώζονται θεμέλια κτιρίων. Προφανώς ο συγκεκριμένος χώρος είχε ιδιαίτερη σημασία και διαδραμάτιζε σημαντικό ρόλο στις θρησκευτικές και κοινωνικές δραστηριότητες των Αλαιέων. Οι οικοδομικές νησίδες του ΝΑ. συνοικισμού απαρτίζουν ένα συμπαγές πολεοδομικό σύνολο το οποίο καταλαμβάνει τα σημερινά οικοδομικά τετράγωνα της Βούλας που περιλαμβάνονται μεταξύ των οδών Βάρης και Ηρακλειδών. Περιλαμβάνουν σπίτια,[43] ιερά μέσα σε ιδιαίτερους περιβόλους,[44] κυκλικά κτίρια,[45] συστήματα υδρεύσεως και αποχετεύσεως.[46] Τα σπίτια σε αρκετές περιπτώσεις έχουν κανονικό σχήμα και απαρτίζονται από τρία ή τέσσερα δωμάτια και βοηθητικούς χώρους, τοποθετημένα στις πλευρές ορθογώνιας αυλής (εικ. 8 και 9).

Αντιπροσωπευτικό δείγμα κατοικίας των Αλαιέων αποτελεί το σπίτι που αποκαλύφθηκε σε οικόπεδο της οδού Πατριάρχου Γρηγορίου Ε΄ στο Ο.Τ. 158 της Βούλας (ιδιοκτησία Παπαχαραλάμπους) (εικ. 9-11).[47] Συγκαταλέγεται στα ελάχιστα σύνολα τα οποία είχαμε την τύχη να ερευνήσουμε σε ενιαία ιδιοκτησία, με εξαίρεση αυτά του συγκροτήματος Καλαμπόκα. Τα τέσσερα δωμάτια της αρχικής φάσεως του σπιτιού έχουν εμβαδόν 95 τ.μ. και είναι χτισμένα στις δύο μακρές πλευρές ορθογώνιας αυλής, οι στενές πλευρές της οποίας επικοινωνούν νότια με δρόμο και βόρεια με στενωπό μεταξύ δύο σπιτιών. Στην δεύτερη φάση επεκτείνεται κατά 1.10 μ. η νότια πλευρά του σπιτιού, το οποίο αποκτά εμβαδόν 104 τ.μ., περιορίζεται το μήκος της αυλής με την εγγραφή μικρού μαγειρείου και διαδρόμου — εισόδου στο νότιο άκρο, ενώ επιμηκύνονται τα νότια δωμάτια. Παράλληλα υπερυψώνεται το δάπεδο όλων των χώρων, στο ανατολικό τμήμα της αυλής δημιουργείται στοά, στο ΝΑ. δωμάτιο κατασκευάζεται καπνοδόχος και, πιθανόν, προστίθεται όροφος στο ανατολικό τμήμα του σπιτιού. Τέλος, στην τρίτη και τελευταία φάση, το σπίτι επεκτείνεται ακόμα νοτιότερα, αποκτώντας εμβαδόν 122 τ.μ. Η επέκταση έδωσε την δυνατότητα να επιμηκυνθεί περαιτέρω το ΝΔ. δωμάτιο, να μετατραπεί το μαγειρείο σε αποθήκη και να κατασκευαστεί νέο ευρύχωρο μαγειρείο στη ΝΑ. γωνία,

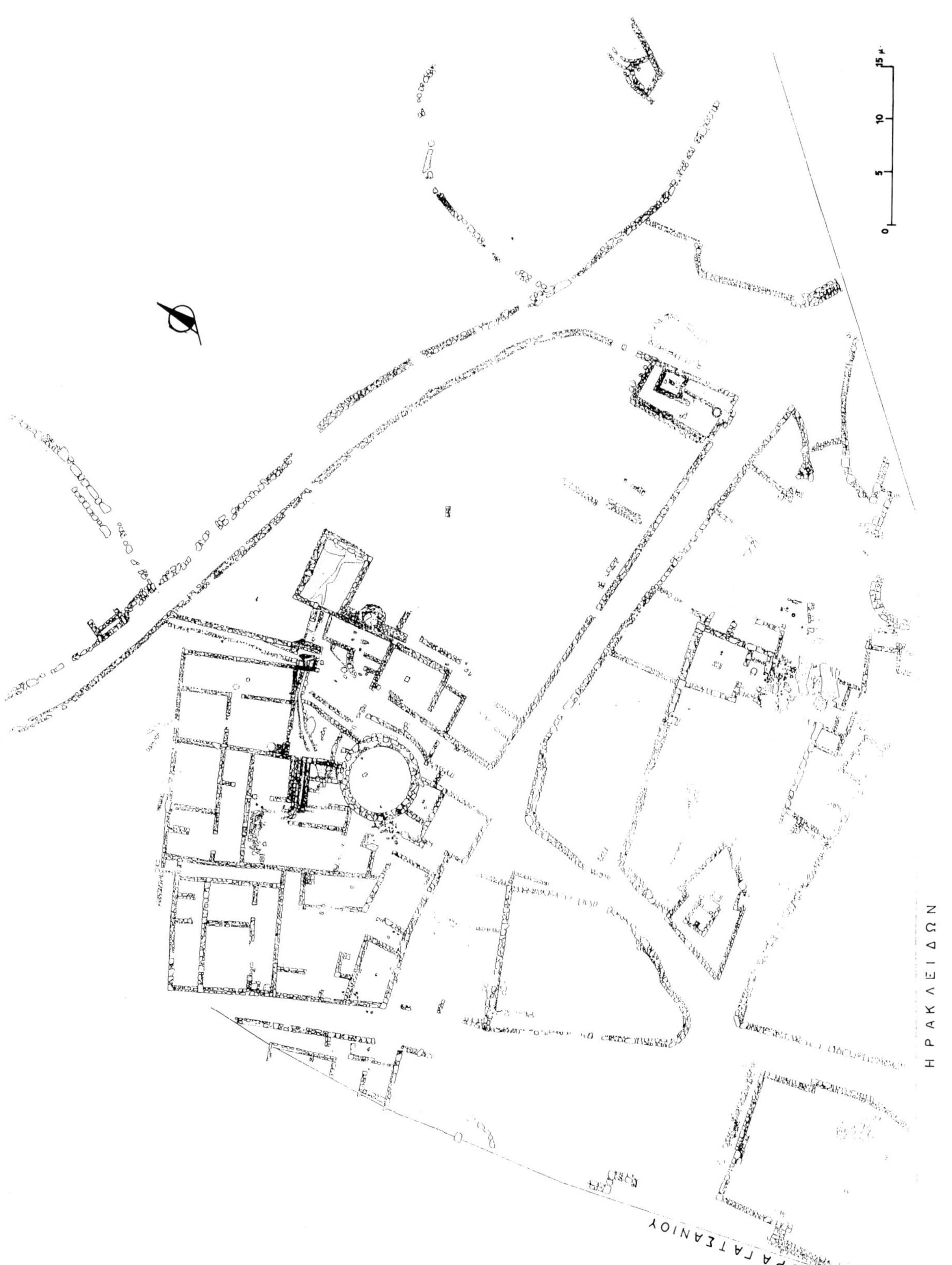

Εικ. 7. Κάτοψη του οικιστικού συνόλου οικοπέδου Καλαμπόκα.

Εικ. 8. Κάτοψη τμήματος του ΝΑ. συνοικισμού των Αλαιέων.

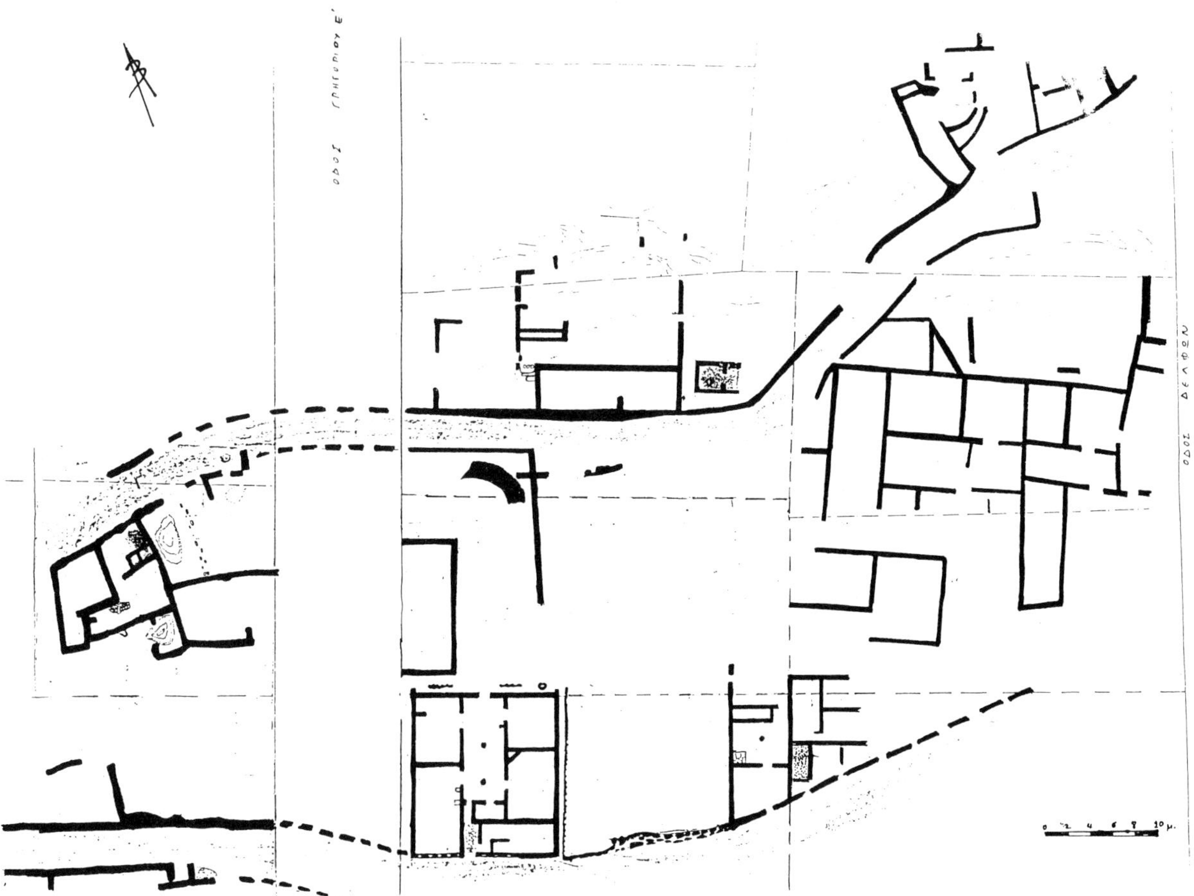

Εικ. 9. Κάτοψη τμήματος του ΝΑ. συνοικισμού των Αλαιέων.

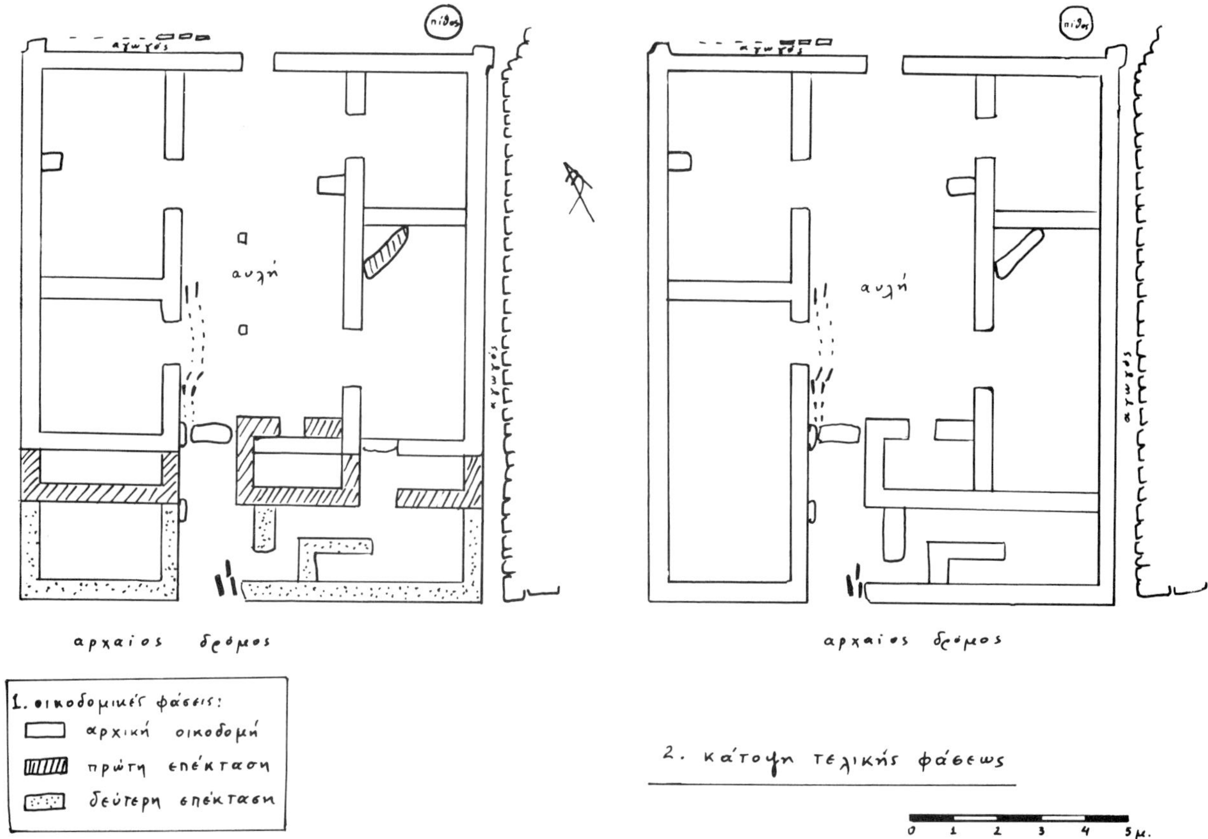

Εικ. 10. Σχηματικές κατόψεις οικοδομικών φάσεων σπιτιού του ΝΑ. συνοικισμού των Αιξωνίδων Αλών.

Εικ. 11. Θεμέλια μελισσοτροφικής μονάδας και αγροτικό ιερό του δήμου των Αιξωνίδων Αλών.

στο οποίο εντάσσεται και μικρότερος χώρος, μάλλον το αποχωρητήριο του σπιτιού. Η κύρια είσοδος διαμορφώνεται σε πλακόστρωτο διάδρομο που καλύπτει αποχετευτικό αγωγό, μέσω του οποίου τα νερά της αυλής μεταφέρονται στον δρόμο. Αγωγοί συγκεντρώσεως και απομακρύνσεως των νερών της βροχής υπάρχουν κατά μήκος της βόρειας και της ανατολικής εξωτερικής πλευράς του σπιτιού. Τα κινητά ευρήματα της ανασκαφής χρονολογούν την διάρκεια χρήσεως του σπιτιού από τα τέλη του 5ου μέχρι τα μέσα του 4ου αι. π.Χ.

Εκτός από τους δύο εκτεταμένους και οργανωμένους συνοικισμούς των Αλαιέων έχουν εντοπιστεί και άλλες οικιστικές μονάδες περιωρισμένης έκτασης, σε διάφορες θέσεις του δήμου. Θεμέλια κτιρίων υπάρχουν στην περιοχή του Αγίου Νικολάου Πάλων, σε μικρή απόσταση από την ακτή (Ο.Τ. 220 Βούλας), τα οποία δεν έχουν ερευνηθεί συστηματικά, ενώ μικρής έκτασης ανασκαφική έρευνα σε συνεχόμενη ιδιοκτησία, αποκάλυψε λείψανα κατασκευών υστερορρωμαϊκών ή και παλαιοχριστιανικών χρόνων (εικ. 1 και 2, θέση α).[48] Θεμέλια ενός ή δύο κτιρίων έχουν εντοπιστεί στην ακτή, μεταξύ των δύο αλιπέδων της Βούλας, τα οποία επίσης δεν έχουν ερευνηθεί και πιθανόν σχετίζονται με λιμενική εγκατάσταση (εικ. 1, θέση β). Σαφή πάντως λείψανα αρχαίων λιμενικών έργων είναι ορατά στο ΝΔ. άκρο της χερσονήσου της Πούντας (όπου οι σημερινές εγκαταστάσεις του ΠΙΚΠΑ), είναι όμως άγνωστο εάν ανήκουν στους Αλαιείς ή στους Αιξωνείς (εικ. 1, θέση γ).

Μία ευρύτερη ομάδα θεμελίων, αποσπασματικά διατηρημένων ή λαξευμένων στον επιφανειακό βράχο, έχει αποκαλυφθεί ανατολικά των δύο συνοικισμών και του δρόμου που τους ενώνει (εικ. 1 και 2, θέση δ). Σ' αυτές τις εγκαταστάσεις πρέπει να αποδώσουμε μάλλον αγροτικό χαρακτήρα, δεδομένου ότι μεταξύ τους περιλαμβάνονται και θεμέλια μελισσοτροφικής μονάδας, δίπλα σε μικρό αγροτικό ιερό του 4ου αι. π.Χ. (εικ. 11). Φαρδείς διπλοί τοίχοι είχαν χρησιμοποιηθεί για την τοποθέτηση πήλινων κυψελών, κομμάτια των οποίων βρέθηκαν *in situ*.[49] Δίπλα στις ίδιες αγροτικές εγκαταστάσεις υπήρχε μία ομάδα 4–5 τυμβοειδών κατασκευών, σωρών δηλαδή από μικρούς λίθους και πολλά όστρακα, διαμέτρου 6–7 μ. (εικ. 12).[50] Οι δεκάδες παρόμοιοι λιθοσωροί που είχαν εντοπιστεί παλαιότερα σε άλλες θέσεις της Βούλας είχαν αποδοθεί είτε σε ταφικά μνημεία, είτε σε προϊόντα καθαρισμού των αγρών που έγινε με παρότρυνση του Πεισιστράτου, είτε, τέλος, σε αποτροπαϊκούς έρμακες.[51]

Ενδιαφέρον παρουσιάζει το συγκρότημα θεμελίων που διατηρείται επιφανειακά στην οδό Μελά (Ο.Τ. 312 και 314 Βούλας) σε μικρή απόσταση από την οδό Ελευθερίας, το οποίο δεν έχει ερευνηθεί συστηματικά (εικ. 1 και 2, θέση ε). Η σπουδαιότητά του πηγάζει από το γεγονός ότι περιλαμβάνει μεταξύ των άλλων κτισμάτων και ισχυρή κατασκευή τετράγωνης κατόψεως, προφανώς πύργο του γνωστού στην Αττική και αλλού τύπου (εικ. 13). Οι διαστάσεις και η όλη κατασκευή του πύργου των Αλαιέων είναι σχεδόν πανομοιότυπες με αυτές του τετράγωνου πύργου του Σουνίου,[52] με μόνη διαφορά την ύπαρξη διαχωριστικού εσωτερικού τοίχου

Εικ. 12. Τυμβοειδής κατασκευή στον χώρο ανατολικά των συνοικισμών των Αλαιέων.

Εικ. 13. Τετράγωνος πύργος ΝΑ. του κύριου νεκροταφείου των Αιξωνίδων Αλών.

στον πρώτο, προφανώς μεταγενέστερη προσθήκη στον αρχικά ενιαίο τετράγωνο χώρο. Η επιμελημένη και παράλληλα ισχυρότατη κατασκευή καθορίζει την χρήση του κτιρίου, η απουσία όμως αδιατάρακτης επιχώσεως καθιστά αδύνατη την συλλογή στρωματογραφικών στοιχείων.

'Ενα ακόμα σύνολο αρχαίων λειψάνων (εικ. 1 και 2, θέση ζ) που διασχίζεται από δρόμο και περιλαμβάνει θεμέλια τοίχων, υπολείμματα λίθινων γεφυριών και πιθανότατα πύργους σώζεται στις δύο πλευρές μικρής χαράδρας, στα ΒΑ. των συνοικισμών των Αλαιέων (εικ. 1 και 2, θέση η). Η θέση βρίσκεται σε αρκετά υψηλότερο επίπεδο (75–80 μ.) σε σχέση με τα υπόλοιπα οικιστικά συγκροτήματα των Αλαιέων (25–30 μ.) και έχει πλήρη εποπτεία ολόκληρης σχεδόν της περιοχής του δήμου και της παραλιακής ζώνης, επομένως συμπληρώνει την αμυντική θωράκιση, καλύπτοντας επί πλέον τις "ορεινές" διεξόδους μεταξύ των δυτικών και ανατολικών υπωρειών του νότιου άκρου του Υμηττού.[53]

Αγροτικές και κτηνοτροφικές ανάγκες πρέπει να εξυπηρετούσαν οι δεκάδες αναλημματικοί τοίχοι που έχουν αποκαλυφθεί στις πλαγιές του Υμηττού και των λόφων στη νότια περιοχή του δήμου.[54] Είναι αμελούς κατασκευής, έχουν πλάτος 0.80–1.20 μ. και συνήθως στηρίζουν πρανή λόφων για να δημιουργηθούν επίπεδοι σχετικά χώροι. Σε μερικές περιπτώσεις αποτελούν όρια ιδιοκτησιών ή ορίζουν χώρους σταυλισμού κοπαδιών ενώ σε άλλες ίσως χρησίμευαν για την τοποθέτηση κυψελών. Ισχυρότερης και διαφορετικής κατασκευής αναλημματικοί τοίχοι έχουν αποκαλυφθεί στην πεδινή περιοχή του δήμου των Αλαιέων. Προορισμό είχαν να προστατεύουν χώρους και κυκλοφοριακές αρτηρίες από πλημμύρες, περιορίζοντας και διοχετεύοντας τα νερά της βροχής προς συγκεκριμένη κατεύθυνση. Σ' αυτήν την κατηγορία των υδρευτικών έργων ανήκει ο επιμήκης τοίχος που αποκαλύφθηκε στο νότιο τμήμα του κύριου νεκροταφείου του δήμου, στην οδό Ελευθερίας.[55] Είχε κατεύθυνση από Α. προς Δ. και, με την βοήθεια δεύτερου μικρότερου τοίχου, συγκέντρωνε τα νερά και τα διοχέτευε, μέσω αγωγού ισχυρής κατασκευής και γέφυρας, δυτικά του αρχαίου δρόμου που ενώνει τους συνοικισμούς των Αλαιέων με το ιερό του Ζωστήρος.

Για τα δημοσίου χαρακτήρα κτίρια του δήμου των Αιξωνίδων Αλών δεν υπάρχουν σαφή ανασκαφικά στοιχεία. Εξαίρεση αποτελούν τα ιερά, τα οποία μπορούμε να κατατάξουμε σε τέσσερις κατηγορίες. Στην πρώτη, των μεγάλων ιερών, ανήκει το ιερό του Απόλλωνος Ζωστήρος, μεγαλοπρεπέστερο από κτιριακής απόψεως και πανattικής τουλάχιστον εμβέλειας από πλευράς λατρείας. Ιδρυμένο στα τέλη του 6ου αι. π.Χ. σε επίκαιρη και ειδυλλιακή ακόμα και σήμερα θέση (στον Λαιμό της Βουλιαγμένης) ως απλός ορθογώνιος σηκός με βωμό, συμπληρώθηκε στον 4ο αι. π.Χ. με την προσθήκη περίστασης, ενώ στους ρωμαϊκούς χρόνους απέκτησε την τελική μορφή του.[56] Σε μικρή απόσταση από το ιερό υπήρχε κρήνη[57] και 150 μ. βορειότερα αποκαλύφθηκε κτιριακό συγκρότημα, το γνωστό ως ιερατική οικία, το οποίο περιλαμβάνει δωμάτια και ισχυρό πύργο μέσα σε περίβολο.[58] Επιγραφές σε αναθηματικά βάθρα και κίονα του ιερού, όπως και

Εικ. 14. Ιερό του ΝΑ. συνοικισμού των Αιξωνίδων Αλών.

επιγραφές από την ιερατική οικία μας πληροφορούν για τα Ζωστήρια, τοπική προφανώς γιορτή προς τιμήν του Απόλλωνος, για τις δραστηριότητες των ιερέων και άλλων επιφανών Αλαιέων, για τις επισκευές του ιερού και για τις οικονομικές δοσοληψίες του.[59] Δύο κυκλικοί πύργοι ΒΑ. και ΒΔ. της ιερατικής οικίας συμπλήρωναν τις εγκαταστάσεις και προστάτευαν το χώρο του ιερού, ελέγχοντας τη θαλάσσια περιοχή για την αποτροπή εχθρικών αποβάσεων στην Αττική.[60] Στους ελληνιστικούς μάλιστα χρόνους πάνω σε χαμηλό λόφο, ΝΑ. του ιερού, κατασκευάστηκε μικρό φρούριο που χρησιμοποιήθηκε για τις ανάγκες του Χρεμωνιδείου πολέμου (εικ. 1, θέση θ).[61]

Αρχαίες πηγές και επιγραφικές μαρτυρίες αναφέρουν παράλληλα με το ιερό του Απόλλωνα Ζωστήρος και άλλα επιφανή ιερά των Αλαιέων,[62] η θέση των οποίων δεν έχει προς το παρόν επιβεβαιωθεί ανασκαφικά. Επίσης, τμήμα επιγραφής που καταγράφηκε ως προερχόμενο από την περιοχή μεταξύ Ζωστήρος και Αλυκής, από το χώρο δηλαδή του δήμου των Αιξωνίδων Αλών, διέσωσε αποσπασματικό κείμενο ιερού νόμου με αναφορά σε ιέρειες του Διονύσου, της Δήμητρος Χλόης, της Ήρας και της Ηρωίνης.[63]

Την δεύτερη ομάδα αποτελούν τά "αστικά" ιερά, όσα δηλαδή εντάσσονται μέσα στον πολεοδομικό ιστό των συνοικισμών των Αλαιέων, ιδρυμένα δίπλα σε δρόμους.[64] Δεν έχουν σταθερό προσανατολισμό, είναι μετρίων ή μικρών διαστάσεων, με εξαίρεση αυτό της οδού Καλύμνου, το οποίο παρουσιάζει και την επιμελέστερη και περισσότερο μνημειακή κατασκευή, όπως τουλάχιστον αποκαλύπτει η ευθυντηρία του. Συνήθως περικλείονται από περίβολο, περιλαμβάνουν πρόδρομο και σηκό και συχνά έχουν εσχάρα-βωμό είτε μέσα στο σηκό είτε εξωτερικά, απέναντι στην είσοδό τους. Σε μερικές περιπτώσεις υπάρχει βάθρο ή θρανίο στο βάθος του σηκού (εικ. 14), προφανώς για την τοποθέτηση αναθημάτων και λατρευτικών αντικειμένων. Σε δύο ιερά εντοπίστηκε και ο αποθέτης, γεμάτος με αγγεία και ειδώλια.

Στην τρίτη ομάδα εντάσσονται τα αγροτικά ιερά. Αυτά έχουν αποκαλυφθεί διάσπαρτα στο χώρο του δήμου, εκτός των συνοικισμών, δίπλα στις βασικές αρτηρίες που τους συνδέουν και, ως προς την κατασκευή, δεν διαφέρουν από τα "αστικά" ιερά. Στο ένα υπάρχει βάθρο μέσα στο σηκό (εικ. 15) ενώ σε μικρή απόσταση από το δεύτερο αποκαλύφθηκε ο αποθέτης του, γεμάτος με ειδώλια γυναικείων μορφών. Σε μέγεθος διαφέρει το ναόσχημο κτίριο της οδού Νικηταρά, το οποίο είχε περίβολο και προσκτίσματα,[65] ενώ προβληματίζει ως προς την ταύτισή της η δίχωρη κατασκευή που ερευνήθηκε στην συμβολή δύο βασικών δρόμων του νεκροταφείου των Αλαιέων (εικ. 16).

Την τέταρτη και εξαιρετικά ενδιαφέρουσα κατηγορία αποτελούν τα ιερά του κύριου νεκροταφείου των Αλαιέων. Παρουσιάζουν την τυπική οργάνωση των άλλων ιερών, είναι επίσης ιδρυμένα δίπλα σε δρόμους, ένα μάλιστα εμφανίζει την μορφή δίδυμου ναού ενταγμένου μέσα σε περίβολο με προσκτίσματα, ακριβώς στο κέντρο του πυκνότερου σε ταφές τμήματος του κύριου νεκροταφείου των Αλαιέων (εικ. 17).[66] Ιδιαίτερο

Εικ. 15. Αγροτικό ιερό των Αλαιέων.

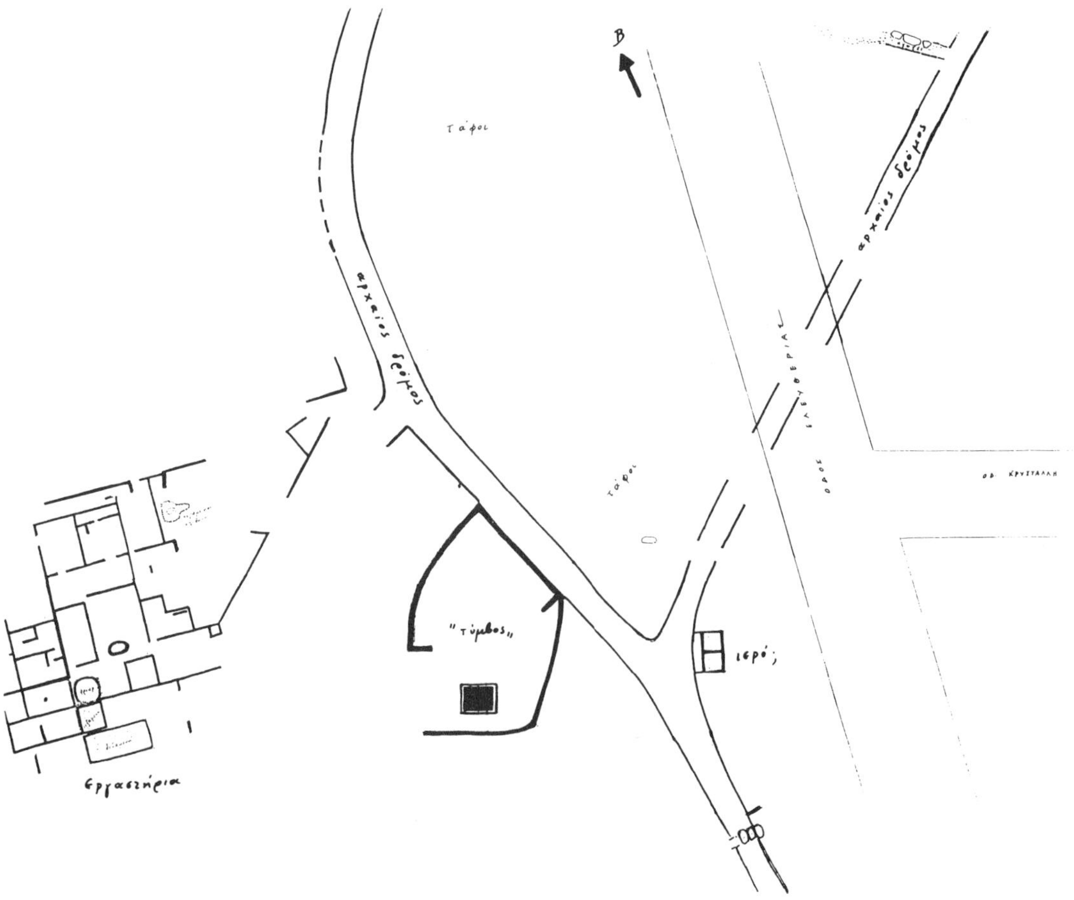

Εικ. 16. Τοπογραφικό τμήματος του νεκροταφείου των Αιξωνίδων Αλών με δρόμους, ιερά και εργαστήρια.

ενδιαφέρον παρουσιάζει μία κατασκευή σε σχήμα βωμού, η οποία αποκαλύφθηκε ενταγμένη σε περίβολο στον χώρο συμβολής δύο δρόμων που διασχίζουν το νότιο τμήμα του νεκροταφείου (εικ. 16).[67]

'Αλλα κτίρια με σαφή δημόσιο χαρακτήρα δεν έχουν εντοπιστεί στον χώρο του δήμου των Αλαιέων. 'Ηδη αναφερθήκαμε στην πιθανότητα αποδόσεως σε δημόσιο κτίριο των θεμελίων που έχουν αποκαλυφθεί δίπλα στο ναό της οδού Καλύμνου, στον ΒΔ. συνοικισμό. Επίσης και ο συνεχόμενος νότια και ανατολικά του ιερού χώρος προσφέρεται για παρόμοιες χρήσεις, όπως κατάλληλος για συναθροίσεις φαίνεται και ο ελεύθερος κτισμάτων χώρος του ΝΑ. συνοικισμού, στο νότιο και ΝΑ. τμήμα του συγκροτήματος Καλαμπόκα, ο οποίος περιλαμβάνει και τους περιβόλους των ιερών (εικ. 10). Στα δημόσια κτίρια πρέπει να συμπεριληφθούν οι πύργοι που έχουν εντοπιστεί στον χώρο του δήμου, όπως και οι κυκλικές κατασκευές που αποκαλύφθηκαν μέσα στους συνοικισμούς, εφόσον δεχθούμε ότι εξυπηρετούν αμυντικούς σκοπούς ή άλλες κοινές ανάγκες. Τέλος, η ανεύρεση δύο τουλάχιστον χορηγικών επιγραφών στις ανατολικές παρυφές του ΝΑ. συνοικισμού των Αλαιέων, αποτελεί ένδειξη υπάρξεως θεάτρου στο δήμο. Η μία επιγραφή, του 380 π.Χ., είναι ακέραια,[68] ενώ η δεύτερη διέσωσε μόνο την λέξη ΕΔΙΔΑΣΚΕ,[69] και οι δύο όμως είχαν μετακινηθεί από την αρχική τους θέση. Γεγονός είναι ότι δεν έχουν εντοπιστεί μέχρι σήμερα λείψανα θεατρικής κατασκευής, έστω και υποτυπωδώς διαμορφωμένα, παρά την σχετική παλαιότερη πληροφορία,[70] δεν αποκλείεται όμως οι Αλαιείς χορηγοί που αναφέρονται στην πρώτη επιγραφή να χρηματοδότησαν παραστάσεις "ἐν ἄστει" και όχι τοπικές.

Εργαστήρια κεραμεικής έχουν αποκαλυφθεί στις δυτικές παρυφές του ΒΔ. συνοικισμού, το ένα σε πλήρη κάτοψη, το δεύτερο αποσπασματικά διατηρημένο.[71] Το σημαντικότερο και πιο εκτεταμένο συγκρότημα εργαστηρίων του 4ου αι. βρέθηκε στο δυτικό τμήμα του κύριου νεκροταφείου των Αλαιέων, σε μικρή απόσταση από την τυμβοειδή κατασκευή με βωμό της οδού Ελευθερίας (εικ. 16). Διατηρούσε κεραμεικό κλίβανο, πηγάδι, δεξαμενές, αποθέτες και απέδωσε, εκτός από την κεραμεική, λίθινα αντικείμενα ημίεργα, κομμάτια λατύπης αλλά και εργαλεία επεξεργασίας λίθου, τα οποία συνηγορούν στην ταύτιση των εγκαταστάσεων με εργαστήριο κεραμεικής και επεξεργασίας λίθου, πιθανότατα συνδεδεμένο με την κατασκευή ταφικών μνημείων και με τις ανάγκες του νεκροταφείου γενικότερα.[72]

Το κύριο νεκροταφείο του αρχαίου δήμου έχει αποκαλυφθεί στην αρκετά ευρύχωρη πεδινή περιοχή, τη γνωστή σήμερα με το όνομα Πηγαδάκια, έχει όμως υποστεί σε ευρεία κλίμακα τις συνέπειες δράσεως αρχαιοκαπήλων ήδη από τον περασμένο αιώνα.

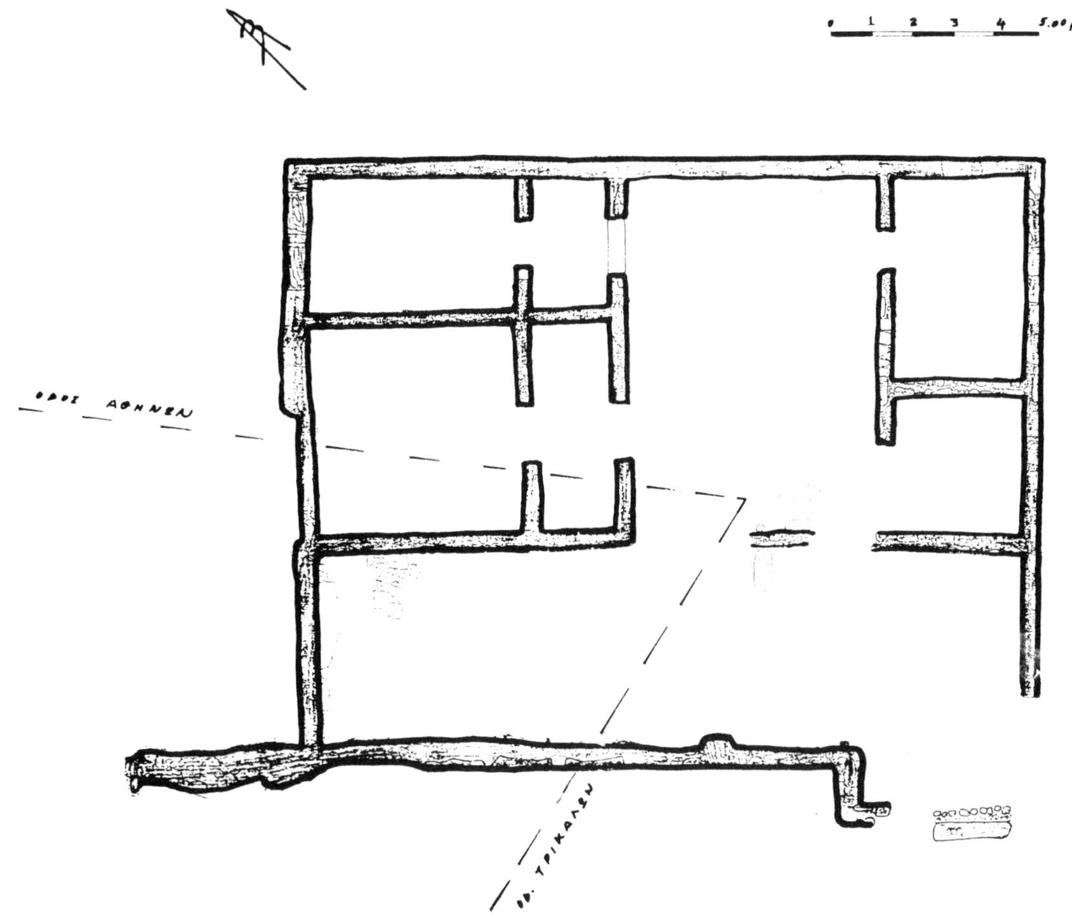

Εικ. 17. Το "δίδυμο" ιερό του κύριου νεκροταφείου των Αλαιέων.

Εικ. 18. Υστερογεωμετρικός τάφος οικογενειακού νεκροταφείου ανατολικά των συνοικισμών των Αλαιέων.

Διασχίζεται από αρκετούς δρόμους, ο σπουδαιότερος των οποίων έχει αποκαλυφθεί κατά μήκος της οδού Ελευθερίας. Σε μνημειακούς ταφικούς περιβόλους ιδρυμένους κατά μήκος αυτού του δρόμου πρέπει να ανήκουν τα επιστήματα που βρίσκονται στο Εθνικό Μουσείο και στο Μουσείο Πειραιώς και διασώζουν τα ονόματα αρκετών Αλαιέων.[73] Πολλοί ταφικοί περίβολοι, εκατοντάδες τάφων και πολλές στήλες, μαρμάρινες λήκυθοι και λουτροφόροι, αποκαλύφθηκαν σε εκσκαφές για θεμελιώσεις οικοδομών, σε εργασίες διαμορφώσεως δρόμων και σε διανοίξεις τάφρων υδροδοτήσεως ή αποχετεύσεως.[74] Αναφέρθηκε ήδη ο μνημειακής κατασκευής περίβολος της οδού Ελευθερίας με την τυμβοειδή διαμόρφωση που περικλείει βωμό (ή ηρώο;). Το μνημείο βρίσκεται σε επίκαιρο σημείο, στην συμβολή του βασικού δρόμου με άλλον που διέσχιζε από ΝΔ. προς ΒΑ. το νεκροταφείο και με τρίτο, μικρότερο, που οδηγούσε στο συγκρότημα των εργαστηρίων (εικ. 16). Ο πυκνότερος ιστός του νεκροταφείου αποκαλύφθηκε στο χώρο που παρεμβάλλεται μεταξύ της ακροπόλεως και του ΝΑ. συνοικισμού. Λάκκοι, πυρές, κιβωτιόσχημοι τάφοι, εγχυτρισμοί, σαρκοφάγοι, λάρνακες, πίθοι, κεραμοσκεπείς τάφοι, από την γεωμετρική μέχρι και την ύστερη κλασσική εποχή, διαφύλαξαν τους νεκρούς Αλαιείς και τα κτερίσματά τους. Στο κέντρο αυτού του τμήματος του νεκροταφείου είχε ιδρυθεί το δίδυμο ιερό που περιγράφηκε προηγουμένως.

Εξίσου ενδιαφέροντα ταφικά σύνολα, περιορισμένης όμως εκτάσεως, αποκαλύφθηκαν στις μεγάλες οδικές αρτηρίες. Κατά μήκος της λεωφόρου Βουλιαγμένης και ιδιαίτερα στους χώρους συμβολής της με τους αρχαίους δρόμους που ακολουθούν οι λεωφόροι Καλύμνου (βόρειο άκρο)[75] και Βάρης (νότιο άκρο),[76] κατά μήκος της λεωφόρου Βάρης,[77] δίπλα στην λεωφόρο Β. Παύλου[78] και στο ανατολικό άκρο της οδού Σπετσών[79] έχουν ερευνηθεί ταφικοί περίβολοι με ποικιλία ειδών τάφων και αποκαλυφθεί υπολείμματα γλυπτού διακόσμου μεγαλοπρεπών ταφικών μνημείων. Ιδιαίτερο ενδιαφέρον παρουσιάζουν επίσης τα μικρά, οικογενειακά μάλλον σύνολα τάφων των γεωμετρικών (εικ. 18), αρχαϊκών και κλασσικών χρόνων που κατά καιρούς εντοπίζονται σε κοιλότητες του φυσικού βράχου ανατολικά της λεωφόρου Καλύμνου.[80] Το μικρής έκτασης αλλά ενδιαφέρον τμήμα νεκροταφείου που αποκαλύφθηκε στην οδό Πρ. Πέτρου της Βούλας, σε μικρή απόσταση από τον χώρο των μυκηναϊκών τάφων, δίπλα σε αρχαίο δρόμο που οδηγούσε από την παραλία προς το εσωτερικό, δεν είναι σαφές εάν χρησιμοποιήθηκε από Αλαιείς ή Αιξωνείς. Δυστυχώς και εδώ οι λαθρανασκαφείς προηγήθηκαν κατά πολύ των αρχαιολόγων, τα ευρήματα όμως της συστηματικής έρευνας έδωσαν τη δυνατότητα χρονολογήσεως των τάφων στους αρχαϊκούς και κλασσικούς χρόνους και αποκάλυψαν ότι οι νεκροί ανήκαν σε εύπορες οικογένειες.[81]

Συμπεράσματα

Τα ευρήματα των σωστικών ανασκαφών στον χώρο του δήμου των Αιξωνίδων Αλών σχηματίζουν αρκετά εύγλωττα το περίγραμμα ζωής και δράσης των κατοίκων ενός αττικού δήμου στον 5ο και 4ο αι. π.Χ. Οι Αλαιείς αποτελούσαν ένα οργανωμένο οικιστικά και παραγωγικά σύνολο, οι δραστηριότητες του οποίου εκάλυπταν όλες τις εκφάνσεις της ζωής και μάλιστα σε αρκετά ανεπτυγμένο επίπεδο. Οι αγροτικές καλλιέργειες (κυρίως δημητριακά, αμπέλια και ελιές) μαζί με την μελισσοκομία αποτελούσαν τις πρωτογενείς παραγωγικές δραστηριότητες, τις οποίες συμπλήρωνε η αλιεία και η παρασκευή αλατιού. Η λειτουργία τριών τουλάχιστον κεραμεικών εργαστηρίων και μίας μονάδας επεξεργασίας λίθου υποδηλώνουν σχετική αυτάρκεια στην βιοτεχνική παραγωγή ενώ η οργανωμένη οικιακή οικονομία αποδεικνύεται από το πλήθος των τριβείων, τριπτήρων, ιγδίων, λίθινων και πήλινων λεκανών, αμφορέων και αγνύθων που βρίσκουμε στα σπίτια των Αλαιέων. Η ύπαρξη πυκνού πλέγματος κυρίων και δευτερευόντων δρόμων εξασφάλιζε την απρόσκοπτη επικοινωνία μεταξύ των οικιστικών και άλλων μονάδων του δήμου αλλά και μεταξύ των Αλαιέων και των γειτονικών δήμων. Το πλήθος των αναλημματικών τοίχων καθιστά φανερή την προσπάθεια εξασφαλίσεως όσο το δυνατόν περισσότερων καλλιεργήσιμων επιφανειών ενώ η κατασκευή αποστραγγιστικών και υδραυλικών έργων αποδεικνύει σοβαρή αντιμετώπιση των προβλημάτων που δημιουργούσαν τα στοιχεία της φύσεως.

Υψηλό θρησκευτικό συναίσθημα υποδηλώνει το σύνολο των μεγάλων και μικρών ιερών που αποκαλύφθηκαν διάσπαρτα στο χώρο του δήμου, όπως και η ύπαρξη βωμίσκων και ειδωλίων στα σπίτια των Αλαιέων. Το ανεπτυγμένο βιοτικό επίπεδο είναι φανερό τόσο στην οργάνωση των σπιτιών (με 3 ή 4 δωμάτια, χρήση κουζίνας, λουτρού και αποχετευτικών εγκαταστάσεων), όσο και στην οργάνωση των νεκροταφείων με τους πλούσια κτερισμένους τάφους και τα επιβλητικά μνημεία. Χαρακτηριστικό εν τούτοις της πρωτογενούς μορφής της οικονομίας του δήμου των Αιξωνίδων Αλών είναι η ανυπαρξία νομισμάτων μεταξύ των κινητών ευρημάτων. Ελάχιστοι μικροί θησαυροί έχουν βρεθεί και μερικά μεμονωμένα νομισματα, κυρίως στην επίχωση των βασικών δρόμων. Αντίθετα, πολλά νοσμίσματα, 4ου κυρίως αι. βρέθηκαν στην ιερατική οικία του Ζωστήρος, γεγονός που επιβεβαιώνει την οικονομική ευρρωστία και τις συναφείς δραστηριότητες του ιερού.

Ολοκληρώνοντας την περιγραφή της γενικής εικόνας του δήμου των Αιξωνίδων Αλών, όπως αυτή σχηματίσθηκε από τα ανασκαφικά δεδομένα, πρέπει να τονιστεί το γεγονός της μοναδικότητάς του. Κανένας άλλος αγροτικός δήμος της Αττικής δεν μας έχει αποκαλύψει την οικιστική οργάνωση και μορφή του σε τόση έκταση και πληρότητα, για μερικούς μάλιστα δήμους, σπουδαιότατους σύμφωνα με τις πηγές, αγνοούμε όχι μόνο την μορφή αλλά και την θέση των οικισμών τους, ενώ τα πενιχρότατα οικιστικά κατάλοιπα άλλων δεν συμβαδίζουν με την ανεπτυγμένη οικονομικά και οικιστικά εικόνα που δίνουν οι πηγές. Οπωσδήποτε η αρχαιολογική σκαπάνη έχει πάντοτε τον τελευταίο λόγο και πιθανόν θα αποσαφηνίσει το θέμα, αποκαλύπτοντας όσα μυστικά εξακολουθεί να κρύβει η αττική γή. Σην περίπτωση των Αιξωνίδων Αλών, η αποκάλυψη και η αποκρυπτογράφηση των αντίστοιχων μυστικών οφείλεται στην εργασία πολλών συναδέλφων που υπηρέτησαν ή υπηρετούν στην Β΄ Εφορεία Αρχαιοτήτων Αττικής και ερεύνησαν περισσότερες από 300 θέσεις. Με την συνεργασία και του υπόλοιπου προσωπικού έχει πραγματοποιηθεί, κάτω από τις γνωστές συνθήκες των σωστικών ανασκαφών, τεράστιο έργο, σχεδόν άγνωστο. Η ομιλούσα χρεώνεται ελάχιστο μέρος του ανασκαφικού έργου, σας παρουσίασε όμως μία συνθετική εικόνα των επί μέρους πορισμάτων των ερευνών με βάση τις ήδη δημοσιευμένες αλλά και τις υπό δημοσίευση εκθέσεις συναδέλφων, τους οποίους και από αυτή την θέση ευχαριστώ.

Σημειώσεις

1. C.W.J. Eliot, *Coastal Demes of Attika, Phoenix* Suppl. 5 (Toronto 1962) 25–26.
2. Α. Κεραμόπουλος, "Ἀνασκαφὴ ἐν Αἰξωνῇ Ἀττικῆς," *Πρακτ* (1919) 34. Ι. Παπαδημητρίου, "Μυκηναϊκοὶ τάφοι Ἁλυκῆς Γλυφάδας," *Πρακτ* (1954) 42–78 και *Πρακτ* (1955) 78 κ.ε.
3. Ν. Κυπαρίσση, "Ἐξ Ἀθηνῶν καὶ Ἀττικῆς," *ΑρχΔελτ* 11 (1927–28) Παράρτημα 44–47. Ντ. Πέππα-Δελμούζου, "Ἐπιστήματα τοῦ τάφου Μενύλλου Ἀλαιέως," *ΑΑΑ* 3 (1970) 235.
4. "Μετὰ δὲ τὸν Πειραιᾶ Φαληρεῖς δῆμος ἐν τῇ ἐφεξῆς παραλίᾳ· εἶθ' Ἁλιμούσιοι, Αἰξωνεῖς, Ἁλαιεῖς οἱ Αἰξωνικοί, Ἀναγυράσιοι· εἶτα Θορεῖς, Λαμπτρεῖς, Αἰγιλεῖς, Ἀναφλύστιοι, Ἀζηνιείς· οὗτοι μὲν οἱ μέχρι τῆς ἄκρας τοῦ Σουνίου ... καὶ μετὰ τοὺς Αἰξωνέας δ' ἐστὶν Ὑδροῦσσα." (Στράβων 9.1).
   "Δῆμοι δὲ οἱ μικροὶ τῆς Ἀττικῆς, ὡς ἔτυχεν ἕκαστος οἰκισθείς, τάδε εἰς μνήμην παρείχοντο Ἁλιμουσίοις μὲν Θεσμοφόρου Δήμητρος καὶ Κόρης ἐστὶν ἱερόν, ἐν Ζωστῆρι δὲ ἐπὶ θαλάσσης καὶ βωμὸς Ἀθηνᾶς καὶ Ἀπόλλωνος καὶ Ἀρτέμιδος καὶ Λητοῦς· τεκεῖν μὲν οὖν Λητὼ τοὺς παῖδας ἐνταῦθα οὔ φασι, λύσασθαι δὲ τὸν ζωστῆρα ὡς τεξομένην καὶ τῷ χωρίῳ διὰ τοῦτο γενέσθαι τὸ ὄνομα." (Παυσανίας 1.31.1).
   "Ἁλαὶ Ἀραφηνίδες καὶ Ἁλαὶ Αἰξωνίδες: δῆμοι, ὁ μὲν τῆς Αἰγηΐδος ὁ δ' Αἰξωνεύς τῆς Κεκροπίδος φυλῆς ... ἔστι δὲ ὁ δῆμος τῆς Ἀραφηνίδος μεταξὺ Φηγέως τοῦ πρὸς Μαραθῶνι καὶ Βραυρῶνος, αἱ δ' Αἰξωνίδες ἐγγὺς τοῦ ἄστεος· ἔστι καὶ λίμνη ἐκ θαλάσσης." (Στέφανος Βυζάντιος).
5. Κ. Κουρουνιώτης, "Τὸ ἱερὸν τοῦ Ἀπόλλωνος τοῦ Ζωστῆρος," *ΑρχΔελτ* 11 (1927–28) 9–52.
6. Στα κατάλοιπα Δ. Θεοχάρη (αρχείο Β΄ ΕΠΚΑ) αναφέρεται: "Ὁ Νεολιθικὸς συνοικισμὸς τῆς Γλυφάδας, ἐπὶ τῆς κορυφῆς τῆς χερσονήσου Πούντας, κεῖται 5 χιλμ. νοτίως τοῦ ΠΕ συνοικισμοῦ τοῦ Ἁγίου Κοσμᾶ. Ἐκεῖνο ποὺ κατορθώθη νὰ διαπιστωθεῖ διὰ προχείρου ἐρεύνης εἶναι ἡ ὕπαρξη ἑνὸς Νεολιθικοῦ συνοικισμοῦ, πιθανῶς ἀναγομένου ἤδη εἰς τὴν ἀρχαιοτέραν Νεολιθικήν."
7. *ΑρχΔελτ* 46 (1991) Χρονικά (υπό έκδοση).
8. *ΑρχΔελτ* 39 (1984) Χρονικά 36 (οικ. Βαλαβάνη).
9. *ΑρχΔελτ* 16 (1960) Χρονικά 40.
10. Βλ. σημ. 2 και *ΑρχΔελτ* 44 (1989) Χρονικά (υπό έκδοση).
11. *ΑρχΔελτ* 34 (1979) Χρονικά 86 (οδός Καβάλας και Λαρίσης). *ΑρχΔελτ* 39 (1984) Χρονικά 35 (οικ. Πετράκη). *ΑρχΔελτ* 44 (1989) Χρονικά (υπό έκδοση, οικ. Γρηγοράκη).
12. *ΑρχΔελτ* 29 (1973–74) Χρονικά 60 (οικ. Σέρρα), 63 (οδ. Ηρακλειδών και Μ. Βασιλείου).

13. A. Furtwängler, *Beschreibung der Vasensammlung im Antiquarium* (Berlin 1885) 4-8.
14. *ΑρχΔελτ* 32 (1977) Χρονικά 42 (οδός Αθηνών-Καβάλας-Θεσσαλονίκης).
15. Κουρουνιώτης (σημ. 5) 49. Φ. Σταυρόπουλος, "Ἱερατικὴ οἰκία ἐν Ζωστῆρι τῆς Ἀττικῆς," *ΑρχΕφ* (1938) 3.
16. *ΑρχΔελτ* 39 (1984) Χρονικά 35 (οικ. Πετράκη). *ΑρχΔελτ* 44 (1989) Χρονικά (υπό έκδοση, οικ. Γρηγοράκη).
17. *ΑρχΔελτ* 34 (1979) Χρονικά 78 (οικ. Σμυρνή, οδ. Σπετσών).
18. *ΑρχΔελτ* 29 (1973-74) Χρονικά 63 (Ηρακλειδών και Μεγ. Βασιλείου), 158 (οικ. Σκαφιδά), 100 (οικ. Ζάκκου). *ΑρχΔελτ* 32 (1978) Χρονικά 58 (οικ. Κοκολάκη-Παναγοπούλου).
19. D. Whitehead, *The Demes of Attica, 508/7 — ca. 250 B.C.* (Princeton 1986) 372.
20. Ο υπολογισμός είναι σχετικός, δεδομένου ότι η αναλογία αριθμού βουλευτών και πολιτών κυμαίνεται από 1:15 μέχρι 1:55 (J. Traill, *The Political Organization of Attica*, *Hesperia* Suppl. 14 [1975] 64 κ.ε.).
21. Ε. Κονσολάκη, *Γλυφάδα, ιστορικό παρελθόν και μνημεία* (Αθήνα 1990) 30-36. Είναι χαρακτηριστικό ότι μόνο σε επτά θέσεις της Γλυφάδας αποκαλύφθηκαν θεμέλια αρχαίων κτιρίων ενώ στη Βούλα ο αριθμός ξεπερνά τις εβδομήντα.
22. Κεραμόπουλος (σημ. 2) 32. Κουρουνιώτης (σημ. 5) 10 και εικ. 2. Παπαδημητρίου (σημ. 2) 72-73. Eliot (σημ. 1) 25-26.
23. *ΑρχΔελτ* 29 (1973-74) Χρονικά 205 (οικ. Τσώλη). *ΑρχΔελτ* 40 (1985) Χρονικά 59 (οικ. Φωκά). *ΑρχΔελτ* 42 (1987) Χρονικά (οικ. Κονσολάκη). *ΑρχΔελτ* 35 (1980) Χρονικά 73 (οικ. Γαλιού). *ΑρχΔελτ* 36 (1981) Χρονικά 50 (οικ. Περδικούρη). *ΑρχΔελτ* 36 (1981) Χρονικά 53 (οδός Αθηνάς-Πολύμνιας-Βορρέου).
24. *ΑρχΔελτ* 37 (1982) Χρονικά 57 (οικ. Πολλέντρι). *ΑρχΔελτ* 39 (1984) Χρονικά 39 (οικ. Μάμαλη).
25. *ΑρχΔελτ* 29 (1973-74) Χρονικά 64. *ΑρχΔελτ* 43 (1988) Χρονικά (υπό έκδοση).
26. *ΑρχΔελτ* 34 (1979) Χρονικά 78 (οικ. Βρυζάκη).
27. *ΑρχΔελτ* 22 (1967) Χρονικά 134 (οικ. Μουτζουβή). *ΑρχΔελτ* 29 (1973-74) Χρονικά 58 (οικ. Τριπολιτσιώτη-Παλαγγιά). *ΑρχΔελτ* 36 (1981) Χρονικά 52 (οδός Βάρης και Καλύμνου).
28. *ΑρχΔελτ* 34 (1979) Χρονικά 78-79 (οικ. Βρυζάκη). *ΑρχΔελτ* 36 (1981) Χρονικά 49 (οικ. Παπαϊωάννου). *ΑρχΔελτ* 38 (1983) Χρονικά 49 (οικ. Αποστολάτου). *ΑρχΔελτ* 42 (1987) Χρονικά 86 (οικ. Γαλανόπουλου).
29. *ΑρχΔελτ* 29 (1973-74) Χρονικά 63 και 160 (οικ. Περβανίδη και Λαμπροπούλου). *ΑρχΔελτ* 34 (1979) Χρονικά 78 (οικ. Κριμήλη-Καλελιοπούλου). *ΑρχΔελτ* 36 (1981) Χρονικά 48 (οικ. Τουλούμη). *ΑρχΔελτ* 37 (1982) Χρονικά 55 και 57 (οικ. Ροδίτη και Πολλέντρι). *ΑρχΔελτ* 39 (1984) Χρονικά 39-40 (οικ. Αυγουστάτου και Μπένου). *ΑρχΔελτ* 42 (1987) Χρονικά 79 (οικ. Σίμωση).
30. *ΑρχΔελτ* 22 (1967) Χρονικά 134 (οικ. Μουτζουβή). *ΑρχΔελτ* 34 (1979) Χρονικά 76 και 79 (οικ. Καμαρωτού και Κόκκοτα). *ΑρχΔελτ* 36 (1981) Χρονικά 49 (οικ. Σιβρίδη). *ΑρχΔελτ* 39 (1982) Χρονικά 34 (οικ. Βούτσελα). *ΑρχΔελτ* 42 (1987) Χρονικά 88 και 90 (οικ. Λώλου και Κανιαμού).
31. *ΑρχΔελτ* 37 (1982) Χρονικά 37 (οικ. Πολλέντρι). *ΑρχΔελτ* 39 (1984) Χρονικά 39 (οικ. Αυγουστάτου και Μπένου).
32. *ΑρχΔελτ* 29 (1973-74) Χρονικά 160 (οικ. Λαμπροπούλου). *ΑρχΔελτ* 42 (1987) Χρονικά 86 (οικ. Γαλανοπούλου).
33. *ΑρχΔελτ* 36 (1981) Χρονικά 49 (οικ. Παπαϊωάννου). *ΑρχΔελτ* 38 (1983) Χρονικά 50 (οικ. Αποστολάτου).
34. Γ. Σταϊνχάουερ, "Έρευνα χώρου αεροδρομίου Σπάτων," *Πρακτ* (1982) 123-126 (και του ιδίου, στα ανά χείρας πρακτικά σελ. 175-189).
35. Travlos, *Attika* 467.
36. *ΑρχΔελτ* 29 (1973-74) Χρονικά 63-64 (οικ. Περβανίδη).
37. *ΑρχΔελτ* 29 (1969) Χρονικά 89-90 (οικ. Καλούμενου).
38. *ΑρχΔελτ* 22 (1967) Χρονικά 134 (οικ. Γιαννάκη). *ΑρχΔελτ* 24 (1969) Χρονικά 89 (οικ. Καλούμενου). *ΑρχΔελτ* 29 (1973-74) Χρονικά 60 (οικ. Σέρρα), 44 (οικ. Χριστοφορίδου και Πρεζάνη), 160 (οικ. Ζήκκου). *ΑρχΔελτ* 32 (1977) Χρονικά 41 (οδ. Βαλτετσίου). *ΑρχΔελτ* 33 (1978) Χρονικά 58 (οικ. Μπούζα και Κοκκολάκη). *ΑρχΔελτ* 34 (1979) Χρονικά 77 (οικ. Μπουρνιά) 78 (οικ. Τρανταλίδη). *ΑρχΔελτ* 39 (1984) Χρονικά 40 (οικ. Κατινάκη). *ΑρχΔελτ* 42 (1987) Χρονικά 73 (οικ. Παναγιωτίδη), 77 (οικ. Απρογέρακα), 85 (οικ. Γιαννακάκη), 86 (οικ. Κίσσα). *ΑρχΔελτ* 43-46 (1988-1992) (υπό έκδοση ανασκαφή νέου τμήματος λεωφόρου Βουλιαγμένης, οικ. Αντωνέλλου, οικ. Σπυρόπουλου, οικ. Σωτηρίου).
39. *ΑρχΔελτ* 24 (1969) Χρονικά 89 (οικ. Καλούμενου). *ΑρχΔελτ* 44 (1990) (υπό έκδοση, διάνοιξη λεωφόρου Βουλιαγμένης). *ΑρχΔελτ* 46 (1992) Χρονικά (υπό έκδοση, οικ. Σωτηρίου).
40. *ΑρχΔελτ* 29 (1973-74) Χρονικά 63 (οικ. Σέρρα). *ΑρχΔελτ* 39 (1984) Χρονικά 40 (οικ. Κατινάκη).
41. *ΑρχΔελτ* 29 (1973-74) Χρονικά 63 (οικ. Σέρρα).
42. Τα αποτελέσματα της συγκεκριμένης ανασκαφής δεν έχουν δημοσιευθεί. Απλή αναφορά γίνεται από τον Travlos (σημ. 35) 467, σχ. 597 και H. Lohmann, "Zur Prosopographie und Demographie der attischen Landgemeinde Atene (Ἀτήνη)," *Stuttgarten Kolloquium zur Historischen Geographie des Altertums* 2, 1984 und 3, 1987 (Bonn 1991) 216 κ.ε., πίν. 9-16.
43. *ΑρχΔελτ* 22 (1967) Χρονικά 134 (οικ. Μουτζουβή). *ΑρχΔελτ* 29 (1973-74) Χρονικά 60 (οικ. Νέγκα), 105-108 (οικ. Ερμογένη, Τσώλη και Κεχαγιά), 158 (οικ. Σκαφιδά), 160 (οικ. Ζίγδη). *ΑρχΔελτ* 33 (1978) Χρονικά 58 (οικ. Γιαννίδη). *ΑρχΔελτ* 34 (1979) Χρονικά 78 (οικ. Χριστίδη), 80 (οικ. Ψάλτη). *ΑρχΔελτ* 35 (1980) Χρονικά 72 (οικ. Καρακίτσου). *ΑρχΔελτ* 36 (1981) Χρονικά 53 (οικ. Τσαντάνη). *ΑρχΔελτ* 39 (1984) Χρονικά 36-39 (οικ. Μάμαλη). *ΑρχΔελτ* 40 (1985) Χρονικά 54-57 (οικ. Λογοθέτη), 57-59 (οικ. Βασιλειάδη). *ΑρχΔελτ* 42 (1987) Χρονικά 76 (οδός Ηρακλειδών-Δαιδάλου), 80-81 (οδός Σερίφου-Δαιδάλου), 82 (οικ. Καραλή), 83 (οικ. Μανωλά). *ΑρχΔελτ* 43-44-45-46 (1988-1992) (υπό έκδοση, οικ. Παπαχαραλάμπους, Δαλιάνη, Αθανασιάδη, Φωτόπουλου, Κιλντένη, Κοιλάκου, Λημνίδη, Σταμάτη, Χοντζόγλου, Ερμογένη, Αυδίκου, Μάντζαρη, Παγουλάτου, Τσαντάνη).
44. Travlos (σημ. 35) και Lohmann (σημ. 42) (οικ. Καλαμπόκα). *ΑρχΔελτ* 39 (1984) Χρονικά 37 (οικ. Μάμαλη). *ΑρχΔελτ* 46 (1991) (υπό έκδοση, οικ. Ερμογένη).
45. Travlos (σημ. 35) (οικ. Καλαμπόκα). *ΑρχΔελτ* 29 (1973-74) Χρονικά 158 (οικ. Σκαφιδά). *ΑρχΔελτ* 39 (1984) Χρονικά 39 (οικ. Μάμαλη). *ΑρχΔελτ* 45 (1990) (υπό έκδοση, οικ. Σταμάτη).
46. Travlos (σημ. 35) και Lohmann (σημ. 42) (οικ. Καλαμπόκα). *ΑρχΔελτ* 29 (1973-74) Χρονικά 105-108 (οικ. Ερμογένη). *ΑρχΔελτ* 44 (1989) (υπό έκδοση, οικ. Παπαχαραλάμπους).
47. Το οικόπεδο ερευνήθηκε το 1989 και η έκθεση ανασκαφής θα δημοσιευθεί στα Χρονικά του *ΑρχΔελτ* 44 (1989).
48. *ΑρχΔελτ* 19 (1964) Χρονικά 72 (Βούλα).
49. *ΑρχΔελτ* 44 (1988) Χρονικά (υπό έκδοση, οικ. Πασχαλινού).
50. *ΑρχΔελτ* 46 (1990) Χρονικά (υπό έκδοση, οικ. Πελοσώφ).
51. Κεραμόπουλος (σημ. 2) 33.
52. J.H. Young, "Studies in South Attica," *Hesperia* 25 (1956) 129, σχ. 6.
53. *ΑρχΔελτ* 39 (1984) Χρονικά 41-42 (οδός Λειψών-Β. Γεωργίου-Λέρου).
54. Ενδεικτικά σημειώνονται μερικές θέσεις (από τις δεκάδες) στην εικόνα 2.
55. *ΑρχΔελτ* 46 (1990) (υπό έκδοση, οικ. Κουστένη).
56. Κουρουνιώτης (σημ. 5) 2-53.
57. *ΑρχΔελτ* 16 (1960) Χρονικά 40.
58. Σταυρόπουλος (σημ. 15) 1-31.
59. Κουρουνιώτης (σημ. 5) 37-43. Σταυρόπουλος (σημ. 15) 23-25.
60. Σταυρόπουλος (σημ. 15) 6-7.
61. Ειρήνη Βαρούχα-Χριστοδουλοπούλου, "Συμβολή εις τον Χρεμωνίδειον πόλεμον," *ΑρχΕφ* (1953-54) Γ' 341-343.
62. Βλ. σημ. 4.
63. *IG* I[2], 135 = *IG* I[3], 144. F. Sokolowski, *Lois sacrées de cités grecques* (Paris 1969) 5, αρ. 18.
64. *ΑρχΔελτ* 24 (1969) Χρονικά 80 (οικ. Καλούμενου). *ΑρχΔελτ* 29 (1973-74) Χρονικά 63-64 (οικ. Περβανίδη). *ΑρχΔελτ* 39 (1984)

Χρονικά 37 (οικ. Μάμαλη). *ΑρχΔελτ* 46 (1991) Χρονικά (υπό έκδοση, οικ. Ερμογένη). Travlos (σημ. 35) 67.

65. *ΑρχΔελτ* 34 (1979) Χρονικά 80–81 (οικ. Σπηλιάδη), όπου περιγράφεται ως κτίσμα με δωμάτια και ανοιχτούς χώρους, η οργάνωση όμως σαφώς ταυτίζει την όλη κατασκευή με ιερό ενταγμένο σε περίβολο. *ΑρχΔελτ* 34 (1979) Χρονικά 77–78 (οικ. Σμυρλή). *ΑρχΔελτ* 44 (1988) Χρονικά (υπό έκδοση, οικ. Πασχαλινού). *ΑρχΔελτ* 47 (1992) (υπό έκδοση, οικ. Κανιαμού-Παναγόπουλου).

66. Το κτιριακό συγκρότημα του συγκεκριμένου ιερού ερευνήθηκε σε δύο φάσεις (*ΑρχΔελτ* 29 [1973–74] Χρονικά 59–60 [οικ. Καρρά] και *ΑρχΔελτ* 36 [1981] Χρονικά 49–50 [διασταύρωση οδών Αθηνών και Καβάλας]) και αποδόθηκε ως οικία. Ο προβληματισμός για την ύπαρξη ενός σπιτιού στο κέντρο του αρχαίου νεκροταφείου και ο συνδιασμός των επί μέρους ανασκαφικών στοιχείων απέδειξε ότι πρόκειται για διπλό ιερό, ενταγμένο μαζί με τα προσκτίσματά του μέσα σε περίβολο.

67. *ΑρχΔελτ* 47 (1992) (υπό έκδοση, οικ. Παναγόπουλου).

68. Α. Παπαγιαννόπουλος-Παλαιός, "'Αττικαὶ ἐπιγραφαὶ 7: Ἔργα 'Εκφαντίδου, Κρατίνου, Τιμοθέου καὶ ἡ Σοφοκλέους Τηλέφεια," *Πολέμων* 1 (1929) 161–163.

69. *ΑρχΔελτ* 36 (1981) Χρονικά 50 (οικ. Περδικούρη).

70. Δ. Παπαγιαννόπουλος-Παλαιός, "'Αττικά, Τὸ θέατρον Αἰξωνῆσιν," *Πολέμων* 4 (1949–1950) 138. Eliot (σημ. 1) 30.

71. Βλ. σημ. 39.

72. *ΑρχΔελτ* 40 (1985) Χρονικά 62–65 (οικ. Μάνη) και *ΑρχΔελτ* 42 (1987) Χρονικά 89 (οικ. Κανιαμού).

73. Βλ. σημ. 3.

74. *ΑρχΔελτ* 29 (1973–74) Χρονικά 158–159 (οικ. Τσίκολη). *ΑρχΔελτ* 32 (1977) Χρονικά 42 (οδός Αθηνών-Καβάλας-Θεσσαλονίκης). *ΑρχΔελτ* 34 (1979) Χρονικά 76 (οικ. Καμαρωτού), 77 (οικ. Νικολαράκου), 78 (οδ. Καζαντζάκη), 81–87 (σκάμματα Ε.Ε.Υ.). *ΑρχΔελτ* 37 (1982) Χρονικά 54–55 (οικ. Βούτσελα), 56–57 (οικ. Μπιρσιτζόγλου), 57 (οικ. Χατζηχριστοφή). *ΑρχΔελτ* 39 (1984) Χρονικά 34 (οικ. Παπαγιαννόπουλου και Πετράκη), 35 (οδ. Λαρίσης). *ΑρχΔελτ* 40 (1985) Χρονικά 65 (οικ. Πρίφτη). *ΑρχΔελτ* 42 (1987) 82–90 (οικ. Χριστοδούλου, Τζίμα, "Ελληνικαί Κατασκευαί", Κανιαμού, Ηλιόπουλου).

75. *ΑρχΔελτ* 43 (1988) Χρονικά (υπό έκδοση, διάνοιξη λεωφ. Βουλιαγμένης).

76. *ΑρχΔελτ* 29 (1973–74) Χρονικά 58–59 (οικ. Παλαγγιά και Τριπολιτσιώτη). *ΑρχΔελτ* 34 (1979) Χρονικά 79 (οικ. Τριπολιτσιώτη).

77. *ΑρχΔελτ* 44 (1989) Χρονικά (υπό έκδοση, οικ. Γρηγοράκη).

78. Ο αρχαίος δρόμος έχει αποκαλυφθεί σε μήκος περίπου 70 μ., τάφοι όμως αποκαλύφθηκαν στην ανατολική πλευρά ενός μόνο τμήματός του, αδημοσίευτοι προς το παρόν.

79. *ΑρχΔελτ* 35 (1980) Χρονικά 73 (οικ. Γαλλιού). *ΑρχΔελτ* 42 (1987) Χρονικά 82 (οικ. Πωλοπετράκη).

80. *ΑρχΔελτ* 33 (1978) Χρονικά 57 (οδ. Αιόλου). *ΑρχΔελτ* 42 (1987) Χρονικά 76–77 (οικ. Μεταξά) 84–85 (οικ. Χριστοδουλόπουλου). *ΑρχΔελτ* 46 (1991) (υπό έκδοση, οικ. Μαυρομμάτη).

81. *ΑρχΔελτ* 44 (1989) Χρονικά (υπό έκδοση, οικ. Μαργαρίτη).

Thorikos During the Last Years of the Sixth Century B.C.

Herman F. Mussche

In Thorikos, as in most places where there was continuity of settlement from the sixth to the fourth centuries, precious little has been preserved from the archaic period. The re-examination of the whole problem was a stimulating challenge for me. Unfortunately I was unable during the summer of 1992 to carry out some checks on the actual material, as the Laurion Museum was closed.

Evidence that Thorikos must have been a major settlement during the last quarter of the sixth century is provided by ceramic finds from a variety of places. First, on the acropolis (Fig. 1) there is an appreciable quantity of good quality pottery in the bothros of the heroic cult in Mycenaean

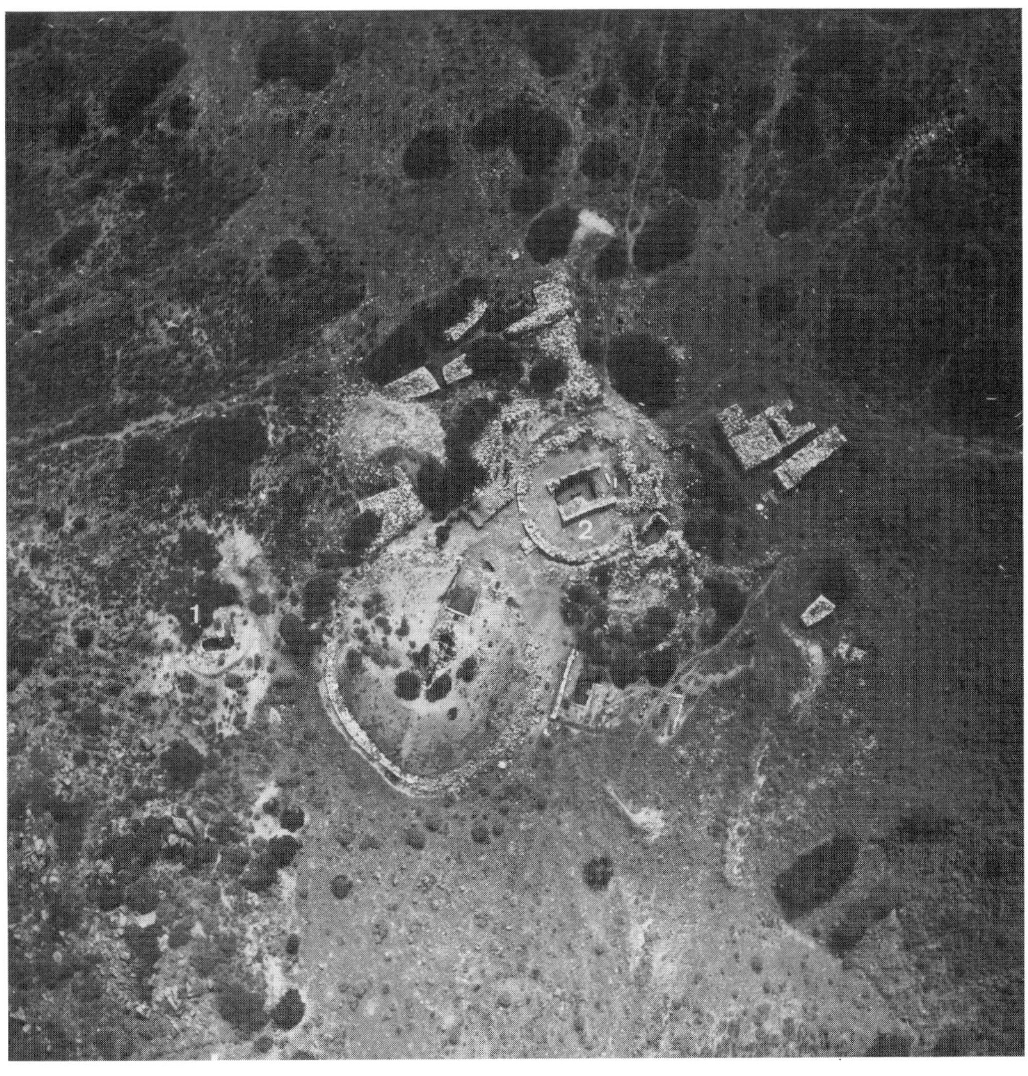

Fig. 1. Velatouri Hill, acropolis: 1. oval tomb I; 2. MH tomb V. Photo W. Myers.

Grave I.[1] Of more interest, but unfortunately very much disturbed, are the remains of a similar but more significant cult over MH Grave V. This shaft grave was excavated by Stais, who then used it as a dump for the stones from the oblong beehive tomb. It was also excavated by J. Servais.[2] It has proved utterly impossible to discover anything further of the original stratigraphy, and because of the untimely death of Servais, the find has remained virtually unpublished. Above this shaft grave a small rectangular cult building has been uncovered, directly related to a quantity of late archaic black- and red-figured sherds which could not possibly have come from anywhere else, such as the sacrificial pit in Grave I.

In the industrial quarter practically no archaic remains have been found *in situ*. But the foundation and levelling layers of the many artificially constructed terraces from the first half of the fifth century have been found to contain hundreds of sherds dating from the last few decades of the sixth century, many of them of good quality. We may assume that in a residential area like the slopes of the Velatouri, earthwork and terracing were confined to what was strictly necessary and earth to be discharged was certainly transported over the shortest possible distance. In other words, maximum use was made of what was available on site. We may conclude that there was a settlement in this quarter at the end of the sixth century and that its traces were, to all intents and purposes, obliterated by the fifth-century residential layer, mainly as a result of the tendency in that century to build the walls directly on bed rock wherever possible.

In the West 4 necropolis, some ten graves dating from the late sixth century have been found; these belong mostly to children.

Having summarized the ceramic evidence I move on to the problems in the theatre area. Noteworthy features here are, first and foremost, the theatre itself and second, the adjoining necropolis (Figs. 2–3). The necropolis is earlier. Discovered in 1963 and partially excavated in 1964,[3] it formed the subject of a number of campaigns undertaken in the 1980s, resulting in the identification of a total of 63 graves (not yet published). The earliest grave, dating from the second half of the sixth century, was excavated as early as 1964. It is true that in 1988 some Proto-Attic sherds were found in another grave, but I would not, on the basis of this discovery alone, venture to conclude that the necropolis could be dated so early, for this grave was disturbed by the construction of the largest southernmost sepulchral monument. It is significant that burials began here in the second quarter of the sixth century and were carried out regularly until the fourth; such continuous use meant locating the

Fig. 2. Theatre-necropolis: 1. retaining wall of the orchestra; 2–8. funerary monuments.

Fig. 3. Area south and west of the theatre: 1. retaining wall of the orchestra; 2–5. funerary monuments; 6. quarry; 7. ore-washery.

graves towards the retaining wall of the orchestra. The largest concentration of graves, however, was in the fifth century. The southernmost and earliest sepulchral monument can probably be dated to the period spanning the late sixth and early fifth centuries; later on about half a dozen smaller monuments were erected between that building and the theatre.

One should note that the present state of the site to the south of the theatre does not reflect its condition in the sixth century. From recent excavations it has emerged that on the east and west sides a substantial quantity of rock was hewn when a quarry was opened in the fifth century in order to get stones for the construction of some components of the theatre. The earliest graves, therefore, were dug in a far narrower and deeper ravine. A final point to be noted is the discovery of various fragments of a peribolos wall of the necropolis.

Although it is always dangerous to draw conclusions before the last square metre has been excavated — and in this case there are about 80 m^2 still to be turned over — several interpretations can be tentatively suggested:

1. the necropolis is not just a casual place of burial but an important cemetery for Thorikos;
2. it was constructed in a rather unusual environment;
3. once the theatre was built, the necropolis was used continuously, even when plays were performed (epigraphically attested in the fourth century), a state of affairs which at the very least can be described as exceptional.

The juxtaposition of theatre and necropolis is thus not accidental but the result of conscious, deliberate choice, for which there must be an explanation. The construction of the theatre itself, directly to the north of the necropolis, started at the end of the archaic period. All that is preserved of this initial phase is the west end of the retaining wall of the orchestra (no longer visible). The east part of the wall collapsed in the first half of the fifth century, swept away by heavy floods, which also deposited a clearly identifiable layer of grout over the whole of the necropolis. The construction of the retaining wall was accompanied by the creation of an orchestra of about 380 m^2, considerably greater than the orchestras of the theatres at Epidauros and of Dionysos in Athens. Furthermore, the orchestra was not round but oblong. This shape too represented a deliberate choice, for according to our calculations there was sufficient room to build a circular orchestra of the same surface area. Whether other structures were in existence at that time is no longer possible to ascertain; unfortunately in the 1950s the mayor of Laurion had the orchestra bulldozed to prepare the ground for a drama festival.

Why was this unusual orchestra built at that time?[4] I think we can reject one hypothesis, namely that plays were performed here in Thorikos in the late sixth century. There remain two other possibilities: it was a place of worship or a political meeting place, or both.

The place of worship hypothesis is supported by some archaeological evidence from the fifth century, when the small Dionysos temple was built in the west parodos, an altar erected on the east side of the orchestra,[5] and a banqueting hall constructed on the east parodos. From a fragment of the *Epigone* by Eratoshenes[6] it would appear that Dionysos landed at Thorikos on his way to the house of Symmachos. Prasiai, further north along the coast, may be associated with this story by confusion with the other landing place, Prasiai in Lakonia, where the plain was known as the Garden of Dionysos.[7] Confusion with the *Homeric Hymn to Demeter* (126) is another possibility; nevertheless in the fifth century and thereafter there was an established cult of Dionysos in Thorikos, as the sacrificial calendar indicates.[8] One might also consider whether there was any relationship between this Dionysos cult and the necropolis, with Dionysos to be interpreted in this instance as a chthonic deity. This might account for the highly unusual proximity of a place of worship to a necropolis. If, as F.J. Frost pointed out,[9] the connection between Peisistratos and the cults of Dionysos is obvious, then we should accept a date for the construction of the orchestra before 528/7 B.C., which seems to me in view of the pottery a bit early, but still possible.

A further hypothesis could be that it was here that a first political meeting place, a simple agora, was laid out after the fall of the Peisistratids in 511 B.C., which would certainly tally with the dating of the wall. Why then was the place selected specifically in the vicinity of a necropolis? It would have been quite easy to lay out a 380 m^2 area elsewhere on the slopes of Velatouri Hill. If the construction could be dated more precisely on the basis of the finds, i.e., before or after 511, a more accurate interpretation could be made, but so far this has not proved possible. Nonetheless, the reconstruction of the site carried out in the fifth century enhanced its function as a place of worship, which very strongly suggests that this was its role in the archaic period. Unfortunately, the sole remaining chance of transmuting hypothesis into certainty lies in those last few square metres.

As far as lead/silver metallurgy is concerned, in the archaic period we must acknowledge that we possess only fragmentary information on the historical development of exploration and that the picture sometimes given of Laurion mines is too static. The documentary sources are concerned mainly with the fourth century and have little to say about the fifth and virtually nothing about what happened before. The archaeological sources are almost entirely of the late fifth or fourth centuries: the mines, the *ergastiria* and a few kilns are all for the most part relics of the last phase of the exploration process.

In only one mine have systematic excavations been carried out, namely, in Mine 3 at Thorikos. We may consider ourselves fortunate that a substantial quantity of pottery and lamps affords a fairly accurate idea of the historical trend of exploitation. It began during the period spanning the Late Neolithic and Early Bronze Age; there was a second phase towards the end of the Late Bronze Age, a third phase in the fourth century B.C. and a final phase in the fifth-sixth centuries A.D. Nothing has been found from other periods. Why? The actual starting point, c. 3000 B.C., was only established as a result of the discovery at that time of very rich ores with a high silver content, comparable to the discovery in the nineteenth century of virtually pure silver at the surface in the Broken Hill and Thakaringa regions of Australia. A primitive form of metallurgy developed from a situation that did not call for any specialized technology. The richest ores were the first to be processed and soon none of them were left. In the Laurion one could find in 86.6% lead sulfide a silver content ranging from 500–5000 gr. Ag. 77.5% lead carbonate (cerussite) is of a lower grade. In favorable cases the ores can be sifted by hand and smelted straight away. This, then, was what was done in the Late Bronze Age and the likelihood is that the Mycenaeans obtained the last high-grade ore from Mine 3.

Once the lead content became too low, the ore could no longer be directly smelted and this meant changing over to concentration, a process for which a whole technology had to be developed, involving the creation of *ergastiria* or washbasins. It is precisely this phase in the historical evolution that is unknown to us. How did the Athenians come to design the highly productive washbasins that we know from the fourth century? Undoubtedly after many and protracted experiments, after a great deal of trial and error, as is evidenced by the multiplicity of minor improvements effected even in the course of the fourth century. Everything that happened before is more or less a closed book for us.

In all probability, the output of the Laurion mines after the end of the archaic period cannot have been so remarkable, for the concentration problem had clearly not yet been solved. Even in the fifth-century deposits in Thorikos there are no traces of plynites. This may also account for the tremendous efforts made after 490 B.C. to uncover further rich ore deposits in the second contact. One must remember that gallery drivage advanced only 10 m. each month. These endeavors were crowned with success at Maroneia in 483 B.C.

Mine 3 at Thorikos was not taken into service again until the fourth century, with a washbasin at hand. The last batch of concentrated ores had a lead content of 51.5% and 190 gr. Ag per tonne — i.e., they were extremely low grade. Nowhere on Velatouri Hill do we find traces of metallurgy in the archaic period or even the first eighty years of the fifth century. At that time mining was being carried on elsewhere in Laurion — precisely where has not been established. Intense exploitation in the fourth century, mainly in the leaner deposits, involved the construction of a large number of wash basins, which produced substantial quantities of plynites, which together with the ecvolades are estimated at about 10,000,000 tonnes, or c. 4,000,000 m^3 over a surface area of barely 15 km^2 — in other words, an activity that must have been devastating for the region.

Notes

1. J. Servais, "Le secteur mycénien sur le haut du Vélatouri, la tombe I," *Thorikos I, 1963 Rapport préliminaire* (Brussels 1968) 29–41. The complete material was published by Michèle Devillers, "An Archaic and Classical Votive Deposit from a Mycenaean Tomb at Thorikos," *Miscellanea Graeca* fasc. 8 (Gent 1988) 78, 23.
2. J. & B. Servais-Soyez, "La tholos 'oblongue' (Tombe IV) et le tumulus (Tombe V) sur le Vélatouri," *Thorikos VIII 1972–1976, Rapport préliminaire* (Ghent 1984) 61–67.
3. T. Hackens, "La nécropole au sud de théâtre," *Thorikos II 1964, Rapport préliminaire* (Brussels 1967) 77–102.
4. H.F. Mussche, "Das Theater von Thorikos. Einige Betrachtungen," in M. Geerard (ed.), *Opes Atticae, Miscellanea philologica et historica Raymondo Bogaert et Hermanno Van Looy oblata* (Steenbrugge, The Hague 1990) 309–314.
5. A new interpretation is to be published by H. Van Looy, "Le théâtre de Thorikos et les représentations dramatiques," in *Miscellanea Graeca* fasc. 9 (forthcoming).
6. J. Powell, *Collectanea Alexandrina* (Oxford 1925) 64: Eἰσότε δὴ Θορικοῦ καλὸν ἵκανεν ἕδος.
7. Brasiai, Pausanias 3.24.4; Prasiai in other authors, Thuc. 2.56.6, 6.105.2; *Schol.* Ar. *Pax* 242; Steph. Byz. s.v. Prasiai.
8. G. Daux, *AntCl* 52 (1983) 152–54.
9. F.J. Frost, "Peisistratos, the Cults, and the Unification of Attica," *AncW* 21 (1990) 3–9.

The Rural Demes and Athenian Politics

Gregory R. Stanton

I. Politics in the Deme

In modern Greek villages, the houses are generally grouped together; there are few isolated farm houses.[1] Rather, people live together and commute out to their work. Even in Attica: the houses at Legrena near Cape Sounion are close together, though there are a few houses scattered along the gravel road north to Kamariza. From the village people walk their goats out to pasture, or drive to the patch of ground where their vegetables are growing. Vari was another example until ten or so years ago, when ribbon development along the road to Voula began to join Vari to Voula. And Varkiza developed nearby. Thiti, near Kitsi, still has a nucleus of houses, but now small properties (what we in Australia call five-acre blocks, despite having changed to hectares twenty-five years ago) are strung out along the minor road – beneath the ridge with the *horos* inscriptions discussed in section IV below – that leads to the Koropi-Aghia Marina main road.

The settlement pattern in ancient Attica seems to have been similar. Each deme had a centre of population, sometimes two. Thus Vari was the place where members of the deme Anagyrous lived.[2] From the cluster of houses people went out to feed their sheep and goats and to grow olives, barley, grapes and vegetables. Sounion had a couple of centres, but the main one – and the only early one – seems to have been in the mining area to the north, though later the harbour at Pasa Limani became important.[3]

There was a major advantage in the members of a deme living in a single population centre: it was easier for them to carry out their business as a deme. Through close proximity to one another they could see who would make a good financial official of the deme; they could discuss political and religious issues that would come up in the deme assembly. By contrast, the family that lived in the Vari Cave House, three kilometres up in the hills, for a generation or two in the fourth, or more likely the third, century B.C.[4] – if, indeed, the house was occupied more than seasonally – would not be well prepared for the debates coming up in the deme assembly, though someone presumably informed them that the meeting was on.

We know what kind of business the demes discussed largely from inscriptions. Eugene Vanderpool published an inscription found near Olimbos which contained regulations for the worship of Demeter and Kore. A hundred years ago an official of a mining company published an inscription which records a deme decision to praise Leukios of another deme for giving the land on which the new agora of Sounion was to be built.[5] It seems that the gifts of such benefactors as Leukios were additional to the regular finances of the deme. Hence the lavish praise, the recompense of honour, the privilege of a front seat at the spectacles, a share in the sacrifices on the same basis as the deme members, the exemption from taxes over which the deme has control – one or more of these rewards were bestowed on such benefactors.[6] The deme nevertheless had its normal payments and receipts to administer and those have been studied by Haussoullier in the last century and by David Whitehead in the 1980s.[7] Another significant obligation of the deme was to select the quota of members for the Council of Five Hundred that met in the city. We owe our knowledge of the deme quotas very largely to John Traill, who in the 60s and 70s studied all the lists of Athenian councillors and published them (with B.D. Meritt) and to his fundamental study *The Political Organization of Attica*. On his successive maps from 1972 to 1986 the numbers in the circles indicate the quotas of the demes.[8]

From the 57th speech of Demosthenes we learn that some local politicians – at least in Halimous – made preparations in advance of deme assemblies. A local leader in Dekeleia named Hierokles seems to have ensured that phratry screenings and ceremonies (and by implication deme assemblies) take place out at Tatoï rather than in the city, as did deme assemblies for Halimous, despite the fact that most Halimousioi still lived in the deme. Nevertheless, local politicians had to campaign for votes both in the deme of Dekeleia and in the city, where members of that deme congregated at a barber's shop near the northwest corner of the Agora.[9]

II. Demes and Trittyes

The demes, we know from the *Athenaion Politeia* attributed to Aristotle, were grouped into thirty units known as *trittyes*.[10] The outstanding work on deme locations done in the last century by Arthur Milchhöfer and in this by Eugene Vanderpool[11] – the latter's work reported and developed by John Traill and other members of the American School (William Eliot, John Camp, Merle Langdon) – has enabled us to outline the shape of most of the *trittyes*. One of the things we have learned from recent research is that the *trittyes* were not regularly-shaped blocks of land. Rather, they were groups of people, each living in their villages, who were forced to associate for certain purposes. The situation is well conveyed by the circles joined by lines on John Traill's maps.[12] The *trittyes* are not blocks of territory but centres of population grouped in what is often an odd-looking way.

In an article published in 1984 I stressed the value of compact *trittyes* for those families that happened to be influential in them. If a particular family belonged to a tribe where the rival families had to attempt to drum up support in demes scattered over a wide area, it had a great advantage over those rivals. The family that controlled, for example, the city and coastal *trittyes* of tribe VII Kekropis (Fig. 1)

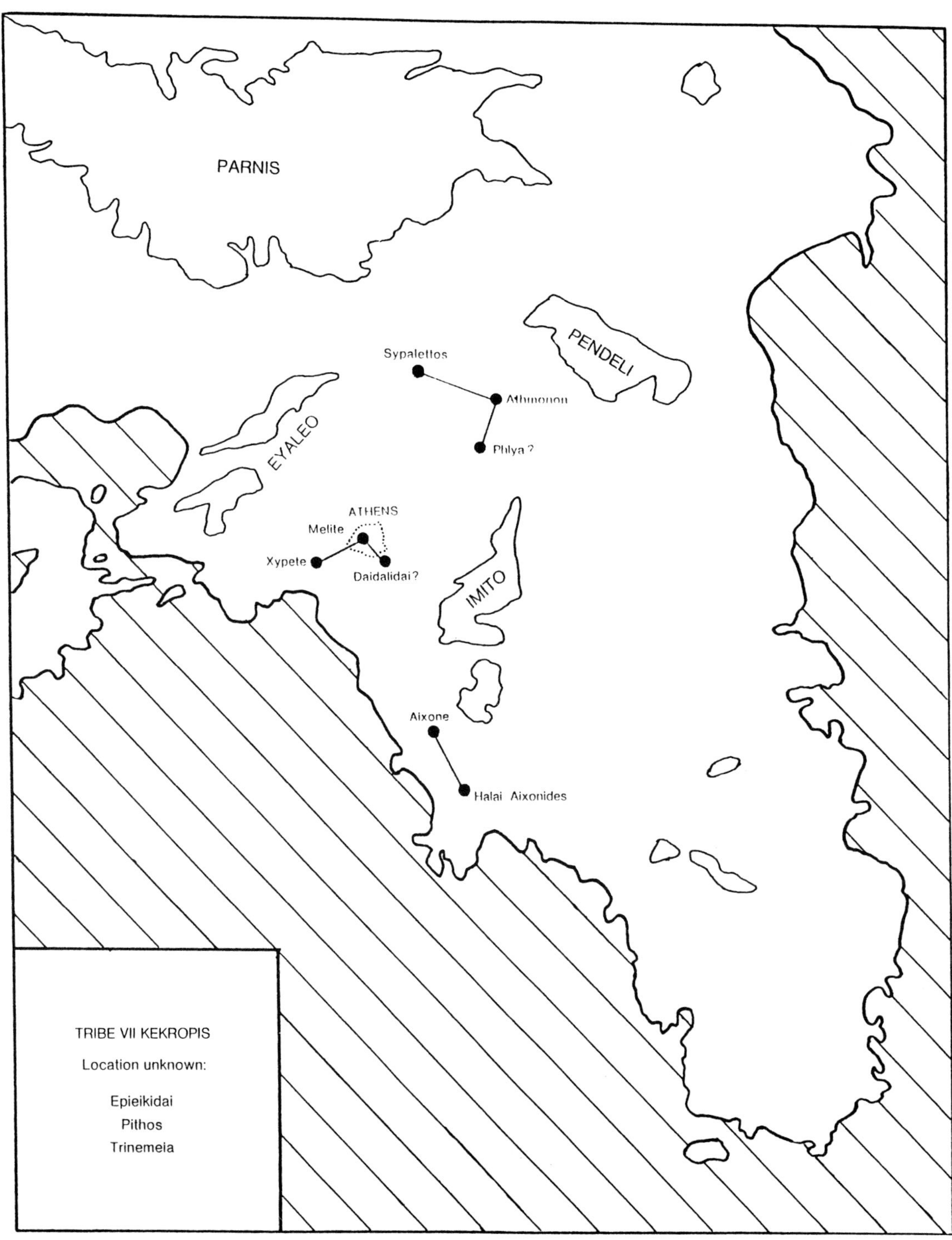

Fig. 1. The demes of VII Kekropis grouped into trittyes.

could hope to rally support for the election of a general from that tribe (at a meeting of the tribal assembly, I believe) or for a motion to be put to the assembly of all Athenian citizens. And do we know of a family which had a foothold in both city and coastal *trittyes* of Kekropis? Yes, the family of Kleisthenes himself, the Alkmeonidai, one branch of which registered in Xypete at the time of Kleisthenes's massive reform of electorates. The Alkmeonidai also had a traditional power base in the southwest coastal region, the Paralia.[13] But the tribe that illustrates most forcefully the advantages to his own family in Kleisthenes's tribal reform is X Antiokhis (Fig. 2). The city *trittys* is maximally compact: it comprises just one deme, Alopeke, in which so many Alkmeonidai are known to have been registered that it may well be called their headquarters. Contrast the inland *trittys*, where any ambitious family would have to muster support from two or three demes north of Pendeli as well as from Pallene at Stavros.[14]

Now, my picture of demes being manipulated for political purposes will be made much more complicated – though not

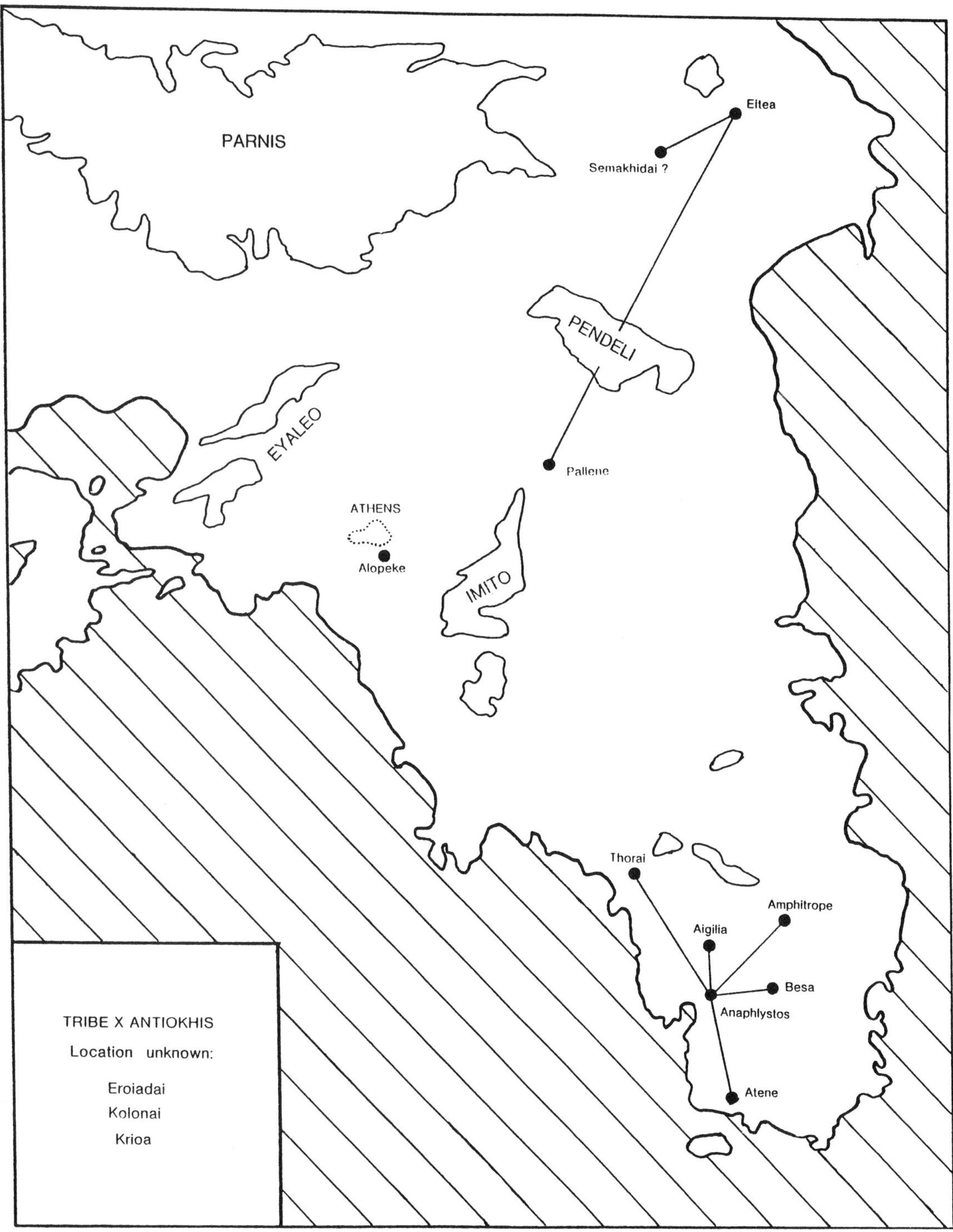

Fig. 2. The demes of X Antiokhis grouped into trittyes.

impossible – if a theory initially aired in the mid-60s and subsequently developed on a large scale by Peter Siewert and by John Traill wins the day. This theory holds that Kleisthenes devised not the topographical *trittyes* I have been illustrating, but 'equal' *trittyes* represented in the Council by either sixteen or seventeen delegates. Thus, in the case of Antiokhis, John Traill would place Eitea, Semakhidai and Kolonai, three demes that are some of the furthest from Athens, in the same *trittys* as Alopeke, just south of the city. Since a major motivation for 'equal *trittyes*' is thought to be ease of military operations, one has to ask why the members of Alopeke, who can saunter up to the Agora in half an hour or so, are linked with demes that will take five or six hours to walk to Athens. One deme, Akharnai, has twenty-two representatives on the Council, too many for a *trittys* with sixteen or seventeen representatives. In his 1986 book John Traill took the radical step of dividing Akharnai into two demes, suggesting that the population centre southwest of Menidhi (Aharnes) was a separate deme represented by six or seven councillors.[15] As one of his reviewers noted, he has yet to meet his first requisite for this new deme, a discernible body of *demotai*.[16] Moreover, the constituent demes of the 'equal *trittyes*' keep changing. In his 1987 reference work Nicholas Jones opted for Siewert's 1982 arrangement,[17] but already John Traill's 1986 book was out with quite different *trittys* affiliations. I owe a lot to John Traill's advice and information, his comments on drafts and his published work, but I naturally hope that in the next century the idea of 'equal *trittyes*' will be looked on as a false lead in the understanding of Kleisthenes's constitutional changes.

Each deme, then, sent a fixed quota of representatives to the Council of Five Hundred every year. It has been inferred that a majority of Athenian citizens enjoyed, or endured, this experience at least once in their lifetime.[18] So the role of rural demes in sending representatives to the Council played an important educational role in the democracy. Deme members dealt with all kinds of issues – ranging from religious matters to foreign alliances and the starting and ending of war – as they prepared the agenda for the Assembly. They also administered financial, judicial and religious matters and dealt with public works and maintenance of the navy.[19] Moreover, for one-tenth of the year each tribal contingent of fifty acted as an executive, as *prytaneis*.[20]

III. Demes and Assembly Meetings

Many of the rural demes, especially in the Sounion and Marathon areas, were so far from the city that members living there and wishing to attend a meeting of the Athenian Assembly must have walked in to Athens the afternoon before the meeting. In these circumstances the deme assembly constituted a valuable training in democratic procedures for members of rural demes.

There is some evidence that members of a deme gathered in the same area on the Pnyx during meetings of the Athenian Assembly. Peter Bicknell and I argued, in an article published in 1987, that in the fifth century B.C. members of *trittyes* were expected – but not compelled – to assemble around signs fixed in the floor of the Assembly place. We were encouraged in this view by the holes for *stelai* (and the remains of one *stele*) in the rock and earth floor at the front of the third stage of the Pnyx (Fig. 3). We believed that the simple *trittys* inscriptions, saying '*trittys* of Kerameis' and so on, belonged to the fifth-century Pnyx (Fig. 4). In particular, a *stele* in the Epigraphical Museum saying '*trittys* of Lakiadai' is still leaded into a huge lump of Akropolis limestone which was presumably used to stand the *stele* upright in the earth terrace at the front of the auditorium. There is another heavy block in the Agora Museum saying '*trittys* of Skambonidai'; it also would not be easily pushed over if sunk in the terrace. But *stelai* for rural demes, whether inland or coastal, must have been sunk directly in the smoothed rock floor of the Pnyx. We have one such *stele* in the Agora Museum, belonging to the *trittys* of Sphettos. We also have records of excavators, Crow and Clarke in the nineteenth century and Kourouniotis and Homer Thompson in the early 1930s, finding slots for *stelai* in the floor of Pnyx I?[21]

In the second stage of the Pnyx, which existed from 404/3 to at least 346 B.C. and possibly later, there was evidently a significant change in the position of the rural demes. Inland demes, it seems, were now at the front of the auditorium, able to heckle speakers and precipitate applause.

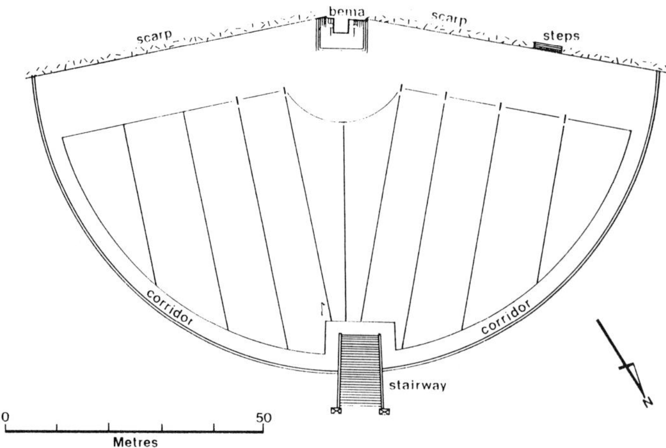

Fig. 3. Slots for stelai *in Pnyx III and suggested grouping by tribes.*

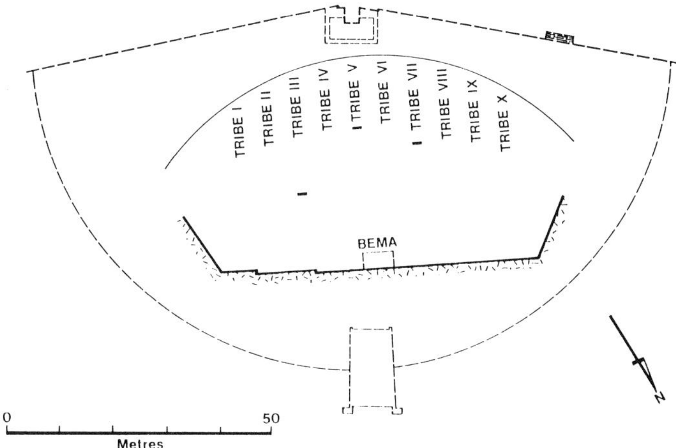

Fig. 4. Slots for stelai *in Pnyx I and suggested grouping by tribes.*

At least, speakers from inland demes were more prominent in the Assembly than their counterparts from city and coastal demes in this period.[22]

IV. Demes and Territory

In the final section of this paper I want to draw attention to increasing concern on the part of demes with what they considered their territory. Thirty years ago William Eliot published a series of inscriptions (discovered by M.T. Mitsos, Eugene Vanderpool and students from the American School) along a ridge near Thiti, all with their feet towards the valley running down to the sea at Aghia Marina. John Traill believes that they separate the demes of Upper Lamptrai and Coastal Lamptrai and, by implication, the inland *trittys* (to which he would assign Upper Lamptrai) from the coastal *trittys* of tribe I. I believe that they tell the members of the deme Pambotadai to the south not to bring their sheep and goats over into the territory of Lamptrai.[23] Not far away, in Kaminia near Vouliagmeni, we now know, thanks to Merle Langdon, that there is a pair of inscriptions saying 'boundary', 'boundary'. Indeed, we confirmed ten days before this conference that there is a third inscription on the ridge saying 'boundary'. The members of two demes, Anagyrous to the east and Halai Aixonides to the west, seem to have agreed to demarcate this sector of their boundary.[24] The most extensive series of such *horoi* known is in Megalo Bafi near Legrena: the deme Atene telling members of the deme in the Legrena valley – possibly Amphitrope, possibly Sounion – to keep off their fertile upland valley.[25] Josiah Ober published another series discovered by Vanderpool above Kesariani; Merle Langdon relocated one of a pair linking Likavitos with Skhisti Petra.[26] Fig. 5 shows this *horos* inscription and Fig. 6 the view from the inscription in

Fig. 5. Horos *inscription to be read in a downward direction on Likavitos.*

Fig. 6. View from Likavitos horos *inscription towards Skhisti Petra.*

the direction of Skhisti Petra. These sets of *horoi* seem to be in many parts of Attica. John Traill once suggested to me that you could set a group of American School students loose almost anywhere in rural Attica and tell them to find rock-cut inscriptions saying *'horos'*. They apparently did just that in 1979 in the Anavissos area, finding two *horoi* near the ravine Ari.[27]

Most if not all of these series of *horoi* must be deme boundaries, and generally they represent attempts by one deme to maintain control of rough pasture for sheep and goats. Sometimes there was evidently agreement between two demes to carve these inscriptions. Again we owe it to John Traill that an impressive dossier of information has been assembled and made public.[28] I hope that Merle Langdon will publish soon the further series that he has been locating. Ten years ago there were just two series of such *horoi* - that is, discounting isolated inscriptions, singletons. Now those two sets have grown to eight. In the second half of the fourth century, then, the rural demes became concerned with control of land and water resources - not just arable land and fishing, but rough grazing land as well.[29]

Two thousand five hundred years ago Kleisthenes or a commission set up under his bill manipulated the demes into *trittyes*. The family of Kleisthenes, in my view, took advantage of this reorganisation by putting a contingent of their supporters - the people in the city and its adjacent coastline who depended on the Alkmeonidai for the continuation of their citizenship - in all tribes, via the city *trittyes*.[30] They also seem to have arranged special advantages for themselves in three tribes - I Erekhtheis, VII Kekropis and X Antiokhis - by putting a city *trittys* in which they had influence together with a coastal *trittys* in which they had a base.[31] The Alkmeonidai, in my view, did not believe in democracy any more than did the Peisistratidai - or, for that matter, Sulla or Caesar.

It is clear to me from the fragments of his poetry that Solon also did not believe in democracy - indeed, he was too early for such ideas.[32] But the steps he took to resolve conflict at the level of clan leaders began the development of Athenian democracy. The tyrant family, by their long dominance of Athenian affairs, pushed other noble families closer to the common people. After the expulsion of the Peisistratidai, Isagoras and Kleisthenes resumed the old game of politics. Kleisthenes added to his faction *en masse* members of the lower classes in the city and its port - partly by a large-scale enfranchisement or re-enfranchisement and partly by a fundamental reorganisation of the citizen body, a reorganisation whose details he could scarcely have spelled out in advance.[33] Herodotos makes clear that by the adhesion of this *clientela* and the passage of the tribal reform Kleisthenes overcame his opponents.[34] Immediate political gain was the intention. But through Kleisthenes his family, the Alkmeonidai, turned out like other aristocrats before them (Solon, the Peisistratidai) effectively to be promoters of the classical Athenian democracy. *Αυτά που έχω πει, είναι όσα εγώ πιστεύω*, as Herodotos said.[35]

Notes

I would like to thank the organisers of this conference and particularly the chairperson of the session, Frank J. Frost, for inviting me to give the oral version of this paper in Athens. The following special abbreviations are used:

Eliot — C.W.J. Eliot, *Coastal Demes of Attika: A Study of the Policy of Kleisthenes* [*Phoenix* Suppl. 5] (Toronto 1962)

Demos — J.S. Traill, *Demos and Trittys: Epigraphical and Topographical Studies in the Organization of Attica* (Toronto 1986)

POA — J.S. Traill, *The Political Organization of Attica: A Study of the Demes, Trittyes, and Phylai, and their Representation in the Athenian Council* [*Hesperia* Suppl. 14] (Princeton 1975)

Thorikos and the Laurion — H.F. Mussche (ed.), *Thorikos and the Laurion in Archaic and Classical Times* [*Miscellanea Graeca* 1] (Ghent 1975)

1. See, for example, J. du Boulay, *Portrait of a Greek Mountain Village* (Oxford 1974) and W.H. McNeill, *The Metamorphosis of Greece since World War II* (Oxford 1978), chapter 4. In 1971 less than 20% of rural settlements comprised fewer than fifty inhabitants: J.M. Wagstaff in R. Clogg (ed.), *Greece in the 1980s* (London 1983) 16. This despite the fact that the smallest category of settlements must grow as rural settlements with fifty or more inhabitants decline: J.M. Wagstaff, *The Development of Rural Settlements: A Study of the Helos Plain in Southern Greece* (Amersham 1982) 14 (on the clustered pattern of settlements: ibid. 86–89). T.M. Whitelaw sought to explore the causes of the shift in settlement patterns in northwestern Keos since the 1920s from a highly nucleated to a more dispersed pattern, in J.F. Cherry et al., *Landscape Archaeology as Long-Term History: Northern Keos in the Cycladic Islands from Earliest Settlement until Modern Times* [*Monumenta Archaeologica* 16] (Los Angeles 1991) 403–54, especially 412–19, 428–30 (428 for the conclusion that dispersed residence was initially only a seasonal phenomenon). In the same volume (383–402) S.B. Sutton attributed the shift in Keos as a whole from a large population concentrated in a single town (Chora/Hora) to a more dispersed settlement distribution (Fig. 20.1 on 386) largely to Keian involvement in national and international forces. For documentation that farmers will walk for five hours or more to the most distant among various scattered fields see J.M. Wagstaff and S. Augustson in C. Renfrew and Wagstaff (eds.), *An Island Polity: The Archaeology of Exploitation in Melos* (Cambridge 1982) 106–133.
2. The case for identifying Vari as Anagyrous, argued by Eliot (35–46) in the 1960s, has recently been re-stated by M.K. Langdon, "The Topography of Coastal Erechtheis," *Chiron* 18 (1988) 43–54. See also G.R. Stanton, "The Tribal Reform of Kleisthenes the Alkmeonid," *Chiron* 14 (1984) 27–28.
3. The deme centre is surely to be placed in the upper Agrileza valley, where the decree of the deme *IG* II^2, 1180 (infra n. 5) was found in the nineteenth century (so Langdon [supra n. 2] 48 n. 20; id., "Two Hoplite Runners at Sounion," *Hesperia* 60 [1991] 311 n. 5). An unpublished excavation of recent years has revealed settlement not far above K.E. Konofagos' excavation of an industrial area (reported in *Το αρχαίο Λαύριο* [Athens 1980] 375–89). For the site at Pasa Limani see M. Salliora-Oikonomakou, "Αρχαία αγορά στο Λιμάνι Πασά του Λαυρίου," *ArchDelt* 34 (1979) [1986] A' 161–73 (using *αγορά* in the title of the article; for the alternative of a depot of the metallurgical trade see J.E. Jones, "The Laurion Silver Mines," *GaR* 29 [1982] 169–83 at 172).
4. Vari Cave House: J.E. Jones, A.J. Graham and L.H. Sackett, "An Attic Country House Below the Cave of Pan at Vari," *BSA* 68 (1973) 355–452. The outside dates of c. 350 – c. 275 B.C. offered by the excavators (ibid. 360, 363–64, 374, 415–18; J.E. Jones, "Another Country House in Attica," *Archaeology* 28 [1975] 6–15 at 14; id., "Hives and Honey of Hymettus: Beekeeping in Ancient Greece," *Archaeology* 29 [1976] 80–91 at 80) should be lowered to the third century in accordance with the redating summarised by S.I. Rotroff in H.A. Thompson et al., *Hellenistic Pottery and Terracottas* (Princeton 1987) 1–6, 185.
5. Olimbos: E. Vanderpool, "A *Lex Sacra* of the Attic Deme Phrearrhioi," *Hesperia* 39 (1970) 47–53; *Thorikos and the Laurion* 21–42 at 25–26. Sounion: *IG* II^2, 1180; finding place: A. Kordhellas, "Λαυρεωτικαὶ ἀρχαιότητες," *AM* 19 (1894) 241; for Kordhellas' position see P. Wolters, ibid. 244.
6. See, for example, *IG* II^2, 1186 (crown worth 1,000 drakhmai, praise, public announcement at the tragedy competition of the Dionysia in the deme, right to a front seat, exemption for self and descendants from taxes controlled by the deme, payment of expenses for the sacrifice, and any other reward desired). I deal with such inscriptions in my paper "The Beginnings of Euergetism in Classical Athens" given at the Xe Congrès internationale d'épigraphie grecque et latine in October 1992.
7. B. Haussoullier, *La vie municipale en Attique: Essai sur l'organisation des dèmes au quatrième siècle* (Paris 1883); D. Whitehead, *The Demes of Attica 508/7 – ca. 250 B.C.* (Princeton 1986). Deme business: Haussoullier, chapter 2 of the first part; Whitehead 111–20. Financial affairs: Haussoullier 62–84; Whitehead, chapter 6.
8. B.D. Meritt and J.S. Traill, *Agora* XV, *Inscriptions: The Athenian Councillors* (Princeton 1974); J.S. Traill, *POA* and *Demos*. Maps 1–2 in *POA*, drawn in 1972, had been replaced by a revised version of Map 2 by the time the book appeared in 1975. Further refinements in our knowledge of deme quotas are taken account of in the coloured map at the back of *Demos*.
9. Halimous meeting in the city: Dem. 57.9–10 (cf. 15, 56, 60 for the name of the deme). Preparations: 57.9–16. Concentration at Halimous: 57.10. Phratry of the Demotionidai to meet in the deme of Dekeleia: *IG* II^2, 1237.52–55. Informal gathering in the city: Lysias 23.2–3; *IG* II^2, 1237.61–64; J. Threpsiades and E. Vanderpool, "Πρὸς τοῖς Ἑρμαῖς," *ArchDelt* 18 (1963) A' 99–114 at 108–10. (The above lines of the Dekeleia inscription are translated in G.R. Stanton, *Athenian Politics c. 800 – 500 B.C.* [London 1990] 191–93.) Display of phratry agenda in both places: lines 121–25 (a later decree). Cf. C.W. Hedrick, Jr., *The Decree of the Demotionidai* (Atlanta 1990) 54–55 (with a translation of the whole inscription at 14–17; id., "Phratry Shrines of Attica and Athens," *Hesperia* 60 (1991) 241–68, especially 243–44, 253–54, 261–64.
10. *Athenaion Politeia* 21.4: διένειμε δὲ καὶ τὴν χώραν κατὰ δήμους τριάκοντα μέρη, δέκα μὲν τῶν περὶ τὸ ἄστυ, δέκα δὲ τῆς παραλίας, δέκα δὲ τῆς μεσογείου, καὶ ταύτας ἐπονομάσας τριττῦς ἐκλήρωσεν τρεῖς εἰς τὴν φυλὴν ἑκάστην, ὅπως ἑκάστη μετέχῃ πάντων τῶν τόπων. "[Kleisthenes] divided the country into thirty parts – ten from the areas about the city, ten from the coastal district, and ten from the inland – each composed of a number of demes. These parts he called *trittyes*, and he assigned three *trittyes* by lot to each tribe in such a way that each tribe had one *trittys* from each of the three regions".
11. A. Milchhöfer, *Erläuternder Text* to E. Curtius and J.A. Kaupert, *Karten von Attika* (Berlin 1881–1900). E. Vanderpool's work is seen, for example, in "The Deme of Marathon and the Herakleion," *AJA* 70 (1966) 319–23; "The Two Attic Demes of Eitea," *ArchDelt* 25 (1970) A' 215–16; "The Attic Deme Phegaia," *Mélanges helléniques offerts à Georges Daux* (Paris 1974) 339–43 and "A South Attic Miscellany," *Thorikos and the Laurion* 21–26. But much of his learning was incorporated in Traill's conspectus of deme locations in *POA* (37–54; although this has been replaced by *Demos* 125–40, Traill's conclusions at *POA* 54–55 still have some force).
12. Maps 1–2 in *POA* and the coloured map at the back of *Demos*, on which, however, the lines joining demes presuppose 'equal', not topographical, *trittyes*.
13. G.R. Stanton, *Chiron* 14 (1984) 1–41, especially 11–16, 33–38. Kallixenos son of Aristonymos, described on one ostrakon as 'of the Alkmeonidai', came from Xypete: G.A. Stamires and E. Vanderpool, "Kallixenos the Alkmeonid," *Hesperia* 19 (1950) 376–90, especially 377–78 and 389; Stanton (supra n. 9) 181–83.
14. Stanton (supra n. 13) 23–25 with map on 22. Alopeke as headquarters of Alkmeonid party: D.M. Lewis, "Cleisthenes and Attica," *Historia* 12 (1963) 22–40 at 23.
15. W.E. Thompson, "Τριττῦς τῶν πρυτάνεων," *Historia* 15 (1966) 1–10; J.S. Traill, "Diakris, the Inland Trittys of Leontis," *Hesperia* 47 (1978) 89–109; P. Siewert, *Die Trittyen Attikas und die Heeresreform des Kleisthenes* [*Vestigia* 33] (Munich 1982); J.S. Traill, "An Interpretation of Six Rock-cut Inscriptions in the Attic Demes of Lamptrai," in *Studies in Attic Epigraphy, History and Topography Presented to Eugene Vanderpool* [*Hesperia* Suppl. 19] (Princeton 1982) 162–71; *Demos*, *passim* (for Antiokhis, 139–40 and coloured map; for Akharnai, 133–34 and 142–44).

16. D. Whitehead, *Phoenix* 41 (1987) 441–43 at 443; cf. *POA* 75–76.
17. N.F. Jones, *Public Organization in Ancient Greece: A Documentary Study* [*Memoirs of the American Philosophical Society* 176] (Philadelphia 1987) 33–35.
18. A.W. Gomme, *More Essays in Greek History and Literature* (Oxford 1962) 185, suggested that between a quarter and a third or more of citizens served in the Council. But the implication of M.H. Hansen's view that about one-fifth served twice (*Demography and Democracy: The Number of Athenian Citizens in the Fourth Century B.C.* [Herning 1985] 51–55, 64, 66) is that the vast majority served once (acknowledged by Hansen in *The Athenian Assembly in the Age of Demosthenes* [Oxford 1987] 114).
19. P.J. Rhodes, *The Athenian Boule* (Oxford 1972), especially chapters 3–4 and 211–13.
20. See especially the lists of *prytaneis* in *Agora* XV (supra n. 8). One is translated with notes in Stanton (supra n. 9) 160–62.
21. G.R. Stanton and P.J. Bicknell, "Voting in Tribal Groups in the Athenian Assembly," *GRBS* 28 (1987) 51–92; Stanton (supra n. 9) 159–60. Cf. J.M. Crow and J.T. Clarke, *Papers ASCSA* 4 (1885/86) 205–60 at 225 and Survey; K. Kourouniotis and H.A. Thompson, "The Pnyx in Athens," *Hesperia* 1 (1932) 90–217 at 104–105, 106, fig. 6. The photograph of the '*trittys* of Lakiadai' *stele* in *Demos* (Plate 10) shows the lump of limestone in which it is embedded.
22. *GRBS* 28 (1987) 80–86, 88, 89–92 (this Appendix partially superseded by P.J. Bicknell, "Athenians Politically Active in Pnyx II," *GRBS* 30 [1989] 83–100 at 85–92). On the interpretation of Aristophanes, *Ekklesiazousai* see further Bicknell 98–100.
23. Eliot 63–64 with map on 57; Traill in *Studies* (supra n. 15) 162–71, reiterated in *Demos* 118–19; G.R. Stanton, "Some Attic Inscriptions," *BSA* 79 (1984) 289–306 at 298–301.
24. Langdon (supra n. 2) 43–54; cf. H. Lauter, "Zwei Horos-Inschriften bei Vari," *AA* (1982) 299–315; Stanton (supra n. 23) 301–303, 305.
25. H. Lohmann, *Hellenika: Jahrbuch für die Freunde Griechenlands* (1983) 98–117 at 99–104. Amphitrope: cf. *Demos* 140.
26. Alepovouni above Kesariani: J. Ober, "Rock-cut Inscriptions from Mt. Hymettos," *Hesperia* 50 (1981) 68–77 at 73–77; M.K. Langdon, "Hymettiana I," *Hesperia* 54 (1985) 257–70 at 257–60; cf. Stanton (supra n.23) 301–303. Likavitos – Skhisti Petra: *Demos* 117, 119–20.
27. *Demos* 117, 120.
28. *Demos* 116–22 with Map 4; cf. my heart-felt comment in *Gnomon* 63 (1991) 29.
29. Stanton (supra n. 23) 304–306.
30. Stanton (supra n. 13) 7, 39–41; id. (supra n. 9) 165–67. Commission: id. (supra n. 13) 3.
31. Stanton (supra n. 13) 11, 38–39; id. (supra n. 9) 150–51, 156–59.
32. Stanton (supra n. 9) 40–49, 52–54.
33. Enfranchisement: supra n. 30. Prior outline of reform: A. Andrewes, "Kleisthenes' Reform Bill," *CQ* n.s. 27 (1977) 241–48.
34. Hdt. 5.69.2 with 5.66.2. Cf. Stanton (supra n. 9) 148 n. 4.
35. Hdt. 2.120.5: καὶ ταῦτα μέν, τῇ ἐμοὶ δοκέει, εἴρηται. My views on the aristocratic promoters of Athenian democracy are outlined in *Ancient Society* (a journal produced at Macquarie University, Sydney, and renamed *Ancient History*) 12 (1982) 5–14.

'Ισονόμους τ' 'Αθήνας ἐποιησάτην: The Agora and the Democracy

T. Leslie Shear, Jr.

ἐν μύρτου κλαδὶ τὸ ξίφος φορήσω
ὥσπερ 'Αρμόδιος καὶ 'Αριστογείτων
ὅτε τὸν τύραννον κτανέτην
ἰσονόμους τ' 'Αθήνας ἐποιησάτην

αἰεὶ σφῷν κλέος ἔσσεται κατ' αἶαν,
φίλταθ' 'Αρμόδιος καὶ 'Αριστογείτων
ὅτι τὸν τύραννον κτανέτην
ἰσονόμους τ' 'Αθήνας ἐποιησάτην

"In a myrtle bough I will wear the sword like Harmodios and Aristogeiton when they killed the tyrant and made Athens a city of equal rights.... Forever will you both have fame on earth, dearest Harmodios and Aristogeiton, because they slew the tyrant and made Athens a city of equal rights."

These stirring verses from the famous Attic drinking song preserve the earliest reference, almost certainly contemporary, to the tumultuous events which brought about the liberation of Athens from tyranny and led to the creation of the democratic government, whose birthday we are here to celebrate after 2,500 years. Commentators on these lines, however, have been at pains to explain how the poetry of the symposium could embrace such brazen falsification of historical fact.[1] Every adult Athenian who sang these verses must have known that Harmodios and Aristogeiton did *not* kill the tyrant Hippias; and far from liberating Athens their assassination of his brother Hipparchos in 514 B.C. caused the tyrant to become even more savagely oppressive. Moreover, it was Kleisthenes, not Harmodios and Aristogeiton, who established the democratic form of government; and both Herodotos and Thucydides were careful to set the record straight less than a century after the events.[2] If popular songs of late archaic Athens could so blatantly disregard the cause and effect of contemporary events, I hope that I, too, may be forgiven for altering likewise, without compunction, the subjects of the dual verb in my title. In our investigation of the archaeology of democracy, two factors, I would suggest, served more than any others to make Athens ἰσονόμους, that is to create the principle of political equality under the laws: the growth of the Agora and the rule of the Demos, these two, a place and an idea. It will be the thesis of this paper that their mutual development was inextricably bound up with each other during the closing years of the sixth century B.C., and that the invention of democracy has left clear traces in the archaeological record.

Students of Athenian topography and monuments have long recognized that the area northwest of the Acropolis, which would in time become the Agora of the classical city, was remarkably slow and late to develop. Only at the very end of the archaic period had the Agora of Athens acquired the architectural appurtenances that one associates with the civic center of a Greek polis: temples and altars, buildings for political functions, offices for the city's magistrates, and large spaces for public meetings and military musters. Indeed, even in the appallingly fragmentary state of our sources, it is plain that the political and constitutional history of Athens is nearly a century older than the archaeological history of her civic buildings. This strange fact must be thought all the more surprising because the archaeological record shows that Athens emerged from the Dark Ages as a flourishing late Geometric community by the end of the eighth century B.C. The high quality of Attic Geometric pottery attests to the prosperity of the ceramic industry, while great funerary vessels from the Dipylon Cemetery marked the ostentatious burials of the richest Athenians. That exquisite gold jewelry was buried with the dead graphically illustrates a re-emergence in the city's wealth. At the same time the importation of precious luxury goods, probably from the Levant, gives evidence of revived commercial contact with distant lands.[3]

Our knowledge of Geometric Athens is, of course, based almost exclusively upon funerary offerings from dozens of excavated burials, and the contents of a few household wells; but the distribution of these deposits in relation to the topography of the city is in itself illuminating. The Geometric cemeteries spread nearly as far to the west, north, and south of the Acropolis as the limits of the later classical city. The low-lying area to the northwest of the Acropolis, where the lower slopes of the Areopagos descend gently to the stream-bed of the Eridanos, had been a region of private fields and scattered dwellings from the Bronze Age, and an unbroken sequence of small family burial plots and the shafts of a few household wells bear witness to the private tenure of this land at the end of the Geometric period. By contrast the area immediately south, southeast, and east of the Acropolis, as far as the Ilissos River, has yielded no Geometric cemeteries.[4] From this circumstance, it seems fair to infer that the most densely occupied part of the early city lay in that quarter, where burial of the dead would then be inappropriate in such close proximity to the dwellings of the living. In this respect, the archaeology of the city is in striking agreement with one of our earliest explicit statements about the topography of archaic Athens. Thucydides (2.15) described the time before the union of Attica under Theseus.

> τὸ δὲ πρὸ τοῦ ἡ ἀκρόπολις ἡ νῦν οὖσα πόλις ἦν, καὶ τὸ ὑπ' αὐτὴν πρὸς νότον μάλιστα τετραμμένον.
>
> "The city consisted of the present Acropolis and the district beneath it looking rather towards the south."

In this region he located many of the city's oldest cults and sanctuaries, among them the shrines of Olympian Zeus, of Pythian Apollo, and of Dionysos in the Marshes.

That some of Athens' most venerable sanctuaries should be sought at the eastern end of the Acropolis has recently received dramatic confirmation in the discovery of a Hellenistic decree honoring a priestess of Aglauros. The text specifies that the marble stele on which it is inscribed is to be erected "in the sanctuary of Aglauros." Since the inscription was found in association with its original base, on the spot where it was first displayed, it now provides formal proof for the location of that famous shrine, where the Persian invaders of 480 B.C. first scaled the Acropolis rock at its steepest cliff.[5] The inscription, however, did not come to light at the caves on the northwestern slope of the Acropolis where the universal opinion of modern scholars had previously placed the sanctuary of Aglauros. On the contrary, the monument lay at the easternmost tip of the citadel (Fig. 1), just outside the great natural cave which overlooks the southeastern quarter of the city.[6] The discovery of

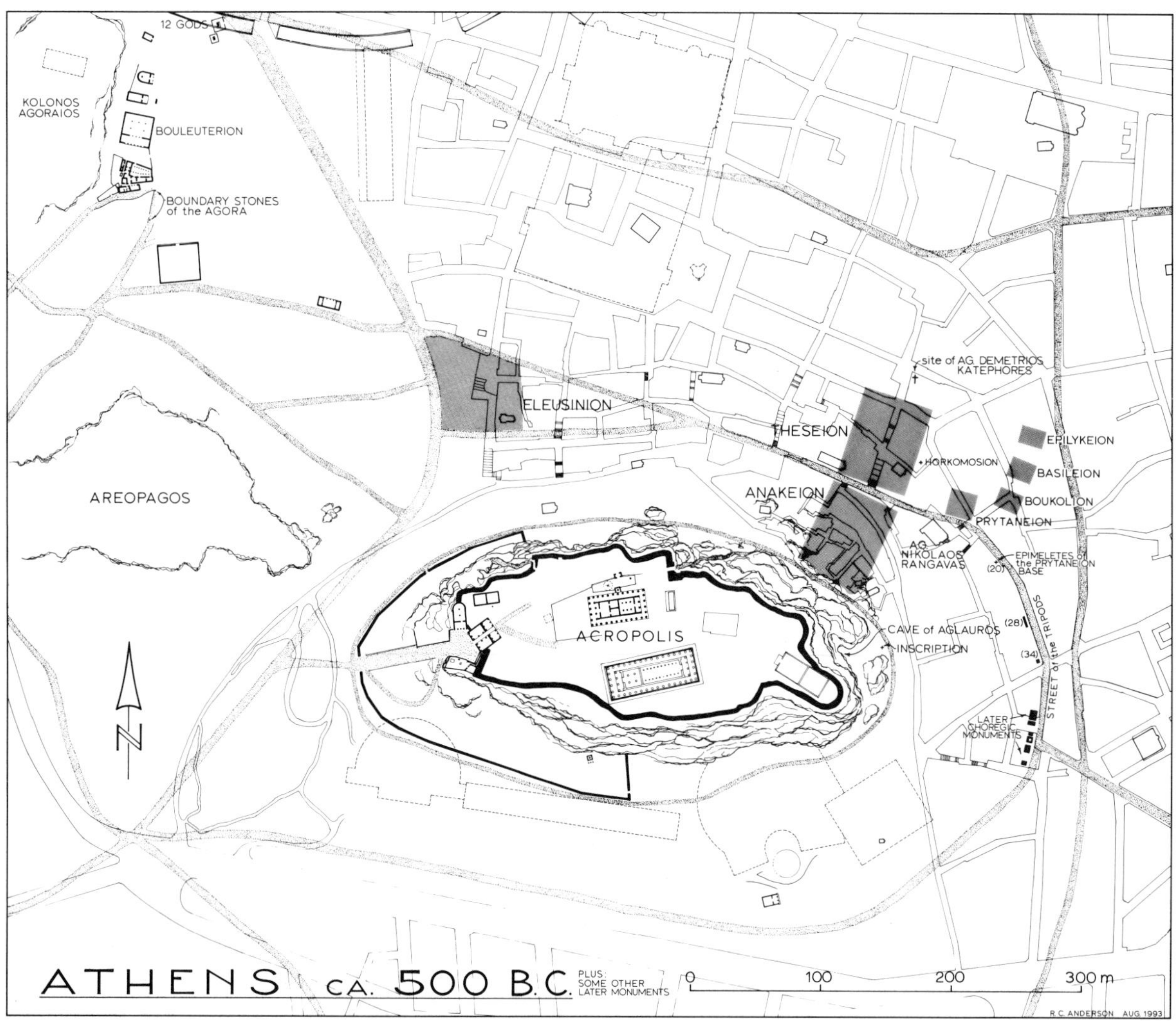

Fig. 1. Acropolis and Agora, ca. *500 B.C., showing locations of earliest civic buildings, sanctuaries, and streets in relation to modern city blocks.*

the true Aglaureion at this spot has, of course, disorganized all scholarly discussions concerning the topography of Athens' most ancient monuments, which some of our American colleagues have long hoped to identify in the diametrically opposite direction.

Positive identification of the sanctuary of Aglauros has important ramifications for our knowledge of early archaic Athens. It forces us to reconsider the location of the city's oldest public buildings, and it affects the way we envision some of the anecdotes of earliest Athenian history. It needs to be emphasized most that the position of the buildings and the locale of the events must now be sought close beneath the eastern cliffs of the Acropolis. Here, Pausanias[7] placed the *temenos* of Aglauros *above* the sanctuary of the Dioskouroi, the so-called Anakeion, where the Acropolis rock was steepest. In a whimsical moment, Lucian[8] depicted the philosophers assaulting the Acropolis from all sides, and some scrambled up the cliff "by setting ladders against the Anakeion." Here, too, Peisistratos, in the celebrated anecdote preserved by Polyaenus (1.21.2), summoned the Athenians to muster under arms at the Anakeion.

> Πεισίστρατος 'Αθηναίων τὰ ὅπλα βουλόμενος παρελέσθαι, παρήγγειλεν ἥκειν ἅπαντας εἰς τὸ 'Ανάκειον μετὰ τῶν ὅπλων. Οἱ μὲν ἧκον· ὁ δὲ προῆλθε βουλόμενος δημηγορῆσαι, καὶ σμικρᾷ τῇ φωνῇ λέγειν ἤρχετο. Οἱ δὲ ἐξακούειν μὴ δυνάμενοι, προέλθειν αὐτὸν ἠξίωσαν εἰς τὸ προπύλαιον, ἵνα πάντες ἐπακούσειαν. 'Επεὶ δὲ ὁ μὲν ἡσυχῇ διελέγετο, οἱ δ' ἐντείναντες τὰς ἀκοὰς προσεῖχον, οἱ ἐπίκουροι προελθόντες, ἀμάμενοι τὰ ὅπλα κατήνεγκαν εἰς τὸ ἱερὸν τῆς 'Αγραύλου.
>
> "Peisistratos, wishing to take away the Athenians' arms, sent word around that they should come armed to the Anakeion. This they did; Peisistratos came forward to make a speech, and began to speak in a low voice. His audience, not being able to hear him, asked him to go to the Propylaion, so that all might hear. Then, while he was talking quietly and they were straining their ears to catch what he said, his bodyguard came forward, took up the arms and deposited them in the shrine of Agraulos."[9]

Mention of the *propylaion*, notably in the singular, not the plural, has caused modern interpreters to localize the tyrant's ruse at the familiar western approaches to the Acropolis; and the chance discovery in the Agora of a fifth-century boundary stone of the Anakeion has long teased American excavators.[10] Both the *horos* and the anecdote must now move eastward, however; for the possibility has to be seriously entertained that the anecdote referred rather to the ancient rock-cut path, which ascended the steep northeastern flank of the hill starting just north of the Cave of Aglauros and entered the citadel by way of the prehistoric postern just east of the present Erechtheion. There is no good reason to disbelieve that the old Mycenaean gate was still open and serviceable in the mid sixth century B.C.[11]

Next after the *temenos* of Aglauros, Pausanias (1.18.3) continues his tour.

> πλησίον δὲ πρυτανεῖόν ἐστιν, ἐν ᾧ νόμοι τε οἱ Σόλωνός εἰσι γεγραμμένοι.
>
> "Nearby is the Prytaneion in which the laws of Solon are inscribed."

From here the traveler descended into the eastern parts of the city as far as the Olympieion, the Ilissos River, and the Stadium. He then returned to the Prytaneion and begins the description of his walk to the Theater of Dionysos and the southern slopes of the Acropolis with the words (1.20.1):

> ἔστι δὲ ὁδὸς ἀπὸ τοῦ πρυτανείου καλουμένη Τρίποδες
>
> "There is a street called Tripods leading from the Prytaneion."

The street of the choregic tripods is, of course, well known today from the monument of Lysikrates (*IG* II^2, 3042) (p. 32, Fig. 1) and the foundations of neighboring monuments which once lined the western side of the ancient thoroughfare curving around the eastern end of the Acropolis between the 80 m. and 85 m. contour lines.[12] A modern street still follows this line, and a part of it still bears the name Tripods. This is of interest because the street shelters several pieces of evidence bearing on the location of the Prytaneion in this immediate region. In the basement of a nineteenth-century building at 34 Tripods Street, on the corner of Thespis, is the foundation for a large choregic monument (p. 34, Fig. 3); further north beneath the building at 28 Tripods Street is preserved the even larger foundation for the northernmost choregic monument as yet found (p. 37, Figs. 5-6).[13] Formerly built into a house one block further north at 20 Tripods Street was a large marble statue base of Augustan date bearing the dedication of Theophilos, son of Diodoros, of Halai who signs as epimeletes of the Prytaneion.[14] This monument that cannot have moved far from its original position was no doubt dedicated in the Prytaneion itself, and it brings us once again to a spot close beneath the eastern escarpment of the Acropolis, and below the great cave now known to belong to Aglauros. In terms of the topography of modern Athens, we shall not be far wrong if we visualize the Anakeion in the district now called Anaphiotika, while the Byzantine church of Aghios Nikolaos Rangavas probably stands very near the site of the ancient Prytaneion (Fig. 1), and only 120 m. distant from the place where the inscription came to light in the sanctuary of Aglauros.[15]

The Prytaneion was Athens' most venerable public building, the foundation of which tradition ascribed to Theseus. It housed the city's common hearth where perpetual fire burned, where ephebes came to sacrifice at their enrolment, and whence colonists and certain religious processions set forth.[16] Worthy citizens and foreign dignitaries might dine there at public expense. Law courts in the Prytaneion tried certain classes of criminal suits;[17] there too were kept the laws of Solon, inscribed on their peculiar wooden *axones*, of which some could still be seen and quoted in the time of Plutarch and Pausanias.[18] In close proximity to the Prytaneion was a nexus of early civic offices (Fig. 1) which were so old by the fourth century B.C., if they still existed, that Aristotle in the *Constitution of the Athenians* (3.5) attributed them to a time before the legislation of Drakon.

> ἦσαν δ' οὐχ ἅμα πάντες οἱ ἐννέα ἄρχοντες, ἀλλ' ὁ μὲν βασιλεὺς εἶχε τὸ νῦν καλούμενον Βουκόλιον, πλησίον τοῦ πρυτανείου (σημεῖον δέ· ἔτι καὶ νῦν γὰρ τῆς τοῦ βασιλέως γυναικὸς ἡ σύμμειξις ἐνταῦθα γίνεται τῷ Διονύσῳ καὶ ὁ γάμος), ὁ δὲ ἄρχων τὸ πρυτανεῖον, ὁ δὲ πολέμαρχος τὸ Ἐπιλυκεῖον (ὅ πρότερον μὲν ἐκαλεῖτο πολεμαρχεῖον, ἐπεὶ δὲ Ἐπίλυκος ἀνῳκοδόμησε καὶ κατεσκεύασεν αὐτὸ πολεμαρχήσας, Ἐπιλυκεῖον ἐκλήθη), θεσμοθέται δ' εἶχον τὸ θεσμοθετεῖον. ἐπὶ δὲ Σόλωνος ἅπαντες εἰς τὸ θεσμοθετεῖον συνῆλθον.

> "The nine archons were not all together; the Basileus had what is now called the Boukolion, near the Prytaneion (an indication of this is the fact that even now the union of the wife of the Basileus with Dionysos, and their marriage, takes place there); the Archon had the Prytaneion, the Polemarch the Epilykeion (this was formerly called the Polemarcheion, but when Epilykos rebuilt and repaired it after being made Polemarch, it was named Epilykeion); the Thesmothetai had the Thesmotheteion. But in Solon's time the archons all came together in the Thesmotheteion."

In early times then, all of Athens' most senior magistrates had their offices near the Prytaneion at the east end of the Acropolis.[19] In addition to the offices enumerated by Aristotle, beside the Boukolion was a building called the Basileion in which the old Phylobasileis, or tribal kings of the four Ionian tribes, held their meetings. Perhaps nearby was the Bouzygion, the field of sacred ox-ploughing, which according to Plutarch was below the Acropolis.[20]

In this region there were in archaic times large open areas that could accommodate public gatherings of the Athenian citizenry; for when Kimon founded the hero-shrine of Theseus in 476/5, there was enough land available immediately adjacent to the Anakeion so that a spacious *temenos* could be laid out. καὶ κεῖται μὲν ἐν μέσῃ τῇ πόλει παρὰ τὸ νῦν γυμνάσιον; "and it lies in the middle of the city beside the present gymnasium," as Plutarch later described it.[21] Moreover, the best archaeological evidence for the site of the Theseion comes from four inscriptions listing the victors in the games of Theseus. All four were removed from the late Roman fortification wall by the church of Demetrios Katephores, a mere 150 m. directly down hill from the Anaphiotika where we have seen reason to locate the Anakeion (Fig. 1).[22] It is possibly a relic of common archaic practice that both civic meetings and military musters took place in the *temene* of Theseus and the Dioskouroi during the classical period. In the time of Aischines, the Thesmothetai conducted the annual allotments of public offices in the Theseion, which implies the gathering of large crowds of people.[23] In the panic that ensued on the day after the mutilation of the Herms in 415 B.C., the entire citizen levy of Athens slept under arms in public places. Everyone who lived between the long walls was ordered to report to the Theseion, and the entire cavalry, presumably between 700 and a thousand men and a like number of horses, slept in the Anakeion.[24] At another moment of crisis during the revolution of 411 B.C., the main hoplite force of the army marched up from Peiraieus and took up a position in the Anakeion, intending to confront the oligarchs of the Four Hundred.[25]

From these scattered references to buildings and incidents, one gains the impression that many functions which we associate with the agora of a Greek polis were in early archaic Athens localized beneath the east end of the Acropolis. Moreover, a single tantalizing reference actually speaks of the ἀρχαία ἀγορά, the "ancient agora." The lexicon of Harpokration, under "Pandemos Aphrodite," quotes the Athenian historian Apollodoros (second century B.C.).

> Ἀπολλόδωρος ἐν τῷ περὶ θεῶν πάνδημόν φησιν Ἀθήνησι κληθῆναι τὴν ἀφιδρυθεῖσαν περὶ τὴν ἀρχαίαν ἀγορὰν διὰ τὸ ἐνταῦθα πάντα τὸν δῆμον συνάγεσθαι τὸ παλαιὸν ἐν ταῖς ἐκκλησίαις, ἃς ἐκάλουν ἀγοράς.

> "Apollodoros in his work *On the Gods* says that the title Pandemos was given to the goddess established in the neighborhood of the ancient agora because all the Demos gathered there of old in their assemblies which they called *agorai.*"

Although interpretation of this statement is not free of topographical problems, it plainly preserves the recollection of an "old agora" on a different site from its classical successor; and it is possible that this too should be brought into relation with the early shrines and public offices that we have already considered.[26]

Let us return now to the familiar ground northwest of the Acropolis where sixty years of excavations have revealed in detail the archaeological history of the civic center. That this is the Agora of classical Athens is a central fact in the archaeology of the city. From the fifth century B.C. until the Roman conquest, the area between the Areopagos and the Eridanos River teamed with the political, cultural, and commercial activities that made Athens the greatest polis of Greece. The pertinent questions for this investigation, however, are when and in what circumstances this district became the Agora. The private fields and family cemeteries of the Geometric period gave way only gradually over time to the public space and open square of the classical market place.[27] That process implies the expropriation of private property and its conversion to public land; and the earliest architectural remains illustrate this precisely. At the southwest corner of the square (Fig. 2), lay the ruinous foundations of a long, narrow building bordering the archaic

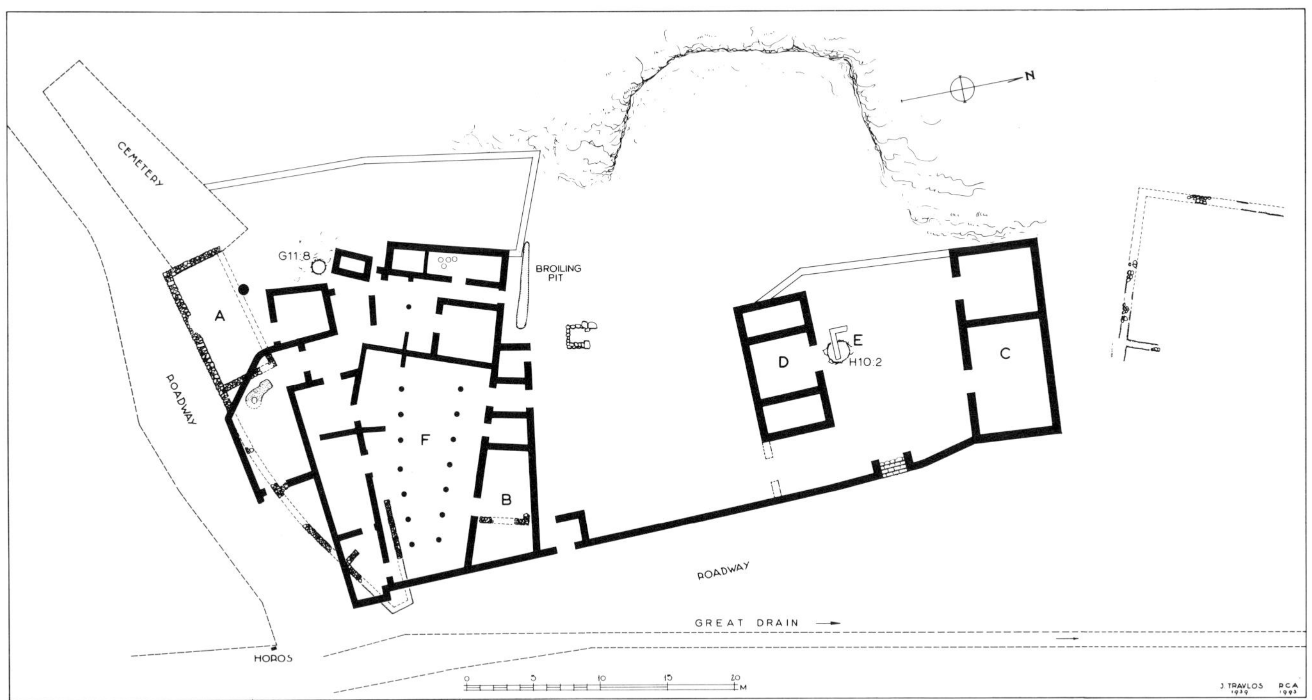

Fig. 2. Earliest buildings at southwest corner of Agora, restored, ca. *530 B.C.*

street beneath the later Tholos and its predecessors Buildings F and J. The building probably goes back to the mid seventh century, and its private ownership is certainly attested by the small potter's kiln in its open courtyard. The scrappy remains of another private industrial establishment for working iron were found under the northeast room of Building F.[28] At the southeast corner of the square, parts of two private dwellings of the early sixth century have come to light in the vicinity of the archaic fountain house (Fig. 3). Since the fountain house was built directly over one room, one infers that the private structure was demolished to make way for the public building.

To the first quarter of the sixth century belongs another building on the site of the later Bouleuterion and Metroon, a small rectangular structure of two rooms opening on a low terrace to the south (Fig. 2). The date of this Building C, not far removed in time from Solon's political reforms, and its location on a site occupied by the Boule and its archives throughout the later history of Athens beguiled the original excavator, H.A. Thompson, to suggest that it might have served in some way the operations of the old Solonian Boule of 400.[29] Thompson's identification of this so-called "Primitive Bouleuterion" has been cheerfully accepted by a number of scholars,[30] but closer examination raises serious doubts. The building was far too small to have accommodated more than a fraction of the 400 Councillors even on its southern terrace. Furthermore, there is nothing about its plan, style of construction, or scale (7 × 15 m.) to distinguish it in any way from the private house under the archaic fountain. The latter also preserves two rooms measuring 5 × 13 m. overall, and other rooms extended out in at least two directions. More indicative are the contents of a deep circular pit at the southern edge of the terrace. This was probably the well that provided water for the building, and it produced a group of pots typical in every way of Athenian domestic table ware of the period 575–525 B.C.: ten drinking cups, an oinochoe, fragments of a column krater, and a household lekane.[31] The only aspect of Building C that is public in character is the building that succeeded it on the same site. Were it not for the fact that Building C was demolished to make way for the Old Bouleuterion, nobody would have considered it anything but an ordinary domestic establishment equipped with an ordinary household well. Moreover, immediately north of Building C were traces of a light wall enclosing the courtyard of the neighboring house, some 10 m. square, which later yielded up its site to the two late archaic temples.[32]

The closing of household wells is indeed a significant phenomenon in the area of the Agora just before and just after the middle of the sixth century. In a separate study, I have drawn attention to the 17 wells of this period that were filled in and went out of use.[33] Since the abandonment of wells implies the removal of the households that used them for their water supply, their number illustrates an apparently deliberate effort to enlarge the area of the public square by the expropriation of private dwellings along the east side, at the southeast and southwest corners, and significantly at several points within the central area of the later Agora. The existence of these

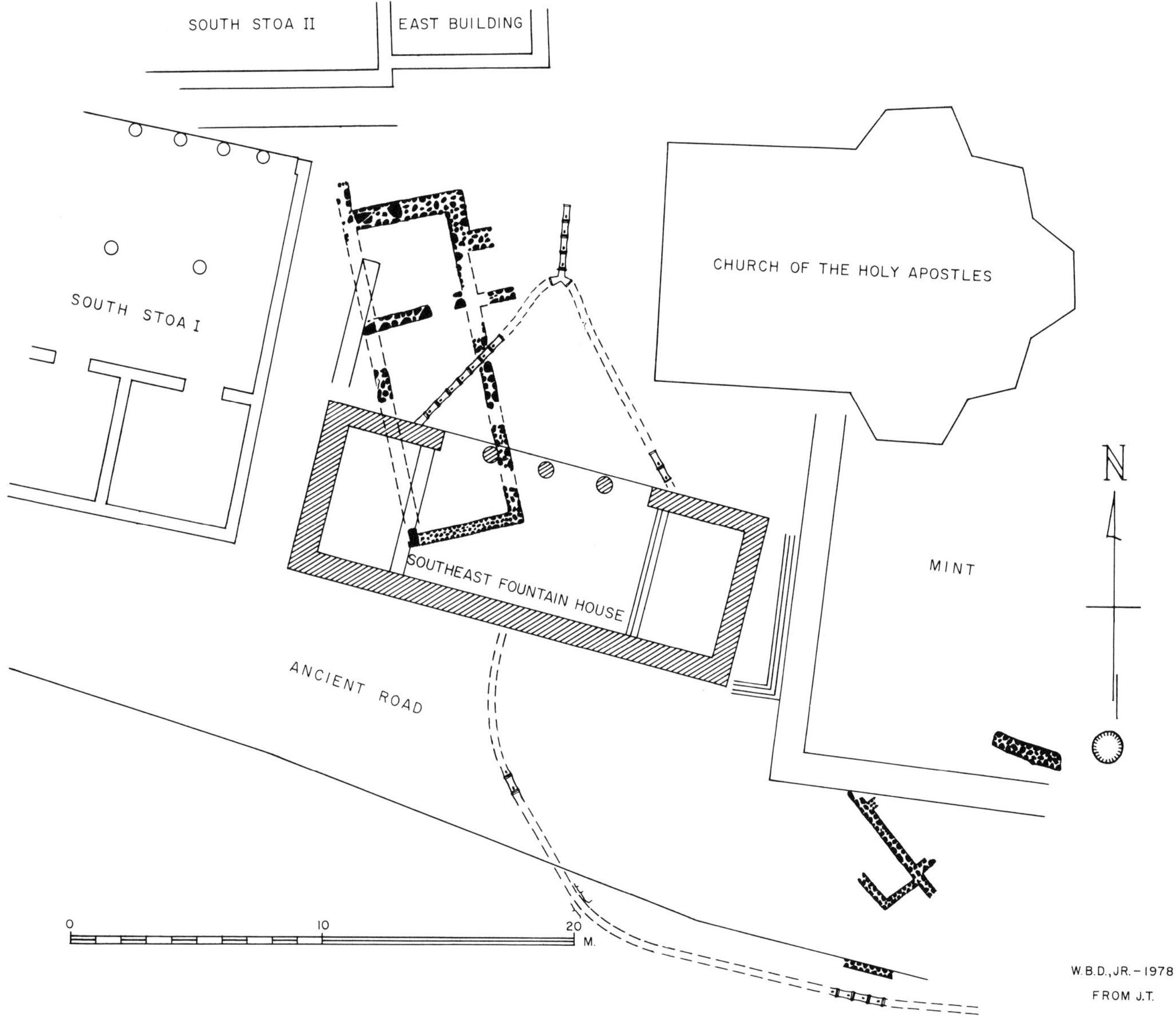

Fig. 3. Private house beneath archaic fountain at southeast corner of Agora, ca. *525 B.C.*

wells, however, is a useful reminder that a considerable part of the public square was still held in private hands as late as the middle of the sixth century.

In the third quarter of the sixth century, another building was erected beside the early structure (Building C) on the site of the later Bouleuterion. A small building of three rooms (D) closed off the terrace on the south and faced north toward the entrance of the earlier structure (Fig. 2). Farther south a larger and more complex building arose on the site of the later Tholos (Building F, G, H, I) consisting of many rooms surrounding on three sides a large colonnaded courtyard (Fig. 2). A smaller courtyard to the west was likewise enclosed by rooms which had a clearly domestic character. One was equipped with storage jars for commodities; another is possibly to be identified as a bake oven. Beside it was a household well and nearby was a broiling pit for cooking meat on spits over charcoal. A black-figured oinochoe found near the bottom of the well shows that the building was already in use early in the third quarter of the sixth century, while the latest pottery from the well of Building C provides a *terminus post quem* for the construction of Building D not much earlier than 530 B.C.[34]

The residential character of Building F has been noticed by several scholars, but its large size and elaborate plan have suggested a function more grandiose than a private dwelling.[35] In his original publication of the remains, H.A. Thompson proposed to identify the building as the official residence of the prytaneis of the Council. His argument ran that the various buildings succeeded each other both chronologically and in function on the same site. Building C was replaced by the Old Bouleuterion, just as Building D was followed by Building F, which in turn yielded the site to the Tholos, a building known to have been the seat of the prytaneis throughout antiquity.[36] On architectural grounds alone, however, it is difficult to believe that Building F succeeded Building D. The great differences in plan and dimensions suggest rather that the two were designed to fulfil entirely different functions. Furthermore, they were built very close together in time, and in fact more recent analysis of the pottery from the two wells indicates that Building F may well have been in use before the construction of Building D. The whole complex taken together has the look of a great house and its outbuildings on either side of a common courtyard.

To suppose that the building was originally built as the residence of the prytaneis in the third quarter of the sixth century is a total anachronism. The institution of a rotating committee of prytaneis presiding over the Boule surely implies the ten tribes of the Kleisthenic democracy. The earliest appearance of the prytany in the preamble of official documents is to be found in the Phaselis Decree (*IG* I³, 10) of the second quarter of the fifth century. The Hekatompedon Decree of 485 B.C. mentions a prytanis in the singular who is otherwise unattested; and it regulates the duties of the Treasurers of Athena by the days of the lunar calendar, which implies that the Bouleutic calendar based on the prytanies was not yet in use.[37] Indeed, P.J. Rhodes has convincingly demonstrated that the prytany system was not introduced until the constitutional reforms of Ephialtes in 462 B.C.[38] It should be obvious, then, that Building F can have had nothing whatever to do with the prytaneis of the Council in the third quarter of the sixth century.

The evident domestic character of the establishment, taken together with what is at this early period an almost palatial grandeur in scale and plan, has led to the interpretation of the building as the residence of a prominent personage. It was the attractive suggestion of H.A. Thompson, first put forward tentatively some years ago, and adopted more recently by J.S. Boersma, that Building F was built for Peisistratos to be the residence of the tyrants.[39] Indeed, the date of its construction, in the years after 550 B.C., agrees closely with the date about 546 B.C. which is generally accepted for Peisistratos' final return to Athens and the establishment of his continuous tyranny. Whether or not this conjecture be accepted, it is consistent with the one aspect of the building that archaeology reveals with absolute certainty, its primarily residential function. For all its size, the plan bristles with awkward angles, oddly irregular spaces, and ill-shaped rooms. Light foundations of rubble masonry carried mud brick walls, and thin wooden columns stood on single discs of stone. Materials and construction are wholly characteristic of Athenian private dwellings, and nothing bespeaks the ordered architecture of Greek public buildings.

The earliest architectural remains in the area of the classical Agora appear without exception to have been domestic in character, but it needs to be emphasized that the public space of the open square seems to have been expanded by the expropriation of private property during a period that coincides with the tyranny of Peisistratos. That the tyrants gave initial impetus to the growth of the Agora there can be little doubt. The archaic fountain house (Fig. 3), which Pausanias (1.14.1) called Enneakrounos and attributed to Peisistratos himself, bears witness to their interest in developing the area by the installation of public amenities.[40] Moreover, the earliest religious structure that can be securely dated was also established by the family of the tyrants. The younger Peisistratos, son of the tyrant Hippias, dedicated the altar of the Twelve Gods in the Agora during his year as Eponymous Archon in 522/1 B.C.[41] This monument came to be the central milestone for the Attic roads, and Pindar later called it the "omphalos of the city."[42] The implied centrality of the altar suggests that the stage was set for the development of the classical Agora early in the last quarter of the sixth century; but it is equally clear that no demonstrably public buildings had yet been built.

By the turn of the century, dramatic changes had occurred along the foot of the Kolonos Agoraios (Fig. 4). Above the demolished walls of the earlier archaic buildings, there had arisen three small temples, a civic office, and a great meeting hall, while Building F, having stood for forty years or so, was substantially remodeled. This burst of construction for public purposes signals a major horizon in the city's life. Athenians had changed forever both the location of their seat of government, and more important the structure of their political process; and both of these changes are directly reflected in the monumental architecture of the new public buildings, in their cut stone masonry, and in the Doric order.

The Old Bouleuterion was laid out on a massive scale for its day, and its foundations measure 23.30 m. east to west, and 23.80 m. north to south (Figs. 5, 8). It had thus almost the same dimensions as the archaic Telesterion in the sanctuary of Demeter at Eleusis, a great hall of similar capacity and design.[43] As seen today the building has been reduced to its lowest foundations because the builders of the Hellenistic Metroon set down their own walls precisely along three sides of its great square (Fig. 6). Its foundations were massively constructed of irregular blocks of limestone; and on the east side where the site sloped down sharply, they measure as much as 1.40 m. in width and are still preserved to a depth of 1.75 m. (Fig. 7). The plan, with its broad entrance lobby, five internal columns, and seating ranged along three sides of the main chamber, has been long familiar since Thompson's first publication.[44] The original restoration of the building now needs to be revised in some respects, however, so that its design conforms better both with the literary references and with the architectural parallels. The much later bouleuterion in the agora at Assos is a structure of striking similarity (Fig. 9). Likewise square in plan, measuring 20.59 m. × 20.62 m., its dimensions closely approximate those of the Athenian building. The council house at Assos preserved at the time of excavation a single shaft and most of the stylobate of its columnar façade, as well as two stumps of interior columns standing on a level floor.[45] Both the façade of five columns and the level floor in the main council chamber have been adopted in the new restoration, in preference to the blank front wall pierced by two doors, and to the banks of stepped seating around the interior (Fig. 8). Since the excavator recognized

Fig. 4. Agora, restored plan, ca. *500 B.C.*

a patch of floor packing for a pebble mosaic at a point on the west side that should have been banked for stepped seats, if they had existed, we may restore with certainty a flat surface for the interior floor.[46] The Councillors no doubt sat on simple wooden benches arranged in rows between the interior columns (Fig. 5). On this principle, the seating plan here adopted makes use of 48 such benches, uniformly 4 m. in length, and placed in eight blocks of six benches. In addition, a bench has been restored against the wall on all sides. This arrangement has the great merit of providing precisely 504 seats at a width of 0.50 m. per seat (as many as 517 people could be seated, if we adopted the stingier dimension used in the later Theater of Dionysos that allowed only 0.487 m. per bottom).[47]

The Council House can now be restored in the Doric order with its frieze of triglyphs and metopes probably running around all sides of the entablature. The evidence for this comes from the débris left on the site after the building suffered heavy damage in the destruction of 479 B.C. The excavator specifically described the original grade level south of the Bouleuterion as spread with chips of yellow poros, with worked and finished surfaces, obviously from the breaking up of building blocks. Most significant are two fragments broken from finished Doric triglyphs, with slots at the sides for insertion of separate metopes. Two other fragments preserve the edges of thin metope panels made of fine, hard, pale tan poros, and their fronts are surfaced with fine, white stucco, a finish that was only applied to the completed masonry of standing buildings. The inference is clear that the surviving fragments came from the original Doric frieze of the Bouleuterion (Fig. 10).

Several classical authors mention that access to the building was controlled by grilles or barriers called

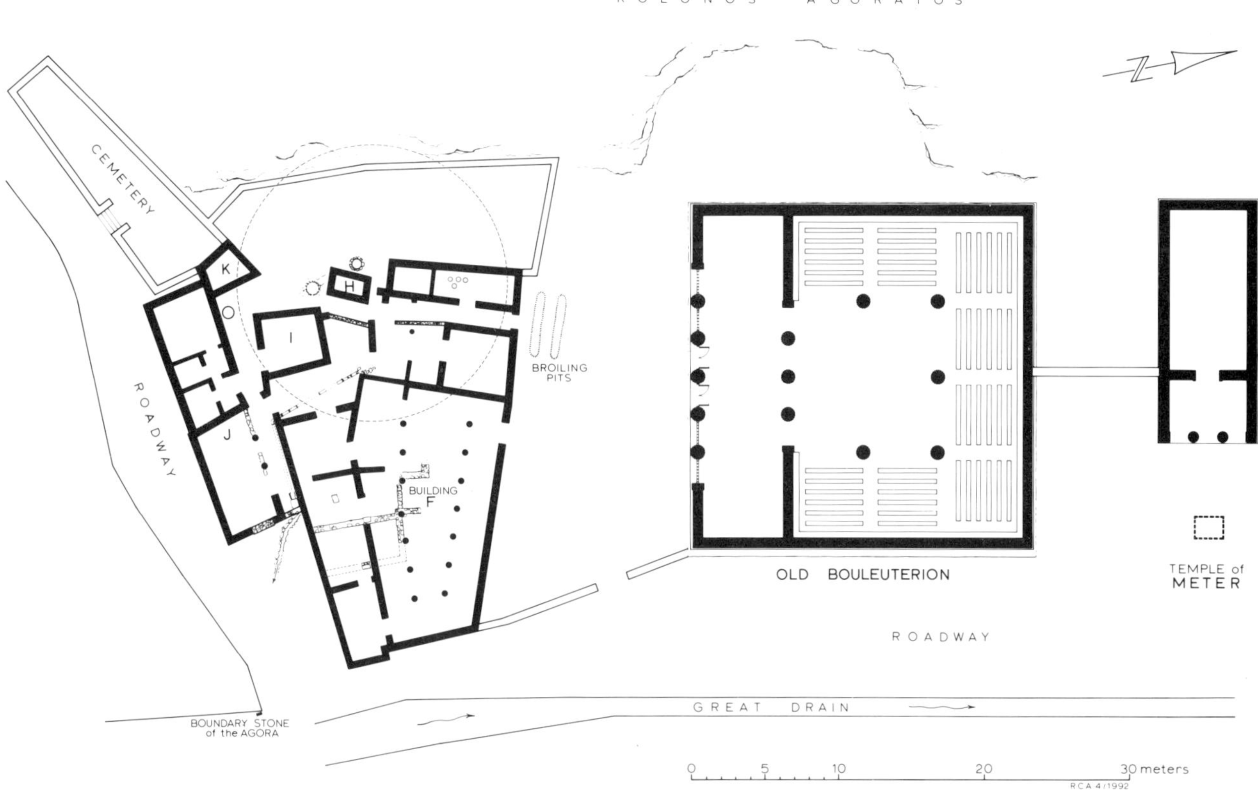

Fig. 5. Building F, Old Bouleuterion, Temple of Meter, restored, ca. *500 B.C.*

Fig. 6. Aerial view of remains of Tholos, Metroon, and Bouleuterion.

Fig. 7. Foundations of Old Bouleuterion beneath porch of Hellenistic Metroon from north.

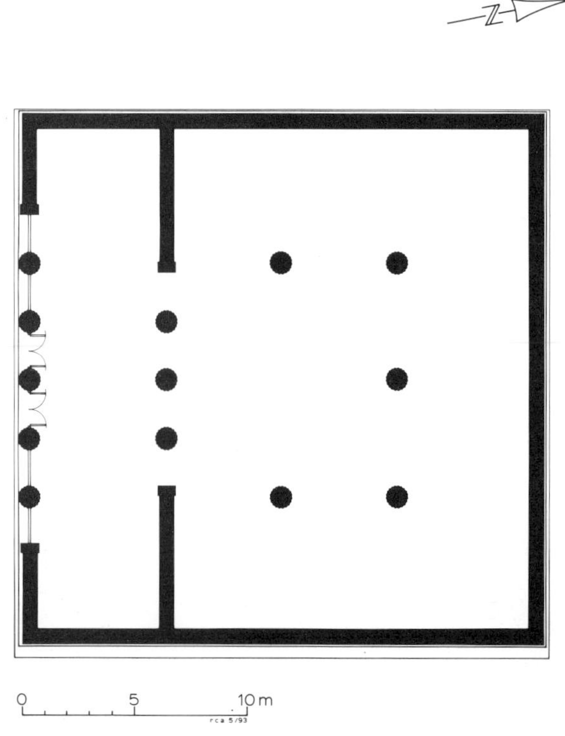

Fig. 8. Old Bouleuterion, restored plan.

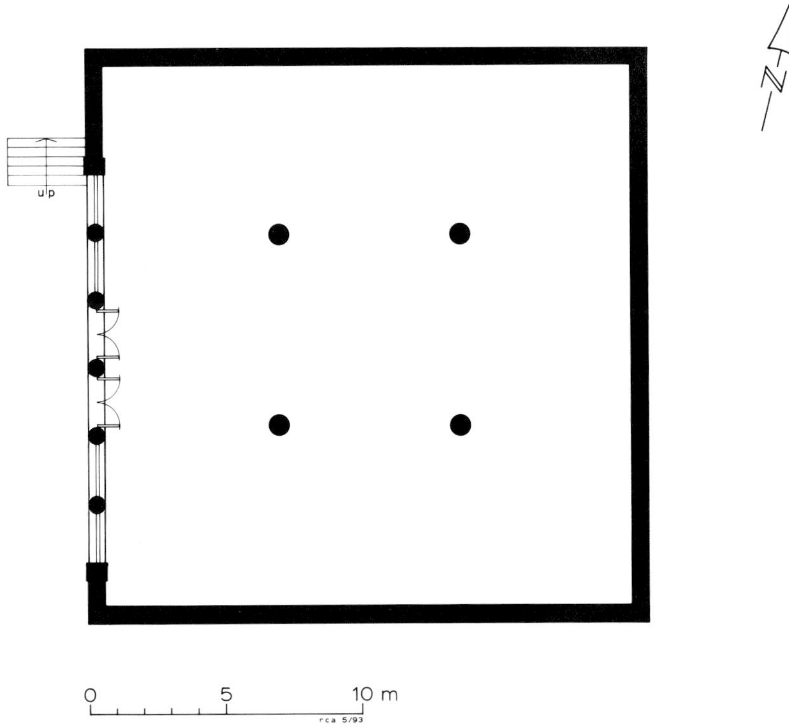

Fig. 9. Bouleuterion at Assos, restored plan.

δρύφακτοι, some of which were fitted with light latticed gates called κιγκλίδες.[48] Once again the council house at Assos provides clear evidence that these grilles should be placed between the columns of the exterior façade. There the standing column has cuttings in which to anchor the original metal grilles; and these were later replaced by marble jambs framing the gates, as we learn from sockets in the stylobate on either side of each column. An entry in the inventories of the sanctuary at Delos gives a graphic description of just such an installation: τρύφακτος λίθινο[ς ἔχων ὀβελίσκους] σιδηροῦς ἕξ, ἐν ὧι ξυλίνη κιγκλὶς καὶ ἥλους σιδηροῦς ἐπὶ

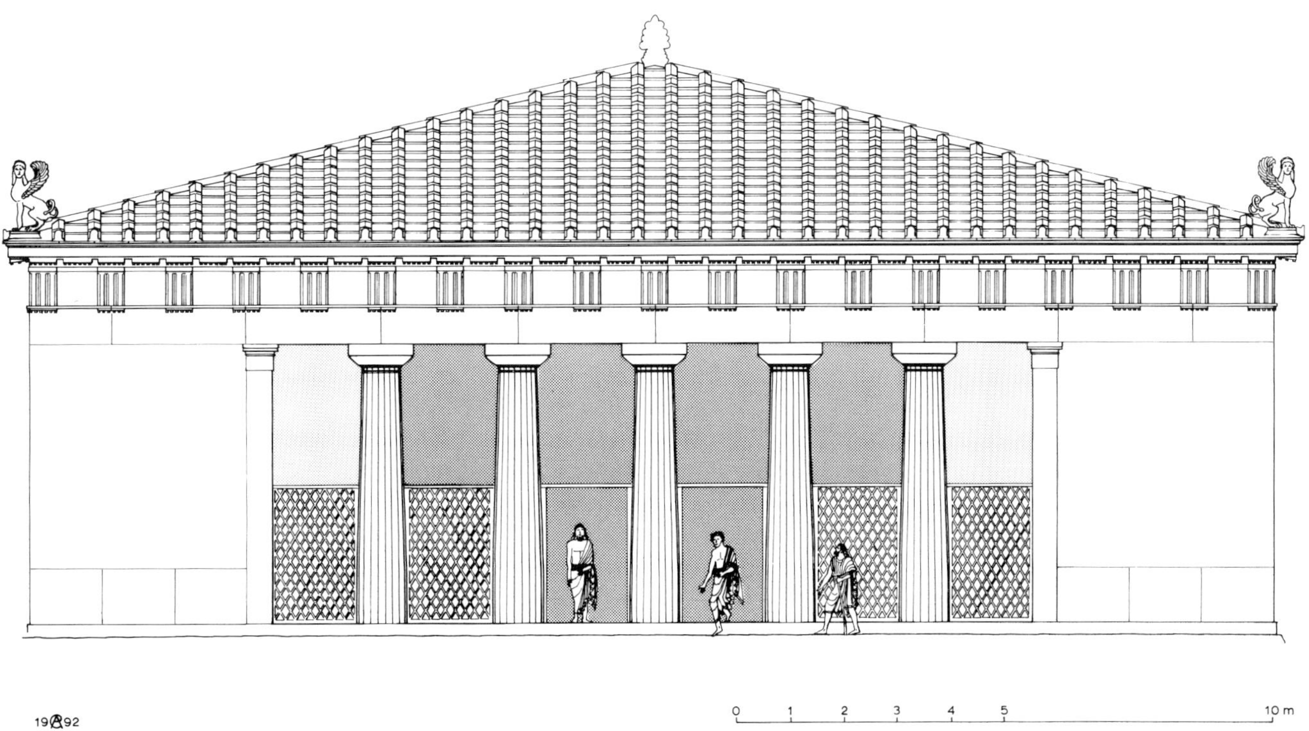

Fig. 10. Old Bouleuterion, restored south elevation.

τοῦ τρυφά[κτου δέκα] τέτταρας· "stone δρύφακτος having six iron rods, in which is a wooden κιγκλὶς and fourteen iron bosses on the δρύφακτος."[49] The specifications for the arsenal of Philo at Peiraieus provide detailed instructions for a similar interior arrangement (*IG* II^2, 1668, lines 63–65): καὶ διαφράξει τὸ μεταστύλιον ἕκαστον ὀρθοστάταις δυοῖν λιθίνοις ὕψος τριῶν ποδῶν, καὶ ἐν τῶι μεταξὺ κινκλίδα ἐπιθήσε[ι] κλειομένην; "And he will close off each intercolumniation with two stone orthostates, three feet in height, and between them he will insert a κιγκλίς; "that can be locked." On the basis of this evidence similar grilles and gates have been restored on the principal columnar façade of the Athenian Council House (Fig. 10).

Of critical importance for this investigation is the date at which the Bouleuterion came to be built at the foot of the Market Hill. The builders set down their foundations through the pre-existing archaic ground level, which had served Building F on the north and east. They then dumped masses of loose, gray, dug bedrock into the open square of their foundations in order to establish the desired floor level inside the building. This building fill proved to have been deposited in three distinct layers of crushed bedrock separated by stone chips and dust from the working of blocks of pale yellow poros. Excavation of these layers inside the southeast corner of the building yielded a total of 1,086 pieces of fragmentary pottery, of which by far the greatest part ranged in date from Late Helladic through the mid sixth century. With respect to the lower limit of the date, which provides the *terminus post quem* for the building's construction, only 47 fragments can be dated to the last three decades of the sixth century, and of these the 16 latest pieces can be placed in the years *ca.* 500 B.C. Not a single sherd from the building fill of the Old Bouleuterion needs to have been manufactured after the turn of the century.[50]

Construction of the Bouleuterion directly affected its older neighbor to the south, Building F. In order to establish level ground in front of the new building's principal façade, the builders created an artificial terrace by dumping more masses of loose, crushed bedrock directly over the earlier archaic ground level to the required depth. The terrace was retained on the east by a low wall that formed a physical link between the old building and the new. The artificial filling behind this wall was found to cover the ruins of the exterior north wall of Building F, and all four rooms of its north wing; but the layer of crushed bedrock stopped abruptly at the south side of each room. Stratigraphy of this kind could have formed only if the builders of the Council House had dismantled the north wing of Building F in order to create a broad esplanade before the main façade of the new building (Fig. 5).[51] Near the southeastern angle of this esplanade, among the débris from the Persian destruction was found a piece broken from the molded rim of a circular marble basin (Fig. 11). Shallow basins of this kind standing on a central post at waist height are among the familiar furnishings of Greek sanctuaries and public buildings. The inscription on the rim, in letters of the end of the sixth century, must surely be restored to read [τ]ô βουλευ[τερίο]. Closely corroborating the date of the pottery, the inscribed basin was doubtless among the building's original furnishings, and it shows that the Boule had begun to function on this site by the turn of the century.[52]

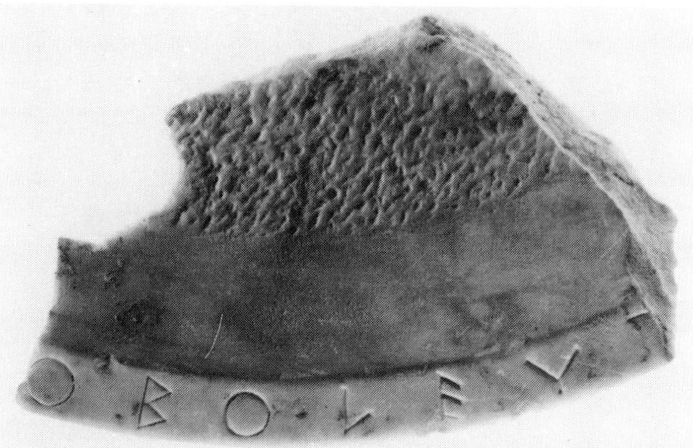

Fig. 11. Agora I 4869: inscribed marble basin from the Bouleuterion.

The remodeling of Building F went beyond demolition of its old north wing. The rooms lost to the terrace of the Bouleuterion were replaced by the construction of Building J along the roadway just to the south (Fig. 5). Half of the long, narrow structure had an open distyle porch, and the other half was subdivided into a suite of small rooms. Evidence for the date of its construction comes from the pottery recovered from beneath the original clay floor of the building. Among the latest pieces are a black-figured plate and a fragment from the floor of a black-figured cup, both of which belong in the years around 500 B.C.;[53] and they show that the refurbishing of Buildings F and J was closely contemporary with the construction of the Old Bouleuterion.

In these same years at the close of the sixth century, another public building arose further north where the diagonal route of the Panathenaic Way made its crossing of the Eridanos River. It was a new civic office for the most venerable of Athenian archons, the Basileus. Small in size, but monumental in scale, the new building took the form of a stoa in the Doric order, and it came to be known to Athenians of the classical period as the Stoa Basileios (Fig. 12). The stoa has chanced to survive in better condition than the other archaic buildings. Its single step and stylobate are preserved intact. The stumps of two Doric columns and both antae stand in their original positions on the stylobate, while part of one internal column is also still in place. Three courses of ashlar masonry in the north wall still display the beautifully dressed stonework of its original fabric (Fig. 15); and surviving blocks of the triglyph frieze and wall-crown, together with fragments of its columns and capitals, allow the superstructure to be restored with certainty. The principal façade in eight Doric columns faced eastward on to the old public thoroughfare that

Fig. 12. Stoa Basileios, view of remains from south.

passed before the building, and within its open porch the interior appointments were of the simplest. At first two interior columns, and later four after a major repair in the fifth century, supported the ridge-pole of the roof (Figs. 13, 14). The only other interior installation from the building's first period was a low stone platform, measuring 0.80 m. in width and 0.50 m. in height. The poros slabs forming the foundation for this were preserved along the foot of the north wall, and shallow trenches from which similar slabs had been removed were found along the west and south walls. The three walls of the stoa were thus at first surrounded by a stone platform that was rather too broad for comfortable sitting, and this was later replaced by an ordinary bench on the old foundations when the building was remodeled at the end of the fifth century.[54]

The evidence for the date of construction of the Royal Stoa parallels exactly that which we have just reviewed for the Old Bouleuterion. That the stoa likewise incurred violent damage early in its history is even more dramatically revealed; for six large fragments of its interior columns and one Doric capital were found together in a pit of discarded débris from the Persian destruction of the city in 479 B.C. Within the foundations of the stoa, excavation of its building fill showed two distinct layers of which the upper had been disturbed by alterations at various times in the fifth century. The lower layer, however, beginning at the level of the bottom of the stylobate, consisted of brown earth, red clay, and much dug bedrock. Throughout this fill were many working chips of poros, as well as larger hunks of the same soft, yellow stone used for all of the superstructure. From the lower building fill came a total of 1,089 fragments of pottery, and the group as a whole bears significant

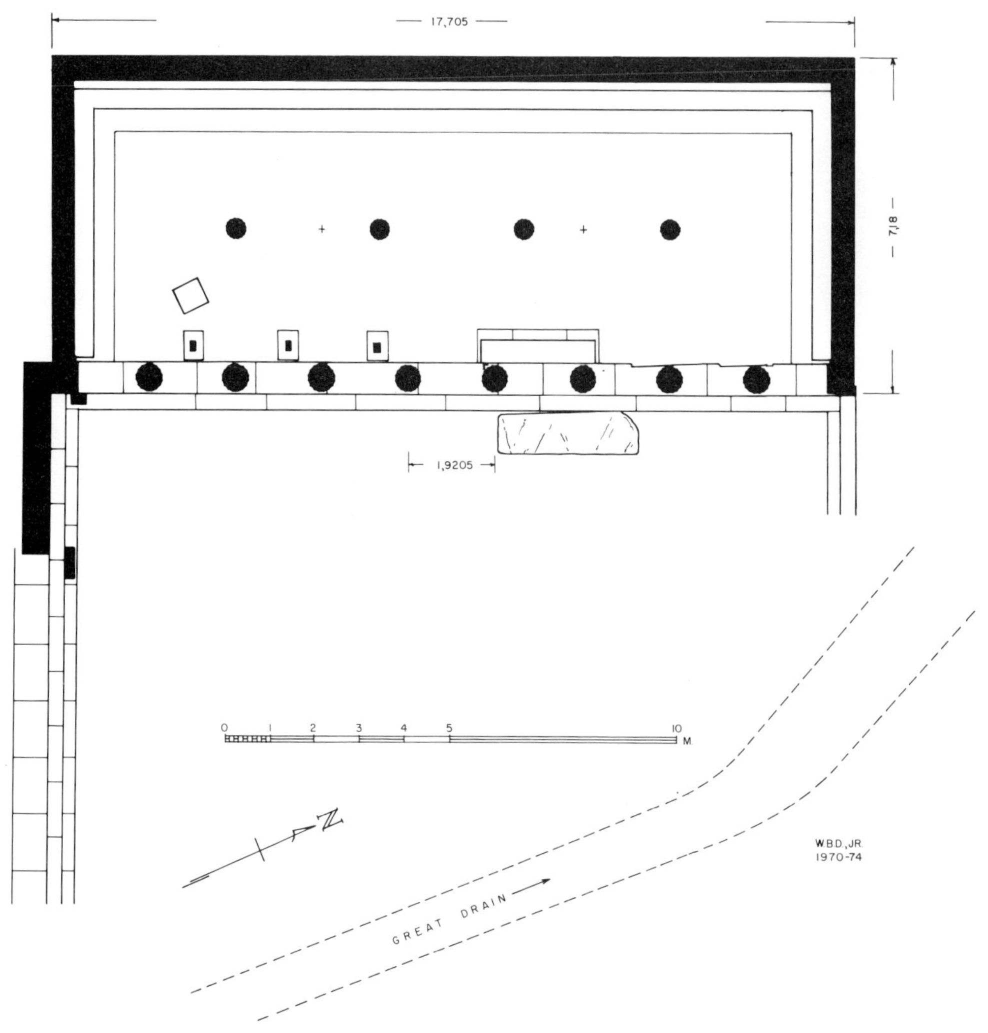

Fig. 13. Stoa Basileios, restored plan, Period 2, as reconstructed ca. *460 B.C.*

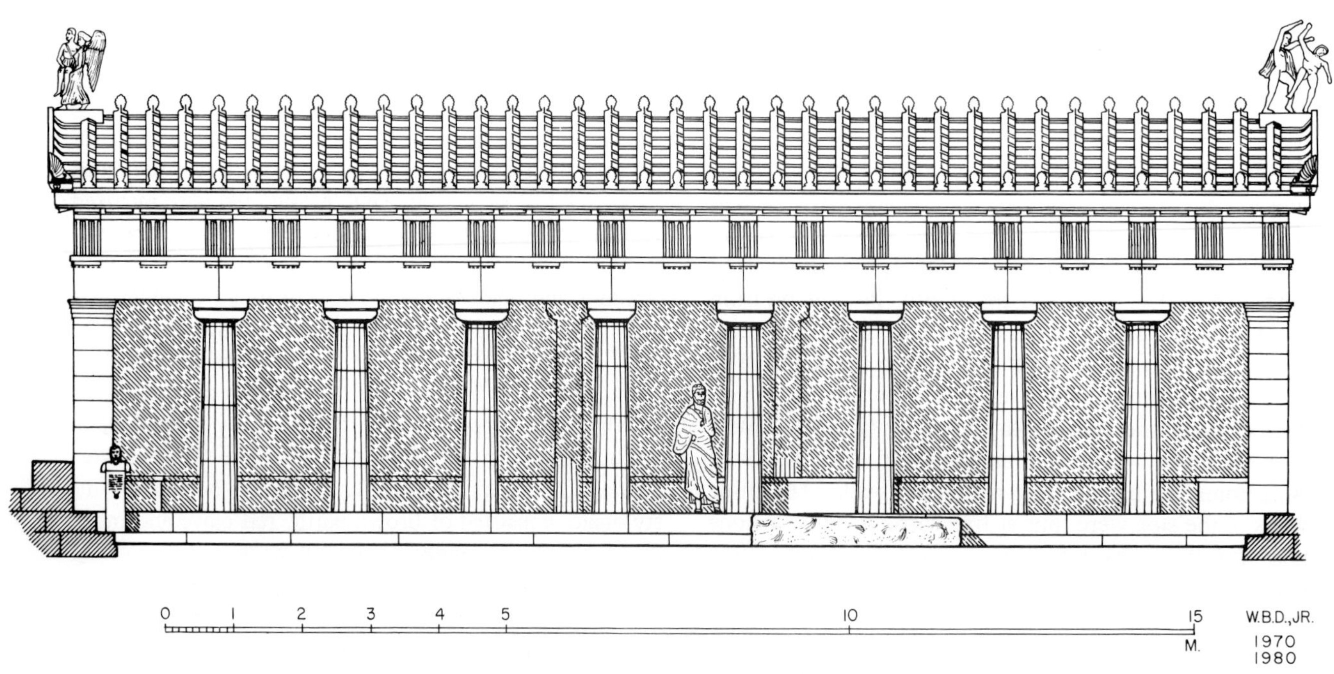

Fig. 14. Stoa Basileios, restored east elevation.

resemblance to the pottery from the building fill within the foundations of the Old Bouleuterion. The incidence of early wares is once again strikingly high, but the 20 latest pieces bring the lower limit of the assemblage to *ca.* 500 B.C., and no later.[55]

Two public buildings, then, arose simultaneously at the foot of the Kolonos Agoraios at about the turn of the century (Figs. 10, 14) . One can scarcely doubt that the immediate impetus for the new construction came in 508 B.C. when Kleisthenes established himself as leader of the common people and promulgated the constitutional reform that created the democratic government.[56] Moreover, one of the new buildings was specifically designed to accommodate that most characteristic institution of the new democracy: the Council of the 500. Boule and Bouleuterion, they were invented for each other; in fact, one might have said that neither could function effectively alone. Beneath the unifying canopy of its roof, the building gathered in the Councillors from all over Attica. Its columnar façade opened to invite their entry, and within its one great hall Athenians from all classes sat down together, a microcosm of the new polis, formed by the designated delegates of the ten new tribes.

The Royal Stoa served as the official seat of the Basileus from the time of its construction throughout the history of public life in Athens, and its functions are attested by numerous ancient authors.[57] Its construction on this site, however, represents a radical relocation. According to Aristotle (*Ath. Pol.* 3.5, above p. 228), the Basileus had formerly occupied the Boukolion among the early civic offices at the east end of the Acropolis, and a building of that name still apparently served certain ritual functions in his own day. From this one infers that the seat of the Basileus was removed from its ancestral site and established on the banks of the Eridanos with the founding of the democracy. For his new office, the King adopted the covered portico of a stoa, a plan not intrinsically well adapted to the conduct of state affairs, where confidential matters would often need to be transacted and a modicum of privacy was always welcome. On the contrary, the Greek stoa is the most quintessentially public form of architecture ever devised: its enclosing walls and roof offer shelter indiscriminately to any comer, while its open colonnade offers unrestricted access to all alike.

Both the stoa and the Bouleuterion are among the earliest examples of their types in Greece; and they are some of the first civic buildings to be embellished with the Doric order, which before that time had been reserved almost exclusively for the sanctuaries of the gods.[58] The columnar order, now removed from its original sacred context, lends a new dignity to the political buildings. The Doric shafts and architraves express the structure of that building, and we see in visual terms the logic of load and support. The alternating triglyphs and metopes, the repeated pattern of regulae and mutules articulate the long horizontal dimensions; and they measure the proper proportion of one part to another, so that the whole façade coheres in structured syntax, which like the grammar of a language is governed by certain laws framed in long usage and tradition. There results that celebrated equilibrium of proportion and monumentality of form unique to the Doric order that has never been surpassed in the subsequent history of architecture. Moreover, when we recall the political functions that the buildings were designed to serve, we see that the abstract language of architectural form could provide no more perfect visual metaphor for the concept of ἰσονομία, political equality subject to laws framed in long usage and tradition. This, as we have seen, was the way Athenians first expressed the novelty of their democratic government. Architectural form and political function thus coalesce in these two buildings, and the Doric order makes a significant contribution of its own to the nascent ideology of democracy.

It is fascinating to observe that the Stoa Basileios and the Bouleuterion, well-known for the free public access of their architecture, became by the fourth century proverbial examples of the orderly decorum ensured by the laws in Athenian public life. The oration against Aristogeiton, preserved in the Demosthenic corpus ([Demosth.] 25. 20, 23), makes the point specifically.

> εἰ γάρ τις ὑμῶν ἐξετάσαι βούλεται τί ποτ᾽ ἐστὶ τὸ αἴτιον καὶ τὸ ποιοῦν τὴν βουλὴν συλλέγεσθαι, τὸν δῆμον εἰς τὴν ἐκκλησίαν ἀναβαίνειν, τὰ δικαστήρια πληροῦσθαι, τὰς ἕνας ἀρχὰς ταῖς νέαις ἑκούσας ὑπεξιέναι, καὶ πάντα δι᾽ ὧν ἡ πόλις οἰκεῖται καὶ σῴζεται γίγνεσθαι, τοὺς νόμους εὑρήσει καὶ τὸ τούτοις ἅπαντας πείθεσθαι ... ἔρανος γάρ ἐστι πολιτικὸς καὶ κοινὸς πανθ᾽ ὅσα, ταξάντων τῶν νόμων, ἕκαστος ἡμῶν ποιεῖ ... ὧν ἓν ἢ δὺ᾽ ἐρῶ παραδείγματος ἕνεκα, τὰ γνωριμώτατα. τὸ τὴν βουλὴν τοὺς πεντακοσίους ἀπὸ τῆς [ἀσθενοῦς] τοιαυτησὶ κιγκλίδος τῶν ἀπορρήτων κυρίαν εἶναι, καὶ μὴ τοὺς ἰδιώτας ἐπεισιέναι· τὸ τὴν ἐξ 'Αρείου πάγου βουλὴν, ὅταν ἐν τῇ βασιλείῳ στοᾷ καθεζομένη περισχοινίσηται, κατὰ πολλὴν ἡσυχίαν ἐφ᾽ ἑαυτῆς εἶναι, καὶ ἅπαντας ἐκποδὼν ἀποχωρεῖν.
>
> "For if any of you cares to inquire what is the motive-power that calls together the Council, draws the people into the Assembly, fills the law-courts, makes the old officials resign readily to the new, and enables the whole life of the state to be carried on and preserved, he will find that it is the laws and the obedience that all men yield to the laws.... Everything done at the bidding of the laws is a contribution made to the state and the community.... One or two of these I will name for the sake of example, choosing the best known. The Council of the 500, thanks to this latticed gate, frail as it is, is master of its own secrets, and no private citizen can enter in. The Council of the Areopagos, when it sits roped off in the Stoa Basileios, enjoys complete freedom from disturbance, and all men hold aloof."

Central to the new democracy was the concept that all citizens enjoyed equal rights before the laws, and the laws applied impartially to all alike. For this ideal to be realized, however, the laws needed to be in written form and displayed in a public place where all citizens could consult them.

This brings us back to the Stoa Basileios and to a controversy that has bedeviled scholars of Athenian institutions from classical times to the present day. Aristotle (*Ath. Pol.* 7.1) writes of the work of Solon:

> πολιτείαν δὲ κατέστησε καὶ νόμους ἔθηκεν ἄλλους, τοῖς δὲ Δράκοντος θεσμοῖς ἐπαύσαντο χρώμενοι πλὴν τῶν φονικῶν. ἀναγράψαντες δὲ τοὺς νόμους εἰς τοὺς κύρβεις ἔστησαν ἐν τῇ στοᾷ τῇ βασιλείῳ καὶ ὤμοσαν χρήσεσθαι πάντες· οἱ δὲ ἐννέα ἄρχοντες ὀμνύντες πρὸς τῷ λίθῳ κατεφάτιζον ἀναθήσειν ἀνδριάντα χρυσοῦν ἐάν τινα παραβῶσι τῶν νόμων· ὅθεν ἔτι καὶ νῦν οὕτως ὀμνύουσι.
>
> "And he established a constitution and made other laws, and they ceased to observe the statutes of Drakon, except those relating to homicide. Inscribing the laws on the *kyrbeis*, they set them up in the Stoa Basileios, and all swore to observe them; and the nine archons, taking an oath at the stone, declared that they would set up a golden statue if they transgressed any of the laws. This is the origin of the oath which they still take."

Now we know from several authors, some of them plainly eye-witness accounts, like the Hellenistic scholars Eratosthenes and Polemon, and later Plutarch and Pausanias, that the laws of Solon were inscribed on revolving wooden *axones* kept in the old Prytaneion.[59] With this information, Aristotle's account appears to be in hopeless conflict, for he says that the laws were inscribed on something called *kyrbeis* and set up in the Stoa Basileios in Solon's time. The matter is further confounded by the report of another fourth-century scholar Anaximenes of Lampsakos, who stated in his *Philippika*, as excerpted by Didymos:[60]

> τοὺς ἄξονας καὶ τοὺς κύρβεις ἄνωθεν ἐκ τῆς ἀκροπόλεως εἰς τὸ βουλευτήριον καὶ τὴν ἀγορὰν μετέστησεν Ἐφιάλτης.
>
> "Ephialtes transferred the *axones* and the *kyrbeis* from the Acropolis to the Bouleuterion and the Agora."

An alternative version of the same incident is reported by Pollux (*Onomastikon* 8.128) and conforms better to the topography given by other authors.

> ἀπέκειντο δὲ οἵ τε κύρβεις καὶ οἱ ἄξονες ἐν ἀκροπόλει πάλαι· αὖθις δ' ἵνα πᾶσιν ἐξῇ ἐντυγχάνειν, εἰς τὸ πρυτανεῖον καὶ τὴν ἀγορὰν μετεκομίσθησαν.
>
> "The *axones* and *kyrbeis* were kept on the Acropolis of old but thereafter in order that all might consult them they were transferred to the Prytaneion and the Agora."

This welter of confusion in antiquity has spawned heated modern argument concerning the *axones* and the *kyrbeis*, whether they were identical, whether they were different kinds of monuments, and if so how they differed, whether they were the same monuments bearing different kinds of text. In all this, it is well to recall that Aristotle had to hand enough information about Solon's laws that he wrote a treatise in five books entitled Περὶ τῶν Σόλωνος ἀξόνων ε΄, *On the Axones of Solon*; yet he reports that the *kyrbeis* were set up in the Royal Stoa.[61] The likelihood is good that he knew what the *axones* were and how they differed from the *kyrbeis*. In his recent analysis of the sources bearing on this problem, R.S. Stroud[62] has argued persuasively that the *axones* and the *kyrbeis* were two discrete sets of monuments, of quite different type and material, but both inscribed with the complete texts of Solon's laws. This conclusion has surprised some scholars because there seemed to be no good reason for two complete texts to exist, and no occasion on which it was desirable for such duplication to be carried out. There was also no ready explanation as to why both sets of monuments should have been on the Acropolis in 462 B.C. when Ephialtes is said to have removed them to the lower city.[63]

I suggest that Aristotle's only error was in his archaeological date for the Stoa Basileios. He knew that the stoa was built to house the inscribed *kyrbeis*, and he assumed that that had happened at the time of Solon's original promulgation of the laws. The quaint old stoa had stood for 175 years when Aristotle wrote and had undergone major repairs on at least three occasions in that time. Aristotle can hardly be blamed for thinking, albeit incorrectly, that the obviously archaic building was a good deal older than it really was.[64] The correct archaeological date for the stoa's construction, *ca.* 500 B.C., shows that the project should be attributed to the new democracy. This provides both the logical occasion and the necessary motivation for duplicating the complete texts of the laws, when the King's office was removed from its ancient site by the Prytaneion and re-established at the foot of the Kolonos Agoraios. It was the prevailing spirit of those very years that the laws should be made available to magistrate and private citizen alike. Indeed, we may go farther and suggest that the form of the Royal Stoa was specifically chosen for the purpose of displaying the *kyrbeis*; and they would have stood, no doubt, on the low, broad platform which ran round the three walls of the building and is certainly part of its original fabric. Here the laws on the *kyrbeis* quite literally surrounded the most ancient magistrate of Athens, but at the same time they were readily available to litigants and witnesses whose law suits brought them to the new stoa. It will be observed also that none of this is in essential conflict with the statement of Anaximenes that the *axones* and *kyrbeis* were brought down from the Acropolis by Ephialtes. He wrote of a time in the second quarter of the fifth century when most of Athens' public buildings were still under repair as the city gradually rebuilt itself after the Persian destruction of 479 B.C. The Stoa Basileios itself was actually in the process of reconstruction during the decade of the 460s,[65] and in light of this it is easy to understand that the *axones* and *kyrbeis* would have been stored for safe-keeping on the Acropolis between the Persian Wars and the time of Ephialtes. There is nothing in Anaximenes' statement to suggest that Ephialtes did anything more than return the old monuments to their original homes in the lower city when the repairs were complete.

Aristotle's mistaken belief that the Stoa Basileios was built in the time of Solon undoubtedly caused another chronological error in his treatment of early Athenian civic offices. Because he knew that the archons had used the old offices in the neighborhood of the Prytaneion before the stoa was built, he dated them to a period before Solon's legislation; but in the time of Solon he says specifically that the archons all came together in the Thesmotheteion (above p.228). We may suspect that he dated the change in the archons' accommodations to the time of Solon for the same reason that he dated the construction of the Stoa Basileios to that early period. In that case, like the construction of the stoa, the relocation of the archons may not actually have occurred until the inception of the democracy at the end of the century.[66] Despite Aristotle's chronological misunderstanding, his treatment of the archons' offices no doubt preserves a vague recollection that the seat of Athenian government was moved from the east end of the Acropolis to the west side of the new Agora on the occasion of the founding of the democracy. It may now be suggested that the place where the archons came together and where they took their meals in common was the building that we know archaeologically as Building F (Fig. 5). That building was certainly equipped with domestic facilities; it was joined to the Bouleuterion by a parapet wall and entered from the south side of their common terrace. Building F was remodeled when the Bouleuterion was built, and it was hastily repaired and kept in service after the Persian destruction.[67] That it served important officials during this period in the building's life there can scarcely be any doubt, and there were none more appropriate than the nine archons themselves. If, indeed, the building had been built in the 540s as a residence for the tyrants, it would have been seen as peculiarly fitting in the last decade of the century that it should house the highest officers of the new democratic government.

The transfer of the civic offices from the area of the old Prytaneion to the foot of the Kolonos Agoraios is no doubt responsible for the curious duplication of offices, sites, functions, and even documents, which is unique to Athens among Greek cities and sowed endless confusion among the later literary sources. The clearest case is to be seen in the two seats of the Basileus, whose office in the archaic period was in the Boukolion near the Prytaneion, and in the classical and later periods was in the Stoa Basileios.[68] So too there was a considerable overlap in function between the old Prytaneion and the later Tholos. Dinners in the Prytaneion at state expense were granted to foreign ambassadors and dignitaries, victorious athletes at the panhellenic festivals, and the oldest living descendant of Harmodios and Aristogeiton; but the prytaneis of the Council and their various servants, secretaries, and assistants always dined in the Tholos.[69] That the Tholos took over some of the functions of the original Prytaneion is also made plain by the ancient nomenclature. During the third and second centuries, numerous decrees of the Boule and Demos conferred honors on the prytaneis and their officers and listed the names of all the bouleutai of the particular tribe. The standard formula of these honorary decrees instructed the prytany secretary to publish the text on a marble stele καὶ στῆσαι ἐν τῶι πρυτανικῶι, "and set it up in the Prytanikon." This site for the erection of the stelai is preserved in the texts of 21 inscriptions and can be restored with virtual certainty in 38 others. Of the 21 documents which preserve the phrase ἐν τῶι πρυτανικῶι, 13 were found in the area of the Tholos, as well as many fragments of the inscriptions in which the phrase can be restored.[70] This evidence long ago led E. Vanderpool to the conclusion that the "Prytanikon" referred to the precinct of the Tholos; and S. G. Miller has referred more recently to the complex of the Tholos as the "Prytaneion-Annex."[71] The similarity of nomenclature then caused later lexica and scholia to assert that the Tholos was called the Prytaneion, and in one instance that the statues of the Eponymous Heroes stood beside the Prytaneion.[72]

Similar confusion seems to have occurred in the case of the Thesmotheteion, the building in which the nine archons are said to have come together in Solon's time (Aristotle, *Ath. Pol.* 3.5). Aristotle alone refers to the building in this form of the name, and clearly in the context of the early offices near the Prytaneion. Plutarch (*Moralia* 714b) called it the Tesmothesion and compared it to the Prytaneion, and the Souda Lexicon (*s.v.* ἄρχων) used the same form of the name. A scholiast on Plato (*Phaedrus* 235d) garbled the name still further to θεμίστιον and a corrupt note in the lexicon of Hesychius (*s.v.* πρυτανεῖον) has reduced it to θεσμοφορεῖον. Another scholiast on Plato (*Protagoras* 337d) appears to equate πρυτανεῖον, θεσμοθέσιον, and θόλος, but it may be that both here and in Hesychius the note is trying to say no more than that those were the names of the official dining places in Athens.[73] There is not a single straightforward statement that a building of this name functioned in the classical period, and it is plain that none of the sources that mention it possessed very much information about it. If, however, as suggested above, it was to the predecessor of the Tholos (Building F) that the archons moved after 508 B.C., then it is easy to see how the later commentators came to confuse it with the Tholos and the Prytaneion. In any event, Aristotle makes a clear statement that the other archons, like the Basileus, moved their offices from one place to another, a change that he dated in the time of Solon.[74] This duplication of the archons' offices and of the functions and nomenclature of the Prytaneion and Tholos thus forms a striking parallel for the replication of the full texts of Solon's laws on the later *kyrbeis*, which included numbered references to the source on the original wooden *axones*.[75]

Critical to the early administration of justice was the assurance not only, as we have seen, that all citizens could consult the laws in written form, but also that the officers and magistrates responsible for enforcing them would not transgress the laws themselves or accept bribes so that others might do so. That assurance was given on the one hand by the public display of the *kyrbeis* inscribed with the laws of Solon, and on the other by the solemn oaths which the nine archons, the Boule, and the dikastic jurors all swore before taking up their responsibilities of office.[76] Aristotle (*Ath. Pol.* 7.1, supra p. 240) states specifically that the oath sworn by the archons in his own day went back to the oath sworn by their distant predecessors at the time when Solon originally framed his laws at the beginning of the sixth century. At *Ath. Pol.* 55.5 a fuller account appears of the swearing-in of archons in the fourth century, and both the procedure and the language sound archaic.

δοκιμασθέντες δὲ τοῦτον τὸν τρόπον, βαδίζουσι πρὸς τὸν λίθον ἐφ' οὗ τὰ τόμι' ἐστιν (ἐφ' οὗ καὶ οἱ διαιτηταὶ ὀμόσαντες ἀποφαίνονται τὰς διαίτας καὶ οἱ μάρτυρες ἐξόμνυνται τὰς μαρτυρίας), ἀναβάντες δ' ἐπὶ τοῦτον ὀμνύουσιν δικαίως ἄρξειν καὶ κατὰ τοὺς νόμους, καὶ δῶρα μὴ λήψεσθαι τῆς ἀρχῆς ἕνεκα, κἄν τι λάβωσιν ἀνδριάντα ἀναθήσειν χρυσοῦν.

"And having been examined in this manner they go to the stone on which are the victims cut up for sacrifice (the one on which arbitrators also swear before they issue their decisions, and persons summoned as witnesses swear that they have no evidence), and mounting this stone they swear that they will govern justly and according to the laws, and they will not take gifts on account of their office, and that if they should take anything they will dedicate a golden statue."

Of particular interest for this study is the stone on which are placed the cut-up parts of the sacrificial victim, and which the archons mount to swear the oath. Several passages mention this stone, always in the singular and always with the definite article (ὁ λίθος), and Aristotle seems to speak of it as a familiar landmark that every Athenian knew.[77] Plutarch (*Sol.* 25.2) also describes the swearing of oaths at the time of Solon's legislation:

κοινὸν μὲν οὖν ὤμνυεν ὅρκον ἡ βουλὴ τοὺς Σόλωνος νόμους ἐμπεδώσειν, ἴδιον δ' ἕκαστος τῶν θεσμοθετῶν ἐν ἀγορᾷ πρὸς τῷ λίθῳ, καταφατίζων, εἴ τι παραβαίη τῶν θεσμῶν, ἀνδριάντα χρυσοῦν ἰσομέτρητον ἀναθήσειν ἐν Δελφοῖς.

"The Council, however, took a joint oath to ratify the laws of Solon, and each of the Thesmothetai swore individually at the stone in the Agora, declaring solemnly that if he transgressed the statutes in any way, he would dedicate a life-sized golden statue at Delphi."

Plutarch's version of the oath shows specific knowledge of *Ath. Pol.* 7.1, for both passages use the rare, perhaps

Fig. 15. "The Lithos" and north wall of the Stoa Basileios, from southeast.

archaic, verb καταφατίζω "to declare solemnly."[78] Moreover, in the immediately preceding paragraph, Plutarch describes the wooden *axones* that he saw in the Prytaneion and says that Aristotle calls them *kyrbeis*. But he also had another source from which he quoted lines from the comic poet Kratinos to show that other early writers called the laws of Solon *kyrbeis*. He also adds two parts of the oath entirely omitted by Aristotle, that an archon who transgressed the laws must dedicate (1) a life-sized statue and (2) at Delphi, details both of which are confirmed as parts of the archons' oath in the fourth century by a reference to them in Plato, *Phaedrus* 235d-e, where however there is no mention of the stone. Aristotle reports that the nine archons swore the oath, while Plutarch says that the Boule swore in common, and the Thesmothetai individually; but both cite the same oath sworn πρὸς τῷ λίθῳ, and both date the swearing of the oath to the time of Solon's original legislation. Aristotle adds that the oath ratifying Solon's laws was the origin of the oath sworn annually by the archons in the fourth century.

The same stone in the Agora figures also in a curious episode that Plutarch recounts at an earlier point in his *Life of Solon* (8.1–2). During the long conflict between Athens and Megara for possession of Salamis, Solon feigned madness in order to circumvent a law prohibiting anyone, on pain of death, from inciting the city to renew the war.[79]

ἐλεγεῖα δὲ κρύφα συνθεὶς καὶ μελετήσας ὥστε λέγειν ἀπὸ στόματος, ἐξεπήδησεν εἰς τὴν ἀγορὰν ἄφνω πιλίδιον περιθέμενος. ὄχλου δὲ πολλοῦ συνδραμόντος ἀναβὰς ἐπὶ τὸν τοῦ κήρυκος λίθον ἐν ᾠδῇ διεξῆλθε τὴν ἐλεγείαν, ἧς ἐστιν ἀρχή·

> Αὐτὸς κῆρυξ ἦλθον ἀφ᾽ ἱμερτῆς Σαλαμῖνος,
> κόσμον ἐπέων ᾠδὴν ἀντ᾽ ἀγορῆς θέμενος.

"He then secretely composed some elegiac verses, and after studying them so that he could recite from memory, he suddenly rushed out into the Agora with a cap on his head. When a large crowd had gathered, he mounted the herald's stone and recited the poem which begins:

> I have come myself a herald from lovely Salamis
> Composing my words as a song instead of a public speech."

It is of interest that the stone is here described as the herald's stone and that Solon himself speaks as a herald in the opening lines of the poem "Salamis" quoted by Plutarch. In the time of Solon, this stone should be understood to lie in close proximity to the old Prytaneion at the east end of the Acropolis, a topographical position which emerges from references to the law court of the Prytaneion. Solon's eighth law on the 13th *axon*, quoted by Plutarch (*Sol.* 19.3), concerns restoration of civil rights and franchises and specifies the exceptions.

Fig. 16. "The Lithos" with raised packing stones visible beneath, from northeast.

"ἐπιτίμους εἶναι πλὴν ὅσοι ἐξ Ἀρείου πάγου ἢ ὅσοι ἐκ τῶν ἐφετῶν ἢ ἐκ πρυτανείου καταδικασθέντες ὑπὸ τῶν βασιλέων ἐπὶ φόνῳ ἢ σφαγαῖσιν ἢ ἐπὶ τυραννίδι ἔφευγον ὅτε ὁ θεσμὸς ἐφάνη ὅδε."

"They shall be restored to their rights and franchises except such as were condemned by the Areopagos, or by the ephetai, or in the Prytaneion by the Basileis on charges of murder or homicide, or of seeking to establish a tyranny, and were in exile when this law was published."

According to Solon's legislation, the Basileus passed judgment from the Prytaneion in certain kinds of homicide cases, and persons who had been condemned in such cases before 594 B.C. were excluded from Solon's restoration of rights. In 352 B.C. Demosthenes (23.76) also had occasion to refer to the curious old court in the Prytaneion, and a scholiast on that passage preserves a few details about the quaint archaic procedure there followed.

ἐπὶ πρυτανείῳ· ἐν τούτῳ τῷ δικαστηρίῳ δικάζονται φόνου, ὅταν ὁ μὲν ἀνῃρημένος δῆλος ᾖ, ζητεῖται δὲ ὁ τὸν φόνον δράσας. καὶ ἀποφέρει τὴν γραφὴν πρὸς τὸν βασιλέα, καὶ ὁ βασιλεὺς διὰ τοῦ κήρυκος κηρύττει καὶ ἀπαγορεύει τόνδε τὸν ἀνελόντα τὸν δεῖνα μὴ ἐπιβαίνειν ἱερῶν καὶ χώρας Ἀττικῆς.

"In the Prytaneion: In this court are tried homicide cases when the victim was clearly killed, but the perpetrator of the crime is missing. One submits the charge to the Basileus, and the Basileus makes proclamation through the herald and forbids the murderer to enter the sanctuaries and the land of Attica."

When a charge of homicide was brought before the Basileus at the Prytaneion, the murderer was debarred from the sanctuaries and the land of Attica by the formal edict of the King publicly proclaimed by the herald. It is surely correct to infer that the King's proclamation was issued by the herald standing on the stone which thus came to bear his name; and common sense suggests that the stone lay in the immediate vicinity of the old Prytaneion, where the court convened, and of the nearby Boukolion, where the King had his seat in archaic times. This was the herald's stone that Solon himself had mounted to recite his poem "Salamis;" and the same stone on which the nine archons had sworn in 594 B.C. that they would govern according to Solon's laws. A memory that solemn oaths were sworn in the neighborhood of the ancient civic offices is also preserved "in the name of the place beside the Theseion which they call *Horkomosion*."[80] Although Plutarch, on the authority of Kleidemos, adduces this as evidence that the mythical war with the Amazons ended in a treaty, *Horkomosion* seems to be no more than a name to Plutarch, who gives no indication that oaths were still sworn there in his time, and who makes no mention of the stone in this context. The name itself, however, *Horkomosion* suggests the formalized ritual of oath-taking which is elsewhere associated with the Lithos; and its location "beside the Theseion" places it among the oldest civic offices of Athens with which this study began.

If the inference is correct that the stone where heralds proclaimed and archons swore in Solon's time should have been located near the Prytaneion and beside the Theseion, then we are led to the startling conclusion that the stone itself must have been removed from its original site and taken to the place that it occupied in the classical Agora. Aristotle mentions the Lithos twice (*Ath. Pol.* 7.1; 55.5), and there can be no doubt whatever that both passages refer to the same stone and the same civic ceremonial. The first oath is that sworn by the archons at the time of Solon's original legislation; the second is the archons' annual oath of office in the latter part of the fourth century. The first passage specifically anticipates the second by the phrase (7.1) ὅθεν ἔτι καὶ νῦν οὕτως ὀμνύουσι; "whence even now they swear in the same way." Pollux (*Onomastikon* 8.86) also gives an account of the *dokimasia* and swearing-in of the nine archons which closely paraphrases the second passage of Aristotle (*Ath. Pol.* 55.5), but Pollux adds a topographical detail of critical importance.

ὤμνυον δ' οὗτοι (οἱ ἐννέα ἄρχοντες) πρὸς τῇ βασιλείῳ στοᾷ, ἐπὶ τοῦ λίθου ἐφ' ᾧ τὰ τόμια, φυλάξειν τοὺς νόμους καὶ μὴ δωροδοκήσειν, ἢ χρυσοῦν ἀνδριάντα ἀποτίσειν.

"They (the nine archons) took the oath at the Stoa Basileios, on the stone on which were the parts of the victims, swearing that they would guard the laws and that they would not take bribes, or they would dedicate a golden statue."

That this is the same oath and ritual to which Aristotle refers (*Ath. Pol.* 55.5) is made plain by the description of the stone "on which are the parts of the victims;" but there is here also the important addition that the stone was "at the Stoa Basileios." In the time of Solon the stone appears to have been near the ancient Prytaneion, but in the classical period it was located at the Stoa Basileios. Like the King's office itself, the stone was originally below the east end of the Acropolis and was later moved to the northwest corner of the Agora.

At this very spot, immediately before the colonnade of the Stoa Basileios, just such a stone has come to light in the excavations (Figs. 15, 16).[81] In all probability it is to be identified with "the Lithos" of which the ancient sources speak. The great slab of poros limestone is rough-hewn on all sides, but its top is worn perfectly smooth by the feet of archons and heralds who mounted it for centuries to swear their annual oaths and to make their proclamations. In its prominent position before the King's office, the stone gives every appearance of having been treated with extraordinary veneration, a civic altar, as it were, sacred to the ancient rituals of Athenian political life. If this discussion is not entirely wide of the mark, it is now possible to suggest why the stone came to be so revered; for it is likely to be the very stone on which the archons first swore to govern according to

Solon's laws in 594 B.C. When the Basileus moved his seat from the archaic Boukolion to the newly built Stoa Basileios, *ca.* 500 B.C., the Lithos was transported to its new site in front of the stoa. Here it served as a very tangible symbol of that sacred trust which the laws imposed on Athenian magistrates, laws that they swore to obey as they stood on the Lithos in front of the actual texts themselves displayed on the *kyrbeis*. The archons of Aristotle's day swore the same oath as they had in Solon's day; and the great stone itself formed the physical link between them and their predecessors and the lawgiver himself.

With King and Council, and possibly the other archons, now established northwest of the Acropolis, the open square that had grown gradually larger in the course of the sixth century had now become effectively the seat of the Athenian government. That fact the Athenians made manifest in the years about the turn of the century when they erected marble pillars at the entrances to the public square. The stones are quite literally signposts that guard the limits of the Agora, and two of these faithful sentinels have stood watch from that day to this.[82] They accost the passer-by and speak out in their own persons, with the wonderful, proud naïveté of archaic thought: "I am the boundary-stone of the Agora." They announce to ancient traveler and to modern student alike that the democratic government had set its stamp forever on the topography and monuments of Athens

.

Notes

1. For discussion of the Harmodios skolia, M. Ostwald, *Nomos and the Beginnings of the Athenian Democracy* (Oxford 1969) 121–136; C.M. Bowra, *Greek Lyric Poetry*² (Oxford 1961) 391–396; V. Ehrenberg, *WS* 69 (1956) 57–69; S. Brunnsåker, *The Tyrant Slayers of Kritios and Nesiotes*² (Lund 1971) 21–29; M.W. Taylor, *The Tyrant Slayers*² (Salem, N.H. 1991) 22–35; G. Vlastos, *AJP* 74 (1953) 337–366.
2. Herodotos 5.55–57; Thucydides 1.20.1–2;6.53.3–59.1; Aristotle, *Ath.Pol.* 18.
3. See J.N. Coldstream, *Greek Geometric Pottery* (London 1968) 29–44; E.L. Smithson, *Hesperia* 37 (1968) 77–116.
4. See J.N. Coldstream, *Geometric Greece* (London 1977) 136–137, fig. 44; I. Morris, *Burial and Ancient Society* (Cambridge 1987) 228–233, and fig. 61.
5. G. Dontas, *Hesperia* 52 (1983) 48–63. The text, dated to the archonship of Polyeuktos (247/6 or 246/5 B.C.), reads, line 30: ἐπαινέσαι τὴν ἱέρειαν τῆς 'Αγλαύρου; line 35: στῆσαι ἐν τῶι ἱερῶι τῆς 'Αγλαύρου. For the Persian ascent at the steepest part of the Acropolis, Herodotos 8. 53; Pausanias 1.18.2.
6. The cave is clearly visible in the photograph, Travlos, *PDA* 407. For the location of the sanctuary of Aglauros, see W. Judeich, *Topographie von Athen*² (Munich 1931) 303; O. Broneer, *Hesperia* 8 (1939) 317–429; Travlos, *PDA* 72 ff., 578; R.E. Wycherley, *The Stones of Athens* (Princeton 1978) 176–177.
7. Pausanias 1.18.2: ὑπὲρ δὲ τῶν Διοσκούρων τὸ ἱερὸν 'Αγλαύρου τέμενός ἐστιν. See N. Robertson, *Historia* 35 (1986) 147–176, and especially 157–169 for discussion of the topography of the early archaic buildings.
8. Lucian, 28 *Piscator* 42: παρὰ δὲ τὸ Πελασγικὸν ἄλλοι καὶ κατὰ τὸ 'Ασκληπιεῖον ἕτεροι καὶ παρὰ τὸν Ἄρειον Πάγον ἔτι πλείους, ἔνιοι δὲ καὶ κατὰ τὸν Τάλω τάφον, οἱ δὲ καὶ πρὸς τὸ 'Ανάκειον προσθέμενοι κλίμακας ἀνέρπουσι βομβηδὸν νὴ Δία καὶ βοτρυδὸν ἑσμοῦ δίκην.
9. Aristotle, *Ath. Pol.* 15.4 describes the same assembly and the same ruse to disarm the citizens, but the story is set in the Theseion instead of the Anakeion, and the tyrant's men are said to have stored the arms εἰς τὰ πλησίον οἰκήματα τοῦ Θησείου.
10. Agora Inv. I 2080: *Agora* XIX, 22–23, H5. Polyaenus 1.21.2 has *propylaion*; Aristotle, *Ath. Pol.* 15.4 has *propylon*; Philochoros placed the Aglaureion near the *propylaia*, *FGrHist* 328 F 105 (= Schol. Demosth. 19.303). Cf. Judeich (supra n. 6); Wycherley, *Agora* III, 115.
11. For the Mycenaean path and postern, Travlos, *PDA* 229; S.E. Jakovidis, *'Η μυκηναϊκὴ ἀκρόπολις τῶν 'Αθηνῶν* (Athens 1962) 97–99, 136–143, assumed that this postern went out of use at the end of the Bronze Age, but cf. J.A. Bundgaard, *Parthenon and the Mycenaean City on the Heights* (Copenhagen 1976) 26–31; Robertson (supra n. 7) 159–160.
12. Judeich (supra n. 6) 183, 305; Travlos, *PDA* 566–567; Wycherley (supra n. 6) 184–185. See now A. Choremi-Spetsieri in this volume, pp. 31–42.
13. See S.G. Miller, *Hesperia* 39 (1970) 223–227; Choremi-Spetsieri in this volume, pp. 34ff.
14. *IG* II², 2877; *Agora* III, 173. The base retains its original dimesions: 0.53 m. wide, 0.20 m. high, and 0.50 m. deep. It was seen at 20 Tripods Street as late as the 1930s, S. Dow, *Prytaneis*, *Hesperia* Suppl. 1 (Vienna 1937) 192; subsequently removed to the Roman Market, S.G. Miller, *The Prytaneion* (Berkeley 1978) 45 n. 20.
15. For the location of the Prytaneion, Robertson (supra n. 7) 160; Miller (supra n. 14) 42–49; P.J. Rhodes, *A Commentary on the Aristotelian Athenaion Politeia* (Oxford 1981) 103–104.
16. Ascribed to Theseus: [Plutarch], *Moralia* 847d,e; Pollux 9.40; Souda *s.v.* πρυτανεῖον; Schol. Thucydides 2.15.2; Schol. Aristeides 3, p. 48, 8 (ed. Dindorf). Colonists set forth from the Prytaneion: *ibid.*; Herodotos 1.146.2. The *orgeones* of Bendis conduct a procession from the hearth of the Prytaneion to Peiraieus: *IG* II², 1283, lines 6–7. Ephebes' sacrifices at their enrolment: *IG* II², 1006, lines 6–7; 1008, line 5; 1011, line 5; 1028, lines 5–6; 1042, lines 2–4.
17. On honorary meals in the Prytaneion, Miller (supra n. 14) 4–13; and the ancient literary and epigraphical references assembled by Wycherley, *Agora* III, 173–174. For homicide cases: Andokides 1.78; Plutarch, *Sol.* 19.3; Pollux 8.120; for trials of inanimate objects: Demosthenes 23.76; Pausanias 1.28.10–11; Pollux 8.120.
18. The *axones* were still intact in the Prytaneion *ca.* 190 B.C. when they were described by Polemon of Ilion, Harpokration *s.v.* ἄξονι. At the beginning of the second century after Christ, Plutarch (*Sol.* 25.1) saw only small fragments (λείψανα μικρά), but these still survived half a century or so later and were seen by Pausanias 1.18.3.
19. Robertson (supra n. 7) 160–163 has rightly seen that the early buildings must have been close together topographically and all in the vicinity of the Prytaneion. Cf. Miller (supra n. 14) 44–49; Rhodes (supra n. 15) 103–106. Aristotle's attribution of the Epilykeion to a Polemarch Epilykos has commonly been doubted, and the name has been thought to refer to some connection between the Polemarch and the Lykeion gymnasium (Travlos, *PDA* 345), but the archaic building should have stood together with the other early offices (Robertson [supra n.7] 163). The Lykeion was outside the eastern limits of the city walls of the fifth century B.C., and it is unlikely that one of the senior archons would have been so far removed from his colleagues in early archaic times.
20. Basileion: Pollux 8.111. The proximity of the Basileion to the Prytaneion is suggested by the fact that the Phylobasileis also presided over certain trials in the court of the Prytaneion, Pollux 8.120. That the Anakeion was also near the Prytaneion is indicated by the ritual meal laid out on a table in the Prytaneion for the Dioskouroi, Athenaeus 4.137e. Behind the Prytaneion was an open lot called the "Field of Famine", Zenobios 4.93. Bouzygion: Plutarch, *Moralia* 144b; see Miller (supra n. 13) 230–231.
21. Plutarch, *Thes.* 36.2; cf. *Kim.* 8.5–6; Pausanias 1.17.2, 6;

Robertson, (supra n.7) 163–168. That the Theseion and the Anakeion were next to each other is indicated by the two versions of Peisistratos' armed muster. Polyaenus 1.21.2 sets the anecdote in the Anakeion; Aristotle, *Ath. Pol.* 15.4 sets it in the Theseion, but in both the meeting moves to the *propylon* of the Acropolis. It is well to note also that a large enough piece of property was still available in the Hellenistic period to allow the Gymnasium of Ptolemy to be erected beside the Theseion.

22. *IG* II [2], 956, line 16; 957, line 11; 958, lines 13–14 state that they were erected ἐν τῶι τοῦ Θησέως τεμένει; *IG* II [2], 968 honors an agonothetes of the Theseia. The church of Demetrios Katephores, demolished in the nineteenth century, stood at the corner of Erechtheus and Kyrrestos Streets, see A. Mommsen, *Athenae Christianae* (Leipzig 1868) 78–81, no. 90.
23. Aischines 3.13; and cf. Aristotle, *Ath. Pol.* 62.1 with the comments of Rhodes (supra n. 15) 689–690.
24. Andokides 1.45; Thucydides 6.61.2 is less precise than Andokides and implies that the whole Athenian levy slept in the Theseion. There were 1,000 active cavalry in 431 B.C. (Thucydides 2.13.6–9). More than a quarter of the active forces (250–300 cavalry) were lost in the years of the plague (Thucydides 3.87), but there will have been some restoration of numbers in the years of peace before 415 B.C. During the civil strife which attended the fall of the Thirty in 403 B.C., the cavalry once spent the night in the Odeion together with their horses and shields, Xenophon, *Hell.* 2.4.24. Since the Odeion measures 62.40 m. on a side, Xenophon's statement suggests approximately the area that would have been needed in the *temenos* of the Anakeion for a similar encampment.
25. Thucydides 8.93.1.
26. See the discussion of Robertson (supra n.7) 163–168; Wycherley, *Phoenix* 20 (1966) 285–293. In the classical period, the naïskos of Aphrodite Pandemos was located on a rock-cut ledge, against the rock face, below the south wall of the Nike bastion; see L. Beschi, *ASAtene* N.S. 29/30 (1967–68) 517–528. Near this spot were found the inscribed epistyle of the naïskos, *IG* II [2], 4596 (*ca.* 320 B.C.) and other inscriptions relating to the cult of Aphrodite (*IG* I [2], 700; II [2], 659). This is the shrine that Pausanias (1.22.3) saw as he approached the entrance to the Acropolis. Scholars have therefore sought to place a "primitive agora" on the western slope of the Acropolis, or on the saddle between the Acropolis and the Areopagos. Cf. Wycherley, *Phoenix* 20, 285–293; id., *Agora* III 224–225; Judeich (supra n. 6) 62, 285; R. Martin, *Recherches sur l'agora grecque* (Paris 1951) 256–261. But Apollodoros' statement may be no more than an attempt to explain the title Pandemos. Harpokration attributes another explanation to Nikandros of Kolophon (second century B.C.) that Solon organized public prostitution at Athens and founded the cult of Aphrodite Pandemos from the proceeds. The same story is told by Athenaeus 13.569d, who quotes both Nikandros and Philemon, the poet of New Comedy. Pausanias 1.22.3, on the other hand, attributes the foundation of the cult to Theseus. There is certainly nothing so old on the site below the Nike bastion, and one wonders if Aphrodite Pandemos is yet another of those early Athenian cults which had two different sanctuaries, one on the slopes close to the Acropolis and one to the east and south. Cf. Apollo Pythios: Travlos, *PDA* 91, 100; O. Broneer, *Hesperia* Suppl. 8, 47–59; id., *ArchEph* (1960) 54–62. Zeus Olympios: *ibid.*; Travlos, *PDA* 91, 402; see opposing views of Wycherley, *AJA* 63 (1959) 68–72; 67 (1963) 75–79; *GRBS* 4 (1963) 166–167. Aphrodite in the Gardens: Travlos, *PDA* 228; Broneer, *Hesperia* 1 (1932) 31–55.
27. See H.A. Thompson and R.E. Wycherley, *Agora* XIV (Princeton 1972) 1–18, 19; J.M. Camp, *The Athenian Agora* (London 1986) 19–60.
28. Buildings A and B of the early structures published by H.A. Thompson, *The Tholos of Athens and Its Predecessors*, *Hesperia* Suppl. 4 (Baltimore 1940) 3–8, pl. I.
29. *Ibid.* (supra n. 28) 8–15; Thompson, *Hesperia* 6 (1937) 117–127; Camp (supra n. 27) 38–39.
30. Travlos, *PDA* 191–193; Wycherley (supra n. 6) 28–30; J.S. Boersma, *Athenian Building Policy from 561/0 to 405/4 B.C.* (Groningen 1970) 15; Martin (supra n. 26) 262–264.
31. Thompson, *Tholos* 12–15. Deposit H 10: 2; the complete inventory of pottery from the well is as follows. Column Krater: P 13346 = *Agora* XXIII, 446. Stand: P 13345 = *Agora* XXIII, 541. Oinochoe: P 13358 (round mouthed) = *Agora* XII, 156. Skyphos: P 13344 (black-figured); P 13352, cf. *Agora* XII, 306; P 13353, cf. *Agora* XII, 309; P 13354, cf. *Agora* XII, 368; P 13355, cf. *Agora* XII, 368. Cup: P 13347 = *Agora* XXIII, 1671; P 13349 = *Agora* XXIII, 1686; P 13350, cf. *Agora* XII, 379; P 13351 = *Agora* XII, 390; P 13356 (one-handled Phaleron cup), cf. *Agora* VIII, 185. Lekanis Lid: P 13357 = *Agora* XII, 1228. Lekane: P 13359 = *Agora* XII, 1751. Aryballos, Corinthian: P 13343. Water Jar: P 13360 (graffito sherd) = *Agora* XXI, D18. Lamp: L 3497 = *Agora* IV, 12; L 3498 = *Agora* IV, 41; L 3499 = *Agora* IV, 28.
32. Thompson, *Hesperia* 6 (1937) 81, pl. VI. Traces of the courtyard wall came to light only 5 m. north of the north wall of Building C.
33. Shear in W.A.P.Childs (ed.), *Athens Comes of Age* (Princeton 1978) 4–5.
34. Oinochoe: P 5463 = *Agora* XXIII, 735; Thompson, *Tholos* 28–29, fig. 21. Also from the period-of-use fill at the bottom of well G 11: 8 came: Amphora: P 6548 = *Agora* XXIII, 56 dated *ca.* 550 B.C. Pelike: P 5459 = *Agora* XII, 24. Household Hydria: P 5461 = *Agora* XII, 1593; P 5460, P 5462 from the same shop. Jug: P 6550 = *Agora* XII, 1692. Thompson, *Tholos* 12–13 saw that the pottery from Deposit H 10: 2 provided a *terminus post quem* for construction of Building D.
35. Boersma (supra n. 30) 16–17; Martin (supra n. 26) 271 n. 2; id., *L'urbanisme dans la Grèce antique* (Paris 1956) 223.
36. Thompson, *Tholos* 42–43.
37. *IG* I [3], 4, A lines 18–19; B lines 23, 24 for the singular prytanis; B lines 17–21 the Treasurers are to open the *oikemata* three times a month, on the last day before the new moon, on the tenth, and on the twentieth of the lunar month.
38. P.J. Rhodes, *The Athenian Boule* (Oxford 1972) 17–19. Cf. the doubts expressed by Miller, (supra n. 14) 62–65 concerning the identification of Building F as the seat of the prytaneis of the Council. Cf. also the criticism of O. Broneer, *AJA* 45 (1941) 127–129.
39. Thompson, *The Athenian Agora, A Guide* [2] (Athens 1962) 21; but the suggestion was later retracted in *Agora Guide* [3] (Athens 1976) 23; *Agora* XIV, 28. See Boersma (supra n. 30) 16–17; cf. the remarks of Camp (supra n. 27) 44–45 and here p. 10.
40. *Agora* XIV, 197–199; Camp (supra n. 27) 42–44 and here p. 10; id., *The Water Supply of Ancient Athens* (Diss. Princeton 1977) 73–94; Travlos, *PDA* 204–209.
41. *Agora* XIV, 129–136; Camp (supra n. 27) 40–42 and here p. 10; Thucydides 6.54.6–7 says that Peisistratos dedicated the altar as archon. For the date, T.J. Cadoux, *JHS* 68 (1948) 71, 111. For revised chronology of the existing remains of the altar, L.M. Gadbery, *Hesperia* 61 (1992) 447–489.
42. The central milestone, Herodotos 2.7.1–2; *IG* II [2], 2640; the "omphalos of the city", Pindar, frg. 75 (ed. Snell).
43. The archaic Telesterion at Eleusis measures 25.30 m. × 27.10 m.; G.E. Mylonas, *Eleusis and the Eleusinian Mysteries* (Princeton 1961) 81.
44. Thompson (supra n. 32) 127–135; id.,*Tholos* 40–44; id., *Agora* XIV, 29–32; Travlos, *PDA* 191–195; Camp (supra n. 27) 52–53.
45. See J.T. Clarke, F.H. Bacon, R. Koldewey, *Investigations at Assos* (Cambridge 1902) 53–59. G. Roux, *BCH* 100 (1976) 475–483 rightly pointed to the similarity between the Old Bouleuterion at Athens and that at Assos. The essential features of the new restoration were adopted by Camp (supra n. 27) 52, but his plan still shows banks of stepped seats. Closer in date to the Athenian building is the larger square hall at Argos of the first half of the fifth century; Roux, *BCH* 77 (1953) 244–248.
46. Thompson (supra n. 32) 130.
47. Cf. A.W. Pickard-Cambridge, *The Theatre of Dionysus in Athens* (Oxford 1946) 140–141.
48. Aristophanes, *Knights* 640–642, 674–675 (424 B.C.) certainly

refers to the Old Bouleuterion. When Aristophanes has the Boule leaping over the δρύφακτοι, the comedy is surely that the δρύφακτοι were too high to leap over, and everybody knew it. The trial of Theramenes (404 B.C.), Xenophon, *Hell.* 2.3.50–56, should be set in the New Bouleuterion not the Old, but this does not invalidate the discussion of the passage by Roux, *BCH* 100 (1976) 475–483. Both buildings doubtless had similar façades. [Demosthenes] 25.23 (quoted infra p. 239) also refers to the later building.

49. *ID* 1403 Bb II, line 19. The same installation is also mentioned in *ID* 1417 A II, line 38; 1426 B II, lines 41–43; 1442 B, line 37. Cf. also *IG* XI, 2, 199 A, lines 76–77. See the useful discussion of F. Salviat, *BCH* 87 (1963) 259–264. Although the Delian inscriptions regularly use τρύφακτος, Hesychius *s.v.* says that the word is the same as δρύφακτος, the regular Attic usage.
50. Deposit H 10: 7. The complete assemblage of pottery fragments has been listed and the deposit has been discussed in more detail in my study, "The Persian Destruction of Athens: Evidence from Agora Deposits," *Hesperia* 62 (1993) no. 4.
51. Thompson, *Tholos* 27; id. (supra n. 32) 130–131.
52. Agora Inv. I 4869: Thompson, *Tholos* 143, a.
53. Plate: P 12235 = *Agora* XXIII, 1418; Cup: P 12236 = *Agora* XXIII, 1795. Cf. Thompson, *Tholos* 34–38. Deposit H 12: 18, lower layer produced 793 fragments of which 38 were datable *ca.* 500 B.C., eight pieces were datable 500–480. The complete assemblage has been listed, Shear (supra n. 50).
54. For preliminary description of the Stoa Basileios, Shear, *Hesperia* 40 (1971) 243–255; *Agora* XIV, 83–90; Camp (supra n. 27) 53–57.
55. This material will receive detailed presentation in the final publication of the stoa, now in preparation. Analysis of the pottery from the lower layer of the building fill now makes it necessary to revise the date of construction downward from the mid sixth century originally proposed by Shear (supra n. 54) 249–250; id., *Hesperia* 44 (1975) 369–370, largely on the basis of the architectural fragments. The pottery now assures a date *ca.* 500 B.C. for the building's construction.
56. Aristotle, *Ath. Pol.* 20–22; Herodotos 5.69–70.
57. The testimonia are conveniently assembled by Wycherley, *Agora* III, 21–25.
58. See J.J. Coulton, *The Architectural Development of the Greek Stoa* (Oxford 1976) 33–34, and the archaic stoas assembled *ibid.*, fig. 20. All buildings in monumental stone architecture, earlier than the Stoa Basileios in Athens, were erected in sanctuaries. Among the 65 bouleuteria catalogued by D. Gneisz, *Das antike Rathaus* (Diss. Vienna 1990) 301–357, only the northern half of the bouleuterion at Olympia is older than the Old Bouleuterion at Athens and in the Doric order, *ibid.* 340–341.
59. Eratosthenes was a student of Zenon of Kition and spent many years in Athens before being called to Alexandria, Jacoby, *FGrH* 241 T1, T10; P.M. Fraser, *Ptolemaic Alexandria* II (Oxford 1972) 463 n. 13; 489–490 n. 205. Polemon's description of the *axones* of Solon in the Prytaneion was quoted by Harpokration, *s.v.* ἄξονι. Plutarch, *Sol.* 19.3 quotes from the eighth law on the 13th *axon*, and later, *Sol.* 25.1–2, describes the *axones* in detail. Pausanias 1.18.3 (quoted supra p. 227) saw the *axones* on his visit to the Prytaneion.
60. Jacoby, *FGrH* 72 F 13; Harpokration, Souda *s.v.* ὁ κάτωθεν νόμος.
61. The title appears in the catalogue of Aristotle's writings found in the *Vita Menagiana*, Aristotle, *Frg.* (ed. Rose) 16, no. 140; see P. Moraux, *Les listes anciennes des ouvrages d' Aristote* (Louvain 1951) 250–251; R. Weil, *Aristote et l' histoire* (Paris 1960) 125–127; cf. E. Ruschenbusch, *Σόλωνος Νόμοι*, *Historia*, Einzelschriften 9 (1966) 40–42.
62. *The Axones and Kyrbeis of Drakon and Solon* (Berkeley 1979); cf. the remarks of Robertson (supra n. 7) 147.
63. For recent studies which conclude that *axones* and *kyrbeis* are two names for the same objects, see Ruschenbusch (supra n. 61) 14–25; A. Andrewes in *ΦΟΡΟΣ, Tribute to Benjamin Dean Meritt* (Locust Valley, N.Y. 1974) 21–28; Rhodes (supra n. 15) 131–134. R. Sealy, *The Athenian Republic* (University Park, PA 1987) 140–145 considers it naïve to suppose that ancient scholars of the *axones* and *kyrbeis* actually described what they saw.
64. Cf. Stroud (supra n. 62) 14–15.
65. Evidence for the date of reconstruction comes from the first layer of earth to gather above the original grade level in front of the Stoa Basileios. This was a thin layer, 0.04 m. to 0.06 m. deep, covering most of the peribolos. Under the south porch this layer was found to cover the step of the stoa and of the stepped retaining wall at the south. Here its top surface was covered with poros chips and dust from the working of poros blocks, and it showed signs of heavy burning. From this layer 832 fragments of pottery were recovered, of which the latest 82 pieces dated to the period 475–450 B.C. Among the pottery was P 30192: Ostrakon of Kimon which might have been cast at any time between 475 and 461 (the year of his ostracism), but cannot have been cast later than that date.
66. An anachronism somewhat analogous to that which dated the Stoa Basileios to the time of Solon occurs at *Ath. Pol.* 15.4. This passage recounts the same anecdote as Polyaenus 1.21.3 (supra p. 227) concerning Peisistratos' disarming of the Athenians. But the assembly under arms is mustered in the Theseion instead of the Anakeion. Aristotle places the story at the time of the final establishment of the tyranny and thus *ca.* 546 B.C. The founding of the Theseion, however, is specifically attributed to Kimon in the years after the Persian Wars, Plutarch, *Thes.* 36; *Kim.* 8.5–6; Pausanias 1.17.6; and Plutarch, *Thes.* 36.1 dates the foundation to the archonship of Phaidon (476/5).
67. Thompson, *Tholos* 27–28.
68. Boukolion: Aristotle, *Ath. Pol.* 3.5 (quoted supra p. 228); Stoa Basileios: Pausanias 1.3.1; Plato, *Euthy.* 2a; *Theaet.* 210d; *IG* I^3, 104, lines 4–8.
69. *IG* I^3, 131; Miller (supra n. 14) 4–11, 38.
70. All are published most recently in B.D. Meritt and J.S. Traill, *Agora* XV, *Inscriptions, The Athenian Councillors* (Princeton 1974). The inscriptions that preserve the formula are as follows (Those marked with an asterisk * were found in the southwest corner of the Agora near the Tholos.): *Agora* XV, 89*, 120*, 130*, 135*, 137, 147*, 168, 170, 174*, 181, 187, 193, 194*, 205*, 206*, 212*, 214, 225*, 240*, 243*, 244. Texts in which the formula can be restored are: *Agora* XV, 76, 77, 78, 84, 86, 88, 100, 104, 115, 121, 126, 127, 128, 129, 132, 138, 141, 158, 163, 171, 175, 178, 179, 184, 189, 191, 192, 199, 204, 211, 215, 216, 217, 223, 226, 232, 234, 236.
71. E. Vanderpool, *Hesperia* 4 (1935) 470–475; Miller (supra n. 14) 38, 60–65.
72. Souda *s.vv.* θόλος, πρυτανεῖον; Timaios Sophistes, *Lexicon Platonicum* 402. For the statues of the Eponymoi said to be beside the Prytaneion, Schol. Aristophanes, *Peace* 1183–1184.
73. See W. C. Greene, *Scholia Platonica* (Haverford, PA 1938) 127; Wycherley, *Agora* III, 168. Cf. also Souda *s.v.* πρυτανεῖον.
74. Aristotle, *Ath. Pol.* 3.5; supra p. 228.
75. Stroud (supra n. 62) 41–42.
76. For the oath of the Boule, see Rhodes (supra n. 38) 190–199; for the oath sworn by the jurors, see id. (supra n. 15) 620–621.
77. Demosthenes 54. 26 refers to arbitrators taking oaths at the stone; and cf. Harpokration, Souda *s.v.* λίθος which both quote Demosthenes and Aristotle.
78. These two passages are the only citations of this word in *LSJ*^{9}, cf. Rhodes (supra n. 15) 136.
79. The same anecdote appears also in Polyaenus 1.20.1. Diogenes Laertios 1.46 says that Solon had the herald read the elegy. Cf. also Demosthenes 19.252, 254–256; Cicero, *De Off.* 1.30, 108; Justin 2.7.9–12; Plutarch, *Poplic.* 27.2; Schol. *Il.* 2.183 = Aristotle, frg. 143 (ed. Rose, p. 121). See the discussion of Robertson (supra n. 7) 165–166.
80. Plutarch, *Thes.* 27.7: ἀλλὰ τοῦ γε τὸν πόλεμον εἰς σπονδὰς τελευτῆσαι μαρτύριόν ἐστιν ἥ τε τοῦ τόπου κλῆσις τοῦ παρὰ τὸ Θησεῖον, ὅνπερ Ὁρκωμόσιον καλοῦσιν. The

sacrificial calendar of Thorikos was apparently to be erected at a place in that deme called *Horkomosion, SEG* 26 (1976–77) 136, lines 62–64 where the name is restored on the basis of lines 12, 52 (cf. *SEG* 28 [1978] 111). Allotted deme officials and their *paredroi* were to swear oaths at their *euthyna*, presumably at the same place, *ibid.* lines 57–64.

81. See Shear (supra n. 54) 259–260; *Agora* XIV, 88; Camp (supra n. 27) 100–104.

82. The two boundary-stones still *in situ* are Agora Inv. I 5510 and I 7039: *Agora* XIX, 27, H25, H26. A third stone of the same series is Agora Inv. I 5675: *Agora* XIX, H 27 found in a late context.

An Appeal by the Greek Ministry of Culture

The heads illustrated below were ***stolen*** from the Acropolis Museum, the Kanellopoulos Museum and the National Museum, Athens, in 1992 and 1993. For any information on their whereabouts, please contact the Directorate of Antiquities, Ministry of Culture, 14 Aristeidou St., GR-101 86 Athens, Greece. Telephone 30–1–3225–158, fax 30–1–3234–239.

1a-b. Acropolis Museum, Athens, inv. no. 13532. Bronze head from the Acropolis. Early fifth century B.C. Height, 0,0304 m. AAA *18 (1985) 173–179.*

2a-b. Kanellopoulos Museum, Athens, inv. no. 1592. Marble head of a girl. Fourth century B.C. Height, 0,125 m, width, 0,094 m.

3. National Museum, Athens, inv. no. 1939. Marble head of a sphinx or kore. Excavated in the sanctuary of Aphaia, Aigina in 1902. Second quarter of the sixth century B.C. Height, 0,22 m. A.Furtwängler, Aegina. Das Heiligtum der Aphaia (1906) pls. 82–83; G.M.A. Richter, Korai *(1968) no. 66, figs. 214–216; J. Floren,* Die geometrische und archaische Plastik *(1987) 310 n. 12.*